Chartered Wealth Manager Qualification

Financial Markets

Edition 6, August 2018

This workbook relates to syllabus version 6.1 and will cover the exams from 7 January 2019 to 4 December 2019

APPROVED WORKBOOK

Welcome to the Chartered Institute for Securities & Investment's Financial Markets study material.

This workbook has been written to prepare you for the Chartered Institute for Securities & Investment's Financial Markets examination.

Candidates sitting the Chartered Wealth Manager titles will be provided with an Information Pack along with the question paper for the exam. This contains taxation rates and allowances for the relevant tax year and tables of gilt market prices.

Published by:
Chartered Institute for Securities & Investment
© Chartered Institute for Securities & Investment 2018
20 Fenchurch Street
London EC3M 3BY
Tel: +44 20 7645 0600
Fax: +44 20 7645 0601

Email: customersupport@cisi.org
www.cisi.org/qualifications

Author:
Tim McCullough

Reviewers:
Catherine Makin
Bob Davidson

This is an educational workbook only and Chartered Institute for Securities & Investment accepts no responsibility for persons undertaking trading or investments in whatever form.

While every effort has been made to ensure its accuracy, no responsibility for loss occasioned to any person acting or refraining from action as a result of any material in this publication can be accepted by the publisher or authors.

All rights reserved. No part of this publication may be reproduced, stored in a retrieval system, or transmitted, in any form or by any means, electronic, mechanical, photocopying, recording or otherwise without the prior permission of the copyright owner.

Warning: any unauthorised act in relation to all or any part of the material in this publication may result in both a civil claim for damages and criminal prosecution.

A learning map, which contains the full syllabus, appears at the end of this workbook. The syllabus can also be viewed on cisi.org and is also available by contacting the Customer Support Centre on +44 20 7645 0777. Please note that the examination is based upon the syllabus. Candidates are reminded to check the Candidate Update area details (cisi.org/candidateupdate) on a regular basis for updates as a result of industry change(s) that could affect their examination.

Workbook version: 6.1 (August 2018)

Learning and Professional Development with the CISI

The Chartered Institute for Securities & Investment is the leading professional body for those who work in, or aspire to work in, the investment sector, and we are passionately committed to enhancing knowledge, skills and integrity – the three pillars of professionalism at the heart of our Chartered body.

CISI examinations are used extensively by firms to meet the requirements of government regulators. Besides the regulators in the UK, where the CISI head office is based, CISI examinations are recognised by a wide range of governments and their regulators, from Singapore to Dubai and the US. Around 50,000 examinations are taken each year, and it is compulsory for candidates to use CISI workbooks to prepare for CISI examinations so that they have the best chance of success. Our workbooks are normally revised every year by experts who themselves work in the industry and also by our Accredited Training Partners, who offer training and elearning to help prepare candidates for the examinations. Information for candidates is also posted on a special area of our website: cisi.org/candidateupdate.

This workbook not only provides a thorough preparation for the examination it refers to, it is also a valuable desktop reference for practitioners, and studying from it counts towards your Continuing Professional Development (CPD).

CISI examination candidates are automatically registered, without additional charge, as student members for one year (should they not be members of the CISI already), and this enables you to use a vast range of online resources, including CISI TV, free of any additional charge. The CISI has more than 40,000 members, and nearly half of them have already completed relevant qualifications and transferred to a core membership grade.

Completing a higher level examination enables you to progress even more quickly towards personal Chartered status, the pinnacle of professionalism in the CISI. You will find more information about the next steps for this at the end of this workbook.

Macroeconomics	1
Financial Statement Analysis	89
Application of Financial Statement Analysis and Accounting Ratios	121
Compounding, Discounting and Bond Maths	167
Liquidity Description, Risk, Return Characteristics	203
Bonds	231
Equities	321
Property and Alternative Investments	351
Derivatives	383
The Securities Market Structure	473
Glossary	547
Syllabus Learning Map	555

It is estimated that candidates will require approximately 200 hours of study time, including study of this workbook, any formal tuition and wider reading, in order to be successful in the examination.

What next?
See the back of this book for details of CISI membership.

Need more support to pass your exam?
See our section on Accredited Training Partners.

Want to leave feedback?
Please email your comments to learningresources@cisi.org

Chapter One
Macroeconomics

1. Classical, Keynesian and Monetarist Approaches (1) — 3
2. Classical, Keynesian and Monetarist Approaches (2) — 27
3. Macroeconomics and Markets — 31
4. Fiscal and Monetary Policy: Inflation, Interest Rates and Exchange Rates — 41
5. Macroeconomic Statistics — 54
6. Financial Markets and Services — 73

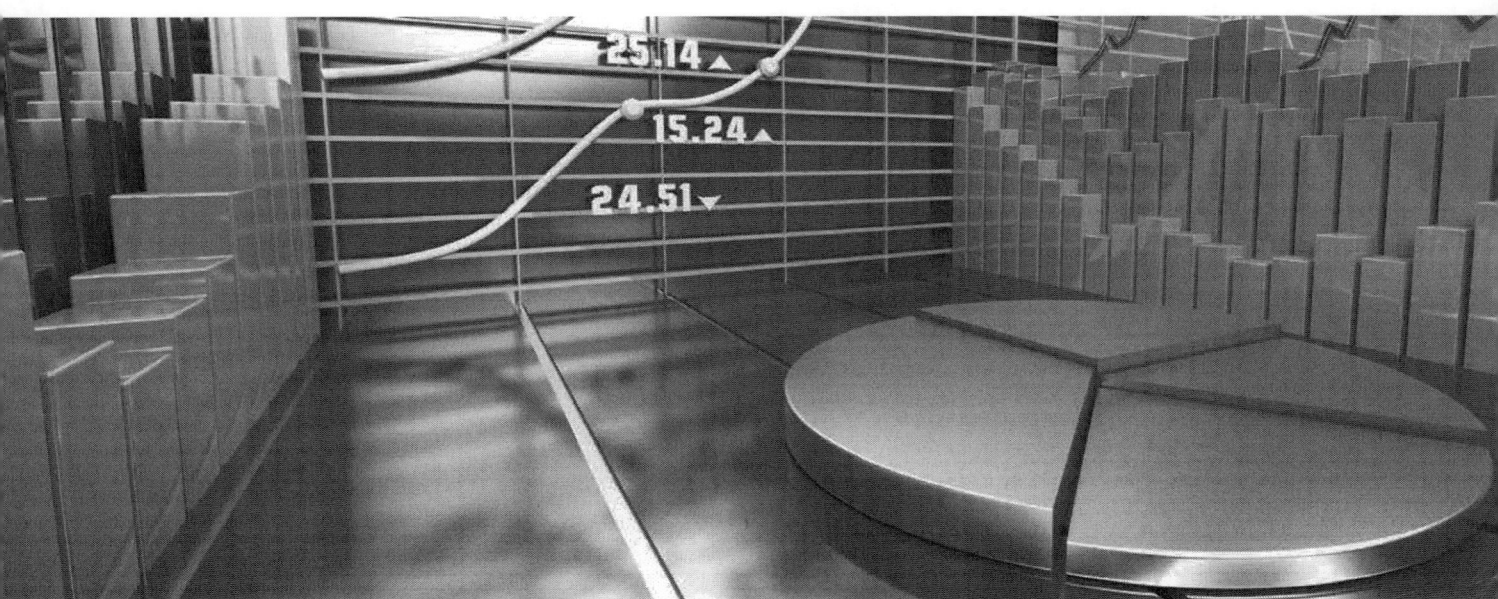

Learning Outcome

Be able to assess the implications of macroeconomics and macroeconomic policy for financial markets

1. Classical, Keynesian and Monetarist Approaches (1)

Learning Objective

1.1 Evaluate Classical, Keynesian and Monetarist approaches in the context of macroeconomic government policy targets and instruments

1.1 Multiple Economic Theories

The broad subject of economics is considered by many to be a social science, in that it studies human behaviour in allocating scarce resources to meet endless demand for goods and services. It is arguably this human behavioural feature which distinguishes it from the natural or physical sciences, where observations legitimise a greater reliance on the identification and application of quantitative and numerical constants. In recent decades, however, possibly due to a perception of relative stability in major economies but exacerbated by rapid advances in computing software, many economists have claimed greater reliability of mathematical models in explaining the interaction of this aspect of human behaviour, leading to the term 'econometrics'. This chapter examines the three major schools of economic theory in the 20th and 21st centuries so far, relating to macroeconomics, before evaluating them in the context of government policies and instruments.

First, it is necessary to distinguish macroeconomics from microeconomics as the two major strands of this social science. Microeconomics studies how individuals and single firms allocate resources efficiently, while macroeconomics considers the aggregate behaviour of a wider population, as they each follow their individual microeconomic goals. It is this aggregation of the behaviour of a larger group, distinguished from other groups by its use of particular economic policies, legal systems or instruments, such as a currency, which allows common features, such as growth, inflation, employment, productivity, government surpluses and deficits, and levels of imports and exports, to be assessed.

It is still possible to find notable instances of disagreement among physical or natural scientists regarding not just the cause of a phenomenon, but even its very existence. Climate change is one example, but the primary causes and optimal treatments of many medical conditions have also been disputed over the years. It should come as no surprise, therefore, that as a social science, macroeconomics too has evolved into several schools of thought, of which the most significant are the Classical, Keynesian and Monetarist. A frequent criticism of macroeconomists is that they remain unable to heal these divisions, which are the basis of sharply different monetary and fiscal policies, affecting the livelihoods of entire populations. Their adoption by varying political persuasions has additionally led to policy reversals in many democracies as one party gains power at the expense of another.

The reason why such distinctions persist is that they are no more than schools of thought derived from theories which are based on assumptions about human behaviour. From these they deduce insights and build models as to how entire economies and their individual participants should be expected to behave. As such, they are prone to revision and improvement when expectations are not borne out in reality. This occurs, most notably, after significant economic events which question the validity of each theory. Keynesianism came sharply into favour in response to the Great Depression of the 1930s, yet gave way to Monetarism following the inflationary problems of the 1970s. Recent advances in behavioural economics and the uncertainty surrounding the radical experiment of quantitative easing, following the global financial crisis of 2007–09, may yet lead to further changes.

The Classical, Keynesian and Monetarist schools are outlined below, with particular focus on the key differences regarding the role and implementation of monetary and fiscal policies within each, but also including illustrations of other notable economic concepts.

1.2 The Circular Flow of an Economy

Before considering differences in macroeconomic principles, it is worth observing an assumption common to all. One example of an economic model which is fundamental to most economic theories is the circular flow between households and firms. This strips out disputed factors, such as the role of monetary and fiscal policies, financial markets, governments and international trade, to represent the core nature of an economy. The provision of goods and services, the funds to pay for them, the provision of labour and the supply of wages all result from the interaction between households and firms. The key distinction between the major economic theories concerns whether it is demand or supply which provides the initial momentum, ie, where the focus of any economic policy should lie.

The Classical, Keynesian and Monetarist models may disagree about the starting point of economic activity (ie, flows from firms to households or vice versa, supply or demand, the chicken or the egg), but the circular flow is illustrated in the following diagram.

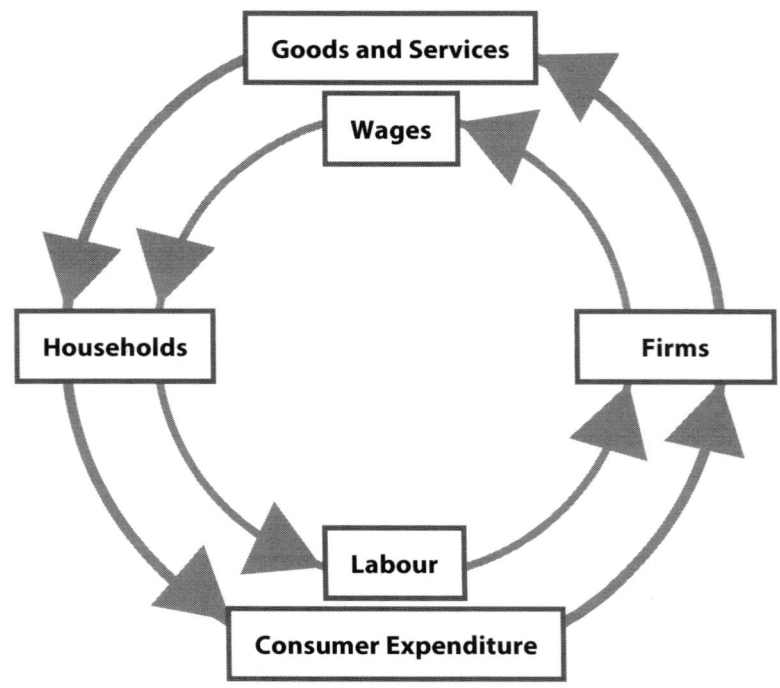

In the outer circle, firms supply goods and services to meet the demand of households in return for payment (consumer expenditure).

In the inner circle, households supply labour to meet the demands of firms in return for wages.

The diagram above is essentially representing a microeconomic model, but applying the metrics in it to a theoretical macroeconomic scenario, under laboratory conditions, offers the following definitions:

1. **national expenditure** – the amount spent by households on goods and services
2. **national income** – the returns of wages to labour, rent for land and income and interest to capital
3. **national product** – the amount received by firms from their production of goods and services.

Economic activity can be measured through observing the money flow at any point in the diagram above, in which there is no introduction or withdrawal of any factor. Flows of money and, thus, of economic activity are equal at any point. In this purest form of an economy, under laboratory conditions, a foundation element of economic theory can be deduced.

$$\text{Output} = \text{Income} = \text{Expenditure}$$

The value of output in an economy can thus be measured in any one of three ways:

1. tallying the value added by each form of economic activity
2. tallying the value of all finished goods
3. tallying the incomes earned by each of the factors of production in the economy.

The totals should be the same.

The table below demonstrates the different methods of computing the output of a highly simplified economy which comprises a lumberjack, a sawmill and a carpenter, and how each creates output, income and expenditure.

	Lumberjack	Sawmill	Carpenter
Sales	100	150	400
Raw Materials		100	150
Labour		20	80
Rent			15
Interest Payment		5	10
Profit	100	25	145

	Rent	Wages	Interest	Profit	Total
Lumberjack				100	100
Sawmill		20	5	25	50
Carpenter	15	80	10	145	250
Total	15	100	15	270	400

The first line of the upper table shows the sales value of the finished goods as they move through the business process. The lumberjack creates £100 of value by cutting a tree from the forest – for which there is no charge, and thus the land provides an input value of £100 into this economy. The sawmill has added £50 of value, and this is reflected in the interim finished good value of £150, and the carpenter then adds another £250 of value to the 'final' finished goods value of £400. The total value created or the total output of this very simple economy is, therefore, £400.

In the same upper table, the lumberjack incurs no costs, so the value created is assigned to 'profit' (assume that they are the sole proprietor; instead of paying themselves a wage, they take the value created in profit). In the next column, the sawmill incurs a raw material cost of £100 (paid to the lumberjack), with a £20 cost for labour and a £5 cost for interest on a loan or financing. The sawmill creates £150 of value, ie, the price that it can charge the carpenter, generating £25 profit after costs. The carpenter thus pays £150 to the sawmill and incurs £105 of other costs as indicated, before selling the finished piece of furniture for £400, generating a profit of £145.

The lower table quantifies the four factors of production: earnings (ie, rent), wages, interest and profit. It then totals these for each of the three participants in this economy, representing their individual contributions to economic output (far right-hand column). In aggregate they equal the £400 from the other perspective.

In terms of the 'output = income = expenditure' model noted above, this economy comprises:

- the total value of the finished goods, ie, furniture created: £400
- the value added by each of the three economic agents (100 + £50 + £250): £400
- the returns to each of the factors of production (£15 + £100 +£15 + £270): £400.

1.3 Modified Circular Flow

In the simple circular flow in section 1.2 above showing output, income and expenditure between firms and households are shown to be equal, with no distortion to the supply of one or the demand of the other. The reality of a modern national economy is far more complex. At any point in the circular flow there are numerous injections and leakages. It is the source and motivation of these additional flows into and out of an economy, together with their subsequent impact, which leads to the distinctive and often contradictory schools of economic thought.

1.3.1 Injections

1. **Exports** – the simplified system outlined above represents a national economy but, in reality, almost all national economies are, to varying extents, 'open' (ie, they interact with other national economies through international trade). When products or services are exported overseas, their value enters the national economy through an injection of expenditure by foreign consumers.
2. **Government spending** – the economic role of government is explored further in a comparison of the major economic schools, but in many economies, the government is both a consumer and producer of goods and services as well as a provider of capital expenditure. The monetary value of government consumption and expenditure represents another injection of funds.
3. **Investment** – the expenditure of firms when they build infrastructure, such as offices and manufacturing plants, is collectively known as investment and is a further injection of funds in.

1.3.2 Leakages

1. **Imports** – these are goods and services which are brought into the national economy from foreign suppliers, causing a monetary flow out of the economy.
2. **Taxation** – the obverse of government expenditure on goods and services is the collection of taxes. Money is removed from the circular flow and transferred to the government. This might be offset by government expenditure, but there is no requirement for amounts to be equal (a balanced budget).
3. **Savings** – the portion of incomes paid to households but not then used for current consumption. An absence of full consumption by households represents a leakage in final demand and a monetary reduction in national expenditure.

It will be seen later that the modified circular flow diagrams and brief outline just given become vital to understanding competing economic theories and economic policy objectives and especially relevant to the discussion of Keynesianism.

1.4 Origins of Keynesian, Classical and Monetarist Economics

It would be wrong to consider the three most important schools of modern economic thought in the western world as being completely distinct from one another, particularly in how they have been implemented by various governments. In their purest forms, there are notable differences based on their core assumptions, but these have been constantly reinterpreted by economists over many decades and, indeed, are currently undergoing considerable reassessment following the global economic crisis of 2007–09.

A brief outline of their evolution in an historical context would be an appropriate starting point before describing them each in more depth in terms of government policy targets and instruments.

The oldest of the three schools is Classical economics, which is generally considered to have started with the ideas of Adam Smith in his 1776 book *'An Inquiry into the Nature and Causes of the Wealth of Nations'* (often referred to as *'The Wealth of Nations'*). The timing reflected significant ongoing changes in how wealth was being created, following the onset of the Industrial Revolution. It is tempting to suggest that each significant evolution from one school to another has followed more dramatic economic events, though these may, in reality, have been mere trigger points for acceptance of concepts which had already been developing for some time. The classical school continued for about a hundred years, with its core principle that economic growth is best achieved through a *laissez-faire* approach of small government relying on the efficiency of free markets. Other notable advocates included Jean-Baptiste Say, Thomas Robert Malthus, David Ricardo and John Stuart Mill. The 1870s, however, are generally regarded as the 'marginal revolution', when William Stanley Jevons, Carl Menger and Leon Walras introduced concepts of marginal utility in response to more socialist and then Marxist theories around the role of labour. This marked a shift into neoclassical economics, which persisted for another 50 years or so.

The Great Depression of the 1930s in western nations marked a further readiness to adopt radical ideas. John Maynard Keynes was a classical economist, but he adapted to the new realities first of hyperinflation in Germany and then of economic depression and mass unemployment in many western economies. Keynes had already been developing his ideas for more than ten years before his most famous work *'The General Theory of Employment, Interest and Money'* in 1936. His views on the role of aggregate demand, especially in the short-run, are described in more detail below, but Keynesian economics became the accepted model for most western nations and remained so in the aftermath of the second world war amongst most social democracies, as government-led demand management, with a primary role of fiscal policy, enjoyed an era of low unemployment and low inflation.

It was another shock, in the form of sharply higher energy prices, rising inflation amidst recession and higher unemployment (stagflation) in the 1970s, which led to the emergence of Monetarist economics. Its most famous proponent was Milton Friedman of the University of Chicago. Although his magnum opus *'Capitalism and Freedom'* was published in 1962, the profile of Monetarism was significantly raised with the elections of Margaret Thatcher as UK Prime Minister (1979), Ronald Reagan as US President (1981) and the appointment of Paul Volcker as chairman of the US Federal Reserve in 1979. Control of the money supply became the key policy in a move away from a more Keynesian active fiscal policy.

Monetarism has not been as widely adopted as Keynesian economics, though some would argue that it has never been adopted in its purest form, due to offsetting of policies and targets between governments and central banks. The issue is discussed in more detail below, but differing interactions have led to a dilution of Monetarist ingredients with Keynesian flavours. The global financial crisis of 2007–09 has thrown up fresh questions of recipe. Historic levels of deflation, which were barely imaginable when Monetarism gained prevalence in the late 1970s, have led to the experiment of quantitative easing (QE), while decisions to expand or reduce significant budget deficits are again being fiercely debated.

The history of economics shows that the Classical, Keynesian and Monetarist schools are not rigid doctrines, but have always been contemporary experiments which are prone to political influences and reactive to circumstance. It is important to consider their forms and to assess their relative success in that context as a social science, rather than as natural sciences.

1.5 Core Principles: Classical, Keynesian and Monetarist Economics

A practical way to ascertain and to compare the essential principles of each school is in a tabulated form. This facilitates a sequential analysis of how macroeconomic government policies are set in accordance to relevant targets. Bear in mind however that this requires relatively crude and arbitrary definitions of each principle, which may not align with how governments choose to adopt and then implement their policies in practice. These policies, the degree of success in their implementation and their impact on financial markets are examined in the rest of this chapter.

	Classical	**Keynesian**	**Monetarist**
Role of Government	Cannot improve market performance, so adopts 'laissez faire' policy	Interventionist via active management of aggregate demand	Similar to classical 'laissez faire', but must control money supply
Fiscal Policy	Less interventionist, aiming for balanced budget.	Key government tool in countering recession via demand stimulation.	Less interventionist, aiming for balanced budget.
Supply	Supply (production) creates demand (income): Say's law. Long-term aggregate supply is inelastic.	Output can be below full capacity even in long-term.	
Demand		Aggregate demand determines economic output. Weakened by paradox of thrift in recession.	
Inflation	Temporary and likely to return to low levels as flexible wages adjust.	Consequence of demand stimulation (to boost employment)	Caused by excessive money supply growth. Must be controlled.
Wages	Highly reactive to changes in demand, to restore full employment	Inflexible, at least in short-term	Theoretically flexible (if no market distortions)
Unemployment	Short-term deviations from full-employment: naturally occurring but self-correcting	Caused by weak aggregate demand. Less desirable than inflation.	Natural rate of unemployment, due to labour market friction and distortion

1.5.1 Classical Economics

Also called 'a free market', 'capitalism', or '*laissez-faire* capitalism', a classical economy is a system in which government stands aside as far as possible, so that prices of goods and services are determined solely by the open market, including consumers in a largely self-regulating model.

In terms of macroeconomic government policy, classical economics is the least interventionist of the three schools. It assumes that consumers and producers are together more capable and more efficient than government in deciding not only at what price goods and services should be bought and sold and at what level of wages labour should be hired, but also what goods and services should be produced and what form of labour should be provided. This freedom of choice means that both prices and wages are fully flexible.

The macroeconomic policy consequences of this are as follows.

The principal role of government is to facilitate the ability of independent buyers and sellers (ie, the private sector) to meet with minimum hindrance, yet with maximum confidence and trust, but otherwise not to interfere. This requires the provision of a legal system protecting the rights of ownership and title, with a judicial system to enforce contracts. This permits buyers and sellers of goods, services and labour to commit to future transactions. At a macroeconomic level, this includes pursuing a free trade policy, without protectionism in the form of subsidy or tariffs, as well as a floating exchange rate policy (discussed below).

Most classical economists would allow for government provision of certain core services, which even the private sector would be unable to provide (eg, defence, law enforcement and judiciary), but any other services would be kept to a minimum, on the principle that private provision can provide a better, more innovative and efficient service than central government planning.

Most other aspects of economic policy are assumed to be managed best by the private sector in a self-regulating manner. Two of the most important principles are that of the 'invisible hand' in Smith's *The Wealth of Nations*' and of Say's law. The former suggests that, at a microeconomic level, each individual acts purely out of self-interest but, at a macroeconomic level, this causes all participants unwittingly to produce the most favourable outcome for everyone, in terms of innovation, quality, efficiency and price. The latter says that an economy which produces (ie, supplies) a certain level of real gross domestic product (GDP) will also generate the income necessary to purchase that level of real GDP. Thus, the demand in an economy can always match its supply, but it is supply which provides the lead (the opposite of Keynesian economics below).

An important caveat of Say's law is that not all the income derived from supply is necessarily spent via demand; demand can thus be weaker than supply. At a microeconomic level, some of the income derived from supplying one good may be spent instead on another. At an aggregate level, this would cause a reduction in subsequent supply for the first good and an expansion in supply for the second, thus restoring the equilibrium of demand and supply for both goods. If some income is instead saved, this causes aggregate demand in the economy temporarily to fall below aggregate supply. In theory, following the microeconomic scenario above, this would cause producers to cut back on production and employment, thus reducing in turn aggregate demand. In reality, if sufficient income is diverted to savings, the accumulative effect will be to cause interest rates to fall. At that point, other investment opportunities will become more attractive (via the 'invisible hand'), which will create a new source of supply, at least as much as before and will thus create at least as much demand. Therefore, not only is the economy restored to its natural level, but it should actually grow, while employment is restored to its natural full level.

One of the consequences of Say's law, therefore, is that the economy should theoretically always be close to full employment, assuming that wages are not kept artificially high and that there are no structural impediments to labour flexibility (eg, specific skill shortages, trade union restrictions). Increased production (ie, supply) rather than demand is the impetus for economic growth, in a direct contradiction to subsequent Keynesian economics. Economic recessions cannot therefore be blamed on an excess or glut of supply; the self-correcting mechanism of a free-market economy will cause any surplus in one good to be offset by a deficit in another, with demand for labour and wages in both industries adjusting accordingly.

A pure *laissez faire* approach generally means a less interventionist fiscal policy. The size of the public sector as a proportion of a national economy is reduced since the government judges that many services can best be provided by the private sector, so less tax revenue is required. The relative lack of government interference also means fewer targets of fiscal interference (to promote or to dissuade activity in one area or another of the economy), which leads to a simpler tax code. This, in turn, can lead to fewer hindrances or distortions to the operation of a free-market economy. The preference for smaller government generally prompts a desire for a balanced national budget even during a recession (a further contrast with Keynesian economics).

The reality of fiscal policy in classical economics, and what is latterly called supply-side economics, is discussed in greater depth below, but is largely based on the idea of the Laffer curve (named after an economic advisor to Ronald Reagan). This states that tax revenue generated when tax rates are 100% of income is the same as when tax rates are 0%, due to the effective disincentive to earn income. It suggests that lowering already high tax rates can actually increase tax revenue, due to the increased incentive to earn and the reduced incentive to seek tax avoidance. The supply-side theory thus proposes lower marginal rate taxes in order to increase investment, thus supply and in turn aggregate demand.

Laffer Curve

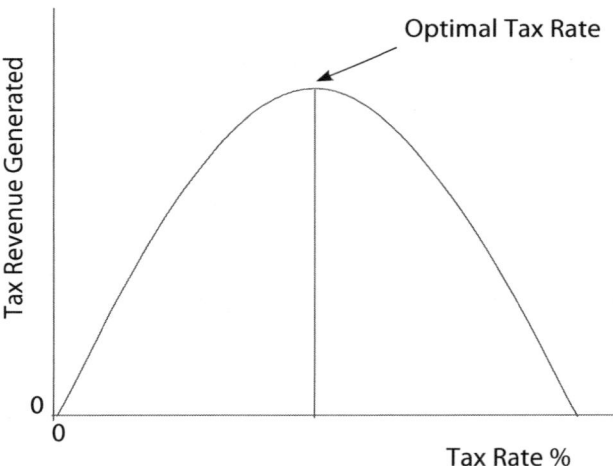

The Laffer Curve is often dismissed as a macroeconomic justification for inherently politically-inspired free-markets policies. It is worth noting, however, that Christina Romer (the former US Chair of the Council of Economic Advisors under President Obama) separately concluded that an exogenous tax increase of 1% of GDP lowers real GDP by roughly 2–3% (http://www.nber.org/digest/mar08/w13264.html). Both inflation and unemployment are assumed to be temporary and relatively self-correcting, as the flexibility of both prices and wages should quickly allow necessary adjustments to occur. In a further example of the theory of demand adjusting to meet supply, an excess of workers would lead to unemployment, if wages were inflexible, yet wage flexibility can instead allow employment levels to remain stable. This leads to the idea that full employment is possible, except where workers refuse to accept wage flexibility, in which case such unemployment is deemed voluntary.

1.5.2 Keynesian Economics

As outlined earlier, although his 1936 publication *'The General Theory of Employment, Interest and Money'* was a radical departure from the principles of classical economics, John Maynard Keynes was an economist originally from the classical school. By seeing the economy as led not by supply but by demand, he proposed however a much greater degree of government intervention.

Aggregate Demand is Determined by both the Private and Public Sectors

Keynes saw that the Classical school of thought was failing to rescue western economies from the depression of the early 1930s, as supply was not generating sufficient demand. This was because decisions taken at a microeconomic level by the private sector can have negative macroeconomic consequences, eg, a weak level of confidence among consumers can become a vicious circle of ever reducing consumer spending in a 'paradox of thrift'. Keynes proposed that government should intervene through active policies to counter such market failures. This necessitates a more mixed economy than in classical economics, guided by the private sector but with government intervention.

Keynes chose to focus primarily on aggregate demand rather than on aggregate supply. Based on the microeconomic behaviour of an individual, he considered what proportion of any additional unit of income would be spent as opposed to saved, in what he called the marginal propensity to consume (MPC).

Private Sector Demand

Income spent by households is considered to be consumption expenditure.

The 'consumption function' expresses how much income will be spent:

$$C = a + cY$$

where:

C = total amount consumed or spent
a = amount consumed when income is zero
c = MPC
Y = total disposable income

Value 'a' is the minimum amount of consumption required by an individual to survive, whereas 'c' is the discretionary factor for what proportion of a person's income will be spent on consumption and, by implication, what remaining proportion will instead be saved.

In graphical terms, the consumption function can be depicted in linear equation where 'a' is the y-intercept (the level of consumption when income is equal to zero) and 'c' is the gradient of the slope indicating the proportion of income allocated to consumption:

Consumption Function

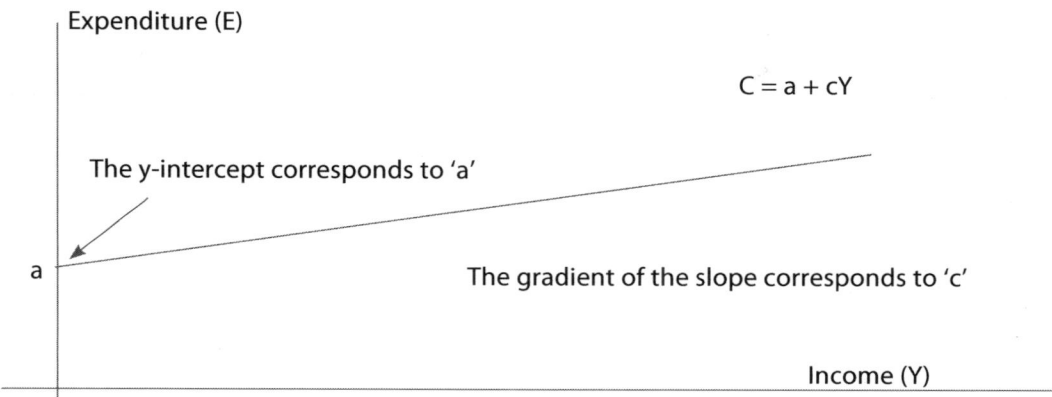

The steeper the slope the greater the propensity to consume and, therefore, the lower the propensity to save.

Although Keynes held that the primary influence on consumption is the level of income, there are additional factors.

- The accumulated net worth or wealth of the individual.
- As people become wealthier and their incomes rise they spend a lower proportion of their incomes.
- The MPC is not a constant; it can change due to the confidence level of individuals and due to their appetites, which Keynes called 'animal spirits'.
- During periods of uncertainty and recession the propensity to consume diminishes, while total income available for consumption may also decrease.
- The availability of credit influences the MPC. Easy access to credit can lead to excessive borrowing which may boost demand in the short term.
- The level of interest rates affects not only the propensity to borrow but also, due to floating-rate mortgages, the level of disposable income for many homeowners.
- Fears of rising inflation can increase the willingness to consume, as individuals seek to avoid erosion of savings.

The overall or aggregate level of consumption in relation to national income as illustrated in the following diagram.

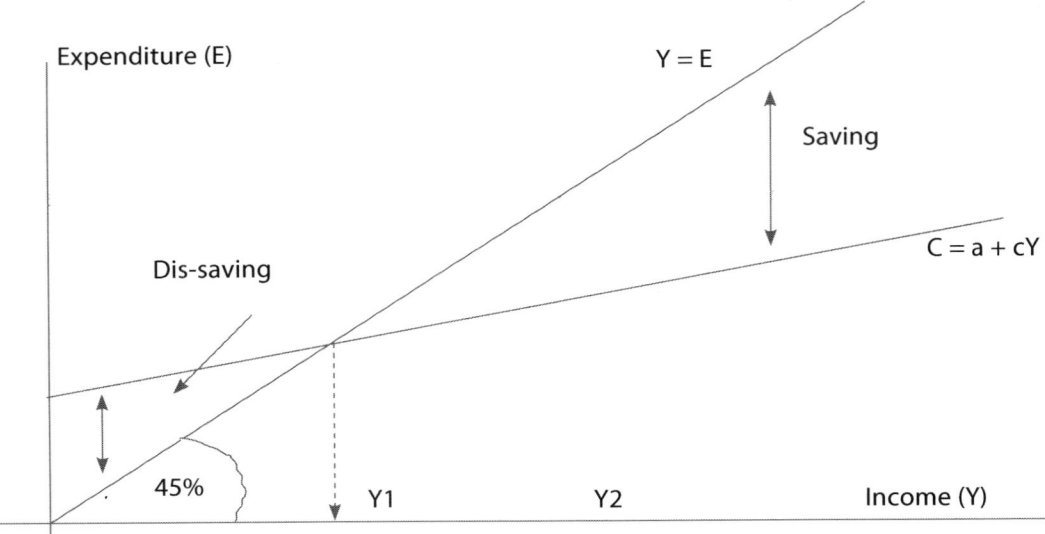

For Keynes, savings was simply that portion of income that was not used for consumption.

The marginal propensity to save (MPS) must therefore be equal to 1− the marginal propensity to consume, or formally:

$$MPS = 1 - MPC$$

Short-term changes in the level of savings can be influenced by the level of interest rates, relative to expectations of inflation, in addition to the same level of confidence which affects the MPC. In the longer-term, however, concerns regarding pensions can also have a significant impact. In the UK, this can involve fears about the value of retirement income from the persistent reduction in recent years in the availability of defined benefit in favour of defined contribution pension schemes, together with potential longer-term effects of government intervention to introduce auto enrolment into employee pension schemes and the gradual extension of the retirement age.

The level consumption in relation to national income is illustrated as follows.

Expenditure: Income minus Savings

The 45° diagonal line Y = E demonstrates an economy where all income is consumed (income = expenditure).

The consumption function line (C = a+cY) shows how much is actual expenditure.

At Y1 income equals expenditure.

At Y2 income exceeds expenditure. Where the expenditure line is below the Y=E line, saving is taking place.

Where (C = a+cY) lies below (Y = E), expenditure is less than income, implying that the remaining income is diverted to savings.

Where (C = a+cY) lies above (Y = E), expenditure exceeds income, implying dis-saving. Consumption is funded by previous savings, fresh debt or from some external source, eg, government assistance.

The greatest short-term effect of a change in aggregate demand is on output and employment, not on prices.

Aggregate Monetary Demand

Keynes recognised the importance of the private sector, yet focused on aggregate demand, ie, including government expenditure.

$$AMD = C + I + G + (X - M)$$

where:

- AMD = aggregate monetary demand
- C = planned consumer expenditure
- I = planned investment expenditure by firms and entrepreneurs
- G = planned government expenditure in its current budgetary policy
- X = planned exports
- M = planned imports
- Therefore (X – M) = planned net exports

According to Keynes, there is no natural tendency for an economy to operate by utilising all available resources (ie, at full employment). He maintained that the public sector alone is incapable of generating full employment. He believed instead that it is the role of government (ie, the public sector) to increase national income through managing aggregate demand.

Demand Management

According to the Keynesian macroeconomic framework, demand management (and specifically, the increasing of national income during a recession) can be achieved via increasing government expenditure, in turn stimulating private sector investment, increasing exports (reducing imports) or by decreasing savings and taxation.

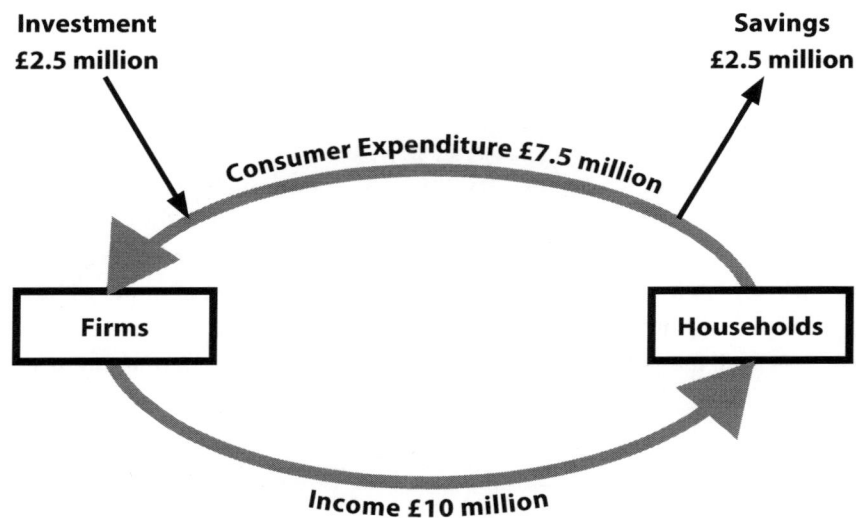

Demand management can be viewed in terms of the earlier circular flow diagram. The flow of national income in this simple model amounts to £10 million and the £2.5 million saved by households is offset by the £2.5 million of investment. Keynes's point was that if the households in this model were withdrawing money from aggregate demand (ie, expenditure), then it was up to government to replace that funding of investment.

The Multiplier Effect

Multiplier effect in a closed economy = $\dfrac{1}{1-MPC}$

where MPC is the marginal propensity to consume.

The change in national income produced by an injection into the circular flow, by increased government expenditure for example, equals the value of the injection times the multiplier.

In addition to an injection of income, eg, through a government stimulus package of increased expenditure on public services, national income will grow by more than the size of the injection itself. The economy in a simple circular flow model will thus increase in size.

Equilibrium conditions are thus disrupted by an injection of investment, creating a stepped progression towards a new equilibrium level at which national income will have expanded by more than the original injection. The degree of such an economic expansion is known as the multiplier and can in theory be measured for a closed economy (ie, a domestic economy without the further distortion of any external trade).

The multiplier effect is also used with reference to banking (or Money Multiplier). Please see also sections 1.5.5 and 3.2.3 below for references to the money supply.

This form of 'multiplier effect' affects a country's money supply and can cause the supply to grow. It comes from the normal business of a bank, ie, borrowing and lending. How much of an effect there is will depend upon the policy of the central bank/government (depending upon the country). The central bank will decide how much of each deposit a bank must hold as reserves (to cover, for example, potential withdrawals, runs). Effectively, banks create more money by lending deposits to other customers, ie, the same money is saved and re-introduced to the money supply as lending (it is calculated by dividing total bank deposits by the reserve requirement).

An Example of the Multiplier Effect

In this example, we assume that the reserve requirement is 20%, ie, for every 100 units of currency a bank receives in deposits, it must keep 20 units in reserve to allow for withdrawals and to ensure that the economy is not starved or flooded with money. This means that, having held 20 units in reserve, the bank can lend the remaining 80 units to other bank customers. The 80 units will then ultimately be deposited by these customers into another bank (or by those that the customers pay with the money). The new bank deposits will mean that the new bank will retain 20%, or 16 units, in reserve but can lend out the remaining 64 units.

In tabular form this looks like:

Bank	Deposit	Lending	Reserves
1	100.00	80.00	20.00
2	80.00	64.00	16.00
3	64.00	51.20	12.80
4	51.20	40.96	10.24
5	40.96	32.77	8.19
6	32.77	26.21	6.55
7	26.21	20.97	5.24
8	20.97	16.78	4.19
9	16.78	13.42	3.36
10	13.42	10.74	2.68
11	10.74	8.59	2.15

This continues as people deposit money and banks continue lending it until finally the 100 units initially deposited create a total of 500 units (100/0.2) in deposits. This creation of deposits is the multiplier effect.

Required Reserves

As stated earlier, the reserve requirement is set by the central bank or government (depending upon the country), and the level of reserve may vary dependent upon the size of the bank/financial institution (thus systemically important banks can hold more reserves than a small challenger bank which is just starting in business), eg, in 2016 in the US, institutions with more than $110.2 million in deposits were required to hold 10% of their total liabilities in reserve.

Money Supply and the Multiplier Effect

As stated earlier, there are different methods of deciding upon the money supply figure (M0 or the monetary base is all of the physical currency in circulation within an economy). The M1 and M2 calculations include adding the balances of deposit accounts and those associated with small-denomination time deposits and retail money market shares, respectively.

Thus, in making deposits to an M1 deposit account, the banking institution can lend the funds beyond the reserve to another person. Although the original depositor still owns the money in their deposit, the bank, by lending the balance (after reserve) creates more funds through lending funds. If the borrower then deposits the funds received from the lending institution, this increases M1 even though there is no real increase in the actual amount of currency.

Central government can thus alter the reserve requirement to tighten money supply (a higher reserve percentage, eg, 25%, would result in a total of only 400 units in the original example). This can cause financial institutions to be more selective in their lending as they have effectively less to lend (and may with a higher rate for lending to maintain profits). On the other hand, the lower the reserve requirement, the greater the increase in the money supply, (and financial institutions may be more willing to lend with a larger amount of money available to lend).

Note that during the financial crisis, banks were 'encouraged' to increase their reserve level, thus reducing the money available to lend to the economy (banks were also 'reluctant' to lend to other banks, because of the fear that they would not survive and not be bailed out by the Government (eg, Lehman Brothers in the US)), thus exacerbating the crisis.

Business Cycles

One of the intentions of Keynesian interventionist policies is to smooth out the peaks and troughs of business cycles. Left to itself, the private sector can tend to overshoot as it alternates between terms of consumer and investment optimism and pessimism. Periods of high demand (economic 'booms') are followed by periods of weaker demand with unemployment 'busts'. This makes the significant assumption that governments are not only able to identify accurately and in a timely manner the turning points from one stage of a cycle to another, but are also able to judge how much stimulus might be needed. It additionally assumes that governments have the political discipline to withdraw such stimulus before growth becomes excessive and causes inflationary pressures. The success or otherwise of governments in successful manipulation of such cycles in consumer and investment confidence is keenly debated among economists, often with a high degree of subjectivity on either side of the argument.

The very slow movement in the business cycle, experienced since the financial crisis in 2008, has made it more difficult for investors to decide where to invest. In a normal business cycle with a relatively predictable movement from one phase to the next, it is possible to identify industry sectors which are likely to benefit and, thus, investors can search for companies which show better than average potential. An example of sectors which benefit in each phase is given below.

Macroeconomics

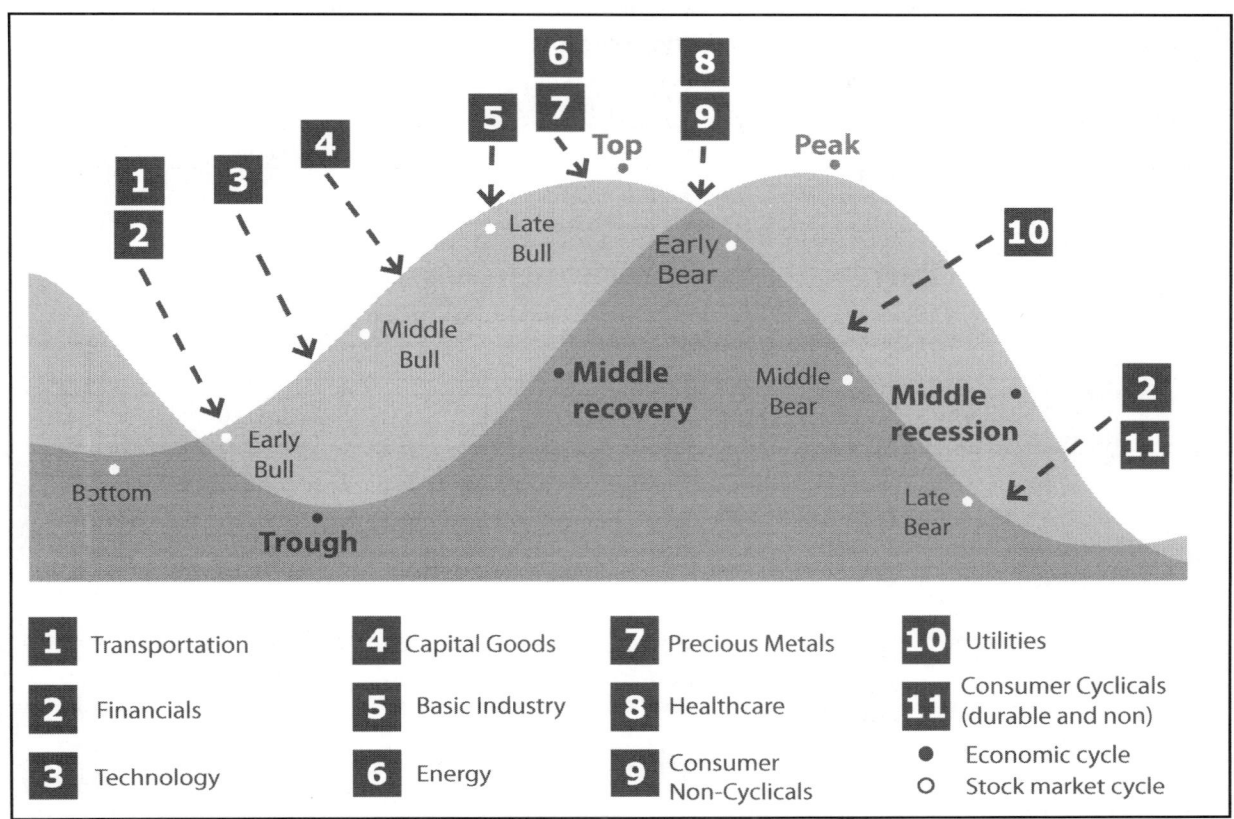

Inflexibility of Prices and Wages

This is in contrast to one of the core tenets of classical economics, in which both prices and wages demonstrate considerable flexibility. A major consequence of the Keynesian belief is that, as the business cycle dips into recession, wages do not decline in order to reflect weakening demand and to offset a new surplus of workers. This can quickly lead to unemployment, which in turn can exacerbate the weakening confidence and accelerate the recessionary amplitude of the business cycle. It is this feature which Keynes believed requires government intervention to offset.

Fiscal Policy

A central aspect of Keynesian economics is the need for an active fiscal policy as a means for government to stimulate demand in periods of weak private sector consumption and investment. The nature of the fiscal intervention depends on the nature of the gap between actual aggregate demand and that level which is needed to generate a full utilisation of resources, including full employment.

A recessionary gap occurs when the level of aggregate demand is lower than that required level.

An inflationary gap occurs when the level of aggregate demand is greater than that required.

Fiscal policy requires interventions in either scenario:

- a budget deficit to correct the under-utilisation of resources resulting from a deflationary gap
- a budget surplus to correct the over-utilisation of resources resulting from an inflationary gap.

Keynesian Model for Fiscal Policy

Keynesian Deflationary Gap

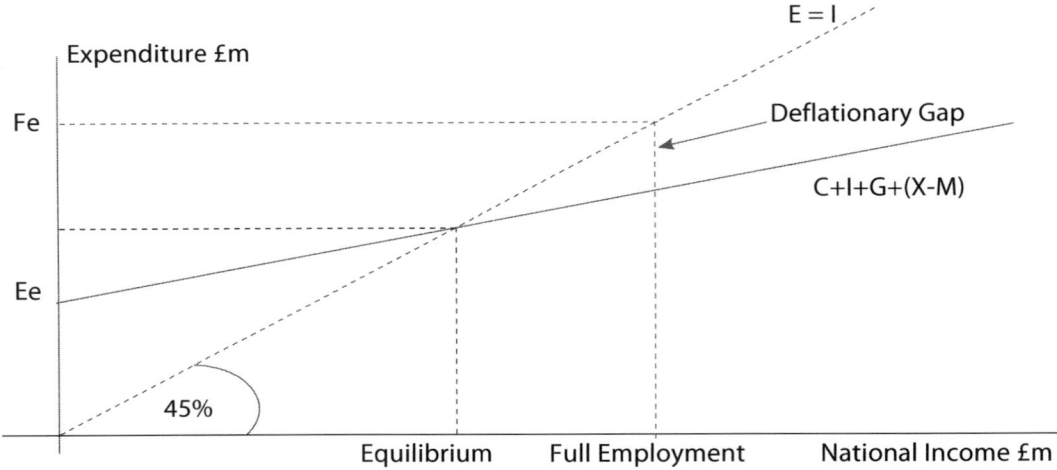

The line E=I represents an equilibrium level of economic activity, where expenditure equals income, in line with the theory of the earlier circular flow model of a closed economy.

The line C+I+G+(X−M) represents the Keynesian level of aggregate demand in the economy, with the same components as outlined above.

Where this line intersects the line E=I, the economy is in equilibrium, but without a full utilisation of resources, including full employment.

The Keynesian solution is to stimulate the level of aggregate demand, so that the aggregate demand line intersects with the equilibrium line at a higher level, ideally at full employment.

The current difference, at the level of full employment, between the equilibrium line and the aggregate demand line represents a deflationary gap.

Assuming such a goal as full employment, a government might increase expenditure by way of a budget deficit to close the deflationary gap, so that the aggregate demand line rises to meet the equilibrium line.

In the short term, the principal method for increasing aggregate demand is to increase the G component of the equation, which may take the form of a stimulus or injection into the economy from increased expenditure in public services and public infrastructure projects.

Keynesian Inflationary Gap

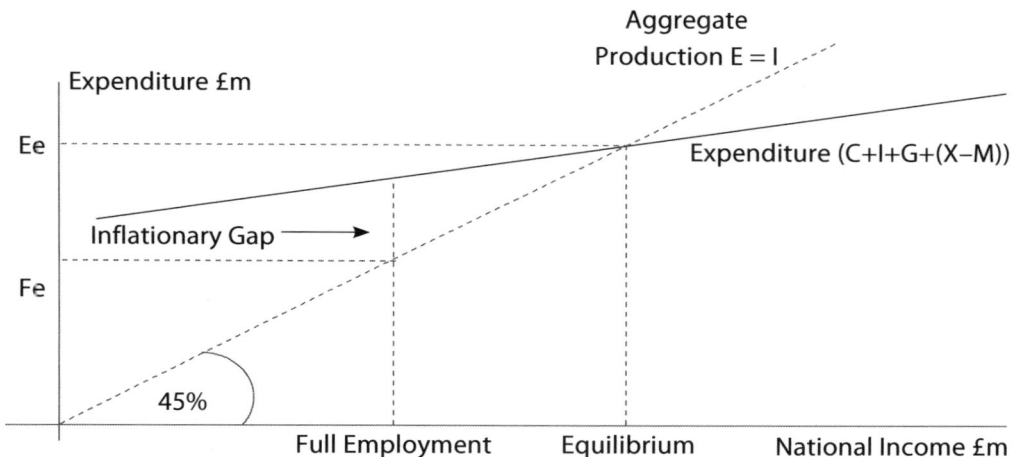

The alternative scenario, which is seen less frequently, is where aggregate demand (C+I+G+(X-M)), intersects with aggregate production, E = I, at a level which is beyond full capacity and full employment. This can eventually reflect inflationary pressures in the economy, although Keynes believed that changes in aggregate demand have a more immediate impact on output and employment than on prices or wages.

A government should implement a tighter fiscal policy which reduces aggregate demand. If the economy is operating beyond full capacity then net government expenditure should be reduced and the inflationary gap closed.

1.5.3 Employment and Inflation: Phillips Curve

An inverse relationship between unemployment and inflation, as devised by A.W.H. Phillips after Keynes published his *General Theory*, has been adopted by many Keynesian economists, despite being challenged over the last 30 years or so by Monetarists on the grounds of weakening evidence (see the following diagram). It was based on nearly 100 years of UK inflation and employment data in the 19th and 20th centuries.

The Phillips Curve

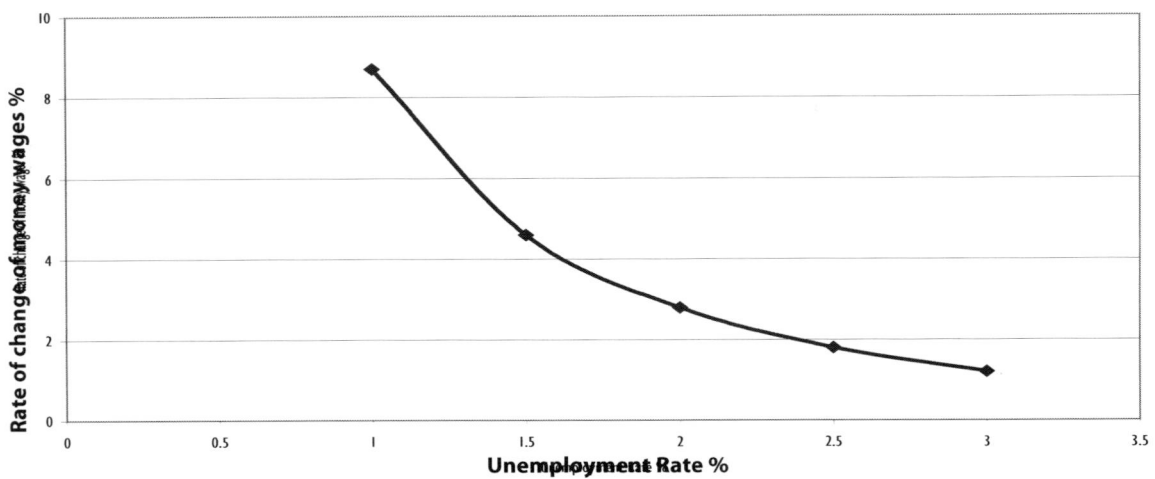

Phillips Curve

The broad nature of the supposed relationship is that if unemployment is high, then wages rise only moderately, while if unemployment is low, then wages rise more strongly. Wage inflation is often taken by economists to represent inflation in general.

The rationale is that in times of low unemployment there is less surplus labour available, so firms must pay more to attract the scarcity of supply. This price pressure weakens when unemployment rises and firms no longer need to pay as much to attract workers. Phillips plotted this inverse relationship to produce a curve to illustrate it at different levels of unemployment over a typical business cycle. This relationship can vary in terms of scale among different national economies, although following the same principle, allowing governments to treat it as a model for setting bespoke economic policies. If, for example, an overriding policy is to keep unemployment below a certain % threshold, the precise level can theoretically be set with apparent confidence in how much inflation would ensue.

The Phillips curve is only viable as a macroeconomic tool of government if it is accepted that aggregate demand can increase real GDP, in line with Keynesian principles. This would cause firms to employ more workers, causing wage inflation as the economy approaches full capacity (ie, lower unemployment).

The phenomenon of stagflation (rising unemployment and inflation) in the 1970s defied the previous evidence of the Phillips curve however, which in turn led to the adoption of Monetarist theories (see below) that inflation is caused primarily by a rise in the money supply. The original study was based on around a century of data, so it is futile to argue whether the principle is relevant or not on samples of just a few years here or there. It is notable however that there is no evidence that any of the leading monetary authorities in the world are currently explicitly targeting both employment and inflation in line with the Phillips curve, even though some consideration to it may arguably have been implicitly given by the Bank of England in recent years.

1.5.4 Monetarist Economics

It can generally be said that most monetarists have more in common with the *laissez faire* beliefs of classical economists than with the aggregate demand-led and interventionist tendencies of Keynesian economics, yet many classical economists reject the key tenet of monetarism: that the most important policy is to maintain control of the money supply.

As observed earlier, while Keynes had been devising his economic theory before the Great Depression of the 1930s, it was the failure of classical economics to cope with the weakness of that environment which prompted his ideas to be adopted widely in preference to the orthodoxy of nearly two centuries. Likewise, Milton Friedman and others at the University of Chicago had been formulating the principles of what is known as monetarism for some time before it became clear that Keynesian economics was unsuited to the 'stagflation' (high levels of inflation amidst weakening or even negative growth). It might be argued that each successive school of thought is adopted not only due to the strengths of its argument, but also due to the perceived failure of the prevailing theory.

1.5.5 Inflation and the Money Supply

The Chicago school of monetarism maintains that there is a close and stable link between inflation and the money supply. Inflation results from excessive growth in the money supply, and can only be regulated by controlling through central banks.

Friedman questioned the use of fiscal policy as a tool of demand management, and held the view that the government's role in the guidance of the economy should be severely restricted.

Friedman was a keen student of economic history and wrote extensively on the subject of the Great Depression of 1930s, which he called the 'Great Contraction'. He argued that it had been caused by an ordinary financial shock whose duration and seriousness were greatly increased by the subsequent contraction of the money supply caused by the misguided policies of the Federal Reserve, the US central bank. Most recently a former chairman of the Federal Reserve, Ben Bernanke, also a student of 1930s' economics history, has published material agreeing with Friedman on this diagnosis of the mistaken policy of money supply tightness during that period.

During the 1980s under the political leadership of President Reagan and Prime Minister Thatcher, together with the chairmanship at the US Federal Reserve of Paul Volcker, monetarism gained the upper hand over Keynesian thinking.

Monetarism focuses on the impact of inflation as a distorting influence in the marketplace. Inflation must be controlled before any other economic problems can be solved.

A problem with inflation is that if it is either too high or too low it may produce fears of a recession, leading to reduced economic activity and higher unemployment.

Impact of Excessive Inflation
- Reduced spending power for individuals, especially those on fixed incomes.
- Erosion of confidence that future returns on investments will cover the costs of capital.
- Higher effective export prices, possibly offset by a lower exchange rate.
- Increased price instability and **volatility** surrounding price movements.

- Higher nominal interest rates, increasing the perceived cost of financing but eroding real value of **bond** assets.
- Relatively lower real interest rates, reducing incentives to lend.

Impact of Insufficient Inflation or Deflation

- Given the prolonged periods in economic history when inflation has been relatively high, it has traditionally been unusual for economists and policymakers to be too concerned about deflation.
- Deflation, when prices are actually declining, is often perceived as a problem every bit as serious as inflation. Economists argue that deflation will lead to reduced demand as consumers delay expenditure, reducing potential returns to businesses and investors causing further declines in income and consumption in a downward spiral which is known as the liquidity trap, 'a deflationary spiral'.
- A further concern about deflation, is that repayment of personal and public debt becomes more onerous in a deflationary rather than inflationary environment where the real value of the debt is eroded as nominal wages and prices increase. Others express concerns about the alternative view and suggest that an inflationary stance towards easing the debt burden can lead to a debasement of currencies.

Monetarism is not a new doctrine. It is based upon the Fisher equation of money, which derived originally from Copernicus, and was acknowledged by both Marx and Keynes, but it has been adopted more fervently by monetarists. Monetarism was nevertheless a challenge to Keynes's focus on short-term in terms of demand management, in that it incorporated the Fisher equation into a coherent explanation of how an economy operates in both the short and long term.

Using the Fisher equation, and a number of assumptions, monetarists developed a model that explains inflation. The key assumption is that the velocity of money is a constant.

Quantity Theory of Money

This was refined by Irving Fisher in the early 20th century and subsequently became a foundation stone of the work of Milton Friedman.

$$MV = PT$$

where:

- M = money supply (stock of money)
- V = velocity of circulation (number of times a unit of money is exchanged)
- P = average price of transactions in a period
- T = total volume of transactions in a period

Assume that M equals £5 million and that the following transactions of a typical consumer are representative for the economy as a whole.

The consumer buys £5 of goods from a retailer and the retailer then spends this £5 on two types of products or services for herself, eg, a newspaper and a cup of coffee. The original purchase of £5 has effectively paid for a total of £10 of goods. Money supply is measured in terms of the total value of all transactions taking place, ie, £5 + £2.50 + £2.50. The velocity of circulation can be simply measured as £10 ÷ £5 or 2.

The number of transactions that take place in this simplified model is three and if this typical pattern were extrapolated to a million consumers the total number of transactions, T, that would take place during a week, would be three million.

The average value of the transactions, P, would be:

$$\frac{£(5 + 2.5 + 2.5)}{3} = \frac{£10}{3}$$

Putting the figures together in the quantity theory of money equation gives:

$$£5 \times 2 = \frac{£10}{3} \times 3, \text{ ie, } £10 = £10$$

As it stands, the theory does not appear to reveal too much beyond the fact that money spent in a period must equal the receipts during that same period. When the theory becomes more valuable is in an examination of the parameters to the equation.

Monetarists, like Friedman, argued that the velocity of circulation, V, tends to be fairly stable over time. Monetarists propose that the total volume of transactions, T, is subject to slow and incremental growth as the productive capacity of the economy expands gradually. So, if both V and T, from their perspective, are relatively stable, the relationship between M and P must be the most critical to determining the level of prices.

The key idea of monetarism is that excessive growth in the money supply, brought about by excessive intervention of governments within the economy, causes inflation. This leads to one of the principal areas of difference between monetarists and Keynesians in their view of the role of government stimulus, and it arose especially, according to Friedman, with regard to the explanations and remedies proposed for unemployment. In particular, monetarists have a view on what they refer to as natural unemployment.

1.5.6 Natural Unemployment

Natural unemployment in monetarist theory, arises because of a misperception by employers as to the true supply conditions of labour in the marketplace. More specifically unemployment can often be explained through frictions and distortions in the labour market such as immobility of labour, inadequate training, the power of trade unions, lack of information about jobs available and seasonality. This differs from cyclical unemployment, which occurs when there is not enough aggregate demand in the economy to provide jobs for everyone who wants to work, in line with the ebb and flow of the business cycle.

Supply side theory (closely aligned with monetarists) believes that by removing the frictions and inefficiencies on the supply side of labour the economy can move closer to true full employment, unlike the Keynesian view, which is that this is only attainable through demand management.

Monetarists believe that demand management will not only not produce full employment, but that through demand-side interventions in the economy, the money supply will be expanded beyond its 'normal' equilibrium levels, thereby creating inflation.

In opposition to Keynesian thinking, which suggests that even if labour markets were perfect there could be high levels of unemployment, and as implicit criticism of this view and an endorsement of the classical view of free markets, the factors already mentioned (the power of trades unions, for example) will bring about a mispricing of labour and, therefore, unemployment.

Natural Unemployment

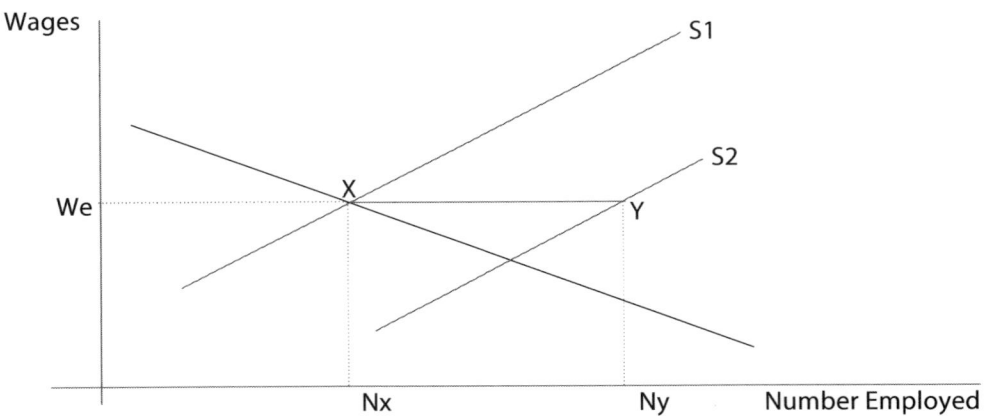

Natural unemployment is the difference between Ny and Nx

Natural unemployment arises because of a misperception by employers as to the true supply conditions of labour in the marketplace. In the diagram above, the downward-sloping line represents the demand for labour. The supply of labour is complicated by factors such as immobility and restrictions imposed by trades unions such that S1 is the supply curve that is presented to employers, whereas the true supply curve would be to the right and is indicated by S2. The equilibrium reached in this market is not a true clearing price for labour, which would be obtainable if the market did not have the supply-side imperfections.

The demand for labour and the equilibrium wage are set at point X and are equal to We on the vertical scale. The supply side argument is that this wage is an artificially created level, based upon the restricted supply of S1, whereas under true market conditions, the numbers employed at this wage level can be extended to the point of intersection of We on the line S2 at Y. The difference between Ny and Nx is the outcome of this supply side restriction and is the underlying cause of unemployment, and attempting to remedy this natural level of unemployment without removing the restrictions and frictions on the supply side will lead to inflation and market distortions.

This critique of imperfections in the labour market gave rise to an associated school of economic thinking advocated by monetarists, known as 'supply-side economics'. The key notion to this body of thought, which was influential during the 1980s, was that markets should be as free as possible, and that removing all kinds of supply-side frictions – not only in the labour market but also with regard to taxation and customs duties on international trade, for example – eliminates many distortions in the marketplace and allows the forces of supply and demand to work properly.

Exercise 1

Outline three principal changes to economic policy that the UK Government can make to help raise demand in the economy.

The answer to this exercise can be found at the end of this chapter.

2. Classical, Keynesian and Monetarist Approaches (2)

Learning Objective

1.2   Appraise the effectiveness of Classical, Keynesian and Monetarist approaches in the context of macroeconomic government policy targets and instruments

In natural sciences, it is normally possible to assess the role and importance of individual constituents in any experiment. This is because each component can be defined and quantified with precision and consistency and can thus be observed in isolation, often under laboratory conditions. Economics, especially macroeconomics, is no natural science however. As described in section 1, the three main schools of economic thought have never been completely distinct from each other, particularly in their implementation. Macroeconomic theories may be devised by economists, but they are implemented by politicians who operate in an environment of compromise and psephology (a statistical study of elections and voting trends).

Politicians from the left and the right often respond to criticism of the effectiveness of their policies by saying that they have been unable to implement the purity of their particular theory of choice. Without constant distortions of short-term political necessity, they claim they could deliver much more of what they promise. The same could be said of macroeconomists, who have even less control over applying their processes. Macroeconomics, like politics, is a social rather than a natural science.

2.1   Political Compromise

In many developed economies, there are nowadays two barriers to a pure application of any of the major economic theories. One of these is the political necessity for compromise, whether within coalition governments or between factions of a majority party. In theory a government which has been elected in a democratic process can claim to have a clear mandate to implement in full the economic policies set out in its manifesto. In reality, such mandates rarely exist. Consider the recent history in the US and UK.

2.1.1 The US

In the 20th and 21st centuries there have been numerous instances of presidents having to win support from opposing majorities in at least the Senate, if not also the House of Representatives. This affected in particular, Dwight Eisenhower, Richard Nixon, Gerald Ford and George HW Bush from the Republicans, but also to varying degrees Ronald Reagan, Bill Clinton, George W Bush and Barack Obama, especially in the later years of their administrations.

Notable recent examples of the contrast between Congressional support and opposition in terms of economic policy implementation can be found with Obama (2009–17). With Democratic Congressional support at the outset, he launched a Keynesian USD 787 billion economic stimulus, including temporarily nationalising major car companies and stimulating new car purchases. Later, Republican Congressional control severely impacted policies, including raising the debt ceiling and significant healthcare reforms.

It is perhaps no coincidence that the benchmark implementation of Keynesian economics occurred during the Democratic presidency of Franklin Roosevelt (1933–45), supported by strong Democratic majorities in Congress, thus helping to enact the economic policies of the 'New Deal'. It may appear striking therefore that Reagan (1981–89) was able to implement many of the tenets of Monetarism in the 1980s, despite Democratic control of the Senate for much of his presidency, but this was largely due to the compatible monetary policy of Paul Volcker (Chairman of the Federal Reserve), as described below.

2.1.2 The UK

Apart from in the US, Keynesian economics was most widely adopted in the UK. Following World War II, the Labour government introduced the welfare state, including the National Health Service (NHS), as well as the privatisation of the Bank of England, railways, coal mines and other significant industries and utilities. Both Labour and Conservative governments, in what amounted to a national economic consensus, continued to implement various forms of mixed model Keynesian policies for three decades of relatively strong economic growth and low unemployment, which have been described (perhaps ironically) as the Golden Age of Capitalism.

Just as the UK was a good example of the success of Keynesian policies at first in a relatively closed economy, so too was it an example of their weaknesses as the economy became less competitive internationally. Although some of the problems were arguably due to industrial policies and poor trade performance, including strong government control over investment, one dramatic consequence was the 14% devaluation in sterling in 1967. Arguably this cured the symptom of the trade deficit rather than the underlying issues of low productivity, which reflected instead the Keynesian approach of government control rather than a free-market or *laissez-faire* Classical approach; it is impossible to prove one way or the other. It was, however, finally the onset of stagflation in the 1970s which introduced Monetarism as an alternative model.

The administration of Margaret Thatcher (1979–90) is closely associated with Monetarism, given the emphasis on controlling inflation via the money supply at the expense of initially sharply higher unemployment and a deep recession. This was combined with, in time, a looser fiscal policy of reduced taxes as well as an increase in *laissez-faire* economics through the privatisation of many industries which had been nationalised under earlier Keynesian policies. Yet despite relatively comfortable parliamentary majorities, Thatcher faced continuous opposition within her own party over the political aspects of Monetarist policies. This arguably allowed the more Keynesian welfare state to remain largely intact, especially in healthcare and education.

It is harder to argue for any defined economic profile of subsequent governments, whether Labour, Conservative or coalition. The 'third way' policies of the Blair governments (1997–2007) broadly attempted a Keynesian return to government demand-led intervention, running budget deficits, and a national minimum wage, though not involving widespread renationalisation as in the post-war period. Yet they also attempted to retain monetary discipline through an immediate decision to assign responsibility for monetary policy to the newly-independent Bank of England. The principle aim of this has been to meet an inflation target (set by the government), with secondary aims to support government economic objectives for growth and employment. The significance of this was to bring the UK in line with other major economies, who had already assigned monetary policies (and in some cases monetary targets) to their own independent central banks, but it also removed the ability of governments to pursue comprehensively Keynesian policies in the future. Both the Brown government of 2007–10 and the Conservative/Liberal Democrat coalition government of 2010–15 were in economic terms dominated largely by the global financial crisis. Brown dramatically increased public debt, nationalising two major banks, whereas the coalition aimed to reduce the budget deficit by dramatically cutting public spending, in an anti-Keynesian policy of ignoring demand-led economic growth.

2.1.3 Open versus Closed Economies

The second issue with assessing the success of economic models is that it is easier to assess these in national economies which are relatively closed (ie, less dependent on foreign trade and investment), as they are less prone to any impact from other economies as well as to currency fluctuations. One reason why Keynesian economics remained effective in the US and UK for so long may have been that his ideas were initially implemented at a time of exceptionally low international trade during the Great Depression of the 1930s and subsequently during World War II. Keynes was notably one of the proponents of capital controls and pegged exchange rates at the 1944 Bretton Woods Agreement. For a while, this notionally insulated each national economy from the uncertainty of capital flows and volatile exchange rates, allowing widespread Keynesian policies to persist.

Some economists would argue that this not only papered over the cracks of developing differences in productivity and competitiveness, but may have exacerbated them. This period highlighted another practical problem in assessing economic theories under static, laboratory conditions: innovation. In order to circumvent capital controls, financiers devised the eurodollar market to raise US dollar financing outside the jurisdiction and regulation of the US, thus weakening the Keynesian restriction. The Bretton Woods system of capital and exchange controls persisted until 1971, despite the effects of both such innovation and growing economic imbalances. At that point, President Nixon cancelled the convertibility of the US dollar into gold, thus effectively bringing an end to the Bretton Woods system of pegged exchange rates. Exchange rates between major currencies quickly began to float, which undermined further the relative purity of Keynesian national economic models. Capital controls were lifted in major economies over the next few years, including the UK in 1979.

As globalisation has increased over recent decades, many economies have become more open to international trade as a significant component in their GDP. Many western countries adopted this many years ago, with more recent manifestations in countries such as China and South Korea, but this has

applied also to countries whose major exports are commodities (eg, Russia and Brazil). Such economies are vulnerable not only to volatility in commodity and currency markets, but also to more global investor sentiment in their fiscal policies. Growing dependence on international funding of fiscal deficits reduces the scope for purer forms of Keynesian economic policies, if these show the slightest signs of weakness, as the cost of funding those deficits can very quickly rise.

Realistic assessment has become harder in recent decades, due to increasing globalisation in trade and the development of financial markets, especially in countries regarded as emerging economies. Both have had the effect on the one hand of neutralising to varying extents the impact of largely domestic economic policies, whilst also highlighting the differences in policy of countries which pursue radically different policies (eg, a fixed exchange rate, more overtly Keynesian policies such as full employment at the expense of rising inflation, rising budget deficits). Any reliance on debt issuance to fund such deficits (especially via short-term debt requiring frequent reissuance) makes it harder to maintain long-term economic policies which may be out of favour with short-term international investors.

In theory, it should be easier for countries to adopt purer forms of one economic theory or another, where they are apparently insulated from exchange rate fluctuations against their major trading partners, for example, in the eurozone area.

Even in countries which share a common currency but which adopt different economic and fiscal policies, there is no real insulation from the same effect of actual currency volatility on the ability to maintain a truly national economic policy of one kind or another. In the eurozone for example, it is no longer possible to devalue the currency in one member state where it is effectively overvalued. Before the euro was introduced in 1999, international investors could pass judgement on the relative strength of currencies within the European Monetary System (forerunner of the euro) by buying one (typically the Deutschmark) and selling another. This alone made it harder for any of these countries to implement and assess any pure economic theory (especially Keynesian) in isolation from other European trading partners, though it did allow some countries to rely on devaluation to alleviate some of the pressures of domestic economic underperformance. Since 1999, however, investors have found a proxy to selling overvalued currencies by instead selling the government bonds of that country and buying the bonds of other governments (eg, the German Bund), ie, trading the **spread** between government bond yields. The effect is to raise the cost of borrowing for the weaker country to reflect the perceived risk of being able to compete on global markets and thus to repay the debt.

The Bretton Woods system was designed partly to insulate member states from international currency flows and exchange rates, thus allowing Keynesian economic policies to operate with greater effectiveness at a national level; the eurozone is likewise designed to reduce pressures on national economies from other member states. Both instances demonstrate instead the resourcefulness of markets to devise means of assigning the scarce economic resources to where they are most effective, whether through the eurodollar market in the past or through trading European government bond yield spreads. This shows the limits of the longer-term effectiveness of some economic models (Keynesian) and the resilience of others (*laissez-faire* Classical).

3. Macroeconomics and Markets

Learning Objective

1.3 Analyse the impact of macroeconomics on the behaviour of markets, sectors, companies and investment themes

Economic policy pursued by governments has, as one of its principal objectives, the preservation of the purchasing power of the currency, although other objectives are also common. It has been asserted by the US, for example, that China has brought about a deliberate weakening in its currency (the yuan) in recent years, in order to maintain a substantial trade surplus with western countries. Prior to the introduction of the euro in 1999, several southern European countries similarly relied on currency weakness for many years to maintain trade competitiveness, which enabled them to defer politically difficult structural reforms to improve productivity. In the case of the UK, the government, through its fiscal policies and the Monetary Policy Committee (MPC) of the Bank of England (BoE), with the exercise of monetary policy, is mindful of the need to avoid heightened volatility in the purchasing power of sterling and to ensure its continued perception as a store of value. The main force of erosion to sterling's purchasing power within the international economy will be the rate of inflation.

Governments and central banks have learnt that there is a close but subtle relationship between the rate of inflation and the prevailing rates of interest, especially short-term rates.

To provide a historical overview of the subject of this section, the following diagram provides a very useful insight into the relationship between the CPI, as a measure of inflation, and the average base rate, as a measure of interest rates seen in the UK from January 2003 to January 2017.

UK Inflation and Bank Rates (January 2003–January 2017)

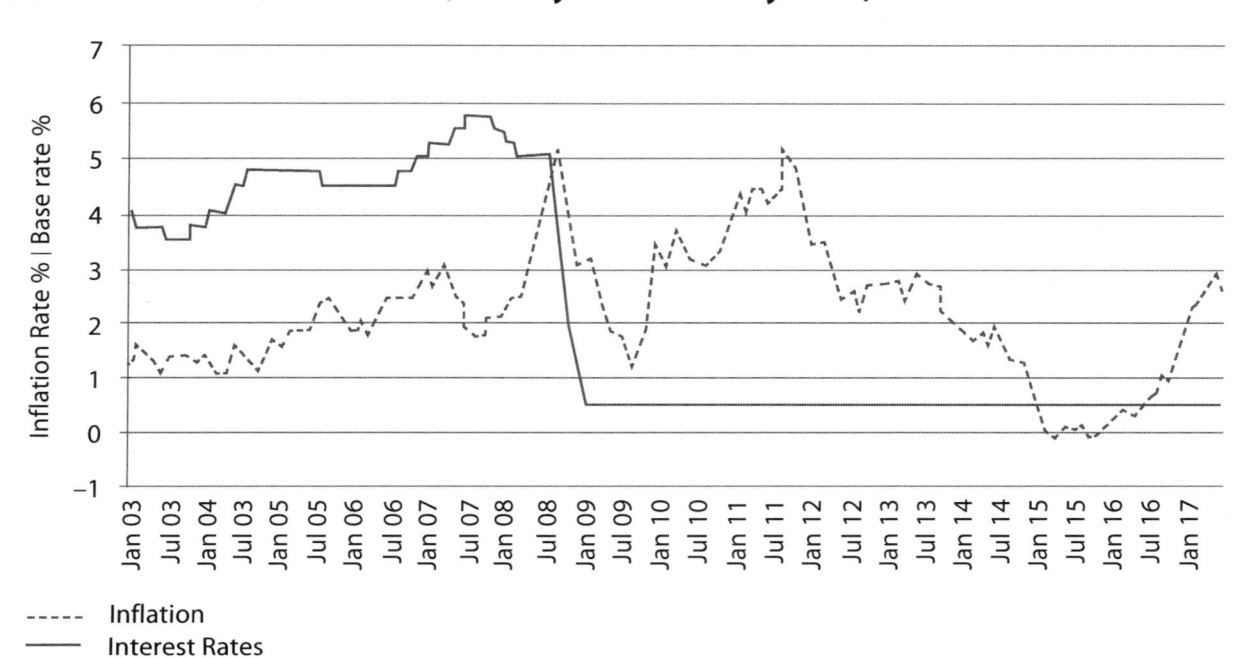

----- Inflation
——— Interest Rates

Source: economicshelp.org, ONS D7G7 \\ BoE

In 1991, the rate of inflation was 14% per annum with a base rate of 8%.

As the CPI dropped during the 1990s the base rate tracked downwards as well but not at the same rate. The direction of the two rates has been well correlated even if the magnitudes of the changes have not. In more recent years, when the rate of inflation has been a lot tamer and closer to a 3–4% annualised average, the base rate has itself remained subdued.

In 2016, the base rate of interest was set by the BoE at 0.25% – its lowest level ever, with inflation moving up slightly to around 1% in late 2016. In November 2017, the BoE increased the official rate of interest from 0.25% to 0.50% – the first increase since July 2007; at the same time, inflation was around 3%. The mechanism by which the UK Government sets the target, around which the MPC must aim to maintain inflation, is discussed further in section 4.2 of this chapter.

In order to explain the manner in which inflation and interest rates have moved historically and the policy implications, some of the standard terminology and economic theory is first examined.

3.1 Measures of Inflation

3.1.1 Consumer Price Index (CPI)

In December 2003, the Chancellor of the Exchequer changed the UK inflation target to a new base, the CPI, which was based on the European Union (EU) harmonised index of consumer prices (HICP). This index has gradually been used more and more as a benchmark inflation rate by the government and other institutions relative to a previous measure, the retail price index (RPI).

The CPIY is the CPI but without indirect taxes, eg, value added tax (VAT), stamp duty and excise duty. The aim is to give the underlying inflation figure, ie, after any effect of indirect taxes has been removed. The result usually shows the underlying inflation rate to be lower than the headline rate.

The CPI-CT includes indirect tax rates, but keeps them constant at the rate which was in effect at the beginning of the year.

The graph below illustrates inflation from the period between March 2007 and March 2017, as demonstrated by the CPI and the older RPI measure. The reason for the variation in the graph lines relates to the way in which each index is calculated differently.

UK Inflation (March 2007 to March 2017)

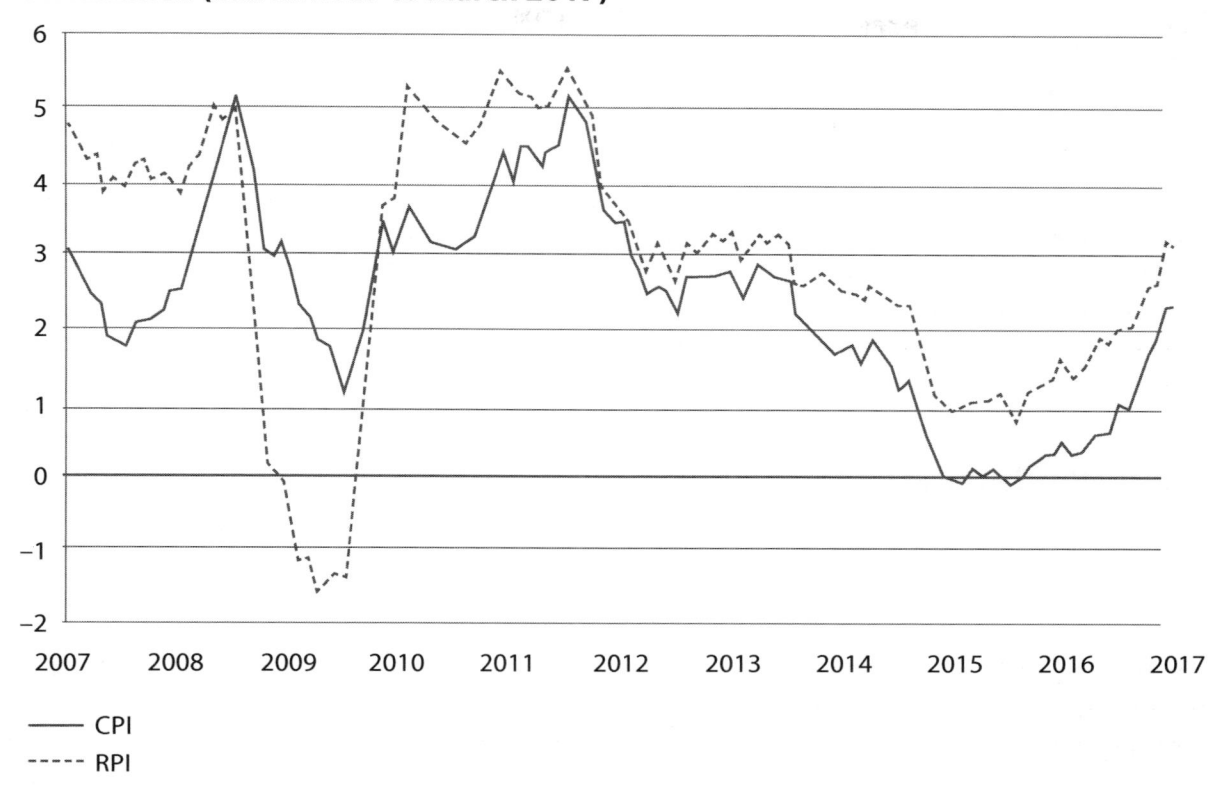

Source: ONS

— CPI
----- RPI

The level of the CPI inflation target for the BoE's MPC was set at 2% in December 2003. Note, that state pensions, and many state benefits, have now moved to being increased in line with the CPI, while some investments, such as index-linked gilts, continue to be calculated, with reference to the RPI.

The CPI is calculated each month by comparing the price of a sample of goods and services that a typical household might buy and pay for, including heating, household goods and travel costs, with the price of the same goods and services one year ago. The UK's inflation rate fell to 0% in August 2015, and was almost flat for most of the year. Inflation has failed to increase due to a sharp fall in oil prices and a continuing supermarket price war. However, in September 2016, the rate of inflation began to increase following the UK referendum to leave the EU and a level of unexpected economic growth.

HICPs were originally developed in the EU to assess whether prospective members of the European Monetary Union (EMU) would pass the required inflation convergence criterion, and then to act as the measure of inflation used by the European Central Bank (ECB) to assess price stability in the eurozone.

There are significant differences between the CPI and the RPI. The CPI excludes a number of items that are included in the RPIX (which is the RPI, excluding the impact of mortgage payments), mainly related to housing. These include council tax and a range of owner-occupier housing costs such as mortgage interest payments, house depreciation costs, buildings insurance and estate agent fees.

The CPI covers all private households, whereas the RPIX excludes the highest earners and also pensioner households, who derive most of their income from state benefits.

The CPI also includes some items that are not in the RPI, such as unit trust and stockbroker charges, university accommodation costs and student tuition fees. Although, in most cases, the same underlying price data is used to calculate the two indices, there are some specific differences in price measurement. For example, different methods are used in the CPI and RPI to adjust prices for quality improvements in new cars and personal computers.

The two indices are also calculated differently. The CPI uses the geometric mean to combine prices within each expenditure category, whereas the RPI uses arithmetic means. The different techniques used to combine individual prices in the two indices tend to reduce CPI inflation relative to RPIX (one major exception being the 2008 recession); this is known as the 'formula effect'. When the Chancellor announced the changeover in target measure, the annual rate of RPIX exceeded the CPI by more than 1%.

3.1.2 Producer Price Index (PPI)

Producer price index (PPI) measures inflationary pressures at an earlier stage in the production process. Input prices measure the change in prices going into the production process. This will include raw materials and other inputs. Changes in commodity prices will directly affect this number.

Output or factory gate prices measure the changes in the price on goods as they leave the production process and enter the retail sector. There is obviously a very strong relationship with input price variation.

Historically, any rises in raw material prices have tended to pass on through the productive process and result in higher retail prices. In recent years, the generally low level of inflation, coupled with the more competitive nature of the labour market, has made it increasingly difficult for producers to pass on price increases. Consumers are now used to stable prices and are unable to force their wages up in order to compensate for higher prices.

3.2 Interest Rates

3.2.1 The Classical View of Interest Rates

According to the framework of classical economics, the approach taken by this school of economic theory analyses and accounts for the determination of interest rates based on the supply and demand of loanable funds. The theory makes a few assumptions follows:

- Supply of loanable funds in this context refers to the funds available for borrowing, which in turn is determined by the quantity of savings.
- Savings are interest rate-elastic, in other words the volume of savings or postponement of consumption depends to a large extent on the interest rate paid to those with savings.

Diagrammatically we should expect to see an upward-sloping curve for savings, ie, loanable funds, based on the rate of interest.

Macroeconomics

Supply Curve for Loanable Funds

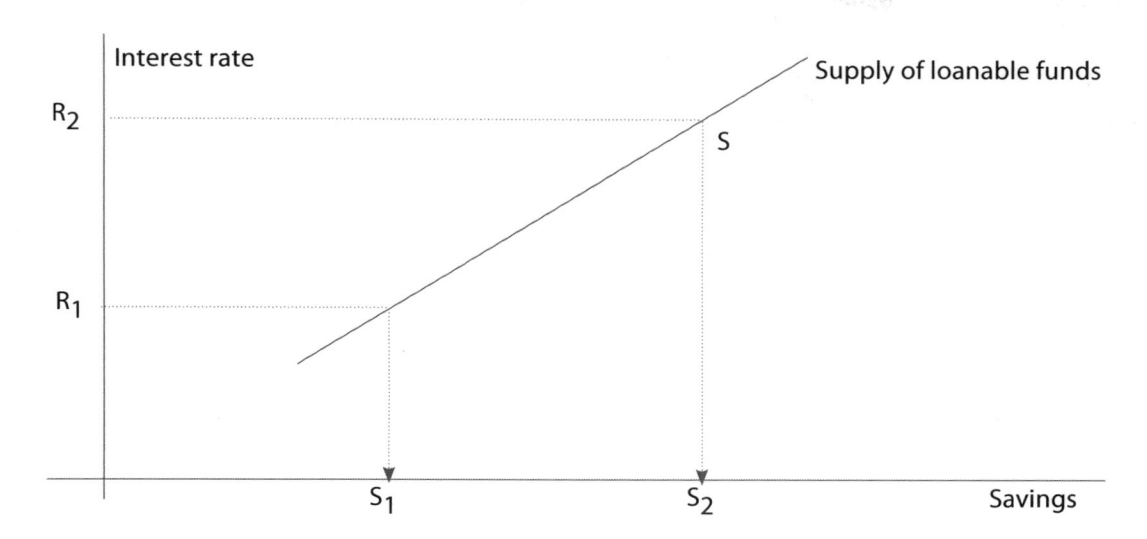

The higher rate of interest being offered at R_2 will intersect with the supply of funds as reflected in the line S at a point which will lead to a higher rate of savings (S_2) than would be applicable at the lower rate of interest (R_1).

The demand for loanable funds comes from the propensity of firms to invest in new business undertakings, as well as consumers' requirements for mortgages and similar products. The main assumption is that investment is interest rate-elastic and that the curve will be downward-sloping.

Demand Curve for Loanable Funds

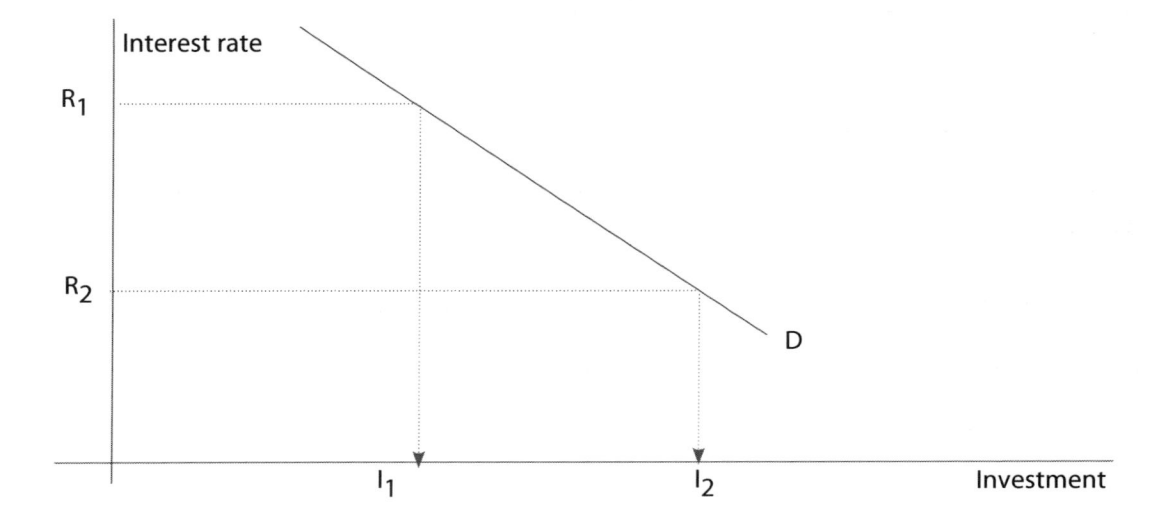

The demand for loanable funds (D) falls as interest rates rise so that at an interest rate of R1 the volume of investment will be I_1, whereas this will expand as the interest rate declines to R_2.

Bringing together the equilibrium level for the supply and demand for loanable funds will result in the setting of a price for such funds – in other words, the interest rate and funds loaned are at equilibrium.

Supply and Demand Equilibrium

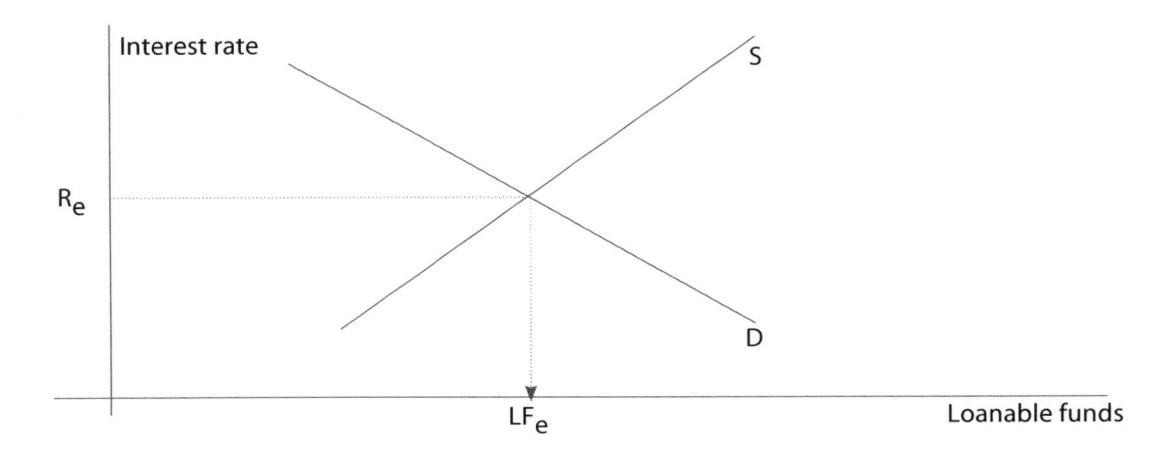

[Graph showing supply curve S (upward sloping) and demand curve D (downward sloping) intersecting at equilibrium point, with R_e on the interest rate axis and LF_e on the loanable funds axis.]

The classical view of interest rate determination is unsurprising given the reliance on market forces, but in terms of macroeconomic issues which affect supply and demand, and of external forces outside the perfect markets presumed by economists, the model has limits in terms of explaining how interest rates are actually set.

3.2.2 The Keynesian View of How Interest Rates are Determined

For Keynes, one of the key notions behind the manner in which interest rates are determined is to take the perspective of the individual investor or saver and examine their so-called liquidity preference.

Liquidity

- Cash is the most liquid asset because it is immediately available and acceptable.
- Government securities are easily converted to cash as there is a deep secondary market for them.
- Many large stocks traded on major exchanges are liquid.
- Assets like property, art and antiques are very illiquid as it may take considerable time to find someone willing to pay an acceptable amount of cash for the asset.
- Liquidity crises can arise when only cash is sure to be readily acceptable, eg, Long-Term Capital Management (LTCM) hedge fund crisis of 1998, when it collapsed the global financial system due to poor trading strategies, and the banking crisis of October 2008.
- As liquidity increases, ie, the asset becomes more like cash, the interest paid on the asset will tend to decrease.

Keynes maintained that investors prefer liquid, low interest-bearing assets rather than less liquid ones that may generate more income such as long-term corporate and government bonds. This is known as the 'liquidity preference theory'. Three cornerstones for Keynes as to this preference for liquidity were the following:

- There was something Keynes called the 'transactions motive' which reflects the convenience of having liquidity available conveniently to take immediate advantage of appealing opportunities.
- Secondly, there was the 'precautionary motive' which reflects the desire to have funds available for contingencies (emergencies).
- The other principal motive for wanting liquidity is the 'speculative motive', which is the desire to have funds available for speculation rather than committed to long-term assets.

So for Keynes, the rate of interest is, unlike the notions presumed by the classical theory, not achieved through the equilibrium level sought out by the supply and demand for investable funds. Rather it is to be perceived as a reward for parting with liquidity. One of the advantages of the Keynesian explanation of how interest rates are determined is that it provides the dimension of risk aversion to the factors affecting the appetite for those willing to supply loanable funds, as well as those wanting to use them for investment purposes.

This premise also lays the foundation for an explanation of the different rates of interest that are required by investors and savers, depending on the following factors which are not readily explainable under the classical view:

- The duration of the commitment of the funds being loaned out.
- The credit risks of the borrower.
- The opportunity cost for the funds – what other returns are available for the use of funds?
- What are the expectations with regard to the future direction of interest rates?
- What are the expectations with regard to the business cycle, the level of economic growth and unemployment?
- What are the expectations with regard to the future course of inflation?

3.2.3 Do Markets or Central Banks Set Interest Rates?

Although the formal procedures for setting the base rate have been described as the outcome of a process of deliberation by the MPC of the BoE for the UK and sterling money markets, there is a market background to these deliberations. The members of the MPC will be aware of the activities of traders and institutions in the money markets who are continually expressing a view on the appropriate level of interest rates and their future direction.

The opinions of traders around the world concerning exchange rates, bond rates and prices for short-term money market instruments are based on the perception of the views of other traders concerning the macroeconomic background and, specifically, their outlook for gross domestic product (GDP) growth, employment and most especially, inflation.

If participants in the money markets are becoming apprehensive about the risk of inflation, they will be pushing up the rates required on making funds available to the borrowers and investors as they will want to be compensated by a real rate of return which will include a **premium** to cover the expected erosion of purchasing power due to inflation.

The term money market (or bond market) vigilantes has arisen to describe the powerful constituency of interests in the money markets which is constantly assessing the future direction of global GDP growth, cost pressures, inflation in general terms, and the size of the premium to be paid in the calculation of the rate of interest for so-called inflation risk.

A recent view (in early 2018) held by some institutional investors and traders in financial markets is that central banks are beginning to lose control of interest rates. It is believed that when they set official rates they are really in effect echoing the views which have already been expressed by the decision-making processes that take place on a daily basis in the relevant markets which trade government bonds, **derivatives** and short-term money market instruments. The allegation is held to be especially the case with regard to longer-term interest rates for government bonds, for example, but is even becoming a widely held view, especially in times of volatility, with regard to the setting of short-term rates as well.

One reason to doubt this hypothesis, however, is the fact that central bank deliberations are closely monitored by the markets, and central banks, from time to time, have shown their capacity to surprise markets with decisions on the exact levels of interest but also by other expressions of monetary policy. Although a more detailed analysis will be laid out in section 4 of this chapter, it will be useful to review in summary form the manner in which central banks can affect the money supply and availability of credit, which is a major determining factor in setting interest rates.

Money Supply

The money supply is the stock or quantity of money that is present in the economy at a specific time. However, we need to distinguish between 'narrow' and 'broad' money supply. Narrow money measures aim to control the money supply that is actually held for use in transactions. Broad money includes narrow money, but also includes money that may be held as a store of wealth. UK measures are as follows:

- Narrow money is that which is highly liquid and used for current spending – notes and coins, cash with banks, known as M0.
- M0 plus retail sterling deposits with banks and building societies is known as M2.
- Broad money includes narrow money, but also includes balances held as savings. One definition only includes retail savings (ie, small deposits held by individuals), the other includes wholesale savings which are much larger and usually held by companies and financial institutions.
- The BoE monitors the ranges of both M0 and M4 (see below) which is the broadest monetary aggregate.

Globally, money supply can be described as follows (but beware that many countries apply unique criteria to each measure, so the overview below is approximate and will vary in precise national compositions):

- **M0** – in some countries, such as the UK, M0 is shown to include bank operational deposits with the central bank; therefore, it can also be called the monetary base (or narrow money).
- **M1** – M0 but excluding bank reserves.
- **M2** – M1 plus 'close substitutes' (eg, short-term time deposits held in banks, plus 24-hour money market funds), ie, it is a wider description.
- **M3** – M2 but also includes large and long-term deposits; the US has not used M3 since 2006.
- **M4** – M3 but also includes commercial paper.

Macroeconomics

Money Supply Equilibrium

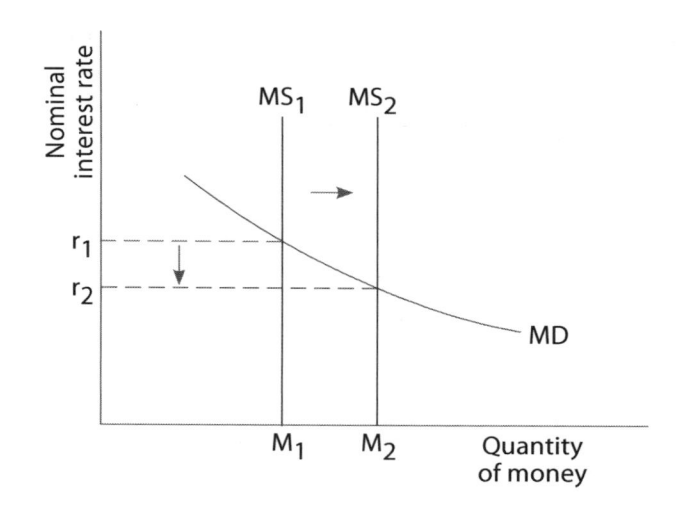

The diagram shows, from a classical point of view, how the ability of the central banks to alter the money supply can drive, from the viewpoint of simple supply and demand, the applicable rate of interest.

MD represents the demand for money and is assumed in this simple model to remain stationary (ie, the demand curve does not move). MS_1 represents the money supply at one moment in time and this is then increased to MS_2. The equilibrium rate of interest given MS_1 is equal to R_1 and with the expanded money supply of MS_2, the equilibrium rate of interest is lower at R_2. Tightening the supply of money would have the converse effect of moving the rate of interest upwards.

Examining how central banks can affect the monetary environment through their control of the money supply and their *de facto* ability to set short-term, official interest rates suggests that, in answer to the question posed earlier, the feedback of signals and influences between the markets and the central bankers is a complex one in which perhaps both entities have to be considered as co-determining interest rates.

Another important consideration with regard to the relationship of interest rates and inflation is seen in what is termed the yield curve.

Yield Curve or Term Structure of Interest Rates

As already indicated there is a pattern to interest rates in the monetary environment and this is well represented by the different interest rates that are in effect at any time across the spectrum of maturities for loan or debt instruments. Specifically, in the market for government securities, there is usually a notable difference between the rate that is paid on a 30-day Treasury bill and a 30-year Treasury bond or gilt.

Here are some of the chief characteristics of the yield curve:

- The yield curve is the relationship between the interest rate and the time to maturity of government securities.
- It is currency-specific, for example, there is a sterling yield curve and a US dollar yield curve.
- It is closely watched by economists and traders, and is commonly plotted in a graphical format which depicts the 'shape' of the yield curve.

- More formal mathematical descriptions of this relation are often called the 'term structure' of interest rates.
- The yield curve is normally upward-sloping with longer-dated securities having a higher yield than shorter-dated securities. This would follow from the Keynesian liquidity preference theory.
- However, the yield curve can also be flat or downward-sloping (inverted).

Shape of the Yield Curve

The shape of the yield curve is believed to be a combination of three theories acting together:

- expectations theory
- liquidity preference theory
- market segmentation theory.

In general terms, the precise shape of the yield curve encapsulates the market's expectations of the future direction of interest rates.

A steep upward-sloping yield curve suggests that the market believes that interest rates will rise in the **future**. A borrower in such circumstances may not want to enter into long-term borrowing arrangements with variable rates as the cost of servicing the borrowing is likely to increase.

Expectations Theory

- The shape of the yield curve varies according to investors' expectations of future interest rates.
- A steep upward-sloping curve suggests investors expect rates to rise in the future.
- Buyers of bonds will defer the purchase of longer-dated securities as they will expect to receive higher yields in the future.
- A downward-sloping curve or inverted curve suggests that markets believe that rates will fall.
- Bond purchasers will be keen to lock in higher yields now as the expectation is that they will decline in the future.
- A flat yield curve suggests that the market thinks that rates will not materially change in the future.

Liquidity Preference Theory

- This is the view expounded by Keynes which is that investors have a natural preference for holding cash rather than a government security (even if the latter also has low **credit risk**).
- Investors need to be compensated for holding longer-dated securities with marginally higher yields as the holding period increases.
- The theory leads to the conclusion that the 'normal' shape of the yield curve will be upward-sloping.

Market Segmentation Theory

- This theory rests on the view that investors have different time frames of reference and different approaches to risk and the volatility of bond prices.
- Typically, banks will invest in shorter-term securities, while pension funds and insurance companies will be buyers of longer-term securities (in UK gilts) to reflect the nature of their liabilities.
- The two ends of the yield spectrum are driven by different interests and perceptions.
- The above is sometimes used to explain the tendency for there to be a wiggle in the middle of the curve (ie, the five-year holding period).

4. Fiscal and Monetary Policy: Inflation, Interest Rates and Exchange Rates

Learning Objective

1.4 Evaluate the effect of fiscal and monetary policy on inflation, interest rates and exchange rates

There are several different policy options which can be employed by central banks and governments to influence and regulate the macro-economy. Governments will tend not to use these in isolation but may decide to place more emphasis on one broad kind of policy at different times in response to particular economic circumstances. The three broad kinds of policy which we shall review are fiscal policy; monetary policy; and exchange rate policy.

In the UK, there is currently no specific strategy for influencing the exchange rates of sterling against other major currencies. The determination of these rates, as will be seen later, results from the daily trading in the **foreign exchange (FX)** markets. By adjusting monetary policy, for example, by increasing/decreasing the base rate, the BoE might hope to influence the exchange rates which prevail in the markets, but there is currently no mandate to attempt this, so any such effect is a byproduct of more general monetary policy.

In the past, however, governments have, at times, attempted to target exchange rates as specific policies. The last occasion was during UK membership of the Exchange Rate Mechanism (ERM), which was abandoned in 1992. Since then the external value of sterling has been allowed to 'float' (see section 3.3) and to be set by the markets.

4.1 Fiscal Policy

Fiscal policy refers to the manipulation of government spending and taxation for the achievement of macroeconomic aims. Before Keynsianism and monetarism, policy was set according to the theory that the economy would self-balance. It was believed that the level of employment and the public budget would reach a state of equilibrium, where taxes and public expenditure were in harmony.

The next section considers the monetarist view of the fundamental limitations of this view that the macro-economy is self-regulating, but the main motivation behind Keynesianism was to address the shortcoming of the classical view and its manifest failure to explain and provide the necessary policy objectives to move the world economy out of the Great Depression of the 1930s.

Keynes advocated in his work *The General Theory of Employment, Interest and Money* that governments had to play a far more interventionist role in the economy and that this role should be primarily implemented through fiscal policy. In essence, the revival of Keynesian thinking among economists and policymakers following the near financial meltdown of 2008, and the subsequent global recession, stems from the view that governments have to inject stimuli into the economy to boost demand for economic activity and that this requires the governments to engage in fiscal stimuli (as well as requiring supporting monetary policy).

Governments in the UK, the US and other major economies confronted an initial rise in unemployment and a drop-in demand for goods and services after the 2008 financial crisis by increasing their public expenditures and by running fiscal deficits. That is, they have been allowing public deficits – the difference between tax revenues and public expenditure – to rise. Some commentators are becoming increasingly anxious that the size of deficits in the public finances are unsustainable and could be sowing seeds for a crisis in the public finances of certain economies.

The UK Government's public sector net borrowing requirement is known formally as the public sector net cash requirement (PSNCR) – often expressed as a percentage of GDP. The chart below shows how this moved from a modest surplus, even before the 2008 financial crisis, to a deficit above 15% in 2010; since then, however, it has steadily decreased. The latest Government policy changed following the 2017 general election; it is no longer seeking to eliminate the deficit entirely.

UK Public Sector Net Borrowing (excluding public sector banks) 1993-2018

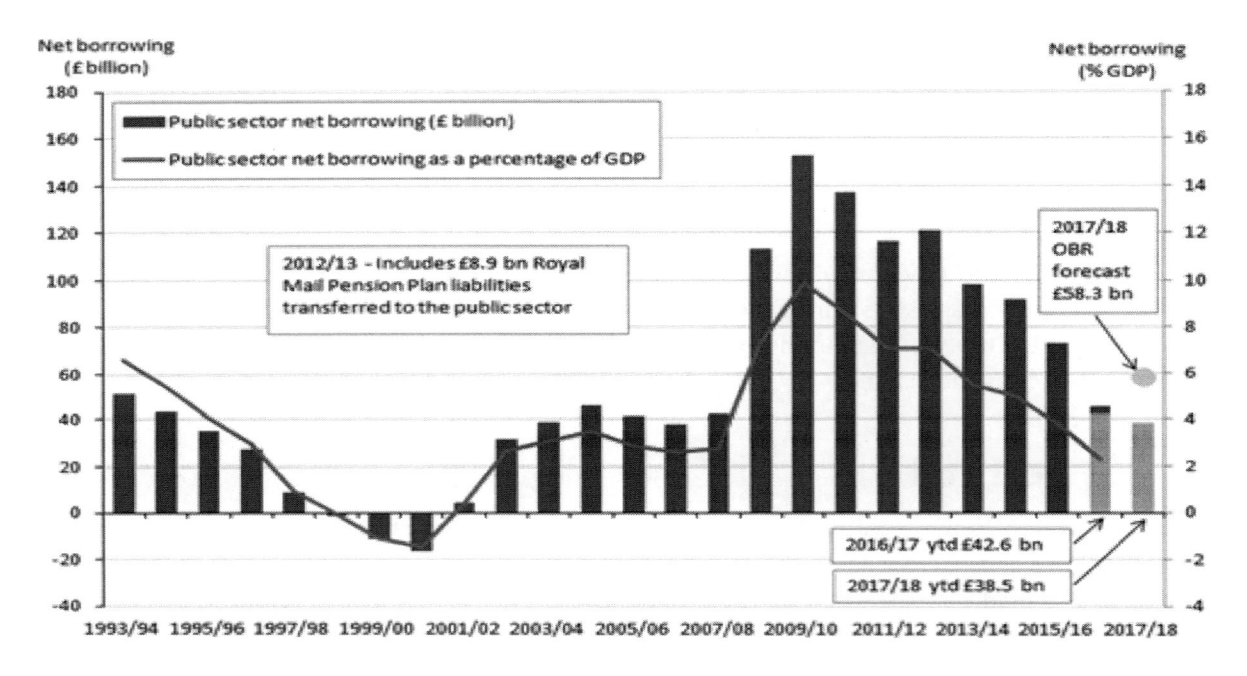

Source: ONS

The desirability of undertaking such large-scale borrowing is a source of much contentious debate among economists. Broadly speaking, the Keynesians believe that it is vital to stimulate the economy and to increase final aggregate demand and are less concerned about the size of the PSNCR than the risk of a deflationary spiral which could potentially lead again to the levels of unemployment seen in the 1930s. On the other hand, the monetarists believe that, in the longer term, the creation of such massive deficits and borrowing by the central government runs the risk of higher inflation after the recovery and higher interest rates to pay for the deficit, which will also impact on the private sector's appetite for capital investments. The Office for Budget Responsibility (OBR) was created in 2010 to provide independent and authoritative analysis of the UK's public finances. It is one of a growing number of independent fiscal watchdogs established around the world.

4.1.1 Definitions of Terms

Fiscal policy can be conducted in a variety of ways. For example, increased government expenditure which has been fully-financed by increased taxation revenue is a 'balanced-budget' increase in expenditure, whereas increased government expenditure which has not been financed by increased taxation revenue is an example of a 'deficit-financed' increase in expenditure. The following are the possible outcomes of fiscal policy:

- **Budget surplus** – government income > government expenditure.
- **Budget deficit** – government income < government expenditure.
- **Balanced-budget** – government income = government expenditure.

4.1.2 Principles of Taxation

Adam Smith in *The Wealth of Nations* described the four canons or principles of taxation:

- **equity** – taxes should be levied according to the taxpayer's ability to pay
- **certainty** – there should be unequivocal rules with regard to the levying and administration of taxes
- **convenience** – should not be wasteful and confusing
- **economy** – the tax should be easy and inexpensive to administer.

Direct and Indirect Taxation

- A direct tax is one levied on income or wealth, eg, income tax.
- An indirect tax is one levied on expenditure, eg, value added tax (VAT).
- An ad valorem indirect tax is levied as a percentage of expenditure, eg, VAT at 20%.
- A specific indirect tax is levied as a fixed amount per unit, eg, taxes on petrol.
- A regressive tax is one when the proportion of tax decreases as income, wealth or expenditure rises.
- A progressive tax is one when the proportion of tax increases as income, wealth or expenditure rises.
- A proportional tax is one when the proportion of tax paid is the same regardless of income, wealth or expenditure.

Overview of Types of UK Taxes (2018–19)

- **Income Tax** – direct and progressive:
    - The personal allowance is £11,850, reduced by £1 for every £2 that an individual earns over £100,000, until the personal allowance reaches nil.
    - The basic rate is 20% payable on the first £34,500.
    - The rate on taxable income from £34,501–£150,000 is 40%.
    - There is a top rate of 45% on taxable income above £150,000.
    - Numerous other allowances are available.
    - Different rates and allowances can apply in Scotland.
- **National Insurance Contributions (NICs)** – direct, with multiple levels and conditions.
- **Corporation Tax**:
    - This applies to corporate profits, is 19% from 1 April 2018.
    - Please note that there is a 20% special rate for the entire profits of unit trusts and open-ended investment companies (OEICs).

- **Capital Gains Tax (CGT)** – this applies to gains made from the sale of assets, although there are exclusions, eg, primary residences. The annual exemption is £11,700 for individuals. The tax rate is 10% for basic and starting rate taxpayers, and 20% for higher and additional rate taxpayers.
- **Inheritance Tax** – the threshold is 325,000, with varying rates.
- **Council Tax** – direct; however, as it is based on the value of the property, and not necessarily reflective of the income levels of occupants, it can be (from the point of view of income) a regressive tax, meaning that it takes a larger percentage of income from low-income earners than from high-income earners.
- **VAT** – indirect and regressive.

4.2 UK Monetary Policy

Monetary policy refers to the decisions with regard to the level of interest rates and the money supply. In the UK, these are the responsibility of the MPC of the BoE. The BoE defines monetary policy as *'the process by which the BoE sets the interest rate – and sometimes carries out other measures – in order to reach a target rate of inflation'*. As well as the base rate, it uses less conventional tools, such as quantitative easing (QE), to meet this target. Subject to the inflation target, the monetary policy objective is to support the Government's economic objectives, including those for growth and employment.

The BoE was given formal responsibility for this by the UK Treasury in the Bank of England Act 1998. It now has operational independence to manage monetary policy, previously within the domain of the Chancellor of the Exchequer, but within a band of 1% either side of an inflation rate target which is still set by the Chancellor in a formal annual remit. This target has been 2% since 2003, measured since 2016 as the CPI. Although this is set as a forward-looking and medium-term (undefined) target, the Governor of the BoE must send an open letter of explanation to the Chancellor if the CPI breaches either side of the target band.

The MPC comprises nine members (the Governor, three Deputy Governors for Monetary Policy, Financial Stability and Markets and Banking, the Chief Economist and external members appointed by the Chancellor) who meet eight times a year.

4.2.1 Overseas Monetary Policies

European Union (EU)

It is important to remember that each jurisdiction, with its own independent currency maintains its own monetary policy. Therefore, within the EU, those 19 countries which are members of the eurozone have a collective monetary policy under the ECB in Frankfurt. They each retain their own national central bank, but their responsibilities are now largely restricted to regulatory roles and to managing national reserves. The remaining nine non-eurozone EU members (ie, UK, Sweden, Denmark and several from Eastern Europe) still, however, have their currencies and, therefore, their own monetary policies. Some are committed to eventually joining the eurozone as part of their EU membership, so their monetary policies are in varying degrees of convergence with that of the ECB. Both Sweden and the UK have long been exempt from the eurozone, so both countries have far greater independence in their monetary policies, in the UK's case even before its decision to leave the EU.

Like the BoE, the ECB has operational independence, but it also enjoys political and legal independence. No EU institution or government can attempt to influence its decisions, yet it is accountable to the European Parliament. It is widely regarded as the most independent of the world's major central banks, in that it both sets and implements its own monetary policy. It has only one primary objective: to maintain price stability by keeping the Harmonised Index of Consumer Prices (HICP) close to but below, 2%. Note that, unlike the BoE, this target is asymmetric, ie, there is a ceiling but no formal floor.

4.2.2 Direct Credit Controls

- Historically, the BoE has from time to time, especially during the 1970s, implemented a policy of direct credit controls.
- Credit controls are mandated curbs or limitations on the ability of the commercial banking sector – which is known as the credit transmission system – to provide additional credit facilities to their customers.
- In theory, the Bank could reintroduce formal credit controls to limit the rate of growth of certain aspects of the money supply and the ability of commercial banks to grant credit.
- These controls directly target the banking system through the regulation of loans. Since this does not fit ideologically with the monetarist approach to the free market it is seldom advocated as a means of monetary control.
- Credit controls have been a technique of monetary control employed by the ECB.

4.2.3 Quantitative Easing (QE)

Quantitative easing (QE) is a rather unorthodox method of boosting the money supply, which in 2009 was adopted as a part of the monetary policy repertoire of the BoE. The aim is to get money flowing around the UK economy when the normal process of cutting interest rates is not working – most obviously when interest rates are so low that it is impossible to cut them any further. This has also been adopted in Europe and also in the US, Japan and Switzerland.

In such a situation, it may still be possible to increase the quantity of money. In the UK, the way to do this is for the BoE to buy assets in exchange for money. In theory, any assets can be bought from anybody. In practice, the focus of QE is on buying securities (like government debt, mortgage-backed securities or even equities) from banks.

So the obvious question might be: where does the BoE get the money to buy all these securities? The answer, to put it rather bluntly, is that it just creates it. There is not even a requirement for it to turn on the printing presses and actually increase the monetary base of notes in circulation. The BoE can just increase the size of the commercial banks' accounts at the central bank. These accounts held by ordinary banks at the central bank go by the name of reserves. All banks have to hold some reserves at the central bank. But when there is QE, they build up excess reserves.

If banks swap their securities for reserves, the size of their own balance sheets shrinks just as the central bank's balance sheet expands. The supposition is that the commercial banks, with reduced pressure on their own balance sheets, will be able to lend more to their customers, which in turn will increase the liquidity available in the economy and thus promote higher aggregate demand.

Nevertheless, QE is not considered to be a conventional form of monetary policy. Practically, the BoE creates new money to buy financial assets such as government bonds or shares. This process aims to directly increase private sector spending in the economy and return inflation to target (2%). In reality, this has resulted in an increase in both bond and stock prices by around 20%, but has not yet resulted in the expected increase in spending.

4.2.4 Summary of Recent Monetary Policy

The BoE's MPC sets monetary policy to meet the 2% inflation target in order to help sustain growth and employment in the UK economy. In 2016, it voted for a package of measures designed to provide additional support for growth, and to achieve a sustainable return of inflation to the target. This package comprised a 25 basis point cut in the Bank Rate to 0.25% (although interest rates were increased to 0.5% in November 2017), a new term funding scheme (TFS) to reinforce the pass-through of the cut in the Bank Rate, the purchase of up to £10 billion of UK corporate bonds, and an expansion of the asset purchase scheme for UK government bonds of £60 billion, taking the total stock of these asset purchases to £435 billion. The last three elements will be financed by the issuance of central bank reserves.

Following the UK's decision in June 2016 to leave the European Union (EU), the exchange rate has fallen and the outlook for growth in the short- to medium-term has weakened markedly. The fall in sterling is likely to push up on CPI inflation in the near term, as for instance, imports become more expensive, hastening its return to the 2% target and probably causing it to rise above the target in the latter part of the MPC's forecast period, before the exchange rate effect dissipates thereafter. In the real economy, although the weaker medium-term outlook for activity largely reflects a downward revision to the economy's supply capacity, near-term weakness in demand is likely to open up a **margin** of spare capacity, including an eventual rise in unemployment. Consistent with this, surveys of business activity, confidence and optimism suggested that the UK was likely to see little growth in GDP in the second half of 2016.

These developments have created a 'trade-off' for the MPC between delivering inflation at the target and stabilising activity around potential. Part of the MPC's remit requires it to explain how it has balanced that trade-off. Given the extent of the likely weakness in demand relative to supply, the MPC judged it appropriate to provide an additional stimulus to the economy, thereby reducing the amount of spare capacity at the cost of a temporary period of above-target inflation. The MPC thought that not only would such action help to eliminate the degree of spare capacity over time, but because a persistent shortfall in aggregate demand would pull down on inflation in the medium term, it should also ensure that inflation does not fall back below the target beyond the forecast horizon. Thus, in tolerating a temporary period of above-target inflation, the MPC expected the eventual return of inflation to the target to be more sustainable.

The MPC believed that the cut in Bank Rate would lower borrowing costs for households and businesses. However, as interest rates are already near zero, it will be a challenge for some banks and building societies to reduce deposit rates much further, which in turn might limit their ability to cut their lending rates. In order to mitigate this, the MPC is launching a TFS that will provide funding for banks at interest rates close to the Bank Rate. This monetary policy action has been designed to help reinforce the transmission of the reduction in the Bank Rate to the real economy to ensure that households and firms benefit from the MPC's actions. In addition, the TFS is intended to provide participants with a cost-effective source of funding to support additional lending to the real economy, providing insurance against the risk that conditions tighten in bank funding markets.

The expansion of the BoE's asset purchase programme for UK government bonds is intended to create a monetary stimulus by lowering the yields on securities that are used to determine the cost of borrowing for households and businesses. It is also likely to trigger portfolio rebalancing into riskier assets by current holders of government bonds, further enhancing the supply of credit to the broader economy.

Purchases of corporate bonds could provide more stimuli than the same amount of gilt purchases. Given that corporate bonds are higher-yielding instruments than government bonds, investors selling corporate debt to the Bank could be more likely to invest the money received in other corporate assets than those selling gilts. In addition, by increasing demand in secondary markets, purchases by the Bank could reduce liquidity premia, and such purchases could stimulate issuance in sterling corporate bond markets.

The MPC expected that, by its three-year forecast horizon, unemployment will have started to reduce and most of the economy's spare capacity will have been reabsorbed, while inflation will be a little above the 2% target. In its projections, the cumulative growth in output is still around 2.5% less at the end of the forecast period than in the MPC's projections. Much of this reflects a downward revision to potential supply that monetary policy cannot offset. However, monetary policy can provide support as the economy adjusts.

The MPC believed that the package it announced contains a number of mutually reinforcing elements, all of which have scope for further action. The MPC can act further along each of the dimensions of the package by lowering the Bank Rate, by expanding the TFS to reinforce the monetary transmission mechanism further, and by expanding the scale or variety of asset purchases.

In August 2016, the MPC agreed that a policy stimulus was warranted, and that the Bank Rate should be reduced to 0.25% and be supported by a TFS. Eight members supported the introduction of a corporate bond scheme, and six members supported further purchases of UK government bonds. These measures have been taken against a backdrop of other supportive actions recently taken by the BoE.

4.3 Exchange Rate Policy

The users of the FX market fall into two broad camps, those using it for international trade and those who speculate in the FX market.

4.3.1 International Trade

FX transactions are essentially driven by international trade. If a Japanese company sells goods to a US customer, it might invoice the transaction in US dollars. These dollars will need to be exchanged for Japanese yen by the Japanese company and this is the FX transaction. The Japanese company may not be expecting to receive the dollars for a month after submission of the invoice. This gives it two choices:

1. It could wait until it receives the dollars and then execute a **spot** transaction.
2. It could enter into a **forward** transaction to sell the dollars for yen in a month's time. This would provide them with certainty as to the number of yen it will receive and assist in its budgeting efforts.

4.3.2 Speculation in the FX Market

Another major factor which accounts for FX transactions is for speculative transactions. If an investor felt that the US dollar was likely to weaken against the euro, they could buy euros in either the spot or forward market to profit if they are right.

Generally, exchange rates around the world are quoted against the US dollar.

Technically speaking, a cross rate is any foreign currency rate that does not include the US dollar. For example, the GBP/JPY (Great Britain pound/Japanese yen) is a cross rate. However, the term has become more loosely used to describe the exchange rate between any currency pair.

Speculators and traders in currencies can participate in the FX market by opening accounts with brokers who will enable them to do one or more of the following:

- Trade in the spot market with or without leverage.
- Trade in the futures markets for currencies which are listed on some futures exchanges, eg, the CME.
- Trade via a derivative, such as an **option**.

Unlike markets which are organised around the opening hours of a particular central exchange, the FX market, being decentralised and truly global, trades 24 hours a day and five days a week.

4.3.3 Main Characteristics of the FX Market

FX is by far the largest type of capital market in the world, in terms of cash value traded, and includes trading between large banks, central banks, currency speculators, multinational corporations, hedge funds, governments, and other institutions.

The Bank for International Settlements (BIS) provides the most useful information on the size and turnover of the global FX market and it has conducted a triennial survey since 1986 with the most recent conducted in April 2016 (with the results published in September 2016).

According to the BIS, the objective of the survey is

'to provide the most comprehensive and internationally consistent information on the size and structure of global foreign exchange markets, allowing policymakers and market participants to better monitor patterns of activity in the global financial system'.

Below are the highlights from the most recent survey which is available from the BIS's website:

Turnover on the Global FX Market

- Trading in the global FX markets averaged $5.1 trillion per day in April 2016. This was down from $5.4 trillion in April 2013, a month which had seen heightened activity in the Japanese yen against the background of monetary policy developments at that time.
- For the first time since 2001, spot turnover declined. Spot transactions fell to $1.7 trillion per day in April 2016 from $2.0 trillion in 2013. In contrast, the turnover of FX swaps rose further, reaching $2.4 trillion per day in April 2016. This rise was driven, in large part, by increased trading of FX swaps involving the yen.

- The US dollar remained the dominant vehicle currency, being on one side of 88% of all trades in April 2016. The euro, yen and Australian dollar all lost market share. In contrast, many emerging market currencies increased their share. The renminbi (RMB) doubled its share, to 4%, to become the world's eighth most actively traded currency and the most actively traded emerging market currency, overtaking the Mexican peso. The rise in the share of renminbi was primarily due to the increase in trading against the US dollar. In April 2016, as much as 95% of renminbi trading volume was against the US dollar.
- The share of trading between reporting dealers grew over the three-year period, accounting for 42% of turnover in April 2016, compared with 39% in April 2013. Banks other than reporting dealers accounted for a further 22% of turnover. Institutional investors were the third largest group of counterparties in FX markets, at 16%.
- In April 2016, sales desks in five countries – the UK, the US, Singapore, Hong Kong SAR and Japan – intermediated 77% of FX trading, up from 75% in April 2013 and 71% in April 2010.

4.3.4 Determination of Exchange Rates

Historically, in the post-World War II era, exchange rates were fixed as part of the 1944 Bretton Woods Agreement and not subject to market forces. Resetting or changing these exchange rates took place, as it did in the UK in the 1960s, by a formal devaluation whereby the rates which had been set in 1944 were modified. The UK Government undertook a devaluation of the pound against the dollar from £1= $2.80 to £1 = $2.40 in 1968.

The era of fixed-exchange rates came to an end during the 1970s, largely as a result of a currency crisis for the US dollar and the end of 'official' convertibility currencies into gold which was abandoned in August 1971. There have been attempts by governments to reintroduce managed exchange rates, but these efforts have essentially failed and the current regime of freely floating exchange rates is now accepted as the only feasible way for the FX market to function effectively.

There are exceptions, such as some currencies of Middle Eastern countries, which are pegged to the US dollar.

Questions with regard to regarding the determination of the FX rates by the markets comes down to several related issues concerning the demand and supply for individual currencies, monetary and interest rate policy and issues relating to purchasing power parity (PPP).

4.3.5 Demand and Supply Conditions for Each Currency

Factors Affecting Demand for Sterling
- Foreigners will need sterling to pay for exports of UK goods to overseas markets.
- Overseas investors will want to invest capital in the UK.
- **Speculation** – if currency is expected to increase relative to one or more other currencies.
- Currency rate management activities of central banks including the BoE.
- Demand will be downward-sloping with respect to price – less demand for exports and less interest from foreign investors as sterling advances relative to other currencies.

Factors Affecting Supply of Sterling
- When UK importers purchase foreign currencies to pay for imported goods arriving in the UK, they are increasing the supply of sterling into the markets.
- UK residents wishing to invest in overseas assets will have to sell sterling to buy foreign currency.
- Speculation – if the UK currency is expected to decrease relative to one or more other currencies, they will sell sterling.
- The BoE may sell the domestic currency to purchase additional foreign currency reserves in order to influence the exchange rate as part of macroeconomic policy.
- Supply will be upward-sloping with respect to price.

Floating Exchange Rates
The FX system which has emerged during the last ten years has elements of some degree of management of rates by central banks and governments but is largely a system which is described as free-floating.

- Pure free float would be when no government intervention takes place and only market forces rates determine rates.
- The present-day system is largely based upon the activities of the large banks and other institutions which are conducting transactions between themselves in the FX market.
- The central banks can issue policy statements and from time to time may intervene directly into the market to buy or sell their currency or another currency from their reserves.
- Central banks will attempt to 'guide' the markets with respect to determining factors such as interest rates, trade policies and other capital market incentives.

In contrast to (more or less) freely floating exchange rates there are alternative models which have been used historically and which could conceivably reappear in the future.

Managed Floating
- If market forces are interspersed with intervention by government via central banks, the term used is 'managed floating'.
- When sterling was within the EU's Exchange Rate Mechanism (ERM) in the early 1990s, the BoE had to intervene to keep the currency within specified bands which were laid down by the European Monetary System (EMS). This was the arrangement for currency arrangements between the EU member states prior to the establishment of the euro currency in 1999.
- Bands were established around a target rate and each member state currency was 'managed' so that the markets knew that violations of the bands would not be acceptable.
- In September 1992, on a day which has become known as Black Wednesday, sterling went through a critical episode with regard to the ERM. Despite concerted efforts by the BoE to preserve the 'bands', sterling dropped below its threshold levels and the decision was taken to exit the ERM.
- To keep a currency within specified bands, interest rates can be manipulated to induce foreigners to either buy or sell the currency.
- Exchange controls can be applied – ranging from direct controls on the flow of currency to withholding taxes and export controls.
- Retaliation and administration costs/losses from speculation are big costs involved in interventionism.

Fixed Exchange Rates

The post-1945 era saw a period of rigid fixed exchange rates in which no floating was permitted. There was a rigid regulation of the market forces to ensure that currencies were pegged. This was less arduous in that era as there was nothing like the free movement of capital around the globe as seen today.

- Under such a fixed-rate regime all central banks cooperated to achieve fixed rates.
- Sometimes if market forces become too misaligned countries are forced into devaluations or revaluations.
- Sterling was devalued on 19 September 1949, as the pound/dollar rate was reduced by 31%, from US$4.03 to US$2.80.
- In the mid-1960s the pound came under renewed pressure, since the exchange rate against the dollar was considered too high. In the summer of 1966, with the value of the pound falling in the currency markets, exchange controls were tightened by the Wilson Government. That restriction was lifted only in 1979.
- The pound was eventually devalued by 14.3% to US$2.41 in November 1967.
- Since then the currency has floated with respect to the US dollar.

Consequences of Floating Exchange Rates

- Free floating allows for 'natural adjustments' to disequilibrium in the balance of payments.
- Market forces eventually become so overwhelming that governments cannot control the exchange rate.
- In response to the burgeoning US China trade deficit, for example, the US administration has been pushing China to revalue its currency and many in Washington have been demanding a target of 10–15% appreciation of the Chinese currency. On 11 August 2015, the People's Bank of China (PBOC) surprised the markets by changing its daily fixing mechanism, which led to a more than 3% devaluation of the renminbi against the US dollar. The most common reason for devaluating one currency against another is to make the country's products cheaper for foreign buyers, thus boosting exports and economic growth (as net exports are a fundamental part of GDP growth).
- Having to maintain a fixed rate of exchange gets in the way of other government objectives.
- Raising interest rates to protect a fixed rate of exchange may be unhelpful from other monetary and fiscal perspectives – as it was in the UK in September 1992.

One issue for the UK in relation to its FX rate policy is the status of sterling with regard to the trading currency of its most important trading partners in the eurozone – the euro. Sterling is outside the eurozone even though the UK is currently a member of the EU. The UK voted to leave the EU on 23 June 2016 but the formal exit will not begin until the UK and the EU have finalised negotiations as to the exact nature of the exit.

The Euro

- The euro (currency sign: €:EUR) is the official currency of many of the EU member states which taken together are known as the eurozone.
- The euro is the single currency for more than 335 million people in Europe.
- Including areas using currencies pegged to the euro, the euro affects nearly 500 million people worldwide.

- The euro was introduced to world financial markets as an accounting currency in 1999 and launched as physical coins and banknotes in 2002. All EU member states are eligible to join if they comply with certain monetary requirements, and eventual use of the euro is mandatory for all new EU members.
- EU countries that are not using the euro – Bulgaria, Croatia, Czech Republic, Denmark, Hungary, Poland, Romania, Sweden and the UK.
- The euro is managed and administered by the Frankfurt-based ECB and the European System of Central Banks (ESCB) (composed of the central banks of its member states).
- As an independent central bank, the ECB has sole authority to set monetary policy. The ESCB participates in the printing, minting and distribution of notes and coins in all member states, and the operation of the eurozone payment systems.

Reserve Currencies

- The euro is widely perceived to be one of two, or perhaps three, major global reserve currencies, making inroads on the widely used US dollar (USD), which has historically been used by commercial and central banks worldwide as a stable reserve on which to ensure their liquidity and facilitate international transactions. Most of the world's major commodities, including oil, industrial metals and agricultural commodities, are by convention priced in US dollars.
- A currency is attractive for foreign transactions when it demonstrates a proven track record of stability, a well-developed financial market to dispose of the currency in and proven acceptability to others. While the euro has made substantial progress toward achieving these features, there are a few challenges that undermine the ascension of the euro as a major reserve currency.
- Persistent excessive budget deficits of EU member nations, economically weak new members and serious questions with regard to expansion threaten the place of the new currency.
- As a new reserve currency, governments sponsoring the euro do receive some substantial benefits. Since money is effectively an interest-free loan to the government by the holder of the currency, foreign reserves act as a subsidy to the country minting the currency.

4.3.6 Summary of Recent Exchange Rate Policy

The government can try to influence exchange rates by buying or selling currencies through its central bank reserves. However, government currency reserves are now relatively small and so such a policy might have to be limited in scope.

Another way the government might wish to influence exchange rates is through changes in interest rates: if UK interest rates are raised, this makes sterling a relatively more attractive currency to hold and so the change should exert upward pressure on the value of sterling. As we have seen, interest rate policy is now determined by the MPC. Interest rate policy is decided in the light of various matters apart from exchange rates, including the inflation rate and the level of house prices.

During the financial crisis of 2008–09 debate sometimes focused on the advantages that the UK has enjoyed in being able to set its own very distinctive monetary and fiscal policy rather than those being practised throughout the eurozone.

- Non-traded goods are commonly 50% of GDP.
    - The forces driving prices of say, wheat, to one world price are not as pervasive for those economic activities and services that are essentially localised and not tradeable, for example hairdressing, car repair and dental treatment.

- There are barriers to trade across countries, including duties and quotas, and these will have the effect of distorting the prices paid for traded goods.
- The flow of international capital in highly integrated financial markets means that exchange rates are very much affected by relative interest rates in different countries.
- The volume of capital movements across countries today is many times larger than the international trade in goods and services.

Exercise 2

'In the UK a fixed exchange rate will always provide stability and economic confidence and should be used in preference to a system of floating exchange rates.'

Evaluate the accuracy of this statement using arguments for and against both approaches.

The answer to this exercise can be found at the end of this chapter.

International Fisher Theory

There are alternative explanations which have been proposed to account for the movements in exchange rates. In particular the 'International Fisher Theory' (named after the US economist Irving Fisher [1867–1947]) states that it is the difference in the 'nominal interest rates' between two countries which will primarily determine the movement of the nominal exchange rate between their respective currencies.

The key insight of the Fisher hypothesis is that the 'real interest rate' in an economy should be independent of monetary variables.

To illustrate, between two different countries with different currencies (ie, not, for example, Germany and France which both use the euro – at the time of writing) the country which has the lower nominal interest rate is expected to have a lower rate of inflation and according to the Fisher hypothesis the real value of its currency should rise over time.

It is an assumption of the International Fisher Theory that capital is allowed to flow freely across borders. In general, the capital markets of most developed countries, especially within economic unions such as the EU, are well integrated. In some less developed countries, currency restrictions and concerns as to the integrity of the local financial system will inhibit the required free flow of capital.

Illustration

$(1+r) = (1+i)(1+R)$

Where:

r = the monetary or nominal rate
i = inflation rate
R = real rate of return

Assume the current spot exchange rate for US dollars into British pounds is $1.6 per pound.

Assume the current short-term interest rate, often known simply as the base rate, is 4% in the US and 8% in the UK.

What would be the expected spot exchange rate of US dollars for sterling rate 12 months from now according to the International Fisher Theory?

Future exchange rates will be based on the relationship in nominal interest rates. Multiplying the current spot exchange rate by the nominal annual US interest rate and dividing by the nominal annual British interest rate yields the estimate of the spot exchange rate 12 months from now ($1.6 x 1.04) ÷ 1.08 = $1.5407.

The International Fisher Theory is arguably one factor in the way that international financial capital markets, and in particular the FX markets, work and helps to explain the way in which currencies will move in the future with respect to interest rate differentials. In essence, the theory proposes that 'exchange rate drift' will be independent of inflation – that is, entirely based on the respective national nominal interest rates.

However, the International Fisher Theory, on its own, does not explain what the **basis** is, in the first instance, for the rate between sterling and the dollar to have reached or been set at $1.60 in the illustration just cited. There must be other factors required, often historical, which provided the starting-out point from which the way that exchange rates move going forward is more easily explicable in terms of the Fisher Theory.

5. Macroeconomic Statistics

Learning Objective

1.5 Interpret macroeconomic statistics

In order to assist in achieving its goals of managing the UK economy, the Government has empowered the ONS with the task of collecting, analysing and publishing a variety of macroeconomic statistics. These different measurements of the state of the economy could be seen as a way for the government and private businesses to take the pulse of the national economy so as to make better decisions with regard to proposed investments and the need for a stimulus or restraint in broad economic policy.

> 'On 26 July 2007, the Statistics and Registration Service Act received Royal Assent heralding a new era of independence for both the Office for National Statistics (ONS) and for the broader UK statistical system. The Act enables the creation of a new independent body, the UK Statistics Authority, which will distance itself from ministers as a non-ministerial department accountable to Parliament.'

Source: The Office for National Statistics

The UK Statistics Authority has a statutory responsibility to promote and safeguard the production and publication of official statistics. It also oversees and ensures the quality, good practice and comprehensiveness of these statistics.

The various measures which will be described in this section, such as CPI and the rate of unemployment, are key parameters which enable economists and business analysts to determine the general trends in the economy and to make forecasts with regard to the future for budgetary purposes. In particular, one of the principal roles of the UK Treasury is to prepare a budget for the conduct of public policy which has to satisfy several different objectives of government policy.

Government economic policies are not commonly set out in terms which allow for easy performance measurement and hence criticism. They are instead couched in more political terms, often as general aspirations. Although the priorities may differ in both absolute and relative terms, UK governments typically include some aspects of the following:

- low inflation
- higher or full employment
- rising economic growth.

Often, there is a trade-off between these objectives as they are not mutually compatible. This can best be seen in relation to the cyclical nature of economic activity and has been previously described by such terms as 'stop-go' cycles and 'boom and bust'.

In simplistic terms the cycle of macroeconomic activity could be said to fluctuate between two extremes of trough and peak:

- Businesses are operating at full capacity, unemployment levels are low, there are inflationary pressures, there is a deterioration in the balance of payments and asset prices become subject to bubbles.
- The business cycle is in a negative or very low growth phase, there is relatively high unemployment, weak retail sales and even, as seen in 2008–09, deflation in both consumer prices and also especially in asset prices such as residential housing.

The diagram below reflects a theoretical view of the business cycle.

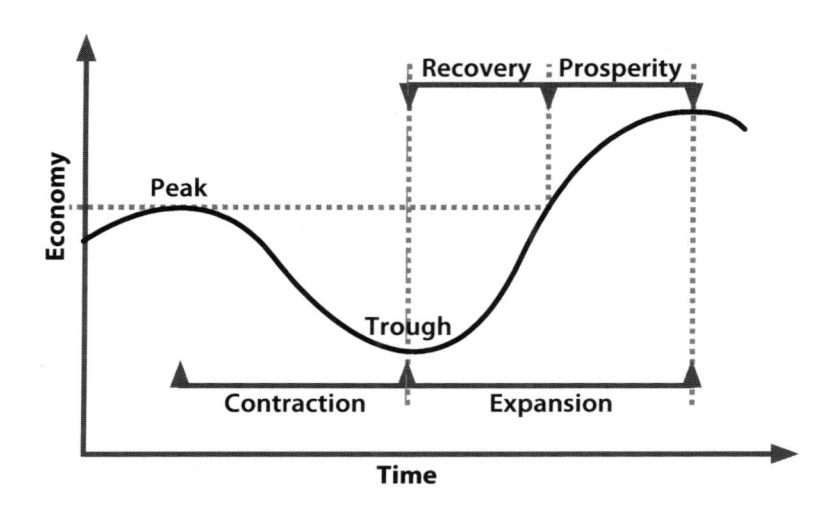

The business cycle could be defined as fluctuations in the general level of economic activity. The business cycle is made up of an expansion phase that culminates in a peak or boom period, when GDP grows rapidly and there are high levels of activity.

The economy then contracts, GDP grows at a slower rate (or even contracts) and unemployment increases. The bottom of the contraction phase is referred to as the recessionary trough. If GDP contracts for two consecutive quarters and unemployment rises, this will be referred to as a recession. In the rare circumstance where GDP contracts by 10% or more, on a year-on-year basis, the term 'depression' can be used.

One of the principal uses of macroeconomic statistics is that it enables policymakers and planners to estimate where the economy is within a business cycle. It is also important to distinguish between economic conditions within a typical business cycle and the kinds of statistical data which were revealed in 2008–09 and which are indicative of a more serious downturn or recession than that seen periodically.

The tasks of economic policymakers are more challenging and require more drastic measures when there is severe economic contraction and deflationary forces at work than in a more generic downturn. The current economic contraction has also been accompanied by record measures of personal and public indebtedness which may indicate that a recovery will not be as simple as that shown in the diagram shown above.

5.1 Measures of Inflation

The main measures of inflation in the UK were covered in section 2.1 of this chapter, but the following is a brief summary:

- **CPI** – this is based on a formula, standard throughout the EU, and, therefore, enables a direct comparison to be made between the inflation rate in the UK and that in the rest of Europe.
- **PPI** – this measures the prices encountered by producers, and is sometimes referred to as measuring inflation at the factory gate.
- **CPIY** – CPI, but does not include indirect taxes, eg, VAT, stamp duty and excise duty. The aim is to give the underlying inflation figure (ie, any effect of indirect taxes has been removed); the result usually is that it shows the underlying inflation rate to be lower than the headline rate.
- **CPI-CT** – this includes indirect taxes, but keeps them constant at the rates which were in effect at the beginning of the year.
- **CPIH** – includes housing costs, such as mortgage interest payments. The owner occupiers cost (OCC) account for 12% of the CPIH weighting.

UK Inflation (CPI) (2008–17)

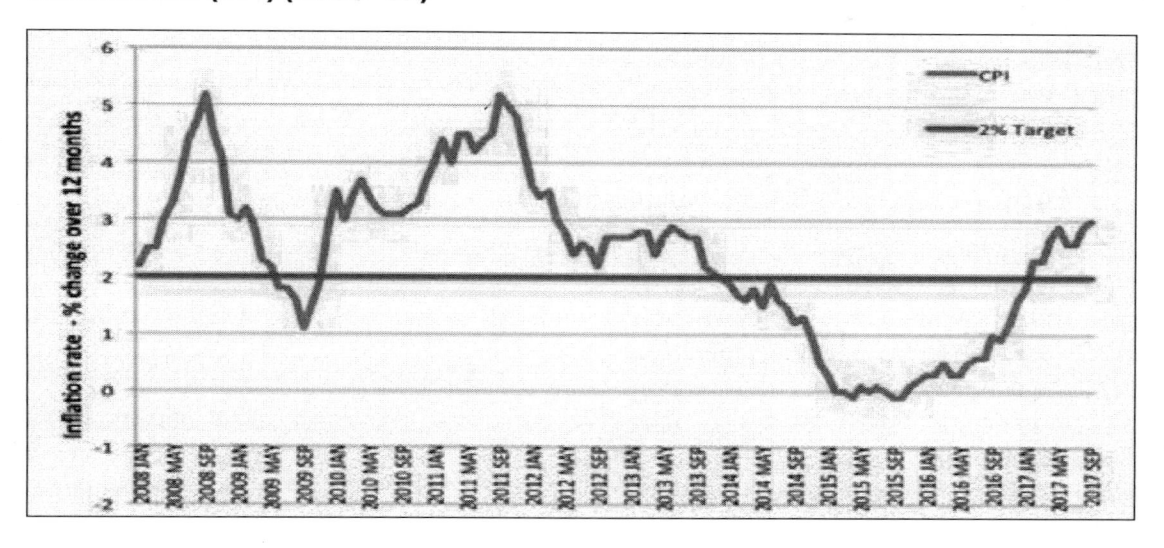

Source: economicshelp.org, ONS – D7G7 – 10 October 2017

The above histogram provides a long-term view of the CPI in the UK, covering the annualised figures for the period from 2008 until September 2017. What is clear from this graph is the decline which has been seen from the levels of 2011, when the annual inflation rate approached 5%, to much lower levels since.

In December 2003, the inflation target was changed to track the CPI and the threshold level was set to 2%, above which the Governor of the BoE has to report to the Chancellor that the inflation target has been exceeded. The CPI was around 0% in 2015 and even dipped into negative figures in some months due to falling oil and food prices. It rose to 0.6% in the year to August 2016, mainly due to air fares and food prices. In 2017, there was a rise in 'cost-push' inflation. The inflationary influences include a number of factors, such as a rise in the price of petrol, food and recreational goods, as well as a devaluation in sterling, making imported goods more expensive, which leads to higher input prices for manufacturers.

UK Inflation – CPI, CPIH, CPI-CT (2010–18)

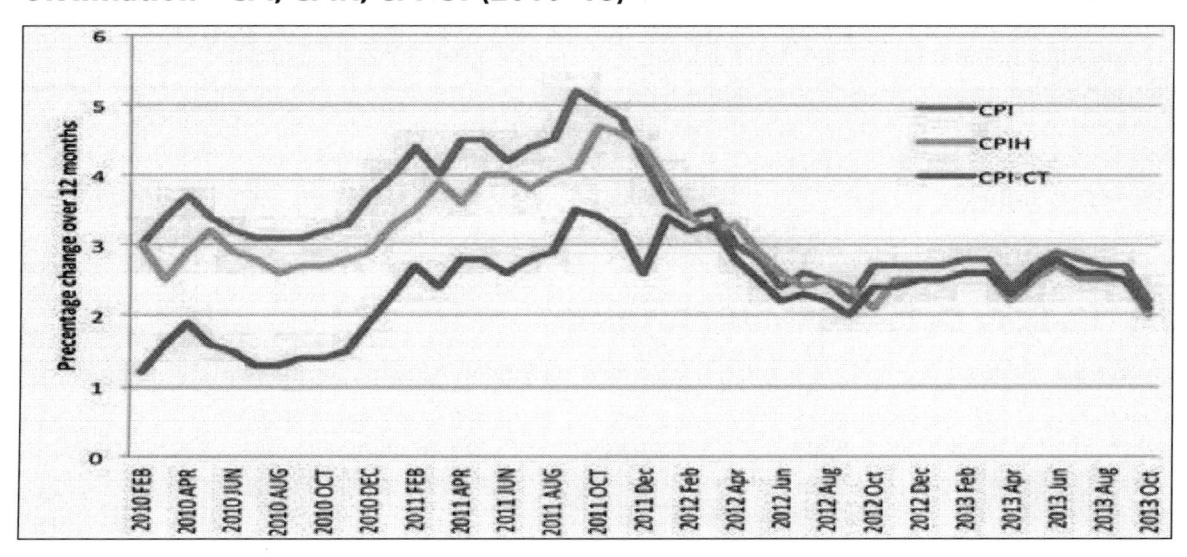

Source: economicshelp.org, ONS D7G7, L550, EAD6

In 2013, the MPC stated that once unemployment had fallen to the 7% threshold, it would assess the state of the economy more broadly, drawing on a wide array of indicators, one of them being the interest rate level which was expected to rise. The current unemployment rate (July 2018) is 4.2%. The MPC interest rates were maintained at 0.5% as at June 2018.

5.1.1 Negative Consequences of Inflation

- Business confidence is undermined – planning and investment becomes even more prone to risk and error.
- Living standards erode due to the diminution of the purchasing power of incomes which do not keep pace with the increases in the general level of prices.
- Inflation discourages savings – in turn investments are less attractive.
- Historically periods of high inflation such as the 1970s have been very bad for capital markets and in particular equities and bonds.
- Inflation will harm the competitive position for exports if inflation is relatively high in the domestic economy.
- In more serious cases of what is sometimes referred to as hyperinflation there can be a collapse of confidence in the domestic currency as was the case for the German mark in the 1920s and the Argentine peso in the 1990s. Some Latin American economies have suffered from flights of capital to the safety of other reserve currencies due to the instability of their currencies caused by persistently high inflation. The mismanagement of the Zimbabwe economy has led to rampant inflation which has effectively destroyed all savings and private wealth within that African economy.

5.1.2 Sources of Inflation

Traditionally, and somewhat simplistically, economists have distinguished between two underlying frameworks to explain inflation:

- **Demand-Pull** – this was the traditional notion based on the classical views of supply and demand and was exemplified in the 1960s. In essence, demand and purchasing power supply outstrip causing prices to rise. The traditional remedy is to deflate demand by fiscal and monetary policies.
- **Cost-Push** – this hypothesis explains inflation as a consequence of increases in the prices of factors of production and these costs are passed on to consumers in higher prices for final goods – eg, commodity inflation of the 1970s instigated by the quadrupling in the price of oil.
- **Imported inflation** – arises from a general increase in imported goods caused by a decline in the external value of the currency – may be necessary to try to 'manage' exchange rates but increasingly the realisation has been that markets set exchange rates and not governments.
- **Monetary inflation** – excess money supply. During the late 1970s and early 1980s UK government policy was specifically aimed at decreasing the money supply to 'choke off' inflation.

5.1.3 Labour Data and Unemployment

Alongside inflation the other very closely observed statistical measures relating to the macro-economy is the utilisation of labour in the economy. This measure is designed to show the overall levels of employment, the number of hours worked, the earnings per hour and, most critically, the level of unemployment. This level is expressed in terms of the percentage of people that are seeking employment but are not gainfully employed.

Average earnings measures the rate at which pay to workers (derived from payroll) are rising in the economy. Historically, these indicators have been linked inversely in that, as unemployment fell, earnings rose. Globalisation and other so-called 'supply-side reforms' introduced into the labour market over the last 20 years have made the market much more competitive.

As a result of Thatcherism in the 1980s, significant reforms have included the restriction of union power, leading to the reduction in benefits and the limitation of employee rights. This has made it more difficult for workers to force up their wages in response to inflation. This has therefore weakened the historical relationship between low levels of unemployment and wage inflation derived from the 'Phillips Curve' (defined by the economist A.W. Phillips from data between 1861 and 1957).

The ONS produces monthly reports on the UK labour market. It also produces a range of graphs and information about employment, unemployment, economic activity and other statistics with regard to the UK labour market.

The following are the main points from the ONS November 2017 report. Further detail and charts showing various statistical information can be viewed on the ONS website (https://www.ons.gov.uk/).

- *Estimates from the Labour Force Survey show that, between April to June 2017 and July to September 2017, the number of people in work fell slightly, the number of unemployed people also fell, and the number of people aged from 16 to 64 not working and not seeking or available to work (economically inactive) increased.*
- *There were 32.06 million people in work, 14,000 fewer than for April to June 2017 but 279,000 more than for a year earlier.*
- *The employment rate (the proportion of people aged from 16 to 64 who were in work) was 75.0%, down slightly compared with April to June 2017 but up from 74.4% for a year earlier.*
- *There were 1.42 million unemployed people (people not in work but seeking and available to work), 59,000 fewer than for April to June 2017 and 182,000 fewer than for a year earlier.*
- *The unemployment rate (the proportion of those in work plus those unemployed, that were unemployed) was 4.3%, down from 4.8% for a year earlier and the joint lowest since 1975.*
- *There were 8.88 million people aged from 16 to 64 who were economically inactive (not working and not seeking or available to work), 117,000 more than for April to June 2017 but 20,000 fewer than for a year earlier.*
- *The inactivity rate (the proportion of people aged from 16 to 64 who were economically inactive) was 21.6%, higher than for April to June 2017 (21.3%) but down slightly from a year earlier.*
- *Latest estimates show that average weekly earnings for employees in Great Britain in nominal terms (that is, not adjusted for price inflation) increased by 2.2% both including and excluding bonuses, compared with a year earlier.*

Source: ONS: UK Labour Market: November 2017

5.1.4 The Misery Index

This is a term which has been used by US economists to describe the combination of inflation and unemployment. The notion is that consumers are hit with two unfavourable economic conditions at the same time – the loss of jobs and also the loss of purchasing power caused by the relatively high level of prices. In the following diagram, the period from 1995 to 2010 has been covered. The annual rate of unemployment is added to and the annual percentage rate of inflation are added together creating a third time series known as the misery index.

Misery Indices: Eurozone Situation Worsens (January 1995–January 2010)

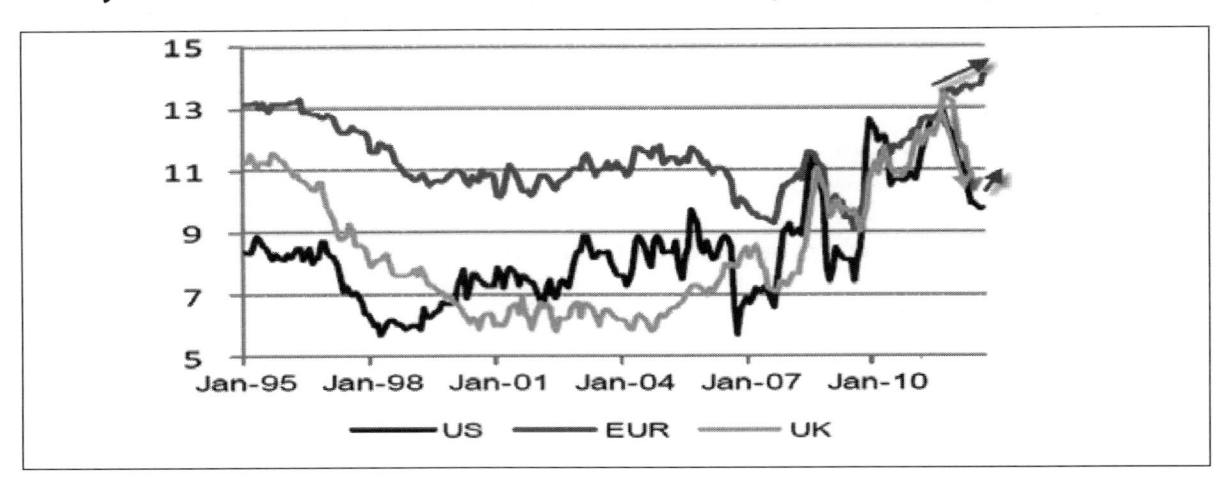

Source: SG Cross Asset Research

The following extract from a Bloomberg report highlights the data from the 2017 'Misery Index', with the UK ranked 44th, and the US ranked 49th, out of 65 nations. The eurozone is ranked 18th, with a Misery Index score of 11 for 2017 and 10.3 for 2016.

2017 Rank	Country	2017 Misery Index (projected)	2016 Misery Index (actual)	2016 Rank (actual)
41	Austria	7.8	6.9	37
41	Germany	7.8	6.6	39
43	Australia	7.7	7	35
44	United Kingdom	7.6	5.6	46
45	Romania	7.5	4.5	53
45	El Salvador	7.5	–	–
47	Norway	7.3	8.3	29
48	Czech Republic	7.1	4.7	51
49	United States	7	6.1	42
50	Hungary	6.9	5.6	46
51	Netherlands	6.8	6.3	41
52	China	6.4	6.1	42
53	New Zealand	6.3	5.4	49

Sources: Bloomberg surveys, national data

Note: Countries without inflation and/or unemployment data for 2016 were not included in the 2016 ranking.

5.1.5 Gross Domestic Product (GDP)

Gross domestic product (GDP) is the monetary value of all the finished goods and services produced within a country's borders in a specific time period.

GDP can be calculated using the following formula:

$$\text{GDP} = \text{Consumption} + \text{Government Spending} + \text{Investments} + \text{Net Exports}$$

$$\text{GDP} = C + G + I + (X - M)$$

Arguably the most important set of data which is released periodically by the ONS relates to UK GDP. This measure is reported in essentially two formats showing the percentage change within the most recent quarter of reference and also the current quarter's relationship to the period one year ago.

The year-on-year statistics are the most useful in assessing the trend of the data whereas those looking for improvements or deteriorations in the trend will be more focused on the changes from quarter to quarter.

The following chart displays the average year-on-year changes in GDP from 2008 to the end of Q3 2017.

Most clearly visible in the chart below are the striking columns for 2009, which reveal a −2% change for one quarter. As can also be seen, the figures for 2016 and 2017 show positive growth, albeit at a minimal level.

UK GDP Quarterly Growth Rate (2008–18)

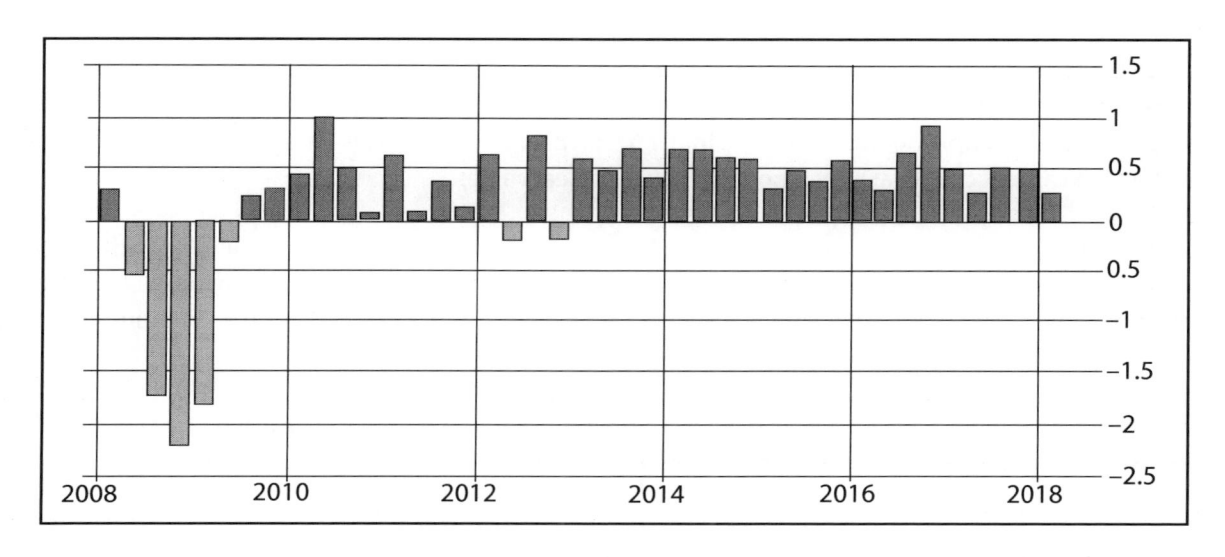

Source: TradingEconomics.com, UK Office for National Statistics

Since 1980 there have been three periods with negative growth or recessions (defined as two consecutive quarters of negative growth). The first is the period of 1980–81 when the top to bottom of the recession produced a similar decline to that being seen in mid-2009, noted above. 2009 shows the largest year-on-year decline since the ONS began keeping records.

In considering the periods other than the recessions there was a fairly consistent period from the mid-1990s through the first seven years of the 2000s when GDP was growing at approximately 3% per annum and this level had been assumed by economists and statisticians to be the expected growth rate looking forward. Whilst not near to this 3%, it is clear that a recovery has been taking place since 2009.

Contrast between GDP and GNP

The key measures of the level of output of the economy are the GDP and gross national product (GNP).

GDP is the total value of output produced in the economy regardless of whom that belongs to. Therefore, it would include the value of cars produced at a Japanese car plant in the UK, but it would not include the value of cars produced within, say, the EU by UK companies.

GNP is the value of output of the participants in the economy and, therefore, includes net property income from abroad.

It is worth noting also that the measure of Gross National Income (GNI) is now recognised by the World Bank instead of GNP. This is defined by the World Bank as the sum of value added by all resident producers plus any product taxes (minus subsidies) not included in the valuation of output plus net receipts of primary income (compensation of employees and property income) from abroad.

Each measure is 'gross' meaning that it is calculated before making allowance for the depreciation in the capital stock of the economy. Every year, a certain increase in output has to take place in order to repair the damage to capital stock in actually producing that volume of activity. The net measures of product are net of allowances for capital depreciation.

The ONS uses different ways to strip out the impact of inflation from the calculation of the GDP figures. One common approach is to create a measure of inflation in the economy, referred to as the GDP price deflator, and after applying this measure (similar to the process used in calculating the CPI and RPI) the gross value can be scaled back from nominal values to real values.

The GDP figure is perhaps the most important barometer of the overall prosperity and growth of the economy. New figures are released quarterly and very often the previous figures will be revised to remove some of the distortions that creep into the estimation process. One of the most important issues is the relationship of the actual data to trend.

Because of the importance of the GDP data and its value as a barometer of the health of the economy, it is also worth looking at a more detailed version of the data.

As seen in the following chart, GDP in the UK grew steadily during the 2000s until a financial market shock affected UK and global economic growth in 2008 and 2009. From the peak in Q1 (Jan to Mar) 2008 to the trough in Q2 (Apr to June) 2009, GDP decreased by 6.1%.

This can be compared with previous economic downturns in the early 1980s and early 1990s, which saw lower levels of impact on GDP. In the early 1990s' downturn, GDP decreased by 2.2% from the peak in Q2 1990 to the trough in Q3 1991. From Q3 (July to Sept) 2009, growth continued to be erratic, with several quarters between 2010 and 2012 recording broadly flat or declining GDP. In the early 1980s' downturn, GDP decreased by 5.6% from the peak in Q2 1979 to the trough in Q1 1981.

UK GDP Annual Growth Rate (1956–2016)

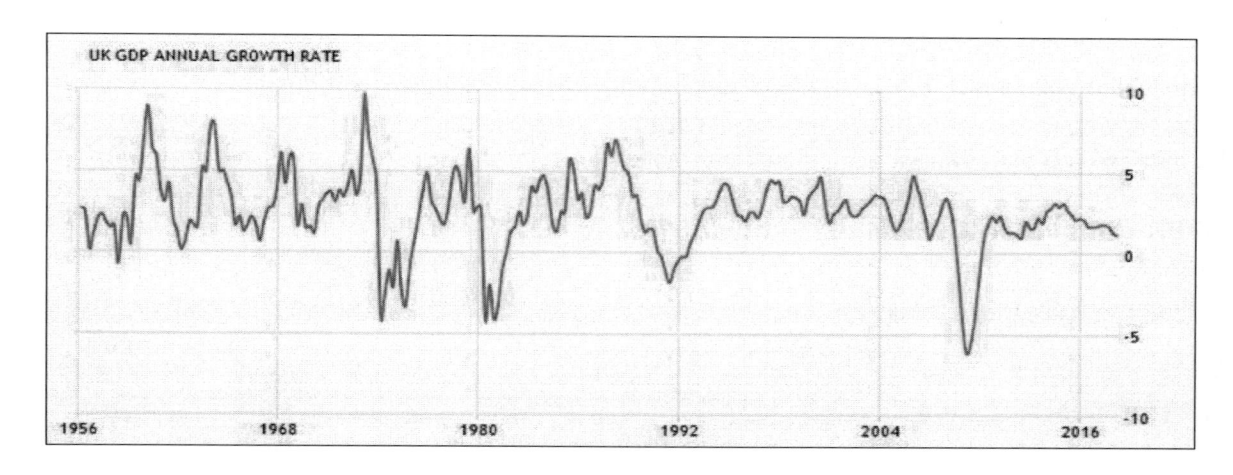

Source: TradingEconomics.com, UK Office for National Statistics

Since 2013, GDP recovered somewhat, with the economy exceeding pre-downturn peak levels in Q2 2013.

As can be seen from the GDP annual growth rates, the UK economy grew only by 1.2% year-on-year in Q1 2018, which was the weakest annual growth rate since Q1 of 2013.

Output Gap

Linked to GDP, another macroeconomic statistic which is significant is the so-called output gap. This measures the extent to which the economy is operating either above or below its capacity constraint. The UK has demonstrated growth at an average trend rate of approximately 2.5% per annum over the last 40 years.

When the economy is operating below capacity, as it was throughout 2009 and during 2010, inflationary pressures tend to be relatively low. If the output gap closes and the economy starts to operate closer to full capacity, then this will put strains on factor markets (eg, labour), and this, according to such hypotheses as that proposed by the Phillips Curve, will allegedly lead to inflation.

5.1.6 Industrial Production

Another time series published by the ONS relates to the industrial production levels of the UK and measures the output from the non-service sector of the economy which is primarily manufacturing activities.

Productivity in the UK rose to 101.50 index points in Q1 2016 from 101 in Q4 2015 and averaged 76.17 index points from 1971 until 2016, reaching a peak of 102.20 in Q4 2007 and a record low of 44.60 in Q1 1971.

The following chart shows the year-on-year percentage changes in industrial production, as determined by the ONS; however, as the UK economy is less of an industrial economy today than it was 30 years ago, this data series is of less importance than it used to be.

UK Productivity (January 2015–July 2017)

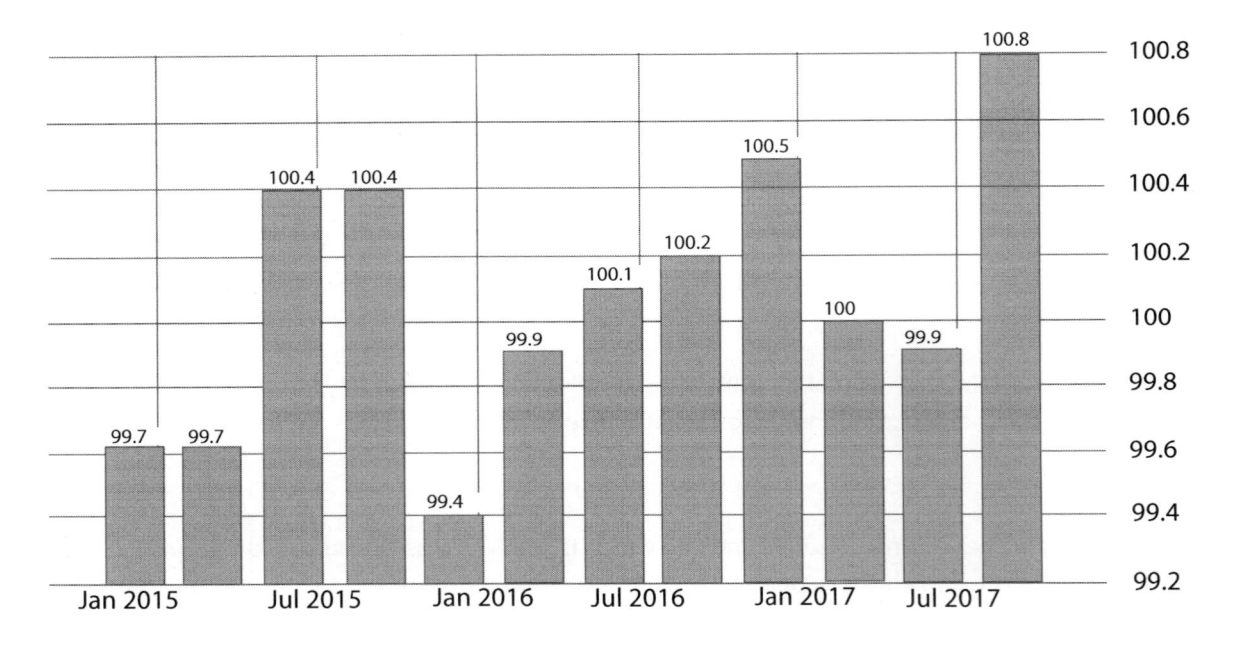

Month	Value
Jan 2015	99.7
(Apr 2015)	99.7
Jul 2015	100.4
(Oct 2015)	100.4
Jan 2016	99.4
(Apr 2016)	99.9
Jul 2016	100.1
(Oct 2016)	100.2
Jan 2017	100.5
(Apr 2017)	100
Jul 2017	99.9
(Oct 2017)	100.8

Source: www.tradingeconomics.com, UK Office for National Statistics

However, there are some economists who believe that the UK economy needs to become less dependent on the services sector, and in particular the financial services sector, and would also like to see a renewed emphasis on the industrial and manufacturing sectors.

5.1.7 Balance of Payments (BoP)

The trade deficit in the UK was £6.5 billion in June 2017.

UK Trade in Goods and Services Balances (seasonally adjusted)

Q3 (Jul to Sept) 2014 to Q2 (Apr to June) 2017

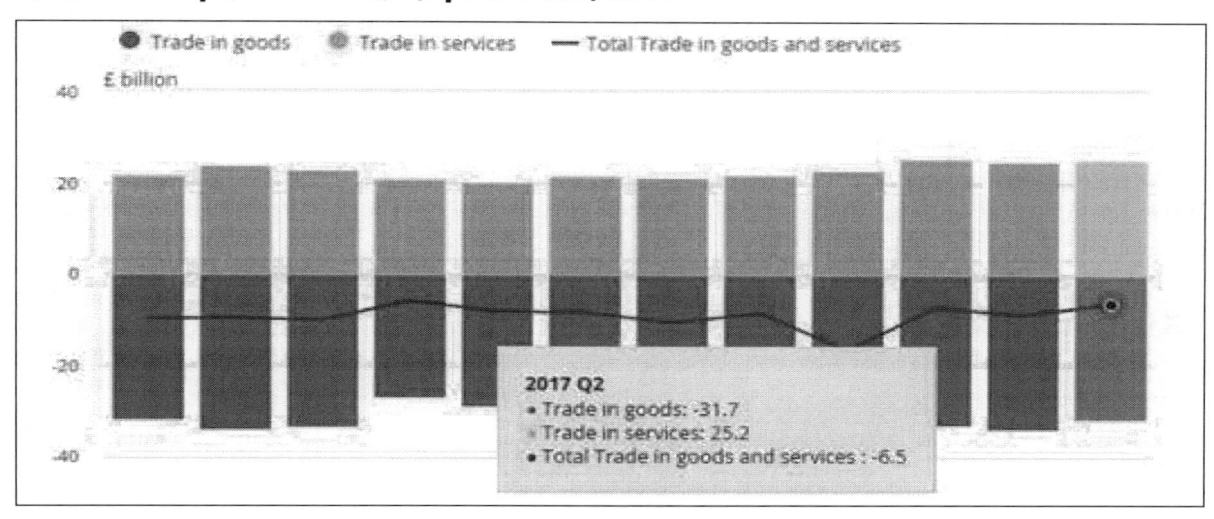

The BoP compares the sterling inflows and outflows of all those exports and imports respectively to provide a balance. A 'positive balance' means that more money is flowing into the UK economy and a 'negative balance' means that more money is flowing out. A detailed analysis will, therefore, enable conclusions to be drawn about international trade, consumption and revenue.

There are three accounts that must balance collectively:

- **Current account** comprises a country's imports and exports of goods, services and capital.
- **Capital account** comprises financial transactions that do not affect income, production or savings, for example a copyright. If and when this attracts income, then the resulting transaction would appear in the current account
- **Financial account** comprises transactions for increases or decreases in international ownership of assets.

A balance of payments deficit or surplus is a deficit or surplus on the current (trade) account of the balance of payments.

The current account is referred to as the balance of trade. The current account records short-term flows of money in and out of the UK. Trade is divided into two blocks – commonly called visibles and invisibles. The visible trade balance reflects the trade in products whereas the invisible trade balance consists of transactions primarily in the services sector.

Over the past 20 or 30 years, the UK BoP has had substantial deficits on its visible trade balance with the rest of the world, hence the UK has consumed more physical goods than it has exported. Fortunately for the UK, as is well known, there is a surplus on the 'invisible account' via the export of services that strengthens the UK's BoP.

UK Balance of Trade

The UK recorded a trade deficit of £1.41 billion in October 2017. The ONS reported that the UK balance of trade averaged –£1,443.26 million from 1955 to 2017, reaching an all-time high of £2,946 million in March of 1981, and a record low of –£6,236 million in September 2016. Since 1998, the UK runs a consistent trade deficit mainly due to an increase in demand for consumer goods, a decline in manufacturing, and a deterioration in oil and gas production. In recent years, the UK has run the biggest trade deficits with Germany, China, and the Netherlands. The biggest trade surpluses, however, were recorded with the US and Ireland.

UK Balance of Trade

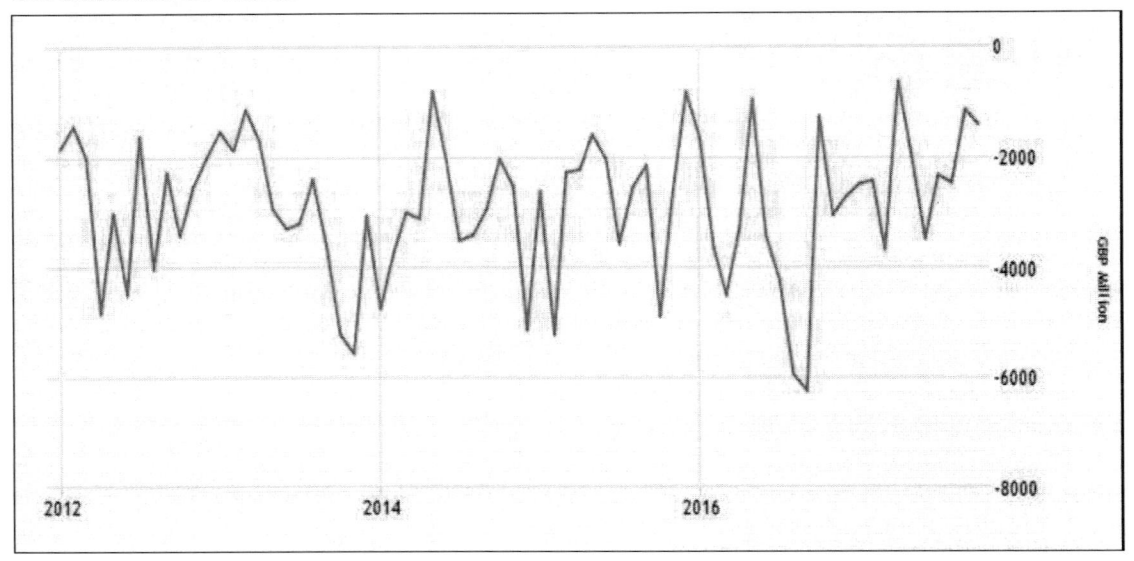

Source: www.tradingeconomics.com, UK Office for National Statistics

General Comments on the BoP

Invisibles are trades in services and income flows. It is here that the UK has been strong over the last 20 years. Included in the invisible earnings of the UK are the activities of the City of London, tourism and other services provided from the UK to overseas individuals. It is the surplus on the invisible trade that offsets the deficit the UK runs on visible trade and which occasionally results in a positive balance of trade overall. Also included within the UK's invisible earnings are flows resulting from income on overseas investments, dividends and interest payments. The UK is one of the world's largest investors overseas, with particularly large stakes in the US.

Transactions in Long-Term Assets and Liabilities

This is the longer-term aspect of the BoP, ie, long-term investment flows either into or out of the UK. In the past, this statement has been referred to as the capital account. The direction of net long-term flows depends on the level of interest expressed by overseas investors in the UK and the opportunities to invest in the UK, which present themselves to UK investors. Obviously, one key determinant of the level of inward investment is the interest rate, particularly the real interest rate.

When interest rates are high, they attract investment and thereby support the exchange rate through the balance of payments.

Overview

If the balance of trade is in deficit, this means that imports exceed exports, and this will eventually have to be corrected, as foreign trading partners will not finance the deficit (eg, through investment in the deficit country) indefinitely. One way of making the adjustment is for the deficit country's currency to fall in value or, through government intervention, to be 'devalued'.

If the domestic currency falls in value, imports become more expensive and exports become relatively cheaper. This automatic mechanism should bring the balance of trade back into line. In reality, economic systems seldom work this efficiently, and the US and UK have maintained trade deficits for a number of years.

Balance of payments statistics are notoriously unreliable, mainly due to the fact that they are based on a series of estimates. There will always be a number known as the balancing item in the balance of payment accounts, which simply ensures that the balance of payments (current account plus capital account) balances overall.

5.2 Consumer Confidence

5.2.1 Confidence Indicators

There are regular surveys conducted of business and consumer confidence. These surveys measure the responses of the sample group to a series of standard questions. As such, the results tend to be relatively volatile. The reaction to the terrorist attacks on 11 September 2001 is a prime example of this. The surveys taken in the aftermath of this tragic event showed a huge collapse in consumer confidence. Much of this collapse was restored within a few months.

Confidence then feeds into other indicators within the economy. If confidence is high, this will often encourage spending and other potentially inflationary forces. However, of itself, confidence is a reflection of other factors.

5.2.2 Retail Sales

The ONS also publishes retail sales data which provides an indicator of the amount of consumer retail expenditure activity – another important indicator of the level of activity in the UK economy. Obviously, it is critically linked to other indicators. If consumer confidence is high, spending is likely to increase. Equally, if asset prices rise, then this will again, via the wealth effect, encourage greater confidence and more spending.

Within these statistics, there are clear feedback loops that can be observed. For example, rising house prices can make consumers feel more confident about the future. If consumers are more confident, then they are more likely to take on major purchases such as property.

This will further stimulate the housing market, thereby forcing prices higher. In this way, asset price 'bubbles' are formed. A bubble is when a market rises too quickly and in effect overshoots its real value. This was the case in the housing markets of the late 1980s and the stock market at the end of the 1990s. The dilemma for policymakers is whether it is a real value or overheated. Equally, there is then the timing and strength of any move to reduce the market.

If the authorities fail to act effectively, then there is a risk of severe economic distortion. A major factor behind the recession of 2008–09 was the bursting of the house price bubble, which became rampant in the period from 2000–06. House prices dropped on average by 19% (and by as much as 25%) across much of the UK (Nationwide house price data), and it has left some homeowners with 'negative equity'; this occurs if the outstanding loan on a property is greater than the value of the property itself, and is quite clearly a huge drag on economic activity.

Retail sales in the UK declined by 0.3% year-on-year in October of 2017, following an upwardly revised 1.3% increase in September 2017. It was the first annual drop in retail sales since March of 2013 amid higher prices. Sales in food stores went down by 2.2% and made the largest downward contribution. Sales at non-food stores also fell, by 1%. Retail sales, year-on-year, in the UK averaged 2.56% from 1997 to 2017, reaching a record high of 9.30% in April 2002 and an all-time low of –4% in February 2009.

UK Retail Sales Year-on-Year (January 2017–October 2017)

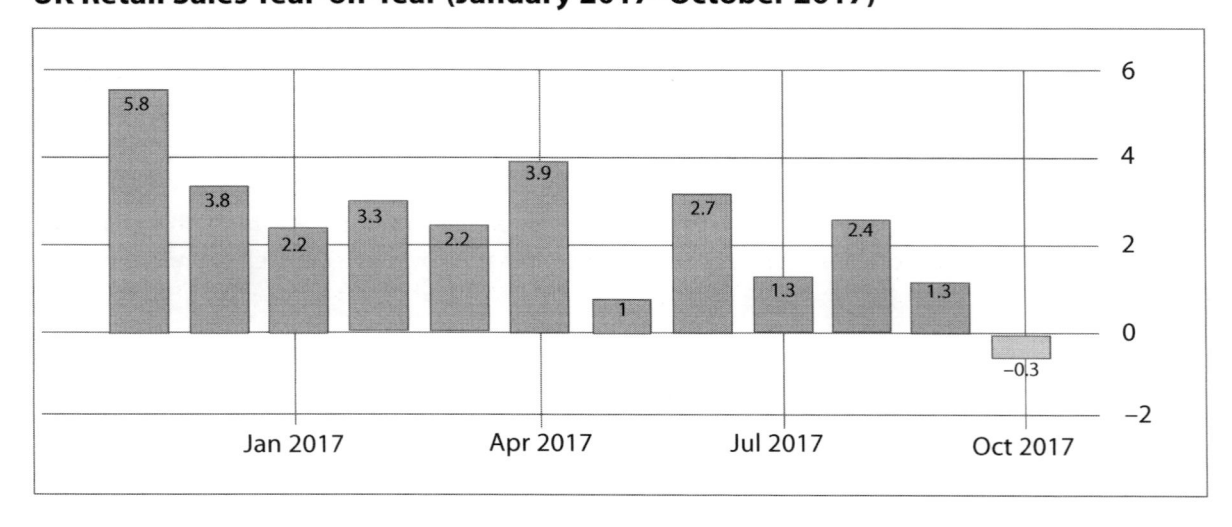

Source: www.tradingeconomics.com, UK Office for National Statistics

5.2.3 Asset Prices

Statistics on asset prices are also of great value to economic policymakers and the assets that are considered of most value are those for property – both commercial and residential – and also the stock market.

In the UK, house prices have historically been the most important in the mind of the consumer. As house prices rise, consumers feel more confident and increase their spending. This is often referred to as the wealth effect. Stock market values can, to a lesser extent, deliver the same effect.

These forces also work in the opposite direction. If asset values fall, the negative wealth effect can be equally powerful in a downward direction. Rapid asset price falls can trigger off a significant contraction of demand. Therefore, the diminution in the wealth effect simply exacerbates the existing contraction of demand.

There are two sources for statistical data on property prices. The first is the Land Registry which is a government agency which maintains a national database of all property transactions including the selling prices at which homes exchanged hands.

The second reliable source for tracking property prices are surveys conducted by private groups such as the one conducted monthly by the Nationwide Building Society. These private surveys are considered to be of more value to economic forecasters than the Land Registry as they publish their data in a more timely fashion and can identify regional trends and differences in the level of asking price to final deal price, for example.

UK Housing Index

The UK Housing Index, otherwise known as the Halifax House Price Index, is the UK's longest-running monthly house price series, with data covering the whole country going back to January 1983.

From this data, a 'standardised' house price is calculated and property price movements on a like-for-like basis (including seasonal adjustments) are analysed over time.

UK House Prices – Year-on-Year % Change (January 2007–October 2017)

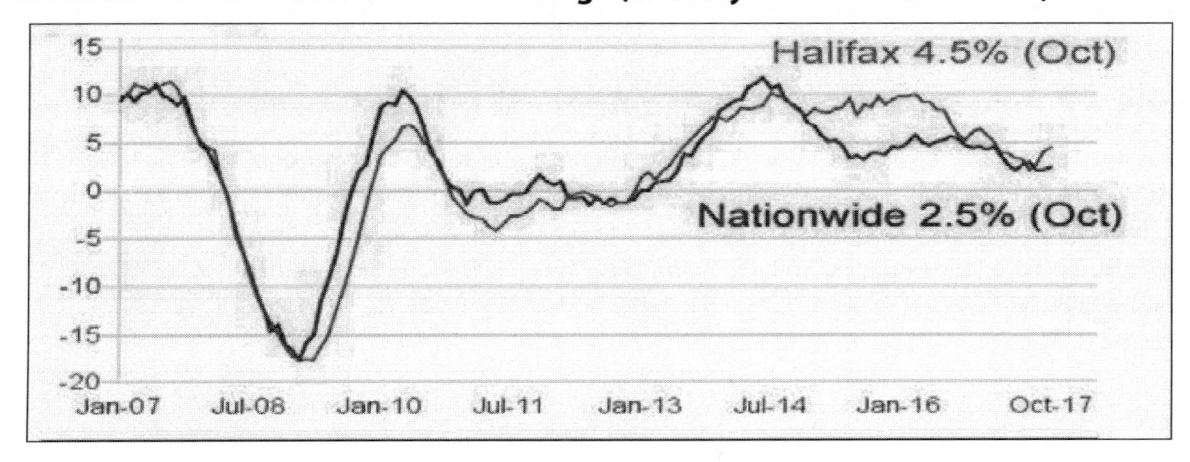

Nationwide – annual comparison by month. Halifax – annual comparison by quarter.
Source: Halifax and Nationwide

The Index increased to 734.1 points in November 2017, from 730.4 in October 2017 (in 1983, the Index was 100).

The diagram above comes from the Nationwide survey and quite clearly reveals the extraordinary growth in the nominal and real value of property prices, and also illustrates the abrupt drop in home prices which has taken place since the peak in Q1, 2007 and which extended into 2013, before picking up in 2014.

Real House Prices (1979–2017)

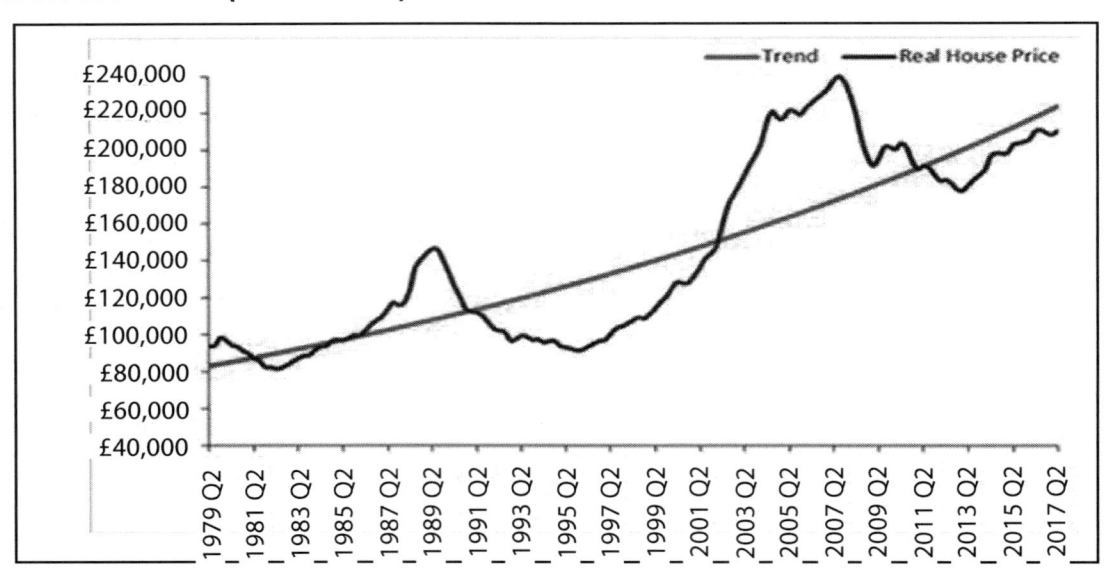

Base 2016 Q2; Trend from 1979 Q2 to present; Trend = c2.6% per annum; Source: Nationwide Building Society

Using inflation-adjusted or real prices, the median value of a house in 1975 was almost £60,000, in mid-2010 it was £168,719, and in mid-2016 it was £204,238. For Q4 2010 to Q1 2013, house prices have corrected following the financial crisis, and the subsequent drop in demand. As the economy started to grow again, prices picked up, with the median value reaching £211,672 in Q3 2017.

5.2.4 Public Sector Net Cash Requirement (PSNCR)

One other vital statistic which is updated by the Chancellor of the Exchequer on a periodic basis is the PSNCR. The requirement is either expressed as the set amount of money that is being raised by the Government, or the percentage it represents of the GDP. Each year in the Budget, the Chancellor sets the PSNCR for the following year and it is then the responsibility of the Debt Management Office (DMO) to issue gilts, or use other measures, to achieve the borrowing required.

The City closely follows the PSNCR figure, as it indicates the amount of money the Government is going to have to borrow from the world's capital markets where it will have to compete with other sovereign borrowers. In 2009, the Government borrowed £175 billion ($254 billion), worth 12.4% of GDP UK. In 2010 it was closer to £150 billion. The current figure is approximately £45 billion (2017), and it should be noted that, since 2009, large quantities of gilts have been purchased under the Government's QE programme (a policy adopted by a number of central banks in one name or another over the same time frame).

UK Central Bank Balance Sheet

The BoE uses its balance sheet for policy purposes. The Bank publishes data on its assets and liabilities on a weekly basis. The new weekly report provides data on all assets and liabilities generated though the Bank's monetary operations. The weekly balance reports can be found at: http://www.bankofengland.co.uk/publications/Pages/weeklyreport/default.aspx.

The UK's Central Bank Balance Sheet increased to £556,078 in 2017 from £422,702 million in 2016. This was largely due to quantitative easing.

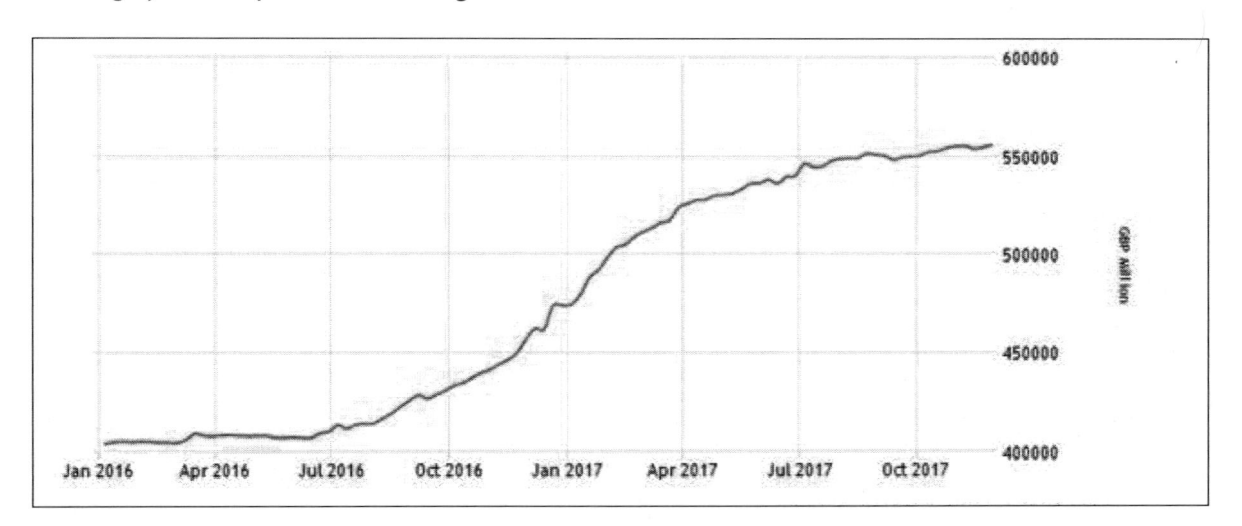

Source: www.tradingeconomics.com, HM Treasury

UK Net Borrowing – % of GDP (1992–2021)

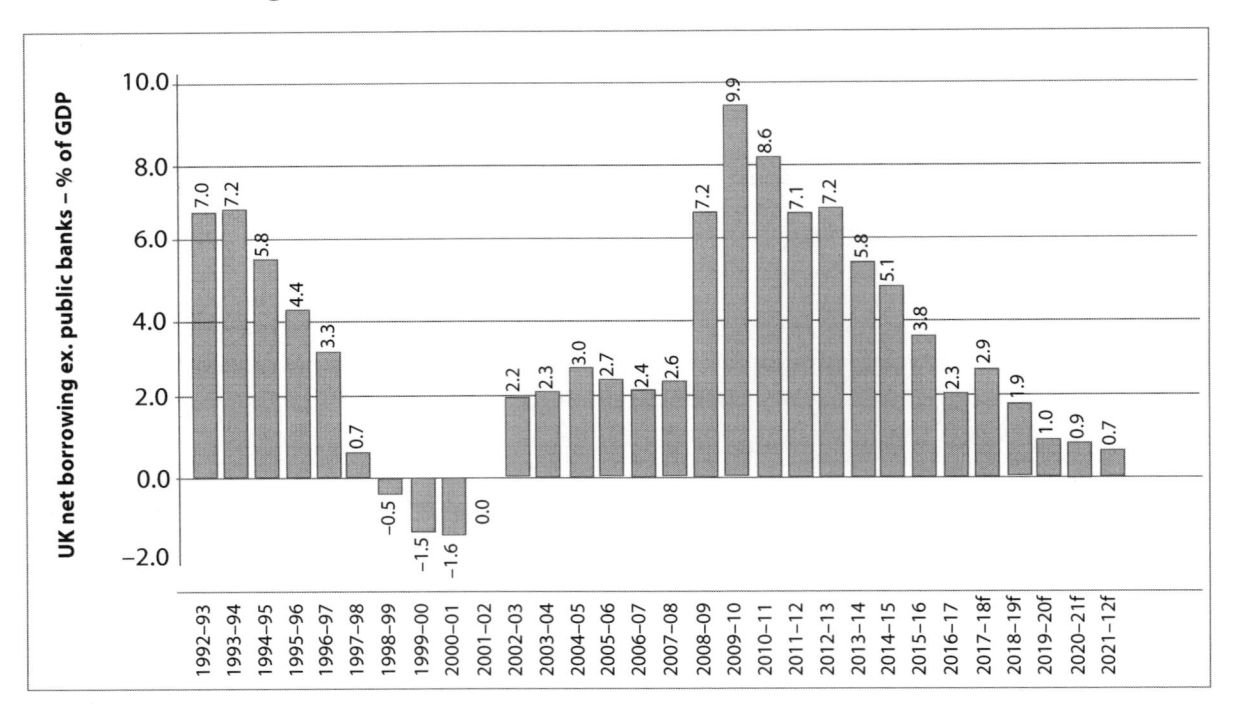

Year	% of GDP
1992-93	7.0
1993-94	7.2
1994-95	5.8
1995-96	4.4
1996-97	3.3
1997-98	0.7
1998-99	-0.5
1999-00	-1.5
2000-01	-1.6
2001-02	0.0
2002-03	2.2
2003-04	2.3
2004-05	3.0
2005-06	2.7
2006-07	2.4
2007-08	2.6
2008-09	7.2
2009-10	9.9
2010-11	8.6
2011-12	7.1
2012-13	7.2
2013-14	5.8
2014-15	5.1
2015-16	3.8
2016-17	2.3
2017-18f	2.9
2018-19f	1.9
2019-20f	1.0
2020-21f	0.9
2021-12f	0.7

Source: www.economicshelp.com, ONS

It is clear that there is a correlation between increases in government spending and, therefore, borrowing in times of economic stress. Candidates should also consider the government commitments to reducing public borrowing and its impact on social programmes that have been cut back. The scaling-back of pension allowance limits from 6 April 2014 is also a direct effect of this 'tightening' of the belt.

Summary

The UK economy is the second largest economy in Europe and the fifth largest in the world with GDP at $2.8 trillion, measured on a PPP basis. In 2017, the country accounted for approximately 3.9% of the gross world product. The UK has one of the highest GDP figures per capita (22nd), estimated in December 2016 at $41,603 (Source: tradingeconomics.com).

There is an enormous amount of statistical data in the public domain which provides the best method of determining the current state of the UK economy as well as that of its competitors.

Useful data on the US economy can be found at the websites of the Federal Reserve and also the US Treasury.

The following are some useful websites for finding updated macroeconomic statistics:

The Office for National Statistics
www.statistics.gov.uk

Historical CPI rates in the UK

www.ons.gov.uk/economy/inflationandpriceindices

Historical Unemployment Rates in the UK

www.ons.gov.uk/employmentandlabourmarket/peoplenotinwork/unemployment

Historical GDP (Quarterly) since 1980

www.tradingeconomics.com/Economics/GDP-Growth.aspx?Symbol=GBP

For views on the residential property data in the UK:

www.nationwide.co.uk/hpi/

6. Financial Markets and Services

Learning Objective

1.6 Explain the role of financial markets and services within the economy

Financial intermediation is a term which can be used to describe in very general terms the main function performed by markets and those institutions, known collectively as financial services companies, which are most active within the capital markets. As a general observation, there is often a distinction made between the capital markets and the money markets.

Both types of market allow market participants to deal in capital, but the usual distinction that is made is that capital markets are used for raising and investing largely long-term capital (usually defined as one year or more), whereas the money markets are financial markets for lending and borrowing with a focus more on the short term. The distinction is not rigorously observed and it is common for people to use the terms interchangeably.

6.1 Role of Capital Markets

When examining the role of capital markets, in general it is useful to make a distinction between what could be called their primary market activities on the one hand, and their secondary market activities on the other.

The two kinds of activities themselves can take place within the operations of the same institution or exchange but have quite separate purposes.

An institution such as the London Stock Exchange (LSE) can function as a primary market and a secondary market. But let us examine each role in turn.

Primary markets are used for the issuance of new securities either as loan stock (or bonds) and also for allowing new companies, or existing ones, to issue new shares or equity. These are known as initial public offerings (IPOs) in the case of an offer to the public or private placement. The reason behind the issuance of equities and bonds is the same, which is to raise new capital for firms to invest in their businesses. In the case of bonds, the issue is in the form of debt, whereas the shares or equity are issued in the form of risk capital. These different kinds of capital will be explained in Chapters 5 and 6.

Secondary markets, such as the LSE or the New York Stock Exchange (NYSE), allow traders and investors to buy and sell securities that have already been issued, and in the case of bonds, which are not yet at maturity. If an investor wants to purchase 1,000 shares of Vodafone they would place an order with a brokerage which is a member firm of the LSE and which would then purchase those shares from another shareholder who wishes to sell 1,000 shares. The deal would take place through the LSE's exchange mechanism and would then be one of the trades registered during the course of a trading session and which would contribute to the ongoing pricing of shares of Vodafone which are reported daily in the financial media.

This secondary market function not only allows traders and investors to move quickly on their desires to buy and sell securities, but also provides vital liquidity to capital markets. The presence of liquidity in financial markets is one of the most important conditions for transactions to take place. Economists have really not provided a satisfactory account of liquidity but rather assume that it will be present in markets. The term refers to the depth of interest from both buyers and sellers for a security and if, as occurs from time to time – as in Q4, 2008 – there is an absence of interest from buyers in many securities, a market will become lopsided and the desire by many to sell their shares and bonds at the same time causes disorderly market behaviour and results in rather sudden and abrupt drops in prices of securities. In its more extreme form, this can be referred to as a market crash. The classic example of such an event took place in October 1987 when global markets dropped precipitously and the NYSE fell by more than 20% in a single session on Monday 19 October of that year, with other indices such as the LSE registering similar falls.

In addition to its better-known function of providing a secondary market for the trading and exchange of shares, the LSE provides a market for the trading of government bonds, local authority loans and some overseas stocks. In order for a company's securities to be traded on the LSE they have to be listed with the exchange and have to satisfy rigorous regulations and compliance requirements.

The vital role of liquidity has been touched upon and it is worth pointing out the different motives of the investor and the speculator or trader. The investor, such as a pension fund or unit trust manager may be purchasing (or selling) securities as part of a long-term portfolio management exercise. The speculator or trader may be interested in trying to profit from short-term movements in the prices of securities without the intention of holding the securities for an extended period. Speculators and traders help to provide liquidity to a market which would see less activity if it was just long-term investors that were conducting the activity. Trading activities create larger volumes in the markets, and thereby enhance the ability of the long-term investors and allocators of capital to buy and sell without moving the market excessively. This is a somewhat controversial topic, as there are some who would argue that the activity of speculators, rather than providing greater liquidity and acting as a way of smoothing price fluctuations, may actually lead to larger movements in prices or volatility, which has the consequence of destabilising markets.

6.1.1 The Changing Face of the Stock Market

Although there are a number of individuals who are quite active in the stock market and who are non-professionals or retail investors, direct public participation in the stock market has been declining for many years. However, many individuals have exposure to the stock market through institutional vehicles such as through purchasing via a collective investment scheme, such as a unit trust or indirectly through the fact that their pension fund will hold the bulk of its assets in the form of tradeable securities. It is perhaps worth mentioning the fact that when stock markets decline the asset valuations of large pension funds and insurance companies will also suffer large drops. This can create potential problems for these institutions which need to provide future income and payouts to their clients.

During the 1980s, the privatisation of industries, under the Thatcher Government, produced first-time equity owners who purchased shares in companies, such as British Telecom and British Steel (later to become Corus). Also during this era, there were several tax incentives introduced designed to encourage savings and share ownership – personal equity plans (PEPs) and ISAs. PEPs merged with ISAs in 2008.

6.1.2 Buying and Selling Shares

Equities are a form of capital which is used by companies to finance their activities. The original seller of equity is the company which issues shares and the buyer could be an investor who purchases the shares at the IPO. Subsequently, the buying and selling of shares takes place through various exchanges where the securities are listed.

As a principal involved in a transaction for shares, the purchaser or seller will conduct the trade through a brokerage firm which will be a firm which is a member of the exchange. Brokers act as an agent to represent the principal and will execute the trade according to the instructions of the client. The broker will present the client with the 'bid' and the 'ask' for the security and the principal will place an order with the broker and this may specify the limits of the price to be paid or received from a sale.

As an example, let us examine the following.

Example

The purchaser is a small pension fund and it wishes to buy 500,000 shares of Vodafone. This company's shares are listed on the LSE and the pension fund may instruct its broker to provide the bid price, which is the price at which someone wanting to buy Vodafone shares currently is prepared to offer.

The ask price or offer price is the amount that someone is willing to sell the shares at. In the case of a large transaction there will be several potential sellers providing offers which may be slightly at variance with the current market price.

Let us suppose that for a smaller number of shares, the current bid is £1.80 and the current ask is £1.82. The difference between the bid and the ask is known as the spread and in the case of large companies traded on liquid exchanges the spread is likely to be narrow. There might be a willing seller for the whole block of 500,000 shares who is willing to sell at £1.81 – slightly below the current ask for a smaller transaction. The fund manager decides to accept this price and accordingly, instructs the broker to purchase all of the shares with a bid of £1.81 per share. The deal is made and the size of the trade and the price are registered in the LSE's computer systems.

At the very moment when the trade is made it could be said that the market price for Vodafone shares was £1.81. But this will be a fleeting price as the next trade which could take place just seconds later may be for a different amount.

Prices of individual shares are constantly updated in real time and redistributed electronically and are seen on the trading screens of hundreds of thousands if not millions of traders and investors across the globe instantaneously. Another consequence of all of the transactions similar to the one just described is that there is a continuous adjustment taking place to the values of a major stock market index such as the FTSE 100. This index is calculated from the price performance of the 100 largest companies in the UK and will be discussed further in chapter 6.

As Vodafone is one of the largest components of the FTSE 100 index, the changes in price of its shares will automatically require a recalculation of the value of the overall index. Of course the other constituents of the index are also changing as well. The movements of all of the prices of the 100 shares in the index are constantly recalculated in real time and this provides the current pricing of the FTSE 100 Index, which is itself a very closely watched benchmark and which can be traded separately from the actual constituents.

As a general comment about the views of investors and traders in the financial markets, they have traditionally been divided into two camps. The view that the market is headed higher is a bullish view and is held by **bulls**; the view that the market is headed lower is a bearish view and is held by **bears**. The terminology has become widely applicable across markets which trade different assets. Associated terminology is the distinction between a **long** position in the market and a **short** position in the market.

Let us suppose that your view of the FTSE 100 Index is bullish and that you believe that it is likely to rise by 5% in the next six months. There are various market instruments, including derivative products, such as contracts for differences (CFDs), which would enable you to take a long position in the FTSE index. If the direction in the market is upwards the long position which you established would be profitable. Being long of a market is essentially the same thing as being a buyer with an expectation that the price will be moving upwards. If on the contrary you have a bearish view of Vodafone and believe that the price will decline by 5% in the next six months you could establish what is called a short position in the stock. Traditionally the manner in which one would go short of Vodafone is to borrow shares in the company (from a broker) and sell them at the prevailing price in the marketplace. If your expectation about a price decline turns out to be correct, then after six months the price of Vodafone is indeed 5% lower and you would buy the shares at the lower price and return them to the broker from whom you borrowed them. Your gain would be 5% as the replacement costs would be 5% less than the price you obtained when you initially sold them. Interest charges would also have to be paid to the broker for the loan of the stock (this will be covered in greater detail in the following chapters), but in effect, being short, it is profitable for a security which goes down in price in very similar fashion to being profitable with a long position of a security which goes up in price. Trading with derivatives has simplified matters for short sellers and there are many traders and investors that will have short positions in securities such as the FTSE 100 index. This is sometimes done for hedging purposes as will be discussed later in the workbook.

It is also worth drawing attention to the fact that during the very difficult market conditions that were faced in Q4, 2008, the Financial Services Authority (FSA), which is the former regulatory body empowered to supervise the conduct of the financial services industry (superseded by the Financial Conduct Authority (FCA)), imposed a ban on short selling.

The following statement was published by the FSA with regard to the restrictions on short selling:

> 'The Board of the Financial Services Authority (FSA) today (Thursday 18 September) agreed to introduce new provisions to the Code of Market Conduct to prohibit the active creation or increase of net short positions in publicly quoted financial companies from midnight tonight.
>
> In addition, the FSA will require from Tuesday 23 September daily disclosure of all net short positions in excess of 0.25% of the ordinary share capital of the relevant companies held at market close on the previous working day. Disclosure of such positions held at close on Friday 19 September will also be required on Tuesday 23 September.
>
> The FSA stands ready to extend this approach to other sectors if it judges it to be necessary.
>
> These provisions will remain in force until 16 January 2009, although they will be reviewed after 30 days. A comprehensive review of the rules on short selling will be published in January.'

In addition, the news release contained the following quotation from Hector Sants, who was at the time the chief executive of the FSA:

> 'While we still regard short-selling as a legitimate investment technique in normal market conditions, the current extreme circumstances have given rise to disorderly markets. As a result, we have taken this decisive action, after careful consideration, to protect the fundamental integrity and quality of markets and to guard against further instability in the financial sector.'

The role of brokers when acting as agents for clients has been outlined in the preceding discussion, but brokers can also conduct proprietary trading and investment activities as well as acting as market makers. The role of a market maker is to provide liquidity for third-party traders who wish to buy or sell in the market quickly and when there may not be a willing counterparty to a trade immediately available. Traditionally, the specialist on the LSE and the NYSE became responsible for maintaining an orderly market for specific companies. Thus, on the NYSE, there would be a specialist who would have a specific remit for a company such as General Electric (GE) and who had to stand ready to buy and sell potentially large amounts of the stock from the public and investment community – even when markets were moving abruptly. The market maker function is similar and is found on electronic exchanges such as the Nasdaq, although increasingly this role is being replaced by automated trading.

The large banks and brokers also conduct proprietary trading in which they risk their own capital to engage in trading and investing in different assets. A company like Goldman Sachs, which is one of the world's largest banks, has become hugely profitable as a result of its remarkable track record in proprietary trading.

Questions have been raised in the wake of the rescue operations mounted by central banks and governments around the world, following the collapse in confidence in the banking system in 2008, as to whether banks should be allowed to risk capital which has been largely underwritten or guaranteed by the public sector balance sheet.

6.1.3 Other Capital Markets

Some markets are centralised and have a hub of operations, such as the LSE and the NYSE, whereas others are decentralised and there is no specific exchange or hub at the centre of the trading activities. An example of the latter is the Nasdaq market in the US which has been established for many years and where stocks are traded on a decentralised basis, which essentially means that the transactions take place on a distributed platform with many nodes rather than a central hub.

Other examples of a centralised market are the commodity markets in the US. The CME and the NYMEX are the exchanges where futures trading in a variety of commodities takes place. Futures contracts are specialised instruments which enable buyers and sellers to make deals for the future purchase and **delivery** of agricultural, industrial and financial products and commodities. The method of trading futures at these exchanges was traditionally known as the 'open outcry method', as it consisted of several hundred traders face to face in what was known as a 'trading pit', and the prices of the commodities were determined in real time by the frantic interaction of these traders, known as 'locals'. Electronically placed orders can enter the pits from outside but the actual process of price discovery takes place entirely within the trading pits during designated hours of the exchange. Many of these exchanges have, over time, migrated to electronic formats; but some markets, such as US equity options, are still traded via **open-outcry**.

In the UK, the futures markets also used to run in a similar manner to those in Chicago and New York when they were part of the London International Financial and Options Exchange (LIFFE) but they have since been switched to screen-based trading only at the exchange, now known as ICE Futures Europe.

The AIM (Alternative Investment Market) is owned by the LSE in the UK, and was opened in 1995. It is available for companies that want to have their shares traded but do not want to satisfy full listing requirements of the LSE. It is easier to qualify for listing as regulations are less stringent about criteria such as market capitalisation and the length of trading history. As previously observed, all of these markets can operate with listed member firms which can act as brokers, market makers and specialists and they are increasingly being electronically driven.

6.1.4 Capital Market Instruments

These will be covered in much greater detail in chapter 6 but these are the principal kinds of securities or financial instruments that are available in the capital markets:

- **Ordinary shares** – these are the most fundamental kind of capital and are to be found at the bottom of the capital structure of any company. Initially they are made available through a rights issue and they are at the bottom of the pile in terms of a liquidation or bankruptcy. The holder of an ordinary share may receive a dividend from the company but that is at the discretion of the company and it is not a fixed amount and may often be zero.
- **Preference shares** – these are more senior in the capital structure and have special preferences in the case of a liquidation and they also will pay a fixed dividend.

- **Debentures or bonds** – these are effectively debt issuances by a company and can either be secured or unsecured.
- **Convertible securities** – can be converted into common equity or ordinary shares. Effectively a bond which can be traded as such till conversion. Normally, receiving a lower coupon rate because of the conversion **option**.
- **Derivatives** – these are securities which derive their value from the movement in price of an underlying security and they come in many flavours, some of which are highly complex. Some of the most widely used and better-known examples of derivatives are as follows:
    - **Options** – calls and puts which confer the right but not the obligation to buy or sell the underlying security.
    - **Futures and forward contracts** – relate to setting prices for transactions that will occur at some point in the future.
    - **Asset-backed securities** – these are based on mortgages, for example, and are known as collateralised debt obligations (CDOs).

Money Markets

In contrast to the infrastructure for the capital markets, which has been examined, the money markets are to a large extent decentralised without any obvious physical locations. Rather, the money market should be seen as a number of interconnected wholesale markets for short-term funds. Their existence is more similar to a virtual network of dealers and intermediaries that are providing the financial economy with the necessary liquidity and short-term funding to operate smoothly and efficiently.

Within the UK, the primary network for the money market is the sterling interbank market, which is the market where wholesale funding takes place between banks wishing to either borrow or lend money on a very short-term, often overnight basis. The rates of interest charted nowadays are known as the overnight repo rate and the sterling overnight index average (SONIA), used as the reference for the sterling overnight index swap (OIS) market and have become a key money market rates.

It is worth pointing out that the interbank market became effectively frozen during Q4, 2008 and much of Q1, 2009 and there was a seizing up of the normal liquidity provided by this vital sector of the money markets – not only in the UK but throughout the global money markets. Banks were unwilling or unable to participate in their short-term financing operations and the central banks – including the BoE – were required to become the lender of last resort to the commercial banks.

The **London Interbank Offered Rate (LIBOR)** scandal in 2012 was a series of fraudulent actions connected to the LIBOR and the resulting investigation and reaction. LIBOR is an average interest rate calculated through submissions of interest rates by major banks across the world. The scandal arose when it was discovered that banks were falsely inflating or deflating their rates to profit from trades, or to give the impression that they were more creditworthy than they actually were. The methodologies both for collating the submitted rates and then for calculating LIBOR have been substantially revised since then.

In addition to being the centre for the sterling interbank market, London has become the dominant financial centre of the euro-currency market. Euro-currency markets are traditionally those where the conducting of business occurs with an asset denominated in a 'foreign' currency, but when the transaction takes place outside the jurisdiction which is the home territory of that currency. This is not to be confused with the market in assets denominated in the euro-currency which was, relatively speaking, a more recent development, dating from the late 1990s. Historically, this market developed during the 1960s and 1970s when the large offshore dollar market began to develop as foreign owners of US dollar-denominated assets conducted dollar-based transactions, including the issuance of eurobonds (which will be discussed in in chapter 5), outside the US financial system and jurisdiction. Since the early days the euro-currency markets have extended to cover most currencies and this market has most major currencies with sizable deposits outside their home markets.

In addition to the interbank market there are other money markets which enable companies to borrow money in the wholesale markets and this is known as the commercial paper market. Effectively companies issue IOUs to banks and other financial intermediaries and can borrow at more advantageous rates than would be available on a more formal structured loan basis. This market was also a major casualty of the financial crisis of 2008 and its activities essentially shut down and are only slowly being revived.

Other kinds of instruments which can provide short-term liquidity within the money market are certificates of deposit (CDs), the market for financing the short-term needs of local authorities; and the much larger market for trading in central government short-term securities which are known as Treasury bills and where the primary pricing structure uses a discounting mechanism.

Discounting will be discussed further in chapter 5, but essentially, the UK Treasury will issue a bill with a specified face value at maturity but when the price to be paid now is at a discount to the value in the future.

Treasury bills, or T-bills, are sold in terms ranging from a few days to 52 weeks. 52-week Treasury bills are rare (usually terms are for six months). Bills are typically sold at a discount from the par amount (also called face value). For instance, you might pay £990 for £1,000 worth of Treasury bills. When the bill matures, you would be paid £1,000. The difference between the purchase price and face value is interest. It is possible for a bill auction to result in a price equal to par, which means that the Treasury will issue and redeem the securities at par value.

In 2009, the US Government made it far easier for small investors to participate in the purchase of Treasury bills. They can be purchased from the website Treasury through non-competitive bidding. Treasury Direct permits accounts for both individuals and various types of entities including trusts, estates, corporations and partnerships.

One further mechanism which is widespread throughout the money markets is the notion of repurchase agreements. A repurchase agreement (also known as a repo or sale and repurchase agreement) allows a borrower to use a financial security as collateral for a cash loan at a fixed rate of interest. In a repo, the borrower agrees to immediately sell a security to a lender and at the same time agrees to buy back the same security from the lender at a fixed price at some later date.

The cash transaction results in transfer of money to the borrower in exchange for legal transfer of the security to the lender, while the promise to repurchase – known as a **forward contract** – ensures repayment of the loan to the lender and return of the collateral of the borrower. The difference between the price which is laid out in the forward contract committing the borrower to repurchase is known as the forward price and the difference between it and the spot price provides, in similar fashion to the discounting mechanism, the implicit rate of interest on the loan, and the settlement date stipulated in the forward contract is the maturity date of the loan. The BoE is a principal participant in the repo market and will accept qualified collateral – Treasury bills for example – as part of a repurchase agreement.

It is worth observing that a consequence of the liquidity crisis which arose in 2008 is that central banks in general, especially the Federal Reserve in the US and the BoE have relaxed the requirements on the quality of the collateral which is acceptable under a repo agreement with the central bank. Commercial banks were permitted to use many kinds of asset-backed securities, which had previously been considered to be below the acceptable standards in terms of credit risk and quality, in their repo agreements with central banks. This was one method used by central banks and policymakers to provide greater financial liquidity during the banking crisis.

6.1.5 The Bank of England (BoE)

The cornerstone of the money market in the UK is the central bank – the BoE.

It was established in 1694, and was nationalised in 1946.

Since being given operational independence in 1997, the BoE has been solely responsible for the conduct of monetary policy – a role which had previously been under the control of the Chancellor of the Exchequer (this is described in section 4.2 of this chapter).

The Bank additionally advises the DMO (part of the Treasury), on the issue and redemption of government securities.

The Bank acts as lender of last resort by lending money to the commercial banks if absolutely required – as has been the case in the aftermath of the financial crisis of 2008.

Responsibility for overall banking supervision was transferred to the FSA in 1998, and to the PRA in 2013, which was created by the Financial Services Act 2012 and is now part of the BoE, operating a close working relationship with other parts of the Bank, such as the FPC and the Special Resolution Unit, as well as the FCA. These regulatory areas are covered in more detail in chapter 9.

The Bank is the sole issuer of notes and coins.

The BoE has the function of controlling the money supply and the amount of credit available through its activities in setting rates and also through open market operations. The Bank can decide to purchase government securities in the open market, which has the effect of adding cash and liquidity to the market, or if it wishes to decrease the availability of credit and restrict the growth in the money supply it will sell government securities into the market which has the effect of removing the monetary base available to the commercial banking system. In recent years this has been a major area of activity, through the introduction of QE (see section 4.2.3 of this chapter).

The BoE can also request special deposits to be placed by the commercial banks with the Bank and this will also have the effect of reducing the Bank's ability to increase the credit available in the financial system.

The BoE's framework for its operations in the sterling money markets is designed to implement the MPC's interest rate decisions while meeting liquidity needs, and so contributing to the stability of the banking system as a whole.

The BoE is the sole issuer of sterling central bank money, the final, risk-free settlement asset in the UK. This enables the Bank to implement monetary policy and makes the framework for its monetary operations central to liquidity management in the banking system as a whole, and by individual banks and building societies.

The Bank's market operations have two objectives, stemming from its monetary policy and financial stability responsibilities as the UK's central bank.

The following outline of the framework's main elements comes from the BoE's own account of these vital parts of its policy, in terms of liquidity insurance facilities for participants in the sterling monetary framework:

- **Contingent term repo facility** – routine monthly operations for firms with predictable needs for liquid assets. They can bid for reserves against the full range of eligible collateral.
- **A discount window facility** – this is a bilateral, on-demand facility for firms experiencing individual or market-wide shocks. Eligible banks and building societies may borrow gilts, for up to 30 days, against a wide range of collateral in return for a fee, which will vary with the collateral used and the total size of borrowings.
- **Indexed long-term repo (ILTR) open market operations** – regular monthly market-wide ILTR operations are aimed at banks, building societies and broker-dealers with a predictable need for liquid assets. The BoE offers funds via an ILTR operation once per calendar month.

6.1.6 Bank for International Settlements (BIS)

Described colloquially as the 'central banks' central bank', the BIS is an organisation which is owned by 60 central banks to serve their pursuit of monetary and financial stability; it is based in Basel in Switzerland.

It coordinates and advises on strengthening resilience and stability in the global financial system via the Basel Committee on Banking Supervision (BCBS). This currently focuses on strengthening the regulatory framework by:

- improving the quality of banks' Tier 1 Capital (minimum 4.5% + 1.5% Additional Tier 1, as a ratio of risk weighted assets)
- increasing the level of capital requirements to enable banks to withstand losses
- revising the risk-weighting of capital in calibrating market risk, counterparty credit risk and securitisation
- introducing capital buffers to handle cyclical losses and systemic industry exposures
- specifying minimum leverage ratio requirements to constrain excess leverage
- introducing an international framework to mitigate liquidity risk.

The capital adequacy ratio is defined as the ratio of a bank's capital to its risk-weighted assets.

Two types of capital are measured:

- **Tier one capital** consists largely of shareholders equity and disclosed reserves.
- **Tier two capital** comprises undisclosed reserves, revaluation reserves, general provisions, hybrid investments and subordinated debt.

Applying minimum capital adequacy ratios serves to protect depositors and promote the stability and efficiency of the financial system as a whole.

From an international point of view, ensuring capital adequacy is the most important problem between central banks, as speculative lending based on inadequate underlying capital and widely varying liability rules causes economic crises.

6.1.7 Financial Intermediaries

Previously, we have reviewed the role played by a broker in providing financial services to an end customer who wishes to buy or sell shares. In general we can look at the role of other companies performing similar functions.

A financial intermediary is a business entity which brings together providers and users of capital. As in the case of brokers, other financial intermediaries such as banks can act as either an agent acting on behalf of a client or they can act as a principal conducting financial transactions for their own account.

Financial intermediaries develop the facilities and financial instruments which make lending and borrowing possible. Financial intermediaries provide the means by which funds can be transferred from surplus units (eg, someone with savings to invest in the economy) to deficit units (for example, someone who wants to borrow money to buy a house).

If lending and borrowing or other financial transactions between unrelated parties takes place without financial intermediation, they are said to be dealing directly.

Here is a list of the better known financial intermediaries:

- Clearing banks, including retail (high street) banks provide basic banking services for individuals and businesses.
- Wholesale or merchant banks which are now better known as investment banks and which provide more specialised financial services on behalf of large corporate clients and even governments.
- Building societies specialise in providing mortgages for residential home buyers.
- Insurance companies, pension funds, unit trust companies and investment trust companies.
- The Government's National Savings & Investments (NS&I).
- Investment and unit trusts (in the US these are known as mutual funds).
- Venture capital firms provide risk financing for new businesses and one of the largest, 3i, is itself a publicly traded company on the LSE.

In spite of competition from building societies, insurance companies and other financial institutions, banks arguably remain the major financial intermediaries in the UK. Following the banking crisis of 2008–09 there have been several significant changes to the financial landscape in the UK, including governmental financial intervention in the banking system to avoid its systemic collapse. The government became a major shareholder in banks, such as RBS and, for a time, Lloyds Banking Group; the latter was involved in a merger with Halifax Bank of Scotland at the time of the credit crisis.

The Chancellor of the Exchequer amended the deposit guarantee and has now guaranteed 100% of the first £85,000 worth of deposits per individual per banking licence (from 30 January 2017). In addition, temporary cash balances of up to £1 million are protected (eg, from house sale proceeds).

Role of Financial Intermediaries

- To act as agents for principals engaged in capital formation and capital transfers.
- To provide collective investment products which enable retail investors more access to risk and portfolio diversification.
- Unit trusts, for example, give investors an opportunity to follow the advice of investment professionals, ie, 'don't put all your eggs in one basket'.
- Other collective investment vehicles, discussed in more detail in chapter 7, allow individuals to have broad-based exposure in many kinds of asset markets.
- Financial products can be structured to assist in risk management and transfer, enabling the development of structured products designed to suit the risk profiles of different customers.
- The role of many financial intermediaries is considered to be one of financial engineering when highly quantitative techniques are employed to develop financial instruments and techniques which (allegedly) help to reduce the degree of risk within a specific financial transaction and to reduce the likelihood of systemic risk.
- Hedging, for example, is often provided in the form of **swap** arrangements which allow one party to offset an exposure in a particular asset to a counterparty that is prepared to assume the risk.
- Financial derivatives and other techniques have been developed at the 'cutting edge' of financial innovation by certain banks and these instruments are sold to market participants on the premise that they will enable the bank's customers to better manage their risks.

6.1.8 Summary of Financial Services

The financial services sector covers a multitude of intermediation activities within complex money-based economies. At the national level, the various money market participants discussed previously including the BoE have the role of ensuring that the credit system which underpins banking financial services available to businesses functions smoothly and without creating unnecessary risks to the financial system.

To the extent that the public sector has had to assume many of the liabilities of the private banking system, the money market mechanisms have not been functioning effectively for some time and there are several government reviews as to changes required to the regulatory system and the practice of certain kinds of finance to make the financial system less prone to crisis.

The financial services sector also operates within an international framework, resulting from both the multinational nature of many financial services activities and from various international agreements and regulatory influences.

Macroeconomics

Example Exam Questions on Economic Policy

Questions about economics can appear throughout the exam and are often asked, so it is important that you can understand and interpret the information being presented to you. Usually, you will be asked to discuss a particular theme or concept or relate it to a specific situation, such as how economic events affect the markets and the investments they deal in.

Some examples are shown below:

Question 1

If a government accepts Keynes' view on tax and spending in a recession, discuss the likely effect on bond prices and interest rates. (5 marks)

Question 2

Explain the injections/leakages/modifications that need to be made to the circular flow of income to reflect the workings of the real economy. (5 marks)

Question 3

a. Following the UK Government reorganisation in July 2016, there has been discussion of the policy which will now be adopted by the new Chancellor of the Exchequer. It appears that the austerity target has eased and new policies will be introduced. One of the major potential policy changes could be the use of fiscal policy and more Keynesian economics. Mr Sandilands, a client, has asked you to a) Discuss what this means, and how it could impact on the equity and bond markets (in your opinion). (15 marks)
b. Explain to him why economists are worried about too low a level of inflation. (5 marks)
c. Following the UK's EU referendum, the Bank of England has stated that it may expand the use of Quantitative Easing (QE), he is also interested in hearing what this means and how the market could be affected in your opinion. Discuss the use of QE and the possible impact on the stock and bond markets. (8 marks)

Exercise Answers

Exercise 1

1. Outline three principal changes to economic policy that the UK government can make to help raise demand in the economy.

Answer

Any three from the following:

- Reduce taxes – including insurance premium tax (IPT), VAT.
- Reduce income and corporation taxes and excise duties.
- Encourage lower interest rates to stimulate spending (the BoE currently has independence in setting monetary policy, within parameters set by the Government).

- Increase Government spending – increased borrowing may raise capital to inject into the economy and stimulate demand.
- manipulating a weaker exchange rate – this will result in relative changes to the cost of exports compared, stimulating demand from overseas.

Exercise 2

'In the UK a fixed exchange rate will always provide stability and economic confidence and should be used in preference to a system of floating exchange rates.'

Evaluate the accuracy of this statement using arguments for and against both approaches.

Answer

Exchange Rates

An exchange rate is the price of a currency expressed in terms of how much that currency can buy of another. This rate can have an effect on industry as it will dictate how competitive businesses are across international boundaries and how much they can be affected by imports from other countries.

Floating Exchange Rates

In a floating system rates are determined by the supply and demand for sterling on foreign currency markets.

Supply and demand for sterling is driven partly by the movement of UK imports and exports where currency is required to buy and sell goods either in sterling or to use sterling to purchase foreign currencies.

Several factors determine the value of the pound:

- balance of payments
- speculation
- confidence
- interest rate differentials
- difference in inflation rates.

Fixed Exchange Rates

In a fixed rate system the government does not allow the rate to fluctuate freely with market forces. Instead, the government uses policies designed to maintain the exchange rate at a pre-arranged level. The government or central bank fixes exchange rates.

The system may only allow one rate or allow small fluctuations within defined limits. The ERM of the EMS has allowed some small fluctuations.

The government can intervene in order to manage the exchange rate in two ways:

- **Interest rate policy** – demand for sterling can be controlled by changing the interest rate. An increase in rate would increase potential returns on accounts of sterling and this would increase demand and push up the sterling exchange rate.

- **Foreign currency reserves** – the BoE holds reserves of foreign currency. If there is downwards pressure on the pound these reserves could be sold in order to buy sterling and increase demand. If there was a chance that the target could be overshot then the government could sell sterling.

Arguments for and against Fixed and Floating Rates

Under a floating system the market (including supply and demand) dictates the rate and market forces will ensure that the correct level is found.

In a floating system the country is not forced into a rate it does not feel comfortable with.

A fixed rate forces external discipline on firms meaning that a devaluation bailout is not an option. It forces companies to become competitive and carefully manage costs and wages as the government cannot intervene if they cannot work within the fixed rate set.

Floating rates can cause uncertainty but a fixed rate will ensure that decisions on exports and investment can be made with more certainty.

In September 1992 (Black Wednesday) the UK left the ERM and economists cite this as the best reason not to use fixed exchange rates. This was reinforced by the following arguments:

- **Safety valve** – a floating rate acts as a safety valve in times of economic pressure when growth and competitiveness lead to unemployment and recession.
- **Balance of payments** – in a floating exchange rate any issues around a country's balance of payments should be short-term as the ability of the rate to fluctuate will affect imports and exports to redress any imbalance. A fixed rate will not allow this to happen in the short term and takes many years to correct.
- **Losing control of monetary policy** – a government will lose control of its ability to control the growth of the money supply and counteract the threat of inflation.
- **Bucking the market** – history has shown that most fixed-rate systems eventually collapse since the government does not have the strength to fight off market forces forever. No government can buck the market.

Chapter Two
Financial Statement Analysis

Introduction	**91**
1. Core Accounting	91
2. Construction of a Balance Sheet (Statement of Financial Position)	98
3. Construction of an Income Statement (Statement of Comprehensive Income)	107
4. Cash Flow Statement (Statement of Cash Flows)	110
5. Accounting Standards	114

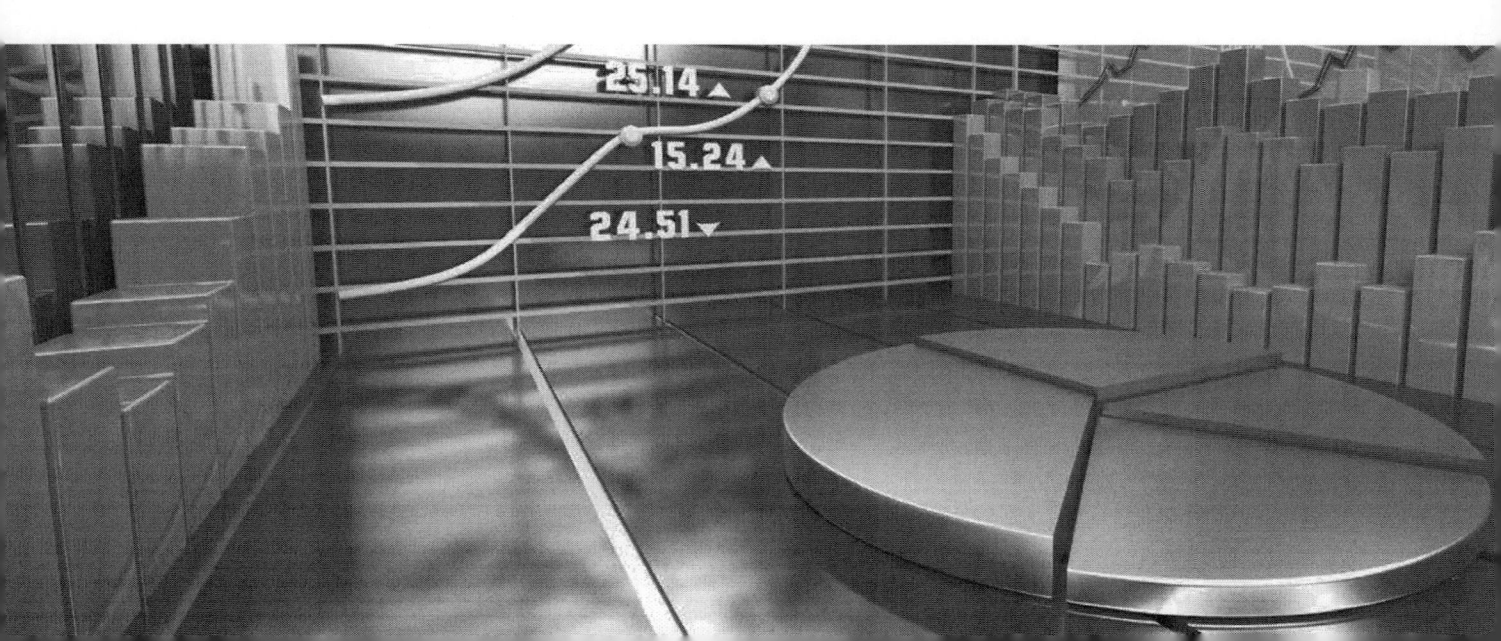

Financial Statement Analysis

Learning Outcome

Be able to explain the structure and content of financial statements issued by companies and their impact on the valuation of securities

Introduction

This chapter is designed to introduce the general principles involved in preparing a set of accounts and the standard form and content of a set of financial statements. All companies are required to complete an annual set of accounts at a minimum and most sizable companies will be producing such statements on a quarterly basis.

This introduction to basic accounting principles is not intended to be a rigorous overview of accounting, but rather to enable the reader to understand the basic elements within accounting and the issuance of financial statements which will assist in a better understanding of the valuation of financial securities.

1. Core Accounting

Learning Objective

2.1 Explain the core accounting concepts: dual aspect; money measurement; entity; going concern; asset management; accruals basis; matching principle; prudence; consistency and comparability; accounting for subsidiaries and overseas business

1.1 Dual Aspect Concept

In accounting, the dual aspect concept states that there are two aspects or ways of looking at all financial transactions, one represented by the assets of the business and the other by the claims against them. Implicit in the concept is the notion that these two aspects are always equal to each other. This derives from the fundamental accounting equation:

$$\text{Assets} = \text{Liabilities} + \text{Capital}$$

The dual aspect concept is also known under the moniker of the double entry book keeping system. Assets are what the company owns, liabilities are what the company owes against those assets or, more precisely, the mode of financing used to obtain the assets. The surplus or shortfall which results from subtracting the liabilities from the assets is known as the equity in the company, or the net worth of the company.

The dual aspect or double entry system is based on the principle that for each transaction there are two entries: a debit entry and a credit entry. This can be summarised by the following simple rule of thumb:

- A **debit entry** represents an increase in an asset or a decrease in a liability.
- A **credit entry** represents an increase in a liability or shareholders' funds or a decrease in an asset.

Example

Robert decides to start an engineering business. He first buys some machinery with £100,000 of his own money. The dual aspect of this transaction is as follows:

	DEBIT (Asset) £		**CREDIT (Liability) £**
Machinery	100,000	Share capital	100,000

The table above demonstrates that the business now has an asset, the machine, and Robert, the owner, has a claim of £100,000 against this asset. Putting this into the accounting equation above:

Assets (machinery £100,000) = Liabilities (£0) plus Capital (£100,000).

Robert then borrows £400,000 from the bank to buy premises. This alters the firm's accounting records as follows:

1. £400,000 increase in cash on DEBIT (Asset) side.
2. £400,000 liability demonstrates that the bank can make a claim against the asset.

	DEBIT (Asset) £		**CREDIT (Liability) £**
Cash	400,000		400,000
Machinery	100,000	Share Capital	100,000

This is expressed in terms of the accounting equation as:

Assets (machinery £100,000 plus cash £400,000) = Liabilities (£400,000) plus Capital (£100,000).

1.2 The Money Measurement Concept

In accounting, every recorded event or transaction is measured in terms of money. If it is not possible to specify the monetary amount of an event then it is not considered a material event or transaction and is not recorded in the company's accounting records.

A monetary amount is a quantitative measurement of value in the accounts, as opposed to qualitative features which cannot be measured and thus are not recorded in financial statements. Examples of qualitative features include:

- skill level among employees
- loyalty among employees
- value of a proprietary brand
- quality of customer service, including after-sales
- administrative efficiency.

Each of these can indirectly impact the revenue, costs, assets or liabilities of a company, both in the short and long-term, and so will be reflected indirectly in the financial statements but cannot be stated separately. The exception is a description in the disclosures alongside the financial statements, where particularly relevant, but this would not include a monetary value.

Modern accounting standards require the disclosure of all current and potential liabilities in these disclosure notes, primarily to give a true and fair account of the company's affairs. There is, however, no requirement to include current and potential assets since there would be a temptation to include highly speculative claims with little substance to back them. The result is that companies tend to under represent qualitative advantages and over represent potential liabilities.

One of the basic principles in accounting is the measuring unit principle: the unit of measure in accounting shall be the base money unit of the most relevant currency.

1.3 Accounting Entity Concept

The accounting entity is the unit for which accounting records are maintained and for which financial statements are prepared. The accounting entity concept (or entity concept or separate entity concept) is the principle that financial records are prepared for a distinct unit or entity regarded as separate from the individuals that own it.

This will often be a limited company when that is a separate legal entity and has its own legal obligations to prepare a tax return, for example, and to file financial statements. The precise form of the business entity and its obligations will depend on the jurisdiction and company law for where the entity is incorporated.

For sole traders and partnerships, accounts are also prepared to reflect the transactions of the business as an accounting entity, not those of the owner(s) of the business.

In the case of a sole trader or one-person business, the entities should be distinct from an accounting perspective in the sense that the sole trader should separate their business activities – for example, drawing a salary from the business – from their purely personal activities. Despite it being their business and apparently their money, there are still two aspects to the transaction: the business is paying out the funds and the individual is receiving them. The affairs of the individuals behind a business must be kept separate from the affairs of the business itself.

1.4 Going Concern Concept

This concept is the underlying assumption made by an accountant when preparing a set of accounts, ie, the business under consideration will remain in existence for the foreseeable future. As well as being a traditional concept of accounting, it is also a legal requirement in many countries, eg, in the UK.

In accounting, going concern refers to a company's ability (or intention, eg, a specific project entity) to continue functioning as a business entity. It is the responsibility of the directors to assess whether the going concern assumption is appropriate when preparing the financial statements. A company is required to disclose in the notes to the financial statements whether there are any factors that may put the company's status as a going concern in doubt.

Financial statements are prepared on the assumption that the entity is a going concern, meaning it will continue in operation for the foreseeable future and will be able to realise assets and discharge liabilities in the normal course of operations. Different bases of measurement may be appropriate when the entity is not expected to continue in operation for the foreseeable future. When a company is not a going concern, the break-up basis is used when all assets and liabilities are stated at net realisable value (NRV). The NRV is generally the selling price of the inventory goods, less the selling costs (completion and disposal).

An auditor who concludes that such a doubt exists is required to issue an opinion reflecting this – a modified opinion if the company has appropriately disclosed the doubt and risks and a qualified opinion if the company has not made appropriate disclosures.

1.5 The Accruals Concept

Financial statements for businesses are generally prepared under the accruals concept of accounting. This concept recognises income and expenses in the trading periods in which they arise, ie, when the transactions occur. It can therefore mean that income and expenditure will be accounted for in one trading period, even though actual payments might be made in another.

Example

Company A sells 100 units of its product to company B with an attached invoice for payment. Using the accruals basis, Company A would have to account for the invoiced sale in its current trading period even though Company B may not pay them for, say, 30 days, by which time, a new accounting year has started for Company A.

As well as being accounted for on the income statement, such 'accrued' income will also be treated as an asset on Company A's balance sheet for the accounting period in which the sale is made, but not in the following period when the cash is actually received from Company B.

Similarly, Company A may incur expenses against the materials needed to make the 100 units of its product sold to Company B. As with the actual product sale, these materials may be invoiced to Company A by a supplier on credit terms. As a result, Company A does not pay for the materials until the next trading period. The expense needs to be accounted for on the income statement when it arises, not when it is paid. Equally, it will be regarded as an 'accrued' expense (liability) on the balance sheet for the current year, but not in the next period when Company A actually makes payment for the supplies.

Prepaid income must not, however, be shown as income in the accounting period in which it is received. It must instead be presented in the subsequent accounting period during which the relevant services are actually delivered.

A prepaid expense must likewise not be shown as an expense in the accounting period in which it is paid. It must instead be presented in a subsequent accounting period during which the relevant services are actually performed.

The accruals basis of accounting ensures that expenses are 'matched' with the income earned in an accounting period. The accruals concept, therefore, works closely alongside the 'matching principle'.

The alternative to the accruals basis is cash accounting, where transactions are recorded in the firm's books only when cash is either received or paid out.

1.6 Matching Principle

The matching principle only exists alongside accruals accounting. The principle requires that revenues and related expenses are matched and reported at the same time. Going back to the example of Company A above, it can justifiably match the actual expense incurred in producing 100 units of its product against the sale of those units to Company B.

If, on the other hand, Company A bought extra materials in anticipation of making further units of its product, but did sell those additional units until a later trading period, the purchase of the additional materials would be regarded as a 'prepaid' expense and only recorded on the income statement of that later period.

With cash accounting, expenses are recognised when cash is paid out, no matter when related sales of the items produced take place.

The matching principle therefore provides a more realistic evaluation of actual profitability, reducing the timing mismatch between when costs are incurred relative to when sales are made.

1.7 Prudence

This is the principle that accounting should always exhibit conservatism. Whenever there are alternative procedures or values, an accountant should choose the one which results in a lower profit, a lower asset value and a higher liability value. The concept is summarised by the phrase *'anticipate no profit and provide for all possible losses'*.

Accountants are expected to take a realistic view of business activity rather than an optimistic view. In other words, revenues and profits have no place in an income statement until they have been realised in the form of cash or other assets for which the ultimate cash value can be assessed with reasonable certainty (which is contrary to the 'accrual accounting' discussed in section 1.5). At the same time, a prudent accountant provides for all known and feasible expenses and losses, whether their amounts are known with certainty or are best estimate in the context of the information available.

Prudence and accruals can be mutually exclusive on occasions. For instance, credit sales are recognised on an accruals basis, although it might be more prudent to wait until payment is actually received.

1.8 Consistency and Comparability

Methods employed in treating certain items within the accounting records may be varied from time to time, so the concept of consistency must be applied.

The consistency concept is important because it allows comparability; it enables users of financial statements to assess reasonably the financial statements of a company.

Example

Company A has been using the reducing balance method of depreciation for the machinery it owns to produce its goods (see section 2.4 below). With the consistency concept, Company A should continue to use this same method in respect of depreciation in subsequent trading periods.

If the company wants to change to a straight-line basis of depreciation, its financial report should provide a justifiable reason for the change, the nature of the change and the impact on the wider accounting statements. In this case, there would be a consequential effect on items such as accumulated depreciation.

Normal or historic cost accounting assumes that transactions occurring over a period of time are measured in terms of a consistent measuring unit, ie, only one currency. It is vital when comparing accounts between different companies and for different time periods that the same unit of account is consistently used for realistic comparison.

1.9 Subsidiary Company Accounting and Overseas Business

Subsidiary companies have separate accounting records. Even though each is a separate incorporated entity, consolidated financial statements are usually prepared for financial presentation purposes. Consequently, the subsidiary's assets and liabilities are combined with the parent.

Such common ownership presents issues in preparing a fair and informative presentation of a consolidated entity's financial condition for reporting and tax purposes.

With regard to overseas subsidiaries, the principal issue is the basis on which the foreign currency of an overseas subsidiary is converted to the reporting currency of the parent company. The rule of consistency should apply, so transactions should be booked either at the rate of exchange at the time of the transaction or on the basis of an annual or quarterly currency conversion.

Some companies use a currency as the basis for all of their accounting which is not the currency of the jurisdiction where the headquarters are situated. It is not uncommon for UK companies to elect to use the US dollar as the basis for all accounting.

The cover method refers to the method of accounting for capital investments from a parent to an overseas subsidiary.

Example

XYZ plc reports its financial statements in sterling. It also has a US subsidiary, XYZ (US Holdings) Inc, whose share capital is denominated in US dollars. The subsidiary is initially a shell company with a share capital of only $100. On 1 September 20X3, XYZ plc increases the share capital of the company to $200 million to fund the purchase of a US trading company. The equity investment is partially financed by a $150 million bond issue, which also takes place on 1 September 20X3.

The company draws up accounts to 31 December 20X3. On 1 September 20X3, the GBP/USD exchange rate is 1.5625 on 31 December, it is 1.5267.

The initial cost, in sterling terms, of the equity investment made on 1 September is £128,000,000. The company retranslates the investment at the closing rate, giving a carrying value of £131,001,507 at 31 December 20X3. The exchange gain of £3,001,507 is taken to reserves.

In sterling terms, the company has a liability to bondholders of £96,000,000 on 1 September and £98,251,130 on 31 December – an exchange loss of £2,251,130. This is also taken to reserves and offset against the exchange gain to give a net movement of £750,377.

Assuming that no other exchange gains or losses are taken to reserves, the notes to the accounts include, under reserves:

	Profit and loss account	
	£'000	£'000
At beginning of year		X
Exchange gains for the year	3,002	
Offset of loss on hedging liability	2,251	
Net movement on exchange gains		750

A similar disclosure of the total exchange gain, and the amount of the loss on the liability that had been offset, occurs in the statement of other comprehensive income (OCI).

2. Construction of a Balance Sheet (Statement of Financial Position)

Learning Objective

2.2 Explain the principles behind the construction of a balance sheet

2.1 Construction of a Balance Sheet

The 'balance sheet' is a snapshot of a company's financial position at a particular moment. It is split into two halves which must always balance each other exactly, hence the name. The key information it provides to shareholders, customers and other stakeholders is what the company owns (its assets), what the company owes others (its liabilities) and the extent to which shareholders are providing finance to the company (equity).

Under the Revised International Accounting Standards (IAS 1), the previous term 'balance sheet' has been renamed the 'statement of financial position'. This new term is not mandatory, and so the more familiar term of 'balance sheet' is used here.

The balance sheet should reflect all of the reporting company's assets and liabilities but, over the years, companies and advisors have often developed creative structures to enable certain items to remain 'off-balance-sheet' rather than 'on-balance-sheet'. The International Accounting Standards Board (IASB) is an independent, private-sector body that develops and approves International Financial Reporting Standards (IFRSs). It aims to ensure that everything relevant to the balance sheet is categorised as on-balance-sheet, and those items that can legitimately be considered as being neither assets nor liabilities of the company can remain off-balance-sheet.

The typical format of the balance sheet is provided below for a fictitious company XYZ plc. There is further discussion of the actual performance of this company in chapter 3, examining separate entries on the balance sheet and income statement for XYZ plc and, in particular, financial ratios which facilitate financial analysis.

The balance sheet of XYZ plc is drawn up as of 31 December 20X2, in accordance with its financial year, ie, the annual period selected for its accounts. Although this also happens to be the calendar year, companies may elect to use a different annual period as their financial year.

This chapter considers the balance sheet for XYZ plc in terms more of its structure and format than of its specific contents.

Financial Statement Analysis

XYZ plc Balance Sheet for year to 31 December 20X2			
All amounts are in £'000			
	20X2		20X1
ASSETS			
Non-current assets			
Investments	903		720
Plant and equipment	4,107		3,219
Property	10,968		9,396
		15,978		13,335
Current assets			
Cash	45		60
Trade and other receivables	4,683		3,573
Inventories	3,723		2,859
		8,451		**6,492**
Total assets		24,429		19,827

LIABILITIES			
Current liabilities			
Bank overdraft	(3,201)		(2,232)
Trade payables	(2,550)		(2,133)
Tax payable	(606)		(579)
Provisions	(420)		(345)
Accruals	(339)		(279)
		(7,116)		(5,568)
Non-current liabilities			
Debenture	(6,500)		(4,250)
Unsecured loan	(2,500)		(2,500)
		(9,000)		**(6,750)**
Total liabilities		(16,116)		(12,318)

Net assets		8,313		7,509

Equity			
Ordinary 1 million shares at 25p each (NV*)	250		250
Retained earnings	7,238		6,434
Share premium account	825		825
Total attributable to ordinary equity shareholders of the company		**8,313**		**7,509**

* NV = notional value of issued shares (ie, par value on the share certificates)

The remainder of this chapter examines the principles behind the construction of a balance sheet, and the separate headings found in the statement. This proforma balance sheet uses the 'net assets = equity' layout traditionally used for UK companies and companies in some other jurisdictions. Alternative presentations, such as 'assets = liabilities + equity', are also permitted.

Assets

An asset is anything which is owned and controlled by the company and confers the right to future economic benefits. Balance sheet assets are categorised as either non-current assets or current assets.

Non-Current Assets

Non-current assets are those in long-term, continuing use by the company. They represent the major investments from which the company hopes to make money. Non-current assets are categorised as:

1. tangible
2. intangible
3. investments.

Tangible Non-Current Assets

Tangible non-current assets have physical substance, such as land, buildings, plant and machinery. These are initially recorded in the balance sheet at their actual cost, or book value. Although such assets will generate income for the company over several accounting periods and not just in the accounting period of purchase, the value of all tangible non-current assets with a limited economic life must be depreciated (see section 2.4 below).

Intangible Non-Current Assets

The recognition of an item as an intangible asset requires a firm to demonstrate that it meets:

a. the definition of an intangible asset, and
b. the recognition criteria.

This refers to costs incurred initially in acquiring or internally generating an intangible asset and those incurred subsequently to increase, replace or service it.

An asset is identifiable if it either:

a. is separable, ie, can be separated or divided from the firm and sold, transferred, licensed, rented or exchanged, either individually or together with a related contract, identifiable asset or liability, regardless of whether the firm even intends to do so, or
b. arises from contractual or other legal rights, regardless of whether those rights are transferable or separable from the firm or from other rights and obligations.

An intangible asset shall be recognised if, and only if:

a. it is probable that the expected future economic benefits that are attributable to the asset will flow to the firm, and
b. the cost of the asset can be measured reliably.

'Purchased goodwill' arises when the consideration, or price, paid by the acquiring company for a target company exceeds the **fair value** of the target's separable, or individually identifiable, net assets. This is not necessarily the same as the book, or balance sheet, value of these net assets:

Purchased goodwill = (price paid for company − fair value of identifiable net assets)

Purchased goodwill is capitalised and included in the balance sheet. Once capitalised, purchased goodwill cannot be revalued.

Many company balance sheets do not include some of their most valuable assets. For instance, some commercial brands are not included because they do not meet the strict accounting definition of an intangible asset (see above).

Investments

Non-current asset investments are long-term investments held in other companies. These investments might be equity investments or investments in debt instruments. They are recorded in the balance sheet at cost less any impairment to their value.

Current Assets

Current assets are those purchased with the intention of resale or conversion into cash, usually within a 12-month period. They include stocks (or inventories) of finished goods and work in progress, the receivables balances that arise from the company providing its customers with credit and any short-term investments held. Current assets also include cash balances held by the company and prepayments. Prepayments refer to a company prepaying an expense.

Example

XYZ plc draws up its balance sheet on 31 December each year. Just prior to the year end, XYZ pays £25,000 to its landlord for the next three months' rental on its offices (to the end of March in the next calendar year).

This £25,000 is not an expense for the current year – it represents a prepayment towards the following year's expenses and is, therefore, shown as a prepayment within current assets in XYZ's balance sheet.

Current assets are listed in the balance sheet in ascending order of liquidity and appear in the balance sheet at the lower of cost or net realisable value (NRV).

2.2 Liabilities

A 'liability' is an obligation to transfer future economic benefits as a result of past transactions or events; it is effectively 'money owed to someone else'. Liabilities are categorised according to whether they are to be paid within, or after one year.

Note the following terms and their definitions:

- **provision** – a liability of uncertain timing or amount
- **contingent liability** – a possible obligation depending on whether some uncertain future event occurs, or a present obligation whose payment is not probable or whose amount cannot be measured reliably.

Non-Current Liabilities

This comprises the company's borrowing which is not repayable within the next 12 months. This could include bond issues as well as longer-term bank borrowing.

A separate subheading exists for liabilities which have resulted from past events or transactions and for which there is an obligation to make a payment, but the exact amount or timing has yet to be established. These are commonly referred to as provisions, eg, obligations which may arise as a result of the company undergoing a restructuring.

Given the uncertainty surrounding the extent of such liabilities, companies are required to create a realistic and prudent estimate of the monetary amount of the obligation once it is committed to taking a certain course of action.

Current Liabilities

This includes the amount the company owes to its suppliers, or trade payables, as a result of buying goods and/or services on credit, any bank overdraft and any other payables, such as tax, which are due within 12 months of the balance sheet date.

2.3 Equity

Equity refers to shareholders' funds, owners' equity or capital. Equity usually consists of three sub-elements: share capital, capital reserves and revenue reserves. Additionally, when group accounts are presented, there may be non-controlling interests within the group equity figure.

Share Capital

This is the nominal value of equity and preference share capital which the company has in issue. This may differ from the amount of share capital the company is authorised to issue as contained in its constitutional documents since the company may have only called up some of its authorised share capital.

Capital Reserves

Capital reserves include the share premium account. Share premium reserves arise when the company issues shares at a price above their nominal value. Capital reserves are not distributable to the company's shareholders in the form of dividends, as the share premium accounts form part of the company's capital base, although they can be converted into a bonus issue of ordinary shares.

Revaluation Reserves

The revaluation reserve arises from the upward revaluation of non-current assets.

Revenue Reserves

The major revenue reserve is the accumulated retained earnings of the company – this represents the accumulation of distributable profits that have not been paid to shareholders as dividends, but have been retained in the business. Retained earnings should not be confused with cash that the company holds or with the income statement which shows the entry of retained, or undistributed, profit in a single accounting period was arrived at.

Non-Controlling Interest

Non-controlling interests arise when a parent company controls a subsidiary company, but does not own all the share capital. The equity attributable to the remaining shareholders is the non-controlling interest and this is reflected in the balance sheet.

In summary, equity is the total of the called-up share capital, all the capital reserves and the revenue reserves:

$$\text{Equity} = \text{Share Capital} + \text{Reserves}$$

Called-up share capital refers to shares issued to investors, on the understanding that the shares will be paid for at a later date, or in instalments.

2.4 Depreciation and Amortisation

'Depreciation' is applied to tangible non-current assets, such as plant and machinery. An annual depreciation charge is made in the year's income statement. This charge spreads the cost of the asset over its useful economic life. This helps match the cost of the asset with the revenue it helps to produce. Economic life is the expected period of time during which an asset is useful to the average business. This requirement does not, however, apply to freehold land and non-current asset investments, since their economic life is not limited and so they are not usually depreciated.

The annual depreciation charge is calculated first by subtracting its estimated disposal value from its cost to give the depreciable amount. This value is then written off over the asset's useful economic life by employing the most appropriate depreciation method. The most common is the 'straight-line method'.

The straight-line method simply spreads the depreciable amount equally over the economic life of the asset using the following formula:

$$\text{Straight-Line Depreciation} = \frac{\text{Cost} - \text{disposal value}}{\text{Useful economic life in years}}$$

The annual depreciation charge is an accounting book entry, or a non-cash charge. No cash actually flows from the business as a result of the charge: it is simply an accounting entry in the income statement to reflect the estimated cost of resources used over an accounting period. The balance sheet value of the asset is its cost, less the accumulated depreciation to date, and is termed the net book value (NBV). This NBV does not necessarily equal the market value of the asset.

Straight-Line Depreciation Example

A machine purchased for £25,000 has an estimated useful economic life of six years and an estimated disposal value after six years of £1,000. Calculate the depreciation that should be charged to this asset and its NBV in years one to six, using the straight-line depreciation method.

Solution

$$\text{Straight-Line Depreciation} = \frac{\text{Cost} - \text{disposal value}}{\text{Useful economic life in years}}$$

$$\text{Straight-Line Depreciation} = \frac{£25,000 - £1,000}{6 \text{ years}} = £4,000 \text{ per annum}$$

Year	Opening net book value	Depreciation	Closing net book value
1	£25,000	£4,000	£21,000
2	£21,000	£4,000	£17,000
3	£17,000	£4,000	£13,000
4	£13,000	£4,000	£9,000
5	£9,000	£4,000	£5,000
6	£5,000	£4,000	£1,000

By reducing the book value of a tangible non-current asset over its useful economic life, depreciation matches the cost of the asset against the periods in which the company benefits from its use.

On occasion, tangible assets, such as land, are not depreciated but periodically revalued. This is done on the basis of providing the user of the accounts with a truer and fairer view of the assets, or capital, employed by the company. To preserve the accounting equation (total assets = equity and liabilities), the increase in the asset's value arising on revaluation is transferred to a revaluation reserve, which forms part of the equity.

Closely linked to the idea of depreciating the value of a tangible asset over its useful economic life is the potential need for intangible assets to be amortised over their useful economic lives. Amortisation, like depreciation, is a book entry whose impact lies in the company's reported income and financial position, not in its cash position. Any intangible assets with indefinite useful economic lives do not undergo amortisation.

Reducing Balance Method

It might be deemed more appropriate for the depreciation method to provide for a higher depreciation charge in the first year of an asset's life and then a more gradual depreciation charge in subsequent years. This requires an alternative to the straight-line method. Such alternatives are 'accelerated depreciation methods'. These may provide a more realistic reflection of any particular asset's actual expected lifetime of usage, as many assets are most effective when they are new, while their usefulness declines more rapidly than assumed in the straight-line approach. One popular accelerated approach is the 'reducing balance method' in which the book value of an asset is multiplied by a fixed depreciation rate:

Annual Depreciation = Depreciation Rate x Book Value at Beginning of Year

The reducing balance method is largely used by HMRC to provide large tax allowances at the beginning of the asset's life in order to encourage investment in non-current assets.

The most common rate used is double the straight-line rate.

Reducing Balance Depreciation Example

A business has an asset with an original cost of £10,000, a scrap value or disposal value of £1,000, and a useful life of five years. Since the asset has five years' useful life, the straight-line depreciation rate would be 20% per year (100% ÷ 5). With the 'double-declining-balance method', double the rate (ie, 40%) is used as the depreciation rate.

The following table illustrates the double-declining-balance method of depreciation. Book value at the beginning of the first year of depreciation is the original cost of the asset. At any time, book value equals that original cost minus accumulated depreciation.

Book Value = Original Cost – Accumulated Depreciation

Book value at the end of one year becomes book value at the beginning of the next. The asset is depreciated until the book value equals the disposal value, or scrap value.

Book Value Beginning of Year Original Cost	Depreciation Rate	Depreciation Expense	Accumulated Depreciation	Book Value End of Year
£10,000	40%	£4,000	£4,000	£6,000
£6,000	40%	£2,400	£6,400	£3,600
£3,600	40%	£1,440	£7,840	£2,160
£2,160	40%	£864	£8,704	£1,296
£1,296	£1,296 – £1,000	£296	£9,000	**£1,000**
				Scrap Value

The process continues until the salvage value, or the end of the asset's useful life, is reached. In the last year of depreciation, a subtraction might be needed in order to prevent the book value from falling below the estimated scrap value.

Writing Down Allowance

HMRC generally does not allow expenditure on assets such as cars, tools or machinery to be deducted from trading profits. A capital allowance can be claimed instead for that expenditure.

Capital allowances are also available for certain building-related capital expenditure, for capital expenditure on qualifying research and development, for donations of used business assets to charity, and certain other capital expenditure.

The aim is to give tax relief for the reduction in value of qualifying assets that are bought and owned for business use by allowing their cost to be written off against the taxable income of your business.

Capital allowances are available to sole traders, self-employed persons or partnerships, as well as companies and organisations liable for corporation tax.

Exercise 1

Construct a balance sheet from the information provided in respect of Company A ltd:

Asset/liability	£
Stock (inventory)	37,000
Property	150,000
Creditors (trade payables)	22,000
Accrued expenses	5,000
Cash	25,000
Prepayments	26,000
Tax	21,000
Five-year unsecured bank loan	31,500
Debtors (trade receivables)	34,000
Plant and machinery	21,000
Shareholder funds	172,900
Retained profit	13,600
Dividends due	27,000

Answer at the end of this chapter.

//Financial Statement Analysis

3. Construction of an Income Statement (Statement of Comprehensive Income)

Learning Objective

2.3 Explain the principles behind the construction of an income statement

3.1 Principles behind the Construction of an Income Statement

The income statement summarises the company's income earned and expenditure incurred over the accounting period. The function of this financial statement is to detail how much profit has been earned and how the company's reported profit (or loss) is calculated.

The amount of profit earned over the accounting period impacts the company's ability to pay dividends and how much can be retained to finance the growth of the business from internal resources.

Like the balance sheet, the format of the income statement is governed by law and underpinned by the requirements of various accounting standards. An income statement of XYZ plc is shown below. In practice, comparative numbers for the previous year and explanatory notes would be provided as well.

Revenue

The income statement starts with a key feature: sales revenues. In accounts, sales revenues are generally referred to as revenue, or turnover. It is everything which the company has sold during the year, regardless of whether it has received payment or not. For a manufacturer, revenue would be the sales of the products that it has made. For a company in the service industry, it would be the consulting fees earned, or perhaps commissions earned on financial transactions.

Costs of Sales

The costs of sales are the costs to the company of generating the sales made in the financial year. These items are also sometimes known as the cost of goods sold. They typically include the costs of raw materials used to make a product and the costs of converting those raw materials into their finished state, including the wages of the staff making the products.

Gross Profit

Total sales, less the costs of those sales, results in the gross profit for the year.

Operating Profit

Operating profit is also referred to as profit on operating activities. It is the gross profit, less other operating expenses, that the company has incurred. These other operating expenses might include costs incurred distributing products (distribution costs) and administrative expenses such as management salaries, auditors' fees and legal fees. Administrative expenses also includes depreciation and amortisation charges. Additional items may be separately disclosed before arriving at operating profit, such as the profit or loss made on selling a non-current asset. When a non-current asset, such as an item of machinery, is disposed of at a price significantly different from its balance sheet value, the profit or loss when compared to this NBV should be separately disclosed if material to the information conveyed by the accounts.

Operating profit is the profit before considering finance costs (interest) and any tax payable – so it can be described as profit before interest and tax (PBIT), or earnings before interest and tax (EBIT).

EBITDA (earnings before interest, tax, depreciation and amortisation) is an indicator of a company's financial performance which is calculated in the following manner:

$$\text{EBITDA} = \text{Revenue} - \text{Expenses (excluding tax, interest, depreciation and amortisation)}$$

EBITDA is essentially net income (profit) with interest, taxes, depreciation and amortisation added back to it, and can be used to analyse and compare profitability between companies and industries because it eliminates the effects of financing and accounting decisions.

Interest Expense/Interest Income

Interest costs are generally the interest that the company has incurred on its borrowings, possibly in the form of bonds or bank loans and overdrafts. Interest income is typically the interest earned on surplus funds, such as from deposit accounts.

Profit before Tax

This is the profit made by the company in the period, before considering any tax that might be payable on that profit.

Tax Payable

This is simply the corporation tax charge that the company has incurred for the period. There can also be a deferred tax expense.

Profit after Tax

Deducting tax and financing costs leaves profit after tax. It reflects all the profit earned during the period, less all of the expenditures incurred. This is also the profit attributable to the shareholders of the company because, in theory, it could all be distributed to shareholders as dividends.

Earnings per Share (EPS)

This is an important figure for readers of financial statements and is included at the bottom of the income statement, in pence. Earnings per share (EPS) is the amount of profit after tax that has been earned per ordinary share. EPS is calculated as follows:

$$\text{EPS} = \frac{\text{profit attributable to ordinary shareholders (earnings)}}{\text{number of ordinary shares in issue}}$$

XYZ plc Income Statement for year to 31 December 20X2		
All amounts are in £'000		
	20X2	**20X1**
Revenue	31,311	25,857
Cost of sales	(24,234)	(19,884)
Gross profit	**7,077**	**5,973**
Depreciation and amortisation	(1,485)	(1,206)
Administrative expenses	(1,347)	(1,086)
Selling and distribution expenses	(1,482)	(1,236)
Other income. Profit from sale of fixed assets	24	36
Operating profit	**2,787**	**2,481**
Finance interest costs	(902)	(738)
Interest received	5	6
Profit before tax	**1,890**	**1,749**
Corporation tax	(606)	(579)
Net profit	**1,284**	**1,170**
Extraordinary items	(18)	–
Profit for the year	**1,266**	**1,170**
Ordinary dividends	(462)	(393)
Retained earnings at end of year	**804**	**777**

20X2 EPS = £1,266,000 / 1,000,000 shares = 126.6p
20X1 EPS = £1,170,000 / 1,000,000 shares = 117.0p

20X2 EPS = 126.6p
20X1 EPS = 117.0p

20X2 dividends per share (DPS) = £462,000 / 1,000,000 shares = 46.2p
20X1 DPS = £393,000 / 1,000,000 shares = 39.3p

20X2 DPS = 46.2p
20X1 DPS = 39.3p

Note that there are 1,000,000 shares, each with a nominal value of 25p, as per the balance sheet of XYZ plc (see section 2.1)

Share price as at 31 December 20X2 = £10.26
Share price as at 31 December 20X2 = £9.13

3.2 Capital versus Revenue Expenditure

Money spent by a company will usually fall into one of two possible forms:

- **Capital expenditure** is money spent on buying non-current assets, such as plant, property and equipment. It is reflected on the balance sheet.
- **Revenue expenditure** is money spent that immediately impacts the income statement. It includes wages paid to staff, rent paid on property and professional fees, such as audit fees.

Exercise 2

Construct a simple income statement from the information provided in respect of Company A ltd:

Income/expense	£
Sales	800,000
Administration and distribution costs	545,000
Tax	16,000
Cost of sales	168,000
Interest paid	8,400
Dividends	49,000

Answer at the end of this chapter.

4. Cash Flow Statement (Statement of Cash Flows)

Learning Objective

2.4 Explain the principles behind the construction of a cash flow statement

A statement of cash flows (as a cash flow statement is now known in accordance with the IAS 1 Revised) is required by accounting standard IAS 7 Cash Flow Statements. The revised IAS Standard is effective for annual periods beginning on or after 1 January 2017. The traditional term 'cash flow statement' is nevertheless used below for familiarity and also to illustrate that the new title adopted by IAS 1 Revised is not mandatory.

The cash flow statement is basically a summary of all the payments and receipts that have occurred over the course of the year, the total reflecting the inflow (or outflow) of cash over the year.

The logic of adding a cash flow statement to a set of financial statements is that it enables readers of the accounts to see clearly how cash has been generated and/or used over the course of the year. This is felt to provide easily understood information to users of the accounts to supplement the performance figures provided by the income statement, and the statement of financial position given by the balance sheet.

IAS7 Cash Flow Statements require a company's cash flows to be broken down into particular headings:

- **Operating activities** is cash which has been generated from the trading activities of the company, excluding financing cost (interest).
- **Investing activities** details the investment income (dividends and interest) which has been received as cash during the year, as well as cash paid to purchase new non-current assets, less cash received from the sale of non-current assets during the year.
- **Financing activities** includes cash spent during the year on paying dividends to shareholders, cash raised from issuing shares or borrowing on a long-term basis, less cash spent repaying debt or buying back shares.

The resultant total should explain the changes in cash (and cash equivalents) between the balance sheets. Many short-term investments, such as Treasury bills (T-bills), are classified as cash equivalents.

Consider again XYZ plc and its cash flow statement for the year ending 31 December 20X2. The figures provided include explanatory points.

XYZ plc Cash Flow Statement for year to 31 December 20X2		
All amounts are in £'000		
Operating profit	2,787	
Other additions to cash		
Depreciation and amortisation	1,485	A loss from the sale of an asset is not a cash expense and is added back into the net income for calculating cash flow.
Loss from sale of fixed assets		A loss from the sale of an asset is not a cash expense and is added back into the net income for calculating cash flow.
Decrease in accounts receivable		If accounts receivable decreases, more cash has entered the company from customers paying off their accounts. The amount by which accounts receivable has decreased is an addition to cash.
Decrease in inventory		A decrease in inventory signals that a company has spent less money to purchase more raw materials. The decrease in the value of the inventory is an addition to cash.
Decrease in other current assets		Similar reasoning to above for other current assets.
Increase in accounts payable	612	If accounts payable increases it suggests that more cash has been retained by the company through not paying some bills – the amount by which accounts payable has increased is an addition to cash.
Increase in accrued expenses		For example, deferring payment of some salaries will add to cash.

Increase in other current liabilities (non-cash finance and tax expenses)			Similar reasoning to above for increase in taxes payable.
Total additions to cash from operations	2,097		
Subtractions from cash			
Gain from sale of fixed assets	(24)		A gain from the sale of an asset is not a cash expense and is added back into the net income for calculating cash flow.
Increase in accounts receivable	(1,110)		If accounts receivable increases, less cash has entered the company from customers paying their accounts. The amount by which accounts receivable increases is a subtraction from cash.
Increase in inventory	(864)		An increase in inventory signals that a company has spent more money to purchase more raw materials. The increase in the value of the inventory is a subtraction from cash.
Increase in other current assets			Similar reasoning to above for other current assets.
Decrease in accounts payable			If accounts payable decreases it suggests that more cash has been used by the company through paying bills. The amount by which accounts payable has decreased is an addition to cash.
Decrease in accrued expenses			An increase in prepaid expenses for example, results in a subtraction from cash.
Decrease in other current liabilities (non-cash finance and tax expenses)			Similar reasoning to above for decrease in tax payable.
Extraordinary items	(18)		Extraordinary items expenses result in a subtraction from cash.
Total subtractions from cash from operations	(2,016)		
Total operating cash flow	2,868		Equals net income after tax + total additions to cash from operations + total subtractions from cash from operations.

Enterprise Cash Flow Statement for XYZ plc for year to 31 December 20X2			
All amounts are in £'000			
Total operating cash flow	2,868		
Investment/capital expenditure			
Decrease in fixed assets	69		Sale of a fixed asset, such as a building, leads to an addition to cash.
Decrease in notes receivable			A reduction in notes receivable indicates that cash has been received.
Decrease in securities investments			Securities have been sold, thereby raising cash.
Decrease in tangible, non-current assets			Sale of a patent or copyright leads to an addition to cash.
Total additions to cash from investments	69		

Subtractions from cash for investments			
Increase in fixed assets	(4,173)		Purchase of a fixed asset, such as a building, leads to a subtraction from cash.
Increase in notes receivable			An increase in notes receivable indicates that further credit has been granted and cash has not been received.
Increase in securities investments			Securities have been purchased, thereby reducing cash.
Increase in tangible, non-current assets			Purchase of a patent or a copyright leads to a reduction in cash.
Total subtractions from cash for investments	(4,173)		
Total enterprise cash flow	(1,236)		Equals total operating cash flow + additions to cash from capital investments + subtraction from cash from capital investments.

Financing activities			
Additions to cash from financing			
Increase in borrowing	2,250		Additional net borrowing leads to an addition to cash.
Increase in capital stock			Additional net equity capital paid leads to an addition to cash.
Interest received			
Total additions to cash from financing	2,250		
Subtractions from cash from financing			
Decrease in borrowings			Net reduction in borrowing leads to a subtraction of cash.
Decrease in capital stock			Retirement of net equity capital paid leads to a subtraction of cash.
Interest paid	(897)		
Total subtractions from cash for financing			
Total equity cash Flow		117	Equals total enterprise cash flow + additions to cash from financing + subtractions from cash from financing.
Subtractions from cash for dividends			
Dividends paid	(462)		
Subtractions from cash for tax paid			
Tax paid	(606)		
Total free cash flow	(951)		Equals total equity cash flow – dividends – tax paid out.

5. Accounting Standards

Learning Objective

2.5 Summarise the financial statement accounting standards: legal compliance; application and differences between UK GAAP, IFRS and IAS

The objective of financial statements is to provide information about the financial position, performance and changes in financial position of a business that is useful to a wide range of users in making economic decisions.

Financial statements should be understandable, relevant, reliable and comparable. Relevance is regarded as a key characteristic of useful accounting information. Reliability relates to the requirement that accounting should be free from material error or bias. Financial statements are intended to be understandable by readers who have *a reasonable knowledge of business and economic activities and accounting and who are willing to study the information diligently.*

Stakeholders who benefit from financial statements include:

5.1 Internal Stakeholders

- **Owners, directors and managers** require financial statements to make important business decisions which affect their continued operations. Financial analysis may be performed on these statements to provide management with a more detailed understanding of the figures. These statements are also used as part of management's annual report to the stockholders.
- **Employees** also need these reports in making collective bargaining agreements (with the management, in the case of labour unions or for individuals in discussing their compensation, promotion and rankings).

5.2 External Stakeholders

External stakeholders who have an interest in reviewing the financial statements of a company include potential investors, banks, government agencies and other parties who are outside the business but need financial information about the business for a diverse number of reasons.

- **Prospective investors** use financial statements to assess the viability of investing in a business. Financial analysts often provide a systematic analysis of financial performance and key ratios, enhancing the basis for making investment decisions.
- **Financial institutions** (banks and other lending companies) use them to decide whether, and on what terms, to grant a company fresh working capital or extend debt securities (such as a long-term bank loan or debentures) to finance expansion and other significant expenditures.
- **Government entities** (eg, tax authorities) use financial statements to ascertain the propriety and accuracy of taxes and other duties declared and paid by a company.

Different countries have developed their own accounting principles over time, making international comparisons of companies difficult. To ensure uniformity and comparability between financial statements prepared by different companies, a set of guidelines and rules are used. Commonly referred to as Generally Accepted Accounting Principles (GAAP), this set of guidelines provides the basis in the preparation of financial statements.

More recently, there has been a push towards standardising accounting rules made by the International Accounting Standards Board (IASB). This body develops International Financial Reporting Standards (IFRSs) which have been adopted by over 100 countries, including the UK and the European Union (EU) (for publicly quoted companies only), but not by the US. The US Financial Accounting Standards Board has made a commitment to converge the US GAAP and IFRS over time, but progress has not been rapid to date.

The IASB is an independent, privately funded accounting standard-setter, based in London. The 14 current board members come from numerous countries and have a variety of functional backgrounds. The IASB is committed to developing, in the public interest, a single set of high-quality, understandable and enforceable global accounting standards that require transparent and comparable information in general purpose financial statements. In addition, the IASB cooperates with national accounting standard-setters to achieve convergence in accounting standards around the world.

Standards issued by the IASB are designated IFRSs. There were standards issued by the IASB's predecessor (the International Accounting Standards Committee) that continue to be designated International Accounting Standards (IASs). The IASB has retained the IASs and also issues IFRSs.

The recent history of the IASB can be summarised as follows:

- The IASB was formally established in 2001, with 13 members.
- The aim of the IASB is to develop a single set of high-quality global accounting standards.
- IASB cooperates with national bodies to achieve a convergence of practices/protocols around the world.
- A new standard starts life as a discussion paper (DP).
- The IASB establishes a working group to develop a new standard.
- Comments from interested participants to the DP are taken into account, leading to a financial reporting exposure draft (FRED).
- If adopted, a new IFRS is issued.

UK Generally Accepted Accounting Principles (GAAP) since 2005

In 2002, the EU agreed that it would apply IASs and IFRSs from 1 January 2005 to the consolidated accounts of EU-listed companies.

In 2012 and 2013 the Financial Reporting Council (FRC) revised financial reporting standards for the UK and the Republic of Ireland, effective since 2015. The revision fundamentally reformed financial reporting, replacing almost all existing standards with five Financial Reporting Standards (FRSs), of which the principal three in terms of the new UK GAAP are as follows:

- **FRS 100** sets out the applicable financial reporting framework for entities preparing financial statements in accordance with legislation, regulations or accounting standards applicable in the UK and the Republic of Ireland.
- **FRS 101** sets out a reduced disclosure framework which addresses the financial reporting requirements and disclosure exemptions for the individual financial statements of subsidiaries and ultimate parents that otherwise apply the recognition, measurement and disclosure requirements of EU-adopted IFRSs.
- **FRS 102** is a single financial reporting standard that applies to the financial statements of entities that are not applying EU-adopted IFRSs, FRS 101 or the FRS for Smaller Entities (FRSSE).

Format and Contents of Accounts

The financial statements of listed companies in the UK must contain the following elements:

	Regulation		
	Companies Act 2006	**UKLA Listing Rules**	**IFRSs**
Chairman's statement *			
Chief executive's review *			
Operating and financial review *			
Corporate governance and remuneration report	✓	✓	
Director's report	✓		
Auditor's report	✓		
Financial statements:			
Profit and loss account	✓		
Balance sheet	✓		
Statement of total recognised gains and losses			✓
Cash flow statement	✓		✓
Notes to the accounts	✓		
Accounting policies	✓		
Figures for this year plus previous year's comparatives	✓		
Five-year summary *			

* It is not mandatory to include these items in the accounts of listed companies. However, listed companies will typically include them in their annual accounts.

5.3 True and Fair Concept

Learning Objective

2.6 Critically appraise a valuation based on a number of subjective assumptions – true and fair concept; apply a sceptical and critical approach

Section 393(1) of the Companies Act 2006 requires that directors only approve accounts that give a true and fair view of the assets, liabilities, financial position and profit and loss of a company.

There is, however, no statutory definition of what constitutes 'true and fair', although there are some eminent judgements (commonly referred to as 'the opinions') by Lord Hoffman and two by Dame Mary Arden ranging over a decade (1983–93) that have outlined what this is meant to represent. The Financial Reporting Council (FRC) commissioned a further opinion from Martin Moore QC in 2013, effectively endorsing the previous opinions; it published its own update in 2014 (available at www.frc.org.uk).

The essence of 'true and fair' means that the company's financial statements offer a true and fair view of its factual and actual financial position and that in determining this, the auditor's opinion is based on reasonable assumptions.

This concept has been the subject of some recent debate, with the FRC offering a view on the clarity of the IASB's Conceptual Framework, reporting that the concepts of 'prudence', 'fair value' and 'stewardship reporting' should be better defined and improved. While there may be more discussion around the true and fair concept, for the moment it seems that compliance with accounting standards will result in a true and fair view, but only when considered with a professional, rather than a mechanistic judgement.

The materiality convention states that, where the amounts involved are immaterial, we should only consider what is expedient. This may mean that an item will only be treated as an expense in the period in which it was paid rather than being strictly matched to the revenues to which it relates.

Summary of Chapter Two

The key accounting concepts are: the dual aspect concept; the money measurement concept; the entity concept; the going concern concept; the asset measurement concept; the accruals basis; the matching principle; and the principles of prudence, consistency and comparability.

A balance sheet is essentially a list of all of the assets and liabilities of a business and their value at a particular point in time.

The basic accounting equation is: Net assets = Shareholders' funds.

For any transaction: Change in net assets = Change in shareholders' funds.

Ordinary share capital represents the total nominal value of the equity shares. Other reserves generally represent an apportionment or allocation of profits from the income statement.

The income statement shows in a detailed format how a company has generated its profit or loss for the accounting period. The major changes to the financial state of the business will be reflected in the balance sheet, which can be monitored for the key changes from one period to the next.

Ratios are used in the comparative analysis of accounts (ie, financial statements), including gross profit percentage.

EPS is a figure closely monitored by shareholders and analysts, who are usually looking for EPS to rise year on year. It is explained in more detail in chapter 3, section 6.1.

The balance sheet (statement of financial position) and income statement are prepared on the accruals basis. They do not show whether or not the company is generating cash from its activities: this is shown in the cash flow statement.

There is standardisation of the requirements for financial statements. In recent years, through the efforts of the IASB, there has been a growing convergence of international standards and principles used by the accounting profession in many parts of the world.

However, important international differences in GAAP still exist.

Example Exam Question on Financial Statements

Questions about financial statements can appear throughout the exam. There is a strong probability that a question covering a firm's accounts will be in the longer sections of the exam (Sections B and C) so it is important that you can understand and interpret the information being presented to you. Usually, you will be asked to analyse a pre-prepared set of statements in some depth using a number of the main accounting ratios. We will cover these in chapter 3.

On occasion, you will also be asked shorter questions about financial statements and accounting methods in Section A. The following examples act as practice questions covering all sections of the exam:

Section A

Discuss the importance of 'going concern basis' in preparation of a company's accounts. (5 marks)

Section B

a. Today, many companies have subsidiaries and these require consideration when looking at the accounts of the company. For accounting purposes, explain how a foreign subsidiary using a different currency should be dealt with. (4 marks)
b. During a takeover, something called 'purchased goodwill' can arise. Discuss what this means and how it is handled in the statement of financial position (also known as the balance sheet). (4 marks)

c. Companies must ensure that the value of assets in their accounts reflect their true value. To do this they will use something called depreciation. Discuss the two different ways that this can be calculated. (12 marks)

Exercise Answers

Exercise 1 – Company A ltd Balance Sheet

Balance Sheet Period ending: xx/yy/zz	£	£
Non-current assets		
Property	150,000	
Plant and machinery	21,000	
	171,000	
Current assets		
Stock (inventory)	37,000	
Debtors (trade receivables)	34,000	
Pre-payments	26,000	
Cash	25,000	
	122,000	
Total assets		**293,000**
Current liabilities		
Tax	21,000	
Creditors (trade payables)	22,000	
Accrued expenses	5,000	
Dividends due	27,000	
	(75,000)	
Total assets less current liabilities (capital employed)		**218,000**
Non-current liabilities		
Bank loan	(31,500)	
Net assets		**186,500**
Comprising		
Shareholders' funds	172,900	
Retained profit	13,600	
Equity		**186,500**

Exercise 2 – Company A ltd Income Statement

Profit/Loss	£
Sales	**800,000**
Cost of sales	(168,000)
Gross profit	**632,000**
Administration and distribution costs	(545,000)
Interest	(8,400)
Profit before tax	**78,600**
Tax	(16,000)
Net profit	**62,600**
Dividends paid	(49,000)
Retained profit	**13,600**

Chapter Three
Application of Financial Statement Analysis and Accounting Ratios

1.	Profitability Accounting Ratios	123
2.	Liquidity Ratios	129
3.	The Working Capital Cycle	132
4.	Financial Gearing Ratios	135
5.	Evaluate Growth in Sales, Profitability and Capital	139
6.	Investor Ratios	141
7.	Earnings Yield, Dividend Yield and Dividend Cover	150
8.	Analysis Interpretation	153
9.	Interpretation Tools	157

Learning Outcome 03

Be able to select and apply the principal accounting ratios, and explain their advantages and limitations, in the evaluation and comparison of financial statements

1. Profitability Accounting Ratios

Learning Objective

3.1 Apply the following profitability ratios: return on capital employed; gross and net profit margins; asset turnover and gearing

1.1 The Financial Statements and Profitability Ratios

The financial statements of a company, comprising the balance sheet, profit and loss account and cash flow statement with all the associated notes, can contain a substantial amount of information. They can, however, be perplexing.

Financial analysts interpret the financial statements and devise ratios (eg, a company's profit performance compared to its sales revenue) which add to the understanding of prospective and existing investors. The financial statements are primarily prepared for the shareholders. Other interested parties may, however, include prospective investors or those considering divesting, lenders, creditors, the government and tax authorities.

The primary purpose of this analysis from the point of view of investors is to obtain a deeper insight into the true nature of:

- returns received
- risks faced.

The directors and managers of the business on the other hand wish to assess the efficiency and effectiveness of available assets in terms of:

- **trading performance** – success in generating profit, focusing on the constituents of the profits and the profitability ratios
- **trading position** – available resources in terms of the growth of assets and liquidity issues.

Lenders (in addition to shareholders and management) also consider the breakdown and servicing of financing:

- **financial performance** – the success in generating a return to its providers of finance through ratios, such as return on equity
- **financial position** – the quality of the business's assets, liabilities, and capital as reflected on the balance sheet, encompassing how the company is financed.

A wide range of standardised ratios are commonly analysed to assist these stakeholders.

Types of Accounting Ratios Used in Financial Analysis

Type of Ratio	Description
Profitability	Assess the trading or operating performance of the company
Liquidity	Evaluate the risk of the company becoming unable to pay its suppliers and ceasing to exist as a going concern
Investment Returns	Assess the returns to those providing financing to the company
Gearing	Assess the risks to those providing financing to the company from excessive borrowing or leverage

1.1.1 Gross and Net Profit Margins

Profitability ratios help to analyse the return that the company generates relative to its revenues. The gross profit margin looks at the percentage of revenues that the company earns after considering just the costs of sales.

The operating profit margin describes the percentage of revenues that the company earns after considering costs of sales and other operating expenses (eg, distribution and administrative costs).

The figures for the profitability ratios are drawn from the income statement.

The formulae for the two ratios are:

- Gross profit margin % = (Gross profit ÷ Revenues) x 100
- Operating profit margin % = (Operating profit ÷ Revenues) x 100

Using the example from XYZ plc in chapter 2:

- Gross profit margin % (20X2) = (7,077 ÷ 31,311) x 100 = 22.60%
- Operating profit margin % (20X2) = (2,787 ÷ 31,311) x 100 = 8.90%

1.1.2 Return on Capital Employed (ROCE)

This is a widely used ratio for measuring overall management performance in relation to the capital invested into the business. It shows the operating profit as a percentage of the capital employed.

The amount of capital employed is the equity plus long-term debt. This is money which the company holds from shareholders and debt providers and which it uses to generate profits.

ROCE effectively gives an annual yield for the company's operations relative to its long-term capital employed. This annual return can then be compared to that of other companies or investment opportunities with similar degrees of risk.

The formula is:

$$\text{ROCE \%} = (\text{Operating profit} \div \text{Capital employed}) \times 100$$

Operating profit in this instance is before financing and tax on the income statement, while capital employed is the total equity on the balance sheet plus the total non-current liabilities on the balance sheet.

In the example of XYZ plc (chapter 2):

$$\text{ROCE \% (20X2)} = (2{,}787 \div (8{,}313 + 9{,}000)) \times 100 = 16.10\%$$

ROCE can also be calculated using the trading side of the company balance sheet:

$$\text{operating profit} \div (\text{total assets} - \text{current liabilities}) \times 100$$

The result is the same:

$$\text{ROCE \% (20X2)} = (2{,}787 \div (24{,}429 - 7{,}116)) \times 100 = 16.10\%$$

Evaluating this percentage requires a comparison with the ROCE of other businesses in the same sector, as well as a consideration of prevailing market conditions.

1.1.3 Asset Turnover

Asset turnover measures the efficient use of assets to produce sales. The ratio helps to measure the productivity of a company's assets.

There is a strong link between this ratio and ROCE given that ROCE measures profitability to capital employed, while asset turnover measures sales to capital employed.

$$\text{Asset turnover} = \text{Turnover} \div \text{Assets (capital) employed}$$

For XYZ plc, asset turnover   = 31,311 ÷ (9,000 + 8,8313)

=31,311 ÷ 17,313

= 1.81.

For every £1 of capital employed in the business, £1.81 is generated in sales.

The capital employed equals the total assets, less current liabilities representing the assets turned over.

Generally, the higher the ratio the better. Companies with low profit margins tend to have a higher asset turnover than those with higher margins.

The asset turnover ratio tends to be higher for companies in certain sectors than in others. Retail, for example, is a sector that often yields the highest asset turnover ratios, scoring around 2.

Conversely, firms in sectors like utilities and telecommunications, which have large asset bases, will have lower asset turnover. The financial sector, for example, often trails in its asset turnover ratio.

It is pointless to compare asset turnover ratios for companies which operate in different industrial sectors. Comparing asset turnover ratios for companies within the same sector may, however, provide a more useful comparison of relative asset use efficiency.

Even this kind of comparison may nevertheless be insufficient, since a company's asset turnover ratio in any single year may differ substantially from that in previous or subsequent years. For any specific company, the trend in the asset turnover ratio over a period of time offers a further check on whether asset usage is improving or deteriorating.

Many other factors can affect a company's asset turnover ratio in a given year, eg, the cyclical nature of an industry.

1.1.4 Operational Gearing Ratio

Operational **gearing** is a measure of operational risk, ie, risk to the operating profit figure. It assesses the levels of variable and fixed operating costs in the business.

$$\text{Operational Gearing Ratio} = \frac{\text{Revenue} - \text{Variable Cost}}{\text{Profit}}$$

Variable costs are those whose level varies directly with the level of output; if sales increase (decrease) then variable costs, eg, raw material costs, will increase (decrease).

Fixed costs are those whose level remains constant regardless of output levels, eg, rent, rates, and depreciation.

The greater the level of fixed costs in the business, the greater the variation in the operational gearing as a result of revenue changes.

In the first table below, two separate companies have similar characteristics except that Company A has fixed costs of £30,000 and Company B has fixed costs of £50,000. Each company operates at a level of 10,000 units of output per year and each has the same revenue, ie, price per unit, and each has variable costs of £11 per unit. The difference between the unit revenue and the unit variable cost is £9 and is known as the 'contribution'. This is the amount that each company has available to cover its fixed costs before it generates pre-tax profit.

Applicaiton of Financial Statement Analysis and Accounting Ratios

Gearing		Company A	Company B
OUTPUT (Units)		10,000	10,000
Sales revenue (per unit)	£20	£200,000	£200,000
Variable costs (per unit)	£11	(£110,000)	(£110,000)
Contribution	**£9**	**£90,000**	**£90,000**
Fixed costs		(£30,000)	(£50,000)
Profit before tax		£60,000	£40,000
Operational gearing ratio		1.50	2.25

Company A with a lower fixed cost earns a profit before tax of £60,000, whereas B, with higher fixed costs, generates a profit of £40,000. The operational gearing ratios for each company are as follows:

Company A: (£200,000 − £110,000) ÷ £60,000 = 1.5

Company B: (£200,000 − £110,000) ÷ £40,000 = 2.25.

Company B has relatively higher fixed costs than Company A, so it has a higher operational gearing. In general terms, a company whose fixed costs are higher as a percentage of total costs will incur a higher operational gearing ratio. One consequence of this is that a company with a higher gearing ratio experiences greater sensitivity in its profit relative to sales if there is a change in the level of output and overall revenue.

The table below shows a range of outputs for Company A, ranging from a 25% decrease to a 25% increase.

Adjusting Output for Company A		75%	100%	125%
Output (Units)		7,500	10,000	12,500
Sales revenue (per unit)	£20	£150,000	£200,000	£250,000
Variable costs (per unit)	£11	(£82,500)	(£110,000)	(£137,500)
Contribution	**£9**	**£67,500**	**£90,000**	**£112,500**
Fixed costs		(£30,000)	(£30,000)	(£30,000)
Profit before tax		£37,500	£60,000	£82,500
Operational gearing ratio	1.50			
Ratio of profit to normal output		0.625	1.000	1.375

The effect of the operational gearing ratio on the profit before tax is as follows:

- where output falls by 25%, the profit reduces by that percentage reduction in output multiplied by the gearing ratio, ie, profit falls by 37.5% (−25% x 1.5)
- where output rises by 25% the profit increases by that percentage increase in output multiplied by the gearing ratio, ie, profit rises by 37.5% (+25% x 1.5).

In the third table below for Company B with the higher gearing ratio, the changes to profit from a 25% decrease or increase in output are more severe, with a ±56.3% change to the normal profit level.

Adjusting Output for Company B		75%	100%	125%
Output (Units)		7,500	10,000	12,500
Sales revenue (per unit)	£20	£150,000	£200,000	£250,000
Variable costs (per unit)	£11	(£82,500)	(£110,000)	(£137,500)
Contribution	**£9**	**£67,500**	**£90,000**	**£112,500**
Fixed costs		(£50,000)	(£50,000)	(£50,000)
Profit before tax		£17,500	£40,000	£62,500
Operational gearing ratio	2.25			
Ratio of profit to normal output		0.438	1.000	1.563

This technique requires a detailed knowledge of a company's cost structure and its fixed and variable costs. This information is not usually included in the published company accounts. It may be possible to extract them from a more detailed examination of the income statement.

Operational gearing is a key factor in evaluating a business and its sensitivity to changes in demand for its products. Businesses with high contribution levels are generally more able to withstand declines in their demand and output, while capital-intensive businesses also have relatively high fixed costs due to the depreciation of their non-current assets.

Exercise 1

You are assessing two companies in two completely different sectors. Company A in Sector 1 has a higher ROCE than company B in Sector 2. Explain the significance of these figures when comparing the two organisations.

The answer to this exercise is at the end of this chapter.

2. Liquidity Ratios

Learning Objective

3.2 Apply the following liquidity ratios: working capital (current) ratio; quick (acid test) ratio

It is important to distinguish between solvency and liquidity. The solvency of a company relates to its long-term assets and liabilities, and its commitments to finance its balance sheet. Liquidity concerns its short-term operations and its ability to meet its ongoing cash requirements.

Liquidity ratios aim to determine the following:

- Does a company have the resources to meet its operating requirements from its working capital on a timely basis?
- Can a company realise those resources quickly enough to raise cash when required, to pay off its liabilities as they fall due?

These ratios are relatively crude and arguably lack sophistication, but they are useful for showing trends and are frequently used in loan agreements.

2.1 The Working Capital Ratio or Current Ratio

The purpose of the working capital ratio or current ratio is to determine if the current assets recoverable within one year are sufficient to cover the liabilities that fall due within one year.

As in accounting convention, current assets normally refer to those assets which are recoverable within one year. Some receivables may, however, be recoverable after more than one year. This fact must be noted in the company's accounts, if material.

$$\text{Current Ratio} = \frac{\text{Current Assets}}{\text{Current Liabilities}}$$

With XYZ plc in 20X2, the ratio is: £8,451 ÷ £7,116 = 1.19.

A ratio above 1 indicates that a company has sufficient short-term assets to cover its short-term debt. Any ratio below 1 indicates negative working capital, while anything over 2 suggests that the company might not be investing excess assets in the most productive and yield-generating manner. Analysts often consider a ratio between 1.2 and 2.0 to be desirable. The circumstances of every business vary however, so snap any judgements about an appropriate current ratio are ill-advised.

A stronger ratio indicates a better ability to meet ongoing and unexpected bills, reducing any cash flow pressure. Stronger liquidity can also enable cash discounts to be negotiated with suppliers.

A weaker ratio may indicate that the business faces difficulties meeting its short-term commitments and that additional working capital support is required. This can adversely impact terms of trade, with reduced credit facilities, in which case an overdraft facility could assist. Building a reserve of cash investments may alternatively create a working capital buffer.

Some practical problems arise when calculating or using the current ratio:

- Overdrafts are designed primarily to deal with short-term financing, so are included within current liabilities. Although they are technically repayable on demand, they are, in practice, frequently repayable after more than one year. Banks often allow companies to extend overdrafts for several years.
- Inventory is included within current assets on the balance sheet and is thus assumed to be convertible into cash within one year, but this may not be feasible. In a recession, it may be hard to generate liquidity from inventory other than through a sale at distressed prices.
- The ratio fails to take into account the timing of cash flows within the period. Liabilities might be payable at very short notice, whereas assets may be recoverable in 12 months' time.
- The ratio is static in that it reflects values at a point in time, ie, when the balance sheet is drawn up. A company might contrive to 'window-dress' its accounts on that date so that its ability to meet its obligations appears more favourable.

In order to alleviate criticism that the current ratio is static, a modified form is often advised – the working capital turnover ratio.

The working capital turnover ratio is also referred to as 'net sales to working capital'. It indicates a company's effectiveness in using its working capital. It is calculated as:

net annual sales divided by average amount of working capital during same 12-month period.

Example

If a company's net sales for the year 20X4 are £2,400,000, and its average amount of working capital during the year 20X4 is £400,000, its working capital turnover ratio would be 6 (£2,400,000 ÷ £400,000).

Working capital is defined as current assets minus current liabilities. As indicated above, the average amount of working capital over the year of the net sales should be used.

As with most financial ratios, the working capital turnover ratio can be compared with those of other companies in the same industry and to the same company's past and planned working capital turnover ratio.

2.2 Quick (Acid Test) Ratio

The quick ratio is an adaptation of the current ratio and is designed to remove the problem of inventory; it is alternatively called the acid test ratio or the liquidity ratio.

$$\text{Quick Ratio} = \frac{\text{Current Assets} - \text{Inventory}}{\text{Current Liabilities}}$$

With XYZ plc in 20X2, the ratio is: (£8,451 - £3,723) ÷ £7,116 = 0.664.

The quick ratio measures the ability of a company to use its near-cash or quick assets to cover its current liabilities. Quick assets include those current assets that can be quickly converted to cash at close to their book values.

An alternative formula for the ratio can be expressed more specifically as follows:

$$\text{Quick Ratio} = \frac{\text{Cash + Marketable Securities + Accounts Receivable}}{\text{Current Liabilities}}$$

The quick ratio, since it excludes inventory, is a more stringent test than the working capital ratio. It indicates whether a firm has enough short-term assets to cover its immediate liabilities without selling inventory.

The quick ratio should be 1:1 or better; this, however, varies widely by industry. A company with a quick ratio of less than 1 is not necessarily insolvent and unable to pay off its liabilities. Depending on the type of business, it may be a sign of liquidity problems.

One useful metric is whether the quick ratio is much lower than the working capital ratio. If this is the case, then current assets are highly dependent on inventory. Retail stores are examples of this type of business, which helps to explain why retailers tend to fall victim to recessions.

The term acid test comes from the way gold miners would test whether their findings were real gold nuggets. Unlike other metals, gold does not corrode in acid; if the nugget did not dissolve when submerged in acid, it was said to have passed the acid test. If a company's financial statements pass the figurative acid test this is one indicator of financial well-being.

Exercise 2

Company A has a current ratio of 1.3 and a quick ratio of 0.85. Company B has a current ratio of 1.15 and a quick ratio of 1.0. All other things being equal, which company presents the most liquidity risk?

The answer to this exercise can be found at the end of this chapter.

3. The Working Capital Cycle

Learning Objective

3.3 Apply receivables, payables and inventory ratios

The next three ratios consider the velocity of cash flow within the working capital cycle.

Cash → Raw Materials → Labour → Finished Goods → Sales → Cash

Working capital is the funding available for conducting day-to-day business operations.

Working Capital = Current Assets − Current Liabilities

A company can increase its profitability by improving the efficiency of the working capital cycle by the following means:

- minimising its stock of materials and parts, ie, through a just-in-time inventory
- ensuring that debtors pay in a timely fashion
- delaying payment to creditors as long as feasible without jeopardising relationships.

In practice, a company should aim to maintain at least an equal balance, eg, between the collection period for receivables and the payment period for payables.

If a company faces customer demand to increase its credit period, it should, in turn, negotiate a longer credit period from its suppliers. A cash flow problem will otherwise arise since it will have to settle its liabilities before receiving from its customers. This is a potentially threatening situation; risking a liquidity trap.

Three ratios are commonly considered:

- The receivables collection period shows how soon receivables (ie, cash) will be realised (in days).
- The payables payment period shows the timescale over which suppliers will be paid.
- The inventory turnover ratio measures the speed at which inventory becomes sales (receivables).

Applicaiton of Financial Statement Analysis and Accounting Ratios

3.1 Receivables Collection Period or Debtors Ratio

The receivables (debtors) collection period gives an indication of how quickly, in terms of working days, a company is able to realise the value of its receivables, ie, convert them into cash.

$$\text{Receivables Collection Period} = \frac{\text{Trade Receivables}}{\text{Revenue}} \times 365 \text{ days}$$

With XYZ plc in 20X2, the figure is:

$$\text{Receivables Collection Period} = \frac{4,683}{31,311} \times 365 = 54.59 \text{ days}$$

This is quite a long time. Is this normal for the industry and has the figure improved or deteriorated since last year? It will definitely weaken the cash flow perspective if the firm is paying its creditors more swiftly. This is considered in the next section.

It is assumed that the company is operating on the basis of granting credit to its customers and in such a situation the denominator in the above equation (revenue) represents the total invoiced sales during the year.

The trade receivables amount represents those invoices which are unpaid at the time of preparing the company's balance sheet. Receivables divided by revenue thus illustrate the proportion of the year's sales which are unpaid, ie, the credit period extended to customers.

As with other financial ratios, this is a static number. It could be distorted intentionally, or unintentionally, if either or both of these figures are not representative of the normal trading activities when the balance sheet is prepared.

Such a concern is particularly relevant where sales are seasonal. The level of receivables can fluctuate considerably during a trading year if sales are concentred during certain periods or seasons. The annual revenue figure is the total of all the sales, irrespective of their seasonal nature, which could make a substantial difference to a snapshot of the company's performance, depending on when in the year the balance sheet is prepared.

3.2 Payables Payment Period

The payables (creditors) payment period shows how quickly the company is settling its liabilities.

$$\text{Payables Payment Period} = \frac{\text{Total Payables}}{\text{Purchases}} \times 365 \text{ days}$$

Purchases are often replaced with cost of sales if the purchases figure is unavailable.

With XYZ plc in 20X2, the figure is:

$$\text{Payables Payment Period} = \frac{2,550}{24,234} \times 365 = 38.4 \text{ days}$$

This figure is lower than the receivables collection period, so cash is leaving the firm quicker than it is being received.

The denominator in this ratio is the cost of sales, which is confined to the direct costs of the business incurred in the production or supply of the product or services being sold. Cost of sales or cost of goods sold does not include, for example, general and administrative expenses.

To obtain a worthwhile and valid comparison, the invoiced payables should be compared with invoiced costs.

If a company had £460,000 for total payables, and a total cost of sales on an annual basis of £2 million, the payables payment period would be calculated as (£460,000 ÷ £2,000,000) x 365 = 84 days (rounded to the nearest number of days).

3.3 Inventory Days

Inventory days (or stock days) indicate how quickly a company is selling its inventory.

$$\text{Inventory} = \frac{\text{Inventory}}{\text{Cost of Goods Sold}} \times 365 \text{ days}$$

With XYZ plc in 20X2, the figure is:

$$\text{Inventory} = \frac{3,723}{24,234} = \times 365 = 56.07 \text{ days}$$

The cost of goods sold (COGS) or cost of sales figure shows the total cost value of the goods sold in the year. The average inventory figure shows the cost value, on average, of the goods held during the year in inventory. This ratio therefore shows how often a company can expect to sell its normal holding of inventory.

This ratio should be compared against industry averages. A high number of days implies poor sales and excess inventory. A low number of days implies either strong sales or ineffective buying.

Inventory management is a critical area with regard to its working capital cycle efficiency. High inventory levels are unsatisfactory because there is an opportunity cost in tying up working capital in inventory. Inventory has an effective zero rate of return versus a rate of return available from other current assets, such as short term money market instruments. It also exposes the company to write-downs of current assets if prices for its marketplace begin to fall.

Exercise 3

In addition to the opportunity cost of committing too much capital to inventory, what other financial implications could arise? Could there be any financial implication for a firm not committing enough capital to inventory?

The answer to this exercise can be found at the end of this chapter.

The same problem relating to the static nature of the inventory days' ratio arises as in other ratios earlier. The balance sheet preparation date may give an unrepresentative view of the matter, especially for a business with seasonal demand and hence seasonal inventory levels.

Depending on the information provided in the income statement, it may not be possible to establish an accurate cost of sales figure. In this case, a revenue figure could be used, but this would be computed on a value-added basis rather than a cost basis and will distort the ratio. With this qualification in mind, the more general use of the ratio is to track changes or trends. It is often these that are more important in financial and accounting analysis than any single ratio value itself.

Any observable trend in this ratio from one year to the next may indicate a surplus or deficit of inventory. It is important also to consider the nature of the business as the appropriate levels of inventory and the inventory days' rate varies greatly among industry sectors.

A supermarket would expect a very low number of inventory days for its perishable products such as milk, whereas a vineyard owner whose inventory takes several years to mature would expect a much higher inventory days' rate.

It is prudent to examine the circumstances of a business when interpreting the ratio. Increased inventory turnover may naively be considered as indicative of a well-run business, but may be due to very low levels of inventory, which can result in loss of sales and hence a deterioration in a company's reputation.

4. Financial Gearing Ratios

Learning Objective

3.4 Apply financial gearing ratios for: debt/equity; interest cover; asset cover

Financial analysts are keen to examine gearing ratios for businesses as they consider the capital structure of a company and the relationship between its borrowings and shareholders' funds, which are not an immediate obligation of a company.

The use of gearing or financial leverage is found in many businesses, in particular the financial services sector. High levels of gearing can indicate much greater levels of financial risk.

Consider gearing and leverage in relation to a company which pays an initial deposit to buy office premises and then finances the remaining purchase funds from a bank.

Two different scenarios illustrate the impact of changes in commercial real estate prices. Assume that the company buys a £500,000 office using £125,000 of assets as a deposit and borrows the remaining £375,000:

- **The office price doubles**, ie, increases by 100%.
  Office value: £1,000,000
  Deposit: £125,000
  Unrealised gain: £875,000
  Return: +700% ((£875,000 ÷ £125,000) x 100).

- **The office price halves**, ie, falls by 50%.
  Office value: £250,000
  Deposit: £125,000
  Unrealised loss: £250,000
  Return: –200% (-£250,000 ÷ £125,000) x 100.

The scale and range of returns for a purchaser of property with debt financing with relatively modest gearing can be substantial. These would be amplified with a smaller deposit and a larger debt to fund the same purchase price, which signifies much higher gearing.

4.1 Debt to Equity

The **debt to equity ratio** is a measure of the risk to shareholders of receiving a lower dividend.

$$\text{Debt to Equity \%} = \frac{\text{Interest-Bearing Loans} + \text{Preference Share Capital}}{\text{Equity Shareholders' Funds}} \times 100$$

With XYZ plc in 20X2, the figure is:

$$\text{Debt to Equity \%} = \frac{9,000}{8,313} \times 100 = 108.26\%$$

Liabilities with an interest-bearing component are included. If XYZ plc held any preference share capital, this would also be included on the numerator, as this requires a committed payment from the company.

The preference share capital would also be deducted from shareholders' funds in the denominator where appropriate.

Various questions arise in relation to the debt/equity ratio:

- Should an overdraft be treated as an interest-bearing loans?
  - There is no definitive answer, but an analyst should consider the nature of the overdraft. Is it a short-term trading anomaly or is it used as a means of long-term financing? In the case of XYZ plc, it does not appear to act as long-term financing, so should not be included as an interest-bearing loan in the equation.
- How should a convertible bond be treated in calculating this gearing ratio? Is it debt or alternatively equity, if it is considered likely to convert?

Application of Financial Statement Analysis and Accounting Ratios

- ○ Convertibles can be shown in the balance sheet as a mixture of equity and liability. If it is probable that the convertible will become equity (ie, the conversion terms are favourable to the investor), then it can be treated as equity. Since the fixed-income debt interest must nevertheless be paid in the near term, it may be prudent to consider it as debt.
- Is there a benchmark size of gearing?
  - ○ In general terms no, although it is widely recognised that in the banking and financial services sector, prior to 2008, the degree of gearing and leverage was extraordinarily risky, leading to a subsequent trend to de-lever balance sheets.
  - ○ If there is little variability in operating profit for a company then financial gearing is of little consequence, as the amplification effect of gearing would have little effect in absolute terms.
  - ○ Businesses such as utilities, with typically steady levels of earnings, can tolerate a higher level of gearing than those more volatile sectors such as technology, banking and financial services.
  - ○ As with other ratios, the key approach in interpretation is to observe trends of improvement or deterioration.

4.2 The Net Debt to Equity Ratio

An alternative to the debt to equity ratio is the net debt to equity ratio. This takes account of cash and investments which a business can use to offset the debt.

$$\text{Net Debt to Equity \%} = \frac{\text{Debt (as above)} - \text{Cash and Current Investments}}{\text{Shareholders' Equity}} \times 100$$

With XYZ plc in 20X2, the figure is:

$$\text{Net Debt to Equity \%} = \frac{9{,}000 - 45}{8{,}313} \times 100 = 107.7\%$$

For net debt to equity the figures are all drawn from the balance sheet: net debt is the same debt as in the debt to equity ratio, less the cash and short-term investments which are within the current assets on the balance sheet.

4.3 Interest Cover

Interest cover is a measure of the ability of the company to pay the fixed interest on borrowings out of its operating profits and other income receivables for the year. In general terms, the higher the level of interest cover, the less risk there is to either shareholders or lenders. An appropriate cover ratio varies again across different business sectors, so there is no single optimal level.

$$\text{Interest Cover} = \frac{\text{Operating Profit} + \text{Interest Receivables} + \text{Other Income Receivables}}{\text{Interest Payable}}$$

With XYZ plc in 20X2, the figure is:

$$\text{Interest Cover} = \frac{2{,}787 + 5}{902} = 3.10 \text{ x}$$

4.4 Asset (or Loan) Cover

Lenders to a company are concerned not only with the interest cover but also with the security or likelihood of repayment of the loan itself. They therefore examine the ratio between loans granted and the assets available to repay them.

The asset cover is calculated as follows.

$$\text{Asset Cover} = \frac{\text{Total Assets} - \text{Current Liabilities}}{\text{Loans Payable}}$$

In the case of a number of loans with different priorities of repayment in a winding-up, the asset cover should be calculated for each of them in priority order on a cumulative basis.

With XYZ plc in 20X2, the figure is:

$$\text{Asset Cover} = \frac{(24,429 - 7,116)}{9,000} = 1.92 \text{ x}$$

For XYZ plc, the loans are relatively simple but the order of priority for repayment is as follows:

Debenture	6,500
Unsecured loans and bank overdraft (2,550 + 3,201)	5,751
The cumulative value of the loans is	12,251

For XYZ plc, the total assets less current liabilities excluding any current instalments due on loans (such as bank overdraft) is:

$$£24,429 - (£7,116 - £3,201) = £20,514$$

Hence, the asset cover for each of the above is:

- Debenture = £20,514 ÷ £6,500 = 3.2x
- Bank overdraft and unsecured loans = (£20,514 − £6,500) ÷ £5,751 = 2.4x

Applicaiton of Financial Statement Analysis and Accounting Ratios

5. Evaluate Growth in Sales, Profitability and Capital

Learning Objective

3.5   Evaluate growth in sales, profitability, capital

The way in which fixed costs behave can be depicted as follows:

'F' represents the amount of fixed costs, which is constant irrespective of the volume of activity.

Variable costs vary with the volume of activity.

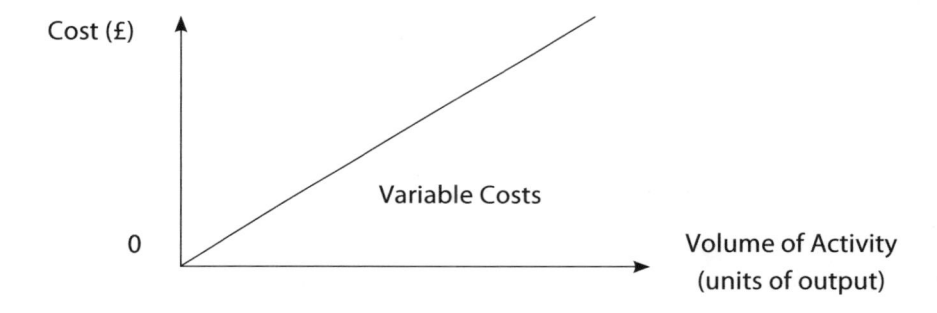

At zero volume of activity the variable cost is zero. The cost increases in a straight line as activity increases.

The straight line for variable cost on this graph implies that the variable cost will normally be the same per unit of activity, irrespective of the volume of activity concerned.

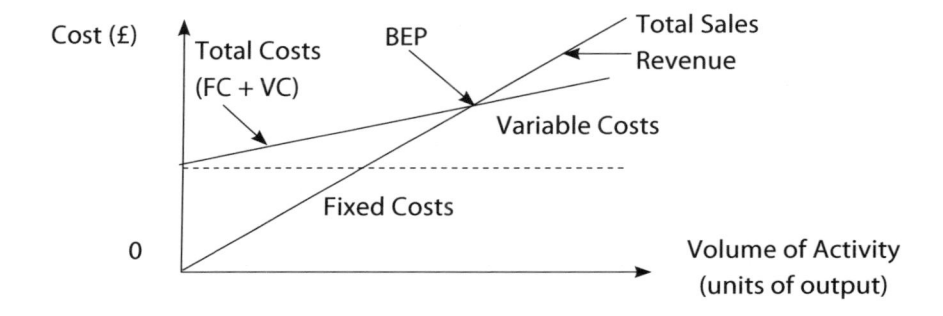

Finding a break-even point (BEP) by graphical means is a laborious business.

$$BEP = \frac{\text{Fixed costs}}{\text{Sales Revenue per Unit} - \text{Variable Costs per Unit}}$$

The denominator of the break-even formula (sales revenue per unit less variable costs per unit) is known as the contribution per unit.

It is called contribution because it contributes to meeting the fixed costs and, if there is any excess, it also contributes to profit.

In cost-volume-profit analysis, a form of management accounting, the contribution margin is the marginal profit per unit sale. It is a useful quantity in carrying out various calculations, and can be used as a measure of operating leverage.

Contribution arises in cost-volume-profit analysis, where it simplifies calculation of net income, and especially break-even analysis.

Given the contribution margin, a manager can easily compute break-even and target income sales, and make better decisions about whether to add or subtract a product line, about how to price a product or service and about how to structure sales commissions or bonuses.

Contribution margin analysis is a measure of operating leverage; it measures how growth in sales translates to growth in profits.

The contribution margin is computed by using a contribution income statement, which is a management accounting version of the income statement, reformatted to group together a business's fixed and variable costs.

Contribution is different to gross margin in that a contribution calculation separates variable costs (included in the contribution calculation) from fixed costs (not included in the contribution calculation) on the basis of economic analysis of the nature of the expense, whereas gross margin is determined using accounting standards.

Contribution format income statements can be drawn up with data from more than one year's income statements, when a person is interested in tracking contribution margins over time. They can even be drawn up for each product line or service. The example below shows a breakdown of three product lines for a fictitious company:

	Line A	Line B	Line C
Sales	£120,400	£202,050	£140,002
Less Variable Costs:			
Cost of Goods Sold	(£70,030)	(£100,900)	(£60,004)
Sales Commissions	(£18,802)	(£40,050)	(£0)
Delivery Charges	(£900)	(£8,084)	(£5,000)
Total Variable Costs	(£89,732)	(£149,034)	(£65,004)
Contribution Margin	£30,668	£53,016	£74,998
Percentage of Sales	25%	26%	54%

Exercise 4

What conclusions can we draw from the information in this table?

The answer to this exercise can be found at the end of this chapter.

6. Investor Ratios

Learning Objective

3.6 Apply investor ratios: earnings per share including adjustments for capitalisation changes, corporate actions and post-balance sheet events

For investors, one paramount set of ratios relate to the earnings of a company. Investors seek good returns, either as income or capital growth, or some combination, and they weigh these returns in relation to potential risks in holding the investment, including the possibility of a partial or complete loss of capital. Note that changes below, such as bonus issues and rights issues, are all examples of corporate actions.

6.1 Earnings Per Share (EPS)

The earnings per share (EPS) ratio is one of the most useful and popular ratios. It is used universally with more or less the same definition in most jurisdictions, but is one ratio with prescribed rules of calculation in the UK. These are laid out in IAS 33, which essentially defines the EPS as:

$$\text{EPS} = \frac{\text{net profit (or loss) attributable to ordinary shareholders}}{\text{average weighted number of ordinary shares outstanding in period}}$$

From the financial statements of XYZ plc in chapter 2, the following calculations can be made:

Profit attributable to the group was £1,266,000 in 20X2 and the number of ordinary shares outstanding during the period was 1,000,000, which gives an EPS of 126.6p.

The EPS ratio is expressed in pence and reveals how much profit made during the year is available to be paid out to each shareholder. Earnings are additionally then divided into the current share price to calculate how many times the EPS must be paid to buy a share. This assesses in effect how expensive (or cheap) the shares are. This reciprocal metric is known as the price/earnings ratio or P/E ratio. In the case of XYZ plc the ratio is share price / EPS = £10.26 / £1.266 = 8.1 x.

There are several variations on the basic earnings per share ratio including, for example, expected growth multiples, but the **vanilla** version from which they derive is EPS. The metric is so widely followed that market analysts will use, for example, the P/E of the FTSE 100 or the Standard & Poor's 500 Index as a critical variable in determining whether stock markets are fairly priced, overpriced or underpriced in comparison to historical norms.

6.2 Capitalisation Issues

In arriving at the EPS ratio, it is important to use the correct denominator in the equation, ie, the number of ordinary shares outstanding. If there have been no changes in the number of shares during the course of a year, there should be no problem in restating the amount at the year end.

If there have, however, been modifications to the capital outstanding during the course of the year, then pro rata adjustments to the number of shares to reflect the changes in capitalisation are required. The purpose of the adjustments is as follows:

- To ensure the ratio for the current year is valid by comparing the full year's earnings to the representative number of shares in issue during the year, not just the number of shares in issue at the year end. For example, the value for the number of shares outstanding would be distorted by an issuance of new shares close to the preparation of year-end statements.
- To provide a consistent view of a company's accounts and profitability trend by ensuring that the previous year's EPS figures have been calculated on a similar basis. It is often necessary to restate a previous year's EPS figures.

The following capitalisation changes are possible:

6.3 Full-Price Issue

- When shares are issued at full value during the course of a year, then the new finance raised at that point is available to generate new profits from that point in the year. Hence, the level of earnings and number of shares rises from the date the shares are issued.
- In order to ensure a like-for-like comparison in the EPS calculation, it is necessary to compare the earnings for the year with a representative number of shares throughout the year as opposed to just the year-end number. This representative number is the weighted average number of shares in issue during the year.
- In the case of a full price issue, it is not necessary to adjust the prior year's figures, as shares were not in issue and will have no impact on the previous year's performance and profitability per share.

6.4 New Share Issue to Acquire a Subsidiary

- If shares are issued as part of the consideration to acquire a subsidiary, the treatment is exactly the same as a full price issue.
- From the date when the subsidiary is acquired it is necessary to consolidate into the group accounts the profit of the subsidiary. In other words, from the date of acquisition the enlarged group's earnings will rise by the earnings generated by the subsidiary.
- It is necessary to apply a weighted average number to the shares as and when they are issued and, therefore, become outstanding.

6.5 Bonus Issues and Share Splits

- In the case of a bonus issue there is no fundamental alteration to the operating assets of the business. There is a restructuring only of the accounting lines which comprise shareholders' funds.
- As a bonus issue does not provide any additional cash, it does not generate new earnings.
- From a balance sheet perspective a bonus issue has the effect of increasing share capital and reducing reserves, ie, restructuring shareholders' funds; it does not change the total shareholders' funds or total net assets.
- From an operational viewpoint, these bonus shares can be considered as if they were issued at the same time as the underlying shares on which they are now being paid.
- In terms of accounting procedure, the bonus issue can be backdated as if the shares had always been in issue.
- Similar considerations apply in the case of a share split where, for example, all existing shareholders are given another share in a 2 for 1 split. Following such an event there are a greater number of shares but since the split is on a pro bono basis, no new finance has been raised.

A pure bonus issue requires an adjustment to the number of shares previously in issue by using the bonus or split fraction as follows:

$$\text{Bonus fraction} = \frac{\text{Number of shares after the issue}}{\text{Number of shares before the issue}}$$

6.6 Illustration of the Effects of a Bonus Issue – or a Share Split

Assume that on 1 January 20X2 XYZ plc has one million outstanding ordinary shares in issue. If it then makes a 1 for 4 bonus issue on 31 August (XYZ plc's year end is at 31 December), the bonus fraction would be as follows:

Bonus fraction = 1,250,000 ÷ 1,000,000 since one new share is issued for every four currently in issue. The calculation of the weighted average number of shares is 5/4 or 1.25.

From this, the weighted average can be calculated as follows:

Dates	Total Number	Bonus Fraction	Time Apportion	Weighted Average
1 Jan to 31 Aug	1,000,000	1.25	2/3	833,333
31 Aug Issue 1 for 4	250,000			
1 Sept to 31 Dec	1,250,000		1/3	416,667
				1,250,000

The practical effect is not significant to the year-end amount of shares outstanding, but demonstrates the protocol for new financing, such as in a rights issue.

One necessary adjustment is to update the previous year's EPS for XYZ plc.

In effect, the EPS should be scaled down by spreading the 20X1 earnings over the larger notional amount of shares outstanding.

When the EPS has to be restated for a bonus issue, the adjustment is:

$$\text{Restated EPS} = \text{Original EPS} \times \frac{1}{\text{Bonus Factor}}$$

6.7 Rights Issue

The purpose of a rights issue is to raise new financing for a company. Shareholders are not obliged to subscribe to a rights issue; as an incentive, the rights issue is therefore usually made at a discount to the current market price.

With a rights issue conducted at a discount to the current price, the increase in earnings will be less than if it had been a full price issue, since less cash is raised per share.

A rights issue at a discount can be considered from the point of view that the company requires new investors to pay the full price for a proportion of the shares but then provides them with additional shares on a pro bono basis (ie, for free). A rights issue at a discount is equivalent to the following:

- Part of the issue being at full share price.
- Part of the issue being a bonus.
- The weighted average number of shares this year at full price is calculated.
- The bonus element is then backdated to the original date of issue and the previous year's EPS figures are adjusted by using the formula of 1 / bonus factor.

Applicaiton of Financial Statement Analysis and Accounting Ratios

The full issue is split into a bonus component and a discount component. The bonus element is calculated by use of the following formula:

Bonus fraction = $\dfrac{\text{Actual price before the issue (cum-rights price)}}{\text{Theoretical price after issue (ex-rights price)}}$

Example

In the following scenario involving XYZ plc, the balance sheet shows ordinary share capital outstanding at 31 December 20X1 of 1 million shares, all issued at a par value of 25p each.

At the beginning of 20X1, XYZ plc had 800,000 ordinary shares issued on the same basis. Assume that it had a rights issue on 31 August 20X1 on the basis of 1 for 4 and that the rights issue was priced at £4.80 (whereas the actual share price on 31 August was £8.80 per share).

	Number of shares	Price £	Value £
Before	40	8.80	352.00
New Issue	10	4.80	48.00
After New Issue	50		400.00

The table shows a theoretical ex-rights price (price after the issue) of £8 (ie, 50 shares valued at £400). The bonus fraction is therefore derived as follows:

Bonus fraction = £8.80 (actual share price) ÷ £8 (theoretical share price) = 1.1

A shareholder is in exactly the same position following either a rights issue or the bonus issue plus full price issue. The outcome from either path is 50 shares worth £8 each.

Logical Validation of Bonus Fraction

Using the bonus fraction, the rights issue is the equivalent of a 1 for 10 bonus issue, plus a full price issue for the remainder of the shares.

A shareholder with 40 shares before the rights issue would take a bonus of 4 shares and pay the full price for 6 (taking his year-end holding up to 50 shares, just as in the case of the 1 for 4 rights issue). The effective share price under this alternative method is the same as above and hence the two are equivalent.

	Number of shares	Price £	Value £
Held	40	8.80	352.00
Bonus	4		
	44		352.00
Full Price	6	8.00	48.00
After	50		**400.00**

As a result of the bonus element of the issue, the share price falls to £8 (ie, £352 ÷ 44 shares in the table above), which is the price for the full price element of the issue.

A shareholder is in exactly the same position following either a rights issue or the bonus issue plus issue at full price. The outcome from either path leads to 50 shares worth £8 each.

6.7.1 Tail-Swallowing

Also known as a cashless take-up, this is a situation where an investor is unwilling, or unable, to make any payment to purchase the full rights issue entitlement. The investor will instead sell some of the rights in order to raise sufficient cash to take up the remaining rights and purchase those shares. No actual cash expenditure is required.

Example

Cally plc shares are trading at £3, and it decides to sell new shares as rights at £1.85.

If it is a 1 for 4 rights issue and an investor has 400 shares, then the entitlement is 100 extra shares. In this example, the 100 rights could be worth £1.15 each (£3 less £1.85).

A shareholder could therefore sell 65 rights for £74.75. If the fees are £10 (for example), this would leave £64.75.

The shareholder can thus buy the remaining 35 shares for £64.75, without investing any new cash.

6.8 Post-Balance Sheet Events

When a share issue between the date of the balance sheet and the date on which the accounts are approved impacts the number of ordinary shares, the basic EPS must be changed to take account of this.

The total number of shares must include the extra shares in issue after the event, when the company undertakes a bonus issue, share split or consolidation, or when there is a bonus element to another issue (eg, a rights issue).

For issues that have an impact on earnings, only shares with no earnings impact should be included in the EPS calculation, eg, the 'bonus' element of a rights issue.

6.9 Diluted Earnings per Share

The purpose of publishing a diluted EPS figure is to warn shareholders of potential future changes in the EPS figure as a result of events which hypothetically might take place. 'Hypothetically' is used in this context because there is only a possibility; certain legal rights have been granted which could be exercised and therefore require further issues of shares. The prudent method of accounting is to assume, from the point of view of share dilution, the worst-case scenario.

Two possible factors could cause share dilution and need to be considered in the conservative method of calculating a true and accurate EPS. A company may have either or both of the following kinds of securities outstanding:

- convertible loan stock or convertible preference shares
- options or warrants.

Each of these situations could result in additional shares being issued and, therefore, qualifying for a dividend in future years which would then dilute the current EPS.

The diluted EPS calculation is theoretical, based on a potential scenario. Due to its significance to the reader of the accounts, its calculation and disclosure is required by IAS 33 – *Earnings Per Share* (GAAP in the UK).

6.10 Convertible Preference Shares and Convertible Loan Stock

Convertibles (either loan stock or preference shares) when issued by a company as part of its capital structure confer to the holder, at their option, the opportunity to convert the convertible security into ordinary shares. Hence, the number of ordinary shares will be increased if the conversion option is taken up.

According to the offering prospectus, the number of shares into which a convertible security may convert into ordinary shares does not remain static but changes over time.

In general terms, the number of shares resulting from a convertible security falls the longer the convertible is held, assuming that the share price rises over that time.

In accordance with prudence and conservatism, the maximum amount of conversion into ordinary shares should be assumed and integrated into the calculation of EPS on a fully diluted basis. This is to alert current shareholders to the maximum possible dilution from any conversion of loan stock or convertible preference shares in existence at any year end.

The number of ordinary shares to be issued and remain outstanding must always assume the maximum possible number that convertible securities could convert into in the future.

The existence of convertibles also affects the earnings figure. A company is already paying interest on any convertible loan stock, and if it has issued any convertible preference shares it is currently paying a preference dividend.

Since the earnings figure is profit after tax, minority interest and preference dividends, the required adjustments are as follows:

Add to the basic number of shares, the greatest number of equity shares that may be issued in the future upon conversion of the loan stock or convertible preference shares in issue at the year end.

6.11 Illustration of Dilution with Convertible Security

Assume that the debt financing of XYZ plc at the year-end 20X1 included £250,000 of 10% convertible loan stock, issued on 30 June 20X0. The terms of conversion for every £100 nominal value of loan stock on the following conversion dates are as follows:

- 30 June 20X1 – conversion ratio is 120:1
- 30 June 20X2 – conversion ratio is 115:1
- 30 June 20X3 – conversion ratio is 110:1

Since the £250,000 of convertible loan stock is still in issue at year end 20X1, the convertible stockholders have not taken the option of converting at a conversion ratio of 120:1 shares.

If the conversion does occur on the next conversion date (30 June 20X2), how much extra profit could be generated by XYZ plc in that trading year (assuming corporation tax of 20%)?

XYZ plc Fully Diluted EPS Calculation			
Basic Earnings as of 31 December 20X2			
Conversion is exercised on 30 June 20X2:			
	Interest saved for one half year		
	£250,000 x 10% x 6/12	£12,500	
	Tax at 20%	(£2,500)	
Additional net earnings following dilution event			**£10,000**

By converting the loan stock at a rate of 115 shares per £100 nominal, we assume the most dilutive possibility as required by IAS 33. This will be the maximum number of new ordinary shares that can be issued, ie, (£250,000 ÷ 100) x 115 = 287,500 shares.

The dilution in this example is assumed to have occurred for six months, since the conversion takes place halfway through the trading period of 20X2. The calculation of fully diluted ordinary shares for the trading period is therefore:

Number of Shares Pre-Dilution			**1,000,000**
	Conversion of £250,000 of loan stock at 115/100	287,500	
	Time apportioned by 6/12		143,750
Fully diluted shares for period 20X2			**1,143,750**

In subsequent years, the dilution calculation would assume dilution for the whole year.

Using the XYZ plc profit figures from Chapter 2, pre-dilution, the EPS for 20X2 is £1,266,000 ÷ 1,000,000 shares = 126.60p per share.

Fully diluted EPS for 20X2 is £1,266,000 ÷ 1,143,750 shares = 110.69p per share.

6.12 Options and Warrants

The other types of dilutive securities to be considered in relation to IAS 33 are options and warrants. These instruments are considered in more detail in chapter 9, sections 2 and 6. Essentially, an option or **warrant** issued by a company to an investor permits, but does not oblige, the holder to purchase additional shares in the company by exercising that option on predetermined terms, involving the price to be paid and the number of securities to be purchased. Often employees of companies may have options to purchase their employer's stock.

If a company has options or warrants in issue, the calculation of diluted EPS must assume the exercise of all outstanding warrants or options.

There are two parts to consider. The first relates to the proceeds which would be received by the warrant or option issuer if the holder exercises the warrant or option to purchase new shares. The second relates to the number of new shares which would then be issued and which would cause a dilution of earnings in the EPS calculation.

The difference between the number of shares issued and the number of shares that would have been issued at fair value is treated as an issue of shares for no consideration.

The fair value of the shares should be based on the average market price of the shares over the year.

Since any shares issued at fair value would also cause an increase in earnings, they are excluded from the diluted calculation on the premise that any increase in earnings would exactly counterbalance the increase in shares, causing no net change to EPS and, therefore, no dilution.

The dilution effect is calculated as follows:

basic number of shares outstanding

+

number of shares that would be issued on exercise of the warrants or options

−

number of shares issued at fair value, due to the proceeds received by the company on exercise.

Example

Assume that XYZ plc has granted options which allow the holders to purchase 1 million new ordinary shares at an exercise price of £8.00 per share.

Assume that the average share price over the preceding year has been £10.00.

There is no material impact to the earnings of XYZ plc in 20X2, so these are left unchanged at £1,266,000.

Assuming that the options are exercised, the company would receive £8 million (1 million shares at £8 each). Using the £10 average share price over the year, this represents an issue of 800,000 shares at fair value. This replicates an issue of 800,000 shares at a fair value price of £10 and of 200,000 for free.

6.13 Disclosure

IAS 33 requires the disclosure of basic and diluted EPS in the income statement, both for net profit or loss for the period and profit or loss for continuing operations. Any additional information, such as alternative methods of calculating the EPS, can only be disclosed by way of a note to the accounts.

A note needs to be included in the accounts detailing the basis upon which the calculations are carried out, specifically the earnings figure and the number of shares used within the calculation, both for this year and for the comparative year.

7. Earnings Yield, Dividend Yield and Dividend Cover

Learning Objective

3.7 Calculate earnings yield, dividend yield and dividend cover

7.1 Earnings Yield

The earnings yield expresses the most recent EPS as a percentage of the current market price for ordinary shares.

$$\text{Earnings yield \%} = \frac{\text{Earnings per share}}{\text{Current market price per share}} \times 100$$

With regard to XYZ plc, the EPS in 20X2 was 126.6 pence and the price per share assumed previously was £10.26. The earnings yield is calculated as:

$$\text{Earnings yield \%} = \frac{£1.266}{£10.26} \times 100 = 12.34\%$$

The earnings yield is effectively the inverse or reciprocal of the P/E ratio, and accordingly, the qualifications expressed in connection with that ratio also apply to the earnings yield.

As noted previously, comparisons between different companies with respect to the accounting ratios are more pertinent when the companies are in the same sector and share similar characteristics.

Assuming that the median earnings yield for XYZ plc's industry sector is 10%, a yield of 7% for XYZ plc would suggest that its shares are in relatively high demand. This might arise because a rapid growth of earnings is expected and investors and traders are 'discounting' this possibility in advance by buying shares in anticipation.

A company with a much higher earnings yield (eg, 16%) might reflect a company which is not currently in favour with investors, who may anticipate poor earnings or other potential weakness.

Investment managers often compare the earnings yield of a broad market index (such as the FTSE 100 or the S&P 500) to prevailing interest rates, such as the current yield on ten-year gilts or US Treasury notes in order to measure the equity risk premium.

Traditional investment theory suggests that investors in equities typically demand an extra risk premium of several percentage points above prevailing risk-free rates (such as T-bills) in their earnings yield to compensate them for the higher risk of owning stocks over bonds.

7.2 Dividend Yield

The dividend yield of an ordinary share is calculated as follows:

$$\text{Dividend yield \%} = \frac{\text{Dividend per share}}{\text{Current market price per share}} \times 100$$

In the case of XYZ plc, the dividend paid for each ordinary share in 20X2 was 46.2 pence; assuming the share price to be £10.26, the dividend yield is:

$$\text{Dividend yield \%} = \frac{£0.462}{£10.26} \times 100 = 4.5\%$$

Long-term investors in equities are often influenced by the dividends paid by a company, as this is a vital part of the total return from holding equities. The income stream from ordinary shares via the payment of dividends cannot be relied upon in the same way as dividend income from either a bond or preferred stock. Dividends can be reduced or eliminated even by large and established companies.

An issuer of a bond or preferred share is obliged to pay the dividend or coupon payment specified in the offering prospectus, whereas the decision to pay a dividend and if so, how much, is entirely at the discretion of the board of directors of the company.

An ordinary shareholder has no guarantee of any dividend at all and nor is there a specific amount that can be relied upon from companies which have historically paid dividends.

During the economic downturn of 2008-09, many companies abandoned the payment of dividends completely or reduced the amounts paid substantially.

Many new companies, and those which are still at a stage of rapid growth, may decide not to pay any dividend as their shareholders would consider that earnings could be better invested in further growth of the business.

There is no obvious relationship between the dividend yield and the perception of the company in the marketplace. A high dividend yield could arise because a company elects to pay a high dividend amount per share or it could also arise, as is often the case, because the shares are currently valued by the market at a low multiple to earnings and dividends. This could be because investors are risk-averse or believe that the market prospects in general are unfavourable.

In general terms, a company with good growth prospects would tend to see an increase in its share price and reduction in yield. This implies that companies with high P/E ratios have a tendency to deliver low dividend yields and those with low P/E ratios have a propensity to provide high dividend yields. A well-regarded company will have a high price relative to high dividend as well, ie, both the numerator and denominator will change.

7.3 Dividend Cover

The board of directors decides what proportion of profits are paid out to shareholders as dividends. The amount, if any, depends on a variety of factors, including their outlook for the future success of the company. One guide to this can be the 'dividend cover', which indicates the stability and growth of dividends. It measures the earnings per share as a multiple of the dividend.

$$\text{Dividend cover} = \frac{\text{Earnings per share}}{\text{Net dividend per share}}$$

From the 20X2 income statement of XYZ plc, the EPS was 126.6 pence and the net dividend per share was 46.2 pence, which means that the dividend cover was 2.74x (126.6 / 46.2).

An unusually high dividend cover implies that the company is retaining the majority of its earnings, presumably with the intention of reinvesting for further growth. This is common among companies which are still in a high growth phase rather than more mature companies which are often expected to pay regular dividends.

If a company pays a dividend which is greater than the year's earnings and the ratio is less than 1 x, the company is funding part of its dividend from past reserves and is said to be paying an uncovered dividend.

Generally speaking, a dividend cover of 2x or higher is considered prudent, in that the company is perceived to be able to afford the dividend. A ratio below 1.5x might however suggest a less sustainable dividend.

If the ratio is below 1x, the company is already using its retained earnings from a previous year to pay this year's dividend and is more likely to be a cause for investor concern.

Exercise 6

Using the information provided in the financial statements for XYZ plc in chapter 2, calculate the earnings yield, dividend yield and dividend cover for the company in respect of the 20X1 year. How have the figures changed in 20X2 and what do they indicate?

The answers to this exercise can be found at the end of this chapter.

8. Analysis Interpretation

Learning Objective

3.8 Interpret the implications and limitations of the analysis in the context of: circumstances of the business; accounting policy and practice; distorting effects

8.1 Benefits and Limitations of Financial Ratio Analysis

The various ratios in this chapter have brought insight into how a business works, in both an absolute sense and relative to its peers and competitors. Professional financial analysts examine such ratios constantly to provide insight to investors and lenders.

Shareholders and managers can benefit from these techniques to understand better the company's performance and how it might improve. Companies with publicly traded debt or equity are usually keen to reveal their performance to the financial community in the best possible light. They therefore often set internal performance targets which are designed to produce favourable ratios.

This chapter introduces some of the most widely-used ratios in financial analysis but there are many other more esoteric examples. Many of the components used in the calculation of these ratios are loosely defined and so can vary from one jurisdiction, or even analyst, to another. The precise factors for calculating dividend cover, for example, and dilution for EPS can vary between the US and the UK. Apart from EPS, as defined in the UK by IAS 33, none of the ratios discussed in this chapter have exact definitions. This can cause doubt as to what exactly is being measured in each case, especially when comparisons are drawn with ratios with the same labels but prepared by different analysts.

Despite this methodological warning, financial ratios are a valuable tool, especially if they are compiled consistently for the same company on a regular basis. They allow trends or anomalies in performance or risk to be identified, eg, problems of efficiency or liquidity. The specific components of the relevant ratio can then be examined in depth to pinpoint the source of any concern.

Some of the most common concerns regarding performance and risk are set out below.

Profitability

Each company has its own business model. This describes the key strategic direction of a company, which can vary dramatically depending on its sector, stage of maturity and ambition. Some are suppliers to mass markets, while others occupy more specialised niches. Some seek a large market share in their sector and work on the principle of low margin and high volume; others prefer the converse model of high margin and relatively low volume.

Given the diverse range of business models in a modern complex economy, it is not surprising that there are few consistent principles regarding profitability in terms of financial ratios.

Although each company has individual scope to outperform or underperform its peers, all companies within a given sector, and to some extent the same economy, are prone to the same macroeconomic forces. A rising tide floats all boats, with some adjustment for individual buoyancy.

To a large extent, most companies have earnings and costs which fluctuate depending on economic factors such as growth, employment, inflation, consumer confidence, interest rates, exchange rates and sometimes commodity prices.

Many of the common financial performance and risk ratios were devised during periods when macroeconomics was dominated by Classical, Keynesian or Monetarist principles (or blends of these) in varying conditions of growth, inflation and employment. The events of the last decade have led some economists to question whether this will continue or if fresh conditions and principles may emerge and persist. This may challenge some of the assumptions about key company financial indicators and hence the relevant ratios. There is already a view that EPS for companies is cyclical and that during a recession the expected rate for a typical company will fall, but as soon as the financial markets begin to discount (ie, anticipate) that a recovery is imminent, the EPS values return to their long-term trend.

The most obvious flaw in placing too much reliance on financial ratios is that the data behind them is always historical. They can be highly useful in identifying companies at relatively greater or lesser risk than those in the same sector from a given change in the macroeconomic environment, but they do not predict that change itself.

So long as financial ratios are based on valid macroeconomic thinking, they at least provide benchmarks for acceptable performance and risk across sectors, both nationally and internationally. Supermarkets for example largely provide necessities, so in a sustained global downturn their profits should remain relatively stable, as measured by traditional ratios. Those same ratios may not however be able to reflect some of the competitive pricing pressures from discount grocery stores. As new industries emerge (eg, social media), it can take time to establish not only relevant data for high-growth companies, but also to establish a benchmark against which individual performance can be analysed.

Liquidity

The 2008–09 financial crisis revealed that the issue of liquidity for the financial services sector had been vastly underrated. Banks which had operated for many years with high gearing were suddenly exposed with respect to their liquidity. The business models of funding long-term obligations with short-term capital from previously highly liquid money markets turned out to have been out of step with dramatically changing conditions.

The liquidity of any business depends to a large extent on the wider monetary environment. Any business has to monitor and manage its own liquidity with reference to those conditions on its own absolute merits; there is no point identifying its own liquidity risk as in the best 10% of its peer group, if the entire group is failing to remain solvent.

Accounting Policies

The accounting policies adopted by any company can significantly impact on its ratios. For example, if non-current assets are revalued then depreciation charges will be higher, leading to lower profits. On the balance sheet however, more non-current assets means a higher capital employed figure, leading to a lower ROCE (lower profits divided by higher capital employed).

In comparing one company which revalues non-current assets and another which does not, or in comparing one company to a previous year when current assets have been revalued in-between, some distortion between the ratios should be expected as a result of this accounting policy.

Window Dressing

Any interpretation of the accounting ratios should take into account the timing of events on a company's balance sheet. If an event takes place towards the end of an accounting period, eg, the issuance of new shares, then the correct approach is to 'weight' the event so that its impact is spread throughout the year.

Companies sometimes make considerable efforts to portray their accounts and ratios in the best possible light, in a process known as window dressing.

Window dressing transactions, also known as cosmetic accounting, are those designed to mislead the reader of the accounts. The extent of the deception can vary substantially, but two common techniques are as follows:

- **Circular Transactions**
  Company A sells goods to Company B which then sells them back to Company A (if Companies A and B are group companies, the transactions would be netted off in consolidated accounts). This sale and repurchase arrangement is designed to give an inflated turnover but has no commercial authenticity. The company creates a false impression, which could improve its profitability ratios. This is misleading to investors and risks damaging the ethical reputation of the company's management.

  Since such a transaction creates an erroneous impression, it is probable that the transactions would have to be disclosed under rules in IAS 24 pertaining to Related Party Disclosures. This IAS ruling covers other kinds of misleading commercial activities, where there is no 'arm's length' relationship between the parties to a commercial transaction.

- **Bed and Breakfast Transactions**
  This is similar to a circular transaction, except that it occurs over the end of an accounting period. Company A sells to Company B prior to year-end, but then repurchases the goods from Company B immediately after the year end. This would artificially increase Company A's turnover for the first year. It would also inflate its profits, if the goods were sold at a profit in the first transaction.

Both practices are intended to mislead the reader of the accounts. Transactions with related parties must be disclosed in the notes with the accounts, and if the disclosures are not made in accordance with accounting standards the board of directors are in breach of company legislation and could be considered to be defrauding investors, resulting in regulatory censure and potential criminal charges.

Distortions

In calculating accounting ratios, it is always prudent to avoid anything which might distort analysis of the accounts.

Comparing a Full Year's Transactions to Year-End Balances

A common cause of distortion arises because several ratios are calculated with reference to a balance sheet figure only at the end of an accountancy period. Relevant data should instead be analysed against a representative balance throughout the year. For example, in assessing profitability, a full year's profits should be measured against a representative amount of capital employed for an accurate and reliable measure of the ROCE.

It is, however, often difficult to calculate the representative amount of capital employed throughout the year, so it may be necessary instead to calculate the ROCE based on start-of-year or end-of-year capital employed figures.

This problem is not confined to ROCE. The same concerns of distortion arise for any ratio which measures a full year's transaction against a year-end figure, eg, receivables' (debtors') collection period, payables' (trade creditors') payment period or inventory turnover rate.

Consider, for example, the acquisition of a subsidiary near year end. The extra revenue and profits apply only from the date of acquisition and so should have only a marginal impact on total revenues for the year; the changes in capital, however, unless properly adjusted, will misleadingly appear at year end by the full amount.

Any capital raised near the year end suffers from a similar issue. The capital employed is higher when the year-end balance sheet is prepared, but the earnings have increased by only a small amount, due to the short period until year end.

Seasonality of revenues can also produce distortions. A company with seasonal sales patterns shows distortions in its receivables' collection period. When sales are seasonal, receivables may appear significantly large or small, relative to the year's total revenue.

Distortions can also occur when analysing group financial data. Income from an associated entity or affiliate can boost the parent company's profits before tax; this has no revenue implications for the group however, so a crude calculation of profit margins based on profits before tax and revenue can incorporate a distorting effect.

Comparing Like With Like

It is imperative to compare accounting ratios on a like-for-like basis. Depreciation methods, for example, should be consistently applied, while the inventory turnover ratios for a supermarket cannot realistically be compared with those of a high-end retail boutique. Likewise, invoiced payables should be compared with invoiced cost of sales when analysing the payables' payment period, while profit margin analysis should compare profits with those revenues which generated the profits.

Summary

When considering any ratio, the aim should always be to compare like with like, to apply the correct perspective on financing and changes in capital structure during the period under investigation and to have a cautious view in general to overreaching with the conclusions that one reaches from the financial ratios.

9. Interpretation Tools

Learning Objective

3.9   Apply other interpretation tools: trend and common-size statements

Financial ratios are a vital part of a company's analysis of its own key performance objectives, particularly relating to prudent financial management with regard to gearing and liquidity. Analysis is also conducted by banks and investment managers with regard to major lending and investment decisions.

Selecting and producing appropriate and accurate ratios is only the start of an analyst's role. Interpreting the results requires further analysis as well as a deep understanding of the value of such information.

Trend analysis assesses ratios not in isolation, but over time. Analysts observe not only the change in a ratio from one period to the next, but also the development of a trend and in particular any unexpected interruption of that trend.

The following table shows highlights from the income statements of a company over a five-year period. The top line of the table reflects gross revenues from 20X0 to 20X4 and shows that in the period under consideration the revenues doubled between 20X0 and 20X4.

	20X0	20X1	20X2	20X3	20X4
	£'000	£'000	£'000	£'000	£'000
Gross Revenue	800	880	1,040	1,280	1,600
Gross Profit	140	170	200	210	240
Gross Margin	18%	19%	19%	16%	15%
Profit before Tax	130	160	180	200	220
Profit Margin	16%	18%	17%	16%	14%
Dividends	4	5	6	7	10

The second line indicates the gross profit in each year, followed by the gross margin.

Although top-line revenue has grown impressively, gross profit as a percentage of revenue has declined. From 20X2 to 20X4 the gross margin has dropped from 19% to 15%.

A similar deterioration occurs in the profit margin (ie, profit before tax, divided by revenues). In the final line, the company has decided to boost its annual dividend to shareholders by 150%, possibly on the basis that its sales have doubled.

	20X0	20X1	20X2	20X3	20X4
	£'000	£'000	£'000	£'000	£'000
Gross Revenue	100	110	130	160	200
Gross Profit	100	121	143	150	171
Gross Margin	100	110	110	94	86
Profit before Tax	100	123	138	154	169
Profit Margin	100	112	107	96	85
Dividends	100	125	150	175	250

The table above provides a trend analysis for the previous set of data to allow a realistic comparison of key parameters and to identify features of concern or merit.

The 20X0 levels for each of the six variables are used as base amounts. In each case, an index value of 100 is created.

This format shows that revenues have doubled and that profit before tax has expanded by 69% (ie, from 100 to 169). It is also clear that the increase in gross profit has failed to match the increase in revenue.

This method of presenting the data expresses ratio values or percentages in terms of index values. The gross margin has declined from 100% in 20X0 to 86% in 20X4 and the net profit margin has declined by 15% to 85% of what it was in 20X0.

The company is expanding its market share via higher turnover, but underlying profitability is deteriorating. An analyst would seek a detailed analysis of its cost structure and, in particular, its marginal costs.

Note also that the dividend has increased by 150%, above the growth rate in turnover and considerably above the rate of growth in profitability.

Gross Revenue Growth	20X0	20X1	20X2	20X3	20X4
A	100	110	130	160	200
B	100	140	200	220	250
Rates of Growth		20X0 to 20X1	20X1 to 20X2	20X2 to 20X3	20X3 to 20X4
A		10.0%	18.2%	23.1%	25.0%
B		40.0%	42.9%	10.0%	**13.6%**

The table above focuses just on the revenue growth of two companies and uses a combination of the index-based approach with a percentage change for each company.

Company A is the same company which was examined in more detail previously and the gross revenue index levels have been included from 20X0–X4.

Company B has data available in the form of similar index values but not in the form of underlying raw data. It is possible, therefore, that one firm might be significantly larger than the other. Despite this potential weakness in analysis, the trends in both companies can still be analysed in the form of year-on-year percentage changes.

The bottom two rows of the table indicate the rates of growth of Companies A and B from 20X0 onwards, and the rates are clearly different. Company A is growing at an expanding rate, whereas Company B is more erratic and after two years of strong growth its rate of growth in the most recent two-year period is substantially slower.

Common-size analysis (also called vertical analysis) expresses each line item on a single year's balance sheet as a percent of one line item, called a base amount.

The base amount for the balance sheet is usually total assets (the same as total liabilities plus stockholders' equity), and for the income statement it is usually net sales or revenues.

By comparing two or more years of common-size statements, changes in the mixture of assets, liabilities and equity become evident.

On the income statement, changes in the mix of revenues and in the spending for different types of expenses can be identified.

The common-size statement is a valuable tool for identifying changes in the way in which assets employed are financed and the breakdown of the assets employed.

The following table shows a summary balance sheet for ABC ltd at five year ends. It provides an overview of the financial state of the company, but the interpretation of the numbers in each column is helped by comparing each row of the table to the two base amounts. These base amounts are the total assets for each year and the total liabilities for each year. This shows the breakdown or composition of the assets and of liabilities and financing.

Balance Sheet Summary for ABC ltd					
	20X0	20X1	20X2	20X3	20X4
	£000's	£000's	£000's	£000's	£000's
Assets					
Non-Current Assets	400	500	520	600	550
Current Assets	420	460	530	660	650
Total Assets	**820**	**960**	**1,050**	**1,260**	**1,200**
Financing					
Share Capital	200	200	210	300	400
Reserves	120	130	160	200	220
Shareholders' Funds	216	340	300	310	330
Loans	50	150	150	150	50
Current Liabilities	234	140	230	300	200
Total Financing	**820**	**960**	**1,050**	**1,260**	**1,200**

In 20X1, for example, ABC ltd took an additional £100,000 loan and in 20X4, the loan was paid back through an issue of new share capital.

The common-size statement, calculated from the previous table and shown below, demonstrates a steady decline in the ratio of non-current assets to the total assets in the last four periods.

Common-size Balance Sheet Summary for ABC ltd					
	20X0	20X1	20X2	20X3	20X4
	Percentages				
Assets					
Non-Current Assets	49%	52%	50%	48%	46%
Current Assets	51%	48%	50%	52%	54%
Total Assets	**100%**	**100%**	**100%**	**100%**	**100%**
Financing					
Share Capital	24%	21%	20%	24%	33%
Reserves	15%	13%	15%	16%	18%
Shareholders' Funds	26%	35%	29%	24%	28%
Loans	6%	16%	14%	12%	4%
Current Liabilities	29%	15%	22%	24%	17%
Total Financing	**100%**	**100%**	**100%**	**100%**	**100%**

Note: the above table may contain figures which have been rounded up.

In 20X0, the company's £50,000 loan represented just 6% of its liabilities/financing whereas, after taking the £100,000 loan in 20X1, this ratio jumped to 16% of the company's liabilities. When £100,000 of new shares were issued and added to the share capital, the funds partially paid back the loan and the ratio of loans to total financing fell to 4%. This indicates a lower leverage or gearing on its balance sheet.

Common sizing can also be applied to a company's cash flow statement. Financing activities from the financing cash flow statement illustrate the gearing, as all financing debits and credits to the cash account can be seen in the same place.

Example Exam Questions on Principal Accounting Ratios

Questions about accounting ratios can appear throughout the exam. There is a strong probability that a question covering a firm's accounts will be in the longer sections of the exam (Sections B and C) so it is important that you can understand and interpret the information being presented to you. Usually, you will be asked to analyse a pre-prepared set of statements in some depth using a number of the main accounting ratios.

On occasion, you will also be asked shorter questions about financial accounting ratios in Section A. The following examples act as practice questions covering all sections of the exam.

Section A:

When evaluating and comparing a set of financial statements, define two ratios and explain the possible 'distorting effects' that can impact on accounting analysis. (5 marks)

Section C:

Mr Zack Boston is considering purchasing the majority of shares in Zvestya plc but, as an American, he is worried that he may not be interpreting the available information correctly and thus be paying too high a price for the shares. He has asked you to advise him. Some information from the latest published accounts is given below.

Zvestya plc Consolidated Income Statement for the year ended 30 June 20XX

	20XX	20XX
	£'000	£'000
Sales		200		220
Less costs of sales		(90)		(103)
Gross profit		110		117
Less expenses				
Rent and rates	5		6	
Lighting and heating	3		4	
Wages	35		40	
Depreciation of shop equipment	6		8	
Net profit before taxation		61		59
Less interest on loans		(4)		(1)
Profit before taxation		57		58
Taxation		(20)		(20)
Net profit after taxation		37		38
Dividends				
Ordinary (proposed)	3		5	
Retained profit		34		33

Application of Financial Statement Analysis and Accounting Ratios

Zvestya plc balance sheet as at 30 June 20XX and 20XX

	30/6/20XX		30/6/20XX	
	£'000	£'000	£'000	£'000
Non-current assets				
Store equipment at cost		60		90
Accumulated Depreciation		12		20
Net book value		48		70
Current assets				
Stock (inventory)	60		80	
Debtors (trade receivables)	10		21	
Cash	2		1	
	72		102	
Current liabilities				
Trade creditors (payables)	32		26	
Working capital		40		76
Total assets less current liabilities		88		146
Owners capital				
Shares	54		88	
Retained profit for year	34	88	33	121
Long term liability		0	0	25
Shareholders' funds		88		146

a. Calculate the Gross Profit Margin for both years and comment on what this is telling you. (4 marks)
b. Calculate the Earnings per share (EPS) for both years. (3 marks)
c. Calculate the Return on Capital Employed for both years (using both trading and financing side methods) commenting upon what these are telling you about the performance of the company. (6 marks)
d. Calculate the Asset Turnover Ratio (for both years) and again comment on what your calculations are telling you. (6 marks)
e. Calculate the Acid Test for both years and comment thereon (The industry average from the FT is 1.2:1). (4 marks)
f. Assuming the most recent dividend is expected to continue indefinitely at that level, what is the price of the share according to the dividend valuation model. (The market expects a return of at least 6.5% on this type of investment) (2 marks)

g. Using your answer to part f) calculate the Price Earnings ratio for 2016 and comment thereon (The industry average in the FT is 11:1). (4 marks)
h. Calculate the dividend cover. (2 marks)
i. Discuss any other information or ratios that you would wish to have before commenting upon the worth of the company. (4 marks)
j. Based on the information available, what advice would you give to Mr Boston and why. (5 marks)

Exercise Answers

Exercise 1

You are assessing two companies in two completely different sectors. Company A in Sector 1 has a higher ROCE than Company B in Sector 2. Explain the significance of these figures when comparing the two organisations.

Answer

Assessing the operational efficiency of two companies in this way can be misleading. As both companies operate in different sectors, the levels and types of capital they need to employ to produce and ultimately profit from could vary considerably. It would tell us a little more if both companies operated in the same sector where capital requirements are likely to be more comparable.

However, even if comparing companies in the same sector, this ratio on its own does not tell us the whole story as to whether one company is substantially more efficient at generating profits than the other. Other profitability ratios should be considered alongside further information with regard to the companies' ability to sustain profitable operations. Profitability could be affected by a number of factors such as changes to management, liquidity, levels of borrowing and use of working capital.

Exercise 2

Company A has a current ratio of 1.3 and a quick ratio of 0.85. Company B has a current ratio of 1.15 and a quick ratio of 1.0. All other things being equal, which company presents the most liquidity risk?

Answer

Company A. Although it has a higher level of cover in respect of its current assets relative to current liabilities, if stock is removed from the equation, it has insufficient funds to pay those liabilities if they are all called in at the same time. This could lead to stock being sold for much less than book value to make up the shortfall.

Exercise 3

In addition to the opportunity cost of committing too much capital to inventory, what other financial implications could arise? Could there be any financial implication to a firm not committing enough capital to inventory?

Answer

Other financial implications could be higher insurance and storage costs and the possibility of inventory obsolescence.

Too little capital to inventory may mean that customers cannot be served and may choose to go elsewhere.

Exercise 4

	Line A	Line B	Line C
Sales	£120,400	£202,050	£140,002
Less Variable Costs:			
Cost of Goods Sold	(£70,030)	(£100,900)	(£60,004)
Sales Commissions	(£18,802)	(£40,050)	(£0)
Delivery Charges	(£900)	(£8,084)	(£5,000)
Total Variable Costs	(£89,732)	(£149,034)	(£65,004)
Contribution Margin	£30,668	£53,016	£74,998
Percentage of Sales	25%	26%	54%

What conclusions can we draw from the information in the above table?

Answer

Although the table shows only the top half of the contribution format income statement, it is immediately apparent that Product Line C is the company's most profitable one, even though it gains more sales revenue from Line B. It appears that it should emphasise Line C in its product mix. Moreover, the statement indicates that perhaps prices for Line A and Line B products are too low. This is information that cannot be gleaned from the regular income statements that an accountant regularly draws up each period.

Exercise 5

Calculate the enterprise value for XYZ plc from the figures provided in Chapter 2.

Answer

Market Cap: Current share price £10.26 x 1 million ordinary shares = £10,260,000 +

Outstanding long-term debt of £9,000,000

+

Overdraft of £3,201,000

–

Cash of £45,000

= £22,416,000

Exercise 6

Using the information provided in the financial statements for XYZ plc in chapter 2, calculate the earnings yield, dividend yield and dividend cover for the company in respect of the 20X1 year. How have the figures changed in 20X2 and what do they indicate?

Answer

Earnings yield

20X1: (£1.17 ÷ £9.13) x 100 = 12.81%

20X2: (£1.266 ÷ £10.26) x 100 = 12.34% – slight decrease in earnings yield – positive sign

Dividend yield

20X1: (£0.393 ÷ £9.13) x 100 = 4.3%

20X2: (£0.462 ÷ £10.26) x 100 = 4.5% – slight increase in dividend yield – positive sign providing it can be sustained

Dividend cover

20X1: £1.17 ÷ £0.393 = 2.98 x

20X2: £1.266 ÷ £0.462 = 2.74 x – slight fall in dividend cover but still sufficient to accommodate dividend increase

Chapter Four
Compounding, Discounting and Bond Maths

1. Investment Decisions and the Time Value of Money	169
2. Compounding and Discounting	174
3. Standardisation of Interest Rate Expressions	181
4. Effects of Inflation on Cash Flows to Determine the Discount Factor	184
5. Arithmetic and Geometric Annualisation	196

Learning Outcome

Be able to select and apply the techniques and concepts of the time value of money, compounding, discounting and annualising

1. Investment Decisions and the Time Value of Money

Learning Objective

4.1 Select and apply the techniques of time value of money, present value and discounted cash flow to investment scenarios

A major feature of investment decision-making refers to time. Investment involves an outlay of economic value, usually cash, at one point in time, in expectation of economic benefits at a later point in time. The outlay typically precedes the benefits. The outlay is usually a single amount, while the benefits often accrue in a stream of smaller amounts over a subsequent period of time.

Investment decisions are crucial to a business or an investor for the following reasons:

- Significant resources are required.
- Investments can comprise a significant proportion of an investor's total resources. Any mistakes could have significant, if not catastrophic effects.
- It is often difficult and/or expensive to escape from an existing investment.

1.1 Actions of a Rational Investor

A rational investor, who is seeking to increase their wealth, is only willing to make investments which will compensate for the loss of interest and purchasing power of the money invested and for the risk that the expected returns may not materialise. At a minimum, the proposed investment should be expected to yield a return which is greater than the alternative risk-free rate, plus the expected rate of inflation, plus a risk premium. The overall risk premium reflects a range of diverse risks such as credit, liquidity and volatility.

These three factors (interest lost, risk and inflation) are set out in the figure below:

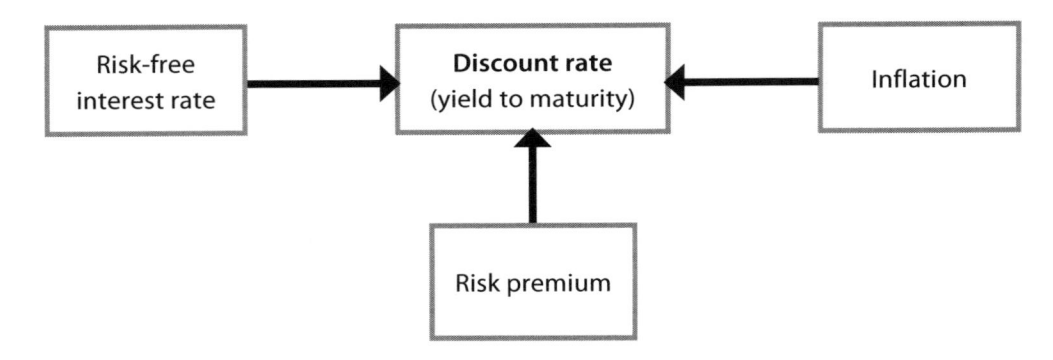

```
   Risk-free              Discount rate
   interest rate  ──────▶ (yield to maturity) ◀──────  Inflation
                              ▲
                              │
                          Risk premium
```

Factors Influencing the Discount Rate Applied to an Investment Project

A decision to invest and the expected return also involves an opportunity cost. An investor with £10,000 to invest faces a number of options, each with its own benefits and potential returns.

It is necessary to evaluate the opportunity cost for each possible decision. If choosing option A means surrendering option B, then the benefits and returns of option B are the opportunity cost for option A.

A comparison of the returns from each option takes into account the money to be received in the future and the timing of those cash flows. Both the amounts of cash received and the timing of those future payments affect the investment evaluation.

The value of future payments should be assessed in terms of their value at present. Consider, therefore, how money invested today can grow in value as the expected return is added to the initial outlay over a period of time:

Principal	£10,000
Term	Five years
Interest	10% annual rate
Frequency	Annual (both principal plus accrued interest are compounded annually at 10%)

The formulae for both simple interest and compound interest are:

Simple interest $FV = PV \times i \times n$

Compound interest $FV = PV \times (1 + i)^n$

where:

FV = Future value   i = Interest rate
PV = Present value   n = number of periods

Annual Return	Comparison between Simple and Compound Interest					
10%	Simple Interest			Compound Interest		
Year	Starting Balance	Interest	Ending Balance	Starting Balance	Interest	Ending Balance
1	£10,000	£1,000	£11,000	£10,000	£1,000	£11,000
2	£11,000	£1,000	£12,000	£11,000	£1,100	£12,100
3	£12,000	£1,000	£13,000	£12,100	£1,210	£13,310
4	£13,000	£1,000	£14,000	£13,310	£1,331	£14,641
5	£14,000	£1,000	£15,000	£14,641	£1,464	£16,105

After five years on a simple interest basis, the £10,000 principal grows to £15,000, whereas on a compounded basis, it grows to £16,105.

The compounding formula can be reversed to calculate the present value of future payments. This applies the inverse logic of discounting rather than compounding. If the compound balance after four years is £14,641, but the initial principal is unknown, that FV can be discounted back to a PV, which should be the initial £10,000 principal.

The present value (PV) formula has four variables:

$$PV = \frac{FV}{(1+i)^n}$$

where:

PV is the value at time = 0
FV is the value at time = n
i is the rate at which the amount will be compounded each period
n is the number of periods

$$PV = \frac{£14,641}{(1+0.10)^4} = £10,000$$

This PV formula is the cornerstone of financial mathematics and is worth careful study. The concept is that the PV of money is the FV discounted back using the appropriate discount rate.

Illustration

An investor is faced with the following choices or options regarding how to invest a principal sum of £10,000 for the next three years.

Scenario One or Option A

The investor will receive net income of £5,000 at each year-end over the three-year life of this investment scenario resulting in total cash flow of £15,000.

Scenario Two or Option B

The investor will receive a net sum of £16,000 at the end of the third year, in other words there is a single cash flow at the end of the period.

Scenario Three or Option C

The third scenario is for the investor to deposit the principal sum in a bank account, as shown above, with an annual rate of interest of 10% compounded annually. It can be seen from the table above that at the end of the third year the principal will have grown to £13,310.

The question becomes which of the three scenarios is preferable by delivering the highest rate of return and, in the process, we will be revealing the opportunity cost of both Options A and B with respect to the low-risk Option C.

In the cases of the three scenarios, the future value or terminal value is known for Option B and Option C but not for Option A.

We need to examine the future value or terminal value of Option A and this can be displayed diagrammatically as below. The assumption is made that each of the payments received are deposited with the bank to earn interest on a compounded basis at 10%. The final payment received in year three will not of course earn any interest as the cut-off date for this illustration is the end of year three.

10%	Compound Interest		
Year	Starting Balance	Interest	Ending Balance
1	–	–	£5,000
2	£5,000	£500	£10,500
3	£10,500	£1,050	£16,550

Terminal or Future Value of Option A = £16,550
Terminal or Future Value of Option B = £16,000 (as shown above under scenario two)
Terminal or Future Value of Option C = £13,310 (as shown above under scenario three)

From this it can be seen that the terminal or future value for Option A is the highest and this would qualify as the most attractive investment opportunity. The opportunity cost in considering both A and B versus the bank deposit would be £13,310 and clearly under both scenarios the result is a higher FV than the simple option of investing the principal in the bank account. These differences can be quantified in terms of what is known as the **net terminal value (NTV)**.

Net terminal value of scenario one is £16,550 – £13,310 = £3,240
Net terminal value of scenario two is £16,000 – £13,310 = £2,690

It is worth observing that if either of the investment scenarios registered a zero NTV, then they would not have exceeded the opportunity cost of leaving the money in the bank, and should be eliminated from consideration.

Let us now consider the two scenarios from the point of view of a cash flow analysis and, in reverse, take the steps from the future or terminal value and see how the process can be used as an alternative (and perhaps more intuitive) method of calculating the net terminal value of each scenario.

Option A	Interest available from bank deposit = i			10.0%
Time	Cash Flow	Compound Formula	Compound Factor	Terminal or Future Value
0	(10,000)	$(1+i)^3$	1.331	(13,310)
1	5,000	$(1+i)^2$	1.21	6,050
2	5,000	$(1+i)$	1.1	5,500
3	5,000	1	1	5,000
			Sum of all cash flows	3,240
Option B	Interest available from bank deposit = i			10.0%
Time	Cash Flow	Compound Formula	Compound Factor	Terminal or Future Value
0	(10,000)	$(1+i)^3$	1.331	(13,310)
1	–	$(1+i)^2$	1.21	0
2	–	$(1+i)$	1.1	0
3	16,000	1	1	16,000
			Sum of all cash flows	2,690

In both cases, the cash flow analysis is debited with the initial outlay of £10,000. In the case of Option A there are positive cash flows of £5,000 at the end of each of the three years whereas with Option B there is simply one positive cash flow of £16,000 which is received at the end of year three.

The compound formula indicates the terminal value or future value which has been foregone by not depositing the cash flows in the interest-bearing account and therefore evaluates each of Option A and B versus the obtaining of a low-risk return.

It can be demonstrated that Option A generates a higher net terminal value than Option B and that both have exceeded the opportunity cost of the low-risk option of leaving the money on deposit in a bank account.

This rather simplified analysis benefits from the fact that the net terminal values all coincide on the same date for valuing the terminal values and, as later sections of this chapter will reveal, the techniques for comparing investments with different maturity dates require some additional calculations.

2. Compounding and Discounting

Learning Objective

4.2 Select and apply discounting and compounding in: perpetuities; continuous, annual and non-annual time periods

2.1 Compounding and Discounting

As discussed in section 1 there is an important distinction between compound interest and simple interest. When money is invested at compound interest, each interest payment is reinvested in addition to the principal amount, so that interest on an increasing sum is accrued in subsequent periods.

2.2 Annuities

An annuity is an investment product which pays out regular cash flows each year and is similar to option A that was considered in section 1 (eg, the payments received from a pension plan by someone in retirement). The table below illustrates projected cash flows for an annuity of £50,000 and also how the discounting formula determines the present value of each cash flow. The sum of the present values of all the cash flows represents the PV of the annuity.

Annuity	Yield to Maturity (Discount) Rate			8.00%
Time	Cash Flow	Discount Formula	Discount Factor	Present Value
1	£50,000	$1/(1.08)^1$	0.926	£46,296
2	£50,000	$1/(1.08)^2$	0.857	£42,867
3	£50,000	$1/(1.08)^3$	0.794	£39,692
		Totals	2.577	£128,855

The discount formula which is applied at the end of each period is $1/(1+i)^n$ (an alternative is to divide each cash flow by $(1+r)^n$ which gives the same answer). Assume a rate (i) of 8%.

Because the cash flows are equal, there is a simpler formula to calculate the present value after n years:

Annuity discount factor = $1/r \times [1 - (1/(1+r)^n)]$

Substituting the values above into this gives a multiple which can be applied to the annual cash flow:

$$\frac{1}{0.08} \times [1-(\frac{1}{1.08^3})] = 12.5 \times (1-0.79383) = 2.5771$$

2.5771 is then multiplied by the £50,000 annuity payment to give the same PV of £128,855.

Note also that the sum of each of the periodic discount factors is also equal to the multiple: 2.577.

The sum of each of these present values (PVs) in the table is the net present value (NPV) of the cash flows.

If the annuity is one which is 'growing' by a set percentage each period, the formula is changed to where A is the annuity amount and g is the amount by which the annuity will grow each year.

Algebra allows the same formula to be adapted to calculate instead the compound interest rate if an initial investment of PV returns a value of FV after n accrual periods:

$$i = \left(\frac{FV}{PV}\right)^{\frac{1}{n}} - 1$$

This can be applied to the compounding interest calculation in section 1.1. Assume the same principal amount, ie, PV of £10,000 and a balance after five years of £16,105. The compounding rate of interest is calculated as follows:

$$i = \left[\frac{£16,105}{£10,000}\right]^{\frac{1}{5}} - 1 = 10\%$$

2.3 Calculating a Time Period through Compounding

The FV, PV and rate of interest (return) can be calculated for an investment using compounding. The amount of time or number of compounding periods requires a different calculation however.

The most straightforward approach is through logarithms. These provide the exponent ('to the power of' number) in a compound interest calculation. The 'log' function is available on most good financial calculators.

The number n of compound periods is:

$$n = \frac{\log(FV) - \log(PV)}{\log(1+i)}$$

Using the scenario from earlier in this section:

$$n = \frac{\log(16105) - \log(10000)}{\log(1.1)} = \frac{4.2070 - 4}{0.0414} = 5 \text{ compound periods}$$

2.4 Periodic or Non-Annual Compounding

Cash flows occurring only at precise annual intervals rarely occur in reality. Cash flows and interest rates are instead commonly required on a non-annual basis.

The three key factors in periodic compounding or discounting are:

- cash flow value
- cash flow timing
- discount rate.

The same formula for an individual cash flow above provides the discount rate.

This formula applies where n is a whole year or a partial year, eg, 1½ years or ¼ of a year.

Example

An investment product requires an initial outlay of £100,000 and results in a series of cash flows of £30,000 at the end of each quarter. The cost of capital or opportunity cost of leaving the outlay on deposit at a bank is 10% per annum. What is the NPV of the cash flows?

	Interest Available from Bank Deposit = i			10.0%
Time	Cash Flow	Discount Formula	Discount Factor	Present Value
0	(100,000)	1	1.000	(100,000)
1/4	30,000	$1/(1.10)^{1/4}$	0.976	29,294
1/2	30,000	$1/(1.10)^{1/2}$	0.953	28,604
3/4	30,000	$1/(1.10)^{3/4}$	0.931	27,930
1	30,000	1/1.10	0.909	27,273
			Sum of cash flows (NPV)	13,101

The NPV of the cash flows is £13,101, which reveals that this investment is more attractive than depositing £100,000 in a 10% interest-bearing account (assuming no difference in risk between the two investment choices). The discount formulae applied in calculating the PV of each cash flow is in the third column from the left and the actual discount factor in numerical form is shown in the fourth column.

The quarterly payments above require a quarterly discount rate which is equivalent to the 10% annualised discount rate.

The discount factor for a period $n = 1/(1+r)^n$

r = rate
n = time period

The $1/(1.1^{1/4})$ discount rate at the first cash flow period can be substituted for n:

$1 + r = (1.1^{1/4})$

$1 + r = 1.0241137$

Therefore, $r = 2.41137\%$

2.41137% compounding quarterly is equivalent to 10% compounding annually.

Now adjust the formula for a simple annuity with one annual cash flow and calculate the discount factor for an annuity which pays quarterly with a compounding rate of 2.41137%.

$$\text{Annuity discount factor} = \frac{1}{0.02411} \times \left[1 - \frac{1}{(1.02411^4)}\right]$$

This gives a quarterly discount factor of 3.77%.

The quarterly discount factor can be applied to the periodic amount due each quarter. This gives the correct NPV and shows that the equivalent rate applies to non-annual payments.

	Interest Available from Bank Deposit = i		10%
Time	Cash Flow	Discount Factor	Present Value
0	(100,000)	1.000	(100,000)
1–4	30,000	3.770	113,100
		NPV (sum of cash flows)	13,100

The equivalent period interest rate for a non-annual period is derived from the annual rate as follows:

Equivalent rate = $(1 + r) = (1 + R)^n$

where:

r = rate for the non-annual period
R = annual rate
n = portion of year(s) in one non-annual period

Exercise 1

Calculate the discount factor in order to discover the NPV of the following cash flows received from a deposit account over the period of a year:

Annualised equivalent rate: 8%. Interest paid monthly. Each monthly payment is £20,000.

The answer to this exercise can be found at the end of this chapter.

Advantages of the Net Present Value (NPV) Method

- It assumes that money received in the future will not be worth the same (less) as money received today. A cash flow received in the future is discounted back to its present day value to find its true value.
- It uses currency amounts to show how profitable an investment/project will be allowing for risk and time, for example.
- The minimum discount rate is the cost of capital – this rate is the starting point and then, for example, inflation and risk can be added to the rate.
- NPV assumes reinvestment. This is different from the assumption for IRR which assumes that the cash flow will be reinvested at the IRR rate (almost impossible to achieve in reality).
- It can work where monetary cash flows are received in both positive and negative forms, eg, year one is a return of 100, year two is a loss of 200 and year three is a return of 500. This is no problem when using the NPV method but cannot work in an IRR calculation.
- Unlike some calculations, eg, payback (which only says how quickly the investment is repaid and ignores further returns), all cash flows are included in the calculation and so the total return is shown for comparison purposes.
- It is, therefore, a good measure of profitability when an investor is trying to decide which investment out of many to choose (IRR may show a higher return, but the project may be small and so the overall return is less).
- All risks are factored into the discount rate, eg, business risk, financial risk and operating risk.

Disadvantages of the NPV Method

- The future cash flows may need to be guessed, eg, what the dividend will be in five years?
- What is the true cost of capital for this investment? This is not always known fully until the money is actually being used.
- It has problems where the investments are for different periods or amounts, eg, large projects would normally be expected to have a higher NPV, however, the actual return percentage may be less than a smaller project (this can be overcome using the profitability index – PI – where the PV is divided by the outlay and the figure can then be compared against other investments irrespective of size).
- If comparing projects with different life spans, eg, three and five years, how do you decide on the comparison? Guessing the investment rate for the two years following the end of the shorter investment?
- No allowance is made for non-quantitative factors.
- The final discount rate will be based on the decision (guess) by an individual and may be wrong, therefore, is the risk level high? If too high, this will kill the investment losing profits, if too low it will see it accepted, but perhaps at a loss.
- The initial outlay, if incorrect, will have a dramatic effect on the result.
- Any sunk costs are ignored, eg, any diligence costs paid to an auditor to help evaluate a takeover bid will be ignored in the outlay figure.
- The cash flow guesses may be optimistic/pessimistic – this will make the returns incorrect and the answer will, therefore, be inaccurate.

Regardless of the above disadvantages, NPV is widely used and is preferred by many over IRR and other evaluation techniques.

Compounding, Discounting and Bond Maths

2.5 Perpetuities

A perpetuity is an annuity in which periodic payments begin on a fixed date and continue indefinitely, without any obligation to repay the principal. It is sometimes referred to as a perpetual annuity.

The UK Government has issued perpetuities in the past, in the form of war loans, and they are known and still trade as consols. As of 2015, it has redeemed all of its perpetual bonds.

Fixed coupon payments on permanently invested (irredeemable) sums of money are other examples of perpetuities. Preference shares' dividends paid perpetually also fit the definition of a perpetuity.

The value of a perpetuity is effectively finite because payments which are anticipated far in the future have an extremely low PV (PV of future cash flows). Unlike a typical bond, because the principal is never repaid, there is no PV for the principal. The PV of a perpetuity is equal to:

The amount of periodic payment (A) ÷ Required rate of return (r).

$$PV = \frac{A}{r}$$

Alternatively, the yield or return on a perpetuity can be expressed as:

$$r = \frac{A}{PV}$$

ABC plc has in issue a 4% irredeemable preference share which is trading at a discount of 50% of its par value (£10.00). When it was issued, interest rates were 4% and it was issued at 100% of its par value. Currently, the market is seeking a yield (return) of 8% on this type of investment, meaning that the irredeemable share is trading at a discount (effectively at £5.00). This means that the face value of the preference shares is £10.00 and the annual dividend payment is £0.40, so the present market value of the share is £5.00 as the market interest rate (ie, the discount rate) are 8%. Note: this means that the 40p dividend has become a return of 8% on the new value of £5.

Suppose that someone wishes to endow a scholarship at a university and the current rate of interest or discount rate is 10% and the intention is to provide £10,000 per year in perpetuity. The amount that would need to be set aside today is as follows:

$$\text{Present value of perpetuity} = \frac{A}{r} = \frac{10{,}000}{0.1} = £100{,}000$$

The benefactor then realises that to provide for inflation, the amount of the scholarship should be subject to an annual increase (after the first year) of 4%. So, the benefactor has had to provide £100,000 in year 1 and £100,000 * 1.04 in year 2 and so on. Assuming a growth rate g, the present value of this stream of cash flow is as follows:

$$PV = \frac{C_1}{1+r} + \frac{C_2}{(1+r)^2} + \frac{C_3}{(1+r)^3} + \frac{C_n}{(1+r)^n}$$

ie, the formula that has been used previously, or

$$PV = \frac{C_1}{1+r} + \frac{C_1(1+g)}{(1+r)^2} + \frac{C_1(1+g)^2}{(1+r)^3} + \frac{C_1(1+g)^{n-1}}{(1+r)^n}$$

Note that we used 'A' previously in this section (standing for annuity payment). This has been replaced above by the letter 'C' to denote a simple cash flow from any source.

The formula above applies where variable cash flows are growing by a set percentage and need to be discounted.

A more simplified formula can solve the sum of this geometric series. If r is greater than g, (ie, the required rate of return is greater than the growth rate), the formula becomes:

$$\text{Present value of a growing perpetuity} = \frac{C_1}{r-g} = \frac{10{,}000}{0.1 - 0.04} = £166{,}667$$

NB: If the rate r is less than rate g (the growth percentage) then this will not work. The same formula is applied to value a company (see chapter 7).

2.6 Continuous Compounding

The continuous compounding calculation shows the interest earned on an investment which is constantly compounded. Continuous compounding effectively leads to an infinite amount of compounding periods. This concept is important for investment products as some derivatives are priced on the basis of continuous compounding.

The continuous compounding formula takes the effect of compounding to the furthest limit. Instead of compounding interest on a monthly, quarterly, or annual basis, continuous compounding reinvests gains perpetually.

Continuous compounding requires a natural log and an exponential function, which conveniently scales easily over multiple periods.

Continuous compounding can be considered in terms of infinitely small compounding periods. It effectively takes the limit of n to infinity. In non-mathematical terms, continuous compounding is the process of earning interest on interest. The interest is earned constantly, and earns interest on itself.

The relevant equation has a helpful mnemonic 'Pert':

A (final amount or result) = Pe^{rt}

- P = principal amount
- e = a mathematical constant and base of the natural logarithm (numerically expressed as 2.718)
- r = rate per period
- t = time (in the same units as the rate's period)
- A = final amount.

An amount P, invested at a continuously compounded rate of r, will grow to e^r (= 2.718^r) at the end of the first year. By the end of t years it will grow to e^{rt} (= 2.718^{rt}).

Example

Invest £1 at a continuously compounded rate of 10% (r=0.10) for 1 year (t=1).

The value at the end of the year is e^{10} (= £1.105).

Investing at 10% a year, continuously compounded, is equivalent to investing at 10.5% a year with annual compounding.

Exercise 2

If you have a starting amount of £1,000, what will be the final amount after two years with a continuous compounding rate of 11%?

The answer to this exercise can be found at the end of this chapter.

3. Standardisation of Interest Rate Expressions

Learning Objective

4.3   Select and apply standardised interest rate calculations: APR; AER

When a financial services firm quotes an interest rate, it is not always immediately apparent how much it is paid. Different firms may quote monthly or annual interest rates, making it difficult to compare accounts easily.

Some lenders offer cashback on some mortgages or charge upfront fees on others, with interest rates adjusted accordingly, making it hard to compare costs.

The two types of annual rates used for compounded interest are the annual equivalent rate (AER), the interest rate applied to savings; and the annual percentage rate (APR), the interest rate for mortgages, credit cards and personal loans.

Both AER and APR are calculated in the same way across providers and the rules for their calculation and expression are governed by statute. When trying to compare different financial products it is advisable to look for these, rather than the headline rate.

3.1 Annual Percentage Rate (APR)

An APR is a measure of the cost of borrowing money. It is quoted by mortgage lenders and companies offering personal loans and credit cards. The APR includes any fees charged by the lender, spread over the period for which the money is being borrowed.

The APR shows the cost of borrowing over the course of a year, as a proportion of the amount borrowed. So, borrowing £100 at an APR of 9% will cost £9 in interest and charges over the first year.

In loan advertisements, a provider may quote a 'typical APR', because many lenders set the actual interest rate according to a borrower's credit record and personal circumstances. A bank has to have offered its typical APR (or a better rate) to at least 66% of potential customers.

In mortgage advertisements, a lender usually quotes a headline rate as well as the APR. Most lenders charge administration fees on mortgages, so APRs tend to be much higher than the headline rates.

The effective APR is sometimes called the mathematically true interest rate for each year.

The calculation for the effective APR (the fee plus compound interest rate) varies depending on whether upfront fees, such as origination or participation fees, are added to the entire amount or treated as a short-term loan due in the first payment.

In the US and the UK, lenders are required to disclose the APR before the loan (or credit application) is finalised although, confusingly, the definition of APR is not exactly the same in the two countries (US APRs can manipulate finance charges). Credit card companies can advertise monthly interest rates, but they are required to state clearly the APR before an agreement is signed.

An effective annual interest rate of 10% can also be expressed in several ways:

- 0.7974% effective monthly interest rate, because $(1.007974^{12}) - 1 \times 100 = 10\%$
- 9.5688% annual interest rate compounded monthly, because $12 \times 0.7974 = 9.5688\%$
- 9.0909% annual rate in advance, because $10\% \div 1.1 = 9.0909\%$

These rates are all equivalent, but to a consumer who is not trained in the mathematics of finance, this can be confusing. APR helps to standardise how interest rates are compared, so that a 10% loan does not look cheaper by being called 'a loan at 9.1% annually in advance'.

3.2 Equivalent Annual Rate (EAR)

Like the APR, an equivalent annual rate (EAR) is quoted for borrowing money, but only in the form of an overdraft. Unlike an APR, it does not include any fees for going overdrawn, but it indicates remaining overdrawn for a whole year.

The calculation taking into account the rate of interest being charged, the frequency it is charged, and the effect of compounding over the year.

EAR should not be confused with AER below.

3.3 Annual Equivalent Rate (AER)

Some savings or investment products pay interest more than once a year; others pay less frequently. The annual equivalent rate (AER) shows the notional rate of interest payable as if the actual frequency were adjusted to a standardised annual payment.

$$\text{Annual Equivalent Rate (AER)} = \left[(1+r)^{\frac{12}{n}} - 1\right] \text{ or } \left[(1+r)^{\frac{365}{y}} - 1\right]$$

where:

r = rate of interest for each time period
n = number of months in the time period
y = number of days in the time period

The gross rate paid on an account offering monthly interest may be lower than the gross rate on an account offering only one interest payment a year, but when interest is compounded it may offer higher returns than the annual payment account.

A building society savings account offering a rate of 6.25% (paid annually) may appear more attractive than an account paying 6.12% with monthly interest payments. The AER on the monthly account however is 6.29%, as opposed to an AER of 6.25% on the annual payment account.

The 6.12% nominal rate for a monthly compounding basis effectively means a monthly rate of (6.12% ÷ 12) or 0.51% per month. Substitute this value into the AER formula above for the AER rate of [$(1.0051)^{12/1}$) –1] or 6.29%. This is higher than the rate for the annual payment account.

If a bank offers depositors a nominal 12% per annum, with interest payable quarterly, the effective rate of interest would be 3% compound every three months, which is:

[$(1.03)^4 - 1$] = 0.1255 = 12.55% per annum.

If there is a charge for withdrawing your money, the AER will take this into account. If, for example, a penalty of 30 days' interest is charged for a withdrawal, this is reflected in the AER.

Example

A building society offers investors 8% per annum interest payable half-yearly. If the 8% is a nominal rate of interest, the building society pays 4% every six months, compounded so that the annual equivalent rate of interest is:

[$(1.04)^2 - 1$] = 0.0816 = 8.16% per annum.

If a bank offers depositors a nominal 10% per annum, with interest payable quarterly, the annual equivalent rate of interest is 2.5% compound every three months, for example:

[$(1.025)^4 - 1$] = 0.1038 = 10.38% per annum.

If an account includes an introductory bonus for a few months, it must be specified whether or not this is included in the AER. If it is not, the AER enables an accurate comparison with an account which offers the same rate of interest all year.

4. Effects of Inflation on Cash Flows to Determine the Discount Factor

Learning Objective

4.4 Evaluate the effects of inflation on cash flows to determine the appropriate discount factor

A useful concept from economics relates to the purchasing power of money and it hinges on the nominal value which refers to any price or value expressed in terms of the money of the day, as opposed to real value, which adjusts for the effect of inflation.

Several indices are used in the UK to track the rate of inflation and the best known are the consumer price index (CPI) and the retail price index (RPI) (see chapter 1, section 3).

For example, if the base year for the RPI was 2010, and the value at that time is 100, then a value of 109 in year 2016 would show that prices have increased by 9% since the base year. The purchasing power of money would accordingly have declined during that period. The real rate of return (ROR) on a series of cash flows has to be calculated by discounting the nominal cash flows in accordance with the rate of inflation.

As a rule of thumb, if rates of interest were at 8% per annum and inflation at 5% per annum, we would know that we could gain a real return of approximately 3% (8%–5%). The general and more accurate formula for converting nominal cash flows at a future period to real cash flows is:

$$\text{Real cash flow} = \frac{\text{nominal cash flow}}{(1+ \text{inflation rate})^n}$$

The table below illustrates the effect of inflation over a longer time frame, but if we start with £1,000, and the nominal return is 8%, we shall have £1,080 at the end of year one. However, the real value of this ending balance, when adjusted for inflation at 5%, is that the purchasing power of that balance will be only equal to £1,028.57.

To determine the real ROR, we need to adjust the nominal ROR, so that it has constant purchasing power or is reduced by the rate of inflation.

$$\text{The real rate of return} = \frac{(1 + \text{nominal rate of interest})}{(1+ \text{inflation rate})}$$

For a nominal rate of 8% per annum and an inflation rate of 5% per annum, the real ROR will be ((1+0.08)/(1+0.05)) – 1 which is 2.857%.

The table illustrates the nominal and real cash flows, over a ten-year period, for a starting amount of £1,000 invested at 8% interest, compounded annually, and with an inflation rate of 5% per annum.

Nominal Rate of Interest (Rnom)				8%
Rate of Inflation (Rinf)				5%
Real Rate of Return (Rreal) = $\left(\frac{(1+Rnom)}{(1+Rinf)}\right) - 1 \times 100$				2.857%
Starting Balance Principal				£1,000
Year	Starting Balance	Interest Earned = Starting Balance x Rnom	Nominal Ending Balance = Principal x $(1+Rnom)^n$	Real Ending Balance = Prior Real Ending Balance x $(1+Rreal)^n$
1	£1,000	£80	£1,080.00	£1,028.57
2	£1,080	£86	£1,166.40	£1,057.96
3	£1,166	£93	£1,259.71	£1,088.19
4	£1,260	£101	£1,360.49	£1,119.28
5	£1,360	£109	£1,469.33	£1,151.26
6	£1,469	£118	£1,586.87	£1,184.15
7	£1,587	£127	£1,713.82	£1,217.98
8	£1,714	£137	£1,850.93	£1,252.78
9	£1,851	£148	£1,999.00	£1,288.58
10	£1,999	£160	£2,158.92	£1,325.39

After ten years, the nominal ending balance would be £2,158.92 but in constant purchasing power, ie, related to the purchasing power today, this will only be worth £1,325.39.

In section 4.1, it must be noted that the discussion in centred on the net present value (NPV) and not the discounted cash flow (DCF). This is because:

NPV = Initial cash outlay – DCF

Therefore, DCF is the present value of the expected cash flows and NPV is the net return on the investment, ie, the future cash flows less the initial outlay. This means that it is only necessary to discuss one because of their similarity.

4.1 Discounted Cash Flow (DCF)

In finance, the discounted cash flow (DCF) approach describes a method of valuing a project, company or asset using the concepts of the time value of money. All future cash flows are estimated and discounted to give their present values (PVs). The discount rate used is generally the appropriate cost of capital and may also include a risk premium to take into account judgements of the uncertainty (riskiness) of the future cash flows.

The following table illustrates the DCF approach for valuing a bond which has an annual coupon of 8% of the face amount of the bond. The bond was purchased for £100 and the payments are made annually for 12 years and the principal is redeemed or paid back at the end of the twelfth year in conjunction with the final coupon payment.

The annuity discount formula from section 2.2 has been used to value the present value of the cash flows including the redemption amount in year 12:

$$\text{Annuity discount factor} = 1/r \times [1 - (1 / (1 + r)^{\wedge n})]$$

For the purposes of clarification, the desired yield or internal rate of return (IRR) of the bond has initially been set at the same rate as the coupon value, ie, 8%. As can be seen from the bottom right-hand cell of the table, the price which one should be prepared to pay for this bond is the face value, since the desired yield is equal to the IRR or yield to maturity of the bond. Just to clarify, if we subtracted from the cash flow the original £100 to purchase the bond, this would also be an illustration of the circumstances discussed in the previous section, where the IRR is at a level where the NPV of the cash flows would be zero.

Current Bond Price	Annual Coupon	8.00%	Assumed GRY	8.00%
Timing of Cash Flows	Cash Flow in £	Discount Factor at	Discount Factor at Desired Yield	Present Value
Coupon Cash Flow Years 1–12	£8.00	$\dfrac{1}{0.08}\left[1 - \dfrac{1}{1.08^{12}}\right] = 7.536$	7.5361	£60.29
Redemption In Year 12	£100.00	$\dfrac{1}{1.08^{12}} = 0.3971$	0.3971	£39.71
			Bond Price	£100.00

This illustration is revealing, in that it confirms that the DCF method in the case of valuing a bond – just like any other stream of cash flows – reveals not only the yield to maturity (IRR – see section 4.2 below) but also the price which one should be expected to pay for such a bond given its coupon characteristics, redemption date and the desired yield. Therefore, in the case just seen, we would, not surprisingly, expect to pay £100 for the bond.

What should we be prepared to pay for a bond with a similar maturity and annual coupon payments of just 5% but when the desired yield remains at 8%?

Current Bond Price	Annual Coupon	5.00%	Assumed GRY	8.00%
Timing of Cash Flows	Cash Flow in £	Discount Factor at	Discount Factor at Desired Yield	Present Value
Coupon Cash Flow Years 1-12	£5.00	$\dfrac{1}{0.08}\left[1-\dfrac{1}{1.08^{12}}\right]=7.536$	7.5361	£37.68
Redemption In Year 12	£100.00	$\dfrac{1}{1.08^{12}}=0.3971$	0.3971	£39.71
			Bond Price	£77.39

Applying the discount factor to the cash flows for the desired yield of 8% shows that the bond should be priced at £77.39.

Intuitively, this demonstrates that we will need to be compensated for the fact that, each year, the coupon is only producing a 5% nominal yield and we desire an 8% yield. In order to be compensated, the initial outlay for the bond will have to be reduced. Upon redemption we will receive the face value of the bond of £100, and this difference, when seen in the context of the discounting model, 'makes up' the lost ground on the annual coupon payments.

Exercise 3

Calculate the price of a corporate bond paying a regular annual coupon of 5% per £100 of nominal stock over ten years. Current required gross redemption yield (GRY) (IRR) is 6.5% per annum.

The answer to this exercise can be found at the end of this chapter.

4.1.1 Reinvestment Rates

The fundamental difference between NPV and IRR is the assumption made about reinvestment rates.

Under NPV, we implicitly assume that surplus funds generated can be reinvested to earn a return equal to the discount rate.

IRR assumes that surplus funds will be reinvested to earn a return equal to the IRR which may be considerably higher than the applicable discount rate.

In conclusion, the NPV method seems to be the more realistic and reliable because the often generous assumptions about returns available within an IRR model do not seem justifiable.

4.2 Calculating the IRR

The IRR is also called the discounted cash flow rate of return (DCFROR) or rate of return (ROR).

The IRR is the annualised effective compounded return rate which can be earned on invested capital. Looked at from a different perspective, the IRR for an investment is the discount rate that makes the NPV of the investment's cash flow stream equal to zero.

Example

Let us consider a simple example to demonstrate the relationship between NPV of an investment and IRR.

If £1,000 is invested producing a coupon of £40 per annum for three years with repayment of the £1,000 at the end of year 3 and the required ROR (IRR) from the market is 4% per annum compound, then the following calculation of NPV would take place:

Initial investment: – £1,000 PV of cash flows:

£40 ÷ 1.04 = £38.46

£40 ÷ 1.042 = £36.98

£40 ÷ 1.043 = £35.56

£1,000 ÷ 1.043 = £889.00

PV of future cash flows: £38.46 + £36.98 + £35.56 + £889 = £1,000 NPV of cash flows minus initial investment: £1,000 – £1,000 = £0 The NPV result of £0 proves the IRR to be 4% per annum.

A project is a good investment proposition if its IRR is greater than the ROR that could be earned by alternate investments of equal risk (investing in other projects, buying bonds, even putting the money in a bank account). Thus, the IRR should be compared to any alternate costs of capital including an appropriate risk premium.

In general, if the IRR is greater than the project's cost of capital, the project will add value for the company.

The above example gives us the IRR. So, what happens when we need to work the IRR out? In the context of savings and loans, the IRR is also called the effective interest rate.

$$NPV = C_0 + \frac{C_1}{1+IRR} + \frac{C_2}{(1+IRR)^2} + \frac{C_3}{(1+IRR)^3} + ... + \frac{C_t}{(1+IRR)^t} = 0$$

As can be seen from this equation, the method for calculating the IRR is not susceptible to an easy solution and, unless one uses a spreadsheet program, such as Microsoft Excel, it has to be performed by an iterative process of trial and error. Also beneficial in guiding such an iterative procedure is the use of a technique of linear interpolation.

The best way to understand the interpolation method is to consider a table of cash flows and to sum the PV of the sum of these cash flows applying different discount factors. The target value for the correct discount value is where the sum of the PVs of all of the cash flows is equal to zero. What one is investigating is the space between a discount rate which will have sum of NPVs which is above zero and another discount rate at which the sum of the NPVs is below zero.

Example

In the table below there is an initial outlay on the project of £800,000 and this is represented by the −800 value in the second column of the table in year zero. This is followed in the next three years by a series of positive cash flows. The actual cash flows need to be discounted back to PV by applying the discount factor as discussed previously, ie:

Discount factor = $1/(1+r)^n$

r = rate

n = time period

In the first table, it can be seen that a discount rate of 5% has been used, and substituting it into the formula above, it can be seen that the discount factor in year 1 is 0.952 and in year 2 it is 0.907, and so on.

	Discount Rate		5.0%
Year	Cash Flow (£'000)	Discount Factor	PV (£'000)
0	(800)	1	(800.00)
1	400	0.952	380.95
2	300	0.907	272.11
3	200	0.864	172.77
Profit	100	NPV =	25.83

The sum of the PVs of the sequence of cash flows is seen in column four of the table and is a positive value of £25,830, known as the Net Present Value (NPV).

As a very rough guide to estimating at what rate of interest the NPV might be close to zero, the following approximation can be used:

$$\frac{2}{3} \times \left[\frac{\text{profit from project}}{\text{initial outlay on project}} \right]$$

Using the example in the table the profit is equal to £100,000 and the initial outlay is £800,000, which provides a rough guide to the appropriate discount factor as follows:

$$\frac{2}{3} \times \left[\frac{100,000}{800,000} \right] = 0.0833 \text{ or approximately 8\%}$$

If we try using a discount rate of 8%, the following table illustrates the result:

	Discount Rate		8.0%
Year	Cash Flow(£'000)	Discount Factor	PV(£'000)
0	(800)	1	(800.00)
1	400	0.926	370.37
2	300	0.857	257.20
3	200	0.794	158.77
Profit	100	NPV =	(13.66)

From the above, it can be seen that, whereas an assumed 5% IRR leads to a positive NPV, the application of the 8% assumption in the table above leads to a negative NPV. From this we can deduce that the rate is somewhere between 5% and 8% and is in fact closer to 8%, so let us try one more iteration of this trial and error approach by assuming the IRR to be 7%.

	Discount Rate		7.0%
Year	Cash Flow(£'000)	Discount Factor	PV(£'000)
0	(800)	1	(800.00)
1	400	0.935	373.83
2	300	0.873	262.03
3	200	0.816	163.26
Profit	100	NPV =	(0.88)

The table above reveals that the assumption of an IRR of 7% is very close to the objective required of delivering an NPV of 0. It can be seen that 7% is just slightly higher than the actual IRR value, since the NPV is very slightly negative. By using Microsoft Excel, it can be determined that the exact IRR for this series of cash flows is in fact 6.93%.

Compounding, Discounting and Bond Maths

If one does not have access to Microsoft Excel, there is an alternative method which can be used to calculate the IRR which, although somewhat laborious, is still superior to a repeated trial and error process. The intuition behind the technique, which is known as 'interpolation', is shown in the table below. Several rates for the IRR within a reasonable spectrum of possibilities are sampled, and for each assumed rate we record the NPV; one can then create a graph of the results. For the data given, here are the corresponding NPVs for several rates:

Discount Rate	ΣPVs
3%	54.16
4%	39.78
5%	25.83
6%	12.28
7%	(0.88)
8%	(13.66)
9%	(26.09)
10%	(38.17)

As can be seen, the NPV is still positive at 6% and then becomes slightly negative at 7% which advises us that the rate will be between these two parameters and will be closer to the upper parameter than the lower parameter. The results can be illustrated graphically and, from the graph, it can be seen more clearly where the actual IRR which returns a zero NPV is to be found.

Sum of NPVs Plotted against Different Discount Rates

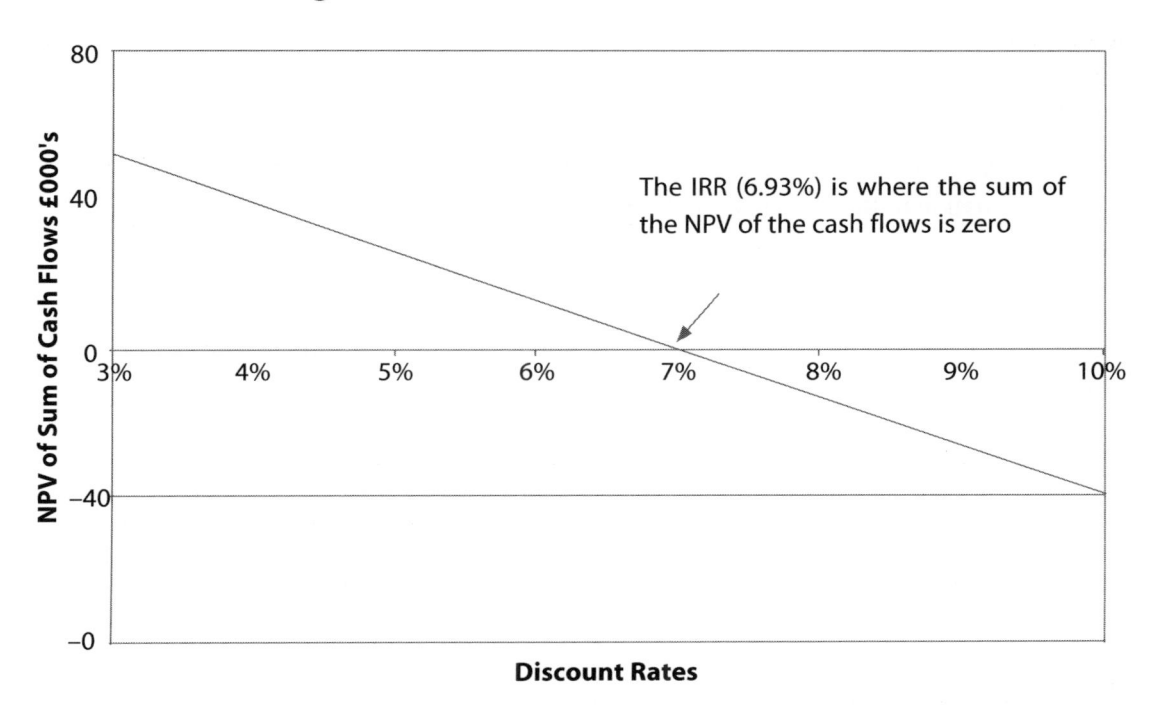

The IRR (6.93%) is where the sum of the NPV of the cash flows is zero

(Graph: NPV of Sum of Cash Flows £000's plotted against Discount Rates from 3% to 10%, showing a downward sloping line crossing zero at approximately 7%.)

Although visual inspection of the graph above will lead us to the conclusion that the appropriate IRR rate is very close to 7%, we can improve on this by using a simple process of interpolation which will give us a more exact result.

4.2.1 Interpolation

The method that we have been using above is described as interpolation and can be stated more formally in the following method for calculating the IRR:

$$\text{Internal Rate of Return (IRR)} = R_1 + \left[\frac{N_1}{N_1 - N_2} \times (R_2 - R_1) \right]$$

where:

R_1 = first selected discount rate (ie, giving a positive NPV)
R_2 = second selected discount rate (ie, giving a negative NPV)
N_1 = NPV of the investment when discounted at R_1
N_2 = NPV of the investment when discounted at R_2

The task of interpolation is made more precise when considering the R_1 and R_2 values which are either side of the interval where the zero NPV is expected to be found. From the data given in the table, we can substitute for R_1 the value of 6% and, for R_2, the value of 7%.

The resulting substitutions would create the following equation which, as can be seen, solves to more or less the value determined by using the IRR function in Microsoft Excel:

$$\text{Internal Rate of Return (IRR)} = 0.06 + \left[\frac{12.28}{12.28 - (-0.88)} \times (0.07 - 0.06) \right] = 6.9331\%$$

As can be seen, the result arrived at by this technique corresponds very well to the true IRR of 6.93%. It is only an approximation to the IRR, since we have assumed that the NPV changes linearly with the rate of interest which, as can be seen from the graph above, is not the case.

If we had selected different values for R_1 and R_2 with a wider interval (eg, 5% and 8% gives an interval of 3%), we would not have come quite as close to the actual value, but since the IRR value is not required to be too precise, we should resist the tendency to aim for spurious accuracy.

Exercise 4

The following cash flows were received from an investment of £600,000 over five years:

Year 1	£250,000
Year 2	£100,000
Year 3	£100,000
Year 4	£150,000
Year 5	£150,000
Profit	**£150,000**

Using interpolation, calculate the IRR of this investment. Use comparative rates of 8% and 9% in order to find a more accurate ROR.

The answer to this exercise can be found at the end of this chapter.

4.3 Uses and Limitations of the IRR

The IRR provides a method for evaluating investment projects when there is an initial cash outflow followed by later cash inflows. The IRR of a project is also known as the yield of the project (and this concept will be explored more fully in relation to bonds when the yield to maturity is equivalent to the IRR of a bond), and if the yield exceeds the cost of financing the investment the project is worthwhile.

There are, however, some significant disadvantages with using IRR in relation to the choice between two competing investments.

When a project has some negative cash flow in between other positive cash flow, the equation of IRR gives rise to more than one ROR, ie, it reaches the trap of 'multiple IRRs'.

The simple value that is obtained from the preceding analysis to determine the IRR will not enable us to determine the actual monetary value of benefits.

Even when comparing two investments with similar initial outlays, although one project may have a higher IRR than another, it will not necessarily have a higher NPV at the relevant cost of capital. This can be readily demonstrated in the following example which shall be examined in some detail.

In addition, the IRR calculation assumes that all cash flows from an investment are reinvested at the same rate (the IRR) which for many longer-term investments is pretty unrealistic.

An Illustration to Demonstrate Limitations of IRR

An investor is faced with a choice between two projects – both of which require an initial outlay of £40,000. It has been determined that Project A yields (has an IRR of) 20% pa, and Project B yields 15% pa. The investor's cost of capital is 6% and we are provided with the sequencing of the subsequent cash flows. Which of the two projects should be undertaken?

As previously observed, the IRR of a project will be equal to the discount rate which, when applied to the sequence of cash flows, realises an NPV of those cash flows of exactly zero. The table below illustrates the process and, as can be seen, the discount rate for Project A which achieves an NPV of zero is 20% and for Project B the comparable discount rate is 15%.

Project A	Discount Rate		20.0%
Year	Cash Flow(£'000)	Discount Factor	PV(£'000)
0	(40,000)	1	(40,000.00)
1	44,000	0.833	36,666.67
2	4,800	0.694	3,333.33
Profit	8,800	NPV =	0.00

Project B	Discount Rate		15.0%
Year	Cash Flow(£'000)	Discount Factor	PV(£'000)
0	(40,000)	1	(40,000.00)
1	8,000	0.870	6,956.52
2	43,700	0.756	33,043.48
Profit	11,700	NPV =	0.00

The next part of the comparison, as discussed with regard to interpolation, is to iterate through several different discount rates – partly in an exercise to discover the IRR, for even though we have been given the information as part of the set-up, it is still useful to check that the rates given do correspond to an NPV of zero, and partly to establish ranges of values which can be depicted graphically for comparison.

The following table shows that for a discount rate stepped at 2.5% up to 30% the NPV values are as indicated and confirms that Project A has an IRR of 20% and Project B has an IRR of 15%.

From reviewing the data, it can be seen that Project A has the higher IRR but has a lower NPV at the investor's cost of capital of 6% than for Project B. This demonstrates that if the yield on a project exceeds the cost of capital, the most favourable circumstance is when the cash flow returns are relatively late in the project life cycle, since the gain in value due to the additional returns exceeds the decay in value resulting from the greater discounting effect as one moves further away in time.

Compounding, Discounting and Bond Maths

Discount Rate	Project A ΣPVs	Project B ΣPVs
2.50%	7,496	9,399
5.0%	6,259	7,256
7.5%	5,084	5,257
10.0%	3,967	3,388
12.5%	2,904	1,640
15.0%	1,890	0
17.5%	923	(1,539)
20.0%	0	(2,986)
22.5%	(883)	(4,348)
25.0%	(1,728)	(5,632)
27.5%	(2,537)	(6,844)
30.0%	(3,314)	(7,988)

Given a 6% cost of capital from reviewing the NPV of cash flows, Project B is preferable. However, at 15%, Project A would clearly be preferred since Project B would then just be breaking even. If we graphically depict the NPV values (on the vertical scale) in conjunction with the different discount rates, it can be seen that there is a crossover point between the two projects.

IRR is affected by both the size of, and the timing of, a project's cash flows. Hence projects with different cash flow patterns can produce different results.

Comparison of IRR for Two Projects

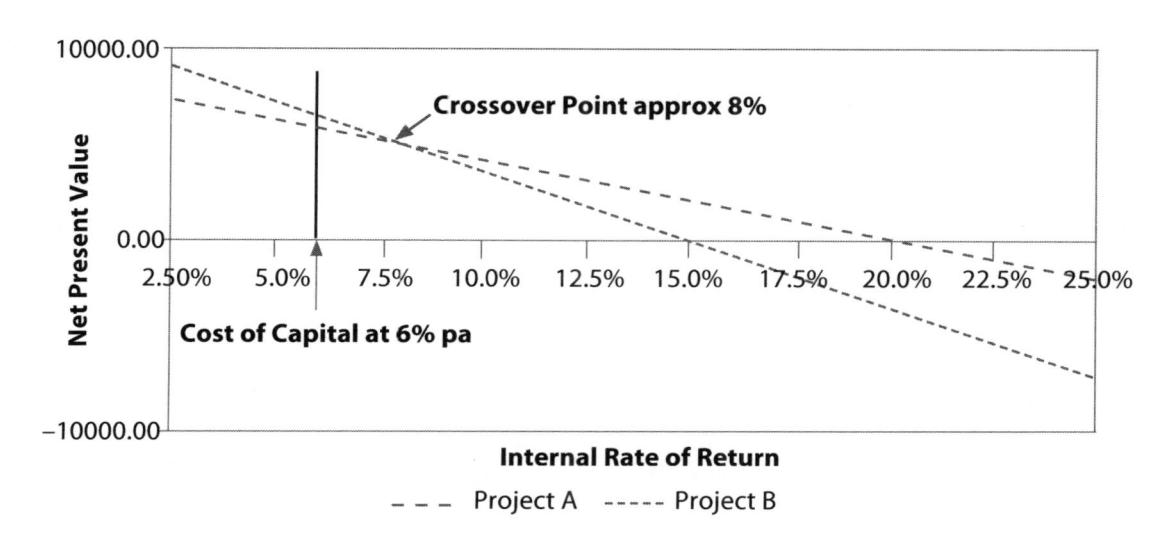

Up to a cost of capital for the investor, the NPV is superior for Project B, but once this point is passed as we move towards the right on the horizontal axis, it can be seen that the NPV for Project A is consistently above that for Project B.

Summary

The IRR (or yield) provides an intuitive method for evaluating individual investments with a prescribed sequence of cash flows, but it is far less useful when comparing projects where there are large differences in the timing of the cash flows or where there is a difference in the scale of the investment opportunities.

5. Arithmetic and Geometric Annualisation

Learning Objective

4.5 Calculate and appraise annualisation techniques

Annualisation refers to the calculation of an investment return over a period longer than one year where the returns in each period are different.

For example, if you invest £1,000 in an asset at the start of 20X0, it might lose 11% in that year, but then gain 17% in 20X1 and a further 8% in 20X2. What is the annualised three-year return?

A simple arithmetic average of the individual returns for each period would suggest a gain of 4.67% ((–11% +17% +8%) / 3), compounded over three years to a gain of £146.74.

This technique works, however, only for returns which are independent of each other. In this case, the return in each period depends on the return of the previous period as a starting point. These returns are therefore interdependent instead of independent. Investment returns must instead be calculated with a geometric rather than arithmetic mean, which allows for the compounding effect of each annual return.

The actual investment returns are as follows.

20X0: £1,000 loses 11%   =   £890.00
20X1: £890 gains 17%   =   £1,041.30
20X2: £1,041.30 gains 8% =   £1,124.60

This represents a substantially lower return than the £146.74 suggested by the arithmetic mean.

The method for calculating the annualised return using a geometric mean is to add 1 to r, the percentage return for each year (so they are all positive), multiply these returns, and then calculate the nth root of this result.

Thus:

$$[(1+r_1)(1+r_2)(1+r_3)\ldots(1+r_i)]^{(1/n)} - 1$$

r = annual rate of return
n = number of years

$$[(1+-0.11)(1+0.17)(1+0.08)]^{(1/3)} - 1$$

$$[(0.89)(1.17)(1.08)]^{(1/3)} - 1$$

$$1.1246^{(1/3)} - 1$$

$$1.04 - 1$$

$$0.04\%$$

This 4% annualised return contrasts with the 4.67% return suggested by the arithmetic mean.

Example Exam Question on Investment Mathematics

Direct questions about investment mathematics are quite rare although one must always assume that any part of the syllabus could be tested thoroughly including this element. In addition, many of the processes and calculations learned under this element are transferable to other sections of the syllabus.

The following examples acts as a practice question.

Example

Explain what is meant by the 'indifference curve' in risk and return. (5 marks)

Example

Mrs Adams understands discounted share prices and allocates her required return quite happily, but often her calculations seem different from the market values. Demonstrate how she can calculate the market required rate using the IRR formula with the following information:

Current share price	£4.00
Anticipated selling price in four years	£4.75
Last dividend paid yesterday	55p

Dividend will grow at 2% per annum for the next 4 years. (8 marks)

Example

What would be the required selling price in three years, of a share which costs £3.25, has a market required return of 7.25% and will pay a dividend of 15p each year? (4 marks)

Exercise Answers

Exercise 1

Calculate the discount factor in order to discover the NPV of the following cash flows received from a deposit account over the period of a year:

Annualised equivalent rate: 8%. Interest paid monthly. Each monthly payment is £20,000.

Answer

The discount factor for 12 months = $1 / (1+r)^{12}$

$1 + r = (1.08)^{1/12}$

$1 + r = 1.00643$

Therefore $r = 0.643\%$ each month

Annuity discount factor = $\dfrac{1}{0.00643} \times \left[1 - \left(\dfrac{1}{(1.00643)^{12}}\right)\right]$

$= 155.52 \times [1 - 0.9260]$

$= 11.51$

Present value = monthly cash flow x ADF = £20,000 x 11.51 = £230,263.08

Exercise 2

If you have a starting amount of £1,000 what will be the final amount after two years with a continuous compounding rate of 11%?

Answer

Substituting these values into $A = Pe^{rt}$

The values are $A = £1,000 \times [e^{(0.11 \times 2)}] = £1,000 \times e^{0.22} = £1,000 \times 1.246 = £1,246$.

Exercise 3

Calculate the price of a corporate bond paying a regular annual coupon of 5% per £100 of nominal stock over ten years. Current required gross redemption yield (GRY) (IRR) is 6.5% per annum.

Answer

Current Bond Price	Annual Coupon	5.00%		Assumed Gross Redemption Yield	6.50%
Timing of Cash Flows	**Cash Flow in £**	Discount Factor		Discount Factor at Desired Yield	Present Value
Coupon Cash Flow Years 1 to 10	£5.00	$1/0.065 \times [1 - (1 / (1.065)^{10})]$ = 7.189		7.189	£35.94
		$\dfrac{1}{(1.065)^{10}} = 0.5327$			
Redemption in Year 10	£100			0.5327	£53.27
				Bond Price	£89.21

Exercise 4

The following cash flows were received from an investment of £600,000 over five years:

Year 1	£250,000
Year 2	£100,000
Year 3	£100,000
Year 4	£150,000
Year 5	£150,000
Profit	**£150,000**

Task

Using interpolation, calculate the IRR of this investment. Use comparative rates of 8% and 9% in order to find a more accurate ROR.

The answer to this exercise can be found at the end of this chapter.

Answer

NPV at 8% = 8.94 (+£8,940.55)

NPV at 9% = −5.5 (−£5,502.36)

The NPV of these cash flows, when using a rate of 8% is calculated as £8,904.55. However, when using a rate of 9%, the NPV becomes negative, calculated as -£5,502.36.

$$IRR = R1 + \left[\frac{N1}{N1-N2} \times (R2 - R1) \right]$$

$$IRR = 8\% + \left[\frac{8.94}{8.94 - (-5.50)} \times (9\% - 8\%) \right]$$

IRR = 8.619%

Example Exam Question Answers on Investment Mathematics

Example

Mrs Adams understands discounted share prices and allocates her required return quite happily, but often her calculations seem different from the market values. Demonstrate how she can calculate the market required rate using the IRR formula with the following information:

Current share price	£4.00
Anticipated selling price in four years	£4.75
Last dividend paid yesterday	55p

Dividend will grow at 2% per annum for the next four years. (8 marks)

Answer

Outlay		(4.00)
Year 1	0.55*1.02/1.05	0.53
Year 2	0.56*1.02/1.05²	0.52
Year 3	0.57*1.02/1.05³	0.50
Year 4	0.58*1.02/1.05⁴	0.49
Year 4	4.75/1.05⁴	3.91
NPV		1.95

Outlay		(4.00)
Year 1	0.55*1.02/1.20	0.47
Year 2	0.56*1.02/1.20²	0.40
Year 3	0.57*1.02/1.20³	0.34
Year 4	0.58*1.02/1.20⁴	0.28
Year 4	4.75/1.20⁴	2.29
NPV		(0.22)

IRR 5+ [1.95/2.17 * 15]

5+13.48

18.48 approximately

Example

What would be the required selling price in three years, of a share which costs £3.25, has a market required return of 7.25% and will pay a dividend of 15p each year? (4 marks)

Answer

$3.25 - 0.15/1.0725 - 0.15/1.0725^2 - 0.15/1.0725^3 = X/1.0725^3$

$3.25 - 0.14 - 0.13 - 0.12 = X/1.0725^3$

$2.86 = X/1.0725^3$

$2.86 * 1.0725^3 = X$

X = £3.53

Chapter Five
Liquidity Description, Risk, Return Characteristics

1. Cash	205
2. Types of Cash Deposits	207
3. Money Markets	220
4. Treasury Bills	226
5. Effect of Inflation	228

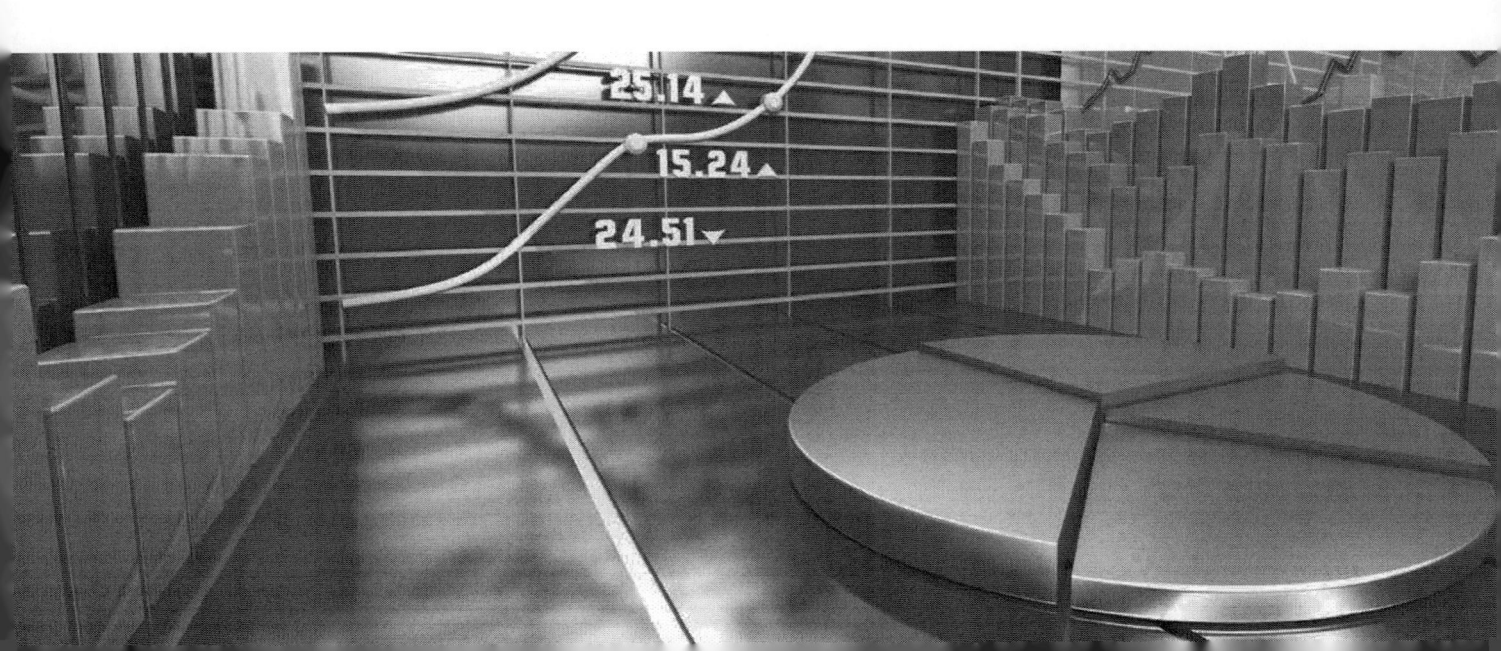

Learning Outcome

Be able to evaluate critically the risks and returns offered by short-term liquid instruments

1. Cash

1.1 What is 'Cash'?

Cash is legal tender, currency or coins, that can be used to exchange goods, debt or services. It may sometimes include the value of assets which can be easily converted into cash immediately, as reported by a company.

1.1.1 Breaking Down 'Cash'

Cash is also known as 'money', in physical form. Cash, in a corporate setting, usually includes bank accounts and marketable securities, such as government bonds and banker's acceptances. Although cash typically refers to money in hand, the term can also be used to indicate money in banking accounts, cheques or any other form of currency that is easily accessible and can be quickly turned into physical cash.

Cash in its physical form is the simplest, most broadly accepted and reliable form of payment, which is why many businesses only accept cash. Cheques can bounce and credit cards can be declined, but cash in hand requires no extra processing. However, it's become less common for people to carry cash with them, due to the increasing dependability and convenience of electronic banking and payment systems.

In finance and banking, cash indicates the company's current assets, or any assets that can be turned into cash within one year. A business's cash flow shows the net amount of cash a company has, after factoring in both incoming and outgoing cash and assets, and can be a good resource for potential investors. A company's cash flow statement shows all incoming cash, such as net income, and outgoing cash used to pay expenses such as equipment and investments.

Money is something that people use every day. They earn it and then spend it. Economists define money as *'any good that is widely accepted as final payment for goods and services'*. Over the centuries money has taken many forms; eg cowry shells, large stone wheels and strings of beads. All forms of money have some things in common.

1. They are store of value. The holder can keep them for an unlimited period before spending, knowing that the value will not change during the period it is held. This is better than holding a commodity which might deteriorate or fluctuate in value eg grain or gold. Note, it is not a perfect way of holding a value as inflation will reduce the buying power over time.
2. It is a unit of account. ie it can be used to value other items using a recognisable unit eg you can compare the price of a computer from store A with one from store B. If you were using barter, one might use grain and the other butter so very difficult to compare. Thus it is easier to where money is the comparison and helps the economy generally.

3. It is a well-accepted medium of exchange. ie most business is happy to accept money as payment for their goods. This is because it is usually backed by the government, eg, in the US paper money states: *'This note is legal tender for all debts, public and private.'* Even if not officially backed by the government, but only by a bank it may still be generally accepted if there is sufficient confidence in the institution, eg, banknotes issued by Banks in Scotland.

Economists tend to believe that the development of money is in the same category as other great inventions like the wheel and the inclined plane. Early forms of money tended to be made of something of value, eg, gold and silver. As time passed and governments were found to be debasing the currency (for various reasons) other types were developed.

These developments included:

Representative Money

A certificate or token that could be exchanged for the actual commodity, eg, gold was kept in the bank and the business person only carried a certificate stating that the bank would give the bearer the gold if asked (in the UK bank note still promise to pay the bearer on demand) the certificate was 'backed' by the gold in the vault. This was quickly accepted as the certificate was easier to carry than the actual gold. Representative money then led another form of cash, fiat money, the type used today.

Fiat Money

Fiat money has no **intrinsic value** and has no backing from an asset in a vault. The value is derived from the backing by the government which declares it to be 'legal tender', ie, it is accepted as having value because the government says it has and people trust the government enough to accept it.

Money replaced the other forms of exchange it has characteristics that makes it more useful. The characteristics of money are:

- durability
- portability
- divisibility
- uniformity
- limited supply, and
- acceptability.

This is best seen by an example of two possible forms of money:

- a camel – used as money historically in some countries
- sterling pound notes (to the value of one camel).

How does each meet the above characteristics?

1. **Durability** – a camel is reasonably durable, but it can fall sick or even die (both reduce the value). Sterling notes are durable and are easy to replace if the start to wear and the value will be constant.
2. **Portability** – the camel can be ridden to a store but if it is a distance, this can be difficult. However currency is much easier to carry (in a wallet/purse/pocket).

4. **Divisibility** – a £50 note can be split, for example, into five £10 notes or ten £5 notes. The camel cannot be split (unless killed which would affect the value).
5. **Uniformity** – camels are all different sizes and shapes thus each has a different value so not uniform. A £50 note is the same as every other £50 note thus they are very uniform.
6. **Limited supply** – in order to maintain its value, money supply must be controlled (by the government). Camels are limited in numbers too, but there is no control of the supply as breeders would produce more if they believed they could sell them.
7. **Acceptability** – camels do have an intrinsic value BUT not everyone will want to accept them in exchange for their goods, eg, would a supermarket accept 20 camels (to feed and store) in exchange for a 60 inch TV? The declaration of legal tender by a government makes the currency acceptable to almost everyone.

Summary

Paper money is a relatively recent type of cash, (from approximately the eighteenth century) The 'value' of cash is determined by its users' faith in the government issuing the currency. This determination of price has a knock on effect in various parts of the economy eg inflation, ie, the more prices rise (inflation), the lower the purchasing power of any currency.

Cheques, debit/credit cards, electronic banking etc have reduced the need to carry actual cash.

2. Types of Cash Deposits

Learning Objective

5.1 Explain the types of cash deposits and their characteristics, including: definition and key properties of cash; risk, price, and return; historic performance of cash; principal problems and liquidity issues, plus implications should liquidity fall; onshore deposit and savings accounts; offshore accounts and tax implications

2.1 Cash Deposits

The most tangible forms of money are banknotes and coins. Keeping money 'under the mattress' (or in a safe) as notes and coins is one option for someone with savings. However, inflation erodes the purchasing power of the money, and no interest is earned. There is also the risk of loss or theft. An alternative is to deposit the money with a sound financial institution such as a bank.

Money is held in cash deposits for the following primary reasons:

- **Security** – banks are generally protected by the Government as evidenced during the 2007–09 financial crisis, when taxpayer funds were used to save some of the UK's biggest banks: RBS, Lloyds TSB (now simply Lloyds) and HBOS (now owned by Lloyds). The Government also rescued the retail savers of the failed Northern Rock and Icesave. See the compensation scheme described in section 2.2 below.

- **Accessibility** – access to cash can be immediate (unless invested for a pre-agreed period), via banks' and building societies' branches, automated teller machines (ATMs) and the internet. Even the mail may still be a method to access the money in a cash deposit. To transfer money from a cash deposit to pay for liabilities, there are also automated banking systems, such as BACS (Bankers Automated Clearing Services), FPS (Faster Payment Service), CHAPS (Clearing House Automated Payment System) and SWIFT (for international payments, via guaranteed messages) that process millions of transactions daily.
- **Liquidity** – liquidity refers to the speed and ease with which one asset can be exchanged for another. It can be measured not only in the number of days in which certain assets could be sold, but also in any discount from their market price or 'fair value', which an immediate sale might bring about. Cash is the most liquid asset under both criteria, followed by instant access deposit accounts.

Accounts for holding cash deposits are generally characterised by a high level of security. Capital is very unlikely to be lost, at least in monetary terms. A UK deposit insurance scheme protects savings up to £85,000 per person per authorised institution (see Financial Services Compensation Scheme (FSCS) in section 2.2 below), and it was made clear by the UK Government's reaction to the 'run' on Northern Rock in August 2007 that no depositors would suffer a loss from the bank's failure. According to the EU Directive 2014/49 on deposit guarantee schemes, the EU member states shall ensure that the coverage level for the aggregate deposits of each depositor is €100,000. Member states which converted the above amount into their national currency initially used the exchange rate prevailing on 3 July 2015 in the conversion, rounding the figure by a maximum of €5,000.

Cash held on deposit is eroded by inflation unless it earns a yield above inflation, resulting in a real rate of return (ROR) for the investor. If the rate of inflation is above the normal savings rate for a sustained period, such a real rate of return cannot be achieved via cash on deposit.

As described above, an important aspect of cash deposits held in instant access accounts is their liquidity. Cash can be required by every type of investor at immediate notice, both regularly and as a contingency; therefore, in terms of financial planning, an investor should hold some cash on deposit to satisfy actual and potential short-term cash flow requirements.

An instant access cash deposit account provides an important instrument for financial planning, whether to make a specific purchase, or an immediate deposit for a leveraged transaction, such as buying property via a mortgage. A cash deposit can also be used for savings towards a regular investment, such as a mutual fund. Cash can be accumulated gradually in a tax-efficient cash deposit account, such as a cash individual savings account (ISA), before being transferred to a stocks and shares ISA when the balance has reached required thresholds for relevant securities.

Investments which offer slightly inferior liquidity include term deposits and certificates of deposit (CDs), since an investor is locked in at a fixed rate for a fixed term, when it might be possible, meanwhile, to obtain more attractive rates from other investments. Such investments also exclude access to cash at short notice for any liquidity needs, except perhaps with a penalty of lost interest or a fixed fee. The overriding principle of short-term investment is that the greater the need for liquidity, the lower the available yield.

2.2 Risk of Cash Deposits

Prior to the establishment of the FSCS in 2001, there had been historical precedents for complete depositor losses when a deposit-taker failed and went into liquidation. The Bank of Credit and Commerce International (BCCI), for example, was closed down in 1991 as a result of fraud on a global scale, causing initial estimated creditor losses of around USD 10 billion (although its liquidators claimed to have recovered around 75% of these by 2013).

If an authorised UK financial services institution defaults or is considered likely to default, the creditor will have recourse to the FSCS. The scheme is administered by the Financial Services Compensation Scheme Limited, a body established by the Financial Services Authority (FSA). It is now governed by the Prudential Regulation Authority (PRA) and the Financial Conduct Authority (FCA). It is not funded by taxpayers, but imposes a levy on the financial services sector depending on its class of activity. It does not accumulate any form of contingency fund, but sets off any surplus from one year's levy against its requirement for the next. It also has the ability to borrow from the financial services sector.

The FSCS is a statutory fund of last resort set up under the Financial Services and Markets Act (FSMA) 2000 to compensate customers of authorised financial services firms in the event of their insolvency. Since April 2018, the scheme now covers deposits, credit unions, pensions, insurance policies, insurance brokering, endowments, investments, mortgages and mortgage arrangement, and debt management. As a result of the financial crisis, it paid out around £21 billion in 2008–09 to cover five bank defaults. This compensated the holders of around 3.5 million bank accounts, but exceeded the levy which had been taken for that period. It, therefore, borrowed the shortfall from the Bank of England (BoE) and HM Treasury, with the relevant class of firm subsequently repaying those loans through subsequent levies.

Although there are various provisions for non-cash investments and insurance policies, the key provision to protect cash deposits is as follows:

> 100% of the first £85,000 per person, per authorised institution, is guaranteed by the FSCS.

The term 'authorised institution' is defined by the FSCS as *'a company, unincorporated body, partnership or individual permitted to carry out a regulated activity by the FCA or the PRA. This term includes a mutual (unincorporated) organisation, for example a friendly society.'* With the exception of insurance claims, this does not extend to firms based in the Channel Islands or the Isle of Man.

Note also that cover is provided only per authorised firm. If an authorised firm operates under several brands, but has only one Firm Reference Number (FRN) from the FCA or PRA, then only one limit applies to products held with all those brands in total.

2.2.1 Portfolio Cash Accounts

An investor may hold their money on deposit with an investment management company or stockbroker that is authorised by the FCA to hold client money. These types of accounts are usually tailored to the client, or to a group of clients, and their interest rates are often tiered by the amount held on deposit. The money is usually readily accessible, with terms and conditions provided in the management agreement. The client money is held by the investment management firm or stockbroker in trust at deposit-takers and will not be directly protected by the FSCS. There is also the risk of the investment management firm or stockbroker not protecting the client money properly, as has been demonstrated by some large FCA fines for client money failures over the last few years for both big and small firms. If the firm does not protect client money properly, then it could be lost or stolen. If a firm were to fail and be placed into the special administration regime, and if the client money has not been adequately protected, there is a risk that the administrators may have too little client money to be able to repay clients and/or may be obliged to use some or all of it to settle creditors' debts and/or allocate it to the wrong clients.

If client money is poorly protected, then circumstantially it is possible that it will not be readily payable to clients. Some examples of this occurring are Lehman Brothers International (Europe), MF Global, Pritchard Stockbrokers and Worldspreads. However, considering the numbers of firms that hold client money, most are protecting it satisfactorily. In addition the FCA is continually developing the client money regime and embedding improvements via enhanced client money rules. Please refer to the CASS Clients Assets Sourcebook (CASS) section of the FCA Handbook www.handbook.fca.org.uk/handbook/CASS/1.

2.2.2 Spreading Risk Across Different Deposit Takers

The ceiling on compensation available through the FSCS leads some investors to consider spreading their capital among a number of banks and building societies in order to reduce the overall default risk. Such diversification should be among institutions which are not part of the same parent group. The benefit of spreading the risk in this way should be weighed against the possible disadvantage of lower rates of interest that may be earned because of the investor missing out on higher rates offered for larger deposits.

2.3 Principal Deposit-Takers

2.3.1 Commercial/Retail Banks

A commercial bank provides services, eg, accepting deposits, providing loans, mortgage lending and basic investment products, such as savings accounts and certificates of deposit. Commercial banks are public limited companies that are regulated, listed on major stock exchanges and owned by their shareholders. Many have traditionally operated with an embedded investment bank which uses the assets (depositors' savings) from the commercial or retail side of the bank. One consequence of the 2007–09 financial crisis in the UK has been the recommendation of the Independent Commission on Banking, chaired by Sir John Vickers, that the largest banks must separate core retail banking from investment banking by 1 January 2019. This 'ring-fencing' process is designed to prevent retail depositors' savings again being put at risk to finance more risky investment bank activities. Relevant legislation includes the Financial Services (Banking Reform) Act 2013 and various Orders and Regulations amending the FSMA 2000. The portion of these large banks which are due to retain their retail and core commercial banking activities will continue to be regulated as authorised deposit-takers by the PRA in accordance with the FSMA 2000 and consistent with the Capital Requirements Directive IV (CRD IV).

A more immediate consequence of the crisis, however, was for governments to become large shareholders in what were previously privately-owned banks. For example, the UK Government still holds around 7% of the equity of Royal Bank of Scotland (RBS) but, in 2017, sold back the remaining tranche of the 43% stake it had to take in Lloyds (following its rescue merger of HBOS). Having nationalised both Northern Rock plc and Bradford & Bingley plc, it continues to recover its rescue funds through sales of some assets and the winding-down of others. The management and disposal of these assets was managed until March 2018 by UK Financial Investments (established by the UK Government specifically to manage its shareholdings in RBS and in UK Asset Resolution, which in turn represented residual mortgage assets in Northern Rock Asset Management and the remainder of Bradford & Bingley). The branch network of Bradford & Bingley was sold to Santander, while the branches of Northern Rock were sold to Virgin Money. Barclays, meanwhile, raised emergency funds from sales of equity to Middle Eastern government investors, therefore avoiding UK government restrictions on paying bonuses and dividends.

2.3.2 Building Societies

Building societies are mutually owned organisations, ie, owned by their members. The members are the holders of savings accounts (often referred to as share accounts) and borrowers. Like shareholders, the members of the society have voting rights. Some building societies have demutualised and become commercial/retail banks, while others have been absorbed in a widespread consolidation of smaller societies in the last twenty years or so. Very few of these retain even their former brand name (eg, Kent Reliance, is now part of One Savings Bank plc).

2.3.3 National Savings & Investments (NS&I)

These are the safest of all deposits in the UK as they are guaranteed in full by the Government – a deposit of up to £2 million is fully protected, unlike any other UK deposit. Accounts are only open to individuals. Although National Savings & Investments (NS&I) savers are predominantly UK residents, as long as an individual has a UK bank or building society account then they can open an NS&I account. The powers governing the way in which NS&I products are structured and managed are derived from specific NS&I legislation and all strategic decisions affecting their products require ministerial consent. Additionally, they are expected by HM Treasury to comply fully with FCA requirements when applicable and appropriate, on a voluntary basis, as well as with the National Savings Bank Act 1971 and the National Savings Regulations 2015. As NS&I holds no capital and has no lending or dealing activities, it is not a bank, hence it is not an authorised deposit taker. NS&I offers primarily simple, deposit-based products and, therefore, some of the detailed rules which make up the FCA regulatory regime are not directly relevant.

2.3.4 Supervision

From 1 April 2013, supervision of the prudential soundness of banks and building societies was changed from the FSA to the PRA in the Bank of England (BoE). Banks will be 'dual-regulated', prudentially by the PRA and for conduct by the FCA (successor to the FSA).

2.4 Deposit Account Types

2.4.1 Instant Access Accounts

As already described in section 2.1 above, an important advantage of an instant access account is its accessibility. Some cash is needed by every type of investor at short notice; it may be for an emergency. These accounts can vary in their flexibility; while some permit unrestricted withdrawals, others may impose restrictions, eg, only two withdrawals per year.

2.4.2 Notice Accounts

Notice accounts are less accessible, ie, the depositor must give notice of perhaps 30, 60 or 90 days to withdraw cash or alternatively suffer an interest penalty. As a result, there is usually a higher rate of interest to offset the disadvantage of the notice period and the relative lack of liquidity.

The quoted interest rate, where interest is paid monthly, is typically lower than on an equivalent account which pays interest annually. This reflects the compounding effect of the Annual Equivalent Rate (see chapter 4, section 3.1).

2.4.3 Term Deposit Accounts

Term deposit accounts (also known as 'time deposit accounts') are for cash deposited over a predefined period for enhanced interest rates. Their inflexibility prohibits early access to the funds and, even if this is permitted, there are normally penalties, such as the loss of all interest and an expensive administrative charge; therefore, they represent a further reduction in available liquidity.

Time deposits are often provided as fixed-rate bonds by a bank. The bond could be offered for a defined period or the issuer may reserve the right to withdraw the offer at any time. Interest is sometimes tiered. For example, a five-year 'step-up bond' might offer a gross rate of interest of 2.0% in year one, 2.5% in year two, 3.0% in year three, rising to 3.5% in year four and a final 4.0% in year five. The issue with fixed-rate bonds, as with fixed-term deposits, is that these are intended to be inaccessible during the investment period and the investor will probably be unable to withdraw any of the cash or may suffer detrimental interest penalties and an expensive administrative charge if withdrawn early.

2.4.4 Money Market Accounts

Certain banks offer money market deposits for individually defined periods (ranging from overnight to five years), interest rates and currencies. The interest rate reflects more closely the current money market rates, such as the London Interbank Offered Rate (LIBOR).

A call account allows the investor to access their money on any working day and by a specified time (normally mid-morning). This is close to the terms of an instant access account and usually pays an interest rate which is aligned to the base rate or LIBOR. A fixed-term deposit combines a fixed-interest rate with a specified period, and is similar to term deposits, but is usually a tailored arrangement to meet a particular investor's needs.

Money market deposits can be appropriate for investors with a large amount of cash to invest, eg, from the proceeds of the sale of a house, pending a later house purchase. There may be minimum investment amounts, but note also that the FSCS now offers compensation for up to £1 million for temporary high balances (less than six months and from particular sources, such as property sales, insurance pay-outs, inheritance, redundancy, compensation and divorce).

2.5 Tax Treatment of Cash Deposits

A UK resident will be subject to tax on bank and building society deposits in the tax year in which the interest is paid at one of the following rates:

Income Tax Rates and Under 65 Allowance

Rate	2018–19 UK (except Scotland)	2018–19 (Scotland)
Tax-free amount of savings income	£1,000 (basic rate taxpayer) £500 (higher rate taxpayer) £0 (additional rate taxpayer)	£1,000 (basic rate taxpayer) £500 (higher rate taxpayer) £0 (additional rate taxpayer)
Personal Savings Allowance	£1,000 (£500 if higher rate taxpayer)	£1,000 (£500 if higher rate taxpayer)
Personal Allowance	£11,850	£11,850
Starting Rate for savings: 0%*	£0–£5,000	£0–£5,000
Starter Rate: 19%	–	£11,851–£13,850
Basic Rate: 20%	£11,851–£46,350	£13,851–£24,000
Intermediate Rate: 21%	–	£24,001–£43,430
Higher Rate: 40%	£46,351–£150,000	–
Higher Rate: 41%	–	£43,431–£150,000
Additional Rate: 45%	Over £150,000	–
Top Rate: 46%	–	Over £150,000
Income limit before Personal Allowance is reduced by £1 for every £2 earned until nil	£100,000 (nil at £123,700)	£100,000 (nil at £123,700)

* Restricted to savings income only, but reduced if taxable non-savings income exceeds Personal Allowance.

The gradual withdrawal of the personal allowance for those with incomes of £100,000 or more, and the restriction of higher rate tax relief for pension contributions for those with incomes of more than £150,000, increases the tax burden on higher-income earners, giving a marginal rate of tax for some of 60%.

From 2016, interest on bank and building society accounts is paid gross of income tax. However, it remains taxable unless held within a tax-advantaged wrapper, such as an ISA.

2.5.1 The ISA Wrapper

There have been several schemes instigated by the UK Government to encourage private savings which essentially provide tax relief or a 'shelter' from taxation for savings that fall within the limits specified in current legislation.

An ISA is a tax wrapper, ie, a tax avoidance scheme, in that any income or capital gains arising from assets held within it attract no tax liability, nor does any capital withdrawal. Details of income and capital gains do not have to be disclosed on the investor's tax return.

There are three main types of ISA available to everyone and one further type available to first-time house buyers only. Cash ISAs and stocks and shares ISAs are covered extensively throughout this workbook, the others less so.

- Stocks and shares ISAs.
- Cash ISAs.
- Innovative finance ISAs.
- Help to buy ISAs (available to first-time buyers only, but being replaced between 2016 and 2019 by Lifetime ISAs).

Additionally, in 2016–17, the concept of the flexible ISA was introduced, allowing investors to withdraw money from their ISA and replace it in the same tax year, without this replacement counting towards their annual ISA limit. This feature can work with a cash ISA, investment ISA, or an innovative finance ISA as long as the investor has a cash holding within them to draw upon. Not all ISA providers may offer this flexibility, so investors should check with their ISA provider before withdrawing any funds.

In order to subscribe, an investor must be:

- aged 18 years or over (stocks and shares ISA, innovative finance ISA), or
- aged 16 years or over (cash ISA)
- and treated as resident and ordinarily resident in the UK for tax purposes.

There is also a mini version for children, called a junior ISA (JISA), which works in a similar way. One anomaly is that 16–18 year olds can open a cash ISA and a JISA in the same year.

An ISA is not itself an investment; it is a tax wrapper designed to incorporate investments. An ISA manager (approved by HMRC) manages the account and ensures all tax relief from HMRC on behalf of the investor. An individual is not allowed to set up their own ISA wrapper without an ISA provider, although individuals commonly manage their own investments within the ISA in the form of a self-select ISA.

An ISA may include investments which fluctuate in value, eg, stocks and shares held either directly or indirectly through a collective investment such as a unit trust, investment trust, open-ended investment company (OEIC) or other undertaking for collective investment in transferable securities (UCITS) such as exchange-traded funds (ETFs).

A cash ISA may, and most commonly does, consist of a cash deposit account. Cash ISAs are simply savings accounts where the interest is not taxed, but there is a limit to how much can be invested into such a wrapper account.

In April 2017, the annual ISA investment allowance was raised to £20,000, where it remains for the 2018–19 fiscal year. That allowance can either be saved in a cash ISA, or in an all-share ISA. It is also permitted to split the allowance between cash and stocks and shares ISAs, eg, invest £3,000 in a cash ISA, and £17,000 in a stocks and shares ISA.

Any savings or investments must be made by 5 April, the end of the tax year. Unused allowances (or portions of them) do not roll over; they are lost for good. This means an ISA should always be the first place any savings go, as after the tax year ends, any savings or investments stay within the tax-free ISA wrapper for the future, where they will continue to earn interest.

2.5.2 Junior ISAs (JISAs)

JISAs are long-term, tax-free savings accounts for children up to the age of 18. The money saved in a Junior ISA can't be taken out until the child is 18.

For UK residents aged under 18, up to £4,260 (2018–19) can be invested each year in an ISA. When cash is withdrawn, the tax advantage is lost. Cash mini-ISAs are available from NS&I. A large number of deposit-taking institutions also provide JISAs.

A child can have a JISA if they:

- are under 18
- live in the UK, and
- are not entitled to a child trust fund (CTF) account.

The child cannot have a JISA if they already have a CTF account. CTFs can now be converted to JISAs however.

Children aged 16 could choose to open an adult cash ISA as well as a JISA.

The money in the account belongs to the child and can't be taken out until they are 18. But there are exceptions to this, for example if the child becomes terminally ill.

Anyone can put money into the account. The total amount that can be paid into a JISA in the tax year 2018–19 is £4,260.

The child can have both a cash and a stocks and shares JISA. If they do, the total amount that can be paid into the two accounts in each tax year is £4,260. For example, £1,000 into a cash JISA and £3,260 into a stocks and shares JISA.

2.6 Offshore Banking

Accounts can be opened at overseas branches of UK banks and building societies by UK residents and expatriates. Cash deposits can be held in sterling or other currencies. Foreign currency accounts are also available at UK mainland branches of some banks. UK residents who require an offshore deposit account will often use a bank or building society in Jersey, Guernsey or the Isle of Man.

There is a narrower choice of accounts than in onshore banking, but offshore accounts are often better tailored to the requirements of international clients, especially for multi-currency transactions and tax efficiency. Typically, the client can select an instant-access, notice or fixed-rate, fixed-term account. Sterling interest rates offered generally reflect UK interest rates. Holders of offshore deposit accounts can normally conduct transactions by internet, post or bank credit transfer.

2.6.1 Tax Implications

Interest earned on deposits with an offshore bank are often paid gross with no deductions for taxation (some countries will tax the accounts). UK residents are obliged under UK tax legislation to declare this income to HMRC and it will normally be taxed at the same rates as UK savings income. For investors who move or retire to another country, without repatriating funds to the UK, offshore bank and building society accounts are likely to be beneficial.

The key test for assessing a liability to income tax on UK savings income is that of residency, although the status of domicile has a further implication which can offer some degree of option about such taxation. There are three criteria to the principle test of residency, the Statutory Residence Test (SRT), which was introduced in 2013. These are a test for automatic non-residency, one for automatic residency and one for sufficient UK ties.

The test for UK residency is based on the number of days spent in the UK in each tax year.

A person is automatically non-resident if they either spend fewer than 16 days in the UK (46 days if they have not been a UK resident for the previous three years) or if they work abroad full-time and spend fewer than 91 days in the UK (of which no more than 30 spent working).

A person is automatically resident, however, if they either spend 183 days or more in the UK or if their only home is in the UK (for at least 91 days in the year and they spend at least 30 days there).

The specific criteria for defining terms such as 'day', 'work', 'home' and 'spend' are not covered here, but can lead to some uncertainty. This leads to the Sufficient Ties Test, with further criteria of family, accommodation, working days and cumulative days over two years and whether more days are spent in the UK than in any other single country.

Even where residency is determined to be in the UK, it has been possible to have an overseas domicile (a non-domicile status). This traditionally follows the domicile of one's father, but numerous countries allow immigrants to establish a new domicile based on citizenship, voting rights, establishing a business or other factors. In the UK, however, a person is now automatically deemed to be UK-domiciled if they have been resident for 15 of the previous 20 tax years, or if they are born with a UK domicile, or even if they acquire an overseas domicile but then return to the UK.

The advantage of being a UK resident but a non-domicile is the option to claim the remittance basis for taxation. Under this option, all income (and gains) earned in the UK are taxed like any other resident, together with any income or gains brought in from overseas. The remittance basis allows, however, any income or gains earned outside the UK but not remitted here to remain untaxed. Such non-domiciles (known as 'non-doms') must now pay a charge for such an exemption (£30,000 if UK resident for seven of the previous nine tax years) or £60,000 if UK resident for 12 of the previous 14 tax years).

2.6.2 Risks with Offshore Banks

The principal risk of an offshore bank, relative to that of an onshore equivalent, is security. Depending on the specific financial centre, there may be little or no compensation offered, whether from the local government or from a mutual insurance scheme, such as the FSCS in the UK. Among those closest to the UK, Jersey, Guernsey and the Isle of Man all have their own compensation schemes which currently secure the first £50,000 per person.

Offshore banks can sometimes provide access to politically and economically stable jurisdictions. This will be an advantage for residents in areas where there is risk of political turmoil, who fear their assets may be frozen, seized or disappear.

Some offshore banks may operate with a lower cost base and can provide higher interest rates than the market rate in the home country due to lower overheads and a lack of government intervention.

Offshore finance is one of the few industries, along with tourism, in which geographically remote island nations can competitively engage. Many islands in the Caribbean, such as the Cayman Islands and Antigua, provide a variety of offshore banking and financial services.

Interest is almost always paid by offshore banks without any deductions being made for taxation. Indeed, many of the most favoured offshore jurisdictions are tax havens in which there are no income taxes applicable. This is an advantage to individuals who seek to exploit international tax avoidance opportunities.

Offshore banking is often linked to other structures, such as offshore companies, trusts or foundations, which may have specific tax advantages for some individuals.

2.6.3 Advantages of Offshore Banking

There are a number of reasons why an investor may consider offshore banking. These include the following:

1. Securing and protecting their capital.
2. Receiving high service levels.
3. Giving themselves convenient and ready access to funds.
4. Depending on country-specific considerations, to save tax on deposits, savings and investments.
5. Allows better access to international investment opportunities.
6. Receive better foreign exchange services.
7. Offers an alternative for lending and credit facilities (perhaps easier access).
8. Lower fees and higher returns.
9. Economic protection.
10. Privacy.

Security

In some countries, bank deposits may not get the same level of protection as, for example, is available in the EU. If these investors use an offshore bank, which is domiciled in a highly regulated, transparent jurisdiction, eg Guernsey, they may feel that their money is more secure. For example, in Cyprus, in 2013, investors were blocked from taking all, but very limited amounts, from their accounts. Had they held offshore bank accounts, this risk would have been removed.

Service

To encourage investors, offshore banks will often offer a very personalised service, eg, giving round-the-clock access to their account 365 days of the year. It is also common for a relationship manager to be appointed for each customer to ensure that investors have a personal point of contact.

Convenience

Investors who travel the world may wish to be able to access their account from anywhere and, thus, offshore banking will meet this need. This is a major reason many accounts are in use.

Tax

Any tax advantage will depend upon the tax regime of the investor's domicile. Often hiding the money is illegal when no tax has been paid but this is part of a much broader tax discussion and beyond the scope of this topic.

For example, the tax benefits might be keeping money outside of the tax jurisdiction of the domicile, thus, protecting it from taxes in the country in which the investor lives. Another reason could be to receive a gross rate of return after tax has been paid at a later date.

Also, money in an offshore bank may be used in inheritance tax planning (which may or may not be legal) as the money may be hidden from the home tax authorities.

Investing

An offshore bank may offer access to different investment funds and investments that are not generally available in the home country, eg, access to a hedge fund will provide you with a wide choice of funds and investments that are not usually available either in your home country or where you are currently living.

Foreign Exchange Services

It is common for offshore banks to offer accounts which accept multi currencies and currency transfers making it very simple and possibly cheaper.

Lending and Credit

The lending and credit facilities offered can potentially be more flexible and tailored to the client's needs.

Fees, Interest and Charges

The fees and charges may be lower than elsewhere (and the interest rate may be higher). Over time, this advantage is diminishing but can still exist.

Economic Protection

If a country is facing a deteriorating economic climate, investors may wish to keep their assets in an offshore bank account. Thus, avoiding the risk of high inflation, currency devaluation or even a coup or war.

Privacy

It may be possible to enjoy greater account privacy by going offshore. For example, Switzerland has historically placed great emphasis on maintaining client confidentiality at all times. This allows investors to protect their assets from court actions.

2.6.4 Disadvantages of Offshore Banking

Offshore banking is a legitimate financial exercise undertaken by many expatriate and international workers. It is usually more accessible to those on higher incomes, because of the costs of establishing and maintaining an offshore account. Simple savings accounts can be opened by anyone, and maintained with scale fees equivalent to their onshore counterparts.

However, offshore banks and other financial firms have been accused of helping various organised crime and terrorist groups and other sources of illicitly acquired funds. The ease with which accounts and trusts could be opened and managed without full declaration of their beneficial ownership has led to suspicions of aiding money laundering and tax evasion. In recent years, two major leaks of confidential papers from offshore legal firms (the Panama and the Paradise Papers) highlighted instances of high-profile individuals from around the world exploiting some of the more aggressive tax avoidance schemes, of which some might even be deemed to amount to tax evasion.

In response to the global prevalence of money laundering and terrorist financing, the Financial Action Task Force (FATF), an independent inter-governmental body, whose objectives are to set standards and promote the effective implementation of legal, regulatory and operational measures for combating money laundering, has made several recommendations. These are considered to be the global anti-money laundering standards, and aim to increase transparency, as well as encourage different jurisdictions to protect their financial services industries from both the reality and the suspicion of money laundering. If transparency on offshore bank accounts and trusts nevertheless increases further, the perceived advantages of offshore banking may appear less obvious.

A clear distinction should be drawn between legitimate tax avoidance schemes and illegal tax evasion and money laundering. The former is perfectly legal, although there is a constant risk that schemes which are clearly contrived to exploit unintended tax loopholes may before long be curtailed and thus transformed into tax avoidance. Some tax avoidance schemes are deemed unethical by commentators, but it should be remembered that although some schemes may be complex, they reflect the often highly specific and contrived tax policies of governments and that even ISAs are just a less complex example of tax avoidance in the UK.

2.6.5 Common Reporting Standard (CRS)

The Common Reporting Standard (CRS), developed by the Organisation for Economic Co-operation and Development (OECD), requires authorities in CRS-participating jurisdictions to obtain information from their financial institutions and automatically exchange that information with other CRS-participating jurisdictions.

The CRS is a global standard for the automatic exchange of financial account and tax information between governments around the world, in the fight against tax evasion. The CRS sets out the financial account information to be exchanged, the financial institutions required to report, and the different types of accounts and taxpayers covered.

The aim of the CRS is to try and reduce, or even prevent, the use of offshore jurisdictions to facilitate tax evasion. Some countries have not yet decided to sign up to the CRS, and exclusions to the list of participating countries include the US. However, the reason for the US exclusion is because the Foreign Account Tax Compliance Act (FATCA) legislation already exists as a mechanism for identifying assets held offshore by US citizens and US tax resident individuals.

3. Money Markets

Learning Objective

5.2 Explain and evaluate the nature and use by investors of the money markets, money market participants, near-cash and short- term money market instruments

3.1 Money Markets

The money market consists of financial institutions and dealers in cash and credit who wish to either borrow or lend for short periods of time, typically up to 12 months. Unlike a centralised exchange, such as the London Stock Exchange (LSE) or the New York Stock Exchange (NYSE), there is no central hub where the activities take place. The money markets are similar to other electronic networks, including the foreign exchange (FX) market, in being decentralised and exist in what is sometimes called a 'distributed form', which is enabled by electronic networks of communication.

The short-term financial instruments which are found in the money markets, and which will be characterised below, are commonly called paper. This contrasts with the capital market for longer- term funding which deals primarily in longer-term bonds and equity.

The core of the money market consists of banks borrowing and lending to each other, using commercial paper, repurchase agreements and similar instruments. These instruments are often benchmarked to (ie, priced by reference to) the LIBOR for the appropriate term and currency.

The normal definition of money market instruments encompasses instruments with a maturity of under one year. However, in reality, longer-dated instruments can also be dealt with in the money market. Given the short maturities of the instruments, there is a tendency for them to be discount securities, issued at a discount to par, rather than carrying a coupon. While it is possible for some of the securities to be in registered form, the conventional approach is for these securities to be in bearer form. The simplest of all money market instruments is cash.

3.2 Money Market Participants

3.2.1 The Bank of England (BoE)

As with the gilt-edged market, which handles the large amounts of government bonds which are used to finance budget deficits, the BoE is a key player in the money markets; however, the Bank's role here is different, focusing much more on the implementation of policy than the raising of finance. It is through open-market operations within the money markets that the bank is able to influence the direction of interest rates and implement its broader monetary policy targets.

The BoE is also known as the lender of last resort, whereby the Bank ensures that the money market will not fail to meet its obligations. The Bank will, however, step in when there is a systemic risk to the market. The Bank acted as lender of last resort to Northern Rock when it got into difficulties during 2007 and provided even more extensive support to the money markets during the financial crisis of Q4, 2008.

3.2.2 Commercial Banks

The principal users of the money markets are the commercial banks, which use the market to trade their own liquidity positions. In very simplistic terms, a bank takes deposits from its customers and then lends the money on to borrowers and makes its profits from the difference or spread between the deposit and lending rates. The BoE and the Bank for International Settlements (BIS) have mandated certain capital adequacy provisions which require that each bank shall retain a proportion of its deposits in the form of liquid assets.

The exact requirements in terms of capital adequacy have been reviewed in the wake of the banking crisis of 2008 and the sovereign debt crisis of 2010–11. The requirements involve somewhat complex accounting principles which go beyond the scope of this workbook (for example, Basel III rules).

There are also many foreign and investment banks which do not have access to a branch network in the UK and therefore need to obtain deposits via the wholesale rather than retail markets – hence, the frequently used term for the money markets, the 'interbank market'.

The role of building societies and smaller banks without a sizeable deposit base, which arises from having an extensive retail network of branches, was one of the contributory factors to the problems faced by Northern Rock which relied on the wholesale money market to fund its liquidity. When the money markets became illiquid owing to the fears that certain institutions might fail, the wholesale money market ceased to function and almost caused a financial meltdown in October 2008.

3.2.3 Companies

In addition to the banks (and financial institutions), large companies, often referred to as corporates, are also involved in the market, partly obtaining short-term flexible finance, but also using the derivative instruments to **hedge** their interest rate exposure. AIG, the large US insurance company, was a major player in the US money market and its collapse created very large problems for the world's derivatives markets and required a rescue by the US government of approximately $200 billion.

3.2.4 Institutional Investors

Pension funds, insurance companies and other fund managers will maintain a portion of the fund in the form of cash and near-cash instruments. The money markets provide an obvious and safe channel through which these liquid assets can be made to generate a return.

3.2.5 Intermediaries

Opportunities always exist for traders to intermediate between buyer and seller, exploiting anomalies in the relative prices of the instruments. The most important intermediaries in the market are the deposit brokers.

These firms act as inter-dealer brokers (IDBs) for the banking market. If a bank receives a large deposit in a particular currency, it may not wish to take the full exposure onto its book. Or indeed, the bank may not be allowed to take the full exposure under the bank's prudential supervision rules. It is able to offload the position through the market via currency deposit brokers (CDBs).

The initial market for these brokers is anonymous. Terms are requested for a borrower, and when a potential lender has provided a rate, this rate is communicated to the underlying borrower. If the rate is acceptable to the borrower, the name is passed to the lender. At this stage, the lender can reject the name on the basis that the lending bank's book is already at its limit to the borrower in question. If the name is rejected, the potential borrower will be informed only that the rate was withdrawn without being told of the counterparty. Once the name has been accepted, the names are passed to both sides of the deal.

With the introduction of the repo market (discussed below) a number of repo dealers have emerged. Most of these intermediaries started as adjuncts to the large bond trading desks at large banks. Initially, they acted as an interface between the needs of the bond trading desks and the larger institutional client of the firm, effectively borrowing funds on a secured basis from the cash-rich institutions. This role then extended to stock-borrowing activity through the reverse repo (also discussed in section 3.4 below).

The secured nature of the repo transaction has led to it becoming one of the principal ways in which the institutions lend their excess cash to the market. Estimates now suggest that over half of the overnight lending which takes place in the market is through repo.

It is from this primarily interbank market that key reference interest rates are produced.

The key reference rate is LIBOR. Thus far, due to the dominance of London as an international banking centre, rate fixing has not been limited to sterling, extending to most internationally-traded currencies. Consequently, many floating-rate deals have been priced off LIBOR rates set in London.

3.3 Money Market Instruments

3.3.1 Bills of Exchange

A bill of exchange (also called a draft) is commonly used in international trade. It is an instrument that is drawn and issued by a supplier or seller of goods to a customer. It specifies an amount to be paid immediately or at some future date. An acceptance of the bill is usually required by the supplier or seller and this acceptance is provided by a bank for a fee. The accepted bill may then be offered by the supplier or seller of the goods on a discounted basis in the money markets.

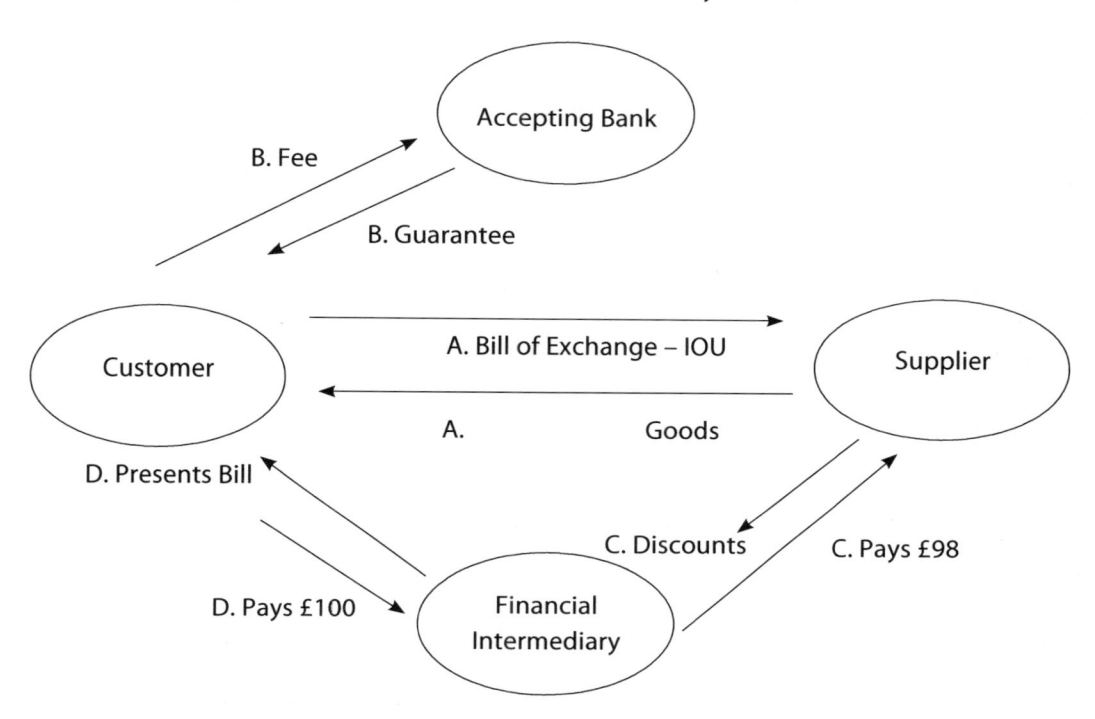

The diagram above shows the manner in which a bill of exchange works and it is instructive to go through the steps involved.

1. A supplier sends goods to a customer who then sends a bill of exchange back to the supplier. Let us assume that the IOU is to pay £100 in 91 days.
2. The supplier has an IOU but no security or guarantee that the bill will be paid. To provide the necessary comfort, the supplier insists that the customer has to get the bill 'accepted'.
3. The bill is accepted when a third party, such as a bank, guarantees to honour the bill if the customer is unable to fulfil the obligation to pay (ie, defaults). The bank will require the customer to pay a fee for 'accepting' the bill and supplying the guarantee.
4. The supplier, having received the accepted bill, could wait for 91 days to receive the £100 from the customer or from the bank in the case of a default.

5. Alternatively, the supplier can sell the bill or the paper into the money market. The supplier would sell the bill at a discount to another participant in the money market who would then wait for the remaining period of the 91 days to collect from the customer or the accepting bank.
6. The financial institution will have a yield exactly identical with the situation described previously for a T-bill, ie, an annualised rate of 8.08%.

3.3.2 Short Gilts

Issued by the government of the UK, short gilts are short term and exceedingly secure as they are guaranteed by the UK government. With their status as relatively risk-free investments, the money market also trades short-term gilts (normally in market terms with less than five years to redemption).

The banks are required to hold a proportion of their assets in the form of liquid investments, and so are active in the short gilts market. This is because, while offering a competitive return, the gilts are also highly liquid, enabling the banks to realise their positions immediately, if necessary.

Other types of low-risk debt are also traded through the money markets, including local authority issues and highly rated corporate issues. Floating rate notes (FRNs), which are linked to the short-term money market rates, are widely traded. The market favours those issued by banks and building societies, since they are perceived to carry less credit risk.

Zero coupon bonds (ZCBs) pay no interest. Instead, they promise to pay just the nominal value at redemption. As there is no other possible form of return, investors will pay less than the nominal value when they buy ZCBs, with their return coming in the form of the difference between the price they pay for the bond and the amount they receive when the bond is redeemed. The bond is said to be issued at a discount to its face value, with the discount providing all of the return on a ZCB.

Commercial paper is a money market instrument issued by a company. Commercial paper is the corporate equivalent of a T-bill. It is typically zero coupon, issued at a discount to nominal value, offering no security and has a life of around three months.

Large companies issue commercial paper to assist in the management of their liquidity. Rather than borrowing directly from banks, these large entities run commercial paper programmes that are placed with institutional investors.

The various companies' commercial paper is differentiated by credit ratings – when the large credit rating agencies, such as Standard & Poor's (S&P), Moody's Investor Services and Fitch Ratings, assess the stability of the issuer.

Asset-backed commercial paper is a short-term investment vehicle with a maturity that is typically between 90 and 180 days. The security itself will be issued by a bank or other financial institution and the notes are backed by physical assets, such as trade receivables or commercial property or even credit card receivables.

Finance companies will typically provide consumers with home loans, unsecured personal loans and retail automobile loans. These receivables are then used by the finance company as collateral for raising money in the commercial paper market. Some finance companies are wholly owned subsidiaries of industrial firms that provide financing for purchases of the parent firm's products.

During the financial crisis in Q4 2008, the commercial paper and asset-backed paper sectors of the money markets became effectively frozen as there was no liquidity in the marketplace. Banks were unwilling to accept any collateral other than government paper because of fears as to the solvency of the issuers of commercial paper.

The BoE, as the lender of last resort, had to intermediate in the money market and accept a wider variety of collateral – such as commercial paper – than it had previously been willing to accept, as security for providing short-term liquidity to the commercial banks and other institutions which required cash and liquidity for their ongoing operations.

3.4 Repurchase Agreements and the Repo Market

A repurchase agreement (also known as a repo or sale and repurchase agreement) allows a borrower to use a financial security as collateral for a cash loan at a fixed rate of interest. Some of the most commonly used securities are gilts which are nearing maturity, T-bills and bank bills which are essentially bills of exchange, that have been accepted by a bank approved by the BoE.

In a repo, the borrower immediately agrees to sell the security to a lender and also agrees to buy back (ie, to repurchase) the same security from the lender at a fixed price at a later date. A repo is equivalent to a cash transaction combined with a forward contract. The cash transaction results in a transfer of money to the borrower in exchange for legal transfer of the security to the lender, while the forward contract ensures repayment of the loan to the lender and return of the collateral of the borrower. The difference between the forward price and the spot price is the interest on the loan, while the settlement date of the forward contract is the maturity date of the loan.

A repo is legally binding for both buyer and seller. For example, a gilt repo is a contract in which the seller of gilts agrees to buy them back at a future specified time and price. In effect, a gilt repo is a means of borrowing, using the gilt as security. The advantage of the very active market in gilt repos that holders of such paper are able to raise finance against the security of the gilts that they hold – potentially, a relatively cheap source of short-term finance. In this way, gilt repo facilitates the smooth running of the secondary market in gilts.

The smooth running of the gilts market is further assisted by the DMO's standing repo facility. This enables any gilt-edged market maker (GEMM) or other DMO counterparty to enter into a reverse repo arrangement with the DMO, perhaps to cover a short position in gilts. This facility is for next-day settlement and the facility can be rolled forwards for up to two weeks. The DMO charges a slightly higher than normal repo rate for firms accessing the standing repo facility.

Although the gilt market has been used as an example, it should be noted that the use of repos is an important liquidity provider for other instruments that are widely accepted in the money market.

3.4.1 Overnight Market

The overnight market is the sector of the money market involving the shortest-term loans. Lenders agree to lend borrowers funds only overnight, ie, the borrower must repay the borrowed funds plus interest at the start of business the next day.

Most of the activity in the overnight market in fact occurs in the morning immediately after the start of business for the day. A typical day at a cash management group for a deposit-taking financial institution begins with forecasting the institution's clients' liquidity needs over the course of that day. If this projection is that the institution's clients will need more money over the course of the day than the institution has on hand, the institution will borrow money on the overnight market that day. On the other hand, if the analyst projects that the institution will have surplus money on hand beyond that needed by its clients that day, it will lend money on the overnight market that day.

Banks are the largest participant in the overnight market, although some other large financial institutions also buy and sell on the overnight market as a way to manage unanticipated cash needs or as a temporary haven for money until the institution can decide on where to invest that money.

4. Treasury Bills

Learning Objective

5.3 Explain, calculate and appraise the investment performance of Treasury bills

Treasury bills, or T-bills as they are commonly known, are short-term loan instruments, guaranteed by the UK government, with a maturity date of less than one year at issue. Generally, they are issued with one month, three months or six months to redemption, with the three-month T-bill the most common. They pay no coupon and, consequently, are issued at a discount to their nominal value, the discount representing the return available to the investor. Gilts are the UK equivalent to US Treasury securities. Gilts generally have longer maturities and also pay coupons twice a year (an equal amount every six months).

Since April 1998, the issuance of UK government debt – T-bills and gilts primarily – is handled by the DMO on behalf of HM Treasury. The DMO took over gilt issuance from the BoE, following the transfer of responsibility for setting interest rates from HM Treasury to the Bank in May 1997.

Sterling T-bills form an important constituent in the DMO's exchequer cash management operations and an intrinsic component in the UK government's stock of marketable debt instruments, alongside gilts. T-bills are zero-coupon eligible debt securities and can be held in CREST and Euroclear.

UK T-bills are issued at weekly auctions, known as tenders, held by the DMO at the end of the week (usually a Friday). These tenders are open to bids from a group of eligible bidders which include the major banks. The bids are tendered competitively – only those bidding a high enough price will be allocated any T-bills and they will pay the price that they bid. The bids must be for a minimum of £500,000 nominal of the T-bills and, above this level, bids must be made in multiples of £50,000. In subsequent trading, the minimum denomination of T-bills is £25,000.

Since they are guaranteed by the government, T-bills provide a very secure investment for market participants with short-term investment horizons. The return on a T-bill is wholly dependent upon the price paid, and the way to calculate the effective yield will be illustrated below.

The T-bill primary participants are banks that have agreed to bid at T-bill tenders on behalf of investors. They are registered financial institutions that are regulated by the FCA and PRA and subject to their rules and guidance in their activities. These firms also provide secondary market dealing levels for T-bills.

Calculating Yields on T-Bills

The principal measures used to evaluate T-bills are as follows:

$$\text{Discount rate} = \frac{100 - \text{Discounted Value}}{100 \times \text{Days}/365}$$

The yield of a T-bill can be derived by using the following formula:

$$\text{Yield} = \frac{100 - \text{Discounted Value}}{\text{Discounted Value} \times \text{Days}/365}$$

An alternative formulation for deriving the yield is:

$$\text{Yield} = \frac{\text{Discounted Rate}}{1 - (\text{Discounted Value} \times \text{Days}/365)}$$

As an example, consider the yield of a T-bill issued at 98 for 91 days:

$$\text{Interest Rate or Yield} = \frac{100 - 98}{98 \times 91/365} = 0.0818 \text{ or } 8.18\%$$

5. Effect of Inflation

Learning Objective

5.4 Explain and evaluate the effect of inflation on the investment risk and return of short-term, liquid instruments

Cash deposits earn interest but there is no capital growth. Interest is commonly paid as a percentage of the capital invested at variable interest rates, or at fixed-term rates over a set period.

Investment performance of a cash deposit should be adjusted by the rate of inflation in order to derive a real rate of return (ROR).

Using an example, if the annual interest is paid at 5%, the rate of inflation is 2%, then the real ROR is in the region of 3%; this means that the purchasing power of the cash investment is increasing at around 3% per annum.

Interest rates on cash deposits tend to move closely with rates of interest on borrowing, assuming a broadly consistent interest rate spread between them. Interest rates move competitively, generally in line with the short-term base rate of interest set by the BoE's Monetary Policy Committee (MPC).

As deposit takers are in competition with each other, their interest rates set on different deposit products will reflect the competitive market conditions which can change even before the official base rate.

A study by Barclays Capital shows that £100 invested in cash deposits since 1899, with income reinvested, would have grown to just £256 by the end of 2016, after adjusting for inflation. The same amount invested in gilts would have grown to £454. £100 invested in equities (shares) with dividends reinvested would have grown to £28,226 over the same period, in real terms. This study does not of course take account of the significantly higher risk associated with investment in equities, compared with gilts or cash.

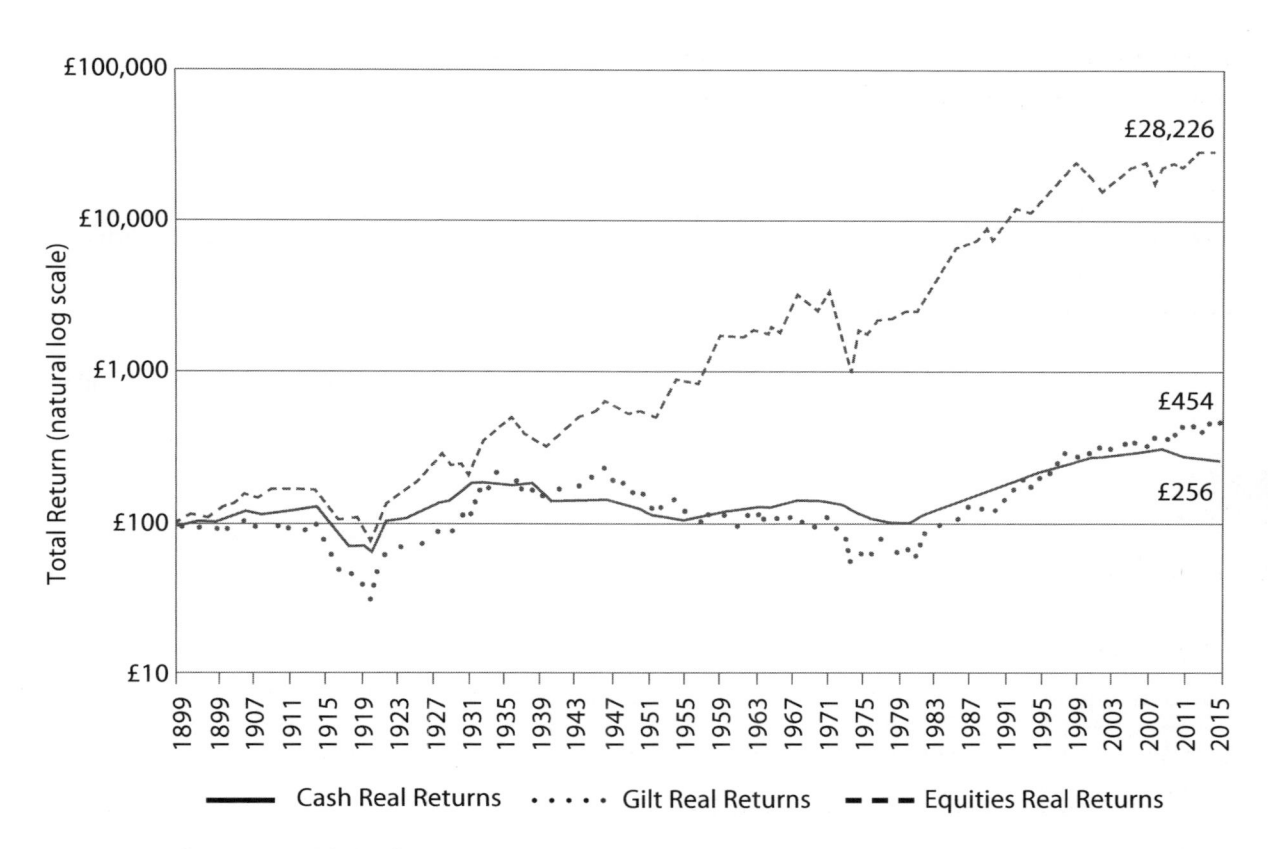

Liquidity Description, Risk, Return Characteristics

[Chart: Total Return (natural log scale) from 1899 to 2015, showing Cash Real Returns (£256), Gilt Real Returns (£454), and Equities Real Returns (£28,226)]

Source: Barclays Equity Gilt Study 2016

However, over shorter-term periods, such as years in which share prices fall, cash deposits may outperform equities. The lower risk of cash deposits can be an important consideration for investments at such times and over short periods, as long as the timing of major price swings in other asset classes is accurately foreseen.

The calculation of real ROR that could be applied to an investment is:

$$\text{Real rate of return} = \frac{1 + \text{nominal rate of return}}{1 + \text{inflation rate}} - 1$$

The nominal rate is the stated rate, or normal return, which is not adjusted for inflation. The rate of inflation is calculated based on the changes in price indices which are the price on a group of goods. A commonly used price index is the consumer price index (CPI). A quick calculation for an approximate real ROR similar to the calculation above is the nominal rate minus the inflation rate. The CPI and nominal rates were discussed in chapter 1.

One of the primary advantages of holding cash deposits with banks and building societies is that of relative liquidity, as explained earlier. This assumes that such cash will, before long, be utilised for some unforeseen need or perhaps for an anticipated investment opportunity. This advantage must be weighed against the minimal real ROR of cash deposits, so both the amounts committed to cash deposits and the length of time invested must be carefully considered.

In recent years, inflation in some countries has turned to deflation, if only briefly. This has caused even nominal rates of return to become negative on some accounts, as some banks have found themselves unable to lend such short-term funds on to borrowers for longer periods at higher rates. This might suggest weak levels of investment confidence, but such negative nominal rates focus attention on what is a normal problem of poor real rates of return. Five central banks have moved their benchmark short-term interest rates below zero (ie, negative) in the last few years (the ECB plus Swiss, Swedish and Danish central banks and the Bank of Japan). These central banks effectively charge commercial banks to deposit cash with them overnight. Since market rates are effectively set by central banks, the effect is, theoretically, to penalise banks for not lending funds at low rates to encourage commercial investment. The reality may, however, be to signal that monetary authorities are running out of policies to stimulate demand for investment and hence recovery from the effects of the global financial crisis.

Exercise Answers

Exercise 1

Two different deposit accounts provide the following ROR:

Deposit A: Pays 2% compound per quarter over two years.

Deposit B: Pays 8.5% compound per annum over two years.

Calculate which account pays the highest overall return.

Answer:

Deposit A: $1.02^8 = 1.1716 = 17.16\%$ return

Deposit B: $1.085^2 = 1.1772 = 17.72\%$ return

Deposit B provides the highest return.

Chapter Six
Bonds

1.	**Characteristics of Bonds**	**233**
2.	**Government Bonds**	**238**
3.	**Corporate Bonds**	**251**
4.	**Bond Pricing**	**261**
5.	**Calculating Bond Returns**	**273**
6.	**Interest Rates and Bonds**	**288**
7.	**Risk Management of Bond Investments**	**302**

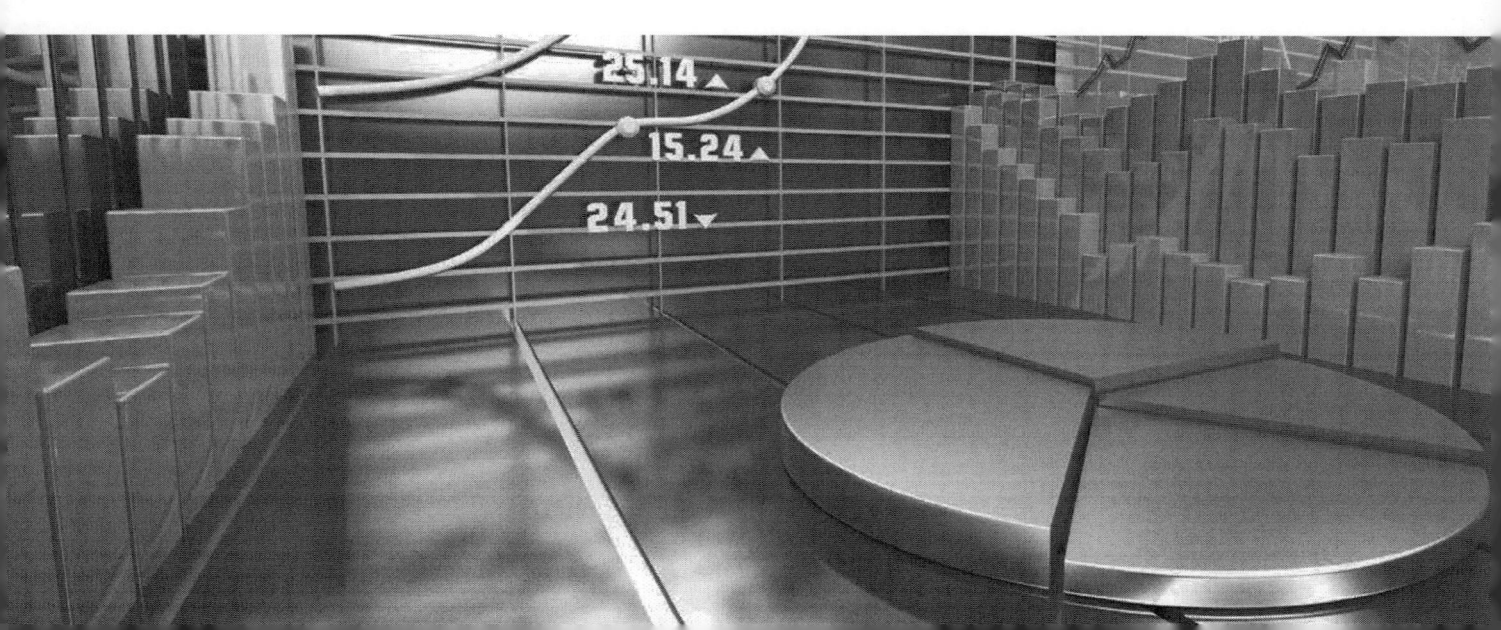

Learning Outcome

Be able to evaluate critically the risks and returns offered by bonds

1. Characteristics of Bonds

Learning Objective

6.1 Explain the characteristics of bonds: definition, types, and key properties of bonds; risk, price, and return; historic performance of bonds; principal problems and liquidity issues, plus implications should liquidity fall; maturities and redemption characteristics; coupons

1.1 Definition, Types and Key Properties

The term 'bonds', 'fixed-income securities', or 'fixed-interest securities', is given to securities that pay a pre-specified or fixed return in the form of capital and income. Following the more widely adopted usage, such securities are also collectively called 'bonds'.

A bond is essentially an IOU issued by a borrower (known as the issuer) in return for the money lent to it by the buyer (known as the holder) for a fixed period and usually with a fixed rate of return or interest. The two principal types of issuer are corporations and governments.

The nominal value of a bond, also known as the face value or par value, is the amount that the issuer will pay back to the holder of the bond at redemption.

The redemption date is when the borrower agrees to repay the nominal value of the bond. It is also referred to as the maturity date.

Bonds provide to the holder a contractual stream of income from the issuer. It comprises a periodic coupon payment (often paid on a semi-annual basis), which is the interest that the borrower pays to the holder, expressed as a percentage rate of the nominal value.

Historically, bonds began as simple negotiable debt instruments, paying a fixed coupon for a specified period, then being redeemed at face value – the term 'straight bond' still describes the plain vanilla version of bonds with the simplest characteristics.

Bonds rank ahead of equities in terms of repayment to creditors in cases of liquidation. As a consequence of this relatively lower risk, the expected returns on bonds are lower than those on equities. Bond are therefore considered investment vehicles for cautious investors and the term 'widows and orphans' is sometimes applied to the class of individuals for which fixed-income securities are deemed most suitable.

The 1970s was a period of momentous changes in the world's financial system, including the abandonment of convertibility of dollars into gold; the end of many fixed currency exchange rates; the emergence of serious inflation which required continuing adjustments of interest rates; the development of the euro currency markets (ie, markets in US dollar and other currency assets based outside of their home jurisdictions); and early innovations in financial markets, including futures, swaps and other derivatives. The volatility in interest rates, commodity prices and currencies enabled global bond markets to emerge as appropriate hedging instruments during the 1970s and, since then, they have become more complex investments, with many variations on the basic straight-bond theme.

1.2 Bond Issuers

Bonds are used by issuers as a means of raising finance. Major bond issuers include:

- Sovereign governments who need to finance budget deficits and to cover national debt obligations. As previously issued bonds reach maturity and are redeemed, these governments issue further new bonds to replace them.
- Local authorities that need to raise finance to help cover any local budget shortfall.
- Companies borrow to fund long-term expansion, particularly as an alternative to diluting existing shareholdings via issuing equities.
- Supranational bodies like the International Monetary Fund (IMF) and the World Bank also issue bonds to fund long-term international development projects.

Regardless of the issuer, there are a number of general characteristics that any bond are likely to share.

1.3 Nominal Value

All bonds are issued with a fixed principal amount or nominal value (also known as face value or par value), which remains with the bond for its life, unlike its market value which fluctuates. On UK bonds, the nominal value is normally £100, and therefore bond prices are quoted on this basis.

The nominal or par value facilitates the calculation of yields, ie, coupon payments are usually a percentage of the nominal value, enabling the calculation of the net present value (NPV) of the cash flows and redemption proceeds.

1.4 Specified Maturity Date

The maturity date is when the nominal value of most bonds is repaid by the issuer. Prior to that date (and to the redemption of the principal), it can be traded on a secondary market.

Over time, variations of these vanilla parameters have been developed, including the following.

1.5 Irredeemable/Perpetual Bonds

These bonds are undated, ie, there is no maturity date and the issuer is under no obligation to redeem the principal sum, though they may have the right to do so if they wish.

- On these bonds, the coupon is thus paid in perpetuity.
- The UK Government has issued such perpetual bonds known as consols.

1.6 Redeemable Bonds

Most bonds redeem at the nominal value only, on the maturity date when the proceeds are repaid.

Occasionally, the issuer may be given the right to repay the bond at an earlier date, or on a range of earlier dates. Such bonds are known as callable, because the issuer has the right to '**call**' the bond back and redeem it prior to maturity. The bond issuer is likely to call the bond back when the cost of replacement finance is cheaper than the interest rate being paid on the callable bond.

The UK Government has issued a particular type of callable bond known as a double-dated gilt. These gilts are issued with two maturity dates and the Government (via the Debt Management Office (DMO)) can give notice and choose to redeem these gilts on any day between the first and final maturity dates.

In contrast to callable bonds, some issuers give the holders of their bonds the right to sell their bonds back to the issuer, prior to maturity. These are referred to as putable bonds.

1.7 Most Bonds Have Coupons

While there is a variety of bond known as zero coupon bonds which are issued at a discount to their face value and do not pay out coupons, the vast majority of bonds are issued with a periodic payment obligation embedded in the instrument. These periodic payments are known as coupon payments.

The basis for the determination of the bond coupon is set before issue, although this does not mean that the value is known at that date. While the vast majority of bonds issued are straights (ie, a fixed coupon), there are a numerous variations.

Some bonds have coupons which vary with economic factors, some are index-linked to protect the bondholder from inflation and some have more esoteric features which can alter the amount of the coupon payment based upon other factors. The majority of bonds are issued with a predetermined value for the coupon, but many are subject to variability in the amount of the coupon payment to be made.

One example of coupons that are subject to some variability is the floating-rate bond, when the coupons are typically linked to a reference interest rate at the time, such as LIBOR. Clearly if LIBOR increases, the coupons will increase and vice versa for falls in LIBOR.

Another example is an index-linked bond when the coupons and usually the principal vary by reference to an index of inflation, such as the retail price index (RPI).

However the amount is calculated, the full coupon for the period will be paid to the holder of the bond on the ex-dividend date. Bonds with predetermined coupons are the most common.

On these bonds, the gross annual coupon (ie, the amount due to be paid in a one-year period, irrespective of the frequency of payment) is specified as a percentage of the nominal value of the bond.

How often the coupon is paid is determined at issue. The frequency is typically every six months or once each year. Occasionally, coupons are paid quarterly, rather than annually or semi-annually.

The frequency tends to be consistent in certain sectors of the bond market. For example, the UK, US, Japanese and Italian government bonds tend to pay coupons semi-annually. The government bonds issued by Germany and France, and most eurobonds, tend to pay coupons annually.

1.8 Stripped Bonds

Normally, the holder of the bond receives all of the asset flows from that bond throughout its life to the maturity date.

The practice has also developed, especially in the US of stripping the coupons and the bond apart, so that the holder of the underlying bond may receive the redemption proceeds, while another person may hold the entitlement to receive the cash flow or coupons. The holder of the redemption amount is in effect in the same position as the purchaser of a zero coupon bond, whereas the person receiving the coupons is in an analogous position to the holder of an annuity.

1.9 Redemption at Maturity

Bonds may be issued that will not redeem at maturity; these are known as an irredeemable or a perpetuity. Most bonds are redeemed, but there are a few variations. The vast majority of bonds are redeemed in cash at maturity. This redemption may be either:

- at **par value** – redeemed at the nominal value of the bond at the redemption date
- at a **premium** – redeemed at a specified premium above the nominal value of the bond at the redemption date.

Other variations exist when instead of obliging the issuer to repay cash at the maturity date the bond may offer the holder the choice between normal cash redemption proceeds and some other asset, such as an alternative bond of a later maturity or shares issued by a corporation.

1.10 Spreads

Commentators often refer to spreads in bond markets. A spread is simply the difference between the yield available on one instrument and the yield available elsewhere. It is usually expressed in basis points, with each basis point representing 1/100 of 1%.

Spreads are commonly measured between the yields on different bonds. For example, if a ten-year corporate bond is yielding 6% and the equivalent ten-year gilt (UK government bond) is yielding 4.2%, the spread over the government bond is 6% – 4.2% = 1.8% or 180 basis points. This spread will vary, mainly as a result of the relative risk of the corporate bond compared to the gilt; so, for a more risky corporate issuer, the spread will be wider. Such spreads are used as indicators of changes in risk sentiment on the basis that the wider the spread versus the risk-free government bond yield, the greater the perceived risk. This applies also in risk sentiment between bond yields of different governments, eg, of eurozone government bonds versus the lower perceived risk of German government bonds.

Spreads are also calculated against other benchmarks, such as the published interest rates represented by LIBOR.

Spreads of bond yields versus equity yields are keenly observed as indicators of changing sentiment and of relative value and are thus actively traded within multi-asset portfolios.

1.11 Convertible Bonds

Some companies or corporate issuers of bonds provide conversion rights with their bond issue and these are known as 'convertible' bonds. A convertible bond gives the holder the right, but not the obligation, to convert the bond into a predetermined number of ordinary shares of the issuer.

In recent years, contingent convertible (CoCo) bonds have become a popular form of issuance, particularly from financial institutions. A CoCo bond is a fixed-income instrument that is convertible into equity if a pre-specified trigger event occurs. Such an event could be the institution, (eg, bank) meeting a certain measure of solvency.

Given this choice, the holder will choose to convert into shares if, at maturity, the value of the shares they can convert into exceeds the redemption value of the bond. However, as there is this upside potential to the value of a convertible bond if the share price rises, and the downside protection of the redemption value if the shares do not perform well, convertible bonds generally trade at a premium to their share value.

The calculation of the premium is shown by the following example.

Example

A convertible bond issued by XYZ plc is trading at £114. It offers the holder the option of converting £100 nominal into 25 ordinary shares of the company. These shares are currently trading at £3.90.

Calculate the premium of the convertible over the value of the shares. For £100 nominal, this is equal to 25 times £3.90 or £97.50.

The bond is currently trading at £114 so the premium at present is £114 − £97.50 = £16.50.

It is common to express the premium as a percentage of the conversion value so this convertible has a premium of £16.50 ÷ £97.50 or 16.9%.

Convertible bonds enable the holder to exploit the growth potential in the equity while retaining the safety net of the bond. It is for this reason that convertible bonds trade at a premium to the value of the shares they can convert into. If there were no premium, then there would be an arbitrage opportunity for investors to buy the shares more cheaply via the convertible than in the equity market.

Usually, convertible bonds are issued where the price of each share is set at the outset and that price will be adjusted to take into account any subsequent bonus or rights issues. Given the share price, it is simple to calculate the conversion ratio – the number of shares that each £100 of nominal value of the bonds can convert into.

$$\text{Conversion ratio} = \frac{\text{Nominal value}}{\text{Conversion price of shares}}$$

If the issuing company has a 1-for-1 bonus issue, then the conversion price would halve and the conversion ratio would double.

1.12 Summary of Influences on Bond Prices

Although this topic is dealt with in more detail below, there are generic factors which affect the pricing of bonds in the secondary market.

In most cases, the income (coupon) from a bond remains the same through its life. However, during the life of the bond, there are many factors, especially inflation and changes in the interest rate environment, that can make it more or less attractive to investors. These factors lead to the price of bonds in the secondary market changing.

If investors see interest rates rising, the prices of bonds will fall. There is thus an inverse relation between the yield of a bond and its price. The reason is that investors require a particular rate of return (ROR), depending upon rates of interest generally. If interest rates rise, investors' required ROR rises. They are prepared to pay less for a particular bond with a fixed-coupon rate than previously. If interest rates generally fall, then investors are willing to pay more for a fixed-rate bond than previously, and bond prices tend to rise.

Investors generally require a higher return if the rate of inflation is expected to rise. Therefore, prices of fixed-rate bonds tend to fall with rising expectations of inflation. However, index-linked bonds have a coupon that is linked to the inflation rate, with the result that the price of index-linked stock will tend to rise as higher inflation is expected.

2. Government Bonds

Learning Objective

6.2 Explain the characteristics of UK and overseas government bonds: issuance; secondary markets; types of bond; repo market; borrowing/lending; trading and settlement

2.1 Government Debt

2.1.1 Introduction

Most developed countries have active markets for bonds issued by their government.

In the UK, for example, gilts are bonds issued by the government to fund its borrowing needs. The UK Treasury has created an executive agency, the DMO, to issue, service and manage gilts on its behalf.

In the US, the US Treasury is the central agency which handles the wide array of securities that are issued by the US Government in the form of Treasury bonds, notes and bills; and US Government debt includes the issue from various government sponsored entities (GSEs) which also involve asset-backed securities.

In the EU, each country retains sovereign control over its own debt, even among members of the eurozone. Prior to the introduction of the euro in 1999, the yields on government bonds issued by countries which appeared likely to be members had been converging towards the yields of bonds issued by Germany, long considered to be the effective European benchmark. This suggested that investors believed not only in monetary union via the euro, but also in eventual economic union through a minimal difference on the perceived risk of holding one country's debt over another's. Immediately prior to the 2007 onset of the global financial crisis, the yields on some European government bonds actually fell briefly below those of Germany. The subsequent change in sentiment towards peripheral European risk (eg, Portugal, Ireland, Italy, Greece and Spain) was quickly reflected in a dramatic widening of the spread between those bonds and the German benchmark. These government yield spreads remain an important benchmark of risk appetite in European markets in general.

As with corporate bonds, UK gilts are issued with a given nominal value that will be repaid at the bond's redemption date and a coupon rate representing the percentage of the nominal value that will be paid to the holder of the bond each year. Different gilts can have different redemption dates and the coupon is payable at different points of the year (generally, at semi-annual intervals).

2.1.2 UK Government Bonds – Gilts (and Sovereign Debt Globally)

Governments, including the UK Government, issue bonds to raise money to cover budget deficits. This results from the government consistently spending more money than the revenue it collects via taxes. As the UK has a high credit rating it is able to borrow substantial amounts from the global investors with a wide range of maturities. Due to the relatively high credit ratings of many countries and huge issuances, the sovereign debt markets are the largest actively-traded bond markets in the world and are considered to have the greatest liquidity.

2.1.3 Credit Ratings of Sovereign Borrowers

Many governments have the highest credit ratings which are issued by the big three global credit ratings agencies – S&P, Moody's Investors Service, and Fitch Ratings. S&P and Fitch Ratings' highest rating is AAA; for Moody's Investors Service it is Aaa. The German, Swiss and Canadian Governments, among others, have the highest credit ratings available from these agencies.

The cutting of a credit rating makes it more expensive for governments to raise money with their sovereign bond issues, as it requires higher repayments to attract investors who may, for example, perceive more risk in a Greek Government bond than in a German Government one.

2.1.4 Sovereign Issuance

Historically, gilts were issued and managed by the BoE on behalf of the UK Government; however, since 1997 this role has been undertaken by the DMO.

Consider an issue which the DMO first offered in September 2016:

Name	Treasury
Coupon	1.50%
Maturity	22 July 2047
Market Price (as at June 2018)	£94.31

Each stock bears a title. Treasury, Exchequer, Funding, Conversion, Consolidated (Consols) and War Loan are names used to indicate the government department that issued the debt.

Example

As another example, consider the 6% Treasury Stock 2028. The 6% coupon indicates the cash payment per £100 nominal value that the holder will receive each year. This payment is made in two equal semi-annual payments on fixed dates, six months apart. An investor holding £1,000 nominal of 6% Treasury Stock 2028 will receive two coupon payments of £30 each, on 7 June and 7 December each year, until the repayment of the £1,000 on 7 December 2028.

In the UK, as in the US, the convention is for gilt coupons to be paid on a semi-annual basis, in equal instalments.

2.1.5 Maturity

Gilt-edged stocks are classified by their maturity dates and the official DMO definitions are below:

- **short-maturity gilts (Shorts)** – instruments with a residual maturity of up to seven years
- **medium-maturity gilts (Mediums)** – instruments with a residual maturity of between seven and 15 years
- **long-maturity gilts (Longs)** – instruments with a residual maturity of over 15 years.

For example, 4.5% Treasury Stock 2034 would be classified as a long-dated gilt because more than 15 years remain until it reaches its redemption date of 7 September 2034.

2.1.6 Dual-Dated Gilts

Previously, the UK Government issued a number of double-dated gilts. These had a range of maturity dates at the option of the Government. The last remaining double-dated stock was redeemed in December 2013.

Example

If issued, 5% Treasury 2030–34 would enable the DMO to choose to redeem the gilt at the earliest in 2030, and at any time up to the later date of 2034.

What would make the government redeem early or late?

The answer is dependent upon the interest rates at the time. If, in 2030, the interest rate that the DMO would have to pay to provide the funds for redemption was only 4%, then it would redeem at the earliest point – saving 1% per annum. In contrast, if the interest rate was greater than 5%, the DMO would not redeem, potentially, until it was forced to do so in 2034.

2.1.7 Undated Gilts

Until late 2014 there existed eight undated gilts. These made up a relatively small percentage of the UK Government's overall debt. They had no fixed maturity date and many of them were very old. The largest, War Loan, was issued in the early 20th century. The redemption of these bonds was at the discretion of the UK Government. They all had relatively low coupons, and for many years there was no incentive for them to be redeemed by the Government. In addition, there was a limited market for these issues due to the levels of their outstanding debt.

In late 2014 and early 2015, the Government gave notice that four of these gilts, including War Loan, would be redeemed in early 2015. The four remaining gilts were redeemed on 5 July 2015.

2.1.8 Price

This is quoted in terms of the amount that an investor would have to pay in order to buy £100 nominal of the stock. The price is quoted in pounds and pence (decimal terms).

2.1.9 Yield

Yield calculations are considered later (see section 5), but in terms of data published daily in the financial media, both the flat and gross redemption yield (GRY) are published. By convention, the yield figure shown for gilts is twice the six-monthly yield, and not the six-monthly yield compounded.

In an example of a 4% gilt, the government pays a fixed coupon at 4% pa until maturity. The market value of a straight, fixed-coupon bond may vary significantly as interest rates vary. This is to be expected since, as interest rates rise and fall, the fixed-coupon rate will become less or more attractive.

2.1.10 Variable Coupon Gilts

The advantage of a floating-rate bond is that the coupon rate is always at a fair level regardless of the prevailing rates of interest which results in the current price of the bond (if purchased or sold in the secondary market) remaining at or around par. Thus, a floating-rate bond protects the nominal value of the investment. There are currently no variable coupon gilts in issue.

2.1.11 Index-Linked Gilts

Index-linked gilts differ from conventional gilts in that the coupon payments and the principal are adjusted in line with a published index of price inflation, such as the UK RPI. This means that both the coupons and the principal on redemption paid by these bonds are adjusted to take account of inflation since the bond's issue. Assuming inflation is positive, the nominal amount outstanding of an index-linked bond is less than the redemption value the government will pay on maturity.

To calculate the inflation adjustment, two index figures are required: that applicable to the stock when it was originally issued and that relating to the current interest payment. For UK gilts, (historically the index is the RPI but may change to the CPI in future issues), the figures used are those applicable eight months before the relevant dates (eg, for a December coupon, the previous April RPI data is used). This indexation lag is required so that the size of each forthcoming interest payment is known at the start of the coupon period, thereby allowing accrued interest to be calculated.

In September 2005, the DMO launched an improved design for any new index-linked gilts; this uses a shorter (three-month) indexation lag than that used in earlier index-linked gilts.

Every six months, the coupon payment on an index-linked gilt (ILG) consists of two elements:

- half of the annual real coupon, and
- an adjustment factor to uplift the real coupon to take inflation into account (as measured by RPI increases post-issue).

The uplifted redemption payment is calculated in a similar fashion, using the RPI from three or eight months earlier, and the RPI applicable to the original issue date.

For example, 2% Index-Linked 2035 pays semi-annual coupons on 26 January and 26 June each year. An investor holding £20,000 nominal will receive 2% of £20,000 x 6 ÷ 12 = £200 each half-year plus the RPI uplift. At the redemption date in 2035, the investor will receive £20,000 uplifted by the RPI increases since issue.

Because these bonds are uplifted by increases in the relevant price index, they are effectively inflation proof. In times of inflation, they will increase in price and preserve the purchasing power of the investment.

In a period of zero inflation, index-linked bonds will pay the coupon rate with no uplift and simply pay back the nominal value at maturity.

2.1.12 Convertible Gilts

Convertible gilts would be issued with an option to convert at a future date (or dates) into longer-dated issues. Alternatively the holder could allow the bond to mature and be repaid the redemption proceeds; however, there are currently no outstanding issues of convertible gilts.

2.1.13 Foreign Currency Debt Issues

The UK Government found it necessary to issue some foreign currency gilts in recent years to finance its foreign currency reserves at the BoE. There are outstanding bonds in US dollars (straight) and also in euros. These bonds are not like ordinary gilts and trade like eurobonds with the same conventions for accrued interest.

2.1.14 STRIPS (Separate Trading of Registered Interest and Principal Securities)

STRIPS is an acronym of separate trading of registered interest and principal securities. Stripping a bond involves trading the interest (each individual coupon) and the principal (the nominal value) separately. Each strip forms the equivalent of a zero coupon bond. It will trade at a discount to its face value, with the size of the discount being determined by prevailing interest rates and time. For example, a STRIPS market has been developed in the UK within the gilts market. Only those gilts that have been designated by the DMO as 'strippable' are eligible for the STRIPS market, not all gilts. Those gilts that are stripped have separate registered entries for each of the individual cash flows that enable different owners to hold each individual strip, and facilitate the trading of the individual strips. Only designated gilt-edged market makers (GEMMs), the Bank of England (BoE) or the Treasury are able to 'strip' gilts.

The key benefits of STRIPS are that investors can precisely match their liabilities, removing any reinvestment risk that is normally faced when covering liabilities with coupon-paying bonds. Furthermore, investors in gilt STRIPS need not worry about the risk that the issuer of the bonds will default – gilt-edged securities are considered to be free of any default risk (also known as credit risk).

2.2 Participants in Government Bond Markets

In addition to the Government's issuing agency, the DMO itself, there are three major groups of participants that facilitate deals in the government bond markets:

- primary dealers – such as GEMMs
- broker-dealers
- inter-dealer brokers (IDBs).

2.2.1 Issuing Agency – Role of DMO

The DMO is the issuing agency for the UK Government. It is an executive agency of the Treasury, making new issues of UK Government securities (gilt-edged securities or gilts). Once issued, the secondary market for dealing in gilts is overseen by two bodies, the DMO and the London Stock Exchange (LSE).

The prime responsibility of the DMO is to ensure that the Government is able to borrow the money it requires to fund the public sector net cash requirement (PSNCR). Issues by the DMO may be for a new gilt with a coupon/maturity dissimilar to any existing issues. Currently, the DMO believes that the range of issues in the market is, if anything, too large and may lead to excessive fragmentation of supply and demand and poor trading liquidity in individual gilts.

In order to avoid this problem, the DMO may issue a tranche of an existing stock. This entails issuing a given amount of nominal value on exactly the same terms as an existing gilt. The DMO refers to this as 'opening up an existing gilt'. The advantages of tranches are that they avoid adding further complexity to the gilt market and increase the liquidity of current issues.

When a tranche is issued, it may be identified by the letter A to indicate that a full coupon may not be paid on the next payment date to reflect the fact that the gilt has only been an issue for part of the coupon period. A small tranche may be referred to as a tranchette.

The DMO is the body that enables certain LSE member firms to act as primary dealers, known as GEMMs. It then leaves it to the LSE to prescribe rules that apply when dealing takes place.

DMO Conducts Auctions for Gilts

Since 1987, the primary method for issuing and selling new gilts became the competitive auctions system. Investors apply for gilts at a price which they are prepared to pay. The DMO issues the gilts to those investors who apply at the highest prices. The key difference to a tender is that all successful applicants pay the price for which they bid, which means that there is not a single price paid as in a tender process.

One of the metrics which is used to judge the 'success' of a government auction is the bid-to-cover ratio which is used to express the demand for a particular security during offerings and auctions. It is computed in two ways: the number of bids received divided by the number of bids accepted, or the total amount of the bids is used instead. It is a metric which is especially followed by financial analysts in the sale of US Treasury bonds and is becoming more of a focus in the DMO's auctions as well.

In general terms, the simple point that needs to be made is that the higher the bid-to-cover ratio in an auction, the higher the demand. A ratio above 2.0 indicates a successful auction comprising of aggressive bids. A low ratio is an indication of a disappointing auction, marked by a higher yield.

Consider the following scenario where the DMO is seeking to raise £10 billion in ten-year notes with a 4.125% coupon.

In order to keep the example simple, and also since the value of the coupon may not have been known exactly prior to the auction, the aggregate number of bids received (which would have been expressed in price terms) would have equated to the following yields shown below:

- £1.00 billion at 4.115%
- £2.50 billion at 4.120%
- £3.50 billion at 4.125%
- £4.50 billion at 4.130%
- £3.75 billion at 4.135%
- £2.75 billion at 4.140%
- £1.50 billion at 4.145%.

The total of all bids received is for £19.5 billion and the number of bids placed when the prices provided by bidders would have equated to a yield at least equivalent to the required coupon value is in excess of the £10 billion on offer. In such a scenario the bid-to-cover ratio can be stated as 1.95 which would be a satisfactory auction result.

Currently, issuance by auction is the DMO's primary funding method. Either new issues or tranches of existing stock can be sold by way of an auction. Running alongside each competitive auction are non-competitive bids when investors can apply for up to £500,000 of nominal value. Applicants through non-competitive bids will receive the gilts they applied for at a weighted average of accepted prices in the auction. Smaller investors can participate in the primary market for gilts, while avoiding the necessity of determining an appropriate price.

2.2.2 Interim Funding or Taps

The Government's current principal method of funding is through regular competitive auctions. However, it may still wish to issue smaller quantities of stock to improve liquidity or improve market efficiency. In such situations, the DMO will sell smaller quantities of stock to investors via the GEMMs.

When tapping stock into secondary markets in this way, the DMO will often introduce a tranche of existing stock, or a tranchette for a smaller amount. Alternatively, it could be as a result of a failed auction when the DMO has not received sufficient applications to account for the nominal value on offer. In such a situation, the remaining stock will be available on tap from the DMO. The DMO defines a tap as an issue of a gilt by the DMO for exceptional market management reasons and not on a pre-announced schedule, so the DMO has the ability to issue gilts in these smaller quantities by tap at short notice, but only for the purposes of market and, therefore, use of taps is restricted to the market management mechanisms in exceptional circumstances.

2.2.3 Gilt-Edged Market Makers (GEMMs)

The GEMM, once vetted by the DMO and registered as with the LSE, becomes a primary dealer and is required to provide two-way quotes to customers (clients known directly to them) and other member firms of the LSE throughout the normal trading day. There is no requirement to use a particular system like the Stock Exchange Automated Quotation System (SEAQ) for making those quotes available to clients, and GEMMs are free to choose how to disseminate their prices.

The obligations of a GEMM can be summarised as follows:

- to make effective two-way prices to customers on demand, up to a size agreed with the DMO, thereby providing liquidity for customers wishing to trade
- to participate actively in the DMO's gilt issuance programme, broadly by bidding competitively in all auctions and achieving allocations commensurate with their secondary market share – effectively, informally agreeing to underwrite gilt auctions
- to provide information to the DMO on closing prices, market conditions and the GEMM's positions and turnover.

The privileges of GEMM status include:

- executive rights to competitive telephone bidding at gilt auctions and other DMO operations, either for the GEMM's own account or on behalf of clients
- an exclusive facility to trade as a counterparty of the DMO in any of its secondary market operations
- exclusive access to gilt IDB screens.

A firm can register as a GEMM to provide quotes in:

- all gilt-edged securities
- gilt-edged securities excluding index-linked gilts
- index-linked gilts only.

There are exceptions to the requirement to customers, including the members of the LSE. The obligation does not include quoting to other GEMMs, fixed-interest market makers or gilt IDBs.

2.2.4 Broker-Dealers

These are non-GEMM LSE member firms that are able to buy or sell gilts as principal (dealer) or as agent (broker). When acting as a broker, the broker dealer will be bound by the LSE's best execution rule, ie, to get the best available price at the time.

When seeking a quote from a GEMM, the broker-dealer must identify at the outset if the deal is a small one, defined as less than £1 million nominal.

2.2.5 Gilt Inter-Dealer Brokers

Gilt IDBs arrange deals anonymously between GEMMs. They are not allowed to take principal positions and the identity of the market makers using the service remains anonymous at all times. The IDB will act as agent, but settle the transaction as if it were the principal. The IDB is only allowed to act as a broker between GEMMs, and has to be a separate company and not a division of a broker/dealer.

2.2.6 Secondary Gilt Market

As with the equities market, gilts used to be traded on the floor of the exchange; however, in 1986, the secondary market in gilts moved to a telephone-driven market supported by GEMMs. The role of the GEMM is to ensure that two-way quotes exist at all times for all gilts. Once accepted as a gilt-edged market maker, the firm is obliged to make a market in all conventional gilts at a size deemed appropriate by the DMO.

As previously observed, the secondary market in gilts, as well as in other sovereign issues, has become an actively traded market in the global capital markets. Government securities are used in combination with other kinds of fixed income products (eg, yield spreads, as described in section 1.10 above) and as part of collateral management (see chapter 9, section 3.2.9).

2.2.7 Interest Rates and Accrued Interest

As seen, government bonds such as UK gilts specify a redemption value (the nominal value of the bond) that will be repaid at the end of the bond's life and a coupon. The coupon is the amount of interest paid to the holder of the bond each year. Gilts are quoted on the basis of the price a buyer would pay for £100 nominal value.

Example

Treasury 6% 2028 might be trading at £126.46, so a buyer would have to pay £126.46 for each £100 nominal value. Why would the buyer be willing to pay more than £100? The answer lies in the available interest rate across the financial markets. If the interest rate available on deposited funds was lower than the coupon rate on the gilt, then that gilt would be a relatively attractive investment and its price would be pushed upwards until the return it offered was in line with other investments.

So, as interest rates across the financial markets decrease, the quoted price of gilts will increase. Conversely, if interest rates increase, the quoted price of gilts will decrease. In summary, there is an inverse relationship between gilts prices and interest rates.

Bonds quoted prices are clean prices, ie, they are exclusive of interest. If a gilt is purchased between interest payments, an adjustment is made to arrive at the amount of cash required to cover the interim interest element as well. This is known as the accrued interest and it is the amount of interest earned by the bond's seller since the last coupon payment. The price including the accrued interest is the dirty price.

Accrued interest is paid to compensate the seller for the period during which the seller has held the gilt, but for which they receive no interest from the bond's issuer. Having only held the gilt for part of the interest-earning period, the seller receives a pro rata share of the next coupon from the purchaser.

So, if the £5,000 nominal of 6% Treasury 2028 mentioned above was sold by the original owner exactly halfway between the semi-annual coupon payments at a clean price of £126.46, the settlement would involve the following sum:

Clean price: £126.46 x £5,000 ÷ 100 = £6,323

Plus, accrued interest: £5,000 x 6% x 6 ÷ 12 x ½ = £75

Dirty price paid by the buyer to the seller = (£6,323 + £75) = £6,398

The accrued interest in the gilts market is calculated using the actual/actual day count convention. In other words, the seller is compensated for the interest on the basis of the actual number of days that have elapsed since the last coupon was paid, divided by the total number of days in the actual period.

The DMO will pay the coupons to the registered holder of the gilt at each coupon payment date. However, because of the possibility of ownership changes just before the coupon payment date, there is a period prior to each coupon payment date when a gilt is dealt without entitlement to the impending coupon payment (known as the ex-dividend period). For most gilts, this period is seven working days prior to the coupon payment date. For the remainder of the year the gilt is described as trading cum-dividend.

2.2.8 Repo Markets

The topic of repo markets has already been discussed in connection with the money markets but not in terms of how this market works for government securities.

A repo is a sale and repurchase agreement. It is legally binding for both buyer and seller. For example, a gilt repo is a contract in which the seller of gilts agrees to buy them back at a future specified time and price. In effect, a gilt repo is a means of borrowing, using the gilt as security.

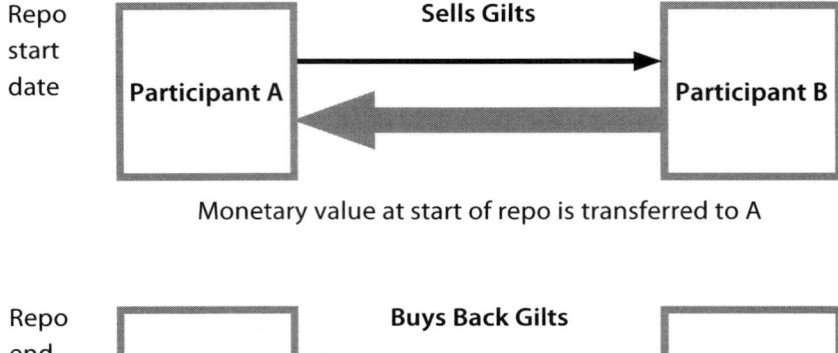

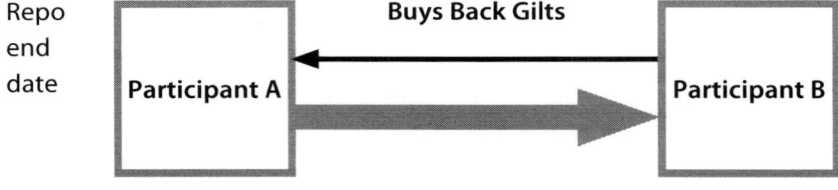

```
Repo         ┌─────────────┐  Sells Gilts    ┌─────────────┐
start        │             │ ──────────────▶ │             │
date         │ Participant A│                │ Participant B│
             │             │ ◀══════════════ │             │
             └─────────────┘                 └─────────────┘
             Monetary value at start of repo is transferred to A


Repo         ┌─────────────┐  Buys Back Gilts ┌─────────────┐
end          │             │ ◀────────────── │             │
date         │ Participant A│                │ Participant B│
             │             │ ══════════════▶ │             │
             └─────────────┘                 └─────────────┘
             Monetary value at end of repo is transferred to B
```

Diagrammatically, both parts of the repo transaction are agreed between the participants at the outset. Participant A has entered into a repo transaction, Participant B has entered into a 'reverse repo' agreement.

The amount of cash paid over by Participant B at the start of the repo will be less than the amount paid back to Participant B at the end of the repo period. The difference between the two amounts, expressed as a percentage, is the effective interest rate on the repo transaction. It is usually referred to as the 'repo rate'.

The obvious benefit to Participant A in the above example is that they are able to raise finance against the security of the gilts that they hold – potentially, a relatively cheap source of short-term finance. If Participant B is considered a conventional bank simply providing finance, then the benefit of using the repo is the security gained by holding the gilts. However, Participant B may be a GEMM that has sold gilts that it does not hold. The repo transaction enables the GEMM to access the gilts that it requires to meet its settlement obligations. In this way, gilt repo facilitates the smooth running of the secondary market in gilts.

The smooth running of the gilts market is further assisted by the DMO's 'Standing Repo Facility'. This enables any GEMM, or other DMO counterparty to enter into a reverse repo arrangement with the DMO, perhaps to cover a short position in gilts. They must first sign the relevant documentation provided by the DMO and then are able to request any amount of a gilt above £5 million nominal. This facility is for next-day settlement, and the facility can be rolled forwards for up to two weeks. The DMO does charge a slightly higher than normal repo rate for firms accessing the Standing Repo Facility.

2.2.9 Stock Borrowing and Lending Intermediaries (SBLIs)

Stock borrowing and lending intermediaries (SBLIs) lend to GEMMs when they take a short position in a gilt, ie, sell more than they currently hold on their books. They must settle the trade and provide the investor with the gilts. The SBLIs have access to large pools of unused blocks of gilts held by institutional investors in the UK as they buy and then hold large blocks of gilt-edged securities, and frequently hold them for years, possibly even to redemption. The SBLIs borrow the blocks of gilts on behalf of the GEMMs and the gilts are transferred to the GEMM who uses them to settle the trade and, in effect, remain short.

The GEMM will need to purchase the gilt in due course to cover the short position, and the blocks of gilts, once bought, will be transferred back to the institutional investor. The SBLI charges commission on the trade of approximately 0.5% and this is split between the SBLI and the institution. This facility is available to all market participants and gives them crucial access to gilt positions that allow them to go short. With the introduction of the gilt repo market in 1996, activity of SBLIs in the gilts market has been minimal as repos achieve a similar outcome, subject to a different mechanism.

With stock lending, the institution does not have to take any action. It simply receives a fee at the end of the process, whereas, with the repo trade, it will have to use the money paid and invest it into the market to make a return, which provides the institution with more opportunity and flexibility.

2.2.10 Settlement

T+1 in CREST, which is part of Euroclear UK & Ireland, the central securities depository (CSD) of the United Kingdom, Ireland, Jersey, Guernsey and the Isle of Man.

In the US, Treasury notes and bonds settle T+1 and Treasury bills settle on the same day (T+0), both through the Fixed Income Clearing Corporation (FICC), which is a subsidiary of the Depository Trust and Clearing Corporation (DTCC).

In Europe, settlement is T+2 via national or international central security depositories (CSDs).

2.3 Bond Prices and Bond Futures

The price of a bond is driven by a number of factors, such as credit rating and required yields. Clearly, the required yield will itself be driven by expectations of future interest rates. A key indicator of the markets, collective expectation of future interest rates is implicit within derivatives of bonds, such as bond futures. As a result, the prevailing price of bonds is, to an extent, driven by the price at which derivatives of those bonds are trading, such as bond futures.

Among the most actively traded global futures contracts is the US 10-year Treasury Note contract which trades on the Chicago Board of Trade (CBOT). This contract has excellent liquidity and provides a vehicle for hedging exposure to a broad variety of fixed-income instruments as well as an opportunity for speculating on the future direction of interest rates and, specifically, as one component in a speculation about interest rate spreads, between, for example, corporate investment-grade bonds or high-yield bonds versus US Treasuries.

The futures contracts can be settled by a cash payment at the time of the contract's maturity or by the owner of a contract delivering certain bonds which are subject to a standardised definition or conversion factor. This gives rise to the practice among participants in the futures and cash markets for bonds of making continuous and precise calculations as to which particular bonds are the 'cheapest to deliver' at the time of settlement of a futures position.

The relationship between the cash market for bonds and the futures markets in government bonds exemplifies the manner in which all cash and derivative markets are driven by a relatively simple arbitrage mechanism. The concept of 'cheapest to deliver' is a vital component in this arbitrage strategy which tends to eliminate discrepancies arising in price between the trading of actual bonds in the cash market and the trading of, for example, US Treasury Note futures. If pricing discrepancies should arise on a temporary basis, these tend to be eliminated as in any arbitrage by selling the relatively more expensive item (ie, the cash bond or the derivative depending on the particular circumstances) and buying an offsetting position in the corresponding alternate position of either the underlying asset or the futures contract.

The interaction between the cash price of bonds and the futures prices is a dynamic two-way process in which prices are constantly being adjusted through arbitrage and through the activities of 'hedgers' as well as speculators.

Exercise 1

Assume that the UK Government issues a gilt in 2018:

Treasury 1.5% 2048

John, a private investor, has asked whether such an investment bears any risks. He has been told that payments from these investments are totally safe.

Outline to John just what key risks he may face while holding the gilt.

See the end of the chapter for the answer.

3. Corporate Bonds

Learning Objective

6.3 Explain UK and overseas corporate bonds: markets; credit ratings; security; redemption; types of bond; fixed/floating coupon structures; covenants and sweeteners; domestic and eurobond issuance; trading and settlement

3.1 The Corporate Bond Market

Just as governments are active within the capital markets, so too are corporations, and the corporate bond market has its own characteristics which are often distinct from that of sovereign bond issues.

Whereas a sovereign issuer does not, de facto, have to pledge any specific security when it borrows in the capital markets, relying on the full faith and credit of the sovereign, the corporate bond market is much more concerned with the nature of the security and the collateral which is supplied to support any borrowings.

The term 'debenture' is used when the lender is provided with some specified security by the borrower (see section 3.4). When no security is provided, the stock is referred to as loan stock or unsecured loan stock (ULS).

There is no requirement for security on a loan, but not providing security will result in the coupon being higher that the company must pay. During the 1980s, a new method of making bond issuance available to companies that wished to borrow in the capital markets but which did not have a strong credit track record became popular. It is known as the junk-bond market or more appropriately the high-yield market. The capital markets have, at most times, developed an appetite for riskier borrowers as long as the coupons being offered by these non-investment-grade credits are sufficiently attractive. When there are general economic/financial difficulties, the yields on such bonds will tend to increase abruptly as fears of default are heightened.

Although many companies have issued ULS in the UK markets, they tend to be companies that have a high credit rating or status.

3.2 Choice of Market

Large multinational firms with high credit ratings are able to access the eurobond or international bond market. A eurobond, covered in section 3.9, is an international bond issue that is underwritten by a syndicate of banks, and sold outside the country of the currency in which it is denominated. Usually denominated in dollars, Europe was the first market for such bonds, hence its name, eurobond.

Smaller companies will be constrained to use the less active domestic corporate bond market.

However, the instruments are fundamentally the same, differentiated only by the pace of innovation that is greater in the euromarkets as is the secondary market liquidity. The basic terms of any issue will be contained in the indenture.

One other major distinction is that the majority of eurobonds are issued in bearer form, whereas domestic issues are required to be in registered form. There is some current speculation that this format may, in time, disappear due to its attractiveness to money-launderers.

It is conventional for issuers in the euromarkets to have a credit rating. While this does not in itself make the company any more secure, it will mean that potential investors have a clearer perception of quality. The role of credit rating agencies in grading corporate bonds is discussed below. It has become a controversial topic since the financial crisis of 2008–09 as the contention is that the agencies were negligent in advising the purchasers of several kinds of debt products, including corporate bonds, of the credit risks involved.

Note
A bond issued in a foreign market by a company is not necessarily a eurobond. It can be a 'foreign' bond issued in a domestic market by a foreign entity, in the domestic market's currency, eg, Tesco issuing a $ bond in the US, known as a 'Yankee' bond.

'Foreign' bonds are regulated by the domestic market authorities and are usually given nicknames that refer to the domestic market in which they are being offered. Since investors in foreign bonds are usually the residents of the domestic country, investors find them attractive because they can add foreign credit to their portfolios without the added exchange rate exposure.

Types of foreign bonds include bulldog bonds (issued in sterling by non-British institutions who wish to sell the bond in the UK) and samurai bonds (a yen-denominated bond issued in Tokyo by a non-Japanese company and subject to Japanese regulations).

3.3   Credit Ratings

Bondholders face the risk that the issuer of the bond might default on their obligation to pay interest and the principal amount at redemption. This so-called credit risk – the probability of an issuer defaulting on their payment obligations and the extent of the resulting loss – can be assessed by reference to the independent credit ratings given to most bond issues.

The three most prominent credit-rating agencies that provide these ratings are S&P, Moody's Investors Service and Fitch Ratings. Bond issues subject to credit ratings can be divided into two distinct categories: those accorded an investment-grade rating and those categorised as non-investment-grade or speculative. The latter are also known as 'high-yield' or 'junk' bonds. Investment-grade issues offer the greatest liquidity. The table below provides an abridged version of the credit ratings available from the three agencies.

Risk	Standard & Poor's	Moody's Investors Service	Fitch Ratings
Investment-Grade	AAA to BBB−	Aaa to Baa3	AAA to BBB−
Speculative-Grade	BB+ to B−	Ba1 to B3	BB+ to B−
High Likelihood of Bankruptcy	CCC to C	Caa to C	CCC to C
Bankrupt or in Default	D		D

Although the three rating agencies use similar methods to rate issuers and individual bond issues, essentially by assessing whether the cash flow likely to be generated by the borrower will comfortably service, and ultimately repay its debts, the rating each gives often differs, though not usually significantly so.

Issues such as asset-backed securities are credit-enhanced in some way to gain a higher credit rating. The simplest method of achieving this would be through some form of insurance scheme that will pay out should the pool of assets be insufficient to service or repay the debt.

During the financial crisis that developed following problems that arose with regard to asset-backed securities in 2007–08 the credit rating agencies were subject to a large amount of criticism for the manner in which they failed to correctly assess the risk of certain kinds of securities that were issued. As a result of the deficiencies of the method of rating credits, there is now increased oversight by regulators of the credit rating function.

Exercise 2

Outline the possible reasons why you think credit rating agencies have come under so much criticism – especially in the wake of the credit crisis of 2008.

See the end of the chapter for the answer.

3.4 Security

Companies have the ability to issue debt which is secured against the company's assets.

There are two types of legal charge that a company can issue over its assets.

Fixed Charge

A fixed charge is a charge over a definable asset of the company. The deed of debenture (the document that sets out the type of charge, ie, fixed or floating) will identify this asset. Normally, the asset, such as land or a freehold building, will be used for the fixed charge, as it can be easily distinguished and the value of it will not significantly reduce over the term of the debenture.

The commercial impact of having a fixed charge is that the company cannot sell the asset without the lender's permission, ie, the debenture holder releasing the charge. The debenture holder is unlikely to do this unless offered an equally good asset on which they can obtain a charge.

If the company fails to pay interest due, or does not repay the capital, the debenture holder can either:

- appoint a receiver and get income from the assets held under charge
- take possession of the asset and sell it, using the proceeds to repay the debentures in full
- return any excess proceeds to the company
- any shortfall will become an unsecured liability of the company.

Floating Charge

A floating charge is a specific type of security, only available to companies. It is an equitable charge on all the company's assets, both present and future, on terms that the company is able to use the assets in the normal course of business.

The floating charge is particularly useful because it allows the company to borrow without pledging specific assets. Company assets covered by the floating-rate charge might be stock, work-in-progress, plant and machinery, vehicles and premises.

The special nature of the floating charge enables the company to continue to use the assets and can also buy and sell them as necessary. It can, therefore, continue business as usual. The charge floats over the assets, rather than specifically fixing on any of them. This carries on until the charge 'crystallises', which will occur when the debenture specifies. This would include any failure to meet the terms of the interest or capital payments, or if the company goes into liquidation, ceases to trade, etc. When the charge crystallises, it fixes on the assets then owned by the company, encompassing any assets obtained up to that date.

When a company is unable to survive, the company will be wound up by a liquidator. The company's assets, if possible, will be sold, the money collected and then used to pay out, in a specific order, the obligations of the company. Fixed charges take priority over floating charges on a winding-up of the company.

3.5 Redemption

A mixture of redemption terms can apply to corporate bonds and, in recent years, there has been a tendency for the ingenuity of some bankers, who are servicing their corporate clients' needs for finance, to become highly inventive.

Early redemptions can be beneficial or disadvantageous to investors, obviously depending on their circumstances, the markets and the issuer's financial position.

Bullets

Most bonds are issued in the form of bullets which essentially means that they have a single redemption date. One of the advantages of this type of redemption is that the task of a financial analyst who has to value the bond is made much simpler. More complex products such as callable bonds, or put-able bonds, where the holder has the right to call for early redemption, are issued but the complexity involved in properly analysing these bonds' current price often dissuades investors from purchasing them.

Serial Notes

A serial note matures annually in instalments of capital and interest over its duration.

Optional Redemption

Optional redemption allows an issuer and occasionally a holder, at their option, to redeem the bonds, albeit there usually need to be circumstances arising for the optional redemption to be exercised, such as timing. This would typically be used for economic reasons. For example, an optional call right would give the issuer the right to apply an earlier redemption; an example of this can be seen in a double-dated bond, where the issuer can redeem at the earlier of two dates, but must redeem by the later date.

Coupons

The type of bond determines the type of coupon. For example, a fixed-rate bond has a coupon that remains the same throughout the life of the bond. Coupons range from simple fixed-rate annual or semi-annual coupons to more complex ones.

Zero Coupon

With a zero coupon bond no coupons are paid out. Instead, investors receive at maturity the difference between the purchase price at issue and the nominal value of the bond, also known as uplift. This then provides the required gross redemption yield (GRY).

Discounted Bonds

A discounted bond is a bond with no coupon (zero coupon bond) or one that is substantially lower than current interest rates. The bonds are issued at a discount to their nominal value, with the discount reflecting the prevailing market interest rate. The longer the maturity of the bond is, the greater the discount against par value.

The earnings from a deeply discounted bond will be treated as income, rather than a capital gain. The advantage to the issuer is that it will not be burdened by the full interest cost in the early years of the debt.

Floating Rate Notes (FRNs)

Floating rate notes are bonds where the coupon level fluctuates comparably with a market rate of interest (often LIBOR – or LIMEAN – London Interbank Mean Rate, ie, the average of the offered and bid rates). The coupon on FRNs consists of two parts: 1) the reference or index rate, for example LIBOR; and 2) a quoted margin, ie, the rate above LIBOR that must be paid. An example of this is a five-year bond with a coupon of LIBOR (the index rate) plus 25 basis points (the quoted margin). A basis point is equal to 0.01%, so 25bps would be equivalent to 0.25%.

Originally margins quoted in corporate bonds were measured in 0.5% and 0.25% but, as a result of competitive pricing, these have reduced to just basis points. The quoted margin is defined at the outset of the deal and indicates the borrower's credit rating and size of the issue, in addition to the market conditions at that point.

Other conditions may be included, such as an interest rate becoming fixed if it falls to a specified level, known as a drop lock.

These are inflexible structures and have often been replaced by floors in which the bond's coupon level must not fall below a certain point, eg, 5%. If the index rate and quoted margin gradually float down to this level then, at the point of 5%, the coupon will be locked, but as the index rate moves up, the coupon could increase back above 5% unlike the drop lock, when once it touches the floor, the bond is locked until redemption.

The minimum rate or floor protects the investor purchasing a floating rate note and is more attractive to the market.

It is possible for the issuer to protect the FRN with a ceiling or a cap on the rate so that as interest rates rise, the coupon also rises, but not beyond the ceiling.

A collared FRN with a floor and ceiling is known as a mini-max bond. This type of FRN collars the interest rate and enables the issuer to offset the cost of the ceiling with the value of the floor.

Inverse floaters pay a variable coupon rate that changes in direction opposite to that of short-term interest rates. An inverse floater subtracts the benchmark from a set coupon rate. For example, an inverse floater that uses LIBOR as the underlying benchmark might pay a coupon rate of a certain percentage, say 6%, minus LIBOR.

Currency of Coupon

It is entirely possible for the coupon and redemption to be in different currencies and these are dual-currency bonds, eg, a bond may pay coupons in dollars and the redemption in sterling. The rate of exchange could either be defined at the outset or the spot rate at the time of the transaction.

Bonds can also be issued with an option to use a mixture of currencies, either at the issuer's or holder's choice.

3.6 Equity Sweeteners

In the same way as for domestic corporate bonds, the issuer of overseas bonds can include equity 'kickers' or 'sweeteners'. These are most obviously provided by either issuing bonds that can be converted into equity ('convertibles') or by attaching warrants that give the bondholder the right to buy a certain number of shares at a pre-agreed price, at a pre-agreed future date. The equity kicker will potentially mean that the bond issuer can pay a lower coupon than would be required in a bond without the sweetener.

Convertibles

A convertible bond gives the holder the right, but not the obligation, to convert into a predetermined number of ordinary shares of the issuer. Given this choice, the holder will choose to convert into shares if, at maturity, the value of the shares they can convert into exceeds the redemption value of the bond. However, as there is this upside potential to the value of a convertible bond if the share price rises, and the downside protection of the redemption value if the shares do not perform well, convertible bonds generally trade at a premium to their share value.

Convertibles tend to be issued with a relatively low coupon.

Warrants

Bonds with an attached warrant entitle the holder to a certain number of shares of the issuer for a set period at a predefined price. The coupon on the bond may be lower than that of comparable bonds without warrants because of the potential benefit of buying shares at an advantageous price. This is like a **call option** to buy shares in the issuer, and is a tradeable security in its own right for the holder.

3.7 Covenants

Invariably, bonds are issued with covenants. Covenants are simply conditions that provide some form of protection for the bondholder.

Common covenants include those limiting further debt and its priority for repayment, those restricting the payment of dividends and those restricting the sale of assets.

3.7.1 Covenants Limiting Further Debt and Priority

These covenants are designed to prevent a bond issuer reducing the value of existing bonds by issuing additional debt of higher priority. This can be achieved by simply prohibiting the issue of debt with a higher priority (the 'negative pledge clause') or, alternatively, by only allowing debt to be issued with a higher priority if the existing bonds are also upgraded to have equal priority (the '*pari passu*' clause).

In addition to restricting the issuance of debt of higher priority, covenants can restrict new debt to a particular monetary amount, or be prohibited unless the firm maintains minimum financial ratios such as earnings tests (income relative to interest charges) and asset tests (tangible assets to debt).

3.7.2 Covenants Restricting the Payment of Dividends

Excessive dividends paid to shareholders could clearly have a negative impact on the value of that company's bonds. To prevent this, bond covenants frequently restrict the payment of cash dividends to shareholders, usually based on levels of earnings and cash. These covenants also place restrictions on the bond issuer using its funds to buy back its shares in the market.

3.7.3 Covenants Restricting the Sale of Assets

To prevent the value of bonds falling due to the issuer selling assets, covenants often state that assets are only permitted to be sold when the proceeds from the sale are used to purchase new fixed assets, or, alternatively, to retire the company's debt.

Some covenants also prohibit the transfer of the whole business, while others require the new owner to assume all of the obligations in the original bond agreement.

Breaching a contractual obligation, such as failing to pay the coupon or principal on the due dates or breaching any of the covenants is known as an event of default. There is often a period of grace after the initial default which gives the bond issuer an opportunity to engage with the bondholders to find a solution. If no solution is found, then the debt becomes immediately repayable.

3.8 Corporate Bond Issuance

The commonest method of corporate bond issuance in the primary, domestic bond market is a placement. In the euromarkets, a more structured approach is needed, to deal with the size of the issues involved.

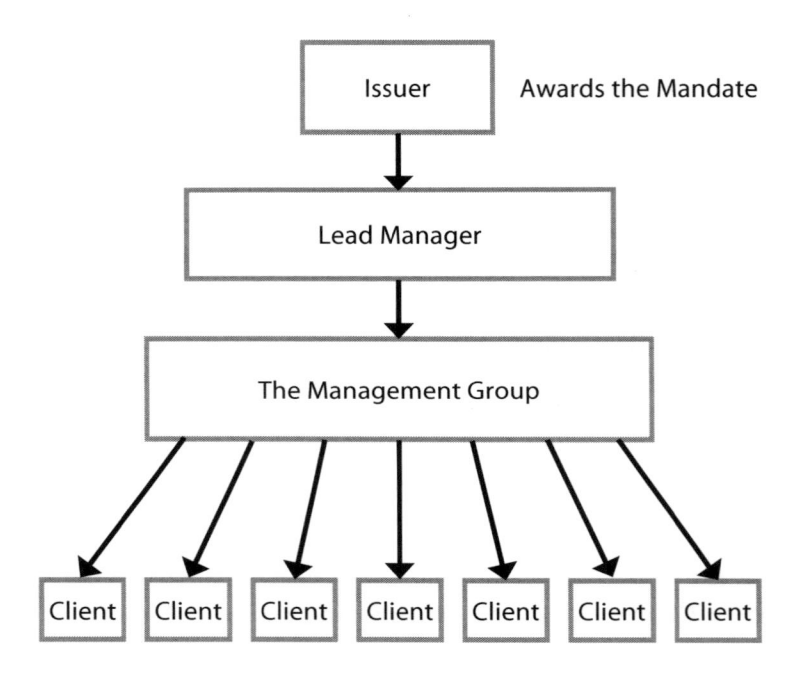

```
              Issuer         Awards the Mandate
                │
                ▼
           Lead Manager
                │
                ▼
        The Management Group
        ╱  ╱  ╱  │  ╲  ╲  ╲
   Client Client Client Client Client Client Client
```

A traditional method of issuing a corporate bond is for an issuer to appoint a lead manager and award them the mandate. With such a mandate the lead manager is empowered and obligated to issue the bond on the issuer's behalf and ensure that the issue is taken up. A failed placement could do serious damage to both the issuer and the lead manager.

The lead manager and issuer will agree terms, including the coupon and the maturity. In normal issues, the lead manager has the ability to amend the terms of the issue as market conditions dictate.

Instead of an issuer relying on the best efforts of the lead manager, the issuer could get the commitment from the lead manager to purchase the entire issue of bonds or shares. This is known as a bought deal. This process transfers the risk of being unable to sell a whole issue at the offer price from the issuer to the lead manager. By putting the issue onto its own balance sheet, the lead manager takes on the underwriting risk.

The lead manager may create a management group that includes other banks or issuing houses and then each one receives a portion of the deal, as agreed with the lead manager. They are obliged to place their commitment to the deal by getting buyers for the deal from their own client bases. However, the lead manager may choose to run the complete book alone, and exclude the other members of the management group.

Variations – under a fixed price re-offer, the members of the management group are not permitted to sell the bonds in the secondary market below the issue price until the syndicate terminates. The syndicate will break when the lead manager believes the majority of the issue has been placed.

Secondary Market

There only exists a limited secondary market in both domestic and euromarkets. The majority of issues are never actively traded. Consequently, the market is not particularly well structured, and has very little involvement from market makers.

3.9 Eurobond Market

Eurobonds are a way for an organisation to issue debt without being restricted to their own domestic market.

Although the first eurobonds were issued in Europe, the term now applies to any bond issued outside the country in whose currency it is denominated. They are, likewise, sold to investors anywhere other than in the country of denomination. For example, a US dollar eurobond could be issued anywhere in the world, except for the US, and sold to investors anywhere, except for in the US. They were devised after the Bretton Woods Agreement of 1944 as a means of avoiding capital controls so that US dollar financing could be accessed outside of the US and without US regulation.

They are generally issued via a syndicate of international banks. Generally, eurobond issuers do not keep a record of the holders of their bonds; the certificates themselves are all that is needed to prove ownership. This is the concept of bearer documents, when the holder of the certificates (the bearer) has all the rights attached to ownership.

The investment banks who originate eurobond issues have been innovative in their structure to accommodate the needs of issuers and investors.

There are plain vanilla, fixed-coupon bonds or bullet bonds that normally pay the coupons once a year. Additionally, there are zero coupon bonds and, as with domestic corporate issues discussed above, other forms of coupons such as floating-rate bonds and bonds with coupons that increase over time (stepped bonds).

For a number of pragmatic reasons, the clearing houses in the euromarkets maintain a form of register of ownership, but this register is not normally open either to government or to tax authorities. Combined with the feature of being bearer documents, an aspect of the eurobond is that, unlike most government bonds, it does not attract withholding tax. Eurobonds pay coupons gross and usually annually.

Eurobonds were originally aimed at wealthy individual investors, but as the market has grown they have increasingly become investments held by institutional investors.

As bearer documents, it is important that eurobonds are physically kept safe, and this is often achieved by holding the bonds in depositories, particularly those maintained by Euroclear and Clearstream.

Bonds which are deposited in these clearing house organisations are described as being immobilised. Immobilisation does not mean that the bonds cannot be transferred in secondary market transactions, it simply means that the bonds are safely held within a reputable depositary and a buyer is likely to retain the bonds in their immobilised form.

As the eurobond market has grown, a self-regulatory organisation has been formed that oversees the market and its participants – the International Capital Market Association (ICMA).

Settlement and accrued interest conventions have been established for the secondary market. Settlement is on a T+2 basis and accrued interest is calculated on the basis of 30 days per month and 360 days per year (30/360 basis).

The following table highlights the major features of eurobonds:

Feature	Detail
Form	Bearer
Interest payments	Gross
Tax	Taxable but untaxed at source
Trades matched through	TRAX system
Trades settled through	Euroclear or Clearstream
Settlement period	Trade day plus two business days
Trading mechanism	Over-the-counter (OTC)

The eurobond market is, in effect, an international market in debt. Companies issuing debt in the eurobond market have their securities traded all around the world and are not limited to one domestic marketplace.

The market only accepts highly rated companies, since eurobonds themselves are unsecured debt.

3.10 Dealing and Settlement

There is no formal marketplace for eurobond trading. The market is based on electronic and telephone contact between the main investment houses which are primarily based in London. The market is regulated by the ICMA which operates rules regulating the conduct of dealers in the marketplace.

Settlement is conducted for the market by two independent clearing houses, Euroclear and Clearstream.

The clearing houses immobilise the bonds in their vaults and then operate electronic registers of ownership.

Settlement in the eurobond market is based on a three-business-day settlement system. Once again, the important feature about the registers maintained by the two clearing houses is that they are not normally available to any governmental authority, thereby preserving the bearer nature of the documents.

The methods of eurobond issuance are identical to those of corporate bond issues in the domestic markets discussed above.

4. Bond Pricing

Learning Objective

6.4 Evaluate bond pricing using: DCF evaluation; clean and dirty pricing of different types of bonds; index-linked issues and STRIPS

4.1 Pricing Bonds

Bonds, most of which have definite schedules of cash flow values with precise timings as to when they will be paid out, are ideally suited to the application of discounted cash flow (DCF) evaluation techniques.

The formula for a DCF evaluation is as follows:

$$PV = \frac{C_1}{(1+r/cf)^1} + \frac{C_2}{(1+r/cf)^2} + \frac{C_n}{(1+r/cf)^n} + \frac{F}{(1+r/cf)^n}$$

where:

PV = the present value of the bond

C = the coupon amount paid on the bond

cf = the frequency of the coupon payment on an annual basis, ie, semi-annual payments would be equal to 2

r is the assumed discount rate (compounded in accordance with the frequency of payments of the coupon and compounding)

F is the face value or redemption amount of the bond

The formula adds together the present value of all of the coupon payments, discounted in accordance with the annual rate of interest (compounded at the frequency rate), and the redemption amount is also discounted in similar fashion.

4.1.1 Annual Coupon Redeemables

If provided with the gross redemption yield (GRY) or yield to maturity (YTM) (also referred to as the discount rate) bonds can be priced using the DCF formula provided above. If, however, the bond is longer-dated, it would be more convenient to apply the idea and calculation of an annuity (see chapter 4, sections 2.2 and 4.1). The GRY is examined further in section 5.3 below.

Consider a bond which pays an annual coupon of 5% and is redeemable at par – a face value of £100 – in five years. The scenarios assume a GRY of 4%, 5% and 6% per annum.

Annual Cash Flows	Annual Coupon	5.00%	Desired Yield	4.00%
	Cash Flow in £	Discount Factor at	Discount Factor at Desired Yield	Present Value
1	£5.00	$[1/1.04]^1$	0.96	£4.81
2	£5.00	$[1/1.04]^2$	0.92	£4.62
3	£5.00	$[1/1.04]^3$	0.89	£4.44
4	£5.00	$[1/1.04]^4$	0.85	£4.27
5	£105.00	$[1/1.04]^5$	0.82	£86.30
			Bond Price	**£104.44**

Each of the five annual coupon payments, supplemented by the redemption value in year five have been discounted using the discount factors shown in the table and the resulting PV of each payment is seen in the right-hand column of the table. The sum of the PVs of the cash flows is seen to be £104.44. The price is higher than the face value of the bond because the desired yield of 4% in this case is below the nominal return of the bond, ie, 5% per annum.

Annual Cash Flows	Annual Coupon	5.00%	Desired Yield	5.00%
	Cash Flow in £	Discount Factor at	Discount Factor at Desired Yield	Present Value
1	£5.00	$[1/1.05]^1$	0.95	£4.76
2	£5.00	$[1/1.05]^2$	0.91	£4.54
3	£5.00	$[1/1.05]^3$	0.86	£4.32
4	£5.00	$[1/1.05]^4$	0.82	£4.11
5	£105.00	$[1/1.05]^5$	0.78	£82.27
			Bond Price	**£100.00**

The second scenario shows that if the desired yield or GRY is 5% and the nominal yield is 5%, the bond should, unsurprisingly, be priced at its par value of £100.

Annual Cash Flows	Annual Coupon	5.00%	Desired Yield	6.00%
	Cash Flow in £	Discount Factor at	Discount Factor at Desired Yield	Present Value
1	£5.00	$[1/1.06]^1$	0.94	£4.72
2	£5.00	$[1/1.06]^2$	0.89	£4.45
3	£5.00	$[1/1.06]^3$	0.84	£4.20
4	£5.00	$[1/1.06]^4$	0.79	£3.96
5	£105.00	$[1/1.06]^5$	0.75	£78.46
			Bond Price	**£95.79**

The third scenario shows that if the GRY is above the nominal yield the price of the bond will be below the par value.

The above scenarios illustrate two key features of bond pricing:

- There is **an inverse relationship between bond prices and interest rates**, ie, as interest rates rise, or specifically the required yield from investors rises, so the present or market value of a bond will fall (and vice versa).
- When the **coupon rate on the bond is equal to the prevailing interest rate (or desired yield), the bond will be valued at par**, as illustrated above when interest rates are at 5%.

These two features are vital for understanding the way in which bond pricing works.

The previous examples were based upon a bond with five annual coupons and while it is perfectly acceptable to use the framework for bonds of longer duration it is simpler and more elegant to use the modified annuity formula for more long-term bonds.

Timing of Cash Flows	Annual Coupon	5.00%	Assumed GRY	8.00%
	Cash Flow in £	Discount Factor at	Discount Factor at Desired Yield	Present Value
Coupon Cash Flow Years 1 to 12	£5.00	$\frac{1}{0.08}\left[1-\frac{1}{1.08^{12}}\right] = 7.536$	7.5361	£37.68
Redemption in Year 12	£100.00	$\frac{1}{1.08^{12}} = 0.3971$	0.3971	£39.71
			Bond Price	**£77.39**

The annuity discount formula is as follows:

Annuity discount factor = $\frac{1}{r} \times \left[1 - \frac{1}{(1+r)^n}\right]$

and the table above shows the manner in which the substitutions into this formula work very well for a longer-term bond. The bond shown has a maturity of 12 years, an annual coupon of 5% and the required yield or GRY is 8%. Each of the coupon payments is subject to the discount factor as shown and the final payment or redemption of the face value which occurs in year 12 is subject to the simpler discount factor shown in the table. As one would have expected from the previous discussion this bond is priced below par as presumably interest rates have moved higher and the required YTM is 8%, which translates into a current price for this bond in the secondary market of £77.39.

4.1.2 Semi-Annual Coupon Redeemables

When we have a semi-annual coupon (eg, as with gilts), we should discount the semi-annual cash flows at the semi-annual rate. The market convention for gilts is to quote the annual yield by simply doubling the semi-annual figure.

The following table shows a hypothetical UK Government bond which has a maturity of five years with the first coupon payment of 2.5% (ie, half of the quoted annual coupon rate) being paid on February 20X1 and continuing until August 20X5 when the bond will be redeemed at its face value. The tabular layout uses the first version of the DCF approach to illustrate the exact nature of the cash flows. Once again for simplification the GRY is assumed to be the same as the nominal yield, resulting in a value whose current price would be at par.

Bond Pricing – Discounted Cash Flow Evaluation			
Present Bond Price	£100.00	**Yield to Maturity (YTM)**	5.00%
Face Value	£100.00	**Coupon Frequency**	2
Coupon Rate	5.00%		
Life in Years	5		
Period	**Date**	**Cash Flow**	**PV Cash Flows (excluding purchase amount)**
	Calendar date when Cash Flow is Paid	Nominal Cash Flow	Discounted Cash Flow = Nominal Cash Flow/ [1+YTM/Coupon Frequency^{Period}]
0		(£100.00)	
1	15 February 20X1	£2.50	£2.44
2	15 August 20X1	£2.50	£2.38
3	15 February 20X2	£2.50	£2.32
4	15 August 20X2	£2.50	£2.26
5	15 February 20X3	£2.50	£2.21
6	15 August 20X3	£2.50	£2.16
7	15 February 20X4	£2.50	£2.10
8	15 August 20X4	£2.50	£2.05
9	15 February 20X5	£2.50	£2.00
10	15 August 20X5	£2.50	£1.95
10	15 August 20X5	£100.00	£78.12
Total		£25.00	£100.00
Sum of present values of coupon payments		£21.88	
Discounted value (ie, PV) of face value		£78.12	
Total sums received at present value		£100.00	

The diagram shows the initial outlay of £100 at time 0 followed by the ten semi-annual payments of £2.50; the redemption amount being paid at period ten, ie, after five years. The PV of each coupon payment can be seen in isolation from the PV of the redemption value.

The nominal value of the coupon payment is as expected £25, ie, ten semi-annual coupons of £2.50 and with a 2.5% discount the PV of the coupon payments is £21.88 and the PV of the redemption amount, when received five years hence, is £78.12.

As one would expect, exactly the same result can be obtained by evaluating the price of the bond using the modified annuity discount factor with the appropriate values shown in the table. The advantage of using this approach is that there is less need to calculate each separate cash flow amount, but rather the NPV of all the coupons can be calculated in one step followed by the calculation of the NPV of the redemption amount.

Estimating Current Bond Price	Annual GRY	5.00%	Desired Yield	5.00%
Semi-Annual Cash Flow Periods	Cash Flow in £	Discount Factor	Discount Factor at Desired Yield	Present Value
T1 to T10 (semi-annual cash flows)	£2.50	$[1/0.025] \times [1-(1/1.025^{10})] = 8.75$	8.75	£21.88
T10 (redemption proceeds at maturity)	£100.00	$[1/1.025^{10}] = 0.78$	0.78	£78.12
			Bond Price	£100.00

NB: Remember to keep the number of cash flows and discount rate the same for the coupons and the capital values.

The next diagram illustrates bonds of long duration during periods of inflation. As interest rates rise, investors demand a higher GRY, possibly considerably higher than the nominal interest rate paid out by the bond through its coupons.

Estimating Current Bond Price	Annual GRY	5.00%	Desired Yield	10.00%
Semi-Annual Cash Flow periods	Cash Flow in £	Discount Factor	Discount Factor at Desired Yield	Present Value
T1 to T20 (semi-annual cash flows)	£2.50	$[1/0.05] \times [1-(1/1.050^{20})] = 12.46$	12.46	£31.15
T20 (redemption proceeds at maturity)	£100.00	$[1/1.050^{20}] = 0.38$	0.38	£37.69
			Bond Price	£68.84

The above bond would exemplify a 10% gilt with ten years' maturity issued with a 5% coupon but where the GRY or desired YTM has risen to 10%, and the bond's price in the secondary market would have to fall to £68.84.

4.1.3 Irredeemables

Evaluating an irredeemable bond means evaluating a perpetuity stream of cash flows.

The value of the perpetuity is effectively finite because the cash flows far in the future will have extremely low PVs. Unlike a typical bond, because the principal is never repaid, there is no PV for the principal. The price of a perpetuity is simply the coupon amount over the appropriate discount rate or yield, that is:

$$PV = \frac{A}{r}$$

where PV = present value of the perpetuity, A = the amount of the periodic payment and r = yield, discount rate or interest rate.

For example, a 3% UK Government War Loan will trade at 50 pence per pound in a yield environment of 6%, while at 3% yield it will trading at par. That is, if the face value of the Loan is £100 and the annual payment £3, the value of the Loan is £50 when market interest rates are 6%, and £100 when they are 3%.

4.1.4 STRIPS

Pricing a STRIP is done using the above methodology (adjusted to reflect the semi-annual convention in the gilts market) as for a zero coupon bond.

Estimating Current Bond Price	Annual GRY	0.00%	Desired Yield	10.00%
Cash Flows	Cash Flow in £	Discount Factor	Discount Factor at Desired Yield	Present Value
0	£0.00	$[1/0.05] \times [1-(1/1.050^0] = 0.00$	0.00	£0.00
T10 (redemption proceeds at maturity)	£100.00	$[1/1.050^{10}] = 0.61$	0.6139	£61.39
			Bond Price	£61.39

A five-year STRIP which pays out no coupons with a desired yield would have to be priced at £61.39, as the above example shows. Note there are no coupons in the table with the redemption taking place five years (ie, ten semi-annual time periods) after the issue date.

4.1.5 Index-Linked Gilt (ILG)

For an index-linked gilt (ILG), all cash returns, both the coupon and redemption proceeds, change with inflation since the issue reference date.

A 5% semi-annual ILG (linked to RPI) which was issued several years previously has just paid a coupon. The RPI at the issue reference date stood at 100. The RPI at the reference date for the coupon just paid stood at 150. To determine the proper pricing of this ILG at the time of the last payment it is necessary to examine the cash flows and appropriate discount factors.

If the RPI was still at 100, in other words there had been no inflation, the coupon and redemption proceeds would be:

The coupon value would be £2.50 (£100 × 5% × ½).

The redemption proceeds would be £100.00.

However the current RPI value of 150 shows there has been 50% inflation since issue and, therefore, the coupon amount and the redemption amounts would have to be adjusted.

The adjusted coupon value would be £2.50 x 150 ÷ 100 = £3.75.

The adjusted redemption amount would be £100 x 150 ÷ 100 = £150.

For all ILGs there needs to be a reference date for measuring the index value which is to be used. That reference date was historically eight months prior to the related cash flow, but for issues since September 2005 this was reduced to three months. For ILGs issued after September 2005, the appropriate values are as follows:

- The issue reference date is three months prior to issue.
- The reference date for any coupon is three months prior to its payment date.
- The reference date for the redemption proceeds is three months prior to redemption.

As the base index figure is the one three months prior to the issue date, and the final reference rate is the index value three months prior to redemption, the holder is compensated for inflation for the three months prior to the issue, but exposed to inflation for the last three months. No real ROR is thus guaranteed in any period due to the time lag involved.

Example

Consider a 5% index-linked gilt issued several years ago which is redeemable in 2½ years. The RPI for the issue reference date was 100, and the RPI for the last coupon (just paid) was 150. Inflation has recently been running at 3% every six months and is expected to continue at this level.

Bondholders require a return of 5% every six months.

Calculate the price of the gilt in the secondary market.

RPI At Issue	100	Original Semi Annual Coupon	Future Semi-Annual Coupon	Current Inflation Rate	Desired Yield
Current RPI	150	£2.50	£2.50 x 150/100 = £3.75	3%	10.00%
Semi Annual Coupon	Inflation-Adjusted	Cash Flow in £	Discount Factor at	Discount Factor at Desired Yield	Present Value
1	£3.75 x 1.03^1	£3.86	$[1/1.05]^1$	0.95	£3.68
2	£3.75 x 1.03^2	£3.98	$[1/1.05]^2$	0.91	£3.61
3	£3.75 x 1.03^3	£4.10	$[1/1.05]^3$	0.86	£3.54
4	£3.75 x 1.03^4	£4.22	$[1/1.05]^4$	0.82	£3.47
5	£153.75 x 1.03^5	£178.24	$[1/1.05]^5$	0.78	£139.65
				Bond Price	**£153.95**

The coupon must be adjusted from its issue value of £2.50 to £3.75 to reflect the change in the RPI from 100 to 150. Using similar reasoning, the redemption amount of the bond must also be adjusted to £150 – as shown in the left-hand column of the table, where the final payment must to be the adjusted coupon of £3.75 + adjusted redemption value of £150, ie, the final payment will need to be £153.75.

The second column shows how these new 'base' amounts as of the evaluation task must then also be adjusted in nominal terms by uplifting them each six months by the level of expected inflation. So each value has to be raised by 1.03 on a compounding basis.

Then apply the standard discounting factor to these nominal cash flows by discounting on a compounding basis at 5% per semi-annual period.

An alternative approach is to discount the real (pre-inflation) flows at real rates.

The required nominal return every six months is 5%, though 3% of this is satisfied by appreciation in the cash flow values due to inflation. The real required return is provided by the Fisher relationship (between inflation and both real and nominal interest rates as defined by Irving Fisher):

$$(1+r) = (1+i)(1+R)$$

where:

r = the monetary or nominal rate (5%)

i = inflation rate (3%)

R = real ROR

Therefore:

1.05 = 1.03(1 + R) and 1 + R = 1.0194 and R = 0.0194 or 1.94%

RPI At Issue	100	Original Semi-Annual Coupon	Current Inflation Rate	Future Semi-Annual Coupon
Current RPI	150	£2.50	3%	£2.50 x 150/100 = £3.75
Desired Semi-Annual Coupon		5.00%	Discount Factor	1.94%
Semi-Annual Cash Flows	Cash Flow in £	Discount Factor	Discount Factor at Desired Yield	Present Value
T1 to T5 (semi-annual cash flows)	£3.75	$[1/0.019] \times [1-(1/1.019^5)] = 4.72$	4.72	£17.71
5	£150.00	$[1/1.019^5] = 0.91$	0.91	£136.25
			Bond Price	£153.95

4.2 Clean and Dirty Prices

The value of a bond has two elements, the underlying capital value of the bond itself (the 'clean price' which is quoted) and the coupon that it is accruing over time (accrued interest). Each coupon is distributed as income to the registered holders on the ex-div date (which for gilts is normally seven business days prior to payment date). The 'dirty price' calculated above using DCF is the price that is paid for a bond, which combines these two elements. Consequently, ignoring all other factors that might affect the price, a dirty price will rise gradually as the coupon builds up and then falls back as the stock is either marked ex-div or pays the dividend.

The dirty price of a bond will decrease on the days coupons are paid, resulting in a sawtooth pattern for the bond value. This is because there will be one less future cash flow (ie, the coupon payment just received) at that point.

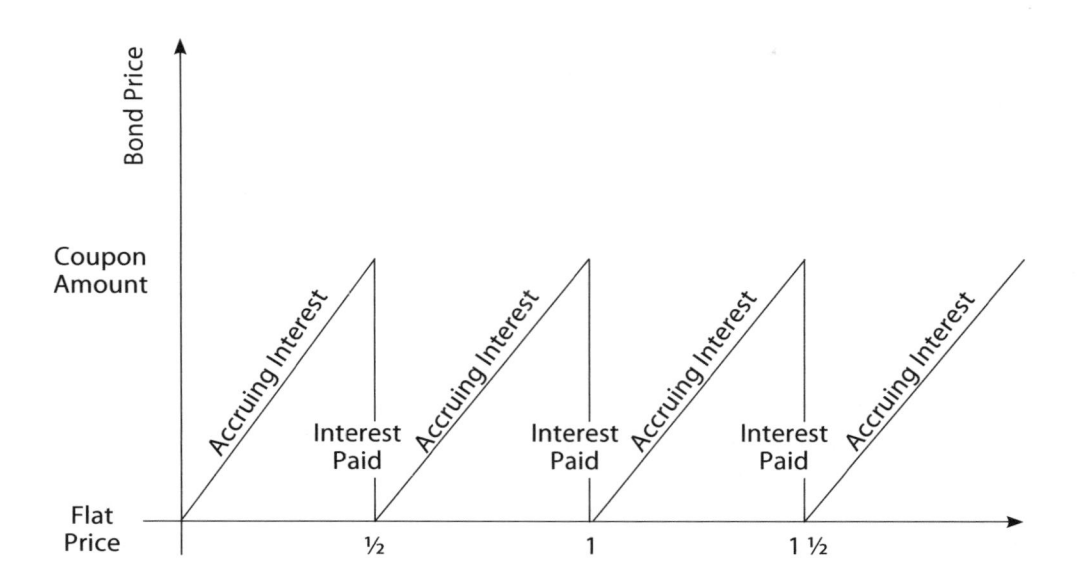

To separate out the effect of the coupon payments, the accrued interest between coupon dates is subtracted from the value determined by the dirty price to arrive at the clean price.

The clean price more closely reflects changes in value due to issuer risk and changes in the structure of interest rates. Its graph is smoother than that of the dirty price. Use of the clean price also serves to differentiate interest income (based on the coupon rate) from trading profit and loss.

It is market practice to quote bonds on a clean-price basis. When a bond settles the accrued interest is added to the value based on the clean price to reflect the full market value.

Historically, investors could sell the bond at the high price just prior to the payment of the dividend, and this gain would be free of tax. This process was known as bond washing. In 1986, the UK moved to a system of clean pricing that separates the two elements.

Under clean pricing, whenever an investor purchases a bond, they pay the quoted price (the clean price), which represents the capital value of the underlying bond with an allowance made for the interest element, allowing the two elements (income and gain) to be taxed separately.

4.2.1 Cum-Dividend Bargains

A purchase made before the ex-div date is referred to as a cum-div bargain. In this situation, the buyer of the bond will be the holder on the next ex-div date and will, therefore, receive the full coupon for the period. The seller, however, has held the bond for part of this period and is, therefore, entitled to a part of that coupon. To account for this, the purchaser of the bond must compensate the seller for the dividend which they have earned.

The purchaser will, therefore, pay the clean price plus the interest from the last payment date up to the purchase date. On the next payment date, the holder will receive the whole of the interest for the six months. However, on a net basis, they will only have received the interest for the period of ownership.

The formula used by the DMO in the gilts market is as follows:

$$\text{Dirty Price} = \text{Clean Price} - \text{Periods Coupon} \times \frac{\text{Days}}{\text{Days in Period}}$$

where:

Days = number of days from the last coupon payment date up to and including the calendar day before the settlement day (next business day following the trade)

Days in period = number of days from the last coupon payment date up to and including the calendar day before the next coupon.

Example

For a particular gilt, the coupons are paid on 1 April and 1 October of each year. On 10 July, an investor buys £10,000 nominal of Treasury 8% at £101.50, for settlement on 11 July. The following are the steps required in the calculations of the clean and dirty pricing:

April	From last coupon (inclusive)	30	30
May		31	31
June		30	30
July	To the day before settlement	10	31
August			31
September			30
	Totals	**101**	**183**

Clean Price	£10,000 at £101.50	£10,150.00
Accrued Interest	(£10,000 x 4% = £400) x 101 days ÷ 183 days	£220.77
Dirty Price		£103.77
Total Amount Payable		**£10,370.77**

4.2.2 Ex-Dividend Bargains

An ex-dividend bargain is one that falls within a period of seven business days before a dividend (coupon) payment date (for all gilts, except a 3½% war loan, which was ten business days). The seller within the ex-dividend period will receive the entire dividend, but must pay a proportion (rebate interest) back to the purchaser. The buyer within this period will not be entitled to the next dividend or pay any accrued interest but will receive rebate interest.

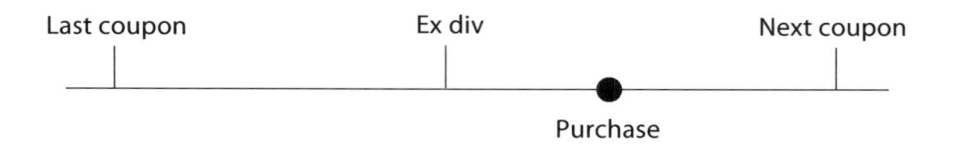

```
Last coupon          Ex div              Next coupon
    |                   |                     |
----+-------------------+---------●-----------+----
                              Purchase
```

The buyer pays the clean price as determined by the market less the number of days' worth of interest that they do not receive.

The formula used in this situation by the DMO in the gilts market is as follows:

$$\text{Dirty Price} = \text{Clean Price} - \text{Periods Coupon} \times \frac{\text{Days}}{\text{Days in Period}}$$

where:

Days = number of days from the settlement day (next business day) to the calendar day before the next coupon payment date (inclusive).

Days in Period = number of days from the last coupon payment date up to and including the calendar day before the next coupon.

5. Calculating Bond Returns

Learning Objective

6.5 Apply the following methods in the calculation of bond returns, understanding their uses and limitation: flat and running yield; gross and net redemption yield; grossed-up equivalent yield; real yields (inflation-linked securities)

In bond markets, the single most important measure of return is the bond yield. There are, however, several different yield measures, each having its own uses and limitations.

- How is the measure calculated?
- How useful is this measure?
- What are the limitations of this measure?

5.1 Flat Yield

The simplest measure of the return used in the market is the flat (interest or running) yield. This measure looks at the annual cash return (coupon) generated by an investment as a percentage of the cash price. It offers the regular annual return generated by the money invested.

The formula for the flat or running yield is as follows:

$$\text{Flat Yield} = \frac{\text{Annual Coupon Rate}}{\text{Market Price}}$$

For example, the flat yield on a 5% coupon gilt, redeeming in six years and priced at £104.40, would be (£5 ÷ £104.40) x 100 = 4.79%.

The flat yield only considers the coupon and ignores the existence of any capital gain (or loss) through to redemption. As such, it is best suited to short-term investors in the bond, rather than those investors that might hold the bond through to its maturity and benefit from the gain (or suffer from the loss) at maturity.

The flat yield shows how a change in interest rates impacts bond prices. If interest rates increase, investors want an equivalent increase in the yield on their bonds. However, because the coupon is fixed for most bonds, the only way that the yield can increase is for the price to fall. This is the inverse relationship between interest rates and bond prices.

When interest rates rise, bond prices fall and vice versa.

The flat yield for an 8% annual coupon bond redeemable at par in four years, can be calculated from its current price (£98.60):

$$\text{Flat Yield} = \frac{£8.00}{£98.60} = 0.0811 = 8.11\%$$

Uses

This measure assesses the annual income return only and would be the most appropriate measure if the bond is an irredeemable, which pays a perpetual coupon but no redemption amount.

Alternatively, the flat or running yield can be useful for short-term cash returns that the investment generates.

Limitations

There are three key drawbacks for using flat yield as a robust measure in assessing bond returns.

Since it only measures the coupon flows and ignores the redemption flows, when applicable, it gives an incomplete perspective on the actual returns from the bond. A bond which has been purchased at a price away from redemption is significantly undervalued when the par value is excluded from the calculation.

The calculation completely ignores the timing of any cash flows and, because there is no DCF analysis, the time value of money is thus overlooked.

With FRNs, the return in any one period will varies with interest rates. If the coupon is not a constant, then using a flat yield basis for measuring returns becomes an arbitrary matter of selecting which coupon amount, among many possible values, to use for the calculation.

For these reasons the flat yield is not a useful measure.

5.2 Japanese Gross Redemption Yield (GRY)

The purpose of the Japanese GRY calculation is to conquer the first limitation of the flat yield, that any gains or losses in connection with redemption are disregarded.

This measure recognises that the total return in any period is a combination of both income and capital components, ie, the coupon received plus any gain (less any loss) for the period.

The Japanese method for calculating the GRY is to use the flat yield, then add the average annual capital gain (or subtract the average annual loss) to redemption, that is stated as a percentage of the current market price.

Hence, we can state the Japanese GRY as follows:

$$\text{Japanese GRY} = \frac{\text{Annual Coupon Rate}}{\text{Market Price}} + \frac{\text{Average Annual Capital Gain to Redemption}}{\text{Market Price}}$$

$$\text{Japanese GRY} = \frac{\text{Annual Coupon Rate}}{\text{Market Price}} + \frac{\left[\frac{\text{Redemption Price} - \text{Market Price}}{\text{Years to Redemption}}\right]}{\text{Market Price}}$$

Consider again the illustration above to calculate the flat yield, which is for the same 8% annual coupon bond redeemable at par in four years, with a current price of £98.6.

$$\text{Japanese GRY} = \frac{8}{98.6} + \frac{(100 - 98.6) \div 4}{98.6} = 0.084686 \times 100 = 8.47\%$$

Uses

The major advantage of this method is to provide an efficient method of assessing the GRY considering all the returns, income and capital. Japanese GRY is a far more useful measure than the flat yield.

Limitations

The calculation completely ignores the timing of any cash flows and the time value of money. This limitation can only be overcome through the use of DCF techniques.

Exercise 3

An investor pays a clean price of £116.80 per £100 of nominal stock with a 6% coupon paid annually. The stock has exactly six years to run until maturity. Calculate the Japanese GRY.

See the end of this chapter for the answer.

Japanese GRY assumes linear capital growth or simple interest rather than the more realistic compound growth. As a result, it is liable to overstate the effects of any capital gain or loss. Furthermore, this inaccuracy increases the further away a bond is from maturity.

5.3 Gross Redemption Yield (GRY)

The gross redemption yield (GRY) is a much fuller measure of yield because it takes both the coupons and any gain (or loss) through to maturity into account. As such, it is more appropriate for long-term investors than the flat yield. In particular, because it ignores the impact of any taxation (hence, GRY), this measure of return is useful for non-taxpaying, long-term investors such as pension funds and charities.

The calculation of the GRY utilises the approach covered in chapter 4 (sections 4.1–4.2) to arrive at the present value of a gilt. It is the internal rate of return (IRR) of the bond. The IRR is simply the discount rate that, when applied to the future cash flows of the bond, produces the current price of that bond.

Expressed in its simplest form, the GRY is the IRR of:

- the dirty price paid to buy the bond
- the gross coupons received to redemption
- the final redemption proceeds.

5.3.1 Mathematical Formulations

Price of bond where GRY = r = $\sum \dfrac{Coupon}{(1+r)^t} + \dfrac{Redemption}{(1+r)^t}$

Price of a bond where GRY = r = $\dfrac{Coupon_1}{(1+r)} + \dfrac{Coupon_2}{(1+r)^2} + \dfrac{Coupon_3}{(1+r)^3} \ldots \dfrac{C_n + R}{(1+r)^n}$

In the above formula, R is the redemption amount and n is the number of years to maturity.

Unfortunately, neither of these formulae can be solved algebraically (except in very rare circumstances) and, therefore, the process of interpolation described in chapter 4, section 4.2.1 represents the only practical method and will be covered again below.

5.3.2 Interpolation Approach

This is founded on the basis that there is an inverse relationship between yields and bond prices, ie, as yields rise, bond prices fall, and vice versa.

To calculate the GRY, select two interest rates and calculate the NPV of the bond cash flows for each rate. These calculations define two reference points in terms of values and rates that can be used to determine a linear relationship between changes in the bond price and changes in interest rates.

Assume the same bond previously used in calculating the flat yield and the Japanese GRY.

The two tables below establish two reference points with regard to homing in on the actual IRR by using the simple annual DCF approach. First, determine the NPV of all the cash flow with an assumed GRY of 7% and debiting the current market price in the cash flow calculation.

	Annual Coupon	8.00%	**Assumed GRY**	7.00%
Annual Cash Flows	**Cash Flow in £**	**Discount Factor at**	**Discount Factor at Desired Yield**	**Present Value**
Current Bond				(£98.60)
1	£8.00	$[1/1.07]^1$	0.93	£7.48
2	£8.00	$[1/1.07]^2$	0.87	£6.99
3	£8.00	$[1/1.07]^3$	0.82	£6.53
4	£108.00	$[1/1.07]^4$	0.76	£82.39
			NPV	£4.79

This provides a reference point at 7%, so then obtain a reference point in terms of the NPV of the cash flows with an assumed GRY of 11%.

	Annual Coupon	8.00%	**Assumed GRY**	11.00%
Annual Cash Flows	**Cash Flow in £**	**Discount Factor at**	**Discount Factor at Desired Yield**	**Present Value**
Current Bond				(£98.60)
1	£8.00	$[1/1.11]^1$	0.90	£7.21
2	£8.00	$[1/1.11]^2$	0.81	£6.49
3	£8.00	$[1/1.11]^3$	0.73	£5.85
4	£108.00	$[1/1.11]^4$	0.66	£71.14
			NPV	(£7.91)

This approach assumes a linear relationship between the NPVs and the GRY so, having established two reference points, a line can be drawn through both points

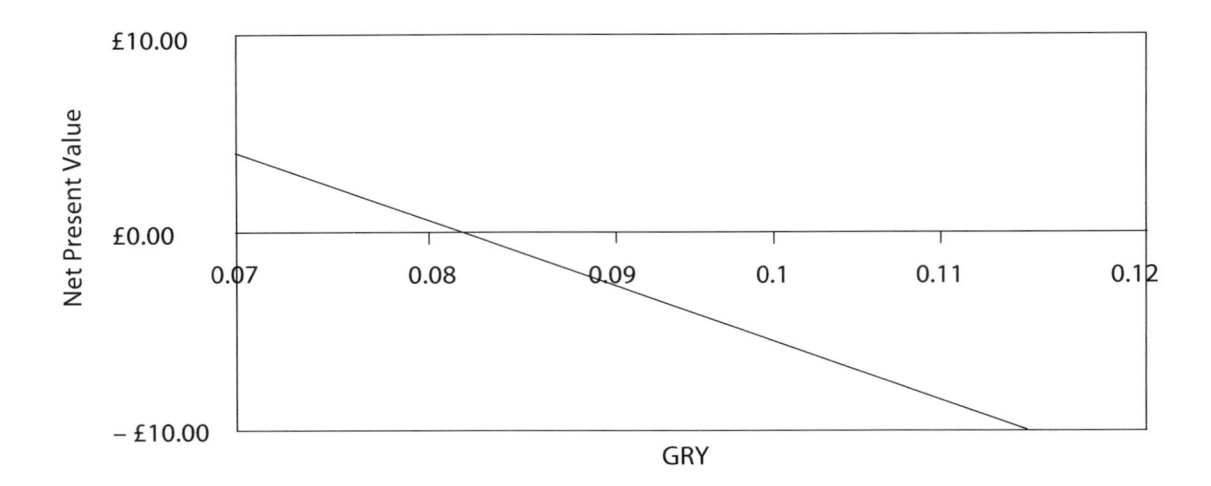

Even though the true relationship between bond prices and interest rates is not linear, using this approach provides a clearer sense of where the approximate range is to refine the intervals and continue with the process of interpolation, as discussed in chapter 4, section 4.2. The graph above suggests a more approximate interval below 8.5%.

The table below shows the annuity formula for discounting cash flows. Select the two much closer reference points which are an assumed GRY of 25 basis points below the 8.5% level and 25 basis points above it.

	Annual Coupon	8.00%		Assumed GRY	8.25%
Timing of Cash Flows	**Cash Flow in £**	**Discount Factor**		**Discount Factor at Desired Yield**	**Present Value**
Current Bond Price					(98.6)
T1 to T4	£8.00	$\frac{1}{0.0825}\left[1-\frac{1}{1.0825^4}\right] = 3.2938$		3.2938	£26.35
Redemption in Year 4	£100.00	$\frac{1}{1.0825^4} = 0.7283$		0.7283	£72.83
				Bond Price	£0.58

Timing of Cash Flows	Cash Flow in £	Discount Factor	Assumed GRY	8.75%
			Discount Factor at Desired Yield	Present Value
Current Bond Price				(98.6)
T1 to T4	£8.00	$\dfrac{1}{0.0875}\left[1-\dfrac{1}{1.0875^4}\right] = 3.2576$	3.2576	£26.06
Redemption in Year 4	£100.00	$\dfrac{1}{1.0875^4} = 0.7150$	0.7150	£71.50
			Bond Price	(£1.04)

As can be seen the NPV of the cash flows for 8.25% is just £0.58, whereas for 8.75% the NPV is below zero and at a negative £1.04. This infers that the rate is closer to 8.25% than to 8.75%, which allows the interpolation calculation.

5.3.3 Conclusion

If the NPV is positive using the first selected rate, then the second selected rate needs to be higher to try to establish a negative NPV, on the basis of the inverse relationship between prices and interest rates. Conversely, if the NPV is negative, then the second selected rate needs to be lower.

In the example above, the rate of 8.25% is too low and 8.75% is too high, hence the GRY must lie between these two points.

The total range of values covered as a result of this 0.5% (8.75% − 8.25%) yield difference is a value of £1.62 (£0.58 − −£1.04). In other words, GRY must lie far enough from 8.25% towards 8.75% that it eradicates £0.58 of this £1.62.

The GRY is, therefore, 8.25% + (58p/162p x 0.5%) = 8.25 + 0.179 = 8.429%.

The actual GRY is 8.428%, hence this calculation is accurate to about one hundredth of a basis point.

5.3.4 Comparing GRY with Flat Yield and Japanese GRY

The Japanese GRY overstates the effect of any gain or loss to redemption. It will overstate the GRY if there is a gain, and understates it if there is a loss.

As above, the Japanese GRY on this bond is 8.49%, ie, higher than the calculated GRY value of 8.429%.

However, there is some value in using either the flat yield or Japanese GRY as quick and ready reference points for the interpolation process.

The relationship between flat yield, Japanese GRY and GRY can be summarised as:

- above par (loss to redemption) flat yield > GRY > Japanese GRY
- below par (gain to redemption) flat yield < GRY < Japanese GRY
- at par flat yield = GRY = Japanese GRY.

The one instance where all three values are identical is when a bond is valued at par. In this circumstance, there will be no gain or loss to redemption and hence, all three measures will produce the same return.

Uses

The GRY measure transcends the main deficiencies highlighted relative to the flat yield and the Japanese GRY. It takes into account all cash returns and precisely when they happen. Therefore, the GRY represents an appropriate measure of the expected overall return from a bond at any point in time.

Limitations

As a measure of predicted return, the GRY based upon the IRR calculation suffers from one major limitation. It assumes that interest rates remain constant throughout the lifetime of the bond and, hence that any coupons could be reinvested at the same rate as the yield. In the highly abnormal circumstance that rates did not deviate from those disclosed by the IRR analysis, the GRY calculated would represent the return achieved. If, as is inevitably the case, the actual rates vary, the return achieved will differ from the GRY.

If the bond is sold at an earlier date and not redeemed at maturity, then the return achieved will be a function of the price of the bond (hence, interest rates) at the disposal date. This can be easily demonstrated by considering again the bond above and assuming that the bond is sold in the secondary market at par. In other words, interest rates have moved to 8% and the bond can be sold at its face or par value.

In terms of cash flow, investors would receive the £8 coupon plus the par value of £100 for a total cash flow return of £108 for a purchase price of £98.6. The GRY for that one year period would be (£108–£98.6)/£98.6 or 19.6%, which would be substantially more than the 8.429% yield return from an IRR analysis.

Conclusion

If interest rates remain stable throughout the period to redemption, then the GRY will represent the return achieved throughout any holding period. If interest rates alter, then the return achieved will alter as reinvestment returns and selling prices (if not held to maturity) change.

In essence, the GRY ignores the fact that the required ROR for bonds will vary and that investors should take into account the term structure of interest rates (see section 6.1 below).

5.4 Net Redemption Yield (NRY)

The net redemption yield (NRY) is similar to the GRY, in that it takes both the annual coupons and the profit (or loss) made through to maturity into account. The NRY, however, considers after-tax cash flows rather than the gross cash flows. As a result, it is a useful measure for tax-paying long-term investors.

The coupon received from gilts is subject to income tax, but any gain made on redemption (or subsequent sale) is not subject to capital gains tax. This makes gilts with a low coupon attractive to higher rate taxpayers, as the price will be lower than par, resulting in a substantial part of the return coming in the form of a tax-free capital gain.

The NRY for individual investors can be formulated as follows in two different formulae:

$$\text{Price} = \sum \frac{C_t(1-T_p)}{(1+r)^t} + \frac{R}{(1+r)^n}$$

$$\text{NRY} = \frac{\text{Annual Net Coupon Rate}}{\text{Market Price}} + \frac{\left[\frac{\text{Redemption Price} - \text{Market Price}}{\text{Years to Redemption}}\right]}{\text{Market Price}}$$

As previously noted, neither one of these formulae can be solved algebraically so, as mentioned previously, to calculate the IRR for NRY an interpolation approach is the only practical method.

As each individual has a different tax position, the NRY will vary for different individuals. The market convention is to compute the NRY at assumed levels of personal tax such as 40%.

Hence the NRY is calculated as the IRR of the:

- dirty price paid to purchase the bond
- net coupons received until redemption (net of the appropriate rate of tax)
- final redemption proceeds which are paid gross at maturity.

Consider again the bond example analysed above, ie, an 8% annual coupon bond with a price of £98.60 and four years to maturity.

Previously, when considering the GRY we used the interpolation method was used with two reference points determined by homing in on the likely interval for the GRY which would produce an NPV of zero for the cash flows. Now simplify matters and look at two reference points for this analysis – the first at 5% which is approximately 60% of 8.25% (the lower reference point from before) and an upper reference yield of 5.5% – since it is not known exactly what interval may be covered and a 0.5% interpolation interval should still deliver quite satisfactory results, as seen when calculating the GRY.

The table below again uses the annuity discount factor and the two assumed GRY rates have been entered for the two scenarios. The important modification that has been made to the cash flows is that the 8% coupon has been netted to a 4.8% coupon (assuming a 40% income tax rate), although the redemption amount of the bond – which is not subject to tax – has been left at its gross value – also its par value of £100.

Timing of Cash Flows	Annual Coupon	8.00%		Assumed GRY	5.00%
	Cash Flow in £	Discount Factor		Discount Factor at Desired Yield	Present Value
Current Bond Price					(£98.60)
T1 to T4	£4.80	$\dfrac{1}{0.05}\left[1-\dfrac{1}{1.05^4}\right]$	= 3.5460	3.5460	£17.02
Redemption in Year 4	£100.00	$\dfrac{1}{1.05^4}$	= 0.8227	0.8227	£82.27
				Bond Price	£0.69

Timing of Cash Flows	Cash Flow in £	Discount Factor		Assumed GRY	5.50%
				Discount Factor NRY Desired Yield	Present Value
Current Bond Price					(£98.60)
T1 to T4	£4.80	$\dfrac{1}{0.055}\left[1-\dfrac{1}{1.055^4}\right]$	= 3.5052	3.5052	£16.82
Redemption in Year 4	£100.00	$\dfrac{1}{1.055^4}$	= 0.8072	0.8072	£80.72
				Bond Price	(£1.06)

As can be seen from the above analysis of the cash flows, the GRY rate of 5% is too low and 5.5% is too high, hence the GRY must lie between these two points.

The total range of values covered as a result of this 0.5% (5.5% – 5%) yield difference is a value of £1.75 (£0.69 – –£1.06). The method of interpolation moves the NRY so far from 5% towards 5.5% that it extinguishes £0.69 of this £1.75 interval.

The GRY is, therefore, 5% + (69p/175p x 0.5%) = 5.00% + 0.19714% = 5.197%.

The actual GRY (which will deliver a zero NPV) is 5.197%, hence this calculation is accurate.

It is possible to get a quick approximation to the NRY by using an approach similar to that for the Japanese GRY, but using the coupon net of tax for the first part of the calculation:

NRY = 0.0487 + 0.0035 = 0.0522 = 5.22%

Although this is less accurate, it is close enough.

Uses of NRY

As it is based on DCF techniques the NRY measure surmounts the major deficiencies highlighted that are relative to the flat yield and the Japanese GRY. It addresses all cash returns and their tax implications for the investor.

Limitations of NRY

The limitations of NRY are as for GRY, ie, it only represents the net return that will be realised if interest rates to maturity remain stable throughout the holding period.

5.5 GRY – Further Considerations

GRY as a measurement of the return a bond will pay has some limitations as in section 5.3.4 above; however, it still provides the best assessment of the potential pre-tax returns from a bond at any point in time and is the main return measure considered when appraising bonds.

GRY calculation methods can cover types of bonds other than the simple annual coupon payment bond so far analysed. These are:

- **bonds** that pay semi-annually (or even more frequent) coupons
- **floating-rate bonds**, where the coupon changes with interest rates
- **index-linked bonds,** where the cash returns change with inflation.

Calculating the GRY for Bonds Paying Semi-Annual Coupons

A similar calculation would apply to a semi-annual coupon, but the coupon would be half the annual amount and would arise twice as frequently (ie, every six months).

For example, using an 8% ten-year semi-annual bond, there would be 20 £4 coupons paid every six months until redemption and also on the date of the 20th coupon payment the bond would be redeemed at its par value – assumed to be £100.

The method of calculation is to use the modified annuity factor for payments which are more frequent than yearly. The table below shows the annuity approach with 20 cash flows, the debit of the current price of the bond and the NPV of the subsequent cash flows from an assumed GRY of 8%.

Estimating Gross Redemption Yield	Annual Coupon	8.00%	Assumed GRY	8.00%
Semi-Annual Cash Flows	Cash Flow in £	Discount Factor at	Discount Factor at Desired Yield	Present Value
Current Bond				(£98.00)
1 to 20	£4.00	[1/0.04] x [1− (1/1.040^20)] = 13.59	13.59	£54.36
20	£100.00	[1/1.040^20] = 0.46	0.46	£45.64
			NPV	£2.00

The table shows that the GRY would have to be more than 8% which can also be inferred from the fact that the bond is trading below its par value implying that the yield required has to be higher than the coupon rate. The NPV of the cash flows shows a positive £2 amount whereas we are seeking a GRY which will effectively give rise to a zero value for the NPVs.

Assume a GRY of 9% for the same bond.

Estimating Gross Redemption Yield	Annual Coupon	8.00%	Assumed GRY	9.00%
Semi-Annual Cash Flows	Cash Flow in £	Discount Factor at	Discount Factor at Desired Yield	Present Value
Current Bond				(£98.00)
1 to 20	£4.00	[1/0.045] x [1− (1/1.045^20)] = 13.01	13.01	£52.03
20	£100.00	[1/1.045^20] = 0.41	0.41	£41.46
			NPV	(£4.50)

In this case, the NPV is negative (−£4.50). Therefore, the actual GRY will lie between 8% and 9% and will be nearer to 8%.

Using the earlier interpolation technique, find the proportionate position within the 8%–9% which matches the position that positive value of £2 is within that interval of £6.50 ie, £2.00 − £4.50.

The method is to express the distance from the lower reference rate of 8% by the proportion of £2 to the interval of £6.50 (ie, (£2.00 ÷ £6.50) x 1% = 0.3077%). This is then added to the lower reference rate of 8%, giving an estimated GRY of 8.3077%.

The market convention is to double the semi-annual yield to obtain the annual GRY. This is assumed in the way that tables are laid out, such that the annualised rate is shown as twice that computed by the discount factor. This does not give a completely accurate assessment of returns, since it ignores the compounding effect of interest rates within any year.

The mathematically correct method of annualising the return is to apply the following simple formula of $(1 + r)^2 - 1$ in the case of semi-annual compounding.

Evaluating FRNs

Floating rate note (FRN) price = $\dfrac{\text{Next coupon + par value}}{(1+r)^n}$

This relationship also applies 'in reverse' to calculate the yield to the next coupon payment date.

Illustration

If an FRN is priced at £104 when we are three months into the annual coupon payment period, what is the GRY assuming interest rates were 8% at the last reset date?

$$104 = \frac{8 + 100}{(1+r)^{3/4}}$$

$$(1+r)^{3/4} = \frac{8 + 100}{104}$$

$$(1+r)^{3/4} = \frac{108}{104}$$

$$= 1.03846$$

$$1+r = \sqrt[3/4]{1.03846}$$

$$= 1.0516$$

$$r = 0.0516 \text{ or } 5.16\%$$

5.6 Evaluating Index-Linked Bonds

The method for evaluating ILGs was covered earlier.

PV of cash flows at real rates $\dfrac{\text{Price}}{(1+i)} = + ... + \dfrac{C}{(1+R)} + \dfrac{C}{(1+R)^2} + \dfrac{C+£100}{(1+R)^n}$

This too can be inverted to calculate the real yield through interpolation. The approach is the normal GRY calculation, except for incorporating the adjusted price (left-hand side of the equation above).

For an ILG, all the cash returns, ie, the coupon and redemption proceeds, change with the inflation index since the issue's reference date.

Example

Consider a notional index-linked bond in issue, with a coupon of 5% paid semi-annually, that was issued several years ago when the index was 100 (three months prior to the issue date) and redeeming in ten years. The reference RPI (three months prior to the payment date) for the coupon just paid is 150. The bond is currently trading at £147.

Calculate the real and nominal GRY when annual inflation is expected to be 5% pa.

The assumed inflation rate of 5% pa corresponds to 2.5% on a semi-annual basis – dividing by two for consistency with GRY assessments.

Given that the RPI has moved from 100 to 150 the value for i in the following equation is 150 ÷ 100 or 1.5 and this determines the pre-inflation value of the bond's price.

$$\frac{Price}{(1+i)} = \frac{147}{1.5} = £98$$

Now use the interpolation method to define two reference yields from which the actual GRY value can be established. If the pre-inflation price is just below par then assume that the discount factor must be above the current coupon rate of 2.5%, so use this as the first reference point. The table below shows the cash flows that include the £98 debit and a discount factor of 2.5%. The resulting NPV shows a positive value of £2, signifying that the actual GRY must be higher than this level, which was already inferred.

Semi-Annual Cash Flows	Cash Flow in £	Discount Factor 2.50%	Discount Factor at Desired Yield	Present Value
0	(£98.00)			(£98.00)
1 to 20	£2.50	[1/0.0250] x [1−1/1.0250^20] = 15.59	15.59	£38.97
20	£100.00	[1/1.0250^20] = 0.61	0.61	£61.03
			NPV of Cash Flows	£2.00

The second reference point for the interpolation process is 2.75% and the results are shown below.

Semi-Annual Cash Flows	Cash Flow in £	Discount Factor 2.75%	Discount Factor at Desired Yield	Present Value
0	(£98.00)			(£98.00)
1 to 20	£2.50	[1/0.0275] x [1−1/1.0275^20] = 15.23	15.23	£38.07
20	£100.00	[1/1.0275^20] = 0.58	0.58	£58.12
			NPV of Cash Flows	(£1.81)

Yield Assessment

The rate of 2.5% is too low and 2.75% is too high, hence the real GRY is between these two points.

Calculating the Real GRY

The total range covered is a value of £3.81 (£2.00 + £1.81), and the real semi-annual GRY is therefore 2.5% + (£2.00 ÷ £3.81) x (2.75% − 2.50%) = 2.6312%.

The real annual GRY would be quoted as twice this, ie, 5.2624%.

Calculating the Nominal GRY

Using the Fisher relationship:

$(1 + r) = (1 + i)(1 + R)$

Providing the nominal semi-annual yield, after adjusting for inflation of 2.5% per semi-annual period as:

$(1 + r) = 1.025 \times 1.026312 = 1.05917$ thus $r = 0.05197$ or 5.2%

The nominal GRY is 10.4% (5.2% × 2).

When the real yield has been established, use it to compare with the nominal yields on offer from conventional gilts.

Further Notes on ILGs

The UK was one of the earliest developed economies to issue inflation-indexed bonds to institutional investors, with the first ILG issue being in 1981. ILGs differ from conventional gilts in that both the semi-annual coupon payments and the principal payment are adjusted in line with movements in the general index of retail prices in the UK (the RPI).

In 2005, the DMO launched an improved design for any new ILGs, using a shorter (three-month) indexation lag than that used in earlier ILGs.

All ILGs first issued prior to 2005 have an eight-month indexation lag, while all issued from September 2005 onwards use a three-month indexation lag.

For example, in a hypothetical three-month ILG, first issued on 20 July 2001, the index ratio for a transaction settling on 5 August 2005 would be:

$$\text{Index Ratio} = \left[\frac{\text{Reference RPI for 5 August 2005}}{\text{Reference RPI for 20 July 2001}} \right]$$

$$= \left[\frac{192.02581}{173.77419} \right] = 1.10503$$

Interest Payments

The semi-annual interest payments per £100 nominal are calculated as the product of the coupon per £100 nominal and the relevant value of the index ratio:

$$\text{Interest Payment}_{\text{Interest Payment Date}} = \frac{\text{Coupon}}{2} \times \text{Index Ratio}_{\text{Interest Payment Date}}$$

Interest payments are rounded to the nearest sixth decimal place per £100 nominal. Using the index ratio in the previous example, and assuming a coupon of 2.5%, the interest payment per £100 nominal that would be due on 5 August 2005 would be:

$$\text{Interest Payment}_{\text{August 5 2005}} = \frac{2.5}{2} \times 1.10503 = £1.381288$$

The redemption payment, per £100 nominal, is calculated in a similar manner:

$$\text{Redemption Payment} = 100 \times \text{Index Ratio}_{\text{Redemption Date}}$$

If the index ratio for the redemption date were 4.38391, then the redemption payment per £100 nominal would be:

Redemption Payment = 100 x 4.38391 = £438.391000.

6. Interest Rates and Bonds

Learning Objective

6.6 Evaluate the impact of interest rates on the term structure of a bond, including: derivation of, and relationship between, yields, spot and forward rates; yield curves; liquidity preference and expectations theory; demand effects; interpretation of yield curves

6.1 The Term Structure of Interest Rates

One of the fundamental precepts of investment appraisal is that if an investor faces a higher risk, then commensurately, there should be provided, and expected, a higher ROR.

The primary notion of risk relates to the variability in the returns or how much volatility might be experienced by an investor in holding one asset rather than another. A further consideration is the greater variability of holding certain bonds rather than others. Volatility and sensitivity to changes in interest rates impacts bonds with different characteristics in several ways. Consider first, the remaining lifetime of a bond or its time to maturity.

The diagram below illustrates a variety of zero-coupon bonds with different periods left to maturity. The benefit of using a zero-coupon is that the full impact of any changes in the required yield, owing to changes in market interest rates, will be expressed wholly in the change in the redemption value, as there are no other cash flows to consider.

Coupon	Maturity (Years)	Bond Price with a GRY (Yield to Maturity) of				Range	Price Range if GRY falls from 10% to 8% (as % of Price at 10% GRY)
		6%	8%	10%	12%		
0%	1	£94.26	£92.46	£90.70	£89.00	£5.26	1.94%
0%	2	£88.85	£85.48	£82.27	£79.21	£9.64	3.90%
0%	3	£83.75	£79.03	£74.62	£70.50	£13.25	5.91%
0%	4	£78.94	£73.07	£67.68	£62.74	£16.20	7.96%

Although a zero-coupon bond does not of course pay any actual coupon, it nevertheless follows the convention of a semi-annual coupon. The GRY must therefore also first be adjusted to a semi-annual basis.

The right-hand column shows the percentage change in the price of the bond if the required yield or GRY moves, for example, from 10% to 8%. The longer the remaining time to maturity (equal to its duration as it is a zero-coupon bond), the greater is this impact on the bond's price. As the remaining time to maturity increases so does the variability. With four years left to maturity, the same zero-coupon bond will see an almost 8% variation in its price as the GRY moves from 10% to 8%.

Returning to the initial theme of this section, it is reasonable that the required return on a longer-dated bond should be at some premium over that of a shorter-dated bond to reflect the additional risk or variability in pricing as circumstances change.

This observation and other tenets of investment theory provide the foundations a term structure of interest rates. The expectation is that yields may rise as investment cash flows extend further into the future. Yet this is not always the case and the term structure of rates can behave counter-intuitively.

6.1.1 Spot Rates

Cash flows at different dates are subject to different risks and should, therefore, be discounted at different rates. However, if the cash flows from a one-year bond should be discounted at a certain rate, then why should the first-year coupon from a five-year bond (received on the same day) be discounted at a different rate (the yield on the five-year bond)? Both represent cash in one year, hence both represent equal risk to an investor.

Various rates of interest appropriate for cash flows at specific dates are needed, regardless of whether they are from a one-year bond or a five-year bond. These are the spot rates.

The spot rate is the rate of interest that the market demands for money from now to a specific future time, ie, the rate for one-month money or one-year money or five-year money.

$$\text{Simple DCF formula} = \frac{\text{Coupon}_1}{(1+r)} + \frac{\text{Coupon}_2}{(1+r)^2} + \frac{\text{Coupon}_3}{(1+r)^3} + \ldots + \frac{\text{Coupon}_n + \text{Redemption}}{(1+r)^n}$$

where r is the GRY of the bond

In the formula above, the same interest rate is applied in discounting the cash flows, regardless of when they arise. For example, this formula can be used for the next one-year period using the one-year spot rate.

A better method of valuing fixed-income securities is to regard a coupon bond as a composite investment made up of several discrete and separate cash flows. For example, an 8% annual coupon bond with three years to maturity can be regarded as a package of four individual flows: £8 after one year, £8 after two years, £8 after three years and the redemption value, £100, also paid after three years.

Diagrammatically, the series of cash flows can be depicted as falling on a single timeline as in the upper part of the following diagram, but they can also be seen as separate and discrete events that follow a single time line of their own. The composite or bundle of the cash flows constitutes the bond's future cash flows but now they are perceived as a series of separate events or STRIPS.

Coupon Bond Cash Flows – 8% Annual – Three-year Maturity

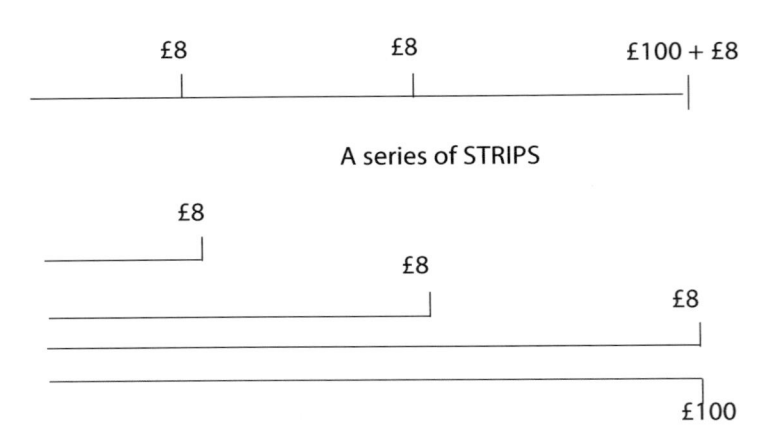

```
        £8           £8          £100 + £8
        |            |            |
_____|_____|_____|

              A series of STRIPS

        £8
_____|
                     £8
_____|
                                  £8
_____|
                                £100
_____|
```

When all the cash flows are considered to be points along the same timeline this is equivalent to the method used in calculating the GRY (among others), ie, applying one rate of interest to all of those flows, to discount them to their PV.

Considered as a series of separate and discrete events, not on the same line, but as a series of timelines which are bundled together, it is more appropriate to regard each flow as an individual zero-coupon bond and value each one at an appropriate rate of interest. The total value of the bond would then be the summation of these individual amounts.

According to this view, in order to correctly value a bond each cash flow should be discounted at the rate appropriate for its timing as a separate event. Using this logic, the simple DCF formula for determining price can be reformulated:

Bonds

$$\text{Spot DCF} = \frac{\text{Coupon}_1}{(1+r_1)} + \frac{\text{Coupon}_2}{(1+r_2)^2} + \frac{\text{Coupon}_3}{(1+r_3)^3} + \frac{\text{Coupon}_n + \text{Redemption}}{(1+r_n)^n}$$

where $r_1, r_2, r_3, ...r_n$ are the relevant spot rates, given the timing of the bond cash flows

Spot rate quotes are available in the money markets, but are only available for relatively short periods, so there are practical considerations in applying a series of spot rates in the UK at present. However, spot rates are more widely available in the US Treasury market.

Spot rates for longer maturities are available from the zero coupon bond or STRIPS market, and these calculations are getting easier in the UK following the introduction of a STRIPS market for government bonds, where it is possible to trade government bonds as either the complete bond or as a series of zero-coupon STRIPS (as in stripped from the bond).

In less fully developed bond markets where these rates are not directly available, the spot rate can still be derived from the normal bond prices.

Derivation of Spot Rates in Less Developed Markets

Spot rates are potentially available from the money markets and the zero coupon bond or STRIPS markets. The US bond market has a comprehensive STRIP yield curve and the availability of future spot rates has emerged from active trading in STRIPS, forwards and the eurodollar futures markets. When dealing in markets where the data is not so prevalent, an alternative is to derive the spot rate from a series of bond prices, if their GRY, coupon value and current price are all known. The process can be illustrated in the table below, which covers a variety of bonds with different periods remaining to maturity:

Maturity	Coupon	Price	GRY	One-Year Spot Rate	Derived Spot Rate
1	9.00%	99.5	9.55%	$\text{Price} = \frac{C+R}{(1+r_1)} \qquad r_1 = \frac{C+R}{\text{Price}} - 1$	9.548%
2	10.00%	98.25	11.02%	$\text{Price} = \frac{C}{(1+r_1)} + \frac{C+R}{(1+r_2)}$	11.098%
3	9.00%	90.56	13.00%	$\text{Price} = \frac{C}{(1+r_1)} + \frac{C}{(1+r_2)} + \frac{C+R}{(1+r_3)}$	13.245%

Note that the one-year yield and spot rate are identical, since this bond simply pays its one cash flow at that date. This can be seen from simple algebra:

$$\text{Price} = \frac{\text{Coupon} + \text{Redemption}}{(1+r_1)} = \frac{100+9}{(1+r_1)} = 99.5$$

When also examining the algebraic solution for the bond with a maturity of two years, it is necessary to use the one-year spot rate calculated in the first part of the equation below, followed by the coupon and the redemption amount in the second year as follows:

$$\text{Price} = \frac{\text{Coupon}}{(1+r_1)} + \frac{\text{Coupon} + \text{Redemption}}{(1+r_2)^2}$$

$$98.25 = \frac{10}{(1+r_1)} + \frac{100 + 10}{(1+r_2)^2}$$

$$98.25 = 9.1284 + \frac{110}{(1+r_2)^2}$$

Rearranging the above gives:

$$(1+r_2)^2 = \frac{110}{89.1216} = 1.23429$$

giving $1 + r_2 = \sqrt{1.23429} = 1.11098$ or $r_2 = 0.11098$ or 11.098%

6.1.2 Forward Rates

The spot rate is a rate of interest agreed today for a deposit or borrowing from today for a fixed period. The forward rate is a rate of interest agreed today for a deposit or borrowing from one future date to another.

The purpose of forward rates is to allow people to lock into rates today for any future deposit or borrowing to avoid the risk of adverse interest rate movements in the meantime.

It is not possible to forecast with certainty what future interest rates will be, hence the borrower or depositor may find the prevailing market rate turns out to be better or worse than the forward rate they have locked into. The point is to hedge the exposure to interest rate risk.

Derivation of Forward Rates

How does a bank determine today the rate at which it will borrow money for one year, starting one year from now?

The solution is in arbitrage. There should be no difference between investing the money for two years and investing it for one year and agreeing now to roll this over in a year's time into another one-year deposit.

Forward rate $= (1 + r_1) \times (1 + {_1f_2}) = (1 + r_2)^2$

where r_1 and r_2 are the one and two-year spot rates, respectively

${_1f_2}$ is the forward rate from Time 1 to Time 2

Time to Maturity	Spot Rate
1	9.548%
2	11.098%
3	13.245%

The table above summarises the results obtained from the previous derivation of spot rates from other data relating to the bond and shows spot rates for maturities stretching from one to three years.

The same formula provides the forward rates:

Forward rate = $(1 + r_1) \times (1 + {_1f_2}) = (1 + r_2)^2$

$1.09548 \times (1 + {_1f_2}) = 1.11098$

$1 + {_1f_2} = \dfrac{1.11098^2}{1.09548} = 1.12669$

$1.12669 - 1 = {_1f_2}$

${_1f_2} = 0.12699$ or 12.7%, ie, the single year rate in the second year is predicted to be 12.7%

6.1.3 Link Between Spot Rates and Forward Rates

Forward rates equate to the term structure of spot rates.

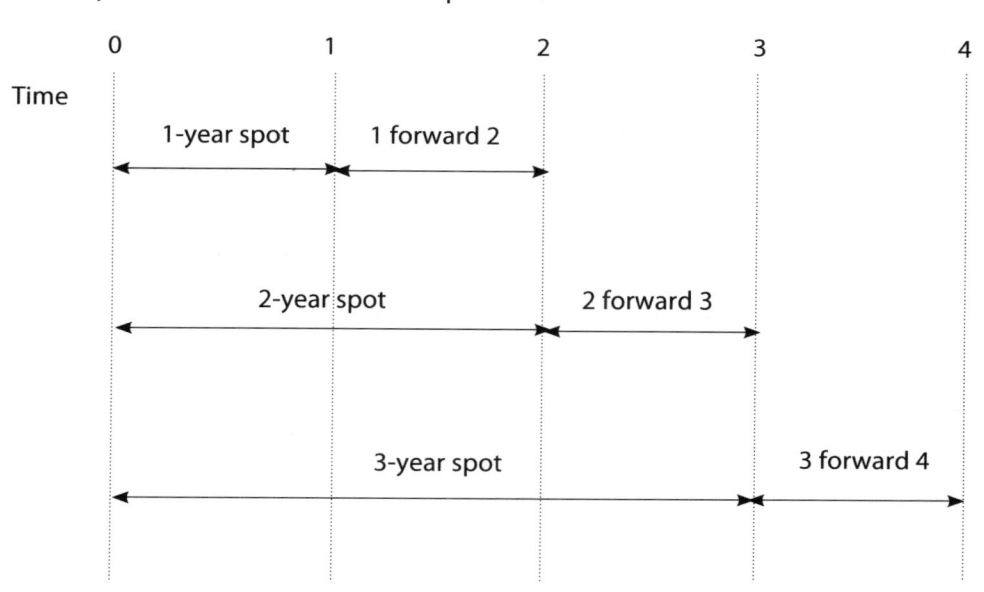

1-year spot $(1 + r_1)$

2-year spot $(1 + r_1) \times (1 + {_1f_2}) = (1 + r_2)^2$

3-year spot $(1 + r_1) \times (1 + {_1f_2}) \times (1 + {_2f_3}) = (1 + r_3)^3$

4-year spot $(1 + r_1) \times (1 + {_1f_2}) \times (1 + {_2f_3}) \times (1 + {_3f_4}) = (1 + r_4)^4$

The formulae above demonstrates the relationship between spot rates and forward rates. From the spot rates for any period of time, the associated forward rates can be derived and vice versa. The question of causality arises however:

- Are spot rates determined first by the consensus view for required returns for given periods from now, from which forward rates may be derived?
- Or are forward rates established first by the consensus view as to future interest rates, from which spot rates may be deduced?

Avoiding the problem of which rate is derived from which for the moment, and simply concentrating on the relationship between these rates, spot rates may be equated to the current one-year spot rate, expanded by the forward rates going out into the future.

For example, the two-year spot rate equates to the current one-year rate and the one-year rate in one year's time, whereas the three-year spot rate equates to the one-year rate multiplied by the one-year rate in one year and the one-year rate in two years. Therefore, the spot rate equates to the geometric mean forward rate.

This causality is resolved later in section 6.1.5.

Exercise 4

Assume the following three-year term structure of spot interest rates:

Rate	1+ Spot Rate
R1	1.04
R2	1.06
R3	1.08

From these spot rates, calculate the implied set of spot and forward rates for the same period.

See the end of this chapter for the answers.

6.1.4 Relationship Between Yields, Spot Rates and Forward Rates

The relationship between yields and spot rates, and between spot rates and forward rates has been discussed informally but there are some useful mathematical relationships between each of the variables.

Consider a series of 10% annual coupon-paying bonds in issue with maturities that are dating from one to ten years, showing the forward rate, the spot rate and the yield:

Year	Forward	Spot	Yield
1	7.0%	7.00%	7.00%
2	8.05%	7.50%	7.48%
3	9.0%	8.00%	7.94%
4	9.0%	8.25%	8.16%
5	9.5%	8.50%	8.38%
6	10.0%	8.75%	8.59%
7	10.0%	8.92%	8.74%
8	9.5%	9.00%	8.82%
9	9.0%	9.00%	8.82%
10	8.0%	8.90%	8.77%

These rates can be plotted on a graph to see how they vary over time:

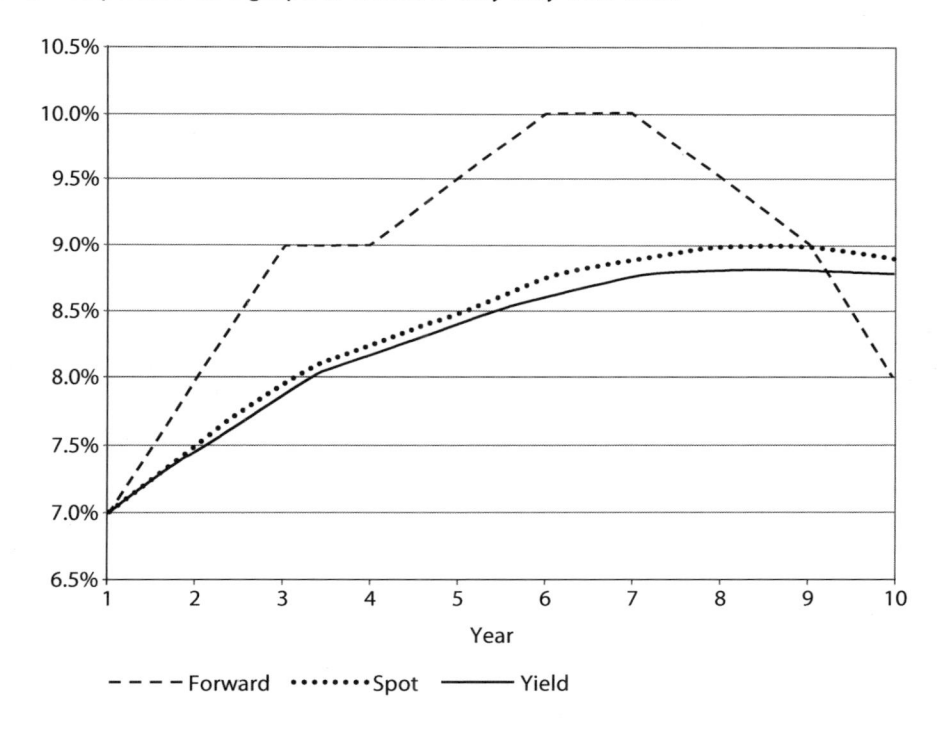

The spot rates equate to the geometric mean of the forward rates and their movements relatively lag behind those of forward rates. Since spot rates are based upon an averaging technique, they smooth out much of the more discursive quality demonstrated by forward rates.

The yield, which is a weighted average of the spot rates, exhibits even less volatility than the spot rates and far less than the forward rates.

Moving along the horizontal time axis, rates rise. Forward rates rise most rapidly, with spot rates next, closely followed by yield curves. For longer-dated stocks, rates begin to fall, again, with greatest volatility in forward rates, with spot rates and yields lagging somewhat. The yield curve shows the least volatility.

Expect to see the following relationships between yields, spots (the term structure of interest rates or zero coupon curve) and forwards.

6.1.5 The Yield Curve

The yield curve above shows the relationship between bond yields and their maturities and is very closely linked to the term structure of interest rates.

The normal shape of the yield curve is illustrated as follows:

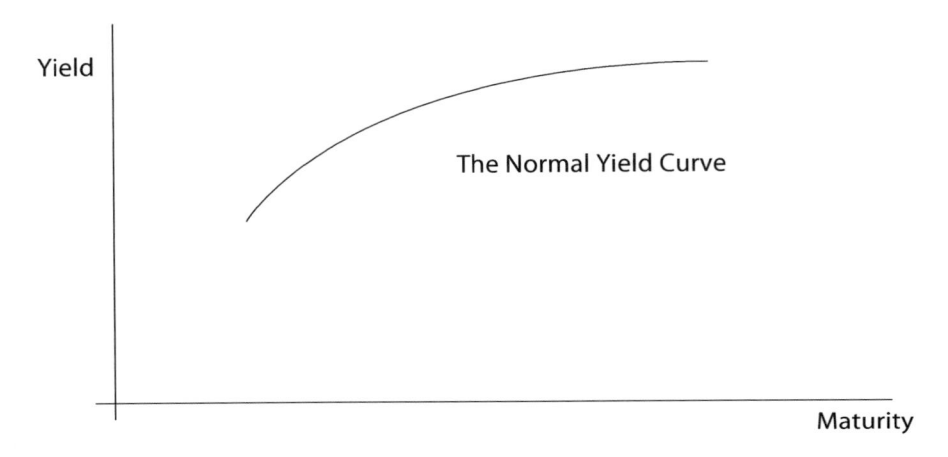

The curve above demonstrates the point made earlier, ie, longer maturity results in higher risk, which results in higher returns or yields.

This relationship is used in evaluating bond issues or trades by establishing the yield to use for discounting the cash flows.

The market value of a bond can be established by applying the relationship where r is the GRY of the bond.

$$\text{Simple DCF formula} = \frac{\text{Coupon}_1}{(1+r)} + \frac{\text{Coupon}_2}{(1+r)^2} + \frac{\text{Coupon}_3}{(1+r)^3} + \frac{\text{Coupon}_n + \text{Redemption}}{(1+r)^n}$$

If an appropriate yield can be established for a bond to use in this relationship, rather than having a single value for r which is substituted across the entire lifetime of the bond, it is possible to value it accurately. This is a daunting task and is complicated by the fact that the term structure of interest rates can have unusual characteristics.

Yield curves do not always have the simple rising shape depicted in the graph above. On occasion, yield curves become inverted with short-term yields higher than longer-term ones.

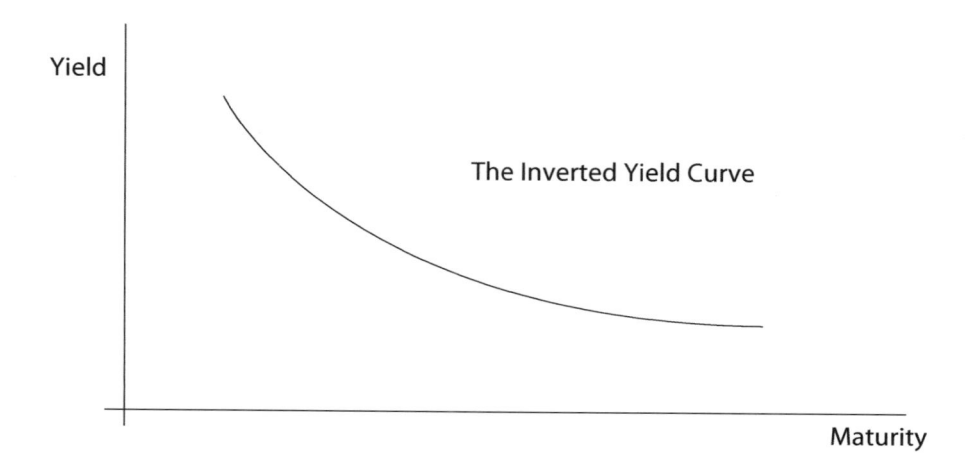

The Inverted Yield Curve

[Graph showing a downward-sloping curve with Yield on the vertical axis and Maturity on the horizontal axis, labelled "The Inverted Yield Curve"]

The downward-sloping curve illustrated above appears to contradict the fundamental principle that potential return rises with an increase in risk.

There are evidently some other factors affecting the yield curve, in addition to the simple risk/return relationship considered so far.

Shape of the Yield Curve

A number of theories have been offered to explain the shape of the yield curve and these are outlined below. As well as the normal and inverted shape, the yield curve can rise or fall steeply or become quite flat depending upon yield expectations. Some central banks even look to manipulate their own yield curve, such as the Bank of Japan (BOJ).

Liquidity Preference

In chapter 1, section 1, the Keynesian concept of 'preference for liquidity' was mentioned as an alternative explanation to the classical economic view that interest rates derive from theories of supply and demand.

Liquidity preference theory proposes that the demand for money reflects not a desire to borrow it, but a preference to keep hold of it (ie, to remain liquid). The rate of interest is, therefore, an incentive to part with money for a period of time (ie, to reduce liquidity). The longer that an investor is prepared to suffer reduced liquidity through lending a sum of money, the higher will be the compensation demanded by the investor in the form of a higher rate of interest or yield.

A consequence of this in terms of the causality within markets is that spot rates that are the core focus of market participants in seeking the best trade-off between liquidity and return. From the determining spot rates, the remainder of the market pricing process then derives forward rates and yields from the spot-rate market.

This theory assumes that that investors have different time frames of reference and different approaches to risk and the volatility of bond prices.

The liquidity preference view is illustrated in a normal upward sloping shape to the yield curve:

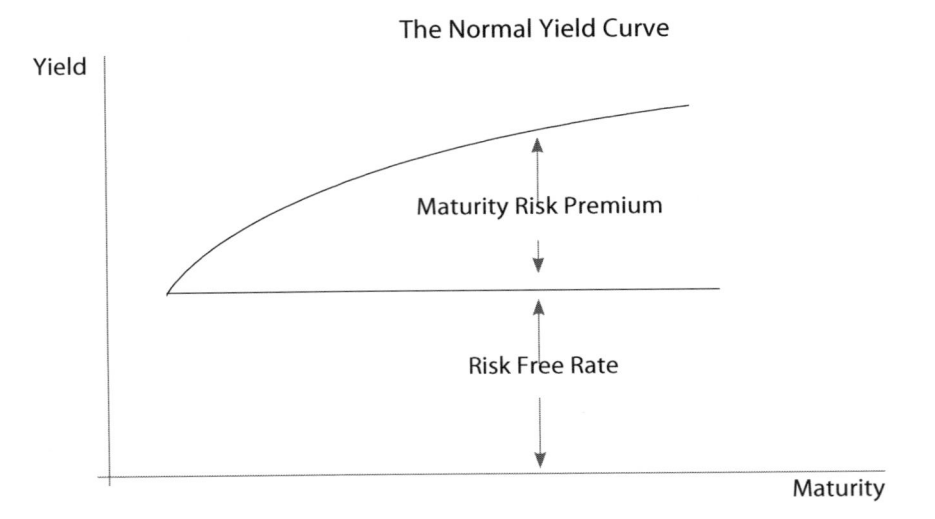

The Normal Yield Curve

[Chart: Yield (y-axis) vs Maturity (x-axis) showing an upward sloping curve. The area between the curve and a horizontal line is labelled "Maturity Risk Premium". The area below the horizontal line down to the x-axis is labelled "Risk Free Rate".]

Expectations Theory

This theory states that the shape of the yield curve varies according to an investor's expectations of future interest rates. A steep upward-sloping curve suggests investors expect rates to rise in the future. There is more demand for shorter-term than longer-term since investors' expect to secure higher rates in the future. From a supply/demand perspective, buyers of bonds will defer purchase of longer-dated securities as they will expect to receive higher coupons in the future.

A downward-sloping curve or inverted curve suggests that markets believe that rates will fall. If the expectation is for lower rates in the future, bond purchasers will be keen to lock in higher coupons now as the expectation is that coupons will decline in the future.

A flat yield curve suggests that the market thinks that rates will not materially change in the future.

Pure expectations theory re-emphasises the inherent interaction between spot and forward rates. It argues that the yield curve is a reflection of spot rates and that spot rates in turn are a reflection of the market's expectation of forward rates. As noted earlier, the yield is the weighted average of spot rates and spot rates equate to the geometric mean of forward rates.

With regard to causality, this theory assumes that forward rates are established by the market from which spot rates, and hence yields, are derived.

Looking back at the data and graph in section 6.1.4 above, the upward slope of that yield curve reflects the market's expectations that interest rates will rise in the short term. The yield then begins to tail off towards the end, reflecting a fall back in interest rates from their peak of 10% down to 8%, giving rise to a mild hump in the yield curve at the longer end.

The steepness of the yield curve would, therefore, also be a reflection of the expected rate of change in forward rates. The faster the expected change, the steeper the yield curve, whether upward or downward sloping.

The only point on the yield curve which can be fixed is immediate short-term rates, set by intervention of the BoE through its operations in the money markets. If short-term interest rates are high, the market's expectation might be that rates will fall. Therefore, this would lead to a downward-sloping or inverted yield curve, whose relationship between forward rates, spot rates and yields is shown in the earlier inverted yield curve diagram.

Another element of the market's expectations will be the expectations of inflation. If the market believes that inflation will rise in the future, the yields on the longer-dated stocks will have to rise in order to compensate investors for the fall in the real value of their money. The expectation of inflation plays a greater role at the long end of the curve than at the short end.

Preferred Habitat and Market Segmentation

The market segmentation theory suggests that there are different categories of investor who are interested in different segments of the maturity spectrum. Typically, banks will invest in shorter-term securities while pension funds and insurance companies will be buyers of longer-term securities (in the UK gilts). The two ends of the yield spectrum are driven by different interests, market participants and perceptions. The preferred habitat or market segmentation view is sometimes used to explain the tendency for there to be a 'wiggle' in the middle of the curve (ie, the five-year holding period). The argument used is that the two ends of the curve react to different sets of business data and are purchased by different market constituencies with different time horizons and requirements.

In the UK, the short end of the market is dominated by the financial sector (maintaining a proportion of their assets in liquid investments) and general insurance companies, whereas the long end is dominated by institutional investors such as pension funds and life assurance companies.

Effectively, this gives rise to two markets concentrated at opposite ends of the yield curve. The impact and relevance of this concentrated demand at these two ends is that prices are driven up and, therefore, yields fall below those that may otherwise have been expected at these points. This may result in a discontinuity or hump in the yield curve.

Supply-Side Factors

Stocks' availability in certain maturity ranges could lead to either an excess or shortage of stock and consequently, an irregular yield on some stocks. This is more often a problem at the long end of the yield curve where governments may be priced out of the issuance market.

During two periods, one being the buy-back period of the late 1980s and the other being the issuance surge of the early 1990s, it is argued the UK Government's funding policy caused considerable pressures on the shape of the yield curve. Specifically, the government held back from issuing at the longer end of the yield curve, due to the belief that longer rates were too high, and this led to a shortage of stock forcing prices up and yields down.

Supply-side issues can also become a factor in complex arbitrage strategies involving the exploitation of small pricing discrepancies between Treasuries with slightly different maturities, as described in the episode below.

A classic example of an arbitrage trade that under most normal conditions should deliver profits with minimal risk is what occurred within the US Treasury market involving the 30-year bond. The situation is described by Roger Lowenstein in his account of the collapse of the hedge fund Long-Term Capital Management (LTCM) *When Genius Failed*.

This trade strategy is normally considered a low-risk arbitrage but contributed spectacularly to the collapse of the hedge fund.

The essential characteristics of the trade involved a difference in the liquidity between the most recently issued 30-year bond (known as 'on-the-run') and the next most recently issued bond, which has perhaps already paid out on one of its coupons; instead of 30 years to run it may only have another 29½ years to run. It is called 'off-the-run' and is typically less liquid than the recently released bond. As Lowenstein remarks:

> 'A funny thing happens to thirty year Treasury bonds six months or so after they are issued: investors stuff them into safes and drawers for long-term keeping. With fewer left in circulation, the bonds become harder to trade… Being less liquid, the off-the-run bond is considered less desirable. It begins to trade at a slight discount (that is, you can purchase it for a little less, or at what amounts to a slightly higher yield). As arbitrageurs would say, a spread opens.' (p 43)

As Lowenstein also points out:

> 'If the spread widens too far then it becomes illogical' (he uses the word 'silly'). 'After all, the US Government is no less likely to pay off a bond that matures in 29½ years than one that expires in 30. But some institutions were so timid, so bureaucratic, that they refused to own anything but the most liquid paper.'

The Theoretical Yield Curve

There are several explanations for the shape of the yield curve, ranging from the pure expectations model which supplies an updated insight into the classical demand/supply theory of interest rate determination, the liquidity preference theory and the more pragmatic preferred habitat or market segmentation theory. The actual explanation for the shape of the yield curve could, of course, be influenced by all three of these factors and others as well.

It is possible to argue that the short term is dominated by expectations of future rates, whereas the medium and long term may be more influenced by the expectations of inflation and the liquidity premium, supplemented by bond purchasers altering their demand and supply for particular long-dated securities dependent on their overall economic outlook.

The expectations theory of the yield curve suggests that the real factor which drives yields and spot rates is the market expectation of future interest rates. Consequently, if the market's expectation of future interest rates is flat, the yield curve, the spot curve and the forward curve would be straight lines running out from the current rate.

In contrast, if there is validity in the liquidity preference theory, which would certainly seem, on the surface, to have a degree of plausibility, then even if the market's expectation of interest rates were that there would be no change, the yield curve should still have an upward slope.

From a purely theoretical point of view, in terms of the mathematical relationships which have been explored in this section it is possible to conclude that whenever the yield curve is upward-loping, the spot rate will lie above it and the forward rate will lie above that.

This would therefore tend to insert an upward bias into forward rates.

An upward-sloping yield curve gives rise to an upward-sloping spot-rate curve and in turn suggests an expectation of forward rates rising, but as in the diagram below, the market's anticipation of forward rates will not be as steep as the forward curve.

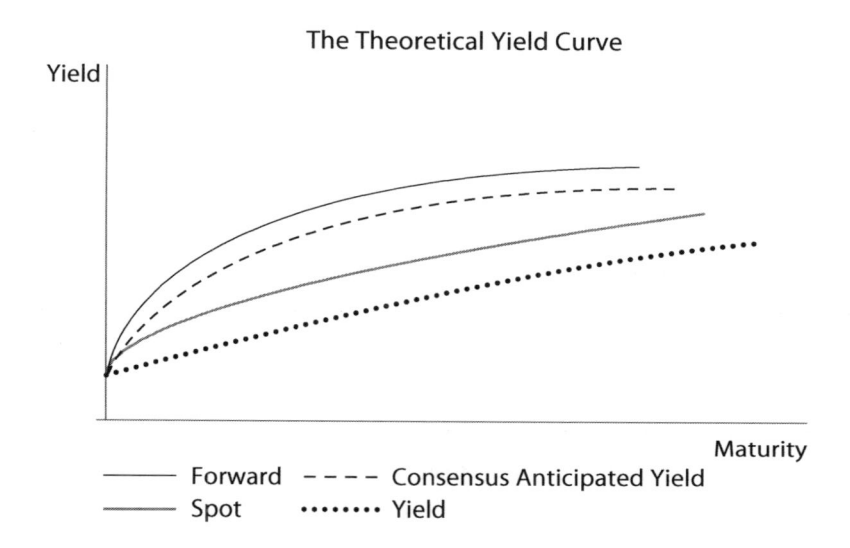

The Theoretical Yield Curve

———— Forward   – – – – Consensus Anticipated Yield
———— Spot   ······· Yield

Forward rates that can be derived as shown are used in the calculation of a variety of interest rate derivative products and, in particular, form the basis of pricing for the short sterling contract available on ICE and the customised **forward rate agreements** (FRAs) available on the OTC market.

However, from these derivations anomalies can arise. For example, the one-year forward derived from current market rates might be 7.5%, whereas the expectation in the market might be 7.25%. In this case, there is a natural advantage for anybody wishing to lock into deposit rates, and a cost to anybody wishing to lock into borrowing rates.

It is possible to argue that the anomaly arises because of the bias whereby borrowers are more keen to hedge their risk than depositors, particularly in an upward-yield environment and consequently, the price they have to pay is slightly above expectation. Therefore, the anomaly of a higher forward rate than expectations might suggest it is the price of such protection.

If so, this undermines the pure expectations theory which suggests that all key rates are driven by forward interest rates and agree with those commentators who argue that the key determinant is the spot rate. They argue that forward rates are merely an arbitrage from spot rates that is used to price a variety of interest rate products.

Alternatively, one could also argue that the forward rate is the market rate and that any consensus simply represents the views of influential economists and which traders are free to reject.

With certain individuals in the market believing one theory and others believing in its alternative, it is likely that their actions, and hence the market, are driven by both.

7. Risk Management of Bond Investments

Learning Objective

6.7 Evaluate the risks of holding bonds and management of this risk, including: interest rate, credit, inflation and other risks; sensitivity, duration and convexity

7.1 Risk Factors

An investor in a fixed-income security is exposed to a number of different risks, and any complete assessment of a bond must include consideration of these factors.

Interest Rate Risk

This is probably the most important risk because of the powerful relationship between interest rates and bond prices. Duration and modified duration (volatility) are a means of measuring this risk. Convexity is a measure of the variation away from the predicted return. Interest rate reinvestment risk can be mitigated by matching the Macaulay duration (in years) of a bond with the term of the investor's liability. Alternatively, FRNs or 'step-up' bonds can mitigate the effect of interest rate changes.

Credit Risk or Default Risk

This is the risk of the issuer defaulting on its obligations to pay coupons and repay the principal. The ratings assigned by commercial rating companies are intended to help assess this risk, although the failures by rating agencies to warn investors of the risk of mortgage-backed securities has caused reputational damage to companies such as Fitch Ratings, S&P and Moody's Investors Service. Default risk could be mitigated by investing in more highly rated bonds (subject to the probable reduced yield, relative to a lower-grade bond, being acceptable to the investor).

Inflation Risk

Inflation risk is linked to interest rate risk, as interest rates have to rise to compensate bondholders for declines in the purchasing power of money. Inflation risk may be reduced by investing in index-linked bonds.

Liquidity/Marketability Risk

The ease with which an issue can be sold in the market will affect the investor's perception of the risk of holding a bond. Smaller issues especially are subject to this risk. In certain markets, the volume of trading tends to concentrate into the benchmark stocks, or the on-the-run stocks, especially in the gilts market, thereby rendering most other issues illiquid. Other bonds become subject to lower volumes of trading as the initial liquidity dries up and the bonds are purchased by investors who wish to hold them to maturity.

The difficulties that can arise in the liquidity and trading conditions of bonds were especially acute during the 1998 crisis which began with the default by Russia on its bonds and led to the collapse of Long-Term Capital Management (see earlier), which traded of fixed-income instruments in a variety of arbitrage strategies.

One of the difficulties that arose during this crisis was the mispricing in the US Treasury market when the most recently issued long-term bond, known as the 'on-the-run' bond, trades at a premium to those bonds which had been issued previously but which subsequently become 'off-the-run' after the next issue. If investors have a preference, during a crisis, for the most liquid instruments, they may hoard 'on-the-run' bonds and force their price to be out of normal alignment with similar bonds which have a slightly different maturity date.

This can result in a breakdown in complex strategies designed to exploit the spreads or price differences across the yield spectrum.

Currency Risk

This risk arises when converting cash flows received from overseas investments, such as foreign stocks and shares, back into the domestic currency of the investor.

Issue-Specific Risk

This can arise from such factors that are specific an individual bond issue, which tend to either increase or decrease the risk, eg, issuer options such as the right to call for early redemption or, possibly, holder options.

Fiscal Risk

This signifies the risk that withholding taxes will increase. For foreign bonds, there would also be the risk of capital controls locking money into the market.

7.2 Macroeconomic Factors Affecting Bond Prices and Yields

A major driver of bond prices is the prevailing interest rate and expectations of interest rates to come. Yields required by bond investors are a reflection of their interest rate expectations. For example, if interest rates were expected to rise, bond prices would fall to bring the yields up to appropriate levels to reflect the interest rate increases. To remain competitive, equities prices would probably also suffer.

The interest rate itself is heavily impacted by inflationary expectations. If inflation was expected to be at 4% per annum, the interest rate would have to be greater than this in order to provide the investor with any real return. The interest rate might stand at 7% per annum.

If market expectations were that inflation was likely to increase further, to say 6%, then the interest rate would increase too, perhaps up to 9%.

The reverse would be true if inflation was expected to fall.

Technically, the interest rate referred to in the preceding paragraphs is the nominal interest rate. The nominal rate is the interest rate including inflation. The interest rate excluding inflation is generally referred to as the real interest rate.

7.3 Summary of Factors Influencing Bond Prices

- Specific issuer factors.
- Macroeconomic or market factors, eg, changes in expectations of prevailing interest rates and inflation.
- The characteristics of a particular issue and the quality of the issuer:
    - issuer's current credit rating (which itself will reflect the issuer's prospects) and highlight the issuer's default risk
    - the structure and seniority of the particular issue, for example, the bonds may carry a higher or lower priority than other securities in the event of default by the issuer and may be structured in a way that gives the bondholders particular priority in relation to certain assets (such as mortgage-backed bonds).
- The above aspects, combined with prevailing yields available on other benchmark bonds (such as government issues in the same currency, with similar redemption dates), will determine the required yield to maturity (YTM) and, therefore, the appropriate price.
- Liquidity – more liquid bonds tend to be more expensive, encompassing a liquidity premium and having tighter bid/offer spreads.

Sensitivity to Maturity

Longer-dated bonds are more sensitive to variations in interest rates than shorter-dated stocks.

The following matrix tracks a hypothetical bond with semi-annual coupon payments, yielding in nominal terms a constant 10%. The variables are the maturity in years and the GRY or required YTM.

Coupon	Maturity (Years)	Bond Price with a GRY (Yield to Maturity) of				Range
		6%	8%	10%	12%	
10%	5	£117.06	£108.11	£100.00	£92.64	£24.42
10%	10	£129.75	£113.59	£100.00	£88.53	£41.22
10%	15	£139.20	£117.29	£100.00	£86.24	£52.96
10%	25	£151.46	£121.48	£100.00	£84.24	£67.22

In this example, it is the price of the 25-year bond which exhibits the widest range as the yield moves through a range of £67.22 from £151.46 to £84.24. The reason is that the longer-dated bond is more exposed to the movements of the GRY, since it has longer to go to maturity. The narrowest range in the matrix is for the bond with only five years to maturity, which demonstrates a price range of only £24.42 as the GRY varies.

Note that when the GRY is equal to the nominal yield, no matter what the maturity of the bond, the price will be at par of £100.

Sensitivity to Coupon

This is demonstrated in the following matrix which tracks a hypothetical bond with a constant maturity of 15 years. The variables are the nominal yields and the variable semi-annual coupon payments and the GRY or the required YTM.

Coupon	Maturity (Years)	Bond Price with a GRY (Yield to Maturity) of				Range	Range as percentage of GRY move from 10% to 8%
		6%	8%	10%	12%		
6%	15	£100.00	£82.71	£69.26	£58.71	£41.29	19.42%
8%	15	£119.60	£100.00	£84.63	£72.47	£47.13	18.16%
10%	15	£139.20	£117.29	£100.00	£86.24	£52.96	17.29%
12%	15	£158.80	£134.58	£115.37	£100.00	£58.80	16.65%

The lower coupon stocks demonstrate the greatest sensitivity to the yield. This may not be immediately apparent from the matrix as the range between the highest and lowest values recorded increases as the nominal yield increases. The right-hand column captures however the percentage change in the price of the bond as the GRY moves from 10% to 8%. The lower coupon bonds are more sensitive, percentage-wise, to changes across the GRY spectrum.

The relationship between the coupon and maturity and the price is not symmetrical (ie, is not equal for a given rise or a fall in GRY). This relationship is known as 'convexity' and is discussed later in this section. Lower coupon bonds have more of their value tied up in the terminal value, as this can be exemplified by the ultimate low coupon bond, the zero-coupon bond, where the entire value is in the final payment.

Impact of the Yield

When yields are especially high, then future flows are worth relatively little when discounted to present value (PV) and their sensitivity diminishes. Conversely, if the yield is low, then the PV of flows in the future is enhanced and the bond is more sensitive to the changing GRY.

Summary

Long-dated greater than short-dated.
Low coupon greater than high coupon.
Low yields greater than high yields.

These simple maxims are useful indicators of the likely sensitivity to changes in the rate of interest, but they do not enable two bonds to be compared.

These maxims are not ranked, which makes it difficult to evaluate the relative sensitivity to interest rates between a low coupon short-dated stock and a high coupon long-dated stock. The solution, devised in the 1930s, was a more composite measure of interest rate risk: duration.

7.4 Macaulay Duration

Named after Frederick Macaulay, Macaulay duration is the weighted average of the PV of all the bond's payments. This can be considered as the average, or effective, maturity of a bond. The seesaw diagram below illustrates this. The fulcrum is placed where the weights of the PVs of the coupon payments balance against the final coupon and redemption payment. The fulcrum is effectively the duration of the bond.

The longer the duration, the longer is the average maturity, and, therefore, the greater the sensitivity to interest rate changes.

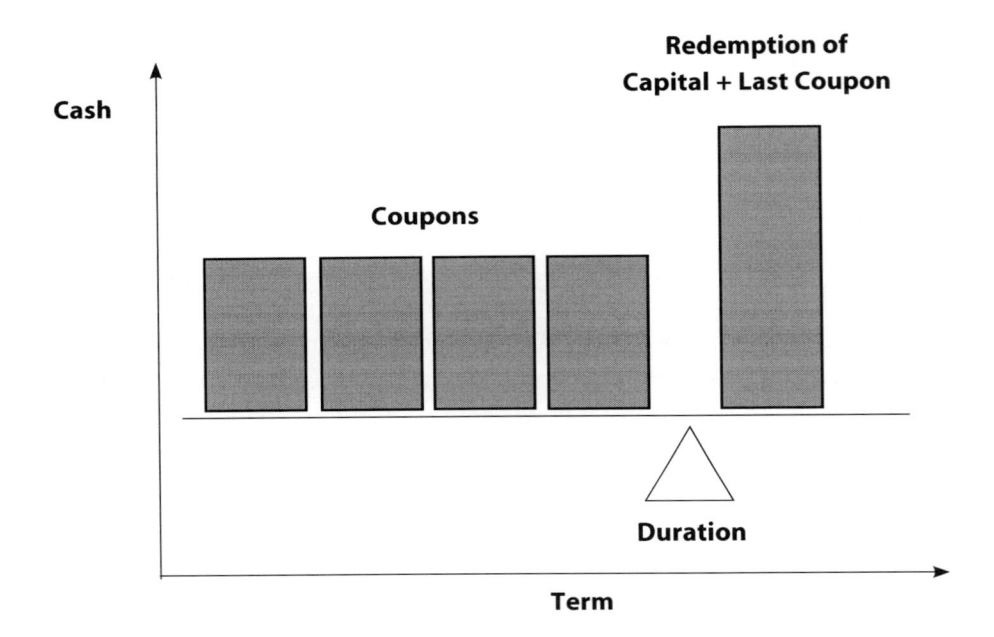

This concept can be illustrated, using a five-year bond with a 7% coupon.

The mathematical formula is:

$$\text{Macaulay Duration (D)} = \sum \frac{(t \times PV_t)}{\text{Price}}$$

$$\text{Macaulay Duration (D)} = \frac{(1 \times PV_1) + (2 \times PV_2) + (3 \times PV_3) + \ldots + (n \times PV_n)}{\text{Price}}$$

where:

PVt = PV of cash flow in period t (discounted using the redemption yield)

n = number of periods to maturity

The table below shows the calculation for a five-year bond with a 7% coupon and a required YTM or GRY of 8%.

	Calculation of Macaulay Duration
Bond Price	£96.01	**Yield to Maturity (YTM)**	8.0%
Face Value	£100.00	**Coupon Frequency**	Annually
Coupon Rate	7.00%		
Life in Years	5		
Period	**Cash Flow**	**PV Cash Flow**	**Duration Calculation**
		Cash Flow/[(1+YTM/Coupon Frequency)^Period]	PV Cash Flow * Period
1	£7.00	£6.48	£6.48
2	£7.00	£6.00	£12.00
3	£7.00	£5.56	£16.67
4	£7.00	£5.15	£20.58
5	£107.00	£72.82	£364.11
	Totals	**£96.01**	**£419.84**
	Macaulay Duration	£419.84/£96.01	4.373

Duration is one of the most useful ways of assessing the risk of holding a bond as the longer the duration of the bond, the greater its risk or sensitivity to interest rates.

As a measure of relative risk for a bond, it is as important as knowing the standard deviation or the beta for a share.

The basic features of sensitivity to interest rate risk are mirrored in the duration calculation. Longer-dated bonds have longer durations.

Lower coupon bonds have longer durations. The absolute low coupon bond is a zero-coupon bond, where the duration is the time to maturity.

Lower yields give higher durations. So, the present value of flows in the future flows drops if the yield increases, moving the point of balance (the fulcrum) closer towards the present day, thereby shortening the duration.

The duration of a bond shortens as the lifespan of the bond decays. However, the rate of their decay is not the same.

In the example above, a five-year bond with a 7% annual coupon has a duration of 4.373 years. In one year's time, the bond will have a remaining life of four years, and a duration based on the same GRY of 3.617 years.

Calculation of Macaulay Duration			
Bond Price	£96.69	**Yield to Maturity (YTM)**	8.0%
Face Value	£100.00	**Coupon Frequency**	Annually
Coupon Rate	7.00%		
Life in Years	5		
Period	**Cash Flow**	**PV Cash Flow**	**Duration Calculation**
		Cash Flow/[(1+YTM/Coupon Frequency)^Period	PV Cash Flow * Period
1	£7.00	£6.48	£6.48
2	£7.00	£6.00	£12.00
3	£7.00	£5.56	£16.67
4	£107.00	£78.65	£314.59
5	£0.00	£0.00	£0.00
	Totals	£96.69	£349.74
	Macaulay Duration	£349.74/£96.69	3.617

The lifespan of the bond will have decayed by a full year, but the duration by only 0.756 of a year.

7.5 Modified Duration/Volatility

At the same time as the Macaulay duration was being promoted as a means of expressing the sensitivity of a bond to movements in the interest rate, Hicks was developing a formula to explain the impact of yield changes on price. Not surprisingly, the two measures are linked.

Hicks' basic proposition was that the change in yield multiplied by his sensitivity measure gives the resultant percentage change in the bond's price, ie, the volatility gives the percentage change in price per unit change in yield.

Modified duration is the estimated percentage change in the price of a bond arising from a 1% change in yields.

The modified duration formula may be derived through the use of calculus, specifically differentiation of the price equation with respect to yield.

Fortunately, there is an easier definition, specifically:

$$\text{Modified Duration/Volatility} = \frac{\text{Macaulay Duration}}{1+\text{GRY}}$$

Some texts do not include the minus sign in the calculation of modified duration but insert it on use. It is included here to emphasise the inverse relationship between prices and yields, ie, as yields rise, prices fall.

Modified duration offers a first estimate of the change in the price of a bond that results from a given change in yields.

Modified Duration = –4.373/(1.08) = –4.0491

This indicates that, for a 1% rise in interest rates, the bond will fall in price by £3.89, or 4.0491% (ie, from £96.01 to £92.12). Note that for a 1% fall in interest rates, the price would rise by an estimated 4.0491% (from £96.01 to £99.90, ie, a rise of £3.89). The actual price should, however, be £100, as interest rates have fallen to 7%, which is the same as the coupon rate of 7%, hence the bond should be priced at par value.

There is an alternative method of calculating modified duration, but this first requires the related concept of convexity.

7.6 Convexity

Duration and modified duration can be the basis for straight-line estimates of the rate of change of price/present value. Convexity is an estimate of the rate of change of duration and measures the curvature of the line which in turn represents the relationship between an instrument's yield and its value.

Modified duration predicts a linear relationship between yields and prices. If the modified duration is 2, then if yields rise by 1%, the price will fall by 2%. If the rise in yields is 3%, then the fall in price would be 6%.

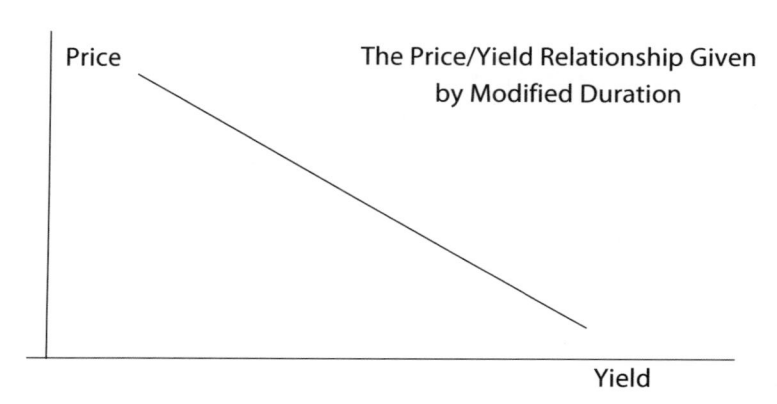

The Price/Yield Relationship Given by Modified Duration

The diagram plots the relationship between price and yield. The slope of the line shows the modified duration.

As yields change, so does the duration. Consequently, the modified duration itself is in flux.

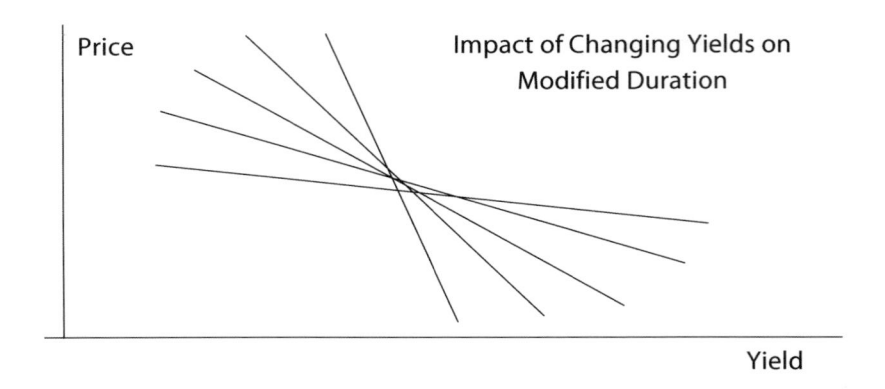

Impact of Changing Yields on Modified Duration

As the yield falls, the duration increases, causing the modified duration to change too. As the modified duration increases, the slope of the line becomes steeper.

The actual relationship between yield and price is given by the convex function of these individual linear relationships. The relationship between bond prices and interest rates is not linear. The actual relationship between prices and yields is curved, with increases in yields resulting in prices dropping, but at a reducing rate.

7.6.1 Definition of 'Convexity'

Convexity is a measure of the curvature in the relationship between bond prices and bond yields that demonstrates how the duration of a bond changes as interest rates change. It is used as a risk management tool, and helps to measure the amount of market risk which a portfolio of bonds is exposed to.

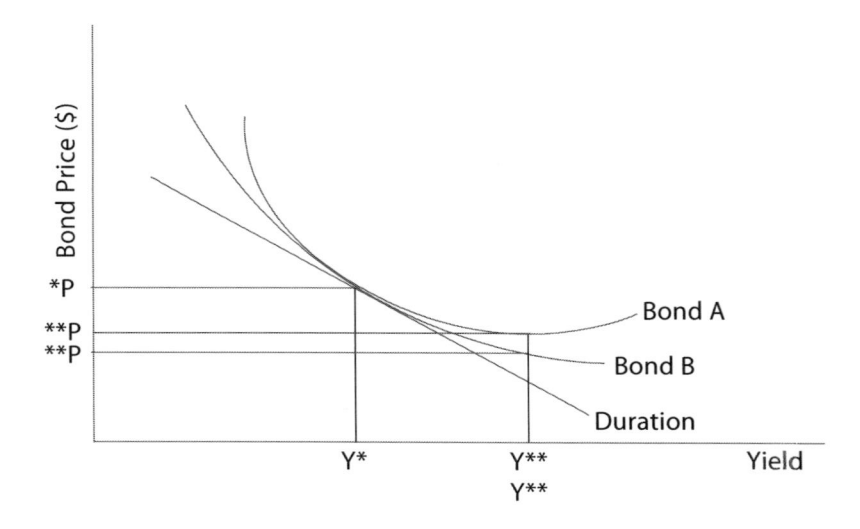

In the example above, Bond A has a higher convexity than Bond B, which means that, everything else being equal, Bond A will always have a higher price than Bond B whether interest rates rise or fall. Where the yield Y* equals the coupon at price *P, the duration of both bonds is the same. At yield Y**, however, the price **P of Bond A is higher than that of Bond B.

As convexity increases, the systemic risk of the portfolio increases. As it decreases, the exposure to market interest rates decreases and the bond portfolio can be considered hedged. In general, the higher the coupon rate, the lower the convexity (or market risk) of a bond.

The relationship between actual convexity and the linear convexity predicted by the modified duration formula can be illustrated as below:

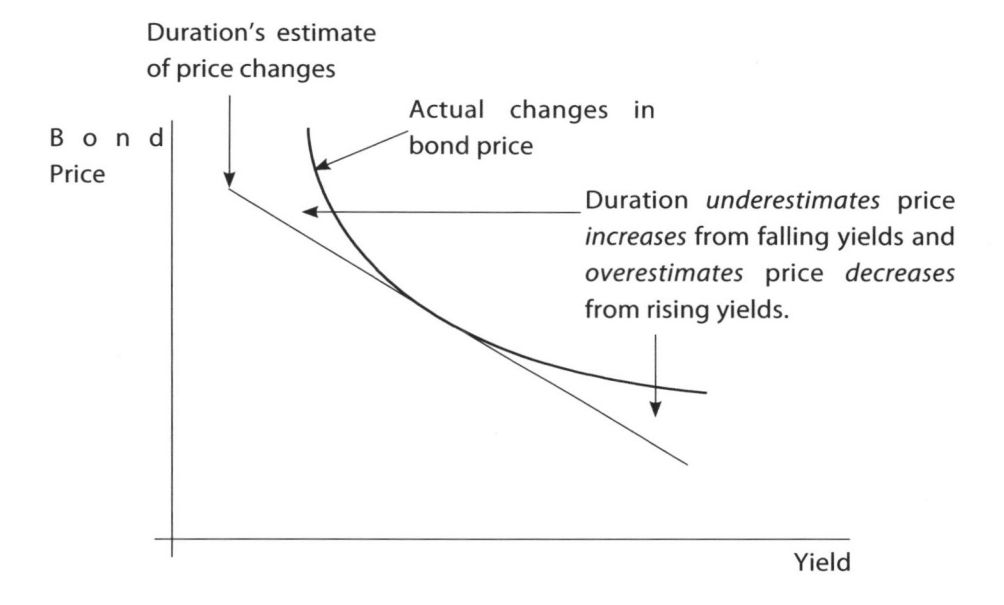

The impact of convexity is that the modified duration tends to overstate the drop in a bond's price and understate its rise. For relatively small movements in the yield, the modified duration will be a good estimate; the accuracy of convexity only diminishes volatility in the yield increase.

Convexity is defined as the change in the modified duration with respect to yields.

$$\text{Convexity} = \frac{\Sigma t\ (t+1)\ PV_t}{\text{Price}\ (1 + GRY)^2}$$

The table below offers an alternative format of the interrelationship of modified duration and convexity.

Consider a three-year bond which pays an annual coupon of 9% and which has a GRY of 8%. The calculation methods are described within the cells in the table:

Calculation of Modified Duration and Convexity				
Bond Price from NPV of Cash Flows	£102.58	**Yield to Maturity (YTM)**	8.00%	
Face Value	£100.00	**Coupon Frequency**	Annual	
Coupon Rate	9.00%	**Life in Years**	3	
Period	**Cash Flow**	**PV Cash Flow**	**Duration Calculation**	**Convexity Calculation**
		Cash Flow/ [(1+YTM/Coupon Frequency)^Period]	PV Cash Flow* Period	1/(1+YTM/Coupon Frequency)^2 *PV Cash Flow* (Period^2+Period)
1	£9.00	£8.33	£8.33	£14.29
2	£9.00	£7.72	£15.43	£39.69
3	£109.00	£86.53	£259.59	£890.20
Totals		£102.58	£283.35	£944.18
Macaulay Duration	2.7623	[Total of Duration Calculation/Bond Price]/Coupon Frequency		
Modified Duration	−2.5577	Macaulay Duration/[1+Yield To Maturity/Coupon Frequency]		
Convexity	9.2043	[Total Convexity Calculation/Bond Price]/(Coupon Frequency^2)		

The sensitivity of bond prices to specified changes in the GRY or YTM are immediately obvious.

The table below shows how a 1% change in the GRY can be easily calculated using the values referenced below. For example, an increase in the GRY from 8% to 9% brings the redemption value of the bond to par or £100, which is £2.58 less than the value which was previously calculated and shown above, when the GRY was at 8%. The table below indicates this as the exact difference after applying the convexity adjustment.

The following calculation shows how the modified duration and convexity adjustment can calculate the new theoretical price of a specified bond when the YTM changes by 1%.

If yield changes by	1.00%			
Bond price will change by	(2.58)			
Modified duration predicts	(2.62) –Modified Duration * Yield Change * Bond Price			
Convexity adjustment	0.05 0.5 * Convexity * Yield Change^2 * Bond Price			
Total predicted change	(2.58)			
Actual new price	£102.58			
Predicted new price	£100.00			
Difference	(£2.58)			

The formula for the convexity adjustment is:

$$\text{Convexity Adjustment} = 0.5 \times \text{Convexity} \times \text{Yield}^2 \times \text{Bond Price}$$

The formula can also be used to explore the change in the bond price from, say, a 2% change in the GRY as follows:

The following method of calculation shows how the modified duration and convexity adjustment can be used to calculate the new theoretical price of a specified bond when the YTM changes by 2%

If yield changes by	2.00%			
Bond price will change by	(5.06)			
Modified duration predicts	(5.25) –Modified Duration * Yield Change * Bond Price			
Convexity adjustment	0.19 0.5 * Convexity * Yield Change^2 * Bond Price			
Total predicted change	(5.06)			
Actual new price	£102.58			
Predicted new price	£97.52			
Difference	(–£5.06)			

The table above shows what happens to the price as the GRY moves from 9%, the par price for redemption, to 10%. In other words, the GRY is increased by exactly 2% from the original assumption of 8% and results in a price of £102.58. Using the formulae outlined in the table, the predicted new price for the bond with a change in the GRY to 10% is £97.52, exactly the difference demonstrated by the convexity adjustment.

Now consider the original bond above, but this time with an assumed 10% GRY.

Calculation of Modified Duration and Convexity				
Bond Price from NPV of Cash Flows	£97.51	**Yield to Maturity (YTM)**	10.00%	
Face Value	£100.00	**Coupon Frequency**	Annual	
Coupon Rate	9.00%	**Life in Years**	3	
Period	**Cash Flow**	**PV Cash Flow**	**Duration Calculation**	**Convexity Calculation**
		Cash Flow/ [(1+YTM/Coupon Frequency)^Period]	PV Cash Flow* Period	1/(1+YTM/Coupon Frequency)^2*PV Cash Flow* (Period^2+Period)
0				
1	£9.00	£8.18	£8.18	£13.52
2	£9.00	£7.44	£14.88	£36.88
3	£109.00	£81.89	£245.68	£812.17
Totals		£97.51	£268.74	£862.57
Macaulay Duration	2.7559			
	[Total of Duration Calculation/Bond Price]/Coupon Frequency			
Modified Duration	2.5054			
	Macaulay Duration/[1+Yield To Maturity/Coupon Frequency]			
Convexity	8.8457			
	[Total Convexity Calculation/Bond Price]/(Coupon Frequency^2)			

The actual price of the bond based upon the NPV of the coupon and redemption payments, discounted at the GRY rate of 10% is within one penny of the value calculated from using the convexity adjustment.

Convexity is a useful value in measuring the sensitivity of a bond to changes in the prevailing interest rate environment.

- It gives a more accurate assessment of the change in the price of a bond from a given change in yields.
- It compares the convexity values of alternative holdings in a bond fund.

- Not all bonds have the same degree of convexity. The general rule is that bonds with a higher duration exhibit the greatest convexity.
- For bonds with the same duration, those with higher coupons have greater convexity.

Illustration

Compare two hypothetical gilts, both paying semi-annual coupons, and both with a maturity of five years.

The first gilt has a 9% coupon and an assumed GRY of 9%. The spreadsheet shows the values for the Macaulay duration, modified duration and the convexity:

Calculation of Modified Duration and Convexity			
Bond Price from NPV of Cash Flows	£100.00	**Yield to Maturity (YTM)**	**9.00%**
Face Value	£100.00	**Coupon Frequency**	Semi-Annual
Coupon Rate	9.00%	**Life in Years**	5
Period	**Cash Flow**	**PV Cash Flow**	**Duration Calculation**	**Convexity Calculation**
---	---	---	---	---
		Cash Flow/ $[(1+YTM/Coupon\ Frequency)^{Period}]$	PV Cash Flow* Period	$1/(1+YTM/Coupon\ Frequency)^2 * PV\ Cash\ Flow * (Period^2+Period)$
1	£4.50	£4.31	£4.31	£7.89
2	£4.50	£4.12	£8.24	£22.64
3	£4.50	£3.94	£11.83	£43.33
4	£4.50	£3.77	£15.09	£69.11
5	£4.50	£3.61	£18.06	£99.20
6	£4.50	£3.46	£20.73	£132.90
7	£4.50	£3.31	£23.15	£169.57
8	£4.50	£3.16	£25.31	£208.63
9	£4.50	£3.03	£27.25	£249.56
10	£104.50	£67.29	£672.90	£6,778.19
Totals		£100.00	£826.88	£7,781.03
Macaulay Duration	4.1344			
	[Total of Duration Calculation/Bond Price]/Coupon Frequency			
Modified Duration	3.9564			
	Macaulay Duration/[1+Yield To Maturity/Coupon Frequency]			
Convexity	19.4526			
	[Total Convexity Calculation/Bond Price]/(Coupon Frequency^2)			

The second gilt is identical, except for a coupon of 5%:

Calculation of Modified Duration And Convexity				
Bond Price from NPV of Cash Flows	£84.17	**Yield to Maturity (YTM)**	9.00%	
Face Value	£100.00	**Coupon Frequency**	Semi-Annual	
Coupon Rate	5.00%	**Life in Years**	5	
Period	**Cash Flow**	**PV Cash Flow**	**Duration Calculation**	**Convexity Calculation**
		Cash Flow/ [(1+YTM/Coupon Frequency)^Period]	PV Cash Flow* Period	1/(1+YTM/Coupon Frequency)^2*PV Cash Flow* (Period^2+Period)
1	£2.50	£2.39	£2.39	£4.38
2	£2.50	£2.29	£4.58	£12.58
3	£2.50	£2.19	£6.57	£24.07
4	£2.50	£2.10	£8.39	£38.39
5	£2.50	£2.01	£10.03	£55.11
6	£2.50	£1.92	£11.52	£73.83
7	£2.50	£1.84	£12.86	£94.21
8	£2.50	£1.76	£14.06	£115.91
9	£2.50	£1.68	£15.14	£138.64
10	£102.50	£66.00	£660.03	£6,648.46
Totals		£84.17	£745.57	£7,205.59
Macaulay Duration	4.4287			
	[Total of Duration Calculation/Bond Price]/Coupon Frequency			
Modified Duration	4.2380			
	Macaulay Duration/[1+Yield To Maturity/Coupon Frequency]			
Convexity	21.4007			
	[Total Convexity Calculation/Bond Price]/(Coupon Frequency^2)			

Both the Macaulay duration and modified duration are longer for the lower coupon bond which causes a higher convexity as well.

Lower coupon bonds have durations which change little with an alteration in the GRY. In the most extreme form, a zero-coupon bond has a duration equal to its maturity and this will not alter as yields move.

Investors may often be willing to pay for convexity. In a volatile market, more convex bonds at any particular maturity outperform those with lower convexity.

Basis Point Value (BPV)

Basis point value (BPV) is simply a finer measure of sensitivity, sometimes referred to as the price value of a basis point or the dollar value of a basis point. This is the change in price if the yield changes by one basis point.

The exact determination of the price expected from a change in yield is a two-step calculation. It involves the calculation of the modified duration for a change in the GRY, which enables a calculation of the difference in the price of the bond resulting from a change in yield, but the second stage, involving the convexity value, gives a more precise price difference in order to determine a more accurate value.

In general terms, more sensitive bonds have a higher BPV.

Exercise Answers

Exercise 1

Assume that the UK Government issues a new gilt in 2018:

Treasury 1.5% 2048

John, a private investor, has asked whether such an investment bears any risks. He has been told that payments from these investments are totally safe.

Outline to John just what key risks he may face while holding the gilt.

Answer

Gilt payments are guaranteed by HM Treasury and are safe unless the Government defaults on its payouts. To date, this has not happened.

It is very likely that John would receive the return of his original investment together with the promised interest payments (coupons).

Providing he buys the gilt at issue and holds it until maturity, he should receive his original investment and regular interest during the term.

However, it's important to understand that, in so far as gilts are safe, they are only safe if they are bought when they are issued and held until they are redeemed. Between times, their price can rise or fall. If he buys or sells at the wrong time, he can lose capital.

The other key market risk for these investments is inflation. If inflation rises, the gilt could provide poor returns in real terms, as it only offers a fixed coupon. The price will adjust to fall in line with the market's view on required yields for bonds of this term and quality.

Exercise 2

Outline the possible reasons why you think credit rating agencies have come under so much criticism – especially in the wake of the credit crisis of 2008.

Answer

A number of explanations of the rating agencies' inaccurate ratings and forecasts have been offered, especially in the wake of the subprime crisis. Some suggestions are outlined below:

- The methodologies employed by agencies have been criticised as being inherently flawed. For example, a 2008 report by the Financial Stability Forum expressed methodological shortcomings such as the use of inadequate historical data. The forum intimated that this led to the underestimating of the risk in structured finance products by credit rating agencies before the subprime mortgage crisis.
- The ratings process has relied on subjective judgments. Governments, for instance, that are being rated can influence credit rating analysts during the review process.
- The rating agencies' desire to make securities issuers happy, as it is they who are the agencies' paying clients. This can create conflicts of interest relative to providing accurate ratings of securities for investors buying the securities. Issuers of securities benefit from higher ratings in that many of their customers are otherwise prohibited from purchasing securities below a certain rating.
- The rating agencies may have not had adequate staff during certain times such as the subprime boom and have, therefore, been unable to properly assess every debt instrument.
- Agency analysts may be underpaid relative to similar positions at investment firms, resulting in a migration of credit rating analysts to other organisations.
- The functional use of ratings as regulatory mechanisms may have increased their reputation for accuracy without the necessary foundation.

Bonds

Exercise 3

An investor pays a clean price of £116.80 per £100 of nominal stock with a 6% coupon paid annually. The stock has exactly six years to run until maturity. Calculate the Japanese GRY.

Answer

Income yield = £6 / £116.80 x 100 = 5.14% per annum

Capital gain / loss at redemption: −£16.80 (ie, a loss)

Annualised loss: −£16.80 / 6 years = −£2.80 per annum

As a percentage of price: −£2.80 / £116.80 x 100 = −2.40% per annum

GRY: 5.14% − 2.40% = 2.74% per annum.

Exercise 4

Assume the following three-year term structure of spot interest rates:

Rate	1+ Spot Rate
R_1	1.04
R_2	1.06
R_3	1.08

From these spot rates, calculate the implied set of spot and forward rates for the same period.

Answer

Rate	Spot/Forward Rates
$_0F_1$	0.04
$_1F_2$	0.0804
$_2F_3$	0.1211

The spot rates in the first table are the geometric averages of the spot/forward rates in the second table. To verify this, consider the general equation where t = 1 and T = 2:

$(1 + R_1)(1 + {_1F_2}) = (1 + R_2)^2$

This yields:

$(1.04)(1 + {_1F_2}) = (1.06)^2$

You can calculate the $_1F_2$ rate by taking $1.06^2 / 1.04 = 1.0804 = 8.04\%$

Check back with your workings: 1.04 x 1.0804 = 1.1236

Square root of 1.1236 = 1.06

Similarly, we can do the same for verifying the three-year spot rate:

$(1 + R_1)(1 + {}_1F_2)(1 + {}_2F_3) = 1.08^3$

To find the ${}_2F_3$ rate:

$(1.04)(1.0804)(1 + {}_2F_3) = 1.08^3$

$(1 + {}_2F_3) = 1.08^3 / (1.04)(1.0804)$

$= 1.1211$. Therefore, ${}_2F_3 = 0.1211 = 12.11\%$

Chapter Seven
Equities

1. **Characteristics of Investing in Listed Equity**   323
2. **Types of Listed Equities**   334
3. **Private Equity (PE)**   343

Learning Outcome

Be able to evaluate critically the risks and returns offered by both equities and derivative investments

1. Characteristics of Investing in Listed Equity

Learning Objective

7.1 Explain and appraise the characteristics of investing in listed equity: definition and key properties of equities; risk, price, and return; historic performance of equities; principal problems and liquidity issues, plus implications should liquidity fall

1.1 The Nature of Equities

The capital structure of a typically large corporation comprises two primary classes of capital. The first, known as 'risk capital', consists of equities or the ordinary shares of the company; the second broad tier is known as 'debt' or 'borrowings'. The debt layer of capital will invariably have more seniority than equity in terms of the claims against the company's assets. In the case of insolvency or the liquidation of a company, whatever value is found in the assets will be distributed according to the seniority of the claims with respect to the capital structure. At the bottom of the pyramid, the ordinary shareholders are the least likely to see full repayment of their stake in the company.

The ordinary shareholders of a company are its owners. The directors of the company have the task of maximising the wealth of the ordinary shareholders. Generally, the ordinary shareholders have the right to a dividend and voting rights on company matters. Among the different classes of holding, ordinary shares are seen as the most 'to vote', in that they are the lowest priority for payment both in terms of the dividend distributions from profits and of capital at the winding-up of a company. Dividend payments depend on the available net profits that the organisation can distribute and are therefore variable in nature with no guarantees. Payment of capital on winding-up depends on the residual capital after all other creditors are paid, including bond and preference shareholders.

A company may or may not have preference shares in its capital structure. A preference share pays a fixed rather than variable amount of dividend, normally half-yearly. Thus, preference shares are similar to loan stock. With loan stock, the interest must be paid even if the company is losing money. With preference shares, the dividend is only paid if there are sufficient post-tax profits. Preference shares do not usually carry voting rights unless the dividend payments fall into arrears.

Many smaller *limited* companies are private companies, which may be owner-managed and cannot offer their shares to the general public. The use of the term 'limited' indicates that shareholders have limited liability: if the company fails, shareholders can lose their entire investment in the company but the company's creditors cannot pursue the shareholders for any further money. However, with many small companies, the kinds of loans that may be provided by banks will often require the personal guarantees of the owners, so they effectively incur a liability for the company, but not directly from their status as shareholders *per se*.

1.2 Listed Shares

Although there a number of very large corporations that have decided to remain as private or unlisted companies, it is common for companies, once they reach a certain size, and have plans to expand their business lines, to raise additional capital by seeking a listing on a stock exchange. They engage an investment bank to act as an underwriter and issuer of an initial public offering (IPO) in which new shares are issued by the company and sold to new subscribers, ie, to new shareholders.

In order to offer shares for sale to the public via an IPO, a UK company must be a plc (public limited company). The kinds of IPOs that can be conducted and the listing requirements of the exchanges vary, and in the case of a large corporation the most likely route for a UK company would be to seek a full listing on the main market of the London Stock Exchange (LSE). If the company is smaller or has less of a trading track record it may join the less closely regulated Alternative Investment Market (AIM).

Overseas companies can also seek listings for their shares on the LSE and, conversely, many UK companies have their shares listed on large international exchanges, such as the New York Stock Exchange (NYSE) and Nasdaq. For example, AstraZeneca plc is listed on both the LSE and the NYSE in the form of an American depositary receipt (ADR), while Vodafone plc is listed on the LSE and Nasdaq.

ADRs represent ownership in the shares of a non-US company (they can be for a part share, single share or multiple shares) and they trade in US financial markets. The stock of many non-US companies trade on US stock exchanges through the use of ADRs. The packaging of non-US domiciled corporate equities enables a US investor to buy shares in foreign companies without the hazards or inconveniences of cross-border and cross-currency transactions. ADRs are priced in US dollars, pay dividends in US dollars and can be traded like the shares of US-based companies.

Both UK and foreign equities are bought and sold by private investors, by large institutions such as life assurance companies and pension funds, and by foreign investors.

There are two principal motivations behind the purchase of shares by an investor:

- To receive income through the receipt of dividends which are paid out by companies from their net earnings.
- To gain from increases in the price of the share in the form of capital gains. While this is a primary motivation for many individuals, there is, of course, no assurance that shares purchased at one time and then sold at a later date will have gained in value – they could have lost in value and a capital loss would be incurred.

1.2.1 Value of a Share

Investment theory leads to the view that the fundamental value of an equity share to the investor is the net present value (NPV) of all the anticipated future dividend payments arising from the share. Essentially, the purchasers of a share are discounting the expected future growth in earnings and dividends, and this comprises the share value. Because the future is extremely difficult to predict, the perceived value of a share can fluctuate sometimes with great volatility.

A company's earnings (profits) can be used either to pay dividends, or to reinvest within the business. Some companies do not pay dividends, perhaps because they have not yet made profits, or because they choose instead to retain their earnings and to reinvest them.

In general terms more mature companies pay dividends and less mature companies – especially companies in their high growth stages such as technology companies often do not pay a dividend but decide to reinvest any profitability into further growth of the business.

Microsoft, a highly profitable company, did not at first pay dividends for many years, but as it has become more mature it has been paying dividends to its shareholders.

A question arises then with regard to share valuation when a company such as Microsoft was not, as through most of its early history, paying any dividends. How does a company command a high stock market valuation, if the value of a share is the NPV of its future dividends but it is not currently paying a dividend?

The suggestion is that investors look ahead to the prospect that the company will be pay significant dividends at some stage in the future. In the case of Microsoft, during many years of reinvesting its earnings it was able to reach a commanding position in the software market and thereby enhance its ability to generate eventual future dividends.

For some companies, a return to shareholders may be achieved when the company is sold for cash in a takeover, through capital gains rather than through payment of dividends.

Dividend Policy

The question of whether shareholders would prefer to receive their return in the form of capital gains or dividends is the subject of the Modigliani & Miller Theorem (also known as the Capital Structure Irrelevance Theorem), named after Franco Modigliani and Merton Miller. The essence is that the value of a firm is the same, regardless of its capital structure, ie, whether it is financed mainly via debt or equity. Shareholders are likewise indifferent to receiving their returns via dividends or capital gains.

If the dividend is higher than expected, then the retained profit will be lower and hence the share price will fall to reflect this. Shareholders could, therefore, sell the surplus dividend received and use the proceeds to buy more shares at the new lower price.

If the dividend is lower than expected, then the retained profit will be higher and hence the share price will be higher too. Shareholders can, thus, sell some shares at the higher price, using these capital gains to make good the reduced cash flow received from the poor dividend.

This theory makes several unrealistic assumptions however, which tend to lead to a clear preference for dividends or capital gains, one way or the other that:

- taxes do not exist (or at least are no different between capital gains or dividends, or in the case of capital structure that interest is not deductible on corporate debt)
- there are no transaction costs, either in the initial share flotation, nor on the sale or purchase of shares
- leverage from higher debt has no impact on the weighted average cost of capital (WACC).

1.2.2 Influences on Share Prices

Prices of equities, in common with most asset classes, move continually during trading hours. Investors differ as to their valuations of security prices based on different time horizons, different economic outlooks and different vested interests.

For markets to work properly there need to be contrasting views, different time horizons and different agendas and priorities among buyers and sellers. While some traders may think that an asset is worth buying at a specified price there must be others who, for various reasons, think that it is worth selling at that price. The two most common frameworks for financial markets are the open-outcry model and the electronic order book and, in both cases, for sustained trading to take place there needs to be a fragmentation of opinions. Assuming that there are a dedicated group of traders that want to trade a particular asset, the more evenly divided opinions are regarding the suitability of the current price the more liquid the market will be. In very liquid markets, buying and selling preferences will show a high degree of non-alignment. Trading stances will be dispersed and there will be no obvious internal coherence to them. But when the fragmentation is replaced by a near-consensus view among traders the liquidity evaporates and markets are prone to behaving in erratic and sometimes dramatic price swings.

Share prices can change as a result of information becoming available to investors about various matters, including:

- earnings prospects and asset values of individual companies
- membership of the board
- adverse factors affecting companies, such as legal action against it, or action by a bank to call in loans
- industry and economy surveys, for example about levels of retail sales, or productivity
- macroeconomic developments, for example: the expected level of interest rates, or where an economy appears to be located in the business cycle
- changes in government policy, for example fiscal and monetary policy
- movements in other stock markets around the world, such as the US, China and Japan
- geopolitical developments including wars, and threats from terrorist groups.

Many companies aim to present a stable and steadily rising pattern of dividend payments from year to year. Sharp changes from the usual pattern may be taken by investors as a signal of a change in the company's fortunes, which may cause a shift in the share price.

One consequence of the global banking crisis of 2008 and the ensuing economic downturn was that many large organisations, especially in the financial services sector, had either to cut their dividends or suspend them entirely. As a result many institutional investors such as pension funds then sold the shares of such companies, creating a downward cycle in share prices. The large US bank Citigroup is, for example suspended payment of a dividend and saw its share price move into low single digits with a corresponding 90% fall in its market capitalisation.

Market capitalisation refers to the value that is placed on a company by multiplying the outstanding equity of a company by its current share price. In some ways it is a flawed notion since it places a value on the entire company from the value of the marginal shares traded during a particular session, which may have been particularly influenced by the wider market.

Investors look for evidence of the quality of a company's management, although such evidence can be difficult to obtain in practice.

Changes in board membership can affect investors' assessment of a company's prospects and the share price may move as a result. If a director resigns, investors are interested in the reason for the resignation. If new directors are appointed, their experience and past track record is of interest.

The prices of some companies' shares are affected more by the state of the wider economy than others. For example, because house purchase decisions are influenced by mortgage rates, house building companies will be particularly sensitive to interest rate changes. If people are moving house less as a result of interest rate increases, businesses such as DIY (do-it-yourself) and carpeting may also face a downturn in demand and therefore earnings.

Given the increasing interdependence of national economies through globalisation of trade and capital flows, share prices tend to be influenced by economic conditions around the world, particularly the state of the economy in the world's largest debtor nation, the US.

Some recent studies have suggested that the interlinkage between global stock markets is becoming much more pronounced than it used to be. Correlation analysis shows a greater degree of co-movement between indices in the US, UK, Western Europe and Japan. This is partly due to the increasing globalisation of trade in recent decades. Some emerging markets have however been less correlated with the more mature market economies, due to idiosyncratic monetary and fiscal policies of certain governments, but also due to regional political tensions which can be hard to dissipate.

On a related theme there is a strong influence between the state of the world economy and final demand and the price levels of major commodities such as oil, copper, and other industrial metals. The emerging markets are greatly influenced by the prices of commodities both as major consumers (in the case of China) and where exports of commodities comprise a substantial proportion of national economic output (in the case of Russia and Brazil).

Equities are no less prone to behavioural weaknesses as other asset classes, such as currencies and commodities. Sometimes, despite prevailing weaker economic sentiment, investors will buy simply because prices have started to rise and they sense that other investors believe they will rise further. In other words they buy in reaction to and anticipation of the actions of others, rather than for any rational investment reason at the time. The opposite occurs, often far more dramatically, when investors sense fear among others, leading to dramatic falls far steeper than that justified by even negative news. The study of behavioural finance in equities as well as other asset classes is a relatively new phenomenon, but gradually growing in popularity.

1.2.3 The Performance of Equities

A study carried out in 2016 by Barclays Capital revealed that equities have produced the best real (inflation-adjusted) returns of all the main asset classes over longer terms of 50 years plus. Over five years, UK equities had produced a real (after inflation) return of around 5% per annum. Over longer terms, this return level is fairly consistent too, hovering above 4% over ten and 20 years and nearer to 6% per annum over a 50-year period. Over short periods, however, equities can be extremely volatile and prone to large losses as much as gains.

Interestingly and much because of a bullish leaning towards government debt in recent times, gilts have outperformed equities over both five and 20 years with annual yields of 5.3% and 5.1% respectively.

What lessons are there for investors seeking exposure to equities? One point is that spreading investment over a period can reduce some of the effects of market volatility. Instead of a single investment of say £10,000 made in 1999, when the US and UK stock markets were at their peak, if an investor had invested perhaps £2,000 per year over the next ten years the principle of cost averaging would have lessened the impact of poor returns for equities in recent years.

The question of buying and holding equities or even index-tracker products such as one based on the FTSE 100 is being questioned by more financial analysts in the light of the more recent data.

Exercise 1

Mrs Bourne has just won £250,000 in the National Lottery and has approached you for investment advice. Having carried out a full fact find, you have suggested some of the money be invested in ordinary shares.

a. What does being a shareholder mean for her?
b. Evaluate critically the risks and returns offered to her by equity investments.

The answers to this exercise can be found at the end of this chapter.

1.3 Equities as Part of a Portfolio

Investors with smaller amounts to invest and who do not wish to build their own portfolio can gain exposure to equity markets through pooled investments such as unit trusts, open-ended investment companies (OEICs) (also called investment companies with variable capital (ICVCs)) or investment trusts.

A number of points of interest from other areas of this workbook are relevant here.

- There is no guarantee of dividends, or of return of capital. Particularly with more speculative investments, it is possible that the whole investment in a particular share will be lost.
- Diversification among different shares with lower or negative correlations helps to reduce the risk of concentrated losses.
- Portfolio managers sometimes use measurements of the beta of a share to measure this risk of high correlation.
- A share with a beta factor of 1 moves in line with the market. If the market (for example, as indicated by a share price index such as the FTSE 100) moves up 5%, the price of this security is likely to move up 5%.
- A share with a beta factor greater than 1 varies more widely than the market. If the market moves up 5%, the price of a security with a beta of 2 is likely to move up 10%.
- A share with a beta factor of less than 1 fluctuates less than the wider market. If the market moves up or down 10%, the price of a security with a beta of 0.5 is likely to move up or down respectively by 5%.
- A share with a beta of 0 does not show any relationship to the movements in the particular market or benchmark it is being measured against, ie, it demonstrates zero systematic risk.

1.3.1 Buying and Selling Shares

Equities are bought and sold through a broker. The traditional notions of the role of a broker, however, are now becoming increasingly obsolete as most institutional and retail investors use with electronic platforms which provide no visibility or intermediation of the broker's platform during the buying and selling of shares.

Historically, and still for some sections of the institutional and retail market for equities the role of the broker could take one of these forms:

1.3.2 Execution-Only Dealing Service

Brokers simply carry out the client's instructions. The client will have agreed, when opening an investment or trading account, not to receive advice on investments.

1.3.3 Advisory or Non-Discretionary Service

Brokers make recommendations, but the client makes the final decision.

1.3.4 Discretionary Service

Brokers will have authority to buy and sell without reference to the client. A carefully worded contract will stipulate the parameters for transactions, for example, the amount of risk the client wishes to take or the types of securities they wish to consider.

1.4 Changing Workflow of Equity Markets

Increasingly, transactions for shares are conducted online through a brokerage platform which clients can access directly. There is no actual human contact with the broker. The brokerage platform may provide clients with a range of services including real-time charting and analysis and also the client can execute trades in real time with a constant updating of the bid and offer prices. In some cases, clients will have direct access to the market order books and can see the order flow which is entering the market.

1.5 Algorithmic Trading

The best way to understand algorithmic trading is to consider the business problem that the technique of trading via algorithms was designed to solve. Large institutional traders leave large footprints in the marketplace. A large unit trust, or mutual fund as they are called in the US, that which decides to place a large buy or sell order into the market's order book runs several risks. The first is that other traders will see the size of the order and know that there is an opportunity for exploitation by front-running the order (trading in advance in the same direction at a more preferable price, in the expectation that the larger order will then drive the market quickly in the desired direction with minimal risk). More of the market risk then lies with the institution with the second, larger trade, which will be trading in a market which may already have started to move.

If another brokerage or affiliated third party sees a large buy order entering the market, there is the possibility for agile traders who may know the size of that order to position themselves quickly to benefit at the fund's expense. In effect, the other participants are buying ahead of the fund, benefiting from the expected uplift that the large order will have on the price for less risk than if they were to buy in a more neutral market. The fund may end up achieving the large purchase that it wished to achieve, but only after moving the market away from the price at which it had intended to execute the trade.

An automated process has been developed to disguise the true intent of these large fund managers. The process, known as algorithmic trading, facilitates the more efficient execution of large orders, by discovering pools of liquidity at certain prices, thereby allowing it to trade without unduly moving the underlying market. For example, if a fund wants to buy large quantity of a particular stock, the order is broken into a series of much smaller sub-orders and then executed over a period of time, in order to achieve actual price executions at the optimal cost.

In other words, algorithms are capable of scattering the original trade objective into a fragmentary process which should no longer be transparent to other market players.

One of the consequences of this innovation is that the micro-structural behaviour of markets is changing. There is far less transparency at the order book level and even when a series of orders do appear on the order screens there is a real question mark as to whether these small 'orders' are in fact part of much larger transactions. Access to the order books was originally seen as a giant step forward in increasing market transparency and levelling the playing field for smaller traders, but as with most innovations there are usually ingenious techniques designed to defeat the purpose. Traders, both large and small, welcome transparency as a great principle, but in practice they would rather be able to operate anonymously and stealthily in the marketplace, increasingly today through what are known as dark pools of liquidity where the complete transaction remains opaque and anonymous.

There has been much innovation regarding the complexity of algorithms that buy-side traders are now using and the motivations have extended beyond the original desire to protect the liquidity of large trades through disguising their size. There have been numerous instances where unexpected, dramatic but short-lived market moves have occurred even in major asset classes in recent years. Consider for example the 36 minute 9% fall and subsequent rebound in US equities on 6 May 2010 or the 40 second 10% fall then recovery in GBP/.USD just after midnight on 7 October 2016. Blame for the former was eventually laid with a UK private day-trader, allegedly manipulating algorithmic systems to generate the extreme volatility, while no satisfactory explanation has yet been found for the latter. The FCA has nevertheless introduced rules (FCA Handbook, MAR 7A) regarding algorithmic trading among both market-makers and speculators, in line with article 17 of MiFID II. The Market Abuse Regime (MAR) is analysed further in chapter 10.

The use of algorithmic trading in different forms of trading venues and their subsequent use to create 'dark pools' of liquidity is also described in chapter 10, section 9.4 but it is important to note that this is a fast-developing area of financial markets and hence of regulation. MiFID II has had a significant impact on investment and intermediary firms' regulation, but was introduced only in January 2018; there will inevitably be unintended consequences before long, leading to revisions and amendments, while technology will to some extent be directed to exploiting loopholes as they are discovered. The incentive of market participants to gain an advantage through technology will remain in constant tension with the reactive desire of regulators to protect end-users and to ensure fair competition in a stable environment, so expect algorithmic trading to persist, but not necessarily in its current format.

1.6 Factors Affecting Share Prices

Investors buy ordinary shares mainly because they expect share values to increase. Over a long period, what causes share prices to rise is the increasing earning power of the companies and their ability to pay higher dividends out of these increasing earnings. However, in the short term, there are many other factors that can distort the picture.

1.6.1 Share Prices Follow a Random Walk

When researchers have examined share price movements for quoted companies, some have claimed that the price movements seem to follow a random pattern, ie, the movement in any one day is uncorrelated to the movement in the previous day. For those who believe in the random walk notion future share price movements cannot be predicted from details of historical movements.

There are a number of other studies which show that there is in fact clustering in stock returns with sharp movements in prices, either up or down, tending to cluster in a fashion which is inconsistent with the notion of a random walk.

Other studies have suggested that there are cyclical and seasonal patterns in stock price movements, which again are inconsistent with the random walk hypothesis, and which could also provide a basis for some degree of predictability in future returns for stocks. It is a lively area of debate among investors and traders.

1.6.2 Share Prices Discount New Information

Share prices are observed to move when new information is received, and will fairly reflect that new information. Professor Eugene Fama, an American economist, developed the efficient market hypothesis (EMH) which, in summary, claims that financial markets are informationally efficient. Therefore, a market would be efficient with respect to an information set if the price fully reflects that information set and the price would be unaffected by revealing the information set to all market participants.

The EMH suggests that all information has been discounted by market participants and that current prices are, in a theoretical sense, the correct prices.

1.7 Behavioural Finance

According to behavioural finance, investors do not behave rationally, which a key assumption of the EMH. The EMH states that new information in the markets is processed quickly and rationally by all participants, leading to little or no chance for investors to make extraordinary returns.

Behavioural finance integrates classical economics and finance with psychology and the decision-making process. It argues that many aspects about asset prices, investor behaviour, and managerial behaviour are best understood in models where at least some elements are irrational, being subject to what psychologists describe as cognitive biases. These biases can result in sub-conscious mental shortcuts, influencing the decision outcome, especially when the decisions are particularly complex or need to be made under time constraints. Examples of this phenomena include loss aversion; investors often appear not to behave rationally, failing to cut losses with a poorly performing stock.

1.7.1 Press Recommendations

Obviously, investment experts will write about their tips, and investors will take note of these. When commentators in the financial media, tip a particular share for whatever reason, it is possible that the price of that share will rise in the short-term. It is worth noting, however, that this may be caused by natural demand or simply by the speculators buying in anticipation of further buying following the press report.

1.7.2 Broker Recommendations

What is true for press recommendations is equally true for recommendations which come from analysts at large brokerage houses or investment firms. If Goldman Sachs or JP Morgan tips a particular share for whatever reason, the price of that share is likely to rise. The same caveat applies as in the case of press recommendations above.

1.8 Market Makers and Speculators

Market makers rely on high volumes of activity in terms of buying and selling to be successful and make their profits. Therefore, when there is minimal activity, there has historically been the temptation to stimulate the market artificially by moving their quoted prices, and possibly sell shares that they do not own. It is however now a breach of the Market Abuse Regime to manipulate markets in such a misleading manner (see MAR in chapter 10, section 8).

Speculators may also use the technique of short selling shares they do not own if they expect the share price to fall. However, other traders may have knowledge of this and then push prices up, creating a phenomenon which is known as a 'short squeeze', as the short-sellers are forced to cut their losses by buying back at higher prices.

1.9 New Share Issues

When a company raises capital by issuing a large number of new shares, the share price may well drop, as at that time there may not be enough willing buyers to buy the number of shares in issue. However, this will very much depend on the reason for the capital raising with the new issue.

Refer also to chapter 3 (section 6.7) and to section 2.5 below for details on how a rights issue at a discount to the current share price can also affect the share price.

1.10 Takeovers

Rumours of mergers tend to push up the share price of the firm being acquired due to the premium normally paid over the share price at the time of the announcement. The risk of failing to generate the returns to justify that premium for the acquisition tends to make it harder however for the share price of the acquirer to rise as much, if at all. When the affected firms are big enough, the wider market may react, particularly in the same sector. It is illegal for those with knowledge of an impending takeover to trade on this knowledge (this action would usually be classed as insider dealing). However, speculation with regard to a potential takeover can still be rife within a market without it being construed as insider dealing.

1.11 Other Factors

There is almost no limit to what could feasibly impact share prices. These derive from a belief that there is indeed a rational explanation in each instance, which goes against some of the ideas of behavioural finance (section 1.7 above). This can lead to any coincidental occurrence being blamed out of convenience, even though there may be other examples of the same occurrence having no or even the opposite impact, in which case they are ignored.

Some of the commonly attributed factors include:

- **Programme Trading**
  The largest single day's fall in the Dow Jones Industrial Average in 1987 was considered to have been greatly exacerbated by computer programmes which were pre-set to sell on each degree of price weakness, without pause. This caused a vicious circle as the momentum of weakness inevitably triggered the next threshold for more selling. Less dramatic instances have been recorded in many other markets.
  Automatic trading curbs have been introduced into many commodity and equity markets, which prompt various degrees of pause in trading, from a few seconds or minutes to several hours or even until the next trading session.

- **Corporate Events**
  Announcements such as share buy-backs, appointments or resignations of directors, changes of dividend policy, profit warnings, credit rating upgrades & downgrades licence approvals (eg, in pharmaceuticals) can all be said to justify price changes. Some hedge fund strategies are even designed specifically around such events.

- **Index Membership**
  There has been an expansion in recent years of passive index trading, where portfolios are constructed to replicate the weighted constituents of an index such as the FTSE 100. Such indices are recalculated periodically to reflect changes in market capitalisation. If it is announced that one company is due to be dropped from an index and replaced with another, such portfolio managers have no choice other than to sell the shares of the departing index member and buy the shares of the new entrant. Other more discretionary investors will however already have identified such changes and would have pre-empted these trades. This leads to the common *'buy the rumour, sell the fact'* phenomenon, where the actual event leads to a price movement which is the opposite to what is expected, as those who moved early take the opportunity to reverse their positions for substantial profits.

2. Types of Listed Equities

Learning Objective

7.2 Explain the types of listed equity: characteristics; rights attached to classes of shares; issuance; equity related investments

2.1 Characteristics

The ownership of shares means that the owner is a member of the company and confers upon the shareholder a number of rights.

Ordinary shares are the most common form of shares issued by companies in the UK.

They represent permanent capital for a company. A public limited company (plc) does not have to redeem the shares, although investors are free to sell their shares to other investors. Shareholders in some private companies may, however, have rights whereby other shareholders have to buy back the shares of those wishing to sell.

Typically, shareholders have no security, although they do usually have voting rights (normally one share, one vote) and can vote at company meetings on matters such as the appointment of directors and auditors, approval of proposed dividends and takeovers.

Dividend payments to ordinary shareholders are discretionary on the part of the company, and can only be paid out of profits and distributable reserves after the preference shareholders have received their dividend in full. Most blue chip companies in the UK pay out dividends either quarterly or semi-annually. This usually takes the form of one or three interim dividends and a final dividend which can be viewed as a balancing payment. Dividends are usually declared with the announcement of the company's interim/half-yearly results, and the final dividend at the announcement of the company's full year-end results. However, payment of the dividend may be delayed for some time after it is declared, although the date on which it is to be paid is usually declared at the same time as the amount.

Ordinary shares are considered to be the risk capital of a business, in that they are the last to be paid in the event that the company is wound up (there is typically nothing left to pay the ordinary shareholders if a company goes into liquidation!). This is the risk taken for being a part owner of the company and having the right to share in the profits of the company.

There are a number of variations on the standard ordinary share:

2.1.1 Non-Voting Ordinary Shares/'A' Shares

As the name implies, owners of these shares do not have the right to vote at company meetings. In all other respects they are identical to ordinary shares.

They are typically issued by founders of companies, particularly family companies, where the existing shareholders do not want to give away any control.

Shareholders are increasingly reluctant to purchase non-voting shares and they are likely to be traded at a discount to the voting shares, despite being entitled to the same level of dividend.

Similarly, a company can issue shares with restricted voting rights.

2.1.2 Deferred Shares

These are shares whereby the holders are not entitled to the payment of a dividend until a condition has been met, such as:

- a specific amount of time must have elapsed since the shares were issued
- the profits have to exceed a certain level
- other classes of shareholders have to have been paid a predetermined level of dividend, before the owners of these shares can be paid.

2.1.3 Golden Shares

These are shares with special voting rights. They may allow the holder to outvote other shareholders in specific circumstances, giving an effective power of veto and often giving the ability to block any one shareholder from acquiring more than a certain proportion of ordinary shares.

They have been issued in the past by companies that the government has privatised, and are held by the government, giving them effective control over the nationalised company. This prevents events such as takeovers and controlling holdings going abroad, on the basis that these industries are of national importance. (This has subsequently been ruled illegal by the EU!)

Another use of golden shares would be family companies that wish to give a trusted, impartial outsider sufficient powers to help resolve conflicts without involving them in running the company.

2.1.4 Redeemable Ordinary Shares

Companies are allowed to issue redeemable ordinary shares, which may be bought back by the company, at either the option of the company or the shareholder, on a date specified at the time of issue, provided the company has at least one other class of shares in issue, which is not redeemable.

2.2 Features of Preference Shares

Preference shares are the second most common form of shares issued by companies, and as with ordinary shares, they come in a variety of forms.

- They pay a fixed rate of dividend unlike the variable/discretionary dividend paid for ordinary shares.
- Preference shareholders are preferred over ordinary shareholders in two respects:
    - a company must pay the preference share dividend in full before paying a dividend to ordinary shareholders
    - in the event that the company is wound up, the preference shareholders are repaid the nominal value of their shares before the ordinary shareholders can be paid (assuming that there is sufficient to pay anything).

- There is no security attached to preference shares.
- They do not usually have voting rights, although there is typically an exception which allows voting rights if the preference shareholders haven't received a dividend for five years or more.

When investors buy preference shares, the dividends are fixed, so they will not benefit from any significant increase in the company's profits, but they are however protected from some of the downside. Variations on the usual form include:

2.2.1 Cumulative Preference Shares

If a dividend is not paid to cumulative preference shareholders because the company makes insufficient profits, the next year a dividend cannot be paid to the ordinary shareholders until any arrears in the payment of dividends to the cumulative preference shareholders has been made up. The rights to be paid a preference share dividend are effectively carried forward. Most preference shares take this form.

2.2.2 Non-Cumulative Preference Shares

With this type of share, if a dividend is not paid, it is lost. The arrears do not have to be made up before a dividend can be paid to ordinary shareholders.

2.2.3 Participating Preference Shares

The owners of these shares have the right to receive additional dividend when the profits of the company exceed a certain level. The additional amount payable is usually expressed and paid as a proportion of the ordinary dividend. Holders of these shares participate more in the risks and rewards of share ownership than normal preference shares.

2.2.4 Redeemable Preference Shares

These are shares that will be bought back by the company at a pre-agreed price on a pre-agreed date. They are identifiable by the fact that they will have a date in their title.

2.2.5 Convertible Preference Shares

Holders of convertible preference shares will, at some point, have the option of converting them into ordinary shares.

Practically, if the company doesn't do well and the share price falls, they can be held as a fixed income investment, and if the share price rises, the investor can convert.

2.3 Shareholders' Rights and Responsibilities

Since the board of directors has responsibility for the day-to-day management of the company, a mechanism is needed to ensure shareholders can exercise some control over them. This is achieved by a series of shareholder rights as laid down in the Companies Act.

- **Basic rights**
  - to receive annual accounts
  - to be notified of annual general and extraordinary general meetings
  - the right to attend meetings and vote
  - the right to share in the profits of the company
  - the right to a share of the surplus on winding up after all liabilities have been paid.
- **Statutory rights**
  - companies must hold annual general meetings at least once a year
  - shareholders with more than 10% of voting rights can call extraordinary general meetings
  - shareholders with more than 5% of voting rights can propose resolutions
  - any shareholder can petition the court on the grounds that the affairs of the company have been conducted in a manner unfairly prejudicial to the interests of some or all of its members.
- **pre-emptive rights (or rights of pre-emption)** – any rights shareholders may have to be offered shares in a company before they are made available to anyone else. They can arise on the allotment, transfer or transmission of shares. Such rights may be important to ensure that a shareholder's proportion of the voting and other rights in the company are not diluted
- **pre-emptive rights on allotment** can arise under the Companies Act or the company's memorandum and articles.

As seen above, the holders of primarily ordinary shares have a right to vote at company meetings.

Voting at these meetings is generally by way of a show of hands where one shareholder has one vote. Larger shareholders can demand a poll, in which case votes are counted in proportion to the number of shares held.

If a shareholder is unable to attend a meeting in person, they can appoint a proxy to vote on their behalf.

When sending out proxy forms, companies usually suggest names of directors of the company who will act as proxies, voting as they see fit unless otherwise instructed.

A representative is sometimes appointed by corporate bodies as an alternative to a proxy. For the duration of the meeting, the representative has the same rights to speak and vote as a member.

The shareholders' responsibilities for the company's financial liabilities are limited to the value of shares that they own but haven't paid for. This is unlikely to happen in plcs – it is more a private company issue.

2.4 Bonus/Scrip/Capitalisation Issues and Their Effects

A bonus, scrip or capitalisation issue is a free issue of shares to existing shareholders, pro-rata their existing holding. The shares are issued without cost, and the companies undertaking such an issue are not raising any additional finance.

The main reason for a company undertaking a bonus issue is to reduce the price of the shares in the market, increasing demand for the shares and therefore making them more liquid.

Convention in the UK is that the company announces the bonus issue in terms of the number of new (free) shares that a shareholder will receive for an existing number of shares. For example, a one for five bonus issue is an issue where shareholders will be allocated one new free share for every five existing shares that they own (the figures can be whatever the company wants). The US convention is to describe the total number of shares instead of just the new shares, so a UK one for five issue becomes a US six for five issue. Unless otherwise stated in this book, assume the UK convention. In the real world you will often have to clarify the convention being used to understand the terms of the issue.

Let's look at an example of how a bonus issue impacts on a company's share price:

Terms of the bonus issue 2 for 5

Current price of each share £7.30

For the purposes of the example, we will assume that the shareholder owns the minimum number of shares needed to participate in the issue, ie, five.

No. of shares		Price	Value
Before the bonus issue	5	£7.30	£36.50
Bonus Issue	2	nil	nil
After the bonus issue	7	£5.21	£36.50

The total value of the shares is now distributed across a larger number of shares, reducing the market price of each share.

This process is also known as a capitalisation issue, because in accounting terms, it is achieved through the capitalisation of the company's reserves. The impact of a £100 million capitalisation issue of shares at £1 each on a company's balance sheet would be as follows:

Before		After	
Net assets	£550m	Net assets	£550m
Share capital 300m @ £1	£300m	Share capital 400m @ £1	£400m
Share premium account	£100m	Share premium account	–
Revenue reserves account	£150m	Revenue reserves account	£150m
Shareholders' funds	£550m	Shareholders' funds	£550m

Equities

2.5 Rights Issues and Their Effects

A rights issue is an issue of new shares to existing shareholders for cash, pro-rata their existing holding. The price of the shares is normally heavily discounted from the current market price. It is a way for companies to raise additional finance.

Pre-emption rights under UK law require that existing shareholders are all offered the same opportunity to buy shares and therefore maintain their proportion of shareholding in the company concerned. This allows them the chance to protect their shareholding from dilution. Although the precise rules vary across European countries, in general, all existing shareholders are also offered the chance to subscribe to the new shares, however there are some exceptions. In France, for example, overseas shareholders outside the EU are normally excluded although, by convention, they receive compensation in the form of proceeds from the sale of their pre-emptive rights (see section 2.5.1 below). In the US, all shareholders have similar rights to subscribe based on their existing shareholding, but not all rights issues offer the same opportunity to sell those rights.

Issues are typically underwritten by investment banks, who guarantee to buy any unsold shares if the issue is not fully subscribed.

Convention in the UK is that the company announces the rights issue in the same way as they do bonus issues, so in terms of the number of new shares that a shareholder will receive, based on the existing number of shares. Broadly, the same arrangement applies in the US and in Europe, in that the number of shares available for subscription by existing shareholders is in proportion to their current holdings.

A four for seven rights issue enables all existing shareholders to buy four new shares in the company for every seven that they already own. As before, the figures can be whatever the company wants.

Let's look at an example of how a rights issue impacts on a company's share price:

> Terms of rights issue: four for seven
> Current price of each share: £4.10

For the purposes of the example, we will assume that the shareholder owns the minimum number of shares needed to participate in the issue, ie, seven.

No. of shares		Price	Value
Before the rights issue	7	£4.10	£28.70
Rights issue	4	£3.30	£13.20
After the rights issue	11	£3.81	£41.90

£41.90 ÷ 11 (known as the theoretical ex-rights price (TERP))

After the rights issue has gone through, the average price of all the shares will reduce, because of the number of discounted shares just issued.

With regard to the actions shareholders should take when faced with a rights issue, they have a number of options:

- **exercise** the rights and buy the shares at the discounted price
- let the rights lapse and do nothing – received lapsed rights proceeds
- sell the rights nil-paid in the market
- split the rights
- sell some of the rights nil-paid, and use the money generated to purchase the remainder of the discounted shares.

2.5.1 Selling the Rights Nil-Paid

If in the example above, our shareholder chose to let the rights lapse and do nothing, the shareholder would be out of pocket after the rights issue had gone through. This is because before the rights issue, the shareholder would have owned seven shares worth £4.10 each, with a value for the total holding of £28.70. After the rights issue, the share price will have fallen. The shareholder will own seven shares, theoretically worth £3.81 each, with a total value of £26.67. The shareholder would suffer a loss of £2.03.

To avoid this loss, the shareholder can sell the right to buy the shares at a discount in the market for a value. This value is known as the nil-paid price, and is calculated as the theoretical ex-rights price (TERP), less the subscription price. In our example:

TERP	=	£3.81
Less subscription price	=	£3.30
Each right	=	£0.51

4 rights x £0.51 = £2.04 (the difference is down to rounding)

2.5.2 Splitting the Rights/Maximum Subscription at Nil Cost

If a shareholder has insufficient money to take up the rights, but is still keen to increase their holding in the company, this might be a suitable option. It involves selling some of the rights nil-paid to generate some money, and using that money to purchase some of the discounted shares.

There is a formula that can be used to calculate the number of rights that need to be sold nil-paid:

$$\frac{\text{number of rights} \times \text{subscription price}}{\text{theoretical ex-rights price}}$$

Apply this formula to the example above and assume that the shareholder has 7,000 shares:

$$\frac{4{,}000 \times £3.30}{£3.81} = 3{,}465 \text{ (the number of rights to be sold nil-paid to fund taking up the remainder)}$$

The sale of 3,465 rights at the nil-paid price of £0.51 will generate proceeds of £1,766.

The shareholder is now free to exercise the remaining rights (4,000 – 3,465), and purchase 535 shares at the subscription price of £3.30 each, total cost £1,766.

As the shares are sold at the minimum of par value, there is no addition to the share premium account.

The impact of a £100 million rights issue of shares at £1 each on a company's balance sheet would be to increase the share capital and total value of the company by £100 million.

Before	
Net assets	£550m
Share capital 300m @ £1.00	£300m
Share premium account	£100m
Revenue Reserves account	£150m
Shareholders' funds	£550m

After	
Net assets	£650m
Share capital 400m @ £1.00	£400m
Share premium account	£100m
Revenue Reserves account	£150m
Shareholders' funds	£650m

2.6 Share Buy Backs and Their Effects

If a company has surplus cash, it can retain the money within the business for future use or return it to its shareholders through either the payment of a dividend or by buying its shares back in the open market.

Shares that have been bought back can be cancelled or retained as Treasury shares. (Treasury shares are bought-back shares, which are not cancelled but held in case they need to be resold. They are sometimes used to fulfil share options as an alternative to a company having to issue more new shares.)

After a share buyback, the profits made by the company are distributed across less shareholders (described as 'earnings enhancing'), often leading to the payment of an increased dividend per share.

In addition, if the company believes that the shares are trading at a value below that of the net assets represented by each share, then the buyback exercise will also increase the value of the company.

Example

Company A has a net asset value (NAV) of £5 per share yet its shares trade at £4 in the market.

The company has 500 million shares in issue:

- total NAV of £2.5 billion
- market capitalisation of £2 billion.

It buys back 100 million shares in the market, for cancellation costing the company £400 million.

- the company then has 400 million shares still in issue
- total NAV of £2.5 billion – £0.4 billion = £2.1 billion.

So now the new net assets per share = £2.1 billion/400 million shares in issue = £5.25.

Although the total market capitalisation of the company is smaller, the company has increased NAV per share by 5% (ie, (£5.25–£5)/£5). One of the main jobs of the directors of a company is to give shareholder return. They have to consider how the cash they have is best invested and it may therefore be that they decide that the best way to give shareholder return is to buy back shares below NAV to boost the NAV of the remaining shares, and consequently the share price.

In addition, the laws of supply and demand suggest that if there are fewer shares available in the market, the price will rise. This rise in the share price gives shareholders the benefit of capital gains as opposed to the income they would have received if the company had paid a higher dividend. Shareholders have a choice as to when to realise this capital gain, and can minimise their tax liabilities in a way which they cannot do if there is a mandatory dividend payment.

Buy-backs can be viewed negatively as they imply that there is nothing more worthwhile that the management of the company could do with the cash in order to grow the company and can therefore be seen as a sign of lack of potential growth in the company in future.

From the company's perspective, if it increased its dividend because it had surplus cash, it would be difficult for it to reduce the dividend in the future as it would be seen as a sign of weakness by the market, and investors relying on a stream of dividends prefer to see stability in the pattern of dividends paid out by a company.

Buy-backs are often undertaken when the senior management of a company consider their shares to be undervalued in the market. There is a widespread suspicion that management engage in share buy backs to increase earnings, and thereby enhance share options and meet targets for bonuses.

3. Private Equity (PE)

Learning Objective

7.3 Evaluate private equity as an asset class: definition and the key properties of private equity; problems due to information asymmetry; risk, liquidity and return; performance of private equity; principal problems and liquidity issues, plus implications should liquidity fall

3.1 Introduction

The term 'private equity' (PE) refers to a particular form of equity that represents a legal entity that is not itself listed on an exchange. It can consist of funds that invest in private companies, or it can refer to the purchase of shares of a public limited company (plc), with the intention of de-listing it into a privately owned entity.

The investment in PE can be provided by both large institutional investors and retail investors. Often, PE investment funds are structured as limited partnerships, and as noted above, are not publicly traded. They are also known for their extensive use of debt financing, enabling large investments to be made, a process known as a leveraged buyout (LBO).

PE represents an important asset class that has received much attention from pension plans, family offices and various investors in the private wealth market. In the UK, there are some exchange-traded products that allow some indirect exposure to PE.

An investment structure that is established as a PE fund will undertake investment activities in a number of pooled investments. Investors buying into a PE investment will invest indirectly in a pool of investment activities that the PE fund is undertaking. The underlying investment activities a PE fund can be involved in range from:

- venture capital startups
- private medium-sized firms seeking expansion finance
- public firms seeking finance for a management buy-out or a leveraged buy-out
- firms in financial distress – known as 'special situations'
- public financing of infrastructure projects.

The size of the PE market has increased substantially in recent years and has been encouraged by:

- potential for higher returns (albeit along with higher risk and lower liquidity in illiquid PE investments)
- development of the limited partnership as an intermediary. This has mitigated some of the problems of investing in PE for many investors, specifically with regard to information asymmetry (see below) and conflicts of interest with regard to incentives
- regulatory changes, permitting more PE investment by pension funds.

3.2 Historical Development of the PE Market

The origins of the PE market can be traced back to 1946, and over the years its development can be followed over a series of boom and bust cycles through to 1981. In recent decades, the development of PE activity has been closely connected with the interest in leveraged buy-outs (LBOs) and the ability to hedge the debt arising from individual investments through ever more sophisticated derivatives.

3.3 Investors in Private Equity

As indicated earlier, PE represents an important asset class to pension plans, firms, family offices and various investors in the private wealth market.

The major motive for investing is to achieve high risk-adjusted returns amidst greater diversification. However, banks and corporations may invest in the market to obtain leverage off their other activities. Entrepreneurial individuals (business angels) may invest in startups. Otherwise, investors tend to be partnerships.

Most institutional investors do not invest directly in privately held companies, lacking the expertise and resources necessary to structure and monitor the investment. Instead, institutional investors will invest indirectly through a PE fund.

Certain institutional investors have the scale necessary to develop a diversified portfolio of PE funds themselves. However, others will invest through a fund of funds (FOF) to create a more diversified approach relative to what a single investor could construct.

3.4 Investment Categories

The main categories of investments are venture capital, distressed companies, LBOs and mezzanine finance. The first category tends to apply specifically towards smaller, newer firms. The remaining three categories may apply to firms of all sizes.

- **Venture Capital**
  - These may be early-stage ventures (either at the startup or early stage production) or later stage (seeking rapid growth in sales or an exit route for some investors). Sales revenue could be up to £50 million. Companies have limited access to bank lending lines if they are small, but greater access if they are larger. Investors are normally partnerships, but business angels may get involved for smaller companies.
- **Distressed Companies**
  - When a company's balance sheet shows high gearing in the form of debt, it is likely that both its shares and bonds will have a high yield. In order to improve the balance sheet, the company may decide to offer new bonds to a new group of buyers. Investors in distressed companies normally seek to influence the negotiations over the restructuring of the debt pile and subsequent strategic direction of the firm.

- With a renewed focus on improving the cash flow within the distressed company, asset sales of non-core businesses are likely to follow, together with a possible improvement in the distressed bond price.
- **Leveraged Buyouts (LBOs)**
  - LBOs normally rely on a large syndicate of banks, hedge funds and PE groups to lend money to an LBO vehicle.
  - In turn, the LBO vehicle normally seeks to buy a controlling interest in a company's equity using a high amount of borrowed capital. The borrowed capital is usually supplied by a syndicate of investors in exchange for LBO bonds. These bonds tend to pay a high yield given the high-risk approach of the investment vehicle.
  - Thereafter, there is potential for the new management team to reduce costs and improve profitability through non-core disposals.
- **Mezzanine Finance**
  - Mezzanine capital is often a more expensive way for a company to raise money, as the debt is not 'secured debt' or 'senior debt'.
  - Mezzanine debt holders normally require a higher yield from their investment relative to the more high-ranking bonds.
  - Mezzanine debt is unsecured in the event of bankruptcy and ranks somewhere between ordinary shares and secured debt if a company defaults.

3.5 Middle Market Companies

This would include profitable companies in stable industrial areas. Such companies may have access to bank credit as well as equity finance. Larger firms may access the private placement market directly. Investors are typically partnerships. The motives for PE finance here may be as follows:

- expansion, either through capital expenditure or acquisitions
- changing capital structure with a refinancing
- changing ownership due to an owner retiring or a corporate spin-off.

3.6 Public Companies

This involves a public listed company buying out the shareholders (partly or entirely) in order to become partly or entirely private. They usually have access to debt markets as well as PE. Investors are typically partnerships.

One example of this was the acquisition of the UK company, Cadbury by the American multinational, Kraft Foods. The final acquisition consideration paid went through different stages as seen in the following paragraph:

> 'On 7 September 2009, Kraft Foods made a £10.2 billion (US$16.2 billion) indicative takeover bid for Cadbury. The offer was rejected, with Cadbury stating that it undervalued the company. Kraft launched a formal, hostile bid for Cadbury, valuing the firm at £9.8 billion on 9 November 2009. On 19 January 2010, it was announced that Cadbury and Kraft Foods had reached a deal and that Kraft would purchase Cadbury for £8.40 per share, valuing Cadbury at £11.5 billion (US$18.9 billion).'

Possible reasons for PE buyouts with public companies are:

- management buyouts (usually companies with strong cash flow)
- LBOs (usually companies with strong cash flow)
- financial distress (turnaround situations if bank credit is not available)
- the desire to avoid company registration costs and public disclosure
- raising funds when the industry is out of favour with public investors.

3.7 Returns

Returns are generally higher in the PE market than for many other asset classes. However, this is counterbalanced by higher risk and low liquidity of investments. Returns tend to be highest for venture capital, followed by distressed companies, LBOs and then mezzanine capital. However, returns will vary depending on economic conditions.

Statistical evidence of how an LBO has fared and what determined its return has been studied by Muscarella and Vetsuypens (Journal of Finance, 1990). They have compared the total value of the firm at the time of the LBO to the value of the firm in a reversed LBO at the time of its secondary initial public offering (SIPO). The median rate of return for 41 firms that went public again was 89% for the entire period from the LBO to the SIPO stage. The mean rate was 69.7%, and the median annualised rate of return in the period was 36.6%.

A working paper by the National Bureau of Economic Research (Ljungqvist and Richardson, 2003) presented more recent return and risk characteristics of PE investment in the US. By analysing data over two decades (1981–2001) they concluded that PE was capable of generating excess returns of the order of 5–8% plus per annum relative to the aggregate public equity market. It was noted that this premium of PE over a stock market could be interpreted as compensation to investors for holding illiquid investment. PE investors tie money in for a lengthy time period from six to ten years.

3.8 Risks

Investments in limited partnership interests are viewed as 'illiquid' investments, and according to the tenets of investment theory they should earn a premium over equities or bonds.

The investor in a PE fund could lose all of their investment if the fund's investments fail. The risk of loss is generally highest for venture capital funds, which invest at the early development stage of companies. Risks are lower for mezzanine capital funds, which invest in companies that have a proven track record but have not yet raised money in a public offering.

The PE investor needs to gauge and control risks in PE through due diligence processes. This will include consideration of the managers' abilities, experience, track record in similar types of investments, commitment and compensation arrangements. There is some evidence that the latter can have a significant impact on the success of a PE investment.

Some of the main points from a risk perspective that need to be considered are:

a. PE investments are illiquid. This means that these investments do not trade in the market and cannot be sold off in the secondary market. Investors have restricted possibilities for withdrawing investments from the fund.
b. There is a long-term commitment required because PE investment takes time to provide the expected returns. Even though marketing literature will promote the benefits of PE investment in terms of risk diversification and return performances of some funds, there is evidence that PE carries higher risks, broadly comparable to publicly traded small cap stocks. PE returns are not guaranteed, and there are reported cases of losses generated especially with new and young businesses.
c. The stand-alone or unique risk of PE investment can be greater. It is therefore an investor's responsibility to make sure that they hold portfolios large enough to be able to diversify some of the unwanted risks from PE investments.
d. An investor will make a fund commitment to supply capital over a period, typically of five years. As a result of this requirement, investors have to be prepared to supply cash on demand over this time.

3.9 Information Asymmetry

In addition to the risks mentioned in section 3.8, information asymmetry can also impact a PE investment portfolio.

Information asymmetry can be broadly summarised as the different degrees of knowledge and information available to the buyers/sellers of a business or investment product resulting from how much they have access to the true nature of the product's merits and demerits. Within PE investment in particular, it can give rise to the following problems:

- **Adverse selection** – owners and managers know far more about their business than potential investors. This is particularly so within PE because a firm is required to make very few public disclosures. A business's good points will tend to be highlighted and its weaknesses overlooked. The true risk of the firm is hidden, and leads to an adverse selection problem for individuals involved in indirect investment through PE funds.
- **Conflict of interest** – after PE financing has been put in place, managers may alter their behaviour and run the business to benefit themselves at the expense of investors, in the absence of regulatory reporting requirements. In this instance, the risk of the firm will increase after investors have committed funds.

To some extent these problems can be mitigated by thorough due diligence before investing and continued monitoring of the company afterwards.

3.10 Differences between PE Investment and Publicly Traded Securities

The deal and the price paid by an accredited investor are negotiated directly with the management of the PE firm or its general partner (GP). PE investments are less visible to the general public, whereas conventional publicly traded securities are transparent in terms of the prices quoted through a highly regulated market-making system.

A PE investor becomes a limited partner. As a result of this status they can request and get access to all information including internal investment plans and policy set by the PE management in the investment project. In conventional investments, this information is only available through publicly released information in the market.

PE investors play an active role in the investment activity throughout the period that they are invested in the investment project. Conventional investors have a more formal principal-agent relationship in which the day-to-day decisions of the board are made by the management of the company.

3.11 Investing in PE Funds

The majority of investors participate in the PE market through PE funds. Among these funds, buy-out funds represent the largest segment (measured either in assets under management (AUM) terms or size of the capital committed).

In buyout funds, the segment can be separated into large-cap buy-out funds and intermediate-cap buy-out funds. Large-cap buy-out funds usually deal with large-cap companies who desire to make an asset sale of a non-performing business unit, or have a spin-off or an equity-carve out business that they want to divest.

PE funds will carry out due diligence on potential candidates and will then take steps to purchase. Once the firm has been purchased, it will then be de-listed as a publicly traded stock. After work has been carried out on the company to restore its profitability, it can later be re-listed in a SIPO process.

Intermediate-cap stocks are often not publicly listed in the first place, and these are purchased without the need to de-list. The intention with these stocks is to improve the performance and capabilities of the firm for it to be listed on the public market.

Buyout firms can realise value gains through a sale of the acquired company, an initial public offering (IPO) or by way of a dividend capitalisation (which involves the issuance of debt to finance a special dividend to the general and limited partners of the PE fund partnership).

Many PE funds require a substantial initial investment (often several hundred thousand pounds) plus additional investment in the first few years of the fund. Investors must be prepared to have their capital locked up for a long period. This disadvantage is offset by the possible benefits of annual returns, which can be up to 30% in some cases.

Most PE fund investment opportunities are only offered to high net worth individuals, or so-called 'sophisticated investors', and institutional investors. The investor will typically become a limited partner in the fund in which they invest.

3.11.1 PE Partnerships

PE partnerships have two major participants:

- **Partnerships** have a life that is fixed by contract, usually around ten years. For the first three years or so, the general partners will invest the partnership's capital. After this, they will manage and liquidate the partnership's investments. Liquidation proceeds will then be distributed to investors.

- **Limited partnerships** would appear to offer problems for investors, since their investments are illiquid over the life of the partnership and investors have little control over the running of the partnership. However, limited partnerships have a valuable role to play in mitigating risks in the PE market.
    - **General partners (GPs)** are the senior managers who manage the partnership's investments. They usually invest only a small proportion of the partnership's capital base (say 1%). They usually have industry or entrepreneurial experience. There may be associates who will hope to become GPs.
    - **Limited partners (LPs)** are institutional and other investors who invest the bulk of the money in the partnership. LPs will tend to run a number of legally separate partnerships at the same time, with some at the investment phase and some in the liquidation phase.

3.11.2 Relationship between Partnership and Portfolio of Companies

When selecting companies, investments are first screened for some basic criteria, and most investments are rejected at this stage. Criteria include the following:

- type of investment, eg, startup versus middle market
- industry area
- location
- whether it is within the partnership's areas of expertise.

Extensive due diligence for a final selection from the initial screening will include:

- visits to the company
- discussions with employers, suppliers and customers
- use of lawyers, accountants and consultants to examine the company
- for new startups, examining the management quality and feasibility of the product
- for established firms, understanding the existing business in detail
- for distressed companies, meetings with lenders
- for management buyouts, focus on succession issues
- for LBOs, focus on cash flow forecasts and the ability to repay debt.

3.11.3 Performance Incentives

The objective of performance incentives is to align the interests of the partnership and the managers of the business.

3.11.4 Direct Control Mechanisms

In addition to the provision of incentives, direct control mechanisms are an effective way of aligning the interests of investors and the management.

- **Board representation** – GPs on the board may have the requisite skills to run the company (due to their backgrounds) and the necessary resources. They can, therefore, exercise significant influence on the company's direction. Voting rights – the partnership's stake may be sufficiently large to give majority control or to give very significant influence. Even if the partnership owns less than 50% of the company, it may ensure that its shares have special voting rights to give it control.

- **Access to additional financing** – the partnership will not give the company all its required funds at the beginning, but have several rounds of financing. This gives the partnership the ability to withhold future funds if it feels this is necessary. In addition the partnership will have the power to inspect company records and information and to receive financial information on a timely basis if requested.

One other form of control retained by partnerships is the right to veto certain transactions.

Chapter Eight
Property and Alternative Investments

1. The Property Market	**353**
2. Types of Property Funds	**354**
3. Commodities	**358**
4. Infrastructure Funds	**363**
5. Hedge Funds (HFs)	**366**
6. Tax-Relieved Alternative Investment Schemes	**376**

Property and Alternative Investments

Learning Outcome

Be able to evaluate critically the risks and returns offered by property

1. The Property Market

Learning Objective

8.1 Evaluate property as a component of a portfolio: definition and the key properties of real estate; risk, price, value, and return; historic performance of real estate; principal problems and liquidity issues, plus implications should liquidity fall

The Investment Association (IA), formerly known as the Investment Management Association (IMA), treats property as a specialist fund category where at least 60% of the assets must be invested directly in property or at least 80% of assets must be in property securities.

As an asset class, property has offered a number of advantages including:

- attractive absolute returns over several years
- portfolio diversification
- relatively low correlation with bonds and equities.

On certain occasions, returns can be volatile however, leading to losses and issues with liquidity. For instance, significant cash outflows from collective property funds during the global financial crisis of 2007–08 and again following the UK's vote to leave the European Union (EU) initially limited the ability of investors to make redemptions.

There are a number of ways in which individuals can invest in property including:

- building a portfolio of directly owned properties
- investing in listed property companies or real estate investment trusts (REITs)
- investing in property unit trusts and similar vehicles
- the issues involved in building and maintaining a portfolio of directly owned properties is beyond the scope of this workbook, which instead considers how this can be achieved through investment funds.

1.1 Features of Property Funds

Unsurprisingly, there is a wide range of property funds available. There is no single classification method in use. They can be differentiated in a number of ways including whether they are:

- listed or unlisted funds
- traded on a stock exchange or direct with the managers of the fund
- open-ended or closed-ended

- low-risk or high-risk
- available to private investors or institutional investors, or
- structured as companies, partnerships, trusts or contractual agreements.

There are three main types of real estate fund:

- core funds
- core plus and value-added funds, and
- opportunistic funds.

Core funds are lower-risk and lower-return funds that are usually open-ended and which aim to produce returns that are benchmarked against an established property index. Investors may have difficulty in realising their positions in open-ended property funds in times of market stress. Core plus and value-added funds use higher gearing and a more active management style to generate higher returns. Opportunistic funds are typically close-ended and exploit opportunities to acquire property from distressed sellers, redevelopments and in emerging markets, and are more similar in nature to private equity funds.

2. Types of Property Funds

Learning Objective

8.2 Explain the characteristics of property investment vehicles and their application in an investment portfolio: performance/risk/reward profiles of direct, indirect and buy to let investment approaches and appraisal methods

2.1 Property Unit Trusts

Property unit trusts can either be authorised by a regulator or unauthorised. Authorised funds are designed primarily for retail investors, while unauthorised funds may only be offered to institutional investors.

Authorised property unit trusts are exempt from capital gains tax (CGT) on any gains they make but the income arising in the fund is liable to corporation tax at (currently) 20%. They are designed for the domestic UK market and their unfavourable tax treatment makes them unsuitable for institutional and overseas investors.

Instead, offshore property unit trusts offer greater flexibility, as they are tax-effective for a greater range of UK and international investors and are less heavily regulated. Offshore property unit trusts are structured to be tax-transparent and so the fund is not liable to income or CGT and instead any entitlements are taxable on the end investor according to their tax position. They may nevertheless incur other weaknesses, such as the need for overseas probate and a weaker level of investor protection than authorised trusts in the UK in terms of governance or compensation.

2.2 Property Authorised Investment Funds (PAIFs)

The aim behind property authorised investment funds (PAIFs) was to introduce a tax-efficient open-ended authorised investment fund for investment in property.

Recently investor confidence in property has begun to improve and property fund managers are looking at the PAIF regime and beginning to convert their funds.

A PAIF must be structured as an open-ended investment company (OEIC) incorporated in the UK.

- It must be authorised and regulated by the Financial Conduct Authority (FCA).
- There is no requirement for a stock exchange listing (which is unnecessary for an OEIC as liquidity is provided to investors by the PAIF itself).
- It may be used by retail, sophisticated and institutional investors in the UK and elsewhere globally.
- If certain conditions are met, and PAIF status is elected, their property investment income is tax-exempt.
- All capital gains are also tax-exempt.
- Income distributions to UK and overseas shareholders are, with some exceptions, subject to UK withholding tax.
- Special UK tax charges are imposed on PAIFs which carry excessive debt or pay distributions from exempt income to any company holding 10% or more than of their shares.
- They are generally entitled to the benefits of the UK's extensive double taxation treaty network.

2.3 Exchange-Traded Funds (ETFs)

There is an assortment of exchange-traded funds (ETFs) that track the performance of a range of European and global real estate indices without the manager selection risk or benefit of an investment fund.

There is a large range of ETFs that track the FTSE European Public Real Estate Association (EPRA)/National Association of Real Estate Investment Trusts (NAREIT) global index series. This series is designed to represent general trends in eligible real estate equities worldwide, and incorporates several indices, including:

- EPRA/NAREIT UK
- EPRA/NAREIT European
- EPRA/NAREIT Asia Pacific
- EPRA/NAREIT Global, and
- EPRA/NAREIT Developed.

ETFs can, therefore, provide investors with exposure to property on a global and regional basis. These could be used to complement investment in domestic property markets and bring diversification benefits or provide a mechanism to invest in a particular region which is expected to outperform.

Property ETFs are traded on the stock exchange as with other ETFs and so offer the benefits of liquidity and should trade close to their net asset value (NAV).

2.4 Real Estate Investment Trusts (REITs)

REITs are well established in the US, Australia, Canada, Japan, Singapore and Hong Kong. The success of the REIT model in Japan has led many Asian countries to adopt the same legislative model, while in Europe, the success of the French REIT model has seen similar legislation passed in the UK and Germany.

In simple terms, a REIT is a company that owns and operates income-producing real estate, which can be either commercial or residential. How they differ from a quoted company that holds a portfolio of property is that the company is not liable to tax on any income or gains made on the property portfolio and instead distributes this as income with any tax liability arising on the shareholder. This avoids the problem of double taxation with the company paying tax and then the shareholder also paying tax on any dividends received.

UK REITs are not subject to CGT on gains made on the disposal of property, providing that they distribute at least 90% of their profits each year to shareholders as dividends.

Investors disposing of a holding in a REIT may be liable to CGT on any gains made, as for any other shareholding. Losses may be offset or carried forward.

REITs are traded on the stock exchange in the same way as any other shares. These means that they are liquid and so are easy to buy and sell and can be readily realised. Their market price is determined by demand and supply as opposed to the valuation of the component assets and so may trade at a premium or discount to the NAV of the underlying property portfolio.

The number of real estate companies globally has expanded dramatically over the last ten years. This has been a result of the strong performance of property.

2.5 Limited Partnerships

Limited partnerships have been an attractive way of establishing unlisted property vehicles. They are complex structures that are established with a general partner who will be the lead investor and who must have unlimited liability. There can be any number of limited partners whose liability is, by nature, limited.

Some of their key features are:

- The investment vehicle is tax-transparent so any gains or income are taxed on the partners.
- They are usually established for a predetermined number of years at the end of which the assets are disposed of and the proceeds distributed, unless the partners vote to extend the life of the vehicle.
- The general partner will appoint an operator to oversee the administrative functions.
- Limited partners cannot be involved in decision-making, otherwise they will lose their limited-liability status.
- Jersey and Guernsey are the home for many limited partnership property funds.

2.6 Investing in Property Funds

The illiquid nature of property makes investment through real estate funds a practical proposition for investors.

Some of the factors that an adviser should consider when investing in real estate funds are:

- asset price bubbles
- relative liquidity of listed vehicles versus investment funds
- permitted levels of gearing
- redemption charges and notice periods.

As with other asset classes, property is cyclical and vulnerable to asset price bubbles as has been seen in Western markets repeatedly in recent decades.

Stock exchange-listed funds can be traded easily on a daily basis and, although pricing is theoretically linked to the NAV of the underlying property portfolio, prices can in practice trade away from NAV. By contrast, investment funds will trade at NAV but cannot necessarily be traded daily as many funds have monthly or quarterly valuation points.

Property funds can have levels of gearing that vary from 0% to 90% with many funds limited to between 50% and 70%. Gearing can enhance returns but brings risk with it. The adviser should be aware of the type of property fund that is being considered and its gearing and assess the risk/reward profile against the investor's risk tolerance.

The adviser should be aware of the frequency at which investment funds can be redeemed with the managers but should also investigate whether the fund manager can impose redemption penalties or notice periods. Recent falls in property values saw a number of property funds impose redemption penalties to deter investors from realising their investment and forcing the property fund to sell at distressed prices. Others imposed notice periods of 12 months, effectively locking investors into the funds.

Example

Mrs Hyatt has invested in equities and bonds in the past but she believes that she should spread her investments into property and commodities to diversify her risks further. She has allocated approximately £2 million to diversify her portfolio.

Discuss Real Estate Investment Trusts (REITs), Enterprise Investment Schemes (EISs) and Enterprise Zone Property Trusts (EZTs), giving your opinion on their suitability for her and how effective they could be in diversifying her portfolio.

Briefly discuss other ways of investing in property that she might consider.

3. Commodities

Learning Objective

8.3 Explain and evaluate commodities as an asset class: definition and key properties of commodities; problems associated with particular types of commodity investment; distinguish between direct and indirect investments in commodities; performance of commodities; principal problems and liquidity issues, plus implications should liquidity fall; price discovery for commodities

---

As non-financial investments, individual commodities are tangible assets that are relatively homogenous in nature. This attribute allows these assets to be standardised as contracts for purchase and sale in futures markets.

Increasingly in recent years many investors have become involved in the ownership of or participation in commodities and natural resources. Commodities can be bought and sold easily in large quantities and held by investors directly in the form of physical assets or indirectly through the functioning of the futures markets.

There are two ways that an investor can access the markets: directly and indirectly.

Investors can gain direct exposure to commodities by purchasing them in cash markets (eg, buying gold coins) or in the futures markets where the delivery of the asset is deferred. Direct commodity investment involves the cash purchase of the asset and taking delivery of it. Space is required to store and insure the asset purchased. Exposure to futures and forwards in the same asset class does not involve taking delivery until the derivatives contracts expire. For example, an investor can buy several thousand barrels of crude oil in the forward market for delivery in December 2022. The future price of the oil is set and the investor may close this contract and take a profit between now and December 2022 when the contract will expire. An increase in oil price will net the investor a return on the deal. Trading in this way is convenient because there is no need for an individual to take delivery of the product.

Alternatively, the investor may prefer indirect commodity investment via for example, commodity-based collective funds or through the shares in commodity-related companies. These are discussed further in section 3.3.

3.1 Three Categories of Commodities

With the notable exception of some agricultural commodities traded on European exchanges and some iron and steel contracts traded on Chinese exchanges, most commodities are denominated only in US dollars, the world's principal reserve currency.

3.1.1 Metals

Metals are generally divided into two categories:

- base (known also as industrial), and
- precious.

Base metals include copper, lead, tin, nickel, aluminium, zinc and various grades of steel and a long list of rarer metals with more specialised industrial uses. They generally require substantial capital expenditure to extract from the ground and then to refine, and are finite resources. Demand for these metals in general is often taken as a bellwether for global economic demand, given their role in industrial production.

Precious metals principally comprise gold, silver, platinum and palladium. Gold in particular has traditionally been used as a hedge against inflation as a store of value. It is also commonly perceived as a safe haven when other investment markets appear unstable, in that it shows inverse behaviour (rising when riskier asset classes fall).

3.1.2 Energy

Energy is traded principally through crude oil and its principal derivative of petroleum (gasoline) as well as natural gas.

Crude oil has two principal benchmarks: West Texas Intermediate (WTI), traded on the New York Mercantile Exchange (NYMEX), and Brent Crude, traded on the Intercontinental Exchange (ICE).

Oil in particular tends to be the largest component of most commodity indices, due to the volumes required by the global economy. Since it is priced in US dollars, it tends to move inversely to the price of the dollar over the medium term. This has been demonstrated in the last decade as first WTI rose to $147 per barrel in 2008 (and near that again in 2011–12), before falling below $40 in 2015. This has generally been accompanied by first weakness in the dollar and then a strong recovery. Given its importance to the costs of global production and transportation, oil is a key component of both inflation and deflationary pressures and has an impact not only on the dollar but also on bond yields.

3.1.3 Softs

Softs comprise agricultural products with different uses. The textile category includes wool and cotton, while major foodstuffs include wheat, rice, oats, cocoa, coffee, soya, and sugar and orange juice. Livestock is most heavily traded in cattle and pigs (pork bellies and lean hogs). Softs have the characteristic of being renewable, usually on an annual cycle. Crops can be grown season after season.

Many soft commodities are however perishable, both before and after harvest. This can make their price highly volatile: if there is a surplus of coffee, relative to typical levels of demand, the price may fall significantly as producers seek to sell as much as they can before the quality deteriorates.

The prices of soft commodities are, as for all assets, driven, among other factors, by the supply and demand.

Supply can be significantly affected by factors such as:

- good/poor harvests
- disease affecting livestock, such as pigs and cattle
- exceptionally good/bad weather
- political unrest in the producing country.

Investors need to bear in mind the short cyclical factors at work in agricultural commodities. A shortage one year leads to increased prices, which can in turn lead to much increased production the following year and a subsequent collapse in prices.

3.2 Direct Investment in Commodities

3.2.1 Cash Market

An investor can buy and sell commodities directly through a commodity broker, or invest in a commodities fund. Dealing in physical commodities is not a practical proposition for most investors because of the minimum quantities that must be traded and the risk of deterioration in quality (especially softs). The cash market is primarily for wholesale and industrial users and producers of commodities rather than for investors.

For non-deteriorating commodities such as metals, however, it is possible and practical to take a direct holding in the commodity, which can be stored in a London Metal Exchange (LME)-approved warehouse. The investor should consider the storage and other costs involved with this option.

Trade on the cash market is for immediate delivery, known as trading physicals or actuals, with the price paid being the spot price. Payment must be made immediately and charges are made for storage and insurance. There is a standard contract size, 25 tonnes for copper, for example, to aid the smooth running of the market. Contracts have precise specifications of quality and grading, to give buyers certainty that they will not receive sub-standard shipments. This in turn provides fungibility to the wholesale market.

3.2.2 Futures Market

A futures contract is an agreement to buy or sell a standard quantity of a specified asset on a fixed future date, at a price agreed today, with buyers obligated to buy and sellers obligated to sell on a specified future date.

Standardised Quantity

Exchange-traded futures are traded in standardised parcels known as contracts. For example, a futures contract on lead might be for 25 tonnes of the metal, or a currency future might be for €20,000. The purpose of this standardisation is so that buyers and sellers are clear about the quantity that will be delivered. If you sold one lead future, you would know that you were obliged to sell 25 tonnes of lead of a known grade.

Futures are only traded in whole numbers of contracts. This limitation is one of the factors which favours swaps, an **over-the-counter** (OTC) alternative to using futures contracts. But on the other hand, futures contracts have the benefit that they are exchange-cleared, which simplifies the **counterparty risk** compared with the counterparty risk inherent in a swap.

Homogenous and Specified Asset

All futures contracts are governed by their contract specifications, and legal documents set out in detail the size of each contract, when delivery is to take place, and what exactly is to be delivered. For example, in the crude oil futures market the contract which is actively traded on NYMEX calls for delivery of oil in terms of West Texas Intermediate Crude, whereas the major contracts traded on ICE call for delivery in terms of Brent Crude.

Fixed Future Date

The delivery of futures contracts takes place on a specified date(s) known as delivery day(s). This is when buyers exchange money for goods with sellers. Futures have finite life spans so that, once the **last trading day** is past, it is impossible to trade the futures for that date.

At any one time, a range of delivery months may be traded and, as one delivery day passes, a new date is introduced. Contracts may be 'rolled over' from one expiry date to another by selling the current contract and moving into a new futures contract with later expiration.

Price Agreed Today

Many people, from farmers to fund managers, use commodity futures because they provide certainty or a reduction of risk. Futures are tradeable, so although the contract obliges the buyer to buy and the seller to sell, these obligations can be offset by undertaking an equal and opposite trade in the market.

Example

Suppose a farmer has sold 1 September wheat future at £140 per tonne. If, subsequently, they decide they do not wish to sell their wheat, but would prefer to use the grain to feed their cattle, they simply buy 1 September future at the then prevailing price. Their original sold position is now offset by a bought position, leaving them with no outstanding delivery obligations.

This offsetting is common in future markets; few contracts run through to **physical delivery**.

3.3 Indirect Investment in Commodities

3.3.1 Shares of Commodity Companies

One approach to indirect investment would be to acquire shares in a commodity-producing company, eg, miners or oil-producing companies. As commodity prices rise, investors could anticipate that the company's revenue, and correspondingly the share price, will rise.

Although all producers will face the same selling price, they will not all face the same cost pressures and hence, though we may expect share prices tend to move in the direction of the underlying commodity prices, the correlation will not be perfect.

There may not be a close correlation between the share prices of oil exploration and refining companies and the price of a barrel of crude oil. The profitability of the major oil companies depends on the margins they earn and they make extensive use of hedging to limit their financial exposure to a volatile commodity price. However, they have flexibility in cutting costs in challenging times. For junior oil exploration companies the field is highly speculative and many exploration companies fail to make the oil finds they expect, while others may sometimes make extraordinary profits.

Mining companies' shares may correlate relatively closely with the price of commodities being extracted if the company is at or near production. As with oil companies, share prices may be volatile and not closely linked with commodity prices, partly due to hedging.

3.3.2 Commodity Funds

Commodities funds offer an investor in real assets a hedge against inflation and look more towards capital growth than income. A retail undertakings for collective investment in transferable securities (UCITS) fund cannot invest in commodities. An investor would however be able to gain commodities exposure through a non-UCITS fund or a qualified investor scheme (QIS).

3.3.3 Other Vehicles for Commodity Investment

Exchange-traded funds (ETFs), which are traded in both the US, on the New York Stock Exchange (NYSE), and also on the London Stock Exchange (LSE), are liquid and focused vehicles which enable investors to gain exposure to different commodities or baskets of commodities. They represent a relatively simple, easily understood and low-charge option for the investor, both institutional and retail.

3.3.4 Advantages of Indirect Investment in Commodities

It enables fund managers and individual investors to participate in a sector which is not closely correlated with certain other asset classes such as bonds.

In the case of most ETFs there is a high degree of liquidity in the shares and they can be traded throughout the trading day.

Some commodity funds pay a dividend unlike any direct investment in the 'physicals'. There are very low holding/storage costs.

The minimum dealing size can be more easily tailored to the fund manager's needs.

3.3.5 Commodity Index Returns

The physical markets for commodities are not centralised, and it is usual for analysts to examine performances of commodities through appropriate benchmarks and indices that have been created to monitor and assess performances. A broad range of indices based on commodity futures contracts is available.

Exercise 1

Briefly outline what roles commodities could play in a multi-asset portfolio.

The answer to this exercise can be found at the end of this chapter.

4. Infrastructure Funds

Learning Objective

84 Evaluate infrastructure funds as an investment vehicle: definition and the key properties of infrastructure funds; problems due to lumpiness and indivisibility; risk, liquidity and return; performance of infrastructure funds; principal problems and liquidity issues, plus implications should liquidity fall; ability of investors to gain access to infrastructure

4.1 Rationale for Private Investment in Infrastructure

Since the 1980s, many countries in the developed world with deteriorating public finances – including the UK, US, Canada, Japan and Australia – have looked to private finance to enhance the quality of ageing infrastructure assets such as roads, railways, seaports, airports and tunnels.

Funding of infrastructure projects has been assisted from the private sector through initiatives such as the Private Finance Initiative and the Public-Private Partnership in the UK. Other European governments are also pursuing similar ways of encouraging private provision of infrastructure.

Banks, pension funds and other private investors have come to view infrastructure as a new long-term inflation-linked asset class which offers a combination of hard assets and long-term earnings.

Sovereign wealth funds – such as those in Abu Dhabi, Singapore and Norway – have also become interested in providing funding and investment in basic power, water and transport infrastructure assets in less developed countries.

4.2 Lumpiness and Indivisibility of Investments in Infrastructure

Investors in infrastructure projects have to contend with a phenomenon which is known in microeconomics as lumpiness or indivisibility of inputs. Lumpy inputs are those financial outlays or business inputs whose quantity cannot be changed gradually as output increases, but rather must be adjusted in large and discontinuous jumps which invariably require substantial capital expenditures. From the viewpoint of economic theory, this category of inputs can exist in either the short run or the long run.

Capacity additions to large infrastructure projects such as the building of extensions to an airport, in the form of a new runway or terminal building, or additions to an existing railway system, are especially subject to such lumpiness.

Example

Building new facilities at a congested airport such as Heathrow would be a classic example of a lumpy investment. Before any increase in capacity by the building of another terminal or runway (leaving aside all issues related to political pressure from environmental groups), the pressure of demand on capacity grows in a variety of forms including the overcrowding of terminals, bottlenecks at landing gates and the lack of any spare capacity for planes to use the existing runways for take-offs and landings. As a result, congestion costs and other external economic costs are increasingly incurred. Theoretically this would justify higher and higher access charges for use of the infrastructure, though in practice non-price rationing has been applied instead. In other words the number of flights (or supply) which the airport can handle has been 'frozen' at a level which is commensurate with the current capacity and safety concerns, but which is far below the potential demand for access to the airport.

Increase in the airport's capacity cannot be gradually increased with demand, but only in very large increments and on a one-off or infrequent basis. If a capacity increase does occur, such as when Terminal 5 was built some years ago, the previously high congestion costs and the appropriate level of access charges fall significantly. For the investor in such an infrastructure enhancement the problem arises that the investment would not be profitable unless it can be underwritten by a public authority such as a national or local government entity.

The challenge for infrastructure projects with a lumpy investment scenario is that the provider may only find it profitable to undertake an economically desirable investment if, in addition to paying a user charge proportional to output, users also have to pay a share of the capital cost. This share must be paid as a fixed amount, not varying with output. If user charges are limited to charges which vary with use (ie, the marginal consumption), there will be some desirable infrastructure investments which simply cannot be made profitable.

Investors in infrastructure companies will often be looking to relevant government authorities to provide the necessary contributions to the capital cost of their investments to ensure the viability of such projects.

4.3 Creation of Infrastructure Funds

There seems to be no shortage of possibilities for the investor who wishes to incorporate infrastructure investment as an asset class in their portfolio. Infrastructure funds are primarily available to the wholesale market; however, there are some funds now quoted on recognised investment exchanges (RIEs) in London and abroad.

Infrastructure investment is illiquid and not divisible into small units. A typical project involves large capital outlay, often with a long payback period. Accordingly, the investors who are typically attracted are those with large amounts of money and who are prepared to be patient. However, there has been success in providing infrastructure funds in the retail market.

Unlisted funds typically invest directly in infrastructure assets. Unlisted funds manage a smaller number of assets, and are usually only available to large institutional investors.

4.4 Risks and Risk Management

As already suggested, because of their relatively weak association with the returns available from investments which are more dependent on business cycles, returns on infrastructure assets have shown an inverse correlation with returns on other asset classes. Investment in infrastructure funds, therefore, offers a means of improving diversification in a portfolio. The fact that many infrastructure funds offer exposure to emerging economies also offers an attractive diversification in another dimension.

An earlier boom of private infrastructure funding in developed countries in the 1990s crashed spectacularly, and many projects were renegotiated, resulting in losses for investors or abandonment. Bearing this in mind, investors may need to be cautious. Part of the reason for this crash was macroeconomic shocks such as the financial crises in Argentina (1997 and 2002) and Russia (1998). Infrastructure projects can also sometimes become quite politically contentious and subject to opposition by local interest groups.

There are sometimes allegations of corruption on infrastructure projects. Host governments may help reduce the possibility of corruption by strengthening incentive systems which create sound public sector management practices and promote transparency and accountability.

Fund managers for infrastructure projects have to accept that not all risk can be managed through project contracts. A strategic management approach is needed, not only to manage technical risks, but also social and political expectations in the host country. Joint-venture style arrangements with host governments can promote trust and cooperation, particularly if financial interests are aligned, for example through profit-sharing arrangements.

In addition to the requirements of the newly emerging markets, there is mounting evidence of degradation in the infrastructure of the developed world. Infrastructure replacement in the mature economies, combined with the growing need for development programmes in, for example, the BRIC nations (Brazil, Russia, India and China) adds to the pool of project financing in which private infrastructure funding may be involved.

5. Hedge Funds (HFs)

Learning Objective

8.5 Evaluate hedge funds as an asset class: definition and key properties of hedge funds; unique features of hedge funds; performance of hedge funds; charges of hedge funds; benefits of fund of funds; principal problems and liquidity issues, plus implications should liquidity fall

The term hedge fund (HF) is very broad, with no precise legal definition. In general it is taken to mean a type of fund which can engage in a wide range of investment strategies, many of them outside the strategies permitted for authorised schemes.

The HF market has experienced strong growth for several decades as more providers have entered the market seeking lucrative fees by offering their own variants. This has resulted in some of the unusually high absolute returns originally offered by the pioneering providers shrinking.

The claims made by HFs are that they deliver positive absolute returns. Most conventional collective investments are focused on delivering returns relative to a well-known benchmark such as the FTSE 100 Index, whose performance they aim to beat. This means that the performance of the benchmark – for example, a share price index – can be as important as the skill of the fund manager.

In order to achieve these goals, HFs have adopted a more flexible and innovative approach base on the underlying notion that they will achieve a positive return despite what the market as a whole is doing.

HFs are often based offshore and are regulated by the Financial Conduct Authority (FCA). Nevertheless their investment strategies may be unauthorised.

HFs have the freedom to invest in almost any type of financial instrument or asset class, using almost any kind of strategy, and are frequently heavy users of derivatives.

The term 'hedge fund' dates back to the 1940s, when a reporter for the *Fortune* magazine, Alfred Winslow Jones, published an article suggesting the investor could achieve high returns if hedging was incorporated in an investment strategy. He set about launching an investment partnership where he incorporated short-selling and leverage into a strategy. His intention was to limit risk and to enhance returns at the same time. During the period 1962 to 1966 he generated an excess return of 85% (after fees) over the top-performing mutual fund of the time. This level of performance attracted interest from high net worth individuals. In addition, Jones also introduced a system of incentive fees of 20% of profits. More recently, however, the hedge fund industry has seen management fees in the region of between 1% and 1.5%, with performance fees in the region of between 14% and 18%.

The possibility of high fee arrangements and lucrative deals also attracted the attention of traditional money managers, who set about constructing their own funds based on the HF principles. However, the historic returns of these managers were the subject of some heavy losses over the mid-1970s period. This was mainly because these managers had dropped Jones's objective of risk management utilising short-selling in a combined leverage play. Instead, some of the new money managers focused just on leverage trades and on long-only strategies. These funds were susceptible to the downturn in the stock market in 1973–74 and suffered huge losses. HFs lost credibility over this time.

Then, in the 1980s, interest was revived in HFs by a small group of funds. One such fund was Jim Rogers and George Soros's Quantum Fund, which was said to have gained $1 billion from speculating on the pound sterling at the time when the UK had to leave the European Exchange Rate Mechanism (ERM) in 1992.

Despite the chequered history of HFs, the possibilities of gaining high fees from these arrangements inspired many money fund managers to leave traditional mutual fund schemes and to set up on their own. As of Q3 2017, the total assets under management for the HF industry amounted to over $3.4 trillion.

5.1   HF Strategies

Sometimes classified as absolute return funds, HFs aim to make a positive return annually, irrespective of the state of the stock markets. They may use shorting, and arbitrage, which involves the simultaneous sale and purchase of securities to take advantage of pricing anomalies, for a known return.

HF strategies can be broken down into non-directional and directional strategies. These are briefly explained along with example strategies below.

5.2   Non-Directional Strategies

A non-directional HF strategy aims to generate a stable return regardless of market performance. In other words, it is designed to deliver positive returns in all market conditions, with low volatility. In essence, fund managers need to get rid of all market risk in order to isolate their funds from market fluctuations. If market risk is neutralised, the fund performance would depend solely on the manager's skill. This type of fund particularly addresses the needs of conservative investors who are typically concerned with risk reduction even if this means sacrificing some return.

Relative Value

Non-directional strategies which exploit the relative values of different securities are focused on the differential between two related securities, rather than taking a specific view of the future direction of either security. The relative value between two securities is often expressed in terms of a spread. For example, the spread between a ten-year gilt and a ten-year German bund could be expressed in terms of basis points, eg, the gilt/bund spread could have a positive value of 50 basis points, meaning that the yield on a gilt is 0.5% higher than the bund.

Such a strategy would aim to profit from an expected change in the spread between these two securities. If the trader thinks that the spread will widen, then the strategy would be to sell the spread. This could be achieved either in the swaps market or by taking a short position in gilts and a long position of equivalent size in bunds. In fact, characteristically, non-directional strategies will entail holding simultaneous long and short positions in related or correlated securities.

With these strategies, the expectation is that market shifts are expected to have a minimal impact on results since the relationship between the two 'legs' of the spread is the critical factor.

Fixed-Income Arbitrage

Arbitrage in fixed-income securities seeks to exploit inefficiencies in interest rate yield curves, corporate spreads and/or pricing of government bonds, swaps, and other derivatives based upon interest rates. Such strategies rely heavily on mathematical and/or statistical valuation models.

Strategies in this category often exploit expected changes in the yield curve. For example, if the yield curve is expected to steepen, with the yields on long-term bonds moving up more than short-term yields, the strategy would be, for example, to buy a two-year gilt and sell a 20-year gilt.

Market Neutral

Market neutral is also sometimes known as equity arbitrage, and the objective of the strategy is to combine long and short positions, while balancing the beta exposure (the degree to which the movements in prices of the security will track movements in the overall market) to ensure a zero or negligible market exposure.

The emphasis is on stock picking as opposed to having a single directional view of the market. One favoured strategy is 'pairs trading', in which one takes converse positions in correlated securities, such as long – a major retailer such as Marks & Spencer – and short – another retailer such as Morrison's, and for this reason the strategy claims to be independent of market movements.

However, in practice, the strategy often turns out to have a lot more directional risk than it is supposed to, as the correlations between the two sides of the pair can be quite unstable and can change suddenly. As with all correlation strategies, there is no intrinsic reason why the path taken by the spread between the pairs cannot be one of a random walk. Correlation does not imply causation, and previously correlated securities may abruptly become uncorrelated securities.

Convertible Arbitrage

Another relative value strategy focuses on those securities which have convertible features. The objective is to profit from mispricing of a convertible security and/or expected trends in factors influencing the price of a convertible security.

Typically the strategy will involve a combination of a long position in the convertible security and a short position in the underlying stock.

In recent years many arbitrage strategies turned out to be far less low-risk than had previously been forecast by advocates of such trades. In general with a convertible there is always the possibility of a sudden dividend payment, and there can be serious risks from the different liquidity features of the convertible securities and the underlying stock. For example, many convertible arbitrageurs suffered losses in early 2005, when the credit of General Motors (GM) was downgraded at the same time that a major investor, Kirk Kerkorian, was making an offer for GM's stock. Since most arbitrageurs were long GM debt and short the equity, they were hurt on both sides.

Statistical Arbitrage

As a trading strategy, statistical arbitrage, which is often abbreviated to StatArb, is any strategy that uses statistical/econometric techniques in order to provide signals for the execution of trades. Signals are often generated through a belief in the notion of 'mean-reversion'. This relates to the idea that if a security has strayed a long way from its mean performance then eventually it will tend to revert back towards its mean performance. The only problem with this belief is in trying to quantify how long 'eventually' may mean. Also involved in StatArb trading are ways of investing in securities which have favourable momentum characteristics that can be determined by statistical measures such as rate of change and other technical characteristics of the price behaviour.

Historically, StatArb evolved out of the simpler pairs strategy previously discussed above. StatArb considers not pairs of stocks but a portfolio of many more stocks (some long, some short) that are carefully matched by sector and region to eliminate exposure to beta and other risk factors.

Because of the large number of stocks involved, the high portfolio turnover and the fairly small size of the mispricings that the strategy is designed to exploit, implementation is usually handled in an automated fashion, and there is much attention placed on reducing trading costs.

Event-Driven

Special Situations

An investment in a 'special situation' is typically an attempt to profit from a change in valuation as a result of a corporate action or takeover, and is generally not a long-term investment. An example of special situation that would prompt investors' attention would be a large public company spinning off one of its smaller business units into a separately tradeable public company. If the market deems the soon-to-be-spun-off company to have a higher valuation in its present form than it will after the spin-off, an investor might buy shares in the larger company before the spin-off in an attempt to realise a quick price increase.

There are many other circumstances that could be referred to as special situation investment opportunities such as tender offers, mergers and acquisitions, and bankruptcy proceedings.

Merger Arbitrage

Merger arbitrage strategies are specialised and seek to profit from the spreads in announced mergers and acquisitions (M&A transactions) or takeovers. Typically, the approach is to buy the stock of the target company in an M&A deal and sell the acquiring company's stock. Profits are realised when the deal is consummated and the stock prices converge. Such strategies are usually considered to be low-risk, but there can be substantial risks if the M&A deal falls through.

Distressed Securities

Distressed securities are securities such as corporate bonds, bank debt, and sometimes the common and preferred stock of companies that are in some sort of distress. Typically, the term 'distressed' in this context means that such companies would appear to be heading toward or in bankruptcy.

When a company is unable to meet its financial obligations, its debt securities may be substantially reduced in value. Typically, a company's debt is considered distressed when its yield to maturity (YTM) is more than 10% or 1,000 basis points above the risk-free rate of return (ROR) available in government securities. A security is also often considered distressed if it is rated CCC or below by one or more of the major debt-rating agencies.

When a company becomes distressed, many investors currently holding its securities will often react to the possibility of bankruptcy by selling those securities in haste at a reduced price. Because their price is reduced, distressed securities are attractive to investors who are looking for a bargain. Typically, these investors think the company that issued the distressed securities is not in as difficult a position as the market believes, and the value of the company's distressed securities may increase, allowing investors holding those securities to profit.

5.3 Directional Strategies

Directional strategies cover the numerous styles of investing which require a view as to the future direction (both short term and long term) of a particular asset class and/or the overall market. Unlike the previous category, which is more focused on relative values between securities, directional strategies require the manager to speculate as to the absolute values of the securities that will be included in a portfolio.

Directional strategies can be subdivided into two categories: equity hedge and tactical trading.

5.3.1 Equity Hedge

Long/Short Equities

The portfolio of a specialist fund using a long/short equity strategy will consist of securities that are on both the long and short sides of the market. The decision as to which securities to invest in will be based on individual judgements about the future direction of each security, rather than the top-down approach.

In essence, the role of the manager practising a long/short equity strategy is to identify securities that are mispriced relative to the manager's internal valuation models, on both the long and short sides of the market. Research methods will often consist of both fundamental analysis and technical analysis of the securities under consideration.

These strategies differ from the non-directional (relative value, event-driven) strategies in that they typically take market direction risk (either long or short) as part of their investment approach.

Market exposure may be net long, net short, or neutral at any given time and is adjusted as market opportunities warrant according to the judgement of the investment manager. The expected returns from the long/short equity approach are that the strategy should outperform in bear markets by aiming to deliver absolute returns, but they will tend to underperform in sharply rising markets.

Emerging Markets

This category of HF investing has come to prominence in recent years because of the outstanding growth statistics of emerging markets. Emerging markets have seen gross domestic product (GDP) growth rates which are far in excess of those seen in the developed economies.

The BRIC economies, in particular, were enjoying strong economic growth, with China leading the way at an annual rate of nearly 10%. India, too, with a large and growing middle class, was making large investment in capital infrastructure. Russia's wealth was dependent on oil and gas prices with its economy enjoying fairly consistent growth and Brazil benefited from strong demand for its agriculture and commodities from countries such as China.

However, there are negatives to consider. In all four BRIC nations there are indications that growth had brought about inflationary pressures and 'overheating' and concerns over the future political direction of Russia, China and Brazil in particular. The equity markets in the BRIC countries and in other emerging economies can also be very volatile; for example, the Chinese stock market in mid-2010 fell by about 60% from its peak in 2007, and also by another 30% in 2015.

Private Placements

These are strategies which focus on the purchase of securities issued without a formal public offering or publication of a full-blooded prospectus.

In the US securities can be issued to 'sophisticated investors' under Regulation D of the Securities and Exchange Commission (SEC) regulations and are known as private placements. The securities which can be quite attractive but which may entail high risk are made available to high net worth individuals who have demonstrated investment experience and are sold without the stringent requirements of a formal public offering prospectus which would be required for an IPO.

Since the Prospectus Directive (PD) was enacted within the European Union (EU), similar opportunities exist for European companies to place securities with qualified investors where the rules on disclosure and the requirements for what needs to be included in a prospectus have been relaxed.

5.3.2 Tactical Trading

Global Macro

Global macro-strategies were brought to prominence by George Soros, a pioneer in the HF industry. His successful strategy was to seek profits from opportunistically trading global markets using financial instruments such as global stock index futures, commodities and large-scale 'bets' in the FX market.

The broad philosophy behind global and macro-investing is to find large-scale themes in the global capital markets, identify trading opportunities and to take large positions on broad indices and currencies. The investment decision-making can be based on a combination of fundamental research, technical analysis and geopolitical evaluation.

Systematic Strategies

Systematic strategies use mathematical models to evaluate markets, detect trading opportunities and generate signals and investment decisions. These strategies can be deployed across all asset classes and in particular are seen in the trading of FX and commodities.

The systems used in this category can be classified as trend-following, which means essentially that the models seek out trends and then 'ride' those trends; or there are other systematic strategies which, for example, look for trading markets at extremes or based on inter-market tactics such as the alignment between certain key FX rates such as the Japanese yen and the Australian dollar and global equities.

Sometimes systematic strategies are known as 'black box' methods because they contain proprietary indicators and analytical tools which the creators do not wish to disclose to investors. In such cases investors will have to consider past performance and other benchmarking criteria in deciding on the merits of the systems.

5.4 General Characteristics of HFs

Historically, investors in HFs are institutions or very high net worth individuals as the minimum investment levels have typically been in excess of £1 million. There are some newer funds where the minimum levels are now considerably lower which makes them accessible to more investors.

Many HFs are based offshore, where regulations and disclosure requirements are lower and where, for example, non-domiciled UK investors may be able to take advantage of tax benefits.

HF managers generally receive a fixed-base management fee, known as the AUM fee. This fee is a percentage (often between 1% and 1.5%) of the value of AUM. In addition they are also rewarded with an incentive fee (often between 14% and 18%) which is related to realised profits. As this cannot be negative if losses are made, there will often be a clause stating that, if losses are made, these losses have to be repaid in any subsequent profits before an incentive fee can be paid.

HFs have a high-water-mark (HWM) provision, which means that the incentive fee is only payable if a certain level of net asset value (NAV) is reached by the fund before the performance fee can be levied. In the early years of trading, once the HWM has been reached and the first incentive fee paid, the HWM is reset on the next highest month-end NAV of the fund.

Many HFs suffered from major redemptions during the turbulent market conditions of 2007–08, and many went out of business. On the other hand some HFs which were positioned to benefit from the collapse of the mortgage-backed securities market made spectacular returns during the same period.

HF investing is quite controversial and there are many who believe that HFs contribute to the volatility in the capital markets. There are others who believe that the opportunity to engage in shorting markets when they are overvalued not only delivers a profitable trading strategy but is also helpful to capital markets by correcting the excesses which lead to 'bubbles' which are ultimately destructive and lead to wealth destruction when the bubbles burst. They thus provide a means to redistribute scarce economic resources towards more productive yet undervalued sectors.

HF investors often take opportunities to withdraw capital from the fund if there are losses and the fund is not able to breach HWMs. It is not unusual for funds that have NAVs trading far below their HWMs to be dissolved. HFs set a minimum lock-in period for investments during which no part of the investment can be withdrawn. These periods can be from one to three years. Further, there is an exit provision when investors can only withdraw funds after the lock-in period within pre-specified exit windows. HFs often charge exit fees levied to discourage withdrawals that would otherwise disrupt the fund manager's investment strategy.

Example

A HF which focuses on global macro-strategies has a base annual management fee of 1%. The incentive fee is 15% for any returns made over and above the risk-free rate. Gross returns during the year were 35% and the risk-free rate is 5%. What is the additional profit-related change?

HF fees = 1% + 15%.

Additional return above risk-free rate = (33% − 3%) = 30%

Effect of incentive fees to return = 30% x 15% = 4.5%

5.5 Fund of Funds (FOF)

Fund of funds (FOF) is the name given to a fund that invests in a selection of HFs.

Benefits

A FOF will invest in a variety of HFs, allowing the investor to diversify.

It provides easy access to investors who may be otherwise unable to use HFs because of the high minimum investments required by many HFs.

There may also be the opportunity to invest in funds that have otherwise closed to new investors.

The manager of the FOF typically claims to have more expertise than the individual investor. They will have better access to information and will be more experienced in the due diligence required prior to investing in a HF. FOFs typically can charge 1.5% management fees plus 10% performance fees.

Disadvantages

- FOFs often struggle to generate returns in excess of a double layer of fees.
- Less visibility of underlying investment funds. Typically a FOF merely reports its top ten holdings.
- Low possibility of interaction between the investor and the underlying HF manager.
- Diversification of HF strategies may be counterproductive.

5.6 Performance Issues

5.6.1 Benchmarking the Performance of Funds

The most important type of benchmarking from the point of view of investors is the benchmarking of the performance of funds and portfolios.

Funds usually choose an index to be their performance benchmark. The index will match the region or sector that the fund invests in. A UK technology fund might choose one of the techMARK indices, whereas an emerging market fund may choose one of the MSCI indices.

The use of indices as benchmarks is one of the reasons why so many different indices exist: they need to match the variety of funds. Even so, some funds and portfolios are better served by using a composite of several indices.

One danger this brings is that it tempts managers to track their benchmark index (and thus avoid the risk of underperforming) rather than genuinely trying to beat it: supposedly actively managed funds thus become closet trackers.

Indices are not perfect benchmarks for performance measurement. Limitations include the range available (although this can be overcome by using **synthetic** indices specially calculated for a specific portfolio). Another problem difficult to resolve is that changes in composition of the index introduce a form of survivorship bias.

5.6.2 Survivorship Bias

This is the tendency for failed companies to be excluded from performance studies because they no longer exist. It often causes the results of studies to skew higher because only companies which were successful enough to survive until the end of the period are included.

For example, a fund company's roster of funds today will include only those that are successful now. Many losing funds are closed and merged into other funds to hide poor performance.

5.6.3 Alpha

Investors' opinions on how to assess performance are thus very much influenced by the relative performance of a fund to its chosen benchmark. It is fair to say that the role of the investment manager is to deliver 'alpha' – an excess return over and beyond the performance of the market overall or the particular sector of the market in which the fund is specialised.

If the fund was 'actively managed', with the fund managers putting a lot of effort into selecting individual investments at some cost to the investor, then the investor might well wonder whether a fund that simply slavishly follows an index – an index tracker fund – would produce better results, at lower cost.

5.6.4 Benchmarking Relative to Peers

The financial press and research companies, such as Morningstar and Standard & Poor's (S&P), produce various rankings of funds according to sector.

Rankings of categories of funds relative to peers over a particular time period are available. Often, quartile rankings will be shown; each quartile includes one quarter of the funds in the category.

Among the metrics which are used to compare performances are not simply the total return of the fund but also some of the ratios discussed in this workbook.

5.7 The Merits and Demerits of HF Investing

Wealth advisers should be cautious of the fact that, despite some funds reporting meteoric returns to their investors, there are a larger number in this category which have consistently underperformed the S&P 500 index over the last decade. Hedge Fund Research (HFR) released a quarterly announcement in which it stated that the global HF industry had continued to surge, with AUM reaching a new record of $3.4 trillion (2017). Prior to this quarterly news by HFR, the *Economist* in a December 2012 article had reported that *'hedge funds had another lousy year, to cap a disappointing decade'*. The publisher recounted the fact that HFRX, a widely used measure of industry returns, was down by 0.6% in 2014, compared to an 13.7% rise in the S&P 500 Index. In 2015, the average HF lost more than 3% compared to a small gain from the S&P 500 of 1.4% (including dividends). The S&P 500 had outperformed its HF rival for more than ten straight years.

This begs the question, then, as to what role is played by HFs in a well-constructed portfolio. Supporters of HFs claim that a small allocation to HF exposures in a traditional equity/bond portfolio can diversify the portfolio during turbulent times. Still, there are many who point to the high 2/20% fee structures charged by HFs in comparison to other cheaper funds such as ETFs, which can equally provide similar diversification benefits to HFs.

Empirical studies have compared the return drivers of traditional investments with alternative investments. The results reveal that, with traditional equity and bond type funds, the underlying market-based risks can have a significant impact on the performances of these funds. However, the traditional focus is on long-only bias, and this presents some constraints when the trends are clearly running against conventional asset classes. As a result of adverse market movements in bonds and/or equities, market-neutral strategies deployed by HFs can help to diversify risks and limit losses. Further, there are HF strategies that have option-like properties when the non-normal or truncated return distributions of these funds can be used to great effect in minimising the risks to conventional investments.

6. Tax-Relieved Alternative Investment Schemes

Learning Objective

8.6 Evaluate enterprise investment schemes, venture capital trusts, woodland, bloodstock, and collectibles as asset classes: definition and key properties; problems due to lumpiness and indivisibility; risk, liquidity and return; performance; principal problems and liquidity issues, plus implications should liquidity fall; ability of investors to gain access at a reasonable price

6.1 Venture Capital Trusts (VCTs)

Venture capital trusts (VCTs) are companies listed on the LSE and are similar to investment trusts. They are designed to enable individuals to invest indirectly in a range of small higher-risk trading companies, whose shares and securities are not listed on a recognised stock exchange, by investing through VCTs.

Investment in VCTs attracts special tax advantages and so the companies need to gain HM Revenue & Customs (HMRC) approval to be treated as such. Once approved, VCTs are exempt from corporation tax on any gains arising on the disposal of their investments. Investors may also be entitled to various income tax and capital gains tax (CGT) reliefs.

VCTs are structured so as to provide investors with preferential tax treatment in a number of ways; this is intended to encourage individuals to provide capital to smaller, start-up companies which might otherwise be unable to find the funding to grow – and to do so through a vehicle which provides the investor with:

- some incentives (the tax relief), and
- a measure of protection (the diversification of a collective investment).

The tax reliefs are only available to individuals aged 18 years or over, with a maximum investment of £200,000, and cannot be claimed by trustees or companies (although there is nothing to stop such investors from holding shares in a VCT).

In terms of income tax, investors benefit from the following:

- Exemption from income tax on dividends from ordinary shares in VCTs (dividend relief).
- Income tax relief at the rate of 30% of the amount subscribed for shares. The shares issued must have been new ordinary shares, and must not carry any preferential rights. They must be held for at least five years.

The relief for dividend income and gains applies whether the shares were acquired at issue or subsequently via a stock exchange trade. The income tax relief is only available for initial subscriptions.

This tax relief at 30% can be set against any income tax liability that is due, whether at the lower, basic or higher rate.

Property and Alternative Investments

The key CGT relief available for VCTs is:

- No CGT on any gain made when the investor disposes of their VCT shares.

VCTs can provide very rewarding opportunities for investors – in part because start-up and developmental/growth companies can, in the right conditions, produce significant growth; and in part because the gains and income are not subject to the same tax drag as less favourably treated investments.

However, because of their nature they also involve a high level of risk. For example:

The companies in which VCTs invest are not listed and so it may be difficult for the VCT to sell them, in order to take advantage of better opportunities. There is liquidity risk. These smaller companies may be more vulnerable to downturns in the markets or the economy. Their share prices may be disproportionately affected by market sentiment. They may also (especially if they have high levels of borrowing) be very sensitive to changes in interest rates.

In some, but not all, cases they may have relatively young and inexperienced management teams and their lack of track record may mean that the best decisions are not always taken.

As with ordinary investment trusts, shares in VCTs are traded on the stock market and their prices are thus determined by supply and demand. Their prices will therefore trade at a discount or premium to the VCT's NAV, as based on a valuation of the holdings in its underlying portfolio.

6.2 Enterprise Investment Schemes (EISs)

Enterprise Investment Schemes (EISs) provide private investors with a way of investing in small- to medium-sized unquoted trading companies in the UK, which would otherwise be difficult to invest in directly.

EISs also offer substantial tax benefits to private investors:

- **income tax relief** – 30% income tax relief either in the tax year in which the funds are invested or the previous tax year
- **CGT deferral** – CGT deferral on gains arising within the last three years or in the next year
- **inheritance tax (IHT) exemption** – qualifying investments will benefit from 100% business property relief under current legislation providing that the investments have been held for at least two years and are still held at the time of death
- **tax-free capital gains** – exemption from CGT on individual holding disposal
- **loss relief** – loss relief to be set against deferred capital gains or income, with an option to defer CGT gains through reinvesting within specified time limits.

Investment Conditions

Income tax relief is available at 30% on EIS investments of up to £1 million in 2017–18, rising by a further £1 million in 2018 for knowledge intensive companies.

To remain qualifying, investments must be held for a minimum of three years in order to ensure that the income is not clawed back.

The size of a qualifying company for an EIS must be fewer than 250 employees and the company must have no more than £15 million of gross assets before the investment. The annual amount that can be raised through an EIS by an individual company is £5 million.

EIS Investment Opportunities

Some EIS opportunities offer the prospect of high returns but with similarly high-risk characteristics.

The considerable tax reliefs available through EIS investments in themselves can provide sufficiently attractive returns and seek investments which place greater emphasis upon return of capital in a timely manner.

A further attraction is an identifiable exit strategy after the minimum holding period. This provides the opportunity for investors to realise their investments if desired or roll over into another EIS in three years' time and obtain a further 30% income tax relief (assuming that the EIS rules still apply at that time).

Risks

It should be noted that an investment in an EIS fund should be regarded as a higher-risk form of investment. Additionally, investments held within an EIS fund may not be readily realisable.

6.3 Seed Enterprise Investment Schemes (SEISs)

Seed enterprise investment schemes (SEISs) complement the EIS. They are predominantly designed to stimulate entrepreneurship and to help smaller, riskier, early-stage UK companies raise equity finance and attract investment, making it easier for these companies to overcome barriers to raising external finance and become established and grow. The scheme applies to smaller companies, under two years old, with 25 or fewer employees and assets of up to £200,000, which are carrying on or preparing to carry on a new business. The companies must not be controlled by other companies.

SEISs enable individual investors to have the opportunity to receive a range of tax reliefs by investing in new shares of companies in the scheme. It makes available tax relief to investors who subscribe for shares and have a stake of less than 30% in the company. Investors can get up to 50% tax relief in the tax year the investment is made, regardless of their marginal tax rate.

SEIS investors can put in up to £100,000 in a single tax year and this investment can be spread over a number of SEIS-eligible companies.

No one company can raise more than £150,000 in total via an SEIS investment. The company must be a UK company that is permanently established in the UK and it must be in a qualifying trade.

A qualifying company can follow a share issue under an SEIS, with further issues of shares under an EIS, or investment from a VCT. However, it must have spent at least 70% of the monies raised by the SEIS issue before it can do so.

6.4 Patient Capital

In 2016, the UK government announced a review into the barriers facing long-term finance for high-growth, innovative firms. As well as identifying current funding availability, it sought to consider the root causes of any barriers from the point of view of investors, as well as considering best practice overseas, before seeking recommendations for changes. This was an industry-wide consultation.

It had been suspected that some of the alternative investment methods listed above (eg, VCTs and EISs) were designed more to obtain tax relief than to provide investment in innovative and thus higher-risk ventures. Some programmes were even marketed as low-risk or offering some degree of capital protection.

There has not been any announcement of curbs to such programmes as yet, but in June 2018, the UK government launched a new £2.5 billion investment programme under the brand name 'British Patient Capital' to be run by the British Business Bank (a government-owned institution which is not actually a bank and is, therefore, not regulated by the FCA or PRA). This fulfilled the Chancellor's 2017 Autumn Budget commitment and followed on from a review of Patient Capital.

At the time of writing (August 2018), it is too soon to be able to discuss this new initiative in any detail, and so candidates should research the topic as it develops in the coming months and years.

6.5 Other Types of Alternative Investment

Alternative investments are often physical assets which tend to be popular with collectors. However, they also have the potential to appreciate substantially in value.

An advantage is that they are not exclusive to wealthy clients and due to the wide variety of options available, even modest investments are possible. The disadvantage is that they often suffer from illiquidity and can be difficult to sell quickly if funds are required for other purposes. They can also be difficult to value due to the size of the different markets. Prices can change rapidly as markets are subject to trends and fashions.

Alternative investments have always been popular with wealthy individuals. They provide an additional level of diversification for a portfolio and have the potential for significantly higher returns.

Other examples of alternative investments include:

- jewellery
- antiques
- books
- art
- classic cars
- coins
- stamps (rare stamps were rated in the top four investments for the 20th century with annual returns of around 10% per annum)
- toys (worth four to five times more if in the original packaging)
- race horses (although more money is made from stud breeders)
- fine wine.

Apart from some advantageous tax relief, such as woodlands relief, below, the main driver for purchasing alternatives is that they cannot be printed like fiat currency, tend to retain their value against the relative purchasing power which is an inflationary hedge, and it could be said to have intrinsic and rarity value.

6.5.1 Woodlands Relief

Woodlands relief relates to forestry and woodlands devoted to growing timber. IHT can be deferred until the timber is cut and sold.

When you die, the beneficiaries of your woodland can ask that the value of the timber – but not the land – be excluded from your estate. However, when the timber is sold, the beneficiaries may have to pay inheritance tax on the value of the sale unless it also qualifies for relief.

If the woodland qualifies for agricultural relief, woodlands relief may not be available and you should claim agricultural relief instead. Business relief may be available on woodland that qualifies as a business asset.

Furthermore, business relief is often more favourable and so this woodland relief is very rarely taken up. This point is made very explicit by the Valuation Office Agency.

Although not the biggest section of the syllabus, questions relating to alternative investments are not uncommon. They could easily feature in any section of the exam so students should be reasonably confident they can discuss the various alternatives in some depth.

Example

The following example acts as practice questions from Section A.

Discuss the risks involved in investing in Private Equity funds.

Example

The following example acts as a practice question from Section C.

Mr Jamieson thinks that the entire market may be going to go through a volatile period for a few years and is therefore considering investing in a hedge fund in distressed companies or infrastructure funds. Critically appraise these potential investments for him.

Exercise Answer

Exercise 1

Briefly outline what roles commodities could play in a multi-asset portfolio.

Answer

The main roles commodities could play are that of effective risk diversifiers – with their low correlative relationships to other assets and their ability to provide a sound hedge against inflation in respect of returns.

Chapter Nine
Derivatives

1. Market Structures, Features, Regulatory and Trading Environment — **385**
2. Range of Derivative Instruments — **390**
3. Principles, Components, Characteristics and Risks — **397**
4. Margin and Collateral — **419**
5. Clearing and Settlement — **426**
6. Exchange-Traded Derivatives (ETDs) — **430**
7. OTC Traded Derivatives — **451**

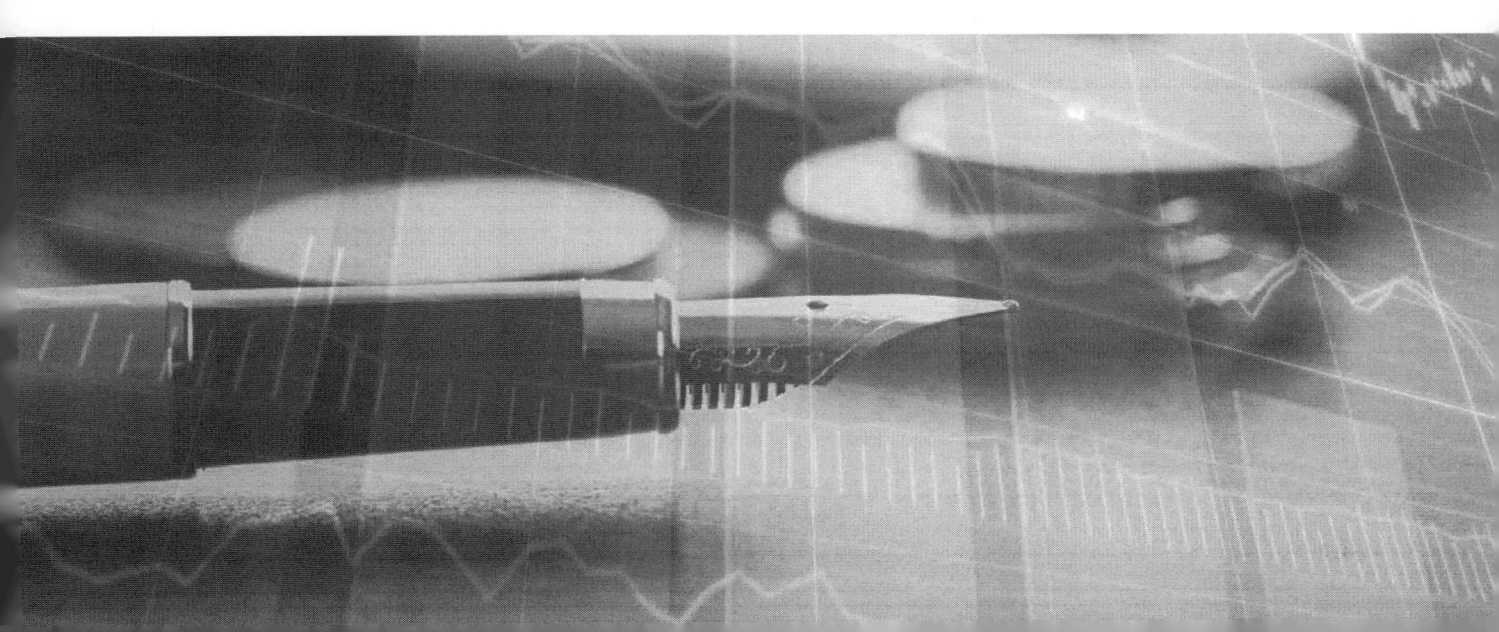

1. Market Structures, Features, Regulatory and Trading Environment

Learning Objective

9.1 Explain derivatives market structures, features and the regulatory and trading environment: role, structure and regulation of global derivatives markets; role or regulators and other supervisory bodies; market terminology; key market participants and roles

1.1 Role and Structure of Global Derivatives Markets

A derivative is a financial instrument whose price is directly linked to the price of a specific underlying market.

Derivatives are used for both hedging and speculation in their respective underlying markets, without the need to trade that market directly.

Liquidity in some derivatives can, in some circumstances be greater than in the underlying market, particularly where the underlying market is an index of assets (eg, equities), whose individual liquidity could be substantially less than that of an index derivative (eg, an index future or option). This can allow large asset allocation changes by fund managers to be executed initially via derivatives in order to secure an overall current price, before later unwinding the derivative as the underlying assets are traded in a manner which impacts their liquidity less.

The use of **initial margin** in futures contracts and of premiums in options (see below) allows both hedging and speculation via derivatives for less initial cost than trading the underlying asset class.

In underlying asset classes which are usually long-only (equities and commodities), derivatives allow short positions to be taken either as a hedge or as speculation. (Note however that in highly turbulent markets, the use of short-selling in equities and in equity derivatives can be quickly banned by the authorities in an attempt to offer stability).

Derivatives are categorised broadly between those traded and settled on recognised exchanges (with fixed contract terms, including contract sizes and maturities) and those traded on an over-the-counter (OTC) basis. The latter offer almost limitless variations of terms of contract, allowing far greater bespoke arrangements, as well as allowing embedding of derivative elements into vanilla assets to form 'structured products'. The settlement of OTC derivatives is increasingly being moved however, to central counterparties, to reduce overall credit risk.

1.2 EU Rules on Derivatives Contracts

A major issue highlighted by the 2008 financial crisis was the lack of regulation for OTC derivatives markets. In response, the European Union (EU) adopted a directive in 2012 called the European Market Infrastructure regulation (EMIR).

EMIR was intended to:

- increase transparency in the OTC derivatives markets
- mitigate credit risk
- reduce operational risk.

1.2.1 Enhancing Transparency

The Directive introduced reporting requirements which were intended to make derivatives markets more transparent. It stated:

- detailed information on each derivative contract must be reported to trade repositories (as well as being available to supervisory authorities)
- trade repositories must publish total positions for each class of derivatives, (market traded as well as OTC)
- the European Securities and Markets Authority (ESMA) had to take responsibility for monitoring and supervising trade repositories (including granting and withdrawing accreditation).

1.2.2 Mitigating Credit Risk

EMIR also tried to reduce the counterparty credit risk attached to derivatives contracts by introducing the following:

- all standardised OTC derivatives contracts must be centrally cleared through central counterparties (CCPs)
- where the contract has not been cleared by a CCP, risk mitigation techniques must be applied
- CCPs must comply with stringent prudential, organisational and conduct of business requirements.

1.2.3 Reducing Operational Risk

Market participants were instructed that they must monitor and mitigate the operational risks associated the trading of derivatives, eg, fraud and human error by using electronic means to promptly confirm the terms of OTC derivatives contracts.

1.2.4 Equivalence Decisions under EMIR

EMIR allows recognition of CCPs and trade repositories which are not based in the EU. Once recognised, EU and non-EU counterparties may use a non-EU-based CCP to meet their clearing obligations and a non EU-based trade repository to report their transactions to.

The recognition is based on equivalence decisions adopted by the European Commission, ie, the legal and supervisory framework for the CCPs or trade repositories are equivalent to the EU regime.

1.3 Role of Regulators

Regulation of derivatives remains under close scrutiny since the global financial crisis of 2007–08. Restrictions have so far tended however not to relate to curbing derivative products themselves (with the occasional exception of short-selling derivatives as noted above), but have focused more on which products may be sold to different categories of clients, with the tightest restrictions on retail clients.

Regulators are greatly concerned however with the risk which derivatives pose to the stability of the global financial system. Total outstanding amounts across all asset classes vary (according to data from the Bank for International Settlements), but over the last couple of years have typically been above USD 500 trillion (OTC) and up to around USD 100 trillion (exchange-traded).

Although the prices of derivatives are in theory driven by their underlying asset, this relationship can reverse, if the respective volumes are also reversed. This can cause unexpected and unwelcome liquidity problems in the underlying markets.

1.4 Market Terminology

There are certain terms which are either unique to derivatives or which have a particular meaning in their context. A list of these is potentially endless, but the most common include:

- **American-style option** – an option that can be exercised at any time, as opposed to a European Style option which can only be exercised at expiry. European Style option contracts can be closed out early, replicating the profitability of American style options in most cases.
- **At-the-money spot or forward** – an option whose strike price is equal to the current, prevailing price in the underlying spot or forward market.
- **Backwardation (see also contango)** – commodities or futures markets where shorter-dated contracts trade at a higher price than longer-dated contracts.
- **Bermudan-style option** – an option that can be exercised at a range of specific times, up to and including the expiry date. It is thus considered midway between an American (anytime) and a European style option (only at expiry).
- **Black-Scholes** – an equation for valuing plain vanilla options developed by Fischer Black and Myron Scholes in 1973 for which they shared the Nobel Prize in Economics.
- **Call option** – a call option gives the owner the right but not the obligation to buy a pre-set amount of the underlying financial instrument at a pre-set price with a pre-set maturity date.
- **Cap** – a financial contract giving the owner the right but not the obligation to borrow a pre-set amount of money at a pre-set interest rate with a pre-set maturity date. Equivalent to a call option.
- **Cash settlement** – derivatives contracts which are settled at maturity (or before maturity at closeout) by an exchange of cash from the party who is **out-of-the-money** to the party who is in-the-money.
- **Collar** – a combination of options in which the holder of the contract has bought an out-of-the money option call (or put) and sold an out-of-the-money put (or call). This locks in the effective minimum and maximum rates that the collar owner will transact in the underlying at expiry.
- **Commodity swap** – a contract in which counterparties agree to exchange payments related to indices, at least one of which (and possibly both of which) is a commodity index.
- **Contango (see also backwardation)** – commodities or futures markets where shorter-dated contracts trade at a lower price than longer-dated contracts.
- **Covered call option writing** – a technique to fund their underlying long asset positions, typically used in equity markets. If an investor sells a call on an underlying asset already in his inventory, then the written call is 'covered' (by ownership of the underlying). Otherwise the investor has sold the call 'naked'.

- **Currency swap (see also interest rate swap)** – an exchange of interest rate payments in different currencies on a pre-set notional amount and in reference to pre-determined interest rate indices in which the notional amounts might be exchanged at inception of the contract and then re-exchanged at the termination of the contract at pre-set exchange rates.
- **Delta** – the sensitivity of the change in the option's price to changes in the price of the underlying asset.
- **European-style option** – an option that can be exercised only at expiry as opposed to an American Style option that can be exercised at any time from inception of the contract. European Style option contracts can be closed out early, mimicking the early exercise property of American style options in most cases.
- **Exchange-traded contracts** – financial instruments listed on exchanges such as the Chicago Board of Trade.
- **Exercise price (see also strike price)** – the price at which a call's (put's) buyer can buy (or sell) the underlying instrument.
- **Exotic derivatives** – any derivative contract that is not a plain vanilla contract and which is typically non-path dependent. Examples include barrier options, average rate and average strike options, lookback options and chooser options.
- **Floor (see also cap; collar)** – a financial contract giving the owner the right but not the obligation to lend a pre-set amount of money at a pre-set interest rate with a pre-set maturity date. It is equivalent to a put option.
- **Forward contracts** – an over-the-counter (OTC) obligation to buy or sell a financial instrument or to make a payment at some point in the future. Examples include forward foreign exchange contracts in which one party is obligated to buy foreign exchange from another party at a fixed rate for delivery on a pre-set date.
- **Forward rate agreements (FRAs)** – a cash-settled obligation on interest rates for a pre-set period on a pre-set interest rate index with a forward start date. A 3×6 FRA on US dollar LIBOR is a contract between two parties obliging one to pay the other the difference between the fixed FRA rate and the floating LIBOR rate observed for that period.
- **Futures** – an exchange-traded obligation to buy or sell a financial instrument or to make a payment at one of the exchange's fixed delivery dates, the details of which are transparent publicly on the trading floor. Contract settlement takes place through the exchange's clearinghouse.
- **Gamma** – the degree of curvature in an option's price curve with respect to its underlying price. It is the rate of change of the delta (ie, delta of the delta) with respect to changes in the underlying price. Positive gamma is favourable. Negative gamma is damaging in a volatile market. Positive gamma is offset by negative theta (time decay). It grows most (ie, is most sensitive) in options which are at-the-money as time moves closer to expiry.
- **Hedge** – a transaction that offsets an exposure to fluctuations in financial prices of some other contract or business risk. It may consist of cash instruments or derivatives.
- **Implied volatility** – option pricing models rely upon an assumption of future volatility as well as the spot price, interest rates, the expiry date, the delivery date, the strike, etc. If all these parameters except for volatility are available as well as the option price, the volatility can be implied mathematically (eg, through the **Black-Scholes** equation).
- **In-the-money – spot or forward** – an option with positive intrinsic value with respect to the prevailing market spot or forward rate. If the option were to mature immediately, the option holder would exercise it to capture its economic value.
- **Interest rate swap** – an exchange of cash flows based upon different interest rate denominated in the same currency on a pre-set notional amount with a pre-determined schedule of payments and calculations. Usually, one counterparty will received fixed flows in exchange for making floating payments.

- **International Swaps Dealers' Association (ISDA) agreements** – in order to minimise the legal risks of transacting with one another, counterparties will establish master legal agreements and sidebar product schedules to govern formally all derivatives transactions into which they may enter with one another.
- **Intrinsic value** – the economic value of an option, as distinct from its time value. For a call option to have intrinsic value, the strike must be less than the current spot or forward price. For a put option, the strike must be greater than the current spot or forward price. Intrinsic value cannot be less than zero.
- **Naked option writing** – selling options without having any offsetting exposure in the underlying cash instrument.
- **Open interest** – the number of outstanding long and short positions, as reported by exchanges in their listed contracts.
- **Option** – the right but not the obligation to buy (sell) a pre-determined amount of an underlying cash instrument at a pre-determined rate on a pre-determined expiration date
- **Out-of-the-money – spot or forward** – an option with no intrinsic value with respect to the prevailing market spot or forward rate. If the option were to mature immediately, the option holder would let it expire. For a call price to have intrinsic value, the strike must be less than the current forward price. For a put price to have intrinsic value, the strike must be greater than the current forward price.
- **Over-the-Counter (OTC)** – any transaction that takes place between two counterparties directly, without involving an exchange. Contracts can be non-standardised, as negotiated between both counterparties.
- **Premium** – the price of an option, referring to the combination of intrinsic value and time value. It is paid by the buyer of an option contract to the seller, usually at the start of the contract.
- **Put option (see also call option)** – a financial contract giving the owner the right but not the obligation to sell a pre-set amount of the underlying financial instrument at a pre-set price with a pre-set maturity date.
- **Put-call parity theorem** – a long put position combined with a long position in the underlying instrument, both for the same delivery date, has the same payoff profile as a long call position for the same delivery date. This can be reversed to create long put positions.
- **Speculation** – taking positions in financial instruments without having an underlying exposure that offsets them.
- **Spot** – the price in the cash market for delivery using the standard market convention. In the foreign exchange market, spot is delivered in most currencies for value two days from the transaction date
- **Strike price** – the price at which the holder of an option exercises their right if it makes economic sense to do so at the appropriate expiry time.
- **Structured notes** – fixed income instruments with embedded derivative products, usually designed to offer an increased yield on the underlying instrument in return for risk incurred from the embedded derivative.
- **Swaptions** – options on swaps.
- **Theta** – the sensitivity of an option's premium to changes in the time remaining to expiry, all other factors staying the same.
- **Time value** – the difference between the intrinsic value and the premium of an option. It is the negotiable part of the premium and includes the factor of volatility. It diminishes at an accelerating rate towards expiry (assuming that implied volatility and the underlying market remain stable)
- **Vanilla** – a derivative in its most simple form, with no unusual features of terms
- **Vega** – the sensitivity of an option's premium to changes in implied volatility, all other factors staying the same.

1.5 Market Participants

The original users of derivatives were those who had naturally offsetting, opposite exposures in the same markets. Three basic examples include:

- **Rates** – a fixed rate borrower (who issues a bond with a fixed rate semi-annual coupon, but whose income comprises semi-annual payments which vary with floating short-term interest rates) can enter into a swap with a floating rate lender,(who receives a fixed rate semi-annual rent for a property lease, but whose long-term debt is payable on a floating rate basis).
- **Foreign exchange** – a UK importer of US dollar-denominated commodities (who faces the risk of a lower GBP/USD exchange rate) agrees to buy US dollars in a strip of GBP/USD forwards from a UK exporter of professional services to companies in the USA (who faces the risk of a higher exchange rate).
- **Commodities** – a wheat farmer (who faces the risk of a lower wholesale wheat price) buys a put option and sells a call option (creating a synthetic collar) for the coming harvest period with a large commercial bread baker (who faces the risk of a higher wheat price). Both are thus protected against extreme movements outside the specified range of the collar.

Nowadays it is far more likely that any non-financial institution wishing to hedge a direct exposure (as above) will find a counterparty more easily among professional market makers, ie, financial institutions. Depending partly on the asset class, the need for bespoke terms and the availability and desire for credit risk, this may be either on an exchange or on a bilateral OTC basis.

Tighter rules regarding capital adequacy since the 2007–08 global financial crisis, together with a range of regulations regarding how risk is measured and allocated, have reduced the appetite amongst liquidity providers to manage such large inventories of risk as before. The long-term impacts are still unknown, but there is a concern that risk appetite is diminishing, which may lead to wider trading spreads and greater volatility as liquidity diminishes. There is some scope for this gap in liquidity to be filled to some extent by asset managers and hedge funds, who can make prices on some of the new trading platforms, but it is too early to predict how much of a difference this might make.

2. Range of Derivative Instruments

Learning Objective

9.2 Explain and appraise the range of derivative instruments and their key features: financial derivatives; commodity derivatives; property derivatives; exotic derivatives; other derivatives

There are two main criteria for categorising derivatives:

- Traded on an exchange (with standard contract terms and credit risk on the clearing house) or traded OTC (bespoke terms and separate credit risk for each counterparty).
- Comprising either a commitment to enter into a transaction at a point in the future or permitting some degree of optionality, which allows one party to transact if advantageous, but obliges the other party to transact at the request of the other?

2.1 Financials (Interest Rates)

OTC	swaps, FRAs, caps, collars, floors, swaptions, convertibles
Exchange	futures (some swap futures now available)
Transaction commitment	swaps, FRAs and futures
Transaction optionality	caps, collars, floors, swaptions and convertibles

2.1.2 Interest Rate Swaps

A swap is an OTC derivative, where two counterparties exchange one stream of floating rate cash flows against another of fixed rate cash flows. These payment streams are the legs of the swap. The cash flows are calculated on a notional principal amount.

In a basic example one party exchanges a floating interest rate obligation for the other party's fixed-rate obligation. The floating rate is then determined at each reset date. In a fixed versus six-month floating swap, the reset date is every six months.

Payments are based on an agreed notional principal sum, with a start date and a set period. The swap specifies particular periods at the end of which the net cash flow exchanges will take place. At each payment date a net payment is made between the two participants based on the difference between floating rate (based on LIBOR) and the fixed rate on the underlying principal sum for the quarter.

In a simple three-year **interest rate swap**, with quarterly payments based on an agreed principal, effective from 1 January 2019, a fixed interest rate is exchanged for a floating interest rate. The first payment is on 1 April 2019, the second on 1 July 2019 and so on.

There are many complex variations of this basic example.

2.1.3 Forward Rate Agreements (FRAs)

This enables a hedger to fix an interest rate in advance. It enables a borrower or lender to take a view on whether rates are rising or falling. No principal amount is borrowed or lent, but a cash flow arises from the difference between the interest rate fixed at the outset (the fixed rate) and the level of the benchmark rate at a second point of time further in the future (the floating rate). One counterparty will pay the difference between these two rates to the other, depending on whether the floating rate is higher or lower than the fixed rate, for a predetermined future period on an agreed principal amount. The benchmark rate most often used is LIBOR.

Therefore an FRA is effectively an agreement to buy or sell an interest rate which is fixed today but starting in the future and which will is revalued against prevailing market rates, using a benchmark rate.

FRAs are traded over-the-counter and can be customised to the hedger's needs.

2.1.4 Futures

Futures are an exchange traded product, traded on both short and long-term interest rate instruments. They are an agreement to buy an agreed number of contracts of a fixed size at an agreed price on a particular date in the future.

Short-term interest rate futures (known as STIR futures) comprise mainly three month interest rate contracts in all major global currencies (eg, short-sterling in the UK, eurodollars in the US, euribors in Germany and euroyen in Japan), as well as some short-term government bills (eg, 3 month US Treasury Bills).

Longer-term futures are based on a range of 5, 10 and 30 year government bonds (the most recent issue in each case), but particularly the ten year (eg, Gilt in the UK, Treasury Note in the US, Bund in Germany and JGB in Japan).

All interest rate futures are quoted as a discount from 100 (eg 93.13 implies an interest rate of 6.87%). Buying a contract therefore reflects a view that interest rates will fall and vice versa for selling futures contracts.

2.1.5 Caps, Collars and Floors

These are the equivalent terms for a call option, a collar and a **put option** in interest rates. They are traded on an OTC basis,

A **cap** protects against a rise in floating rates over a given period, based usually on three month LIBOR. Similar to the interest rate swap above, if at any three month reset date the three month LIBOR is above the specified strike rate, the difference is paid by the cap seller to the buyer on the principal amount for that period. If the floating rate is below the fixed rate, nothing is paid. This continues for the lifetime of the cap. The buyer pays a premium to the sell at the outset.

A **floor** offers the equivalent protection for a fall in floating rates.

A **collar** combines a cap and a floor, where the strike rate on the cap is above that on the floor. The difference between represents the range where neither counterparty is effectively hedged and where no payments will occur. Both counterparties are effectively bound against a move in floating rates outside this range, whether favourable or not. The strikes are often set at levels designed to require offsetting premiums from one counterparty to the other (ie, a zero-premium collar).

2.1.6 Swaptions

A swaption is an option to enter into an interest rate swap at a given date in the future. As in other option contracts, a premium is paid by the buyer to the seller at the outset.

2.1.7 Convertibles

A convertible is an OTC bond which gives the holder the right, but not the obligation, to convert it into the issuer's ordinary shares sometime in the future. The holder should choose to convert into shares if, at maturity, the value of those shares would exceed the redemption value of the bond. As well as the holder's right to convert, the issuer might also have the right to call (ie, redeem) the bond if certain conditions are met. Such multiple embedded options can make the revaluation of convertibles difficult.

A convertible is thus a hybrid of a corporate bond and a warrant. In the case of a warrant, the holder has to pay cash when exercising the right to buy shares, whereas in a convertible the payment is the forfeiture of the bond itself in return for shares.

The holder of a convertible has the security of coupons and repayment prior to conversion, plus the potential for capital growth in the equity post conversion.

2.2 Financials (Currencies)

OTC	swaps, futures, options and CFDs
Exchange	futures and options
Transaction commitment	swap, futures and CFDs
Transaction optionality	options

The scope and size of the FX derivatives market reflects the size of underlying FX as the largest asset class, but the vast majority of derivatives are traded OTC.

- **Exchange-traded futures and options** – these have been available for many years, principally on the Chicago Mercantile Exchange (CME), but their volume and range of contracts has always remained a fraction of OTC availability.
- **Currency swaps** – these always refer to cross-currency interest rate swaps; they should not be confused with FX forwards (simply an agreement to sell one currency for another at a near date and to exchange them back at a far date). Currency swaps can therefore be for fixed v floating interest rates (in different currencies), fixed v fixed or floating v floating. They are traded OTC.
- **OTC options** – in FX these are traded with a vast amount of flexibility in terms of contract terms, leading to an extensive use of 'exotic' options, with highly customised parameters. They are also embedded extensively within structured products. The liquidity in OTC options has allowed their **implied volatility** (derived from the premium of each option) to be traded as a sub-asset class in its own right and is the benchmark for pricing most vanilla options.
- **Contracts for Difference (CFDs)** – CFDs are OTC derivatives to benefit from the capital gains from a long or short position in an underlying currency, commodity, stock index or individual stock, without having to buy or sell that security itself or to pay full value for it. Each party settles the cash difference between the price of the underlying investment when the agreement is made and its price when the agreement is ended.
CFDs have a nominal daily maturity, but in practice are renewed / rolled over at the close of each trading day on request. Positions can thus be maintained indefinitely, so long as margins are paid on a mark-to-market basis. CFD contracts are subject to a daily financing charge, usually applied at a previously agreed rate linked to LIBOR.

2.3 Financials (Equities)

OTC	swaps and warrants (primary issue)
Exchange	futures, options and warrants (secondary issue)
Transaction commitment	swaps, futures and CFDs
Transaction optionality	options and warrants

Most equity derivatives (except for warrants) are available both in the larger single stock equities and in composite equity indices (eg, FTSE 100, S&P 500). This allows exposure not only to specific equities, but to the broader market as a whole. The latter can be particularly useful when making major asset allocation switches, where the initial change of exposure can be implemented with an index derivative, which can later be unwound when the individual portfolio components can be purchased and sold.

- **Equity Swaps**
  These are swaps of anticipated income between a basket of equities and another asset class over a specified time period. This might be swapping the capital performance on equities (equity leg) for the floating rate return on a basket of bonds (floating leg), though many variations are available. Both counterparties maintain ownership of the original assets. They can involve single stock equities or indices and are traded OTC.

- **Futures and Options**
  Futures are traded on both single stock and particularly on indices, on exchanges.

- **Warrants**
  A warrant is a security issued by a company, which gives the holder the right, but not the obligation, to buy new shares in that company at a fixed price on a fixed date in the future.

  Warrants can be issued stand-alone, but are usually attached to a corporate bond as an added incentive of potential equity gain.

  They are issued by the company itself (OTC), which must then issue new shares for purchase if the warrants are exercised. Note the contrast with call options, which are exercised via the purchase of shares already in existence. Warrants thus risk diluting existing shareholdings. Warrants also tend to have much longer maturity terms than call options (years as opposed to months).

  In other respects the pricing of warrants is similar to that of options, in terms of volatility (see below).

  Although warrants are issued by individual companies on an OTC basis, they can then be listed and traded on the London Stock Exchange (LSE).

2.4 Commodities

OTC	options, swaps and CFDs
Exchange	futures and options
Transaction commitment	futures, swaps and CFDs
Transaction optionality	options

Commodity derivatives are heavily skewed towards exchange-traded products across all sectors (energy, metals and softs), with additional contracts available in sectors such as rubber and palm oil. Liquidity is generally greatest in futures, but most commodities are also available in options.

Options and swaps are also commonly traded by investment banks within customised complex hedges for clients on an OTC basis. These commonly occur when embedded into other asset classes in the form of structured products (see below).

2.5 Property

OTC	swaps
Exchange	futures
Transaction commitment	future and swaps
Transaction optionality	none

UK commercial property derivatives are extremely limited in their scope and liquidity. One problem has been liquidity; the strongly trending nature of property for years at a time makes market-makers reluctant to show two-way prices. Another has been the use of a suitable benchmark. The Eurex exchange offers annual futures contracts based on the total returns of the MSCI-IPD UK Quarterly Indices. Whilst these notionally extend beyond 'All Property' to sectors for retail, office and industrial and five further sub-sectors, the reality is that they do not necessarily offer an effective hedge for individual properties, which can be affected by highly localised factors.

2.6 Exotic

Exotic derivatives are variations on the more 'vanilla' derivatives which are available both on exchanges and OTC. By their nature they are non-standardised contracts and therefore available only in the flexibility of OTC markets.

There are many variations on the basic interest rate swap, as outlined in more detail below, such as amortising swaps, inflation swaps etc, but even these are not generally classed as exotic.

Exotic is not a defined term, but refers usually to options which are non-path dependent. Vanilla options can be priced according to well-known models (eg, Black-Scholes, but with many subsequent enhancements since that 1973 introduction), such that the fair value of two options in the same asset class but with different contract terms can be assessed with reasonable accuracy; these are termed path-dependent. Non-path dependent exotic options have additional features which can dramatically change the price and even the existence of an option prior to expiry. These include barrier options (where the payout at expiry can change due to an interim underlying price being traded), binary options (where the price at expiry is either zero or a full given amount, depending on specific factors), cross-asset options (where an event in one asset class can cause a payout in another) and many more.

These derivatives are highly customised by banks for their clients, designed to specific needs of both hedging and speculation. Not only is their pricing far more sophisticated and opaque than for vanillas, but the risk management can at times be highly sensitive to even minor moves in underlying markets.

2.7 Other

There is almost no end to the range of derivatives available (eg, gas emissions, weather), with more being devised and launched constantly, largely to improvements in underlying data and to processing speeds in software.

2.7.1 Credit Default Swaps (CDSs)

The most significant other derivative however is a credit default swap. The most significant risk to a bondholder is that the issuer fails to make the coupon and principal repayments as they fall due, ie, that the issuer defaults.

A CDS allows the buyer to make periodic payments to the seller (similar to insurance premiums). If a separate bond issuer then defaults on a specified bond during the lifetime of the CDS, the CDS seller will make a one-off payment to the buyer.

For example, if an investor buys a CDS from ABC investment bank where the reference entity is XYZ ltd (a company which has issued debt). The investor makes regular payments to ABC and if XYZ defaults on its debt, the investor receives a one-off payment from ABC and the CDS contract is terminated. A default could be more specifically defined, but generally means that a coupon payment is missed, even after a predetermined 'grace' period.

The investor does not even have to own any of XYZ's debt. If the investor does hold XYZ debt, then a CDS can be considered a hedge. But investors can buy CDS contracts on debt which they do not own. This is a naked CDS position and is purely speculative, betting against the solvency of XYZ.

If XYZ ltd defaults, one of two things can happen:

- the investor delivers a defaulted asset to ABC for a payment of the par value (physical settlement)
- ABC pays the investor the difference between the par value and the market price of the debt (**cash settlement**). There is often some recovery value and not all value is destroyed for a bondholder. CDS speculators opt for this method, as they do not own the underlying debt.

3. Principles, Components, Characteristics and Risks

Learning Objective

9.3 Explain and evaluate the principles, components, characteristics and risks of derivatives: relationships to underlying; physically settled versus cash settled; derivatives strategies, risk/reward profiles and payoff diagrams; general pricing principles – futures, options; exercise of options, assignment of obligations, abandonment and expiry; types of contracts on equity, index, currency, bond and commodity assets; risks of derivatives: legal, counterparty, settlement and dealing risks, market and other risks associated with derivative investing

3.1 Relationships to Underlying

The 'derived' nature of their name infers that derivatives have a close relationship with their underlying securities. With the exception of 'exotic' options (above) and structured products (below), it is generally possible with appropriate software to observe and predict with some degree of accuracy the change in price of one with that of the other.

3.2 Physical versus Cash Settlement

Market conventions can vary and are covered in more detail within each asset class (see below), but the general principal is:

- **Physical Settlement**

Interest rates:	swaptions (exercised into swaps), futures and convertibles (into equity)
Foreign exchange	vanilla options and futures (exercised into spot FX)
Equities	futures & options (into existing shares) and warrants (into new shares)
Commodities	futures and options (into warehouse delivery, if specified)

- **Cash Settlement**

Interest rates	swaps, FRAs, caps, collars, floors, CFDs
Foreign exchange	swaps and CFDs
Commodities	swaps and futures & options (cash settlement, unless specified)
Property	swaps and futures
Exotic	contract specific
Other	CDS

3.3 Derivative Strategies, Risk/Reward Profiles and Payoff Diagrams

3.3.1 Futures

A futures contract is an agreement to buy or sell a standard quantity of a specified asset on a fixed future date, at a price agreed today.

There are two parties to a futures contract (a buyer and a seller) whose respective obligations are:

- The buyer of a future is obliged to buy a fixed amount at a specified rate on a specified date.
- The seller of a future is obliged to sell a fixed amount at a specified rate on a specified date.

The outcome for a buyer or seller of a future when it reaches its expiry date is determined by reference to the price of the underlying asset at that time.

A futures buyer commits to buy at a pre-agreed price (eg, £115) and will make a profit if the underlying asset is trading above this price at expiry.

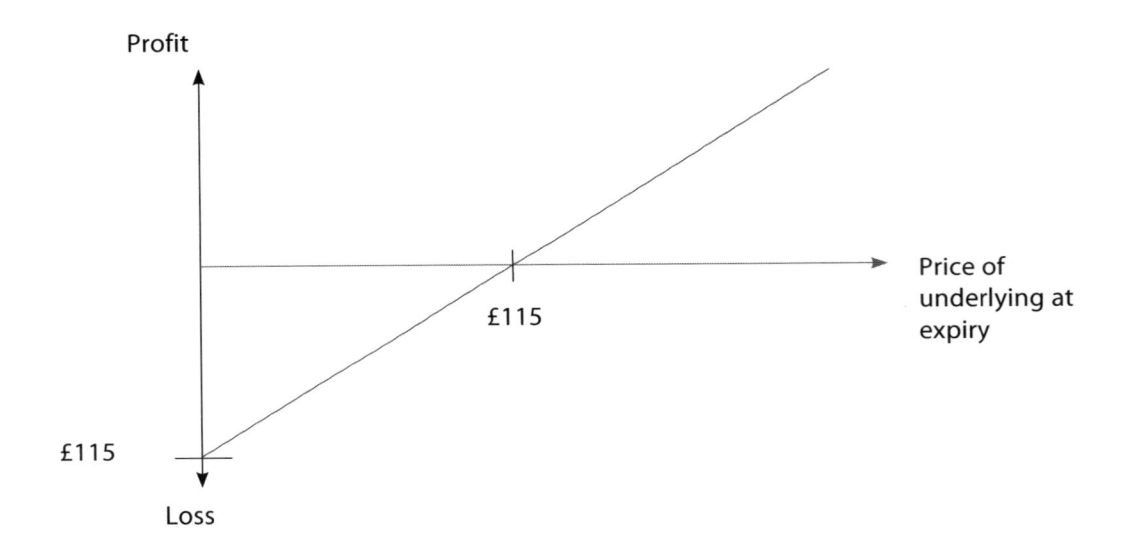

The reward to the buyer is unlimited, but the risk may be limited, if the asset price has a floor of zero (as in equities and commodities). In that scenario the buyer cannot lose more than the market price at the time of trade.

A futures seller has the opposite risk profile. The risk is unlimited, but the reward may be limited, if the asset price has a floor of zero (as in equities and commodities). In that scenario the seller cannot gain more than the market price at the time of trade.

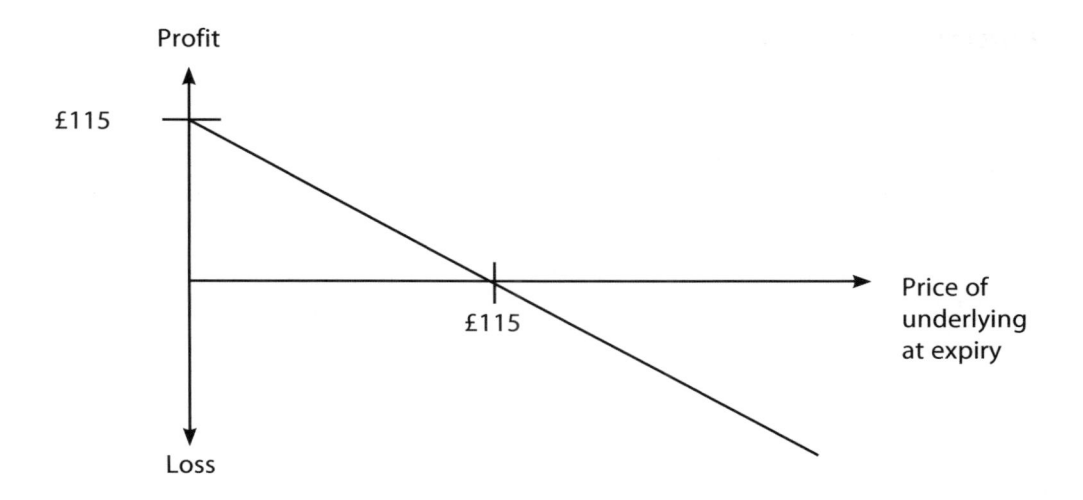

[Chart: Profit/Loss diagram showing a downward-sloping line from £115 profit (at price 0) crossing the x-axis at £115, with axes labelled "Profit/Loss" (vertical) and "Price of underlying at expiry" (horizontal).]

3.3.2 Profit and Loss

The profit and loss on a futures contract is determined by the price at the time of trade versus the price at expiry (or at closure), multiplied by the number of contracts and size of each contract, the size of each **tick** (in terms of price points) and the cash value of each tick.

Example – FTSE 100 Index Future

An investor sells five FTSE 100 futures at 5978 and holds them to delivery. The Exchange Delivery Settlement Price (EDSP), which is the official price at the expiry of the contract, is 5805.

The contract size for the NYSE Liffe FTSE 100 future is the index x £10 per point, the tick size is 0.50 index points and tick value is £5 per tick.

The profit/loss is calculated by taking the number of ticks moved x tick value x number of contracts.

The position has moved into profit by 173 index points (buying at 5805 and selling at 5978).

Since each index point represents two ticks, the movement = 173 x 2 = 346 ticks. Profit = 346 x £5 x 5 contracts = £8,650.

Example – SHFE Natural Rubber Future

A manufacturer buys ten SHFE July Natural Rubber futures at CNY (yuan) 19,650. One month before maturity, the position is closed out at CNY 20,250.

Contract size is five tons, quotation is in yuan per ton and the tick size is five yuan.

The profit/loss is price movement multiplied by contract size and by number of contracts.

Price movement is CNY 600 (buy at CNY 19,650, sell at CNY 20,250).

Profit on each contract is CNY 3,000 (CNY 600 x 5 tons).

Profit = CNY 30,000 (CNY 3,000 per contract x 10 contracts).

3.3.3 Options

An option gives a buyer the right, but not the obligation, to buy or sell a specified quantity of an underlying asset at a pre-agreed price, at a designated time in the future. The seller, in exchange for the upfront payment of a premium, grants the option to the buyer.

The two parties to an options contract are the holder and the writer. The writer confers the right, rather than the obligation, on the holder to either buy (call) or sell (put) an asset at a pre-specified price. In exchange the holder pays a premium for this right. This premium can represent a fraction of the cost of the notional value of the asset.

As the holder is in possession of a right, rather than an obligation, the holder does not have to exercise this right if the transaction ultimately proves not to work in their favour. The option can simply be left to expire with the loss of the premium paid. The writer, however, is obliged to satisfy this right if taken up, or exercised, against them by the holder.

Most exchange-traded financial options are cash settled rather than physically settled. Therefore, if exercised, the cash difference between the **exercise price** of the option and that of the underlying asset, rather than the asset itself, passes from the writer to the holder.

Consider an asset with a current price of £32.23. An investor wishes to buy a six month out-of-the-money call option with a **strike price** of £35 for a premium of £5. The option has no intrinsic value because the current stock price is below the exercise price, so the premium comprises only what is called time premium (ie, effectively the element of uncertainty or risk that the underlying price will rise above the strike price in the remaining 6 months).

The pay-off diagram shows that after the premium is taken into account, the option buyer will only experience a profitable payoff if the stock rises above £40 (£35 strike price + £5 premium). After that the returns to the option buyer show a substantial return owing to the inherent gearing of the option instrument.

Payoff Diagram on a Call Option		
Current Stock Price =		£32.23
Strike Price of Option =		£35.00
Price of the Option =		£5.00
Stock Price	**Payoff**	**Net Payoff**
£20.00	£0.00	(£5.00)
£25.00	£0.00	(£5.00)
£30.00	£0.00	(£5.00)
£35.00	£0.00	(£5.00)
£40.00	£5.00	£0.00
£45.00	£10.00	£5.00
£50.00	£15.00	£10.00
£55.00	£20.00	£15.00
£60.00	£25.00	£20.00

The option will not be exercised if the price is below £40 so the holder only loses the premium by not exercising their right to buy the underlying shares (ie, maximum loss of £5).

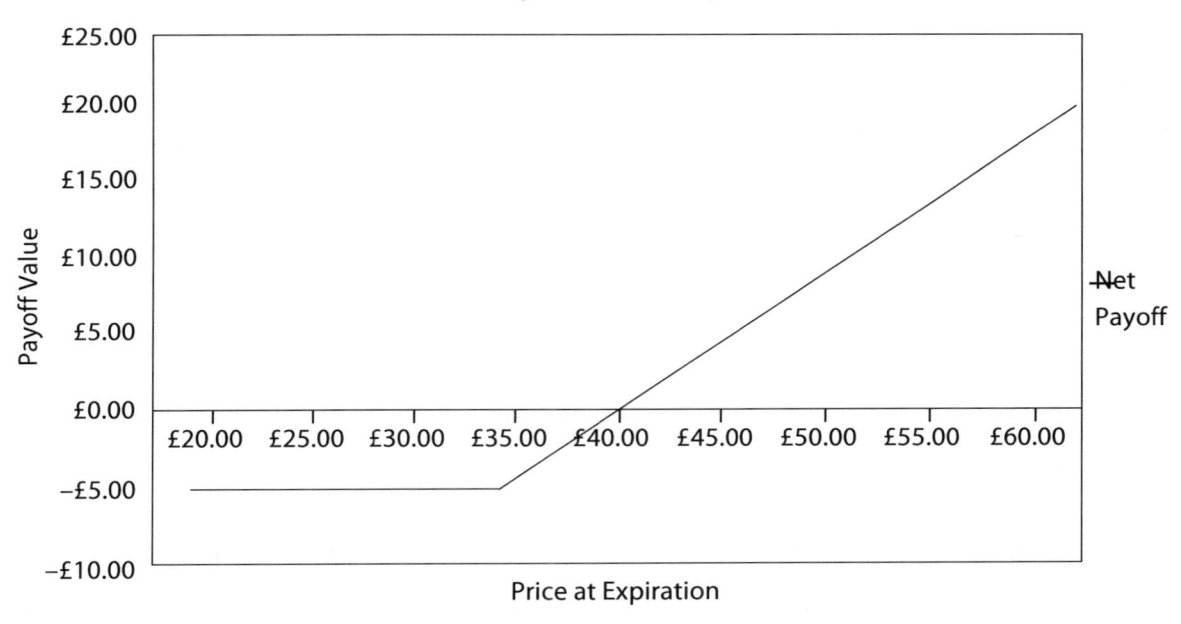

Net Payoff on a Call Option

Equivalent payoff profiles can be observed in the examples below for a wide variety of vanilla options, from the point of view of the buyer and of the seller, both naked and combined with a position in the underlying security. This includes some of the more common combinations of options, creating synthetic directional positions in the underlying security as well as creating exposures directly to the anticipated volatility.

Strategy: Long Call Option

Strategy	Long Call Option	
Motivation	Bullish – believe asset price will move higher	
Implementation	Open purchase of a call option. If very bullish buy out-of-the-money call, if less so buy in-the-money call	
Key characteristics	Maximum risk	Premium paid
	Maximum reward	Unlimited
	Break-even	Premium paid + exercise price
Comments	Position value will decay as time elapses	

Model of Option Payoffs and Profits			Action	Buy	Call
Exercise price	110.00	Premium paid	6.00	Strategy	LONG

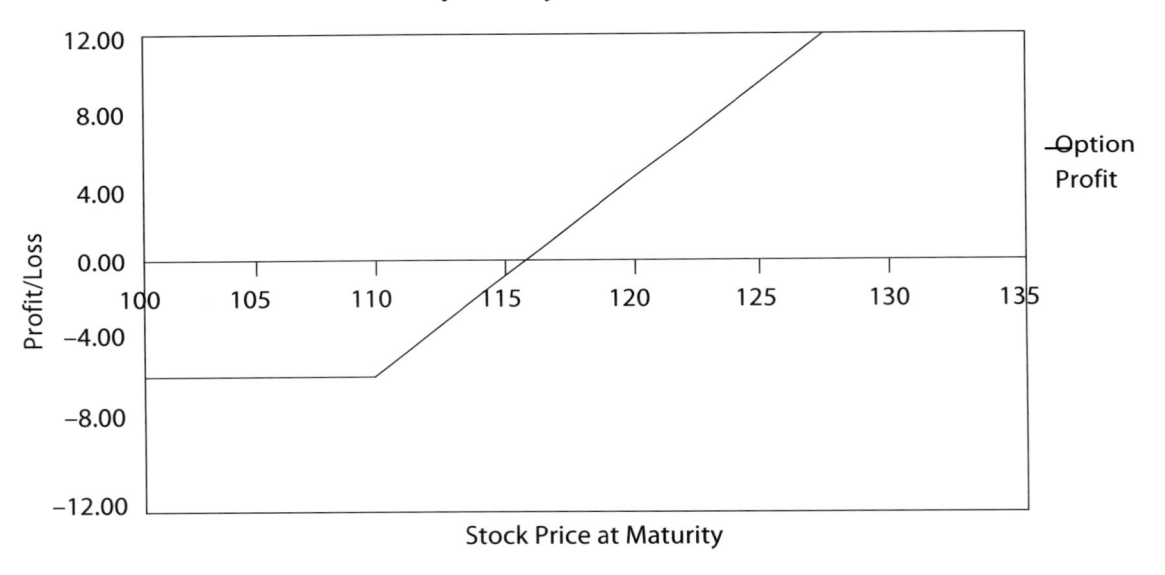

Option Payoffs and Profits

Stock price at maturity	95	100	105	110	115	120	125	130	135
Intrinsic value	0.00	0.00	0.00	0.00	5.00	10.00	15.00	20.00	25.00
Profit/(Loss)	(6.00)	(6.00)	(6.00)	(6.00)	(1.00)	4.00	9.00	14.00	19.00

Strategy: Long Put Option

Strategy	Long Put Option	
Motivation	Bearish – believe asset price will move lower	
Implementation	Open purchase of a put option. If very bearish buy out-of-the-money put, if less so buy in-the-money put	
Key characteristics	Maximum risk	Premium paid
	Maximum reward	The value of the asset less the premium paid, ie, an asset valued at £110 falling to zero, the buyer makes £110 less the premium paid
	Break-even	Exercise price – premium paid
Comments	Position value will decay as time elapses	

Model of Option Payoffs and Profits			Action	Buy	Put
Exercise price	110.00	Premium paid	6.00	Strategy	LONG

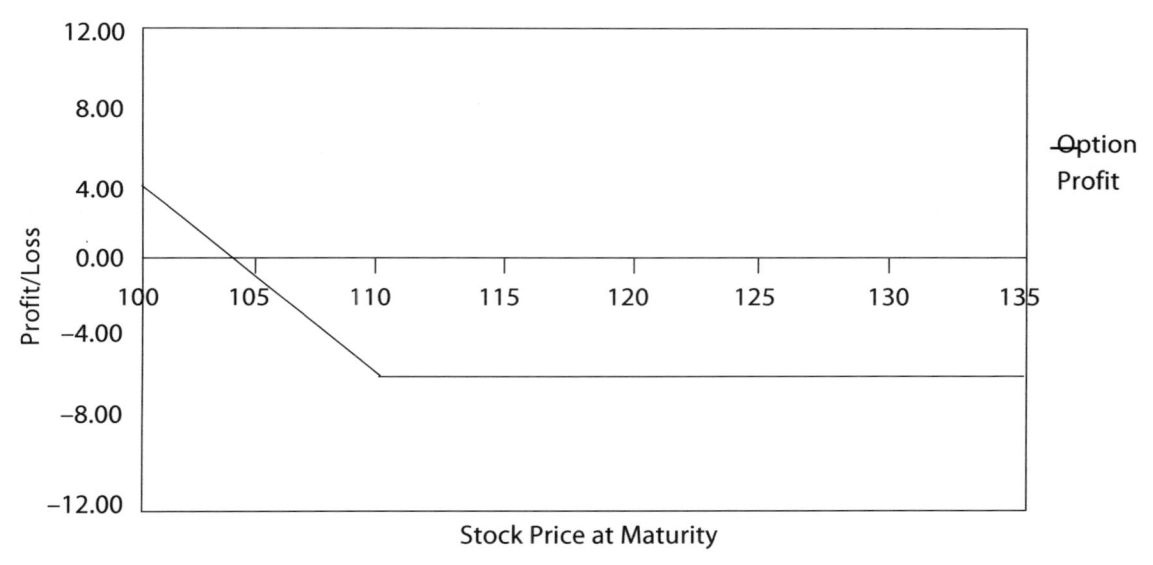

Option Payoffs and Profits

[Graph showing Option Profit line starting at 4.00 at stock price 100, crossing zero near 104, declining to -6.00 at 110, and remaining flat at -6.00 through 135. Y-axis: Profit/Loss from -12.00 to 12.00. X-axis: Stock Price at Maturity from 100 to 135.]

Stock price at maturity	95	100	105	110	115	120	125	130	135
Intrinsic value	15.00	10.00	5.00	0.00	0.00	0.00	0.00	0.00	0.00
Profit/(Loss)	9.00	4.00	(1.00)	(6.00)	(6.00)	(6.00)	(6.00)	(6.00)	(6.00)

Strategy: Short Call Option

Strategy		Short Call Option
Motivation		Bearish – believe asset price will move lower
Implementation		Opening with the sale of a call option. If very bearish sell in-the-money call, if less so sell out-of-the-money call
Key characteristics	Maximum risk	Unlimited, ie, the only limit is any maximum price of the asset, eg, if it rises to £130 the writer has to pay the difference between exercise price and £130
	Maximum reward	Premium received
	Break-even	Premium received + exercise price
Comments		Position value will improve as time elapses

Model of Option Payoffs and Profits			Action	Sell	Call
Exercise price	110.00	Premium received	6.00	Strategy	SHORT

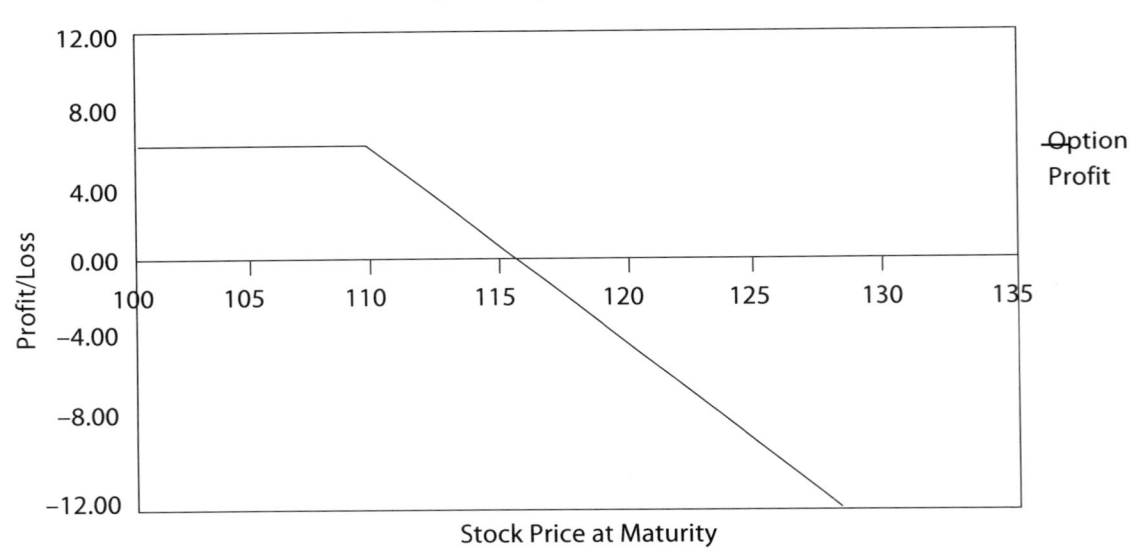

Option Payoffs and Profits

Stock price at maturity	95	100	105	110	115	120	125	130	135
Profit/(Loss)	6.00	6.00	6.00	6.00	1.00	(4.00)	(9.00)	(14.00)	(19.00)

Strategy: Short Put Option

Strategy		Short Put Option
Motivation		Bullish – believe asset price will move higher
Implementation		Opening with the sale of a put option. If very bullish sell in-the-money put, if less so sell out-of-the-money put
Key characteristics	Maximum risk	The entire value of the asset less the premium, ie, an asset valued at £110 could fall to zero and the loss is £110 less the premium received
	Maximum reward	Premium received
	Break-even	Exercise price – premium received
Comments		Position value will improve as time elapses

Model of Option Payoffs and Profits			Action	Sell	Put
Exercise price	110.00	Premium received	6.00	Strategy	SHORT

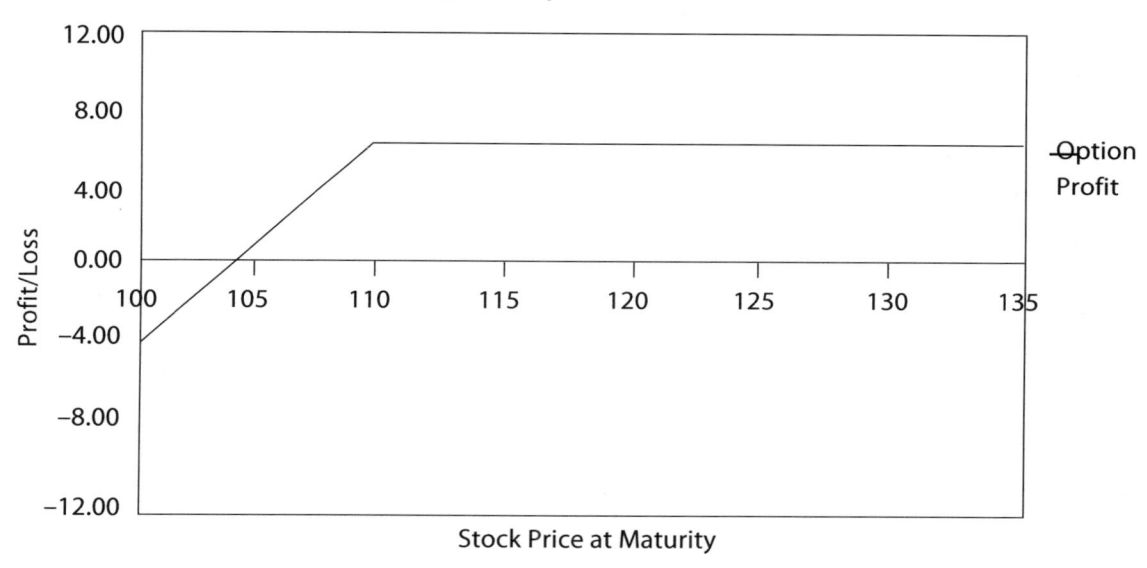

Option Payoffs and Profits

Stock price at maturity	95	100	105	110	115	120	125	130	135
Profit/(Loss)	(9.00)	(4.00)	1.00	6.00	6.00	6.00	6.00	6.00	6.00

Strategy: Covered Call Writing

Strategy	Selling (or Being Short) a Covered Call	
Motivation	Bullish to neutral – subject to chosen strike price Earn premium income from selling a call option, which has the effect of boosting overall returns on the stock and providing a measure of downside protection	
Implementation	Long position in the underlying, eg, a stock or a future, and selling a call option. If the call is sold out-of-the-money the trade has bullish expectations, if at-the-money call is sold the position is relatively neutral	
Key characteristics	Maximum risk	Initial value of underlying – call premium
	Maximum reward	Difference between strike – underlying asset value + call premium received
	Break-even	Initial value of underlying + call premium
Comments	Can enhance the returns in sideways or static markets and also provides a limited protection against falling prices	

Options Trading Strategy	Action	Writing a Covered Call			
First part of strategy	Buy asset			Asset price	110.00
Second part of strategy	Sell call option	Exercise price	110.00	Premium	5.00

Strategy: Being Long a Protective Put

Strategy	Protective Put	
Motivation	Moderately bullish and with limited downside risk This strategy is a hedge against a temporary dip in the stock's value. The protective put buyer retains the upside potential of the stock, while limiting the downside risk	
Implementation	Long position in stock or future and the purchase of a put option	
Key characteristics	Maximum risk	Initial value of stock or future – strike price + put premium
	Maximum reward	Unlimited
	Break-even	Initial value of stock or future + put premium
Comments	This is the classic example of hedging a long position in a stock or future where the underlying is protected to the downside but allows unlimited profit on the upside	

Options Trading Strategy	Action	Buying a Protective Put			
First part of strategy	Buy stock			Asset price	110.00
Second part of strategy	Buy put option	Exercise price	110.00	Premium	6.00

Strategy: Bull Spread with Call Options

Strategy	Bull Spread with Call Option	
Motivation	Moderately bullish – believe asset price will move higher Profit from a gain in the underlying stock's price without the upfront capital outlay and downside risk of outright stock ownership	
Implementation	Purchase of a low strike call option and sale of a higher strike call option	
Key characteristics	Maximum risk	Net premium
	Maximum reward	Difference between strikes less initial net premium
	Break-even	Lower strike + initial premium

Strategy	Action	Bull Spread With Calls			
First part of strategy	Buy call option	Exercise price	100	Premium	8.00
Second part of strategy	Sell call option	Exercise price	110	Premium	4.00

Strategy: Bull Spread with Put Options

Strategy	Bull Spread with Put Options	
Motivation	Moderately bullish – believe asset price will move higher Investors initiate this spread either as a way to earn income with limited risk, or to profit from a rise in the underlying stock's price, or both	
Implementation	Open purchase of a low strike put option and sale of a high strike put option	
Key characteristics	Maximum risk	Difference between strike prices – net premium received
	Maximum reward	Net premium received
	Break-even	Higher strike – net premium

Options Trading Strategy	Action	Long a Bull Spread with Puts			
First part of strategy	Buy put option	Exercise price	100.00	Premium	4.00
Second part of strategy	Sell put option	Exercise price	110.00	Premium	9.00

Strategy: Bear Spread with Call Options

Strategy		Bear Spread with Call Options
Motivation		Moderately bearish – believe asset price will move lower The chance to earn income with limited risk, and/or profit from a decline in the underlying stock's price
Implementation		Open sale of a low strike call option and purchase of a high strike call option
Key characteristics	Maximum risk	Difference between strikes – the premium received
	Maximum reward	Net premium received
	Break-even	Lower strike + initial premium received

Options Trading Strategy	Action	Long a Bear Spread with Calls			
First part of strategy	Sell call option	Exercise price	100.00	Premium	8.00
Second part of strategy	Buy call option	Exercise price	110.00	Premium	4.00

Strategy: Bear Spread with Put Options

Strategy		Bear Spread with Put Options
Motivation		Moderately bearish – believe asset price will move lower Profit from a near-term decline in the underlying stock
Implementation		Open sale of a low strike put option and purchase of a high strike put option
Key characteristics	Maximum risk	Net premium paid
	Maximum reward	Difference between strikes – the initial premium paid
	Break-even	Higher strike price – net initial premium paid

Options Trading Strategy	Action	Long a Bear Spread with Puts			
First part of strategy	Sell put option	Exercise price	100.00	Premium	6.00
Second part of strategy	Buy put option	Exercise price	110.00	Premium	9.00

Strategy: Long Straddle

Strategy	Long Straddle	
Motivation	Expect a large increase in market volatility Profit from increased volatility or a sharp move in the underlying stock's price	
Implementation	Purchase of call and put option with same expiry and same strike prices	
Key characteristics	Maximum risk	Limited to premiums paid
	Maximum reward	Unlimited
	Break-even	Upside: strike price + both premiums Downside: strike price – both premiums

Options Trading Strategy	Action	Buying a Straddle			
First part of strategy	Buy call option	Exercise price	110.00	Premium	6.00
Second part of strategy	Buy put option	Exercise price	110.00	Premium	5.00

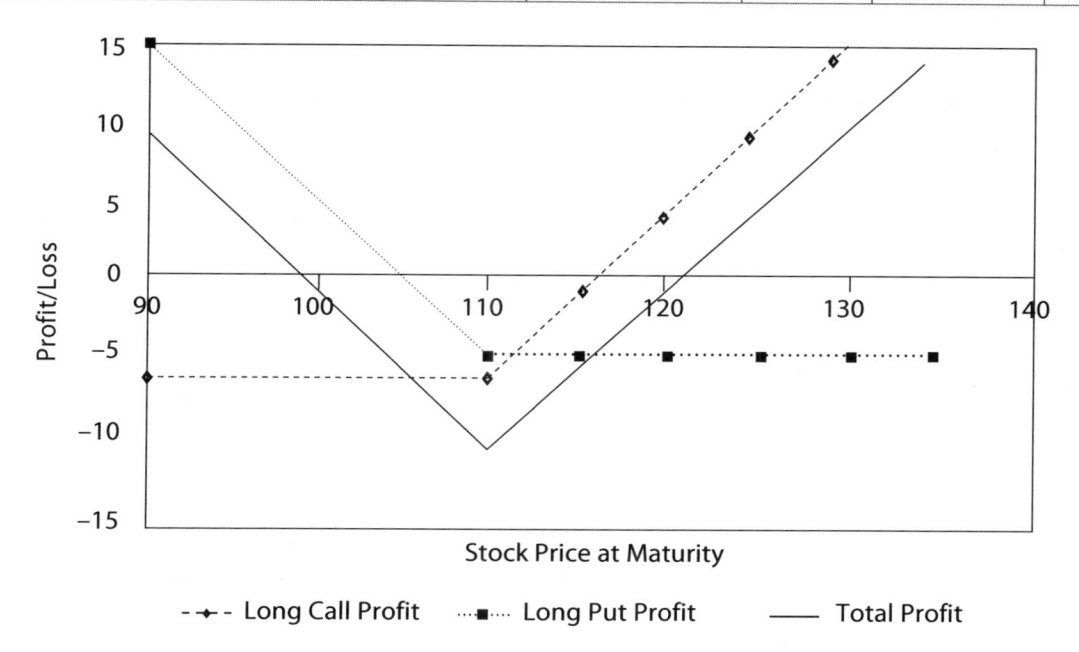

Stock price at maturity	90	110	115	120	125	130	135	140	145
Call option profit	(6)	(6)	(1)	4	9	14	19	24	29
Put option profit	15	(5)	(5)	(5)	(5)	(5)	(5)	(5)	(5)
Total profit	9	(11)	(6)	(1)	4	9	14	19	24

Strategy: Short Straddle

Strategy	Short Straddle	
Motivation	Designed to exploit decreasing volatility Earn income from the sale of options if the stock price and volatility remain steady	
Implementation	Sale of call option and put option with same expiry and strike prices	
Key characteristics	Maximum risk	Unlimited
	Maximum reward	Premium received
	Break-even	Upside: strike price + both premiums Downside: strike price – both premiums
Comments	Benefits from low volatility	

Options Trading Strategy	Action	Selling a Straddle			
First part of strategy	Sell call option	Exercise price	110.00	Premium	6.00
Second part of strategy	Sell put option	Exercise price	110.00	Premium	5.00

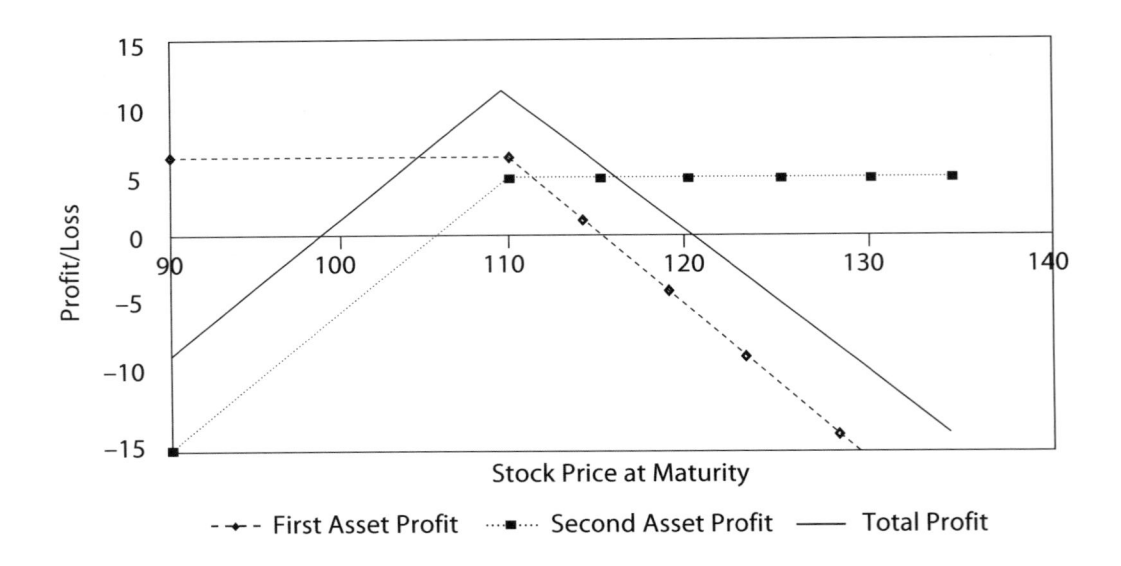

Stock price at maturity	90	110	115	120	125	130	135	140	145
Call option profit	6	6	1	(4)	(9)	(14)	(19)	(24)	(29)
Put option profit	(15)	5	5	5	5	5	5	5	5
Total profit	(9)	11	6	1	(4)	(9)	(14)	(19)	(25)

Strategy: Long Strangle

Strategy		Long Strangle
Motivation		Expect a large increase in market volatility Capture a quick increase in implied volatility or a big move in the underlying stock price during the life of the options
Implementation		Purchase of call and put options with same expiry but different strike prices
Key characteristics – if call strike > put strike	Maximum risk	Limited to premiums paid
	Maximum reward	Unlimited
	Break-even	Upside: higher strike price + premiums Downside: lower strike price – premiums
Key characteristics	Maximum risk	Limited to premium – difference between strikes
	Maximum reward	Unlimited
	Break-even	Upside: call strike price + premium Downside: put strike price – premiums
Comments		A lower-cost alternative to a long straddle – less subject to time decay but the break-evens are further apart

Options Trading Strategy	Action	Buying a Strangle			
First part of strategy	Buy put option	Exercise price	105.00	Premium	6.00
Second part of strategy	Buy call option	Exercise price	110.00	Premium	5.00

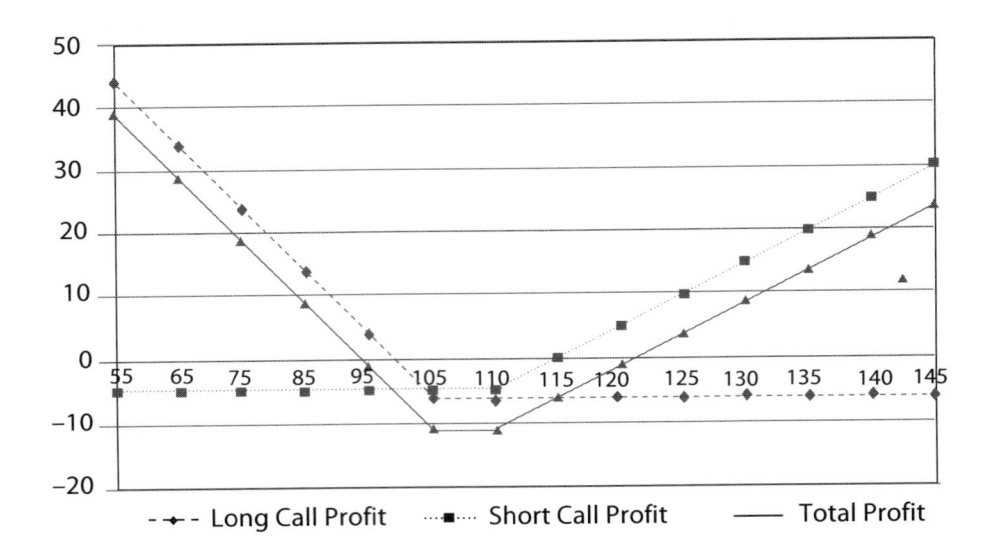

Stock price at maturity	55	65	75	85	95	105	110	115	120	125	130	135	140	145
Put option profit	44	34	24	14	4	(6)	(6)	(6)	(6)	(6)	(6)	(6)	(6)	(6)
Call option profit	(5)	(5)	(5)	(5)	(5)	(5)	(5)	0	5	10	15	20	25	30
Total profit	39	29	19	9	(1)	(11)	(11)	(6)	(1)	4	9	14	19	24

Strategy: Short Strangle

Strategy	Short Strangle	
Motivation	Expect a drop in market volatility	
Implementation	Sell a slightly out-of-the-money put option and a slightly out-of-the-money call option of the same underlying stock and expiry date	
Key characteristics	Maximum risk	Unlimited
	Maximum reward	Premiums received
	Break-even	Upside: strike of short call + premium Downside: strike of short put – premiums
Comments	Alternative to a short straddle – break-evens more widely dispersed and less subject to early losses	

Options Trading Strategy	Action	Selling a Strangle			
First part of strategy	Sell put option	Exercise price	105.00	Premium	6.00
Second part of strategy	Sell call option	Exercise price	110.00	Premium	5.00

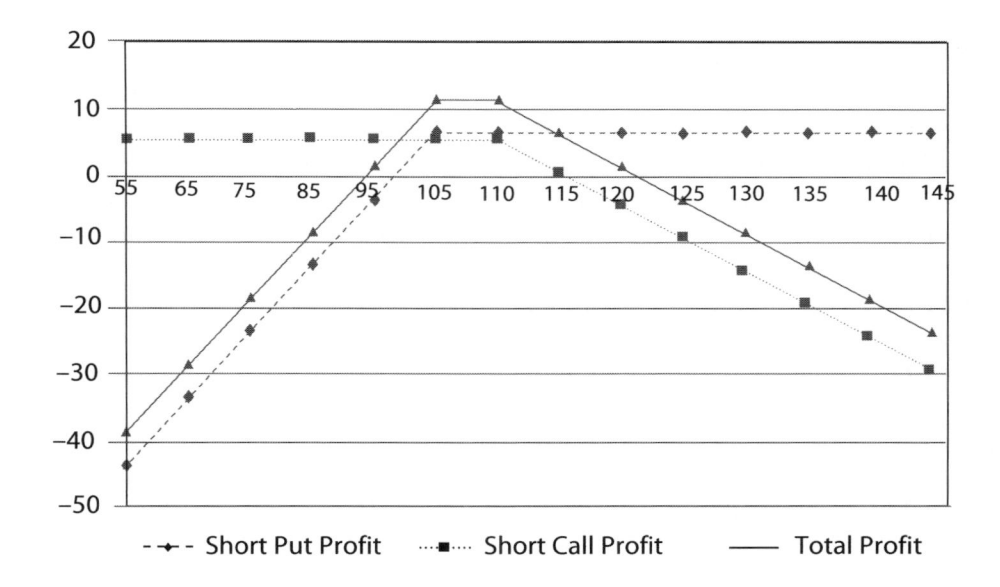

Stock price at maturity	55	65	75	85	95	105	110	115	120	125	130	135	140	145
Put option profit	(44)	(34)	(24)	(14)	(4)	6	6	6	6	6	6	6	6	6
Call option profit	5	5	5	5	5	5	5	0	(5)	(10)	(15)	(20)	(25)	(30)
Total profit	(39)	(29)	(19)	(9)	1	11	11	6	1	(4)	(9)	(14)	(19)	(24)

3.4 General Pricing Principles: Futures and Options

3.4.1 Futures

Pricing of futures is linear, in line with underlying securities. As the price of the relevant security changes by 1%, so does the price of the future.

3.4.2 Options

Intrinsic Value

The premium (price) of an option comprise its intrinsic value and its time value.

- **Intrinsic value** – the observable value of the option if it were to be exercised now. It is a simple measure of how far **in-the-money** the option is (ie, how much higher the current market price is above the strike price of a call option, or how much lower the current market price is below the strike price of a put option).
- **Time value** – at its simplest it is the option premium minus any intrinsic value. It is thus the negotiable value of the option, representing the uncertainty remaining before expiry.

Time Value

Time value in vanilla options is usually calculated using equations based around the Black-Scholes formula of 1973, adapted many times since then for different asset classes. Most of the components are readily observable and thus not subject to negotiation between counterparties:

- **Underlying asset price** – the higher the asset price the more valuable are call options and the less valuable are put options.
- **Strike price** – the higher the strike price the less valuable are call options and the more valuable are put options.
- **Time to maturity** – the longer the term of the option, the greater the risk to the writer that the option may expire in-the-money and thus be exercised. The longer the term therefore, the higher the premium.

The one factor which is not generally observable is implied volatility. While the historical volatility of any security is easily observed, this does not take account of anticipated volatility. This can be distorted by sentiment and supply and demand. This becomes something of a chicken-and-egg situation: the premiums cannot easily be compared for value between two similar options (eg, same security, both calls or puts, same expiry, but perhaps slightly different strike prices), but the implied volatility can be derived from each premium. This implied volatility (known to traders as 'vol') then offers a fairer comparison of value between the two. The 'vols' of many options can then be constructed into 'vol' curves or surfaces, which in turn allow premiums for more options to be calculated more efficiently. In this way implied volatility becomes the key negotiable component in pricing option premiums.

- **Implied volatility of the underlying asset price** – the more volatile the anticipated price of the underlying asset, the greater the chance of the option expiring in-the-money, therefore the higher the premium.

There are two other factors that will affect the option premium the income yield on the underlying asset and short-term interest rates. It should be noted that their effects on option prices are usually fairly minor in relation to the other factors.

- **Income yield of the underlying asset** – the greater the income yield of the underlying asset, the greater the sacrifice being made by the call option holder by not holding this asset, but the greater the benefit to the put option holder. Therefore, the higher the income yield, the more valuable the put option and the less valuable the call option.
- **Short-term interest rates** – the higher the short-term rate of interest the greater the interest income received by the call option holder on the cash not committed to buying the underlying asset. This makes call options more valuable. However, the outlay on a put option not earning this higher rate of interest makes put options less valuable.

3.5 Exercise and Expiry

As described earlier, exercise of an option is the right of the holder, not of the writer. The holder of a call option will only exercise if the market price of the underlying security is above the strike price at the appropriate time of expiry (see American, Bermudan and European expiry definitions above).

The holder of a put option will only exercise if the market price of the underlying security is below the strike price at expiry.

Depending on the market, exercise can be in the form of physical delivery. In this situation the holder of a call option pays the strike price to take delivery of the underlying market, which might be a specified number of STIR contracts (short-term interest rate option), a physical commodity in a warehouse (commodity option) or a specified amount of one currency in exchange for the sale or another (FX option). This form of exercise is clearly set out in the original terms of the option.

Other forms of exercise are in the form of cash settlement. The difference between the strike price and the current market price is calculated. The principal amount of the option (OTC) or the number of contracts and their individual nominal value (exchange traded) are then evaluated in terms of that price difference. The option writer then pays that amount to the buyer.

If the option expires out-of-the-money, then nothing happens. The buyer does not exercise the option (the underlying security can instead be traded separately at the more favourable market rate), so there is neither a physical nor cash settlement. The option is thus abandoned by the holder.

3.6 Risks of Derivatives

3.6.1 Legal

Derivative contracts require legal enforceability.

Exchange traded derivatives require membership of a relevant exchange, including acceptance of their terms and conditions.

OTC derivatives are usually subject to universal legal agreements, of which the most widely-adopted is that of the International Swap Dealers' Association (ISDA). There are various forms and protocols of an ISDA agreement, relevant to different forms of derivatives, which are always negotiated and agreed on a bilateral basis between every pair of counterparties, before trading can commence for the first time.

Perhaps the most disputed area lies in credit default swaps, where the definition of default is open to different interpretation and arguably even manipulation.

Credit events are typically defined to include a material default, bankruptcy, significant fall in an asset's value or debt restructuring for a specified reference asset. If such a credit event occurs, the seller makes a predetermined payment to the buyer, and the swap then terminates.

Credit events typically include:

- **Default** – failure by the reference asset (assets) to make specific debt or other reference payments as defined in the default swap agreement.
- **Significant fall in asset price/value** – most common in basket-based swaps, the swap contract will have a clearly defined valuation level for a specific or basket of assets. Once its/their value falls below this level, the buyer can trigger the swap payment agreement.
- **Bankruptcy** – once the reference asset files for, or is forced into, bankruptcy, most default swaps are automatically triggered for final payment.

- **Debt restructuring** – if the reference asset or its creditors initiate debt restructuring that will change the status or priority of the default swap buyer's asset, if included in the swap agreement, the buyer will receive payment.
- **Merger or demerger** – any change in the owner status or independence of the asset or company is considered a credit event, as is any significant change in the asset ownership structure.

The definition of a credit event is determined in the agreement made between the counterparties to the transaction at the time of the trade. The agreement, which is usually based on the ISDA Master Agreement, will also clearly define the responsibilities and process for notification of a credit event; this is normally done by the buyer or its agent. It also includes the details of the settlement procedures. This is, in effect, an option, and the periodic payments are effectively an option premium.

3.6.2 Counterparty

One of the most significant differences between exchange traded and OTC derivatives is that of counterparty risk.

In exchange traded derivatives, each member of an exchange trades with the exchange itself, settling with its own clearing house. There is no credit exposure to any other member of the exchange. See below for more details on how this counterparty risk is managed in terms of margin and collateral.

In OTC derivatives there is bilateral counterparty risk between both sides to every deal, requiring detailed credit analysis of each counterparty. Further details on margin and collateral are found below.

3.6.3 Settlement and Dealing

Most futures contracts are settled in cash or rolled forward to the next standard delivery date (typically monthly or quarterly).

In option contracts if there is a chance that the option may be exercised, then the holder has the same counterparty risk on the seller as in any derivative which has a confirmed transaction (eg, swaps, futures, FRAs, CFDs). The option seller, by contrast, only has counterparty risk concerning the payment of the upfront premium and concerning the settlement via physical delivery after any potential option exercise (eg, spot FX settlement risk or physical commodity delivery after option exercise). The option seller does not otherwise have any other claim on the buyer.

This settlement risk applies to both exchange-traded and OTC options.

In credit default swaps, if a default occurs, the agreed compensation can be settled by a cash payment or by physical delivery.

- **Cash settlement** – a sum of money is paid in compensation. This might, for example, be determined by the level at which a reference asset (such as a bond issued by the underlying third-party company) trades after the default.
- **Physical settlement** – the buyer of the risk pays the full value of the principal against delivery of the defaulted asset. This could be a specific asset agreed in advance (reference asset or obligation) or any financial obligation of the given issuer, eg, a bond or a derivative contract.

Every credit default swap includes trigger points and notification procedures, such as who has the right to do what, time limits and payment schedules. In most cases, the buyer has exclusive notification / exercise rights, while some swaps have an automatic notification trigger, under certain predefined events. As with all other OTC products, these can be customised to meet the buyer's demands or the nature of reference asset or assets.

3.6.4 Market Risks

Contango and Backwardation

Although cash and futures prices generally move broadly in line with one another, the basis is not constant. During some periods, cash prices move faster than futures. At other times, futures outpace the cash market.

This movement in basis is brought about by a variety of factors. Most important is the relationship between supply and demand. Under normal conditions, futures prices of physical commodities are higher than cash prices. The reasons for this can vary, but when futures prices are higher than cash prices, the market is said to be in **contango**.

However, this normal or contango situation in which futures prices are higher than cash prices can be radically altered if there is some short-term lack of supply. If, for example, there is very little zinc available for delivery, the price demanded for what little is available can be very high indeed.

Markets in which futures prices are lower than cash prices are said to be in backwardation. The terms contango and backwardation are not used in all markets. Sometimes, when futures are higher than cash prices, the market is said to be at a premium, while when futures are lower than cash, it is said to be at a discount.

The availability of supply, and hence the basis, is also subject to seasonal influences. For example, the wheat market will tend to be oversupplied at harvest time and undersupplied at other times. This will reflect itself in futures prices, when you may see certain months in contango and others in backwardation.

Basis Risk

Basis can be defined as the difference between the spot price of a commodity and the relative price of the futures contract for the same commodity.

Changes in basis represent a threat and an opportunity to futures users.

To illustrate this, consider a wheat farmer who has a short hedge (he holds physical wheat and sells wheat futures) to protect himself against a price fall in 20X9.

	Cash Price	Futures Price	Basis
February 20X9	140	150	(10)
July 20X9	120	135	(15)
	(20)	15	
Cash Market Loss	(20)		
Futures Profit	15		
Net Position	(5)		

The hedge is not entirely effective: a £20 loss in the price of physical wheat is only partially offset by a £15 gain in wheat futures. This difference emerges because the cash price has moved further than the futures price. In other words, there has been a change in basis.

When the basis becomes more negative or less positive, as above, it is said to weaken. When the basis becomes more positive or less negative, it is said to strengthen.

Basis changes do occur and represent potential profits or losses to investors. Notwithstanding the fact that the relationship between cash and futures may vary, the risk this represents is smaller than the risk of remaining unhedged.

Option Greeks

Unlike futures prices, option premiums do not move in a linear relationship with the underlying security, due to the mathematical properties surrounding uncertainty and time to expiry.

A number of measurements regarding the sensitivity of an option premium to various parameters have therefore evolved, in each case isolating one market risk on the assumption that all other price parameters remain the same.

- **Delta** – the sensitivity of an option premium to a 1% move in the underlying security price, measured on a scale of 0% – 100%. In vanilla options it can be taken as a rough proxy for the likelihood that the option will eventually be exercised. Thus a 0% delta applies only to an option which is imminently about to expire out-of-the-money, while a 100% delta applies to an option which is certain to be exercised in-the-money (ie, its price now moves in a linear fashion to the underlying security). A 50% delta option is considered at-the-money, so its premium will change at a rate of 50% of any change in the underlying price.
- **Gamma** – the sensitivity of delta to a 1% move in the underlying security price. An option which is at-the-money (ie 50% delta) and almost at expiry will see its delta change dramatically for only a small change in the underlying price, whereas an option close to expiry but either deep in- or out- of the money will have a less sensitive delta. Longer dated options also have less sensitive deltas and thus lower gamma.
- **Theta** – the sensitivity of an option premium to a reduction of one day in the time to expiry. This is a measure of the time decay in an option and is usually directly proportionate to the value of gamma (ie, both theta and gamma are highest for at-the-money options which are very close to expiry).
- **Vega** – the sensitivity of an option premium to a 1% change in its implied volatility. This is a measure of the uncertainty and hence volatility in the market. Unlike gamma or theta, it is higher for longer-dated options, especially those approximately at-the-money.

Please note that there are many 'Greek' terms used in derivatives. The following is by no means exhaustive, but is a list of the most common Greek terms used:

- Delta
- Vega
- Theta
- Rho
- Lambda
- Epsilon – following the 2008 financial crisis, when one major issue highlighted
- Gamma
- Vanna
- Charm
- Voma
- Veta
- Vera
- Speed
- Zomma
- Color
- Ultima.

4. Margin and Collateral

Learning Objective

9.4 Explain and evaluate the characteristics and risks of margin and collateral: purpose, types and application of collateral and margin; parties involved; processing, collection and payment; pricing factors and calculation

4.1 Exchanges

In guaranteeing contracts, an exchange clearing house is taking on a substantial risk, especially on those contracts which have a contingent liability, such as futures contracts and written options. A contingent liability is one where a loss might arise but it is not possible to be certain of its amount – the outcome is contingent upon the price of the underlying asset.

In order for any clearing house to protect itself there are a number of steps that it might take:

- It only permits the clearing members' firms that meet (and continue to meet) its membership and financial criteria. This is the first line of defence – the quality of its membership.
- It only deals directly with clearing members, all of whom have the most onerous financial resources requirements.
- The next line of defence is its margining system, where margin is best defined as the cash (or equivalent) deposited with the clearing house to cover the risk of the clearing member defaulting on its position.
- It relies on its own financial resources and perhaps operates inter alia a default fund; it has lines of credit with a consortium of major banks; and it has insurance policies.

The underlying reason for requiring margin payments is to support the guarantee provided by the clearing house, in other words to reduce or eliminate any counterparty credit risk. This is the underlying purpose of an efficient margin system.

Margin is collected in two ways: initial margin is largely collected when a position is first established, and then **variation margin** may be collected as that position worsens. Margin is demanded by the clearing house separately for the house accounts maintained by the clearing member (which will include any non-segregated client positions) and the segregated client accounts. As an example, ICE Clear Europe will demand margin from each type of account separately, on the basis of the net positions in that account.

The concept and protection provided by margins has started to be applied to a select group of exchange-cleared OTC products. The two types that have been most popular to date have been contracts for difference (which are mainly cash-settled) and certain types of energy contracts. In both cases, the clearing house will swap the OTC contract with an exchange-based equivalent. It can then apply its standard margin requirements to the position, and normal payments and procedures are then followed.

4.2   Types of Margin

There are two types of margin: initial and variation margin.

4.2.1   Initial Margin

Initial margin is a good faith deposit (perhaps in the form of collateral rather than cash), lodged with the clearing house against potential liabilities on an open position. It is returned when the position is closed out.

Initial margin is calculated by the clearing house in respect of clearing members' positions using whatever system it has adopted. The clearing member similarly calculates margin with respect to its clients, and may demand a higher rate of margin (known as broker margin) from its client.

Once a client's trade has been executed, the clearing member or broker that holds the client's account will put the trade in the client's segregated or non-segregated account (depending on its relationship with the client), and at the same time collect the initial margin that is required.

Note that if the new trade was the purchase of an option, no initial margin is collected; instead the premium payment will be collected from the client's account. The reason is that buying an option is not a contingent liability transaction. The maximum loss an option buyer will have is the up-front premium payment.

Initial margin seeks to protect the clearing house (and in turn the broker) from the worst-case loss a position could potentially incur in one day. The actual initial margin rate per contract will be set by looking at the recent price volatility of the contract and will be determined by the clearing house following consultation with the exchange.

Derivatives

Example

For example, by continually monitoring market prices, ICE Clear Europe calculates that the most the price of the FTSE futures contract could move in one day is 300 points. Given the tick size and tick value, this could mean a potential loss of £3,000 per contract on the day on long/short open positions. So the initial margin rate will be set at £3,000 per contract for both the buyer and seller of a future. If the volatility changes up or down, the initial margin requirement may be changed.

Initial margin is re-computed every business day and effectively called first thing in the morning before markets open. After the market has opened, if there is a sudden jump in the volatility, and the clearing house is no longer comfortable with the amount of initial margin held – indeed, if the initial margin amount is exhausted – it can call for an extra intra-day margin which is taken immediately from the clearing members via their PPS accounts.

Initial margin can be provided in cash or covered by acceptable non-cash collateral. Clearing houses have different rules on the forms of acceptable collateral they will accept.

4.2.2 Spreads

Spreads involve more than one position across different delivery months in the same contract (a traderperhaps being long a June FTSE 100 future and short a September FTSE 100 future). The initial margin will be substantially lower than normal in this case because the two positions largely offset each other, and the price movements of each month, although not perfectly, do tend to correlate in their movement. These are known as intra-commodity spreads. Spreads also exist between different instruments that always exhibit correlation in their price movements. These are called inter-commodity spreads and apply to contracts such as ICE Futures Gas Oil and ICE Futures Brent Crude Oil.

Therefore, most exchanges take into account the offsetting nature of these positions when setting the margin requirements. The net result is a reduction in the margin required for the two spreads mentioned above. For example, CBOT, which is now part of the CME Group, has a comprehensive list of the offset that is applied to spreads' margin due to their reduced risk. It depends on the particular contract and varies from $25 to as much as $110 per contract.

As a contract nears its expiry date, its volatility can increase. If physical delivery is required in final settlement of the contract, then only those position-holders who wish, or may wish, to take delivery should maintain their open contracts in the market. Others should close out or roll their positions forward to later delivery months. Therefore, as delivery for that product draws near, the clearing house may wish to minimise the speculative and delivery pressures by increasing the initial margin (this is known as a spot month margin).

This occurs in order to ensure that those position-holders contemplating taking the contract to delivery either have the underlying asset to deliver or have allocated adequate funds to effect settlement. It will also force any less well-capitalised speculators out of the market, thereby reducing short-term speculative pressures.

4.2.3 Variation Margin

Exchanges establish settlement prices every business day in order to provide the price yardsticks for calculation of mark-to-market variation margin and valuation of positions at the end of the day. This procedure is normally conducted at the end of the trading period, so the daily settlement price is also referred to as the closing price. However, some markets do not use the closing price, particularly those that have a global pricing influence (such as the LME), or markets that are in operation for most of the 24-hour day.

The closing range is a measure of the range or spread of prices that are quoted during a specified time just before daily trading ends. Each exchange has its own criteria for determining the closing range; most have different time frames for different contracts and they are usually longer for commodity contracts compared to financial contracts.

Generally, the daily settlement price is then simply the weighted average traded price during the final 30 seconds of the settlement range. However, market supervision has the flexibility to adjust the daily settlement price if the calculated price is not deemed to be a fair reflection of the market price.

At the close of each trading day all positions are marked-to-market, based on the daily settlement price. The profit/loss on the day is measured and must be paid to/received from the clearing house as variation margin by the following day by the clearing members. The same procedure applies between clearing members and their customers by exactly the same process in turn. In this way, profits and losses accruing to positions are accounted for every day.

Variation margin, which must be paid in cash (cleared funds) in the currency of the contract, is calculated as:

$$\text{Variation margin} = \frac{\text{ticks moved on the day (today's closing price - yesterday's closing price)}}{\text{x the contract's tick value x number of contracts of the open position}}$$

Example

An investor is long 20 December Euroyen (LIBOR) Futures on the SGX. The contract closing price is 99.7750, down from its previous closing price of 99.7825. The contract's minimum price fluctuation is 0.0025, which equates to a tick value of JPY 250,000. The investor will have JPY 37,500 debited from their account, for the day's variation margin for this position.

JPY 37,500 = 0.0075 (today's price movement) x JPY 250,000 (tick value) x 20 (number of contracts of the open position)

Note: For this contract the Singapore Exchange has a minimum price movement of 0.0025 or JPY 625. This is based on the contract's specification, where 1 tick or 1.0 price movement equals JPY 250,000. Therefore, a price movement of 0.0025 = JPY 625 (JPY250,000 x 0.0025).

Each clearing member has at least one bank account to which ICE Clear Europe has access via a direct debit system so that variation margin payments can be transferred. These are the Protected Payments System (PPS) accounts.

4.2.4 Maintenance Margin

This is an arrangement between member and client and is not operated by the clearing house. Usually a member firm will expect a client to deposit more than the initial margin. This provides a safety cushion for the member and allows for the payment of some variation margin without referring back to the client every day. Once the credit breaches a preset limit (trigger/maintenance level), the member will issue a margin call (trigger margin), expecting the client to replenish the account to the original amount. This practice is common in the US.

For example, if the initial margin for a long gilt futures contract on NYSE Liffe is set at £5,000 per contract, a broker/clearing member might require that its client deposit an additional 25% of that amount as a maintenance margin. This will ensure that the member is protected from any possible losses, should the client be unable to meet any variation margin payments, particularly in volatile markets.

The level of maintenance margin is usually set at 25–50% of the initial margin payment of any new positions.

4.2.5 Methods of Determining a Margin

Exchanges have developed several different programs to calculate the initial and variation or daily margin requirements for all new and existing futures and options positions.

The level of variation/daily margin required for an existing position is determined by the change in the price of the underlying asset.

For futures, there is a direct relationship, therefore a 3% rise in the price of gold in the cash market will have a similar effect on the margin required for those short gold futures, since the future's price will rise at least that amount.

For options, the relationship between price changes in the underlying and their effect on an option's value is more complex, given the characteristics of an option. An option's delta is used to measure the sensitivity of an option's price to changes in the price of the underlying asset. Since an at-the-money option has a delta of 0.5, a 3% rise in the price of its underlying asset will result in an approximate 1.5% rise in the value of the option. Remember, however, that this is only one of the factors that will influence the option's price; any changes to its volatility and time decay will also be taken into account.

4.2.6 Net Liquidation Value (NLV)

Because margin requirements are based on the net positions held by the member firm, and there may be a variety of positions held at a given time, the calculation of the total margin amount due or to be received is based on the net liquidation values (NLVs) of the constituent parts of the portfolio. This allows for the profits showing on a portion of a member firm's positions to offset the losses of other positions in its portfolio, resulting in one net payment.

4.2.7 Acceptable Collateral

Cover for initial margin can be provided using collateral rather than cash. The following is the full list of assets that some of the major clearing houses accept as payment for initial margin from their members:

- Cash in most major currencies (sterling, euros, US dollars, Swiss francs, Swedish krona, Danish krone, Norwegian kroner and Japanese yen). Most national exchanges accept cash deposits at approved banks in their local currency.
- Bank guarantees from an approved bank in an approved form.
- Certificates of deposit (denominated in Sterling and US dollars).
- Government debt (bills, bonds and notes) from the following countries: UK; US; Germany; Italy; Netherlands; Sweden; Austria; France; Spain; Belgium; Canada; Australia; Finland; Denmark.

However, it is important to note that:

- undated bonds are not acceptable
- the bonds must be denominated in the currency of the issuing country
- Swiss bonds are not acceptable
- collateral is also marked-to-market daily and is subject to a published 'haircut', which means that the full market value is not credited; this has become more common after the downgrading of several government bonds on the list
- the securities that are used as collateral are lodged with depositories and custodians that are acceptable to the specific clearing house.

4.2.8 Credit Lines

Although it is uncommon, some exchanges allow their members to extend credit to their clients to cover margin requirements. Deals requested in the excess of a specified credit line will be rejected by the exchange member firm. These so-called credit lines will be subject to the regulatory rules specifying the circumstances in which lending money to clients is acceptable. For example, the FCA has rules on customer borrowing; under FCA rules, credit may be extended for up to five days without a formal written loan agreement.

4.2.9 OTC Margin and Collateral Management

Collateral management is the process that allows market participants to reduce the counterparty credit exposure that arise from longer-maturity OTC derivative contracts, such as swaps and options.

For example, Company A enters into a ten-year interest rate swap, as a fixed-rate payer, with one of its main banks. As market rates fall, in favour of the bank and against Company A, the mark-to-market profit on the swap represents a loss to Company A and a profit for the bank. This in turn increases the bank's risk exposure to the company, since it has a loss on this swap position.

One way that the banks can reduce the risk exposure created by the swap is to enter into a Credit Support Annex (CSA) or Collateral Support Document (CSD), which contains the details of the conditions and procedures by which collateralisation will occur.

Collateral is something of value. The main types of collateral that are accepted include cash, bank guarantees, certificates of deposit, government bonds or negotiable (ie, tradeable) securities, such as equities with special agreement since they are not accepted by several major exchanges.

Collateral is held against the risk of default by a counterparty. It is important that the collateral is an asset that is easy to liquidate in the case of default.

Collateral management is the process that allows market participants to reduce the counterparty credit exposure that arises from longer-maturity OTC derivative contracts, such as swaps and options.

If a bank considers that the credit risk incurred by trading with a particular counterparty is too great, or has already reached the credit limit in place, then it may ask for collateral from the counterparty in order to continue trading with it.

Cover for initial margin can be also provided using collateral rather than cash.

A bank ensures that it has the most up-to-date and accurate measure of its credit exposure to a counterparty by ensuring that its operations area processes all deal tickets and term sheets (a non-binding agreement which sets out the basic terms and conditions under which an investment or trade will be made; a term sheet is usually used as a template to develop a more detailed legal document) on a timely basis.

The bank assesses the size of the risk it is taking in making the transaction and requires that the counterparty places with it collateral to that value, either at the same time as dealing or beforehand. Typically, the arrangement will allow for the bank to ask for more collateral subsequently (this is known as the delivery amount) if the value of the existing trade or collateral falls during the life of the deal. It might also return some collateral if the value of either the collateral or the trade rises; this is known as the return amount.

If the counterparty then goes bankrupt, the bank can try to use this collateral to offset the loss.

Collateral of this nature is often called margin, and asking for collateral, or more collateral, is making a margin call. It may be that the bank subtracts or assigns a reduced value to the collateral's market value. This is known as a haircut. The size of the haircut reflects the bank's perceived risk of holding the specific asset. In other words, it is applied to protect against any potential movements in the market and potential changes in the collateral's value which might arise before there is time for extra collateral to be transferred from the counterparty. The size of this haircut is directly related to the minimum threshold amount and the price volatility of the collateral.

Depending on the transaction's agreement, collateral or a margin might be called for by either party (ie, by whichever party is currently in mark-to-market profit from whichever party is currently in loss) or by the higher credit-rated party. The agreement may be that margin calls can be made daily, weekly or monthly, or only at the time of an event such as an interest settlement.

5. Clearing and Settlement

Learning Objective

9.4 Explain and evaluate the characteristics and risks of margin and collateral: delivery and settlement

9.5 Explain and evaluate the clearing and settlement of exchange-traded and OTC derivatives: definition and purpose of clearing and settlement; roles and relationships; risks and guarantees; central counterparty clearing; clearing of OTC transactions; transparency and confidentiality; counterparties; documentation; settlement of transactions

5.1 Exchanges

Clearing is the process by which derivatives trades are confirmed and registered. Registration is with a clearing house that becomes legal counterparty to every transaction. The legal process whereby the clearing house becomes the counterparty to all trades is called **novation**. This involves substituting the clearing house as the buyer to every seller and the seller to every buyer. Hence every original exchange contract becomes two new contracts; the original contract no longer exists.

Any currency risk that exists for clearing members with regard to settlement is minimal, since as a member of a clearing house and exchange it must maintain an account in the clearing house's currency. Any currency risk that does arise from the clearing process arises from the exchange rate movements between the member's home currency and that of the exchange's, for the amounts of their net daily margin payments.

This central counterparty structure removes almost all counterparty risk (credit risk) from all clearing members operating within the market. The only counterparty risk faced by clearing members is with the clearing house itself, not with one another.

In addition, the clearing house will monitor all open positions and will facilitate the settlement process by acting as the intermediary with respect to the close-out and delivery of futures contracts and the exercise and assignment of options contracts. In the rare case of default, the clearing house faces one day of market risk, since all members must pay a daily margin payment which is based on their net position's profit/loss relative to the previous day's price movement.

On the rare occasion that the margin payments do not cover the net position's loss, all clearing houses, such as LCH.Clearnet or ICE Clear Europe, for example, maintain a default fund, which is cash that is paid in by its members. In order to ensure that the fund is sufficient, the clearing house runs a wide range of stress tests, so that the fund's size meets worst case estimates of the market's volatility. Note that this fund only covers default by members directly to the clearing house.

One major advantage of a clearing system is that it greatly reduces counterparty risk. The clearing house guarantees the financial performance of the contract and, as long as the clearing house is backed by substantial financial resources, and is thus highly creditworthy, market users and investors can have a

Derivatives

high degree of confidence in the system. Another advantage is that contracts become easy to trade, with the clearing house making it easy to close out a trade by taking an equal and opposite position – because both long and short positions are novated to the clearing house as central counterparty, the previous position is effectively closed.

Settlement risk – the risk that an expected payment of cash or a security will not be made on time or at all – is another risk associated with the delivery/clearing process. The establishment of a **netting** system/ agreement is an effective method of minimising this kind of risk.

5.2 Structure of the Clearing System

The different tiers that make up the clearing system at the exchange level are the clearing house, the clearing members and the non-clearing members. The clearing members themselves can be general clearing members or individual clearing members, which means respectively that they clear either:

- for themselves, for direct clients and for other exchange members, or
- for just themselves and direct clients.

The clearing house is typically owned by its members or by the exchange whose contracts it clears, or both. There are different models. For example, in the case of the Options Clearing Corporation (OCC) in the US, the clearing corporation is jointly owned by several exchanges. On the other hand, the Chicago Mercantile Exchange's (CME's) clearing house is a division of the exchange itself. ICE Clear Europe is owned by exchanges and clearing members.

The tiers are:

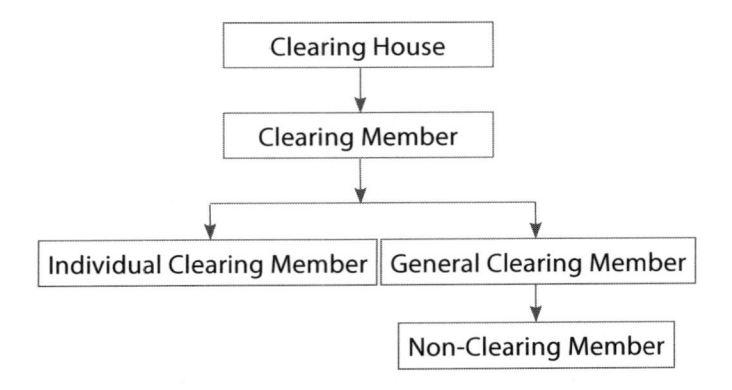

```
                    Clearing House
                          ↓
                   Clearing Member
                          ↓
        ┌─────────────────┴─────────────────┐
        ↓                                   ↓
Individual Clearing Member         General Clearing Member
                                            ↓
                                   Non-Clearing Member
```

To illustrate its different tiers and the clearing process, it is useful to look at a typical trade and the individual steps involved. The example that follows highlights the systems and procedures that are used when a trade initiates on NYSE Liffe, for which ICE Clear Europe acts as the clearing house.

The first part of the clearing process is trade reporting or registration. For most exchanges, such as NYSE Liffe, its electronic trading system automatically reports a trade, once it happens, to the ICE Connect. Once this takes place, the clearing process begins.

Example 1

Step 1. The trade

Mr X. Ample is a client of ABC ltd, a member firm of ICE. He places a market order. ABC ltd will act as broker, executing the trade on the ICE exchange. ABC ltd is not a member of ICE Clear Europe.

Any trade executed needs to be reported to and registered with the clearing house (ICE Clear Europe). The trade will need to be registered via a clearing member, and ABC ltd has an agreement with a general clearing member, KMM ltd, a firm which is a member of both the exchange and ICE Clear Europe.

Step 2. Confirmation and matching

ABC ltd will pass details of the trade to KMM ltd (its clearing member) who will input the details into the confirmation and matching system (known as ICE Connect, used by ICE) where it will wait until the counterparty to the ABC ltd trade enters the equal and opposite details into the system.

Step 3. Registration

Once matched, KMM ltd registers the trade with ICE Clear Europe (via ICE Connect), giving details of the type of account the trade is assigned to. The account will either be in a segregated, 'client' account, or within the non-segregated 'house' account, and the decision as to whether the trade is to be allocated to a segregated client account is the client's to make.

Step 4. Novation

At the point of registering the trade with ICE Clear Europe the contract is novated, resulting in ICE Clear Europe becoming counterparty to two new transactions – one with KMM ltd and the other with ABC ltd's original counterparty. The original contract between ABC ltd and its counterparty no longer exists. In effect, ABC ltd (a non-clearing firm) has committed KMM ltd (its clearing member) to a transaction with ICE Clear Europe (the clearing house).

ICE Clear Europe guarantees the performance of the contract to its immediate counterparty, the clearing member – KMM ltd in the above example. This is known as a 'principal-to-principal' guarantee.

ICE Clear Europe will call on KMM ltd for any subsequent payments (margin) on the contract as necessary. KMM ltd, as a clearing member, will pay any margin due through the Protected Payments System (PPS) – a system used by ICE Clear Europe in conjunction with several leading banks, which will automatically debit members' bank accounts. KMM ltd will collect any payments from ABC ltd, its customer. ABC ltd will in turn call on any payments from its customer, Mr Ample. Each party has a principal-to-principal relationship with the other.

When Mr Ample decides to close the position, the same process takes place. Note that ABC ltd will not have to go back to the original counterparty because the original contract no longer exists. As the contract is standardised, the offsetting trade simply cancels out the trade previously registered with the clearing house, thus cancelling any delivery obligations.

Note also that the clearing house does not give any guarantees to Mr Ample, the client. Mr Ample and his broker (ABC ltd) have a risk on each other defaulting, as does ABC ltd and the clearing member (KMM ltd). So, although the system substantially reduces the risk of default, it does not eliminate it along the whole system.

5.3 Exchange-Cleared Over-The-Counter (OTC) Products

The increased concern over counterparty risk combined with exchanges' desire to expand and diversify has led to exchanges offering clearing facilities and guarantees to a range of OTC derivatives.

The main advantage of having an OTC derivative cleared or substituted by an exchange's clearing house is that it eliminates any counterparty risk. This is particularly attractive for longer-term contracts. Once the OTC contract is cleared, it is subject to the same requirements, such as margin payments and delivery procedures, as any other exchange-traded derivative.

Centrally cleared OTC products are executed and delivered in a process similar to exchange-traded products. For any type of delivery to take place, both counterparties must be exchange members and have either a direct or indirect clearing relationship with the respective clearing house.

Unlike **exchange-traded contracts**, the clearing house does not assign or match buyers to sellers, but it does monitor and guarantee that delivery is made on both side of the trade. The trades are executed between two counterparties and delivery takes place using the respective clearing system.

5.4 Clearing Fund

The clearing fund is a pool of funds contributed by clearing members for use in case of default, for both exchange-traded and OTC contracts that are cleared by the clearing house.

Every clearing member is required to contribute to the clearing fund. The required amount is based on a risk assessment using each clearing member's level of uncovered risk, which is based upon the trading activity. This risk-based payment is reviewed on a regular basis: for example NYSE Liffe exchange recalculates each clearing member's payment on a monthly basis; other exchanges reassess these payments on a quarterly basis.

The clearing fund will be used should a clearing member default in the delivery process. The fund is used only after any margin or other related funds have been utilised.

6. Exchange-Traded Derivatives (ETDs)

Learning Objective

9.6 Explain the main types, characteristics, and pricing of exchange-traded derivatives: convertibles, covered, and uncovered warrants: factors influencing pricing; bases for calculation and actual calculation; significance and uses; futures; factors influencing pricing; bases for calculation; significance and uses; options; factors influencing pricing; bases for calculation and actual calculation; significance and uses

9.7 Describe and explain the trading of exchange-traded derivatives: main UK and international exchanges; trading platforms; mechanisms, procedures, and processes; wholesale trading facilities; standardisation of deals, contracts, and agreements; market transparency, reporting and monitoring; order/instruction flow and order type; input and matching, trade registration processes; maturity, expiry, margin, liquidity, exercise and delivery

6.1 Convertibles, Covered and Uncovered Warrants

6.1.1 Convertibles

As outlined in section 2 above, a convertible is a fixed-income security that gives the holder the right, but not the obligation, to convert it into a predetermined number of the issuer's ordinary shares on a certain date or over a specific period. It is effectively a hybrid between a bond and a warrant (see below), except that the payment at conversion is in the form of forfeiting the bond for shares, rather than paying cash. In the absence of conversion, the holder receives coupons and eventual capital repayment, as in any other bond.

Characteristics of Convertibles

- Pay a low coupon, though this is offset by the option to convert into shares at the conversion date.
- Are subordinated, requiring senior creditors to be paid out in full before any payment can be made to holders in the event of insolvency.
- Are employed as a deferred share. Issuers expect them to be converted into shares at the conversion date.
- Are bonds (ie, loans to companies that react to changes in market yields and interest rates while in issue); which can convert to shares (ie, ownership of the company that allows for participation in its profits).
- Have a conversion entitlement to shares that is expressed in a number of ways.
- Include rights that are normally to convert the debt into ordinary shares of the company in a predefined conversion ratio. For example, £100 nominal is converted into 30 shares (a conversion ratio of 30). The conversion right may exist for a period of time during the bond's life (the conversion window) or may only be available on maturity.

Additional Terms

- A range of conversion ratios can be included at different maturities of the bond:
- The holder of the bond could also be required to provide extra capital on the conversion, eg, £100 nominal of the debt converts into 20 shares and the bondholder is required to pay an additional £2.50 per share. So, each share has an actual cost (assuming the bond is trading at par) of (£100 ÷ 20 = £5) + £2.50 = £7.50.
- Put rights enabling the holder of the bond to force an early redemption of the bond, normally at a premium to the par value.
- Call rights enabling the issuer to call the bond under certain conditions.
- When establishing the terms of the convertible, the issuer will usually avoid unnecessarily complicated terms, since this will confuse and result in dissuading potential purchasers of the bond.

Advantages and Disadvantages

Advantages to the Issuer

Compared to both a bond and a share issue, convertibles offer the following advantages to the issuer:

- at the time of issue, there is no immediate dilution of the current shareholders rights
- a lower coupon is payable than would be the case with a normal, fixed rate bonds structure
- suitable when assets are not available to secure straight finance
- suitable for finance projects with long payback periods.

Disadvantages to the Issuer

- If the company fails to perform, it is still obliged to make the coupon payments and ultimately, redeem the bond for cash if the holder chooses not to convert.
- A firm cannot be sure that it is issuing deferred share capital when it issues a convertible.

Advantages to the Investor

- The holder has the security of a fixed-income instrument, offering downside protection even if the shares fall in value and the opportunity to benefit if the shares perform well. However, as unsecured lower-ranking stock, this advantage could be limited in the event of say, liquidation of the firm.
- Convertibles rank above shares in priority on liquidation.
- Convertibles usually offer higher yields than the underlying shares.
- Convertible bonds tend to be very marketable compared to non-convertible issues.

Disadvantages to the Investor

- Although potentially offering higher yields than the underlying shares, convertibles usually offer lower yields than equivalent straight bonds.
- The attractiveness of a convertible may be tainted by issuer call options.
- If anticipated share growth is not achieved, the holder will have sacrificed yield for no benefit.

Conversion Ratio

Usually, convertible bonds are issued where the price of each share is set at the outset and that price will be adjusted to take into account any subsequent bonus or rights issues. Given the conversion price, it is simple to calculate the conversion ratio – the number of shares that each £100 of nominal value of the bonds can convert into.

$$\text{Conversion ratio} = \frac{\text{Nominal value}}{\text{Conversion price of shares}}$$

If the issuing company has a 1 for 1 bonus issue, the conversion price would halve and the conversion ratio would double.

Valuation of Convertibles

The valuation of convertibles presents the investor and the company issuing them with some complexities as there are trade-offs between the various considerations involved. In terms of the initial pricing and placement of the issue the simple rule of thumb is as follows: if it is too expensive, investors will not purchase the convertible stock and the issue will fail. If the price is too cheap, then the issuer will be obtaining finance on disadvantageous terms, affecting shareholders if the share price drops.

Valuating of convertibles is complex in practice due to the various embedded options that may exist, but an assortment of models have been developed. Three of the most popular ones are the dividend valuation model, the crossover method and the option pricing method.

6.1.2 Dividend Valuation Model

Convertible debt usually provides a fixed rate of interest and gives the holder the option to convert it into equity at a future date, under terms specified by the company. The impact of this is that the ultimate redemption proceeds could either be in cash or shares.

To apply the dividend valuation model, we will need to establish which of these will be preferable at the conversion date and include it as the redemption proceeds in the evaluation.

The table below illustrates the key features of valuing a convertible using the dividend method. A company has a 7% convertible debt in issue which has conversion terms of 40 shares per £100 of nominal value. The current share price is £2, which is expected to grow at 3% per annum. The period of analysis prior to potential exercise of conversion rights is five years.

Valuation of Convertibles: Dividend Method				
Nominal Value	£100.00	Required Rate of Return from Investors = r		10.00%
Current Share Price	£2.00	Conversion Debt terms, ie, Rate of Interest = i		7.00%
Current Dividend	£0.00	Conversion ratio, ie, number of shares per £100 nominal value		40
Expected Growth Rate of Stock Price (g)	3%	Expected Cash Flow from Dividends		£0
Conversion Interest per Nominal Value	£7.00	Future Value of Shares	Current Value *(1+g)^5	£2.32
Period for Analysis (years) t	5	Future Value of Shares	Number of Shares * FV Shares	£92.80
Market Value of Convertible	Cash Flow in £	Discount Factor	Present Value	
Time				
		$\dfrac{1}{0.1}\left[1 - \dfrac{1}{1.1^5}\right] = 3.791$		
1-5	£7.00		£26.54	
5	£92.80	$\dfrac{1}{1.1^5} = 0.6209$	£57.62	
			£84.16	

The current price of the shares is £2.00 and the investors require an ROR – r – of 10% per annum which provides the discount value to apply to discounting the values of the cash flows to their PV.

The dividend on the ordinary shares into which the convertible could be converted shall be assumed as zero in this case, simply to keep the valuation simple and to distinguish it from the second model which will be discussed below. The income from the bond component of the convertible is 7%, which is payable annually. The convention is for the nominal value of the bond to be £100 and all of the calculations are predicated on this nominal value.

Accordingly, the bond income based on the nominal amount will be £7 per annum. There is a convenient formula which can be used for calculating the PV from using a compounding form of the discounting factor:

Annuity discount factor = $1/r [1 - 1/(1 + r)^n]$

Annuity discount factor = $1/0.1 [1 - 1/1.1^5] = 3.791$

The PV of income cash stream from the bond is therefore:

$7 \times 3.791 = £26.54$

The expected growth rate of the stock price – g – can be used to calculate the future value of the shares in the following manner:

Future value of one share = Current Value x $(1 + g)^n$

Future value of one share = £2.00 x $(1.03)^5$ = £2.32

Since the conversion rate is for 40 shares the future cash value of the shares after five years is £2.32 x 40 = £92.80. This value also needs to be discounted by the ROR required, which is calculated as follows PV = FV x $(1/(1+r)^5)$ = £92.80 x 0.6209 = £57.62.

The PV of all the cash flows is £26.54 + £57.62 = £84.16.

Given the convertible's characteristics as provided the market value should be £84.16.

6.1.3 Crossover Method Based on Income Crossover

The crossover method is another technique used to approximate the relative attractiveness of a convertible and its underlying equity. This estimates the date on which the rising common stock dividend will equal the convertible coupon. It is appropriate when there is no predetermined conversion date, but instead the holders have a choice of dates on which conversion can occur and a likely date of conversion needs to be established.

The crossover method assumes the conversion takes place when the income that would be expected as dividends from the shares obtained exceeds the interest from the debt. Therefore, it is also known as the income-based approach.

Illustration

A company has an existing share price of 180p. Dividends are currently 20p and are growing at a rate of 5%. Investors require a ROR of 18%. There is some 10% convertible debt in issue, which has conversion terms of 40 shares per £100 of nominal value. What is an appropriate market value for the convertibles?

Valuation of Convertibles: Crossover Method/Income-Based Approach				
Nominal Value	£100.00	Required Rate of Return from Investors = r		18.00%
Current Share Price	£1.80	Conversion Debt Terms, ie, Rate of Interest = i		10.00%
Current Dividend	£0.20	Conversion Ratio, ie, number of shares per £100 nominal value		40
Expected Dividend Growth Rate g	5.00%			
Interest coupon per Nominal Value	£10.00			

STAGE ONE	Value the convertibles on the basis that they are converted into shares immediately			
	Immediate Conversion	Conversion Terms x Current Share Price (40 shares x £1.80)		£72.00
STAGE TWO	Value the income stream at present value and estimate crossover when dividend income exceeds interest income			
	Value income on	40	shares each paying dividend of	£0.20	£8.00

Year	Interest on Debt (£)	Basic Dividend £	Dividends Subject to Growth Rate Below (£)	Income pickup (£) That is coupon payment minus dividends subject to compound growth	Present Value of Pickup Discounted at Investor's Required ROR
			5.00%		18.00%
1	10	8	8.40	1.60	1.36
2	10	8	8.82	1.18	0.85
3	10	8	9.26	0.74	0.45
4	10	8	9.72	0.28	0.14
5	10	8	10.21	(0.21)	–
				£3.59	£2.80
Simple value of convertible assumes conversion rate * current share price				£72.00	
Present value of the pickup discounted at the ROR required				£2.80	
Total, ie, market value of the convertible				£74.80	

Consider the convertible security that is presented in the table format above.

In this instance, the convertible is providing income in the form of interest at a rate of £10.00 per bond. The dividend income on the ordinary shares into which the convertible security could be converted is paying 11.11% per annum (20p/£1.80) and is subject to an expected annual rate of growth of 5%. Clearly, the income stream being offered by the bond component of the convertible is, in the first instance, paying out a more attractive stream than that which could be obtained from receiving the ordinary share dividend. However, the latter is increasing at an annual rate of 5% per annum and could be expected to eventually surpass the income stream from the bond part of the convertible. Both income streams need to be analysed in terms of their PV using the required ROR as the discount rate in the PV calculations.

The difference between the income earned from the bond coupon and the initial dividend when discounted to PV is shown as £1.36 and remains positive for the first four years. At the beginning of the fifth year, it would make sense for the holder of the convertible to convert the security into ordinary shares because at this point the cash value of the dividend earnings has risen above the level of the cash income from the coupon.

When the discounted pickup income prior to conversion is added together the PV is £2.80 and this can be added to the value of converting the security into ordinary shares at the time of issue using the nominal value conversion of 40 shares per £100.

Using this method of determining when the crossover in income would trigger a conversion the current value of the convertible should be calculated at present as being £74.80.

6.1.4 Option/Warrant Pricing Method

The crossover method of valuation can be useful as a relatively easy way to value a convertible, but it fails to take account of the real nature of the convertible, which is a combination of two separate instruments: a low-coupon bond and an option or warrant to buy the underlying equity of the issuing company. A more appropriate method of valuing a convertible would be to use option, and warrant, pricing techniques, discussed later.

The value of the option or warrant will be determined by a number of factors:

- exercise price of the option
- actual price of the underlying share
- expectations with regard to volatility in the price of the underlying share
- time to expiry of the option
- interest rates
- whether a dividend will be paid on the share in the option period.

An example of this technique would be a convertible currently at expiry date that can either be converted into shares with a value of £120 or redeemed for cash of £100. Clearly, the total value of the convertible is £120. This is made up of its value as straight debt (£100) plus the value of the option to convert into equity, which must be worth an additional £20.

Since the option is already at its expiry date, there is no time value, and the whole of the £20 is intrinsic value. Intrinsic value is the difference between the market price of the shares (£120) and the exercise price of the option (£100). In the case of a convertible, the exercise price of the option is the lost proceeds from holding the instrument as straight debt – in other words, £100.

The value of the convertible prior to conversion will be the higher value of:

- the plain vanilla bond (disregarding the conversion right), and
- the bond – the number of shares that could be obtained at their current market price.

Illustration

Assume the convertible has one year to maturity and will be redeemed for £110 cash. Alternatively, the investor can convert into shares at any time over the next year. The current value of the shares is £125. The debt holder's required ROR is 10%.

The value of the instrument now as straight debt is the PV of the proceeds as debt, ie, £110 ÷ (1+r) or £110 ÷ 1.1 which equates to £100.

The value in terms of the shares that could be created is £125. The current intrinsic value of the convertible will, therefore, be £25, ie, the current value of the shares (£125) less the value of the straight debt of £100.

While this establishes a current intrinsic value, the market value of the convertible would be higher since there is time value left in the option to convert, ie, one year and the possibility that the price of the equity component could move higher (or lower). But with one year to remain, the option has a time premium value which will contribute to a higher value for the convertible than the intrinsic value. The option itself could be sold by the holder as it has market value and is tradeable.

If the current value of the shares was significantly less than the cash redemption option, then the value of the convertible will be closer to its value as straight debt, but with a small additional amount of time value. The option component would have no intrinsic value and, as time passes, the time value will decay until it becomes worthless. This situation is sometimes described as being one of a 'busted' convertible.

6.1.5 Ongoing Valuation of a Convertible

A convertible is basically a combination of two instruments and the valuation reflects this:

$$\text{Conversion price} = \frac{\text{Market value of shares}}{\text{Number of shares into which convertible can be converted into}}$$

Illustration

If a convertible has a market value of £120 (per £100 per nominal stock) and gives a right to convert each £100 of nominal into 40 shares that have a current price of £2.80 per share, then the conversion right only has an intrinsic value (difference between the price per share for which the conversion right may be exercised and the market value of the underlying asset) beyond the point when the share price exceeds £3.00 as demonstrated by the conversion price formula:

$$\text{Conversion price} \quad \frac{£120}{40 \text{ shares}} = £3.00 \text{ per share}$$

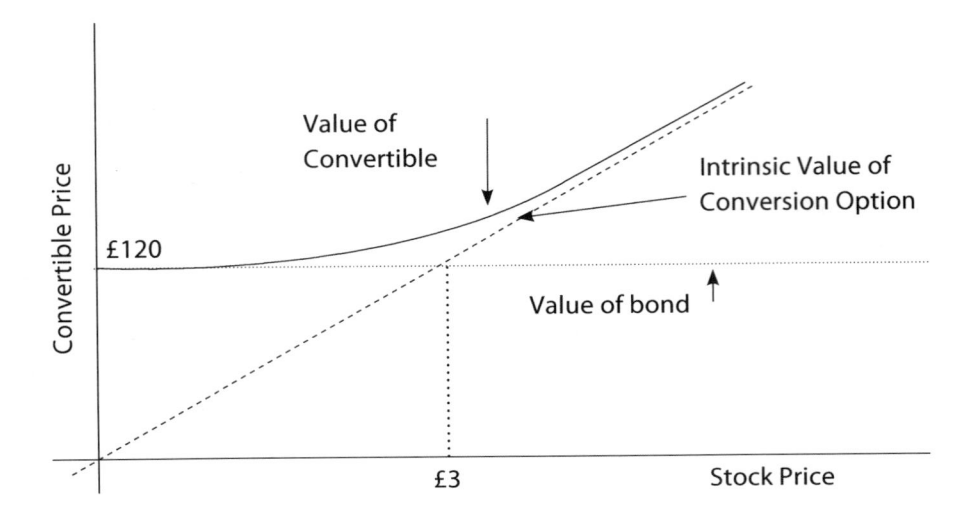

[Diagram: Convertible Price (y-axis) vs Stock Price (x-axis). Horizontal dashed line at £120 labelled "Value of bond". Curve labelled "Value of Convertible" flattens at £120 for low stock prices and rises above the diagonal dashed line labelled "Intrinsic Value of Conversion Option" which crosses at £3 on the x-axis.]

Once the share price exceeds this point, the conversion right starts to attract a value. The market value will be greater than this simple intrinsic value, since it will also reflect the time value of the conversion right.

The diagram above illustrates that the valuation of a convertible is unlike an option when the strike price is fixed; here, although the conversion ratio is fixed, the bond price itself varies, eg, if the price of the bond rises to £140, so the new break-even price would be as follows:

$$\text{Break-even share price} = \frac{£140}{40 \text{ shares}} = £3.50 \text{ per share}$$

The break-even point at the expiry of the conversion option would be the nominal value of the bond divided by the number of shares into which convertible can be converted into.

6.2 Warrants

A warrant entitles the holder to buy a certain number of underlying shares of a company for a set period at a predefined price. This is like a call option to buy the shares. The primary difference is that the warrants are issued by and exercisable on the company, which will issue new shares if exercised. Options are held by investors and relate to shares already in issue; their exercise does not result in new shares being issued.

Warrants have similar characteristics to call options, in terms of their volatility, risk and the way in which they are valued.

6.2.1 Advantages and Disadvantages

Advantages to a Company of Issuing Warrants

- Raising immediate cash without finance needed for dividend payments for new shares.
- Increasing attraction of a debt issue. Many warrants are attached to a debt issue, giving debt investors the added attraction of an equity kicker. This will translate into lower required yields on the debt, meaning that the initial financial burden on the company is lower.
- After debt is issued, the warrants are normally detached from the debt and traded separately in the secondary marketplace (there is a secondary market for some of the more attractive and liquid warrants).
- If the share price drops, then warrants issued are unlikely to be exercised. The company will have received money on issue of the warrants but it will not pay for issuing any new shares.

Disadvantages to the Company

If and when the warrant is exercised:

- new shares are issued by the company, potentially at a significant discount to the then share price
- required dividend payments in total may increase dramatically if the share price is not to be detrimentally affected.

Advantages to Investors

- Geared investment in a company's shares, that are a cheaper alternative to buying the share itself, similar to a call option.
- Way of securing an income yield, while keeping available high equity performance, through buying debt plus warrants from the company. Similar to the principle of buying a convertible debt issue.

Disadvantages to Investors

- Geared investment, so percentage losses can be extreme if the share underperforms.
- Risk of a company takeover. If the company is taken over, the exercise date of the warrants will probably be accelerated to the takeover date. This will destroy any time value in the warrant, meaning that an investor could suffer a major loss. If the warrant is out-of-the-money, having just been issued, for example, then it could become worthless.

Additional Factors When Considering an Investment in Warrants

Note that a warrant holder will not be affected by bonus issues or rights issues because the terms of the warrant will adjust in the same way as the terms of options contracts, outlined above.

Warrants have a number of other characteristics. For instance:

- **Exercising** – a warrant is exercised when the holder informs the issuer of their intention to purchase the shares underlying the warrant.
- **Premium** – a warrant's premium represents how much extra you have to pay for your shares when buying them through the warrant as compared to buying them in the regular way.

- **Gearing (leverage)** – a warrant's gearing is the way to ascertain how much more exposure you have to the underlying shares using the warrant as compared to the exposure you would have if you buy shares through the market.
- **Expiry date** – this is the date the warrant expires. If you plan on exercising the warrant you must do so before the expiry date. The more time remaining until expiry, the more time for the underlying security to appreciate, which, in turn, will increase the price of the warrant (unless it depreciates). Therefore, the expiry date is the date on which the right to exercise no longer exists.

Warrants are longer-dated options and are generally traded OTC.

6.2.2 Secondary Market

Sometimes, the issuer will try to establish a market for the warrant and to register it with a listed exchange. In this case, the price can be obtained from a broker. But often, warrants are privately held or not registered, which makes their prices less obvious. Unregistered warrant transactions can still be facilitated between accredited parties, and in fact several secondary markets have been formed to provide liquidity for these investments.

6.2.3 Comparison with Call Options

Warrants are much like call options, and will often confer the same rights as an equity option and can even be traded in secondary markets. However, warrants have several key differences:

Warrants are issued by private parties, typically the corporation on which a warrant is based, rather than a public options exchange.

Warrants issued by the company itself are dilutive. When the warrant issued by the company is exercised, the company issues new shares of stock, so the number of outstanding shares increases. When a call option is exercised, the owner of the call option receives an existing share from an assigned call writer (except in the case of employee stock options, when new shares are created and issued by the company upon exercise). Unlike common stock shares outstanding, warrants do not have voting rights.

Warrants are considered OTC instruments, and thus are usually only traded by financial institutions with the capacity to settle and clear these types of transactions.

A warrant's lifetime is measured in years (as long as 15 years), while options are typically measured in months. Even the longest equity options available tend to expire in two or three years. Upon expiration, the warrants are worthless if not exercised unless the price of the common stock is greater than the exercised price.

Warrants are not standardised like exchange-listed options.

Illustration

Warrants are available in a (fictional) investment company, Cambridge Investment Trust plc. The company's shares are currently trading at 77p each, and warrants are available giving the investor the right to buy shares at £1 each, up until 2020. The warrants are trading at 4p each.

In the above example, the warrants' expiry date is in 2020 and their exercise price is 100p.

Derivatives

What are the advantages to the company, such as the fictional Cambridge Investment Trust plc encountered above, that persuade them to issue warrants? Clearly, the sale of warrants for cash will raise money for the company, and if the warrants are exercised, then further capital will be raised by the company. Similarly to call options, holding the warrant does not entitle the investor to receive dividends or to vote at company meetings, so the capital raised until the warrant is exercised could be considered as free.

Obviously, warrants offer a highly geared investment opportunity for the investor, and warrants are often issued alongside other investments, rather than sold in their own right.

Illustration

ABC plc is attempting to raise finance by issuing bonds. Their advisors inform them that they could issue bonds paying a coupon of 6% pa, or lower it to 5% pa if they give away a single warrant with each £100 nominal of the bonds. The warrants are detachable from the bonds – in other words, the investors could decide to sell their warrants or keep them, regardless of whether they retain the bonds.

Traditional warrants are issued in conjunction with a bond (known as a warrant-linked bond), and represent the right to acquire shares in the entity issuing the bond. In other words, the writer of a traditional warrant is also the issuer of the underlying instrument. Warrants are issued in this way as a 'sweetener' to make the bond issue more attractive, and to reduce the interest rate that must be offered in order to sell the bond issue.

6.2.4 Warrant Price Behaviour

Warrants (including covered warrants) are highly geared investments. A modest outlay can result in a large gain, but the investor can lose everything. Their value is driven by the length of time for which they are valid (their maturity or period until expiry) and the value of the underlying security.

There is a relatively simple method of looking at the price of one warrant relative to other warrants – using the conversion premium. The conversion premium is the price of the warrant plus the exercise price required to buy the underlying share less the prevailing share price.

Example

Calculating the conversion premium for the Cambridge Investment Trust plc encountered above:

Warrant price	=	4p
Plus exercise price	=	100p
Less share price	=	77p
Conversion premium	=	27p

Note that if the resultant figure was a negative, the warrant would be trading at a conversion discount.

6.2.5 Valuation of Warrants

As a warrant has the same commercial effect for the investor as an option, its valuation can be achieved in the same way.

In undertaking this, however, we need to consider the differences between an option and a warrant: specifically that, when a warrant is exercised, new shares are issued by the company, diluting the value of the shares in existence.

The value of a warrant can therefore be defined as follows:

$$\text{Warrant value} = \frac{A}{1+q} \times \text{Number of shares}$$

where:

A = value of an equivalent option derived from a suitable option pricing model

q = percentage increase in the number of shares in issue once the warrant is exercised (expressed as a decimal)

6.2.6 Warrant Premium and Gearing

The warrant premium is the price by which the warrant price plus the exercise price exceeds the share price. Although it may not be obvious, this is also the time value of the warrant expressed as a percentage of the share price, as can be demonstrated by the following algebraic rearrangement:

$$\text{Warrant premium} = \frac{\text{Warrant price} + \text{Exercise price}}{\text{Share price}} - 1$$

$$\text{Warrant premium} = \frac{\text{Warrant price} + \text{Exercise price} - \text{Share price}}{\text{Share price}}$$

$$\text{Warrant premium} = \frac{\text{Warrant price} - \text{Intrinsic price}}{\text{Share price}}$$

$$\text{Warrant premium} = \frac{\text{Time value}}{\text{Share price}}$$

We have already seen that options are highly geared investments. The same is true for warrants. The warrant gearing ratio indicates how highly geared the warrant is, and it is calculated as follows:

$$\text{Gearing ratio} = \frac{\text{Share price}}{\text{Warrant price}} \times 100\%$$

	Warrant A	Warrant B
Issuer	XYZ plc	XYZ plc
Share Price	180	180
Exercise Price	100	300
Expiry Date	2020	2020
Price of Warrant	160	30
Gearing Ratio	112.50%	600.00%

Warrant A is considered to be deeply in-the-money and Warrant B is deeply out-of-the-money. The price of Warrant A is consequently much higher and will almost certainly be exercised. It is not a highly geared investment, and investing in the warrant will, at current levels, give a little less than the percentage returns of investing in the share itself.

The situation with Warrant B is very different. A change in the share price from 180 pence to 181 pence is unlikely to affect the value of the warrant significantly. If the share price rises significantly, however, then the price of the warrant could also rise significantly, giving a very high percentage return on initial investment. Warrant B is much more highly geared than Warrant A.

6.3 Covered Warrants

Covered warrants are issued by financial institutions and are listed securities on the London Stock Exchange. They provide leveraged exposure to a wide range of underlying instruments, such as equities, baskets, indices, currencies and commodities. They are quoted throughout the trading day and offer all the benefits of transparency and liquidity.

A covered warrant gives the holder the right, but not the obligation, to buy (call warrant) or to sell (put warrant) an underlying asset at a specified price (the strike price or exercise price) by a predetermined date. The price paid for this right is the 'premium' and with covered warrants you cannot lose more than this initial premium paid. They are limited liability instruments so there are no further payments or margin calls required to maintain a covered warrant position. Covered warrants offer a flexible alternative to retail investors who seek to gain the leverage benefits of derivatives, but who wish to limit their risk. When the issuer sells a warrant to an investor, they typically cover or hedge their exposure by buying the underlying instrument in the market. Covered warrants have an average life of six to 12 months, although some have maturities of several years.

The benefits of covered warrants to an investor are, typically, low-cost, flexibility and limited liability.

The cost of the warrants is, as noted above, the premium (which represents the maximum potential loss to the holder). They are exercised at the exercise price and expire at the expiry date.

A call warrant may be purchased as a bet on the price of the underlying asset rising, while a put warrant may be bought as a bet on the price falling.

Example

The ordinary shares of X plc trade at 120p (as at 15 June). An investor who believes the price will rise may be able to buy a call warrant to buy at 150p by, say, 30 September. Let's say this warrant is priced at 5p for each share. If the X plc share price rises to 160p, the warrant can be excised for a profit since 160p – 150p = 10p proceeds, compared with the cost of 5p, providing the investor with an overall profit of 5p per share (10p – 5p). If the share price does not reach 150p by 30 September, the warrant will be worthless on expiry.

A put warrant to sell X plc at 100p by 30 September could be exercised if the share price of X plc falls below 100p. The profit on exercise will depend on how far below 100p the price falls, less the initial warrant cost.

Covered warrants can be sold on in the secondary market before being exercised, in which case, part of their value will be the time value attributable to the hope that the warrant can eventually be exercised at a profit.

6.3.1 Futures

A futures contract is an agreement to buy or sell a standard quantity of a specified asset on a fixed future date, at a price agreed today.

There are two parties to a futures contract – a buyer and a seller – whose respective obligations are as follows:

- The buyer of a future enters into an obligation to buy on a specified date.
- The seller of a future enters into an obligation to sell on a future date.

6.3.2 Tick Size and Value

With all futures contracts, the tick is a fundamental concept which needs to be clearly understood to see how the instruments change in value and the contractual commitment that is undertaken by both parties to the contract.

- The **tick size** is the smallest permitted quote movement on one contract.
- The **tick value** is the change in the value of one contract if there is a one-tick change in the quote.

Example

Consider the FTSE 100 Index Futures contract.

The contract size for this index future is equal to £10 per index point multiplied by the value of the index, so if the index is trading at 7000 the value of the contract would be £70,000. The actual tick size for this contract is 0.5 points of the index, and each tick (0.5 points) is £5, so a sequence of prices traded for the future might be quoted as:

- 7000.0
- 7000.5

- 7001.0
- 7001.5
- 7002.0

The value associated with each index point will be £10 and another way of expressing these two characteristics of the tick and tick value for the FTSE 100 Index is to say that one index point = £10, which is the same as two ticks x £5 per tick.

These two factors are used to calculate the futures profit or loss:

Profit = Quote change in ticks x Tick value x Number of contracts

So, for example, if a speculator buys two contracts of the FTSE 100 Index Futures at 7,000, and sells them shortly after at 7040 exactly, the profit would be:

Profit = 80 ticks x £5 per tick x 2 contracts = 40 index points x £10 per point x 2 contracts = £800

Hedging with the FTSE 100 Index Future

The FTSE 100 Index Future fixes the price at which the underlying index may be bought or sold at a specific future date.

This contract gives exposure to, or hedges exposure against, the index, ie, the stock market in general.

6.3.3 Unit of Trade

Unit of trade = Index value × £10

That is, a contract can be valued by multiplying the index value by £10. If, for example, the index stood at 7200, then one contract would have a value of 7200 x £10 = £72,000.

Under these circumstances a speculator or a hedger may buy – or take a long position in – the index future, or may wish to sell – or take a short position in the index future.

A speculator who believes that the FTSE 100 is about to move upwards could gain long exposure to the index by buying a single futures contract which would in effect give the speculator £72,000 of exposure to the market. Another speculator who believes that the FTSE 100 is going to go down might decide to sell – or go short of – the index as a result of selling a single futures contract which would mean that they would be short of £72,000-worth of the index, and would profit if the market falls.

In contrast to the pure speculator, who is really interested in following hunches about the future direction of the index and is attempting to benefit from making the right call and going either long or short, a hedger is someone who already has a stake in the market and is looking to hedge her risk by having an offsetting position in the futures market. If by chance someone owned exactly £72,000-worth of stocks which were representative of the index, and that person becomes nervous that the market is about to go down then selling a single futures contract would provide an offset or hedge to the loss of value of the actual holdings of equities.

6.3.4 Delivery

This contract is cash-settled. That is, rather than the two parties exchanging the underlying asset and the pre-agreed price at the delivery date, they simply settle up by the payment from one to the other of the difference in value.

6.3.5 Quotation

The quote given is in index (and half-index) points.

6.3.6 Tick

The tick size – the smallest permitted quote movement – is 0.5 index points.

The tick value is £5, ie, 0.5 index point x £10.

Example

You are managing a £36 million pension fund portfolio and you believe that the market is about to fall. The index and the future currently stand at 7200. The alternatives are: to sell the portfolio and move into cash/bonds – this will avoid the market fall, but will clearly incur massive dealing costs – or to set up a short hedge using the futures contract.

6.3.7 Short Hedge

The future is quoted at 7200, hence each contract will hedge £72,000 (ie, 7200 × £10) of the exposure. To hedge the full portfolio, exactly 500 contracts are needed (£36 million ÷ £72,000).

Consider the position if the market (and the futures contract) fall 200 points.

6.3.8 Cash Position

Old portfolio value = £36,000,000

New portfolio value = £36 million × 7000 ÷ 7200 = £35m

Loss = £1,000,000

6.3.9 Futures Position

Sold index at 7200

Bought index to close position at 7000

Points gain: 200 = 400 ticks.

Hence, the total profit on 500 contracts sold short will be:

Profit = Ticks x Tick value x Number of contracts = 400 x £5.00 x 500 = £1,000,000

The profit on the short futures position exactly cancels the loss on the portfolio and hence represents a good hedging strategy.

In the case presented, there was an exact match because the size of the portfolio and the value of the index produce an integer value for the number of contracts required for hedging purposes. If a fractional value is obtained when dividing the size of the portfolio by the current size of the contract (based upon the actual FTSE 100 Index value) then the number can be rounded down to the nearest integer and the hedge will not be a 100% match but will provide an effective way of allowing the portfolio manager to shelter the portfolio from adverse movements in the overall market.

6.4 Hedge Ratio

One assumption made here is that a pension fund portfolio is only as volatile as the index, ie, assumes that the beta (ß) of the portfolio is 1. If this is not the case, then it may be needed to sell more or less contracts to achieve the hedge. The important determinant is the relative volatility.

By definition, the futures contract has a ß = 1. If the portfolio has a ß = 1.3, then a 1% change in the index will cause a 1% change in the value of a future but a 1.3% change in the portfolio value. This will therefore need 1.3 times as many futures contracts to provide sufficient profit to cancel any losses suffered in the portfolio.

When hedging with futures, follow the formula below for determining how many contracts will be required to ensure that the hedging reflects the relative volatilities of the portfolio and the underlying instrument upon which the futures contract is based.

$$\text{Hedging required number of contracts} = \frac{\text{Portfolio value}}{\text{Futures value}} \times h$$

where h is the hedge ratio, which reflects the relative volatilities of the portfolio and the hedging instrument.

In the case of hedging a portfolio against the FTSE contract the value for h – the hedge ratio – is simply found by using the beta value of the portfolio.

$$h = \frac{\text{Volatility of the portfolio}}{\text{Volatility of the futures contract}} = \frac{-\beta p}{\beta f} = -\beta p \text{ since } \beta f = 1$$

6.4.1 Residual Risk in a Hedged Portfolio

A correctly hedged portfolio, ie, one with the correct hedge ratio, should exhibit no risk whatsoever, assuming the portfolio is fully diversified and exhibits no unsystematic risk.

In practice, however, risk in a hedged portfolio may arise due to:

- Using the incorrect hedge ratio as a result of incorrectly assessing the beta of the portfolio.
- Unsystematic risk within the portfolio that the hedge cannot eliminate (hedging with an index future can only eliminate systematic risk, since the index moves with the market, ie, moves with systematic factors only).
- Unsystematic risk can only be eliminated by further diversification within the portfolio.

6.5 UK Gilt Future

One of the financial futures which is widely traded is the contract which allows one to have exposure to the UK gilts market. There are similar reasons behind the motivation to want to trade with this instrument. On the one hand a speculator might have a particular view on the direction of interest rates and wish to benefit from taking a position in the futures market in anticipation of that potential move. On the other hand, someone who has a portfolio which is mainly comprised of UK government securities might be looking for a vehicle to use to hedge against adverse movements in the gilt market.

Unlike the futures contract based upon the FTSE 100 Index which tracks precisely the index in a one-to-one fashion, the futures contract which tracks the direction of UK gilts is less precisely correlated to any single underlying instrument. Over many years, the UK Government has issued a wide variety of gilts with different coupons and different maturities and this raises a question as far as the requirement which is required for futures contracts, which is to have a standard deliverable. What has been developed with regard to a uniform bond which can be delivered against the futures contract is a notional bond which has a nominal value of £100,000, a coupon of 4% and a maturity window of between 8.75 and 13 years.

The actual contract specification can be seen in the following table.

UK Long Gilt Future (ICE Futures Contract Specification)	
Contract size	£100,000 nominal value
Bond characteristic	Notional 4% coupon
Deliverable months	March, June, September, December
Tick size and value	0.01% (1 basis point) and £10
Last trading day	11am – two days prior to the last business day in the month
Delivery day	Any business day in delivery month (seller's choice)
Settlement	List of deliverable gilts published by the exchange with maturities of between eight years and nine months to 13 years

The use of a notional bond with a 4% coupon with a specific period of acceptable maturities allows the exchange, as well as those who have taken a position in the futures contract, to calculate which of the issued gilts will be acceptable for delivery and also at what price the actual bond can be converted to the price of the notional bond.

6.5.1 Unit of Trade

The unit of trade = £100,000 nominal of a notional 4% gilt, ie, gilts with a nominal value of £100,000.

6.5.2 Delivery

The eligible deliverable gilts will have differing maturities and coupons and therefore differing prices and differing interest rate sensitivities. To try to cater for these price and sensitivity differentials, the exchange calculates a price factor or conversion factor for each of the deliverable gilts.

The conversion factor will, in turn, determine the price actually paid for the delivered gilt and the market will seek out the opportunity to deliver those bonds which are the cheapest-to-deliver (CTD) after taking into account the adjustment factor implied by the conversion table.

The relationship between the price of the CTD gilt and that of the future is:

$$\text{CTD gilt price} = \text{Futures price} \times \text{Price factor}$$

The seller of the future also has the choice as to which date during the month of the expiration of the futures contract to make delivery. The seller will therefore decide whether he would prefer to receive the accrued interest from holding the gilt for the month, or hold cash on deposit earning interest.

If interest rates are low compared to the coupon rate, then he will hold the gilt as long as possible, making delivery on the last day. If, however, interest rates are high compared to coupon rates, then he will deliver on the earliest date and hold cash.

6.5.3 Quotation

The quotation is similar to gilts quotes, ie, price per £100 of nominal value.

6.5.4 Tick

The gilt contract is £100,000 in size, so the tick value, (one basis point, or one-hundredth of 1%) is £10.

6.5.5 Hedging with the UK Gilt Future

As we noted with the FTSE 100 contract, in order to achieve a hedge with a future, we must apply the following relationship:

$$\text{Number of contracts} = \frac{\text{Portfolio value}}{\text{Futures value}} \times h$$

where h represents the beta value of the share portfolio (ie, the degree to which the portfolio is more or less volatile than the overall market benchmark – or the FTSE 100).

However, in the case of fixed-income instruments such as bonds or gilts there is a different measure of relative volatility with respect to a benchmark and that is to compare the duration of the bond portfolio with the duration of the notional bond assumed by the UK long gilt futures contract.

$$h = \frac{\text{Volatility of portfolio}}{\text{Volatility of futures}} = -\frac{\text{Portfolio duration}}{\text{Futures duration}}$$

The negative sign for h, in the formula above, indicates going short the future when already long the portfolio of bonds. The duration of a bond portfolio is calculated as the weighted average of the durations of the bonds within the portfolio. However, what is the duration of the futures contract?

This information is made available after an analysis has been performed to determine which is the CTD in the circumstances applicable for the notional UK 4% gilt. Suppose that it is found that the CTD bond for a one-year futures contract is an 8% 12-year annual coupon bond.

Calculate:

- the current bond price when interest rates are either 8% or 9%, and the corresponding one-year futures prices
- the bond price and futures price at the maturity of the futures contract in one year at those same rates.

Under each of the interest rate scenarios above the price of the futures contract today is the same as that of the CTD at the maturity of the futures contract. Hence, the sensitivity of the futures contract to interest rate changes (its duration) is the same as that of the CTD as at the maturity date of the futures contract.

In practice however it is not known which bond will be the CTD until the maturity date of the futures contract, although it should be predictable if it is assumed that interest rates remain constant to maturity. Hence, the position can be assessed now, though this hedge may not be static and may need modifying as economic factors (and the CTD) vary.

6.5.6 Options

Exchange traded options are entirely vanilla in nature.

Their overall use is similar therefore to the vanilla OTC options, in terms of strategies and pay-off profiles, as described in section 3 above.

7. OTC Traded Derivatives

Learning Objective

9.8 Explain the main types, characteristics, risks, and pricing of OTC traded derivatives: forwards and forward rate agreements (FRAs); OTC option products; contracts for difference; swaps – interest rate, currency, equity and commodity, bond; credit default swaps; credit derivatives; structured products

9.9 Describe and explain the trading of OTC traded derivatives: mechanisms, procedures, and processes; wholesale trading facilities; standard and bespoke deals, contracts, and agreements; market transparency, reporting and monitoring; order/instruction flow and order type; confirmation, maturity, expiry, margin, liquidity, exercise and delivery

7.1 Forward Rate Agreements (FRAs)

A forward rate agreement (FRA) enables a company to fix an interest rate in advance. It enables a borrower or lender to take a view on whether rates are rising or falling. There is no principal amount actually borrowed or lent, but a cash flow arises from the difference between the interest rate fixed at the outset (the fixed rate) and the level of benchmark rate at a point of time in the future (the floating rate). The FRA pays out the interest rate difference for a predetermined future period on an agreed principal amount. The benchmark rate most often used is LIBOR.

Therefore a FRA is effectively an agreement to buy or sell an interest rate which is fixed today and which will be revalued against prevailing market rates, using a benchmark rate:

- starting on an agreed future date
- for an agreed future period
- based on an agreed principal amount (a notional amount, ie, used for the calculation but not actually transferred).

The party that pays the fixed rate is the buyer of the FRA, and the party that receives the fixed rate and pays the floating rate is the seller of the FRA.

A FRA is settled on the date when the FRA period starts. In a FRA the settlement amount is subject to discounting. This happens because the FRA payment takes place at the beginning of the FRA period rather than following market convention for other instruments, and paying at the end, or on maturity. The discounting is applied at current market rates, and represents a deduction for the interest which would accrue if the amount paid were to be deposited from the date of payment through to the end of the FRA period.

The benchmark rate, eg, LIBOR, ie, the floating-rate value, is determined on the first day of the FRA period and will then apply through to the agreed maturity. The difference between the level of the benchmark rate and the pre-agreed fixed rate will give rise to a net settlement amount calculated using the following formula:

$$\text{Notional Principal Amount} \times \frac{(\text{ICE LIBOR} - \text{FRA rate}) \times \frac{\text{days in FRA period}}{\text{days in year}}}{\left(1 + \left(\text{LIBOR} \times \frac{\text{days in FRA period}}{\text{days in year}}\right)\right)}$$

The period over which interest is calculated is known as the 'calculation period'. The length of this as a proportion of a year is known as the day count fraction. All day counts are taken from, and including, the first day of the calculation period up to, but excluding, the last day. The denominator in the day count fraction – days in year – is taken as either 365 or 360, depending on the market convention; for example, both euro and dollar use 360, and sterling uses 365.

The calculation of the FRA settlement amount can result in a positive or a negative figure. The amount is transferred from seller to buyer if LIBOR is higher than the FRA rate (negative) and from buyer to seller if LIBOR is lower than the FRA rate (positive).

Example

A company knows that in one month's time it will need to borrow £15 million for a period of six months. The company treasurer is concerned that interest rates might rise in the next month, thereby making its borrowing more expensive. He wants to fix the future borrowing rate today, even though the money isn't needed for a month.

He enters into a forward rate agreement whereby he buys an FRA on £15 million to start in one month's time to run for a period of six months, at a rate of 5.4%. It is agreed that in one month's time the 11.00am fixing of LIBOR, for a six-month maturity, will be used as the benchmark rate.

Suppose that the LIBOR fixing is 5.55%. The seller of the FRA will therefore pay the company 0.15% (the difference between the 5.4% rate agreed and the 5.55% subsequently fixed) on £15 million, for a period of six months.

There is no exchange of principal between these two parties. Instead, the company will borrow the £15 million from its usual lending bank, or some other source, at the prevailing market rate of 5.55% (plus any lending margin which it negotiates with its bank).

The net settlement amount is:

$$€15,000,000 \times \frac{(0.0555 - 0.0540) \times 182/360}{1 + (0.0555 \times (182/360))} = €11,064.54$$

Alternatively, suppose that interest rates had fallen and the LIBOR fixing was 5.25%. The company would have to pay the seller 0.15% on £15 million for six months. However, the actual borrowing from the bank would be at only 5.25% plus margin. The net effect is, therefore, still that the company borrows at 5.40% plus lending margin.

Therefore, a fall below 5.40% does not benefit the company as it must pay the seller the difference but conversely, any rise above 5.40% is offset by the receipt of the difference from the seller.

The FRA described in the previous example is known as a 1 v 7 FRA. This means that it covers a future period which begins one month from today and ends seven months from today.

FRA quoted rates are based on the forward/forward rate; for example, the quoted rate of a 1 v 7 FRA is based on the six-month starting in one month's time; that is the definition of a forward/forward rate. To calculate this you need the current one-month and seven-month reference rates (usually LIBOR).

$$\text{FRA quoted rate} = r_{FRA} = \frac{(r_2 n_2 - r_1 n_1)}{n_{FRA}(1 + r_1 n_1 / 365)}$$

where:

n_1 is the number of days from the dealing date or spot date to the settlement date
n_2 is the number of days from the dealing date or spot date to the maturity date
r_1 is the spot rate to the settlement date
r_2 is the spot rate from the spot date in the FRA contract period
n_{FRA} is the number of days in the maturity date
r_{FRA} is the FRA rate.

Therefore, if the one-month UK rate is 5.55% and the seven-month rate is 5.85%, what is the price of a 1 v 7 GBP FRA?

$$\text{1 v 7 GBP FRA} = \frac{(5.85\% \times 214 - 5.55\% \times 31)}{183 \times (1 + (5.55\% \times (31/365)))} = 5.87\%$$

or:

$$\text{1 v 7 GBP FRA} = \frac{(10.7985)}{183.8626} = 5.87\%$$

Since FRAs are traded in the over-the-counter market, they can be tailor-made to suit a hedger's exposure, since the notional amount, future period, currency and reference rate are flexible. As mentioned above, FRAs are quoted giving the deferred period first, then the notional maturity. Therefore, a 2 v 5 FRA is one for a three-month rate that starts two months in the future.

A series of FRAs that cover future three-month interest rates is similar to a series of three-month interest rate futures contracts, if they both are in the same currency and have the same reference or underlying interest rate. A key difference is that, by being an OTC derivative, the details of the FRA are flexible.

7.2 Contracts for Difference (CFDs)

Contracts for difference (CFDs) are OTC derivatives which allow investors to benefit from the capital gains from a long or short position in a particular underlying index, stock, currency or commodity without having to actually physically own or pay full upfront value for it. The investor enters into an agreement with a CFD provider – usually a stockbroker or a firm offering an online dealing service – to settle the difference between the price of the underlying investment when the agreement is made and its price when the agreement is ended.

The profit or loss is determined by the difference between the prices at which the investor buys and sells the contract and the contract amount. The investor can profit from predicting the correct movement in the underlying asset's price, either up or down, without having to buy or sell the actual asset.

CFDs are cost-efficient, in that an investor buying a CFD on a share does not have to pay stamp duty, nor the broker's fee that is normally associated with share transactions. CFDs also allow investors who are bearish on a share an easier way to profit from the fall in a share's price, rather than physically going short of a share.

CFDs are based on margin trading, so an investor can leverage their position. Most brokers require a margin deposit of up to 30% of the contract's value. This allows investors to increase their risk, based on the size of their initial investment. But many contracts include an automatic stop loss order as part of the contract, which minimises the risk of a large loss. Most CFDs are nominally intra-day trades, since those that are held overnight normally incur interest charges.

CFDs do not have an expiry or maturity date like options or futures. As opposed to having an expiry date, a CFD is effectively renewed/rolled over at the close of each trading day if desired. An investor can keep their position open indefinitely, as long as there is enough margin in their account to support the position. CFD contracts are subject to a daily financing charge, usually applied at a previously agreed rate linked to the London interbank offered rate (LIBOR). The parties to a CFD pay to finance long positions and may receive funding on short positions in lieu of deferring sale proceeds.

Example

An investor is bearish on company ABC plc shares. They are currently trading at 145p. The investor decides to sell a contract for difference on 5,000 shares at that price. The investor's broker requires a 15% margin or £1,087.50.

$$5,000 \times 145p = £7,250$$
$$£7,250.00 \times 0.15 = £1,087.50$$

Just before closing, ABC's shares have fallen to 137p. The investor decides to end the CFD, realising a profit of £400.

$$5,000 \times 137p = £6,850$$
$$£7,250 - £6,850 = £400$$

This is a return of 36.8% on the investment (the margin).

The two key differences between spread betting and contracts for difference are that the latter do not have a fixed maturity/expiration date and that spread betting in the UK is considered gambling and therefore is treated differently as far as tax is concerned, since CFDs are subject to CGT.

7.3 Swaps

7.3.1 Interest Rate Swaps and Swaptions

A swap is an OTC derivative, where two counterparties exchange one stream of a cash flow against another. These payment streams are called the legs of the swap. The cash flows are calculated over a notional principal/asset amount.

For example, a straightforward interest rate swap (a so-called plain vanilla swap) involves one party exchanging a floating interest rate obligation for another party's fixed-rate obligation. The floating rate will be determined on the swap's reset date. For example, for a fixed versus six-month floating swap, the reset date will be every six months. Once the floating rate is determined, the swap will start accruing interest as of its effective date.

The plain vanilla interest rate swap, based on an agreed notional principal sum, will specify a particular start date and run for a set period. The swap will specify particular periods at the end of which the cash flow exchanges will take place; this is known as the swap's 'payment date'.

With the agreement of both parties, and after an evaluation or mark-to-market of the swap's value, either party can initiate action to cancel or end the swap after an agreed payment. When this happens, all calculations of accrued interest are based on the swap's termination date. This is the date that the swap officially ceases to exist.

For example, a three-year plain vanilla interest rate swap might be arranged with quarterly payments based on a principal sum of £6 million, effective from 1 January 2013, exchanging a fixed interest rate for a floating interest rate based on the LIBOR. The first payment under the swap will be at the end of March 2015, the second at the end of June 2015 and so on.

At each payment date a net payment will be made between the two participants based on the difference between floating rate (LIBOR) and the fixed rate on the underlying principal sum for the quarter. If LIBOR exceeds the fixed rate, the difference will be paid to the party that is due to receive LIBOR and pay the fixed interest. The payments will be made in the opposite direction if LIBOR is less than the fixed rate.

A swaption is an arrangement where a buyer pays an up-front sum for the right to enter into a swap agreement by a pre-agreed date in the future. In other words, the buyer of a swaption has the option to enter into a swap. The concept is the same as we saw for options earlier.

Large corporations and other institutions use these interest rate swaps and swaptions to manage risk and, potentially, take advantage of cheaper and more appropriate funding. The arrangements are facilitated by financial institutions. It is a wholesale market not open to the private investor.

As they are OTC instruments, swaps come in a variety of forms. In addition to fixed-for-floating swaps (as illustrated above), there are also floating-for-floating swaps. These are alternatively referred to as 'basis swaps' and might enable a borrower to swap six-month LIBOR rates for three-month LIBOR rates. Basis swaps are considered in more detail shortly. As well as these interest rate swaps that are based on a single currency, there are also currency swaps (where there is an exchange of currency, as well as interest) and equity index swaps.

Following a series of scandals and issues relating to the setting of LIBOR, there are plans in place that will phase out the benchmark gradually. In due course, LIBOR will be replaced by other indices that track the short-term interbank borrowing rates. What effect, if any, this will have on OTC instruments that reference LIBOR, is unclear at present.

Currency swaps were one of the earliest types of swap. One of the first examples was between the World Bank and IBM in 1981. IBM wanted to borrow US dollars and the World Bank wanted to borrow Swiss francs and German marks. However, because the World Bank was already a frequent issuer of European currency debt and IBM was not, the rarity value meant IBM could borrow Swiss francs and German marks more cheaply. So, IBM borrowed Swiss francs and German marks, the World Bank borrowed US dollars and they entered into a swap – the result being that they both saved money on their borrowings.

Currency swaps have continued to develop. It is possible to enter into currency swaps that exchange:

- fixed interest in one currency for floating interest in another currency
- fixed interest in one currency for fixed interest in another currency
- floating interest in one currency for floating interest in another currency, or
- floating interest in one currency for fixed interest in another currency.

Example

A UK company might expect to receive a stream of US dollars from exports over the next five years. It needs to convert US dollars into sterling. Rather than use a series of separate forward FX transactions to achieve this, it could instead use a currency swap. The series of US dollar flows are considered as a package and, in the swap, the company agrees to pay these flows to a counterparty over the five years, in return for a series of sterling cash flows. This would be a fixed-fixed currency swap without principal exchanges. The UK company has protected itself against its UK income being eroded by exchange-rate movements depreciating against the US dollars. Conversely, if exchange rates improve, it will see no benefit.

As seen above, the uses of currency swaps include potentially reducing the cost of borrowing and replacing unpredictable future cash flows (due to exchange rate movements) with predictable cash flows agreed in a swap.

In an equity swap (or index swap), two counterparties agree to exchange the return on an equity index, or a specified basket of shares, for a fixed or floating rate of interest. This enables the creation of a synthetic portfolio of shares without the need to buy all of the individual underlying shares and incur the transaction costs for doing so.

A fixed/floating swap (as described above) is also known as a coupon swap. An alternative is a floating/floating swap, known as a basis swap or index swap, in which each of the two payment streams is based on a floating rate. For example, an organisation might pay three-month LIBOR and receive six-month LIBOR. A basis swap might also be a **currency swap** (see below) – for example, paying three-month LIBOR in one currency and receiving six-month LIBOR in another. The term 'basis swap', therefore, covers a range of possibilities.

For example:

- single-currency swap from one period LIBOR to another period LIBOR
- single-currency swap from LIBOR to an overnight interest rate
- single-currency swap from LIBOR to another interest rate, such as a commercial paper rate
- cross-currency swap from a floating-rate in one currency to a floating-rate in another currency.

7.4 Other Types of Swaps

There are several types of swaps in common use other than the interest rate and currency swaps previously mentioned. Here we will describe the variety of products and types of swaps that are traded in the OTC market. At the end of the chapter, some of the operational complexities that arise are considered.

7.4.1 Asset and Total Return Swaps

An asset swap is a swap that can be used to change the interest rate exposure or currency exposure of an investment. The swap itself can be straightforward. The term 'asset swap' is used to denote the reason for doing the swap, and is also used for the whole package of the asset and the swap together.

An investor might, for example, buy a floating-rate note (FRN) and also transact a swap to receive a fixed interest rate and pay LIBOR. The result would be a synthetic fixed-rate investment. Or, in reverse, he might create a synthetic FRN by buying an underlying fixed-rate investment while paying fixed and receiving floating in the swap.

The advantage of such a structure is that the investor is then able to choose the underlying asset according to such criteria as availability, credit quality, liquidity and competitive pricing. The choice of whether to invest in fixed or floating rate can be separated from the choice of asset.

Example

An investor wishes to buy a ten-year floating-rate note issued by the government (because he wants the highest credit rating possible) but no such issue exists. He can instead buy a ten-year government fixed-rate bond and swap it.

Even if such an FRN does already exist, it might be that the synthetic structure using the swap achieves a slightly better yield, if the two markets are not exactly in line.

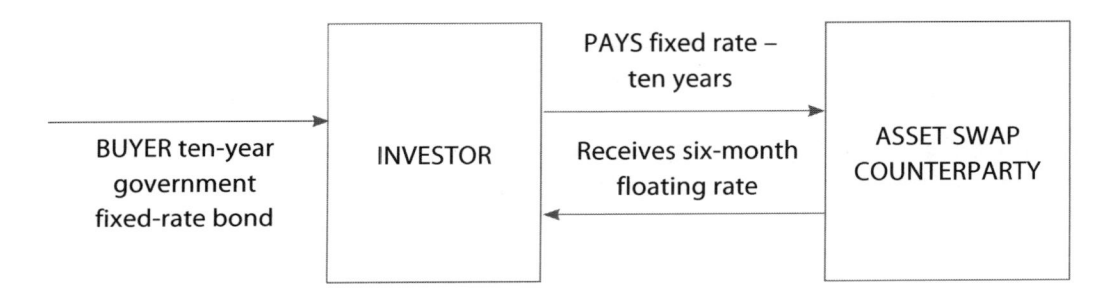

```
BUYER ten-year                          PAYS fixed rate –
government    →    INVESTOR                 ten years          →    ASSET SWAP
fixed-rate bond                                                     COUNTERPARTY
                                        Receives six-month
                                          floating rate       ←
```

In a total return swap, one of the legs pays the total return on a particular financial asset, ie, the total benefit that would have arisen from holding that asset, including all interest payments, fees and capital appreciation. This amount could be negative if the security's value has fallen rather than risen.

For example, the swap could be linked to the value of a particular bond. In this case, one party would pay the other the total increase in value of the bond from the start of the swap to the end of the swap (or receive the total fall in value) and also pay the value of any coupons received on the bond over the life of the swap. The other leg of the swap would typically be a floating-rate interest such as LIBOR.

Example

A UK pension fund wishes to invest in eurozone shares quickly.

One way to do this is to become the receiver of a total return swap (TRS) that has a portfolio of eurozone shares as the underlying instrument.

The price of the TRS will roughly be the same as the cost of a long position of the underlying share portfolio for the pension fund (the TRS buyer), while the seller is financing the position.

The pension fund will receive any increase in the value of the eurozone share portfolio (underlying asset), whilst the seller will receive any fall in the share portfolio's value.

7.4.2 Amortising, Accreting and Rollercoaster Swaps

An interest rate swap is often used by a company to convert the interest rate risk on a borrowing, eg, from floating rate to fixed rate. Suppose that the underlying borrowing arrangement with a bank involves paying the loan back in instalments during its life (an amortising loan). In this case, the swap needs to be amortising also, to match the loan pattern; the notional principal on which the swap payments are based will decrease over the life of the swap.

Other patterns could also be used. For example, the notional principal in the swap might be designed to increase (an accreting swap) rather than decrease. Or it might rise and fall repeatedly, in line with seasonal borrowing requirements (a rollercoaster swap).

7.4.3 Inflation Swaps

An inflation swap involves an exchange of cash flows, with one or both of its legs calculated with reference to an inflation index. It provides investors with protection against rising prices on a notional principal or an asset's future value. An investor who wants protection from rising prices agrees to pay a fixed amount based on the expected rate of inflation.

The swap payments are based on benchmarks such as the Retail Prices Index (RPI) in the UK, the Eurozone's Harmonised Index of Consumer Prices, or the US Consumer Price Index. Maturities normally range from five to 30 years for inflation swaps.

7.4.4 Constant Maturity Swaps (CMSs)

A constant maturity swap (CMS) allows the purchaser to fix the base of received flows on a swap.

The floating leg of a basic interest rate swap is typically reset against a published index, such as LIBOR. The floating leg of a constant maturity swap is fixed against a point on the swap curve on a periodic basis.

It is an interest rate swap where the interest rate on one leg is reset periodically, but with reference to a market swap rate rather than LIBOR. The other leg of the swap is generally LIBOR but may be a fixed-rate or, potentially, another constant maturity rate.

CMSs can either be single-currency or involve two currencies. The prime factor for a CMS, therefore, is the shape of the forward implied yield curves.

7.4.5 Arrears Swaps

In a plain vanilla interest rate swap, the floating interest rate is observed at the start of a period, and paid at the end of that period. In an arrears swap, however, the floating rate is observed and paid at the end of the period.

For example, in a LIBOR-in-arrears swap with semi-annual resets, the six-month LIBOR rate from time ti to ti+l is used to calculate the coupon payment at time ti.

7.4.6 Forward Start Swaps

A forward start swap is one that is agreed today, but the exchange of funds takes place at a future date. It is often priced as two partially offsetting swaps – both starting today, but one ending on the deferred start date of the forward swap. For example, a one-year swap and a five-year swap could partially offset to create a four-year swap, starting in a year's time. Forward start swaps are also known as deferred start swaps or delayed start swaps.

7.4.6 Overnight Index Swaps (OISs)

An overnight index swap (OIS) is a fixed/floating swap (or basis swap) where the floating index (or at least one of them) is an overnight interest rate, eg, a swap to pay 5% fixed for three months and receive the overnight interest rate recorded each day.

In this case, the overnight benchmark interest rate used is not, say, overnight LIBOR, which is the rate at a particular time of day. Instead, the benchmark used is a published overnight index, such as Fed funds effective for USD. This is the average of the overnight interest rate throughout a given day, weighted by the volume of business transacted in the market at that rate. The equivalent published indices for sterling and the euro are the Sterling Overnight Interbank Average Rate (SONIA) and the Euro OverNight Index Average (EONIA) respectively. Some OISs use a tom/next interest rate rather than an overnight interest rate (by buying or selling a foreign amount settling tomorrow and then doing the opposite – selling or buying it back settling the day after).

In order to avoid the expense and administration of many payment transfers, the floating-rate payment is not physically paid each day. Rather, it is accumulated and paid, say, each month. Because this effectively delays the payment, the daily interest rate fixings are compounded to calculate the actual payment, rather than simply added together.

An OIS might be used, for example, by a bank that lends money for three months at a fixed rate but funds itself in the overnight market. The swap described above – pay 5% fixed for three months and receive the overnight interest rate – would hedge the interest rate risk.

Although OIS means 'overnight index swap' in general, it usually refers to a USD OIS in particular. Similarly, although 'TOIS' means 'tom/next indexed swap' in general, it usually refers to a USD TOIS in particular.

The OIS market has grown dramatically in volume. Some of the instrument's various advantages and uses are as follows:

- Liquidity requirements and interest rate risk can be managed separately. Suppose, for example, that a bank wishes to borrow for one year to ensure liquidity but would prefer to fund itself overnight from the point of view of interest rate risk. It can take in a one-year borrowing and transact a one-year OIS to pay the OI and receive one-year fixed.
- An OIS can be used in arbitrage strategies. For example, a dealer might borrow funds repeatedly in the overnight market, lend for, say, a three-month term, and pay fixed/receive the OI in an OIS.
- Credit risk can be reduced significantly. Rather than lend money for one year, a dealer can transact an OIS to pay the OI and receive one-year fixed, and at the same time lend money for only one day in the overnight market and then roll over this overnight cash loan repeatedly for a year. The credit risk on the rolling overnight loan is far smaller than the credit risk would be on a one-year loan. This separates the interest rate decision from the balance sheet decision. The same could be done with a traditional term swap, say for one year against three-month LIBOR, but an overnight credit risk is clearly less than a three-month one and leaves the dealer with greater flexibility in their lending decisions.
- Conversely, an investor can use an OIS for an asset swap, whereby they invest in an attractively priced long-term investment but swaps, the income to the overnight rate (receive the OI and pay the fixed in the OIS).

7.4.7 Mark-to-Market (MTM) Swap

A mark-to-market (MTM) swap is one where settlements are calculated by revaluing the swap (ie, marking it to market) regularly and paying or receiving the mark-to-market loss or gain since the previous settlement. The benefit of this is that it removes, at each settlement date, any credit risk that has built up.

The effect is the same as closing out the existing swap, settling its current value, and putting in place a new swap at the current swap rate for the remaining life of the original swap. This can be done for a single-currency swap or a cross-currency swap (an FX resettable swap).

An FX resettable swap has the characteristics and structure of a basic currency swap and an MTM swap. This includes the fact that all payment dates must be set so that they are business days for both currencies, to avoid any mismatch of payments. Also, as is the case with most basic FX swaps, there will be an exchange of principals at the beginning and end of the swap.

7.4.8 Commodity Swaps

A **commodity swap** involves paying or receiving a cash flow that is determined by the price or returns of a specific commodity. This type of swap has become increasingly popular given the significant volatility in both the supply and demand for most commodities. The users of this type of swap are increasingly interested in hedging their risks. This ranges from airlines that want to lock in one of their major costs – jet fuel – to farmers and other agricultural producers who are looking for a stable income flow from their production.

A fixed-for-floating commodity price swap is one whereby one party periodically pays to the other the cash value of an agreed quantity of the underlying commodity multiplied by a fixed price, and the other party in return periodically pays the cash value of an agreed quantity multiplied by a floating price, indexed to current commodity prices. With this swap there is no exchange of the commodities. This is analogous to a fixed/floating interest rate swap.

Example

An aluminium producer makes regular sales of aluminium and receives the market price for his sales of aluminium. He believes that the aluminium price is going to fall over the next 12 months and wishes to hedge against this risk. He therefore undertakes a swap to receive, from a swap counterparty, an agreed fixed aluminium price each month, based on an agreed quantity of aluminium. At the same time, he agrees to pay that counterparty each month the market price for aluminium, which is then current, based on the same quantity. He will continue to sell aluminium to his customers in the usual way, as the swap is a completely separate transaction from the underlying physical aluminium sales.

The net effect is that the producer will receive an approximately fixed price for his aluminium sales. The two swap parties will need to agree on an aluminium price index for the purpose of the swap settlements. This index will not necessarily be exactly the same as the price received by the producer from his customers from time to time, so that he will be left with a basis risk, but the two should move closely in line. The timing of the swap settlements might also not be exactly the same as for the physical sales but, again, the producer will be better protected than if he had not hedged at all.

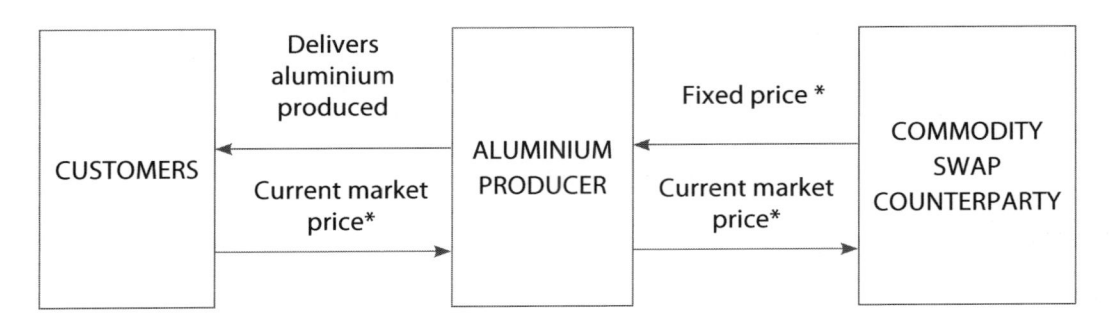

```
                Delivers
                aluminium
                produced                  Fixed price *
              ←───────────              ←───────────           COMMODITY
  CUSTOMERS                ALUMINIUM                             SWAP
              Current market PRODUCER   Current market        COUNTERPARTY
                 price*                     price*
              ───────────→              ───────────→
```

* Aluminium price

A commodity price-for-interest swap is one whereby the value of a fixed amount of the specified commodity is exchanged for a floating-rate interest payment (usually related to LIBOR) or a fixed-rate interest payment.

Commodity swaps can involve any commodity for which a producer wishes to fix the net price he will receive over time, a user wishes to fix the net price he will pay over time, or a speculator wishes to take a view on the price over time. Some particular areas in which such swaps are transacted are:

- bullion swaps (gold, silver, platinum and palladium)
- energy swaps (crude oil, natural gas and gasoline).

7.4.9 Equity, Volatility, Variance and Dividend Swaps

Equity swaps are swaps whose payments on one or both sides are linked to the performance of equities or an equity index. They are sometimes used to avoid withholding taxes, obtain leverage, or enjoy the returns from ownership without actually owning equity.

This type of swap allows an investor or fund manager to exchange the returns on an equity investment (an individual share, a basket or index) for a return on another non-equity or equity-based investment. Its returns are strictly based on the relative volatility of an individual share or index.

The simplest type of equity swap is a bullet swap, in which all payments are made at maturity.

Example

Investor A swaps $10 million at LIBOR + 0.05% (LIBOR + 5 basis points) against the return of the Hang Seng index over six months. Investor A would receive from investor B any percentage increase in the Hang Seng applied to the $10 million notional (if the Hang Seng declined over the year, not only would investor A receive nothing from investor B, but investor A would have to pay investor B the value of the fall in the index, thus synthesising an actual investment in that index).

Let's assume that in six months' time LIBOR is 5.5% and also assume a swap tenure of precisely 180 days. If that is the case, then the floating leg payer/equity receiver (investor A) would owe (5.5% + 0.05%) x

$10,000,000 x 180/360 = $277,500 to the equity payer/floating leg receiver (investor B).

If over the same period the Hang Seng had risen from 23,100 to 25,250 or 9.3%, investor B would have to pay investor A 9.3% of $10 million = $930,000. But if over that same period the Hang Seng had fallen to 22,100 or by 4.3%, investor A will have to pay investor B a total of $707,500 ($430,000 due to the drop in the index and $277,500 for the LIBOR leg of the swap).

A variance swap takes the concept of an equity swap beyond the movement in equity prices. A variance swap allows an investor to hedge or speculate on the future price movements of an underlying asset, which can be a currency, interest rate, commodity or index. In a variance swap, one side's payment will be linked to the realised variance – the price movements of the specific asset over the life of the swap. These prices are recorded on a daily basis, and are most commonly based on the asset's closing price. The other side of the swap will pay a fixed amount, which is agreed up-front.

The main attraction/advantage of a variance swap is that it provides pure exposure to the volatility of the underlying asset's price as opposed to straight call or put options, which may require delta hedging. It is for this reason that variance swaps are more widely used in the equity markets than volatility swaps. The profit/loss of a variance swap depends solely on the difference between implied and actual volatility. The profit/loss of a variance swap depends solely on the difference between implied and actual volatility.

A dividend swap is a swap that consists of a series of fixed payments, which might be based on current interest rates, while the other series of payments is based on the future dividend payments from an individual share, or group of shares or an equity index. Unlike other equity-related swaps, dividend swaps are based solely on the actual dividend payments, without taking into account the underlying share price or index's level.

The holder of the fixed leg will pay their counterparty a pre-designated fixed payment at each interval. The other party – the holder of the floating leg – will pay their counterparty the total dividends that were paid out by a selected underlying, which can be a single company, a basket of companies, or all the members of an index. The payments are multiplied by a notional number of shares, which is agreed when the swap is first entered into.

Like most swaps, the contract is usually arranged such that its value at signing is zero. This is accomplished by making the value of the fixed leg equal to the value of the floating leg – in other words, the fixed leg will be equal to the average expected dividends over the term of the swap. Therefore the fixed leg of the swap can be used to estimate market forecasts of the dividends that will be paid out by the underlying.

7.4.10 Property and Environmental Swaps

Environmental swaps (also known as 'Debt for Nature' swaps) are usually debt swaps which allow the debtor country (usually a less developed country) to have the amount of its debt reduced by the amount that it spends on key environmental projects. These swaps can be structured on a bilateral or tripartite basis. In the bilateral type of swap, the borrower has its debt reduced directly by the creditor for the amount that has been spent on the pre-agreed environmental issue. In a tripartite-based swap, a third party, such as an international organisation, pays the creditor for the amount that the borrower has spent on the environmental project. One of the main purposes of this type of swap is to reduce the debt problems of poorer countries while promoting conservation/environmental issues.

Property swaps are a variation on a total return swap, where the return/payment of one side is linked to the returns (rental income and/or appreciation in value) of a specific property or group of properties or a development. In return, the buyer of the property return will pay a pre-agreed interest rate. While most property swaps are used by investors to gain exposure to the property sector without the cost of physically buying the properties, this type of swap has become popular as a way of making houses affordable in a rising property market.

7.5 Credit Derivatives

An area of derivative products that has grown significantly in recent years is that of credit derivatives. These are instruments whose value depends on agreed credit events relating to a third-party company, for example, a credit downgrading of that company, or an increase in that company's cost of funds in the market, or a default, or bankruptcy. The purpose of such derivatives is to enable an organisation to protect against unwanted credit exposure, by passing that exposure on to someone else. Credit derivatives can also be used to increase credit exposure, in return for income.

7.5.1 Credit Default Swaps (CDSs)

As outlined earlier, in a credit default swap (CDS), the party buying the credit protection makes a periodic payment (or pays an up-front fee) to the other party. In return, it receives an agreed compensation if there is a credit event relating to some third party or parties.

There are three types of credit default swaps:

- **Basic** – based on a specific asset as reference to the credit event. The reference asset is usually the asset or at least is the pricing guide to the obligation that can be delivered, if that is part of the swap agreement.
- **Index** – based on the movements of an index, either a debt-related or equity/market-based index; the buyer will most likely purchase protection if the underlying index falls below a certain level. This type of CDS is closely related to a total return swap.
- **Basket** – based on the default of a basket of securities, such as a portfolio of several airline debts. The terms of this type of credit default swap could be based on the first to default, or any number within the basket to trigger the credit event. The number of securities in the basket can range from three to 20. The greater the number in the basket, the higher the initial premium, given the wider insurance provided.

Every credit default swap includes the trigger points and notification procedures, such as who has the right to do so, time limits and payment schedules. In most cases, the buyer has exclusive notification/exercise rights, while some swaps have an automatic notification trigger, under certain predefined events. As with all other OTC products, these can be customised to meet the buyer's demands or the nature of reference asset or assets.

Most credit default swaps are priced using the reduced-form pricing approach, in which the credit event process is modelled directly into the swap's price based on the probability of the credit event occurring. The most widely used measure of the probability is what is known as the default swap or asset swap spread, which is the premium being paid to investors over LIBOR or another reference rate to hold the asset. The ongoing premium payments made by the purchaser of the default swap are based on this spread, and most likely change on an ongoing basis over the duration of the swap.

Example

ABC Bank has a portfolio of airline leases and is concerned that higher fuel prices will hurt airline profits. It buys a basket credit default swap that is based on a portfolio of aircraft leases for five airlines from a hedge fund. The terms of the basket swap define a trigger credit event when the second of the airlines applies to restructure their leases. When this occurs, ABC Bank notifies the hedge fund of the trigger; it receives the remaining payments due from all of the leases and the hedge fund now owns the leases and is directly exposed to the five airlines.

7.5.2 Credit-Linked Notes (CLNs)

A credit linked note (CLN) is a form of funded credit derivative. It is structured as a security, with an embedded credit default swap allowing the issuer to transfer a specific credit risk to credit investors. The issuer is not obliged to repay the debt if a specified event occurs. This eliminates a third-party insurance provider. Under this structure, the coupon or price of the note is linked to the performance of a reference asset. It offers borrowers a hedge against credit risk, and gives investors a higher yield on the note for accepting exposure to a specified credit event.

Example

A bank lends money to a company, and at the time it issues a credit-linked note, which is bought by investors. The interest rate on the note is determined by the credit risk of the company. The funds the bank raises by issuing the note are invested in high-quality, low-risk bonds.

If the company remains solvent, the bank is obliged to pay the note in full. But, if the company goes bankrupt or is unable to repay the loan, the note-holders/investors become the company's creditors and take on the original loan. The bank in turn gets compensated by the returns on less-risky bond investments funded by issuing credit linked notes.

7.5.3 Credit Spreads

In a credit spread option, a credit spread is first defined as the difference between the yield on a particular asset (eg, the yield on a particular bond issued by a company) and some agreed benchmark (eg, a swap rate or government Treasury bond yield for the same maturity as the bond).

A strike rate is then set for this spread. In the case of a put option, the option buyer then pays a premium up-front and receives any difference between the actual spread and the agreed strike if the spread rises above that strike.

Example

Bank A lends cash to Company XYZ for five years and then wishes to protect against the credit risk of Company XYZ. Bank A purchases a credit spread put option, where the credit spread is defined as the difference between the yield on a particular bond issued by company XYZ and the yield on a Treasury bond. If the spread rises above an agreed level (the strike), Bank A receives an agreed compensation from Bank B to offset the deterioration in its own asset (its loan to Company XYZ).

Credit spread options are designed to hedge against (for the buyer) or capitalise on (for the seller) changes in credit spreads, ie, differences in their respective yields. A reference security is selected and strike spread and maturity are set. The pay-off is based on whether the actual spot or market spread at the exercise date is over or under the spread on the reference security. The transaction may be either based on changes in a credit spread relative to a risk-free benchmark (eg, LIBOR, gilts or US treasuries) or changes in the relative spread between two credit instruments.

Credit spread options may be structured as an American or European option.

The buyer of a credit spread option would be looking to protect, or hedge, against a widening of the spread between the two securities. If a fund manager holds a large position in a non-EU government debt, he might buy a credit spread option with EU government debt as a reference to protect the portfolio from a deterioration in the fund's holding debt's price in the short term, if elections are expected shortly.

Example

A fund manager had a €50 million position in a ten-year non-EU government bond that yields 7%. The manager is confident that the position has good long-term potential, but is concerned that the upcoming elections might cause short-term spreads to widen. Currently ten-year EU government debt is yielding 4.75%.

The fund manager can buy a three-month €50 million spread option on the 7% non-EU government debt versus a 4.75% EU government bond; the fund's bond is currently trading at a 2.25% spread to its EU benchmark.

The fund manager can lock in the 2.25% spread by buying the credit spread option. It is a European-style option. In three months' time, if the spread has widened beyond 2.25%, the fund will receive the equivalent payment that will effectively lock in that spread.

7.5.4 Credit Default Options and Other Instruments

A credit default option is an option to buy protection (payer option) or sell protection (receiver option) on a credit default swap based on a specific reference credit with a specific maturity. The option is usually a **European-style option**, meaning that it is exercisable only at one date in the future at a specific strike price defined as a coupon on the credit default swap.

Credit default options on single credits are extinguished upon default without any cash flows, other than the upfront premium paid by the buyer of the option. Therefore buying a payer option does not provide protection against an actual default, but only against an increase in the credit spread (higher interest rate/lower price for that single credit). This may explain why these options are very illiquid and therefore less popular. Another key feature is that their prices are usually based on very high implied volatilities. A put option that makes a pay-off if the issuer of a specified reference asset defaults is called a default option.

Collateralised debt obligations (CDOs) are a type of structured asset-backed security (ABS) whose value and payments are derived from a portfolio of fixed-income underlying assets. CDOs' securities are split into different risk classes, or tranches, where 'senior' tranches are considered the safest securities. The interest and principal payments are made based on seniority, therefore the junior tranches pay a higher coupon payment (and interest rate) and are quoted at lower prices to compensate for their higher default risk.

A few analysts and investors are concerned that CDOs, other ABSs and other derivatives spread risk and uncertainty about the value of the underlying assets more widely, rather than reducing risk through diversification. The onset of the 2007–08 financial crisis gave substantial support to this point of view. In fact, before the credit crunch, all of the credit rating agencies failed to adequately account for these large risks (this can be seen in the case of the nationwide collapse of housing values) when rating CDOs and other ABSs.

CDOs vary in structure and underlying assets, but the basic principle is the same. To create a CDO, a corporate entity is constructed to hold assets as collateral and to sell the packages of cash flows to investors.

The following is an example of how a typical CDO is constructed. A special purpose entity (SPE, more commonly referred to as a special purpose vehicle or SPV in European markets) acquires a portfolio of underlying assets. Common examples of the types of these underlying assets include mortgage-backed securities, commercial real estate bonds and/or corporate loans. The SPV then issues bonds (CDOs) with different tranches, and the proceeds are used to purchase the portfolio of underlying assets. The senior CDOs, since they pay a higher price, are paid from the cash flows from the underlying assets before the junior securities and equity securities. Losses are first borne by the equity securities, next by the junior securities, and finally by the senior securities.

The risk and return for a CDO investor depends directly on how the CDO and its tranches are defined, and only indirectly on the performance of the underlying assets. In particular, the investment depends on the assumptions and methods used to define the risk and return of the tranches. CDOs, like all other asset-backed securities, allow the originators of the underlying assets to pass credit risk to another institution or to individual investors. Thus investors must understand how the risk for CDOs is calculated. The issuer of the CDO, typically an investment bank, earns a commission at time of issue and earns management fees during the life of the CDO.

A Collateralised bond obligation (CBO) is a derivative security that creates an investment-grade bond from a pool of junk bonds (high- risk). These junk bonds are typically not investment grade, but, because a CBO includes a pool of several types of credit-quality bonds together, they offer enough diversification to be considered 'investment grade'.

In other words, a CBO is a type of asset-backed security that is composed of the receivables/payments from junk bonds. Issuers of CBOs package and sell their receivables on bonds they own to investors in order to reduce their default risk. Returns on CBOs are considered to be a lower risk than the individual bonds backing them. This is based on the view that it is unlikely that all or even most of the junk bonds will default. They are similar in structure to a collateralised mortgage obligation (CMO), but different in that CBOs represent different levels of credit risk, not different maturities.

A synthetic CDO is a form of CDO that invests in CDSs or other non-cash assets to gain exposure to a portfolio of fixed-income assets, as opposed to a basic (or cash flow) CDO which is backed by a portfolio of underlying assets. As with basic CDOs, synthetic CDOs are typically divided into credit tranches based on the level of credit risk assumed. Initial investments into the CDO are made by the lower tranches, while the senior tranches may not have to make an initial investment.

All tranches will receive periodic payments based on the cash flows from the credit default swaps. If a credit event occurs in the fixed income portfolio, the synthetic CDO and its investors become responsible for the losses, starting from the lowest-rated tranches and working up. Synthetic CDOs can offer extremely high yields to investors. However, investors can also be responsible for much more than their initial investments if several credit events occur in the reference portfolio.

Synthetic CDOs were first created in the late 1990s as a way for large holders of commercial loans to protect their balance sheets without actually selling the loans and potentially harming client relationships. They have become increasingly popular because they tend to have shorter life spans than cash flow CDOs.

7.6 Structured Products

Structured products is a term used to describe a series of investment products that are more commonly known as guaranteed growth bonds, FTSE Capital Protected Bonds and a whole variety of other marketing names.

These types of structured product have been around for some time, and their features and terms differ markedly from product to product. There are ones designed for the mass retail investment market, ones that target the high net worth market only, ones that are for the customers of a single private bank, and even ones designed around individuals for the ultra-wealthy.

Candidates should familiarise themselves with the common types of structured product before reading this section. Some have hard guarantees (known as floors) to prevent capital loss, but others have variable levels of protection and are known as structured capital at risk products (SCaRPs). The terms underlying assets and strategy can all vary widely. Some structured products are traded on exchanges while others are arranged privately for customers. The type of structured product is key to its price, suitability, return on capital and customer expectation.

7.6.1 What are Structured Products?

Structured products are packaged products based on derivatives which generally feature protection of capital if held to maturity but with a degree of participation in the return from a higher-performing, but riskier, underlying asset.

They are created to meet the specific needs of high net worth individuals and general retail investors that cannot be met from standardised financial instruments that are available in the markets.

These products are created by combining underlying assets such as shares, bonds, indices, currencies and commodities with derivatives. This combination can create structures that have significant risk/return and cost-saving advantages compared to what might otherwise be obtainable in the market.

The benefits of structured products can include:

- protection of initial capital investment
- tax-efficient access to fully taxable investments
- enhanced returns
- reduced risk.

Interest in these investments has been growing in recent years albeit in a lower leveraged format than was previously popular prior to the 2008 financial crisis. High net worth investors now use structured products as a way of achieving portfolio diversification. Structured products are also available at the mass retail level, particularly in Europe, where national post offices, and even supermarkets, sell investments on to their customers.

Structured products have increasingly been under the glare of the regulatory spotlight since the late 1990s, when so-called precipice bonds led to millions of investor losses and compensation. Since then, the sector has matured (and grown) somewhat, but the onus on the adviser to carefully assess the value for money and the protection premium of a product (the value/cost for having certainty of capital returned, at the expense of potential growth) cannot be underestimated. Recent Financial Ombudsman Service (FOS) cases also highlight the importance of assessing market levels and the potential for growth/income.

7.6.2 Development of Structured Products

Structured products have their origins in the guaranteed bonds marketed by life offices from the 1970s onwards. In recent years, the providers of these products have explored ever more innovative combinations of underlying asset mixes, which have enabled them to offer a wider range of terms and guarantees.

Structured products have offered a range of benefits to investors and generally have been used either to provide access to stock market growth with capital protection or exposure to an asset, such as gold or currencies, that would not otherwise be achievable from direct investment.

Their major disadvantage has been the fact that they have had to be held to maturity to secure any gains. The gain that an investor would make on, say, a FTSE 100 linked bond would only be determined at maturity, and few bonds offered the option of securing profits earlier. Many structured products are set up to run and mature after multi-year terms (two and a half to six years is commonplace). What if market conditions change or the product otherwise no longer meets the client's expectations? The investment manager should be monitoring these products on a regular basis to make sure that they are performing in line with customer expectations and still constitute value for money. The FCA expects firms to be able to justify investing and holding these products via value-for-money testing.

This need for greater flexibility led to the development of listed structured products, and in 2005 the LSE created a market segment to accommodate both primary and secondary markets in them.

7.6.3 Types of Listed Structured Products

There is a wide range of listed structured products, and the terms of each are open to the discretion of the issuing bank. They are known by a variety of names, including certificates and investment notes.

Despite being traded on the LSE, they are not standardised exchange products and the specification will change from issuer to issuer. One key feature they do have, however, is that they are listed, held and settled in CREST.

They do, however, fall into some broad categories that are considered below.

Index-Based Product Trackers

As the name suggests, a tracker structured product replicates the performance of an underlying asset or index. They are usually long-dated instruments or even undated so that they have an indefinite lifespan.

As a tracker replicates the performance of the underlying asset, its price will move in proportion to it. No dividends are paid on the tracker; instead, any income stream is built into the capital value of the tracker over its lifetime.

Where the underlying asset is, say, an index on an overseas market such as the Standard & Poor's 500, an investor may be exposed to currency movements. Some trackers will therefore incorporate features that ensue the tracker is constantly fully hedged for currency risk.

Tracker funds now directly compete with ETFs. The objectives can be similar but the fund structures, tax and costs can vary. Where structured products come into their own is their ability to be used to track other assets such as commodities and currencies or an index representing the same.

Accelerated Trackers (and Boosters)

With an accelerated tracker, the investor will participate in the growth of the underlying index or asset provided that, when it matures, its value is greater than the initial value. If the asset or index is valued at less than its initial value, then the investor will lose the same amount. If the product pays out an income, which is accelerated (often quoted as a ratio) then this is often referred to as a booster.

Example

An accelerated tracker might provide for the investor to participate in 200% of the growth of an index. If an investor buys £1,000 of an instrument and the index it is based on grows by 10%, then they will receive back their initial investment of £1,000 plus 200% of the growth, which amounts to £200 – that is,

£100 growth x 200% = £200.

If the final value of the underlying asset is, say, 10% less than the issue price, then the investor will receive back the initial price of £1,000 less the change in the underlying asset – 10% or £100 – which amounts to £900.

The investor will usually surrender any right to the underlying income stream form the asset in exchange for the right to participate in any performance.

Reverse Trackers

A reverse tracker is similar to a standard tracker except that, should the underlying asset fall, then the value of the tracker will rise. These trackers are also referred to as bear certificates.

Digitals

A digital is a structured product/note that has two reference indices instead of just one as the basis for the payout.

Capital-Protected Trackers

Capital-protected trackers, as the name suggests, allow investors to gain some exposure to the growth of an underlying asset or index while providing protection for the capital invested.

The amount of participation in any growth, and the protection over the capital invested, will vary from product to product and is obtained by surrendering any right to income from the underlying asset.

For example, an instrument might be issued to track the performance of the FTSE 100 and provide participation of 140% of any growth but with 100% capital protection. If the FTSE 100 index is at a higher level at maturity, then the investor will receive back the initial price plus 140% of the growth over that period. If the index is lower than at the start, then the capital protection kicks in and the investor will receive back the initial price.

Structured Capital at Risk Products (SCaRPs)

SCaRPs are products like those above but have variable (or floating) floors rather than a fixed capital protection. Such products often pay out based on barriers, which determine the level of gain or loss. The rate of payout can change as it reaches different barriers, be 1 for 1 (1:1) or a multiple like 1.5:1, 2:1, 3:1 and so on.

OTC Structured Products

An index-linked note is an instrument whose return is determined by a specific index. This index could be an equity index, which can be based on the performance of a single share, or a basket of shares, or a market index, such as the FTSE 100 or S&P 500 index or, for a bond/debt instrument, an inflation index such as CPI (Consumer Prices Index) or RPI (Retail Prices Index). For example, for UK-issued index-linked gilts in 1981, both the semi-annual coupon payments and their redemption value were linked to the UK RPI.

An equity-linked note is a debt instrument whose yield is determined by the performance of an equity product. A company might link the return of its debt to the performance of its share price as a method of lowering the base interest rate.

A capital-protected product (which is also known as a capital-protected borrowing) is generally associated with the purchase and holding of shares or other financial securities, such as single warrants. This type of financial product allows an investor to borrow money or obtain credit to purchase shares or other types of financial securities. These shares and financial securities purchased then become security for the loan. Under the terms of the financial product, if the shares or financial securities fall in value below their purchase price the purchaser can transfer the shares or securities back (a put option), or surrender them to the lender to meet all outstanding obligations under the loan (a limited recourse loan). Therefore, the purchaser/investor is guaranteed a minimum price/value for the shares/securities that are part of the capital-protected product. In effect, it is a loan with an embedded put option for the financed securities.

Capital-protected loans, generally, have higher interest rates and/or additional fees.

7.6.4 Trading and Settlement

Listed structured products will usually be structured as an instrument, such as a zero coupon bond, and will be firstly offered in the primary market where they are made available to investors.

Chapter Ten
The Securities Market Structure

1.	The Structure of the UK Securities Market	475
2.	Issuance: Primary, Secondary and Dual Listing	480
3.	Issuing and Admission to Recognised Investment Exchanges (RIEs)	483
4.	Requirements of NEX, AIM and the Official List	489
5.	Issuing Securities Without a Prospectus	492
6.	Exchange and Over-the-Counter (OTC) Trading	495
7.	Markets for Government and Corporate Bonds	500
8.	Market Abuse Regime (MAR)	505
9.	Alternative Trading Venues	513
10.	Structure of International Markets – Developed and Emerging	521
11.	Clearing, Settlement and Custody Process	529
12.	The Role of International Central Securities Depositories	535
13.	Custody of Assets	537

The Securities Market Structure

Learning Outcome

Be able to explain the securities market structure, trading venues and custody and settlement processes

1. The Structure of the UK Securities Market

Learning Objective

10.1 Demonstrate an understanding of the structure of the domestic market: summarising primary, secondary and dual listing and explain the process of issuing and gaining admission to a recognised investment exchange, distinguishing between the requirements of NEX, the AIM market and the Official List and issuing securities without a prospectus; discriminate between on exchange and over-the-counter (OTC) trading and detail the transparency obligations; Illustrate markets for trading government and corporate bonds; stock lending and CREST

1.1 The UK and the London Stock Exchange (LSE)

1.1.1 The UK is a Major Financial Centre

The Global Financial Centres Index (GFCI) is published by the Z/Yen Group ltd. It also publishes an annual survey of the leading financial centres in the world (the most current version of its survey can be found on their website at http://www.longfinance.net/Publications/GFCI23.pdf.

In its latest 2018 survey, the GFCI shows London is still the leading financial centre overall, although its lead over New York has narrowed, with Hong Kong close behind.

The listing for the centres are compiled based upon various metrics related to the volume of transactions, amount of capital raised and traded, and various qualitative issues which are determined by opinion-researching and questionnaires.

1.1.2 The London Stock Exchange (LSE)

There are over 2,600 companies listed on the LSE (the UK Main Market, the International Main Market, the Professional Securities Market (PSM) and AIM (formerly known as the Alternative Investment Market), with a combined market capitalisation of approximately £4.4 trillion.

Normal trading sessions are from 08:00 to 16:30 Monday to Friday, except holidays declared by the LSE in advance.

The LSE operates in the following primary areas:

- **Equity markets and primary issuance**
    - The LSE enables companies from around the world to raise capital. There are four primary markets; Main Market, AIM, the PSM and the Specialist Fund Market (SFM).
- **Trading services**
    - The LSE provides an active and liquid secondary, highly active market for trading in a range of securities, including UK and international equities, covered warrants, exchange-traded funds (ETFs), exchange-traded commodities (ETCs), real estate investment trusts (REITs), fixed interest, contracts for differences (CFDs), depositary receipts and derivatives.
- **Information services**
    - The LSE provides real-time prices, news and other financial information to the global financial community.
- **Multilateral trading facilities and derivatives**
    - The LSE has a trading infrastructure platform known as 'Millennium Exchange' to provide a capability for processing trades from multilateral trading venues. To this extent, the LSE has begun to resemble the much more distributed nature of an OTC market; however, the trades which take place on the platform still have to meet all of the LSE's transparency obligations as required by the Financial Conduct Authority (FCA) for a registered investment exchange. The ability to process a range of derivatives has also been expanded by the use of this trading platform, and designed to bring the cash equity and derivatives markets closer together. It is fair to say that the bulk of the custom derivatives business is conducted 'off-exchange' by the network of dealers and investment banks that constitute the swaps market.

1.2 Regulatory Structure of the UK Market

The main regulatory, supervisory and trade body framework supporting UK financial markets consists of the following:

- The Bank of England (BoE), including the Financial Policy Committee (FPC).
- The Companies Act 2006.
- The Financial Conduct Authority (FCA).
- The Prudential Regulation Authority (PRA).
- The UK Listing Authority (UKLA).
- HM Treasury.
- The Takeover Panel (POTAM).
- Exchange membership and rules.

The regulatory framework that underlies the way that the financial markets, in general in the UK, and on the LSE in particular, operate includes oversight and compliance with the following fundamental principles:

- Company law – in particular the various Companies Acts and especially the Companies Act 2006.
- Regulations and requirements of the FCA.
- Supervision and vigilance by HM Treasury.
- POTAM.
- Rules of membership laid down by an exchange, such as the LSE rulebook.

The Securities Market Structure

The Companies Act details the requirements for companies generally, such as the requirement to prepare annual accounts, the need to have accounts audited and for annual general meetings (AGMs). Of particular significance to the LSE are the Companies Act requirements for a company to become a public limited company (plc), since this status is one of the requirements for a company to be listed and traded on the exchange.

There have been many versions of the Companies Act over the years, but the 2006 Act provided, at the time, a complete overhaul of the previously enacted legislation. It contains 1,300 sections, 16 schedules and covers many of the key areas including:

- company names
- memorandum of association
- articles of association
- share capital and maintenance of capital
- meetings
- communication with shareholders
- directors' duties
- company secretary and company record, and
- annual reports and accounts.

1.2.1 Financial Conduct Authority (FCA)

The FCA has to give its authorisation before an exchange is allowed to operate in the UK. It has granted recognition to the LSE and, by virtue of this, the exchange is described as a recognised investment exchange (RIE). In granting recognition, the FCA assesses whether the exchange has sufficient systems and controls to run a market. Furthermore, the FCA (through its division – the UK Listing Authority (UKLA)) lays down the detailed rules that have to be met before companies are admitted to the official 'list' that enables their shares to be traded on the exchange.

In April 2013, changes to the UK regulatory structure formally took effect. The UK Government established a macro-prudential regulator, the FPC (within the BoE) to monitor and respond to systemic risks, and transferred responsibility for prudential regulation to a focused new regulator, the PRA, which was established as a subsidiary of the BoE.

1.2.2 UK Listing Authority (UKLA)

The UKLA is the body responsible for setting and administering the listing requirements and continuing obligations for plcs seeking and obtaining a full listing on the LSE. The FSA was appointed as the UKLA in May 2000, before the FCA assumed its responsibilities in 2013.

Each jurisdiction has its own rules and regulations for companies seeking a listing, and continuing obligations for those already listed. The formal description of the UKLA is that it is the competent authority for listing – making the decisions as to which companies' shares and bonds (including gilts) can be admitted to be traded on the LSE.

The UKLA sets the rules relating to becoming listed on the LSE, including the implementation of any relevant EU directives. The LSE is responsible for the operation of the exchange, including the trading of securities on the secondary market, although the UKLA can suspend the listing of particular securities and, therefore, remove their secondary market trading activity on the exchange.

In a similar way in the US, the Securities and Exchange Commission (SEC) requires companies seeking a listing on US exchanges (such as the New York Stock Exchange (NYSE) and Nasdaq) to register certain details with it first. Once listed, companies are then required to file regular reports with the SEC, particularly in relation to their trading performance and financial situation.

1.2.3 HM Treasury

Her Majesty's Treasury (commonly known as HM Treasury) is the economics and public finance ministry, with overall responsibility for fiscal policy as well as providing a supervisory role for the entire financial framework in the UK. It is headed by the Chancellor of the Exchequer, considered to be the most powerful office in British politics after the Prime Minister.

1.2.4 The Takeover Panel (POTAM)

The UK supervisory authority that carries out the regulatory functions required under the EU Takeover Directive is the Takeover Panel, also known as the Panel on Takeovers and Mergers ('the Panel' or 'POTAM'). The Panel's requirements are set out in the Takeover Code that consists of six general principles, and a number of detailed rules (see also section 8.7).

The Code is designed principally to ensure that shareholders are treated fairly and are not denied an opportunity to decide on the merits of a takeover. Furthermore, the Code ensures that shareholders of the same class are afforded equivalent treatment by an offeror. In short, the Code provides an orderly framework within which takeovers are conducted, and is designed to assist in promoting the integrity of the financial markets.

The Code is not concerned with the financial or commercial advantages or disadvantages of a takeover. These are matters for the company and its shareholders. Nor is the Code concerned with competition policy, which is the responsibility of government and other bodies.

Each of the six general principles are reproduced below. Although the detail of each principle is probably outside the syllabus, it is useful to be able to review the principles fully to appreciate the spirit of the Code. At its broadest, the Code simply requires fair play between all interested parties:

- All holders of the securities of an offeree company of the same class must be afforded equivalent treatment; moreover, if a person acquires control of a company, the other holders of securities must be protected.
- The holders of the securities of an offeree company must have sufficient time and information to enable them to reach a properly informed decision on the bid; when it advises the holders of securities, the board of the offeree company must give its views on the effects of implementation of the bid on employment, conditions of employment and the locations of the company's places of business.

The Securities Market Structure

- The board of an offeree company must act in the best interests of the company as a whole and must not deny the holders of securities the opportunity to decide on the merits of the bid.
- False markets must not be created in the securities of the offeree company, or the offeror company, or of any other company concerned by the bid in such a way that the rise or fall of the prices of the securities becomes artificial and the normal functioning of the markets is distorted.
- An offeror must announce a bid only after ensuring that they can fulfil in full any cash consideration, if such is offered, and after taking all reasonable measures to secure the implementation of any other type of consideration.
- An offeree company must not be hindered in the conduct of its affairs for longer than is reasonable by a bid for its securities.

1.2.5 Trade Associations and Professional Bodies

British Bankers' Association (BBA)

The BBA was the leading association for the UK banking and financial services sector, with 200 members from over 50 countries, supporting and promoting policies and initiatives on the full range of UK and international banking issues and engaging with a number of associated professional firms. In July 2017, it merged with several other bodies to form UK Finance.

The Investment Association (IA)

In 2014, the former Investment Management Association (IMA) merged with the Investment Affairs Division of the Association of British Insurers (ABI) to create the Investment Association (IA). The IA is the trade body for the UK's approximate £6.9 trillion asset management industry.

The Chartered Institute for Securities & Investment (CISI)

According to its website

> 'The Chartered Institute for Securities & Investment is the leading professional body for securities, investment, wealth and financial planning.'

Formed in 1992 by LSE practitioners, the CISI has more than 45,000 members in 104 countries. It sets almost 40,000 examinations in 80 countries, covering a range of vocational qualifications.

Personal Investment Management & Financial Advice Association (PIMFA)

PIMFA, previously the Wealth Management Association (WMA), is the trade association for firms that provide investment management and financial advice to help individuals and families plan for their financial life journeys.

According to its website, PIMFA's mission is to create an optimal operating environment so that its member firms can focus on delivering the best service to their clients, and provide responsible stewardship for their long-term savings and investments.

Their objectives are as follows:

1. To represent the diverse range of firms in the investment and financial advice industry with a unified voice.
2. To provide industry thought leadership, consolidating our extensive technical insights and expertise in research and policy work.
3. To lead the debate on policy and regulatory recommendations to ensure an optimal operating environment for firms and clients, maintaining the UK's position as a leading global centre of excellence.
4. Through our advocacy work, we promote the industry as a key catalyst to develop a culture of savings and investment in the UK.
5. To promote a greater understanding of the sector and its role as a beneficial force in transforming the way people save and invest for the future.
6. To facilitate dialogue across industry stakeholders, while developing best-practice guidance.

2. Issuance: Primary, Secondary and Dual Listing

Learning Objective

10.1 Demonstrate an understanding of the structure of the domestic market: summarising primary, secondary and dual listing and explain the process of issuing and gaining admission to a recognised investment exchange, distinguishing between the requirements of NEX, the AIM market and the Official List and issuing securities without a prospectus; discriminate between on exchange and over-the-counter (OTC) trading and detail the transparency obligations; Illustrate markets for trading government and corporate bonds

2.1 Overview of Security Issuance

Recognised stock exchanges, such as the LSE in the UK and the NYSE in the US, are marketplaces for issuing securities and for facilitating the trading of those securities via the trading and market-making activities of their member firms. All stock exchanges provide both a primary and a secondary market.

2.1.1 Primary Issues

The primary market, or the new issues market, is where securities are issued for the first time. The primary markets exist to enable issuers of securities, such as companies, to raise capital and enable the surplus funds held by potential investors to be matched with investment opportunities the issuers offer. It is a crucial source of funding. The terminology often used is that companies 'float' on the stock exchange when they first access the primary market. The process that the companies go through when they float is often called the initial public offering (IPO). Companies can use a variety of ways to achieve flotation, such as offers for investors to subscribe for their shares (offers for subscription).

Offerings can be underwritten by an investment bank which acts to guarantee the sale of a new securities issue by purchasing the securities for resale to the public. Alternatively, the shares sold in an offering may be sold on a 'best efforts' basis by the manager of the IPO. In this situation there are no guarantees that an IPO will succeed in selling all of the shares being offered; if markets are going through periods of adversity and turmoil, for example, it is common for an IPO to be withdrawn. IPOs are covered in section 3.1.3.

A large IPO is usually underwritten by a 'syndicate' of investment banks led by one or more major investment banks (lead underwriter). Upon selling the shares, the underwriters keep a commission based on a percentage of the value of the shares sold (called the gross spread). Usually, the lead underwriters, ie, the underwriters selling the largest proportions of the IPO, take the highest commissions – up to 5.5% in some cases.

The secondary market, not to be confused with secondary issuance, is where existing securities are traded between investors, and the stock exchanges provide a variety of systems to assist in this, such as the LSE's SETS system that is used to trade the largest companies' shares. These systems provide investors with liquidity, giving them the ability to sell their securities if they wish. The secondary market activity also results in the ongoing provision of liquidity to investors via the exchange's member firms.

2.1.2 Secondary Issues

A secondary issue is an offering of shares by a shareholder of the company (as opposed to the company itself, which is a primary offering).

There are two types of secondary issue. A non-dilutive secondary issue is a sale of securities, in which a shareholder of the company sells a large portion of their shareholding. The proceeds from this sale are then paid to the shareholder who is selling their shares.

A dilutive secondary issue involves the company creating new shares and selling these to the public. It is also known as a follow-on offer or a subsequent offer.

2.1.3 Issuing, Listing and Quotation

To offer shares for sale to the public via an IPO, a UK company must be a plc. The kinds of IPOs that can be conducted and the listing requirements of the exchanges vary, and in the case of a large corporation the most likely route for a UK company would be seek a full listing on the main market of the LSE. Mid-cap stocks can now be sold in the high growth segment (HGS) of the LSE, which is part of the LSE's Main Market. It is a transitional segment designed to attract high growth, mid-sized UK and European companies aspiring to an Official Listing over time. If the company is smaller or has less of trading a track record it may join the less closely regulated AIM that is also operated by the LSE.

Companies seeking a full listing on the LSE have to meet stringent entry criteria (see section 3.1.1).

These criteria are known as the Listing Rules and are administered by the FCA in its capacity as the UKLA. They appear in the FCA Handbook: https://www.handbook.fca.org.uk/handbook/LR.pdf

The listing rules are relaxed for technology companies or companies that invest heavily in research and development (R&D) that seek a full listing but lack a three-year trading record. Technology companies often require development capital and can apply for a listing on a separate segment of the LSE known as 'techMARK'.

The advantages to a company of obtaining a full listing include:

- raising its public profile
- increasing the liquidity and marketability of its shares so that they can be more easily traded, and
- gaining easier and less expensive access to new capital.

The disadvantages, however, include:

- the costs and increased accountability associated with obtaining and maintaining a full listing as a result of greater disclosure and compliance requirements
- relinquishing an element of control, and
- becoming a potential takeover target.

Once a company has undertaken a listed offering its share prices will be quoted in the normal fashion for all listed companies, ie, with a bid and ask quotation, and the shares can be traded on a variety of platforms.

2.1.4 Dual Listing

Dual listing refers to the fact that many securities are listed on more than one exchange. This can be the case when a company's shares are listed and traded internationally both on the LSE and another exchange overseas, such as in the case of Vodafone and HSBC. HSBC shares are listed in London and Hong Kong. Its American depositary receipts (ADRs) are listed on the NTSE. Vodaphone has a secondary listing on Nasdaq.

Dual listing can also refer to stocks trading on more than one exchange within the same jurisdiction. Many stocks are traded on the NYSE or the American stock exchanges and on one or more of the regional exchanges. Although dual listing theoretically should improve the liquidity of a stock, thereby benefiting investors, most dual-listed securities trade chiefly on one exchange.

One consequence of a dual listing for multi-national corporations is in reference to the Sarbanes-Oxley Act (often referred to as SOX).

Passed in 2002 by the US Congress, the Act's objective is:

'to protect investors by improving the accuracy and reliability of corporate disclosures made pursuant to the securities laws, and for other purposes.'

It applies to US public companies and their global subsidiaries. It also applies to foreign companies that have shares listed on US stock exchanges.

As a result of their dual listing, SOX therefore applies to some of the UK's largest companies by market capitalisation, such as British Petroleum (BP), HSBC, Prudential, Royal Dutch Shell and Vodafone, as well as many other international companies.

Exercise 1

Outline one benefit and one potential drawback of a company obtaining a dual listing.

The answers to this exercise can be found at the end of this chapter.

3. Issuing and Admission to Recognised Investment Exchanges (RIEs)

Learning Objective

10.1 Demonstrate an understanding of the structure of the domestic market: summarising primary, secondary and dual listing and explain the process of issuing and gaining admission to a recognised investment exchange, distinguishing between the requirements of NEX, the AIM market and the Official List and issuing securities without a prospectus; discriminate between on exchange and over-the-counter (OTC) trading and detail the transparency obligations; Illustrate markets for trading government and corporate bonds

3.1 Overview of Security Issuance

As mentioned earlier, recognised stock exchanges, such as the LSE in the UK and the NYSE in the US, are marketplaces for issuing securities and for facilitating the trading of those securities via the trading and market making activities of their member firms. All stock exchanges provide both a primary and a secondary market.

Listing requirements are the set of conditions imposed by a given stock exchange upon companies that want to be listed on that exchange. Such conditions sometimes include minimum number of shares outstanding, minimum market capitalisation, and minimum annual income.

3.1.1 Requirements by Stock Exchange

Companies have to meet the requirements of a listing exchange in order to have their shares listed and traded there. The requirements vary by stock exchange and for a complete listing of the requirements, which include different permutations of minimum criteria, the reader is advised to check the websites for each of the three major exchanges itemised below. However, the essential requirements are summarised as follows:

LSE

The main market of the LSE has a variety of listing requirements, some of which are fairly specialised, but the principal ones are as follows:

- The market value of the company's issued share capital, or market capitalisation, must be at least £700,000, of which no less than 25% must be made freely available to the investing public to ensure an active market in the shares. This 25% is known as the free float.
- The market value of any company bond issues must be at least £200,000.
- Should a company bring both debt and equity to the market, the total value must, therefore, be at least £900,000.
- All securities issued by the company must be freely transferable, that is, third-party approval to deal in these securities must not be required.
- The company must publish a statement showing that it believes it has sufficient working capital to last at least the next 12 months.

New York Stock Exchange (NYSE)

To be listed on the NYSE there are different methods of meeting the minimum requirements. In broad terms the following apply:

- **Distribution and Size Criteria**
  Under these criteria a firm wishing to list on the NYSE must meet all three of the following:
  - There must be a minimum of 400 separately identifiable holders of the shares.
  - There must be 1,100,000 public shares outstanding in the US.
  - The market value of the public shares has to be at least $100 million.
- **Stock Price Criteria**
  All issuers must have as a minimum a $4 stock price at the time of listing.
- **Financial Criteria**
  All companies seeking a listing must meet one of the following standards:
- **Earnings Test**
  - aggregate pre-tax income for the last three years $10 million
  - minimum in each of the two most recent years $2 million
  - each of last three years must be positive.
- **Valuation with Cash Flow**
  - global market capitalisation $200 million.

Nasdaq Stock Market

Nasdaq has three sets of listing requirements. Each company must meet at least one of the three requirement sets, as well as the main rules for all companies.

Listing Requirements for All Companies

Each company must have a minimum of 1,250,000 publicly traded shares upon listing, excluding those held by officers, directors or any beneficial owners of more than 10% of the company. In addition, the minimum bid price at time of listing must be greater than $4, and there must be at least three market makers for the stock. Companies must also have at least 400 round lot (100 shares) shareholders.

In addition to these requirements, companies must meet all of the criteria under at least one of the following standards:

- **Listing Standard No. 1** – the company must have aggregate pre-tax earnings in the prior three years of at least $11 million, in the prior two years at least $2.2 million, and no one year in the prior three years can have a net loss.
- **Listing Standard No. 2** – the company must have a minimum aggregate cash flow of at least $27.5 million for the past three fiscal years, with no negative cash flow in any of those three years. In addition, its average market capitalisation over the prior 12 months must be at least $550 million, and revenues in the previous fiscal year must be at least $110 million.
- **Listing Standard No. 3** – companies can be removed from the cash flow requirement of Standard No. 2 if the average market capitalisation over the past 12 months is at least $850 million, and revenues over the prior fiscal year are at least $90 million.
- **Listing Standard No. 4** – companies must have a market capitalisation of $160 million, total assets of at least $80 million and stockholders' equity of $55 million.

3.1.2 UK Listing Authority (UKLA)

The FCA, when it acts as the competent authority under Part VI of the Financial Services and Markets Act 2000 (FSMA), is referred to as the UK Listing Authority or UKLA. In this role, the FCA is a securities regulator, focused on the companies which issue the securities traded in financial markets.

By making and enforcing the Disclosure and Transparency Rules, the Listing Rules and the Prospectus Rules, the FCA aims to protect investors and foster appropriate standards of transparency, conduct, shareholder rights and due diligence.

3.1.3 Initial Public Offering (IPO)

For the issuer, the key benefit of an IPO, over other capital-raising methods, is that IPOs can raise substantial sums of capital and generate favourable publicity for the issuing companies. The money raised in the form of an IPO is known as risk capital and the company assets are not encumbered or hypothecated in the same manner as if the capital was raised via a debt offering.

For investors, the benefit of buying shares in a new issue is that, assuming adequate due diligence (ie, fully researched the business plans and risk disclosures in the offering document), they can diversify existing portfolios with shares in a new company.

The early-stage investors who purchased shares in the IPOs of companies such as Microsoft, Intel, Apple and Google could have amassed fortunes if they had retained their shares. The extraordinary capital gains seen in the shares of such companies represents one of the most exciting opportunities for returns in the financial markets.

Of course not all IPOs lead to such success stories. A company may only perform in a mediocre fashion following an IPO, and, as was seen during the 'dot com' mania of the late 1990s many internet ventures, with little or no revenues, were taken to market in a bubble-like mania of IPOs and many of these companies have subsequently disappeared. Others were absorbed by acquiring companies, and, in many cases, the purchasers of shares in an IPO were eventually issued shares in the company which acquired the original issuers. In some cases the returns from these acquisitions have also produced extraordinary returns.

Stages of an IPO

There are three broad stages to an IPO:

- **The decision** – the issuing company (in conjunction with its advisers, particularly the investment bank) makes a decision to raise capital via an IPO. This will involve careful consideration of the pros and cons of a public offer.
- **The preparation of the prospectus** – this is the necessary document that must accompany an IPO, involving the whole team of advisers, including the investment bank, reporting accountants and legal advisers.
  In the US, a prospectus has to be filed with the SEC and strictly follow prescribed procedures and full risk disclosures in accordance with regulations covering new issues. In the UK similar policies are in place and regulated by the FCA.
- **The sale of securities** – the investment bank will manage the sale and may well establish a syndicate of co-managers to assist in selling the securities to its clients.

3.1.4 Structure of the Offering

Consider a hypothetical example of how the IPO is structured in the case of a relatively new technology company, which intends to sell one million shares of its stock in a public offering through an investment banking firm (or group of firms which are known as the syndicate), chosen by the company as underwriter(s).

The underwriters act as broker for these shares and find buyers among their clients. A price for the shares is agreed by the sellers (the company's owners and directors) and the buyers (the underwriters and their clients). A part of the responsibility of the lead-underwriter in running a successful offering is to ensure that once the shares begin to trade publicly, they do not fall below the offering price.

When a public offering trades below its offering price, it is said to have 'broke issue' or 'broke syndicate bid'. This creates the perception of an unstable or undesirable offering, which can lead to further selling and hesitant buying of the shares. To manage this situation, the underwriter initially oversells ('shorts') to its clients the offering by an additional 15% of the offering size. In this example, the underwriter would sell 1.15 million shares of stock to its clients. When the offering is priced and those 1.15 million shares are 'effective' (become eligible for public trading), the underwriter is able to support and stabilise the offering price bid (known as the 'syndicate bid') by buying back the extra 15% of shares (150,000 shares in this example) in the market at or below the offer price). It does this without assuming the market risk of being 'long' of extra 15% of shares in its own account, as it is simply 'covering' (closing out) its 15% oversell short.

The Securities Market Structure

An IPO is usually structured with a base number of shares that the company is planning to issue. However, the issuing company may also reserve the right to increase the number of shares that it issues, if significant levels of demand would remain unsatisfied, if only the base number of shares were issued. The option to increase the number of shares is referred to as a greenshoe.

Greenshoe

A greenshoe option is a clause contained in the underwriting agreement of an IPO. The greenshoe option, also referred to as an over-allotment provision, allows the underwriting syndicate to buy up to an additional 15% of the shares at the offering price if public demand for the shares exceeds expectations and the stock trades above its offering price.

The greenshoe option provides stability and liquidity to a public offering where the offering has such strong demand (as was the case for a number of the 'dot com' IPOs of the 1990s) that the price of the stock immediately goes up and stays above the offering price.

In the hypothetical example above, the underwriter has oversold the offering by 15% and is now technically short those shares. If it were to go into the open market to buy back that 15%, the company would be buying back those shares at a higher price than it sold them at, and would incur a loss on the transaction.

The over-allotment (greenshoe) option allows the company to grant the underwriters the option to take from the company up to 15% of additional shares than the original offering size at the offering price.

If the underwriters can buy back all of its oversold shares at the offering price, it would not need to exercise any of the greenshoe. But if it can buy back only some of the shares before the stock rises, then it would exercise a partial greenshoe for the rest of the shares. And, if it cannot buy back any of the oversold 15% of shares at the offering price ('syndicate bid') because the stock immediately rises and stays up, then it can completely cover its 15% short position by exercising the full greenshoe.

3.1.5 Underwritten versus Best Efforts

Underwriting the offer is generally the responsibility of the investment bank(s) and they typically arrange 'firm' underwriting when there are guarantees in place to buy the securities.

An IPO is underwritten when there is a firm undertaking by the investment bank(s) conducting the offering, that all of the offering will be fully subscribed. In other words, the underwriting bank(s) guarantee that any shortfall by subscribers will be purchased by the bank(s) for their own account.

Investment banks may not provide a 'firm' undertaking to place all of the securities on behalf of their clients. Instead, the lead-underwriter along with the co-managers of the offer may provide a 'best efforts' underwriting in which they will do their best to sell the shares involved in the offering but with no formal guarantee that this will be achieved. In practice, the managers of the underwriting are not committing to purchase any unplaced securities for their own account in an unconditional manner. If the underwriter and the co-managers insert the 'best efforts' undertaking, and there is a failure to complete a full sale of the offering, there is a risk to the underwriter of reputational damage, which could result in the underwriter not being invited to participate in future IPOs.

3.1.6 Price Stabilisation

Stabilisation prevents a substantial fall in the value of securities when a large number of new securities are issued. The lead manager of the issue agrees to support the price by buying back the newly issued securities in the market if the market price falls below a certain, predefined level. This is an attempt to give the market a chance to adjust to the increased supply of securities, by stabilising the market price.

By increasing the demand for the securities in the market at the same time as more securities become available, the price should remain more stable. This will mean the issuing company's securities appear less volatile, and existing investors will be less likely to begin panic selling, creating a downward spiral in the security's price. The securities that are bought back by the lead manager of the issue will then be sold back into the market over time.

There are strict rules laid down by regulators regarding stabilisation practices. For example, the FCA restricts the stabilisation period and requires disclosure to the market that stabilisation is happening, and that the market price may not be a representative one because of the stabilisation activities.

3.1.7 Methods of Issuing Ordinary Shares

Shares issued by companies which are listed on a stock market normally have certain rights (usually not preferential). There are many reasons why a listed company may issue more shares; the most common is to raise more capital share. Where companies are issuing shares to the public for the first time, there can be many reasons why it is doing so and there are a number of ways that it can do this, eg, public offers, offers for sale, offers for subscription, placings and introductions.

Public Offers

Also called an initial public offer (IPO) a public offer is a relatively expensive method for issuing shares to the public; for example, offer prospectuses, documentation and advice are all required (it is commonly used by new companies seeking large amounts of capital to expand/consolidate).

- **Offers for Sale** – the public are asked to subscribe for shares at a price decided by the public. The company will sell the shares for the price which allows all (or most) shares to be sold. Anyone offering less than the final price will receive no shares and, if someone offered more, they will only have to pay the final price.
- **Subscription Offers** – the public are asked to subscribe for shares being issued by a company at a fixed price.

Placings

With placings, shares are offered to specific individuals but are not being offered to the general public. The idea is to target specific investors who are likely to be interested in investing in the company. This is a less expensive method of issuing shares as the full offer documentation is not required.

Introductions

Introductions are used where there are already a large number of shares in the hands of numerous investors, Ie, the rules for listing with regard to ownership are already complied with. Therefore, the shares can be listed without too much administrative formality. It should be noted that no new shares need be issued as this time, but this will allow a market for the shares to be created and possible future issues will be easier to arrange as a market price will exist.

4. Requirements of NEX, AIM and the Official List

Learning Objective

10.1 Demonstrate an understanding of the structure of the domestic market: summarising primary, secondary and dual listing and explain the process of issuing and gaining admission to a recognised investment exchange, distinguishing between the requirements of NEX, the AIM market and the official list and issuing securities without a prospectus; discriminate between on exchange and over-the-counter (OTC) trading and detail the transparency obligations; Illustrate markets for trading government and corporate bonds

4.1 The London Stock Exchange (LSE)

The LSE began life in 1773 when traders who regularly met to buy and sell the shares of joint stock companies in Jonathan's Coffee House voted to change the name of the coffee house to that of the London Stock Exchange.

The LSE is Europe's largest stock exchange; in the rapidly changing financial markets, the LSE has to continue evolving to adapt to the new platforms and technologies of a very competitive global marketplace.

The LSE is a Recognised Investment Exchange (RIE) and, as such, is responsible for:

- providing a primary and secondary market for equities and fixed interest securities
- supervising its member firms
- regulating the markets it operates
- recording all transactions, or bargains, executed on the exchange
- disseminating price-sensitive company information received by its Regulatory News Service (RNS) and distributed through commercial quote vendors, also known as secondary information providers (SIPs).

The LSE operates both a primary and secondary market. As discussed elsewhere, in its guise as a primary market, the LSE will provide facilities for new issuance of securities by existing listed companies and new companies which have satisfied the listing criteria explained below.

In its capacity as a secondary market, the role which comprises the majority of its day-to-day activities, the LSE provides a marketplace, nowadays almost exclusively an electronic market, for the dealing (trading) of a variety of securities.

The LSE provides real-time market information to various organisations around the world which subscribe to the data feeds and trading facilities of the firm. The LSE's website outlines the following three key considerations with regard to membership of the exchange:

4.1.1 Eligibility for Membership

Membership is available to investment firms and credit institutions authorised in the European Economic Area (EEA). You may also be eligible if you are not EEA-regulated and should speak with the membership team for further details. Members may be eligible for stamp duty reserve tax (SDRT) exemption and may apply for this as part of their application.

4.1.2 Connectivity

Firms can connect directly to the exchange's markets. The exchange currently offers several types of connectivity options with varying levels of management and performance. These range from full host-to-host solutions to vendor access network connections.

4.1.3 Clearing and Settlement

If you choose to connect directly to the exchange, you will need to have in place appropriate clearing and settlement arrangements. Members of the LSE benefit from an efficient and competitive clearing and settlement infrastructure across its domestic and international markets.

The major securities which are traded daily on the LSE are:

- shares of domestic listed public companies or plcs which are of two main varieties:
    - companies with a full listing
    - smaller UK plcs admitted to AIM
- exchange-traded funds (ETFs) and other new investment products on its extraMARK exchange
- international equities
- domestic corporate bonds
- UK Treasury issuance, including gilts
- local authority fixed-interest securities
- international bonds, including eurobonds.

4.1.4 Full Listing

The UK Listing Rules and the criteria required by firms are outlined in section 8.8 of this chapter.

The Securities Market Structure

4.2 AIM (Alternative Investment Market)

Gaining admission to AIM is far less demanding than obtaining a full listing, as a minimum market capitalisation, free float and past trading record is not required.

Most AIM companies tend to be those in the early stages of development, typically operating in growth industries or in niche sectors, with a view to applying for a full listing once they become more established.

The criteria to be satisfied to gain admission to AIM include:

- The company will have to appoint a nominated adviser (NOMAD) to advise the directors of their responsibilities in complying with AIM rules. The NOMAD will also have to advise the firm on how to prepare a prospectus that accompanies the company's application for admission to AIM.
- The company will also have to appoint a nominated broker to make a market and facilitate trading in the company's shares, as well as provide ongoing information about the company to interested parties.

4.3 Listing Rules and Compliance

Once companies have obtained a listing they are subject to a strict set of rules and regulations set by the UKLA known as continuing obligations.

Among other things, these require a company to promptly make all price-sensitive information public and issue the annual and interim report and accounts to shareholders within a set timeframe.

Information is price-sensitive if it might be expected to move the company's share price in a material way, once in the public domain. This includes informing details of any significant change to a company's current or forecasted trading prospects, dividend announcements, directors' dealings and any notifiable interests in the company's shares.

A notifiable interest is when a shareholder or any parties connected to the shareholder has at least a 3% interest in the nominal value of the company's voting share capital. If that is the case, they must inform the company of their interest within two business days.

4.4 NEX Exchange (NEX)

Like the LSE, NEX is an RIE under FSMA. It was previously known as ICAP Securities & Derivatives Exchange (ISDX) and, together with the LSE, is another stock exchange located in London. NEX provides a trading platform for securities that are on the full list, on AIM and other securities that are traded on its own market.

NEX operates the following market segments:

- NEX Exchange Main Board (a regulated market). This is the market for larger companies with a track record of three years or more, as well as other issuers who are able to comply with the more demanding requirements of the UK Official List and associated UK corporate governance standards. Membership of this market gives companies access to the widest range of both institutional and retail investors.

- NEX Exchange Growth Market (a primary market for unlisted securities). This is the market for earlier stage, entrepreneurial companies seeking access to growth capital. Its regulatory framework is specifically designed to meet the needs of smaller companies. The admission criteria and ongoing obligations are as simple as possible to allow management to focus on running their businesses and generating returns for their shareholders, while still protecting investors.
- NEX Trading (a secondary trading market for listed or quoted securities admitted to trading on other EU markets). This allows NEX member firms to quote prices and report trades in listed or quoted securities that are admitted to EU markets other than NEX.

4.5 Market Participants

LSE membership consists of all major multinational banks as well as smaller boutique private client banks, brokers, dealers, market makers, clearing firms and other financial intermediaries.

LSE member firms can operate as principal and/or agents and thus be classified as brokers, dealers, market makers or hybrid variations.

Historically, the main buyers and sellers who would be responsible for the bulk of trading activities on the LSE would have been high net worth investors and corporate investors who were investing in the shares and bonds of other companies. Today, the participants in the daily activities of the LSE, in common with all financial markets, is overwhelmingly conducted by institutional investors, such as pension funds, index funds, ETFs, hedge funds, investor groups, banks and other miscellaneous financial institutions.

5. Issuing Securities Without a Prospectus

Learning Objective

10.1 Demonstrate an understanding of the structure of the domestic market: summarising primary, secondary and dual listing and explain the process of issuing and gaining admission to a recognised investment exchange, distinguishing between the requirements of NEX, the AIM market and the Official List and issuing securities without a prospectus; discriminate between on exchange and over-the-counter (OTC) trading and detail the transparency obligations; Illustrate markets for trading government and corporate bonds

5.1 Public Offerings and Disclosures

For most public offerings of securities, a vital prerequisite is a prospectus or offering document which the issuer has to make available to all prospective investors and the exchanges upon which it intends to list its securities. Such a prospectus has to disclose all of the pertinent details with regard to the offering including a detailed business plan, an explanation of how the proceeds from the offering will be used, details of all owners/directors of the entity, and most importantly, a comprehensive disclosure of all of the risks associated with the investment.

There are, however offerings, of securities which are made not to the general public, but a subset of so-called 'sophisticated investors'. Here, the rigorous kinds of disclosures that have to be made in an IPO prospectus (sometimes known in the US as a 'red herring') can be avoided.

In the US, the SEC has special provisions for what are termed private placements. A private placement (or non-public offering) is a funding round of securities which are sold without an IPO, and without the formality of an approved prospectus, usually to a small number of chosen private investors.

In the US, although these placements are subject to the Securities Act of 1933, the securities offered do not have to be registered with the SEC if the issuance of the securities conforms to an exemption from registrations as set forth in the Rules known as Regulation D. Private placements may typically consist of stocks, shares of common stock or preferred stock or other forms of membership interests, warrants or promissory notes (including convertible promissory notes), and purchasers are often institutional investors such as banks, insurance companies or pension funds.

5.2 Prospectus Directive (PD)

Under the Markets in Financial Instruments Directive (MiFID) rules, which are applied throughout the members of the EU, a similar provision have been made for offerings made to a restricted class of investors in Europe when a formal prospectus is not statutorily required, or at least when the disclosures required are far less onerous than those required for a public offering.

The Prospectus Directive (PD) sets out the initial disclosure obligations for issuers of securities that are offered to the public or admitted to trading on a regulated market in the EU. It provides a passport for issuers that enables them to raise capital across the EU on the basis of a single prospectus.

The rules apply to prospectuses for public offers of securities and admission of securities to trading on a regulated market. The key provisions of the directives are:

- **Prospectus requirements** – prescribing the contents and format of prospectuses; allowing issuers to incorporate by reference; allowing the use of three part prospectuses; setting out the exemptions from the requirement to produce prospectuses.
- **Approval and publication of prospectus** – setting out procedures for approval of prospectuses and how and where they must be published.
- **Passport rights** – introduce administrative measures to facilitate the passporting of prospectuses on a pan-European basis making it easier for companies to raise capital across Europe.
- **Third-country issuers** – prospectuses drawn up under a third-country's law can be treated as equivalent to directive requirements. This is determined on a case-by-case basis.
- **Other provisions** – requiring issuers to produce annual information updates and the establishment of a qualified investors register.

One significant provision of the PD, as implemented in the UK, is that issuers/offerors are exempt from the obligation to produce a prospectus when offers of securities are made only to qualified investors (QIs).

5.3 Qualified Investors (QIs)

QIs are legal entities authorised to operate in the financial markets (eg, investment firms and insurance companies), governments, supranational institutions, as well as natural persons and small and medium-sized enterprises (SMEs) that certify that they meet the required criteria.

The PD allows the FCA to maintain a register of QIs which must then be available to all issuers and offerors. The information held on the qualified investor register (QIR) is solely to facilitate the issuance of securities without the requirement to publish a prospectus under the PD.

Natural persons and SMEs can only be recognised as QIs if they meet the criteria specified below and are registered on the QIR.

QIs will be removed from the QIR annually (30 June) and so QIs must specifically request that their details appear on the new register every year. Amendments can be carried out at any time by contacting the Register Team.

5.3.1 Natural Persons Seeking Inclusion on the QIR

Investors wishing to register as a QI need to self-certify. At least two of the following three criteria to qualify for inclusion on the QIR must be met:

- The investor must have carried out transactions of a significant size (at least €1,000) on securities markets at an average frequency of at least ten per quarter for the last four quarters.
- The investor's security portfolio must exceed €0.5 million.
- The investor must work – or have worked for at least one year – in the financial sector in a professional position which requires knowledge of securities investment.

The QIR is only available to issuers/offerors or their agents and exclusively for the purpose of making an offer of securities to a QI.

5.3.2 Small- and Medium-Size Enterprises (SMEs) Seeking Inclusion on the QIR

Small and medium-sized enterprises (SMEs) are also required to self-certify. However, at least two of the following three criteria must be fulfilled to qualify for inclusion on the QIR:

- The average number of employees is less than 250.
- The total balance sheet does not exceed €43,000,000.
- The annual net turnover does not exceed €50,000,000.

5.3.3 Issuers/Offerors Seeking Access to the QIR

The information held on the QIR is to be used solely for issuing securities without publication of a prospectus (see the terms of consent in the application form for inclusion in the QIR and the terms of access in the application form for access to the register).

The following information is included on the QIR for individuals:

- QI's name
- QI unique reference number
- a contact address (this can be the address of their representative/legal, financial or other adviser or a PO Box address) or broker name and identification number with that broker.

The following information is included on the QIR for SMEs:

- company name
- contact name and position, and
- registered office address.

5.3.4 Taxation Issues for Qualified Investor Schemes (QISs)

A qualified investor scheme (QIS) is a type of authorised investment fund (AIF) which is subject to regulation by the FCA. The general treatment of investors in an AIF is designed to recognise that they have bought units in a pooled investment scheme in which the investors have no control over the decisions of the fund manager over when and what investments to buy and sell.

Instead of being charged tax on their share of the income and gains of the scheme, they are liable to tax on the distributions they receive and to capital gains tax (CGT) (or to corporation tax on chargeable gains) on the gains made when they sell their units. This treats their holding of units in a fund (that is units in an AIF or shares in an open-ended investment company (OEIC)) in a similar way to a holding of shares in a normal company.

6. Exchange and Over-the-Counter (OTC) Trading

Learning Objective

10.1 Demonstrate an understanding of the structure of the domestic market: summarising primary, secondary and dual listing and explain the process of issuing and gaining admission to a recognised investment exchange, distinguishing between the requirements of NEX, the AIM market and the Official List and issuing securities without a prospectus; discriminate between on exchange and over-the-counter (OTC) trading and detail the transparency obligations; Illustrate markets for trading government and corporate bonds

6.1 Features of Exchange v OTC Markets

Financial, technological and regulatory innovation to meet the requirements of both hedgers and speculators has been at the heart of the development of both exchange-traded and OTC markets. This process is continuing, causing limited blurring of some distinctions in terms of centralisation, clearing and settlement, though not affecting the core difference between standardisation and flexibility.

Centralisation

As noted earlier, increasing volumes of trades in equities have been migrating from RIEs, such as the LSE to alternative trading venues such as multilateral trading facilities (MTFs), (see section 9 of this chapter). Part of the aim of the latest MiFID regulations (MiFID II) is to regain the transparency, if not the control, of this business, since its relative opacity in terms of anonymity and lack of price discovery can, in some instances, resemble that of OTC markets. It is too early to tell how successful this aim will be.

Clearing and Settlement

Here, the movement is more from OTC towards a variation of the exchange model, in which a centralised clearing house is counterparty to both sides of every trade. There is currently enthusiasm to reduce the enormous amounts at risk between both counterparties on every trade (FX is the largest of all markets with over $5 trillion traded and settled on a daily basis. The model of continuous linked settlement (CLS) reduces net exposures through a central body, while the use of prime brokers has also helped to reduce fragmentation in settlement risk across the entire body of participants. Initiatives such as SwapClear, ForexClear and CDSClear, may in time grow to centralise and control gross OTC settlement risk further.

Standardisation

There is, however, little sign that participants wish to surrender the benefits of contract flexibility in OTC markets. Exchange-traded markets continue to have standard terms, not only for size and tenor, but also for conditions. They can offer none of the flexibility of the many different forms of interest rate swaps, swaptions and their hybrids, let alone the second or third generation of exotic FX options.

Exercise 2

Outline what you consider could be a benefit of OTC trading.

The answer to this exercise can be found at the end of this chapter.

6.2 Futures Markets

Examples of more traditional centralised, exchange-based markets are the futures markets in the UK and the US. In the UK, the London Metal Exchange (LME) is the largest futures exchange in the world for trading in base metals. Another important exchange for futures in the UK is ICE Futures Europe.

Futures contracts are specialised instruments which enable buyers and sellers to make deals for the future purchase and delivery of agricultural, industrial and energy-based commodities as well as for financial products. The former method of trading futures on these exchanges was known as 'open outcry' as it consisted of several hundred traders face to face in what was known as a trading pit. The prices of the commodities were determined in real time by the frantic interaction of these traders, known as 'locals'. However, most futures are now traded electronically on electronic trading platforms.

6.2.1 Transparency of Futures Trading

Futures trades are settled via clearing houses and the trading volumes and price behaviour are fully transparent. In the US, the Commodities Futures Trading Commission (CFTC) publishes weekly analysis of futures trading known as the Commitment of Traders Reports, which give a detailed breakdown not only of all of the transactions completed on the US futures exchanges but also the kinds of participants – speculators and commercials – who are holding different positions.

6.2.2 Characteristics of Futures Trading

The trading of futures contracts calls for the delivery by the seller at a specified date in the future to 'deliver' the item which has been traded. The item could be a physical commodity such as 100 barrels of crude oil, a bushel of corn or 25 tonnes of copper of a specified grade.

Financial futures require the delivery of a bond or gilt of a certain maturity with a specified coupon (there are conversion mechanisms designed to convert bonds with alternative coupon amounts to the standardised form) or a certain amount of a foreign currency in the case of a FX futures contract. In some instances, the buyer of the futures position will request settlement in terms of delivery of the actual commodity – which is known as an **exchange for physicals (EFPs)** or the appropriate kind of bond – but in most cases the manner in which the contract is settled is through a cash settlement. In essence, one party pays to the other the difference between the value of the contract at the time of entry versus the value at the time of exit or settlement.

To contrast the difference between a futures contract for a physical commodity and one for a financial instrument, consider how a futures position in, eg, copper, traded on the LME, differs from a futures position in the FTSE 100 index, traded on the ICE Futures Europe market.

6.2.3 London Metal Exchange (LME)

The LME is the world's largest exchange in options and futures contracts on base and other metals. It offers hedging, worldwide reference pricing, and the option of physical delivery to settle contracts.

The LME offers futures and options contracts for metals such as:

- aluminium
- copper
- tin
- nickel
- zinc
- lead, and
- aluminium alloy.

Producers and traders in the metals listed on the LME can sell the metal to one of the many big warehouses of the LME, all over the world, and receive a warrant. This is a way to share the cost of these warehouses between the many industry participants and make it more efficient, to compete against other products.

Each day, the LME issues detailed figures on how many tonnes of each metal are in its warehouses, which helps producers and consumers assess supply.

6.2.4 ICE Futures

FTSE 100 Index Futures

The FTSE 100 Index contract is designed to represent the performance of the FTSE 100 Index, which comprises the 100 most highly capitalised companies, representing approximately 81% of the UK market. It is used extensively as a basis for investment products, such as derivatives and ETFs.

Contract Specifications

Unit of Trading

Contract valued at £10 per index point (eg, value £73,000 at 7300 index points)

Delivery months March, June, September, December (nearest four available for trading)

Quotation index points (eg, 7300.0)

Minimum price movement (tick size and value) 0.5 point (£5.00)

Settlement

Cash settlement based on the **exchange delivery settlement price (EDSP)**.

6.3 Characteristics of OTC Trades

As outlined in section 6.1, OTC markets have, historically, not been centralised, not had a central clearing counterparty and had full flexibility in terms of contract specifications, such as size, tenor and conditions.

The largest market in the world is FX, which is 98% OTC (there is minimal volume in exchange-traded futures or options); however, 94% of this comprises spot, forward outright and forward swaps (ie, non-derivative). Other OTC non-derivative trades include money markets, including cash deposits, commercial paper and certificates of deposit, but OTC markets also include derivatives of various asset classes.

Some OTC derivatives might at first glance appear dangerous, but it is important to distinguish between 'vanilla' and 'exotic' forms. The structures, pricing and risk management of even vanilla derivatives in interest rates (from forward rate agreements (FRAs) to swaps) and FX (cross-currency swaps and options) can appear complex, yet they are intuitively and mathematically relatively straightforward; many are just building blocks of vanilla derivatives. There is, however, ongoing debate concerning appropriate pricing models and accurate measures of risk in large derivative portfolios, especially relating to unexpected 'fat-tails' in distribution models. New regulations, such as the Fundamental Review of the Trading Book (FRTB, due in 2019) are designed however to align more appropriate and homogenised risk standards across the industry, and to isolate risk within trading books and move it away from the main banking books. The ring-fencing process among the largest UK banks, due to be completed by 1 January 2019, further limits the trading and risk management of such products away from the main commercial and retail balance sheets.

It is, nevertheless, fair to question the appropriateness of some 'exotic' path-dependent options, which are more common in FX. Their pay-out is often linked not in a linear fashion to the level in the underlying market at expiry, but to the path of market movement prior to then, often with dramatic changes in profitability. Pricing is far less mathematically transparent, while their binary features allow otherwise expensive hedge strategies to appear inexpensive. These discounts are often deceptive, however, which makes them generally unsuitable for hedging, or for anyone other than aggressive speculators. For this reason, regulators are currently restricting their use among retail customers amid some instances of mis-selling or even fraud.

Looking into the future, it may be that these OTC contracts will require to be cleared in a similar manner to that seen for futures trading. Clearing firms would essentially be liable for losses if a counterparty defaulted. Because of this liability, the clearing firms would have the ability (and responsibility) to require transparency, margin requirements, and upfront capital to execute these trades.

Clearing firms in the US, including the Chicago Mercantile Exchange (CME) and the Intercontinental Exchange (ICE) operate clearing for some derivatives other than futures when they are essentially paid to monitor risk management practices. ICE clears credit derivative swaps contracts which has helped grow its revenue base. If the US Government were to require all OTC contracts to be cleared, it might have a profound effect on both of these companies.

In the UK, the LCH.Clearnet Group is a leading multinational clearing house, serving major exchanges and platforms as well as a range of OTC markets. It clears a broad variety of asset classes, including securities, exchange-traded derivatives, commodities, energy, freight, FX derivatives, interest rate swaps, credit default swaps, as well as euro and sterling denominated bonds and repos. LCH.Clearnet works closely with regulators and clients to identify and develop innovative clearing solutions.

7. Markets for Government and Corporate Bonds

Learning Objective

10.1 Demonstrate an understanding of the structure of the domestic market: summarising primary, secondary and dual listing and explain the process of issuing and gaining admission to a recognised investment exchange, distinguishing between the requirements of NEX, the AIM market and the Official List and issuing securities without a prospectus; discriminate between on exchange and over-the-counter (OTC) trading and detail the transparency obligations; Illustrate markets for trading government and corporate bonds

7.1 Government Bond Market

In addition to the UK Government itself, via the Debt Management Office (DMO), a branch of HM Treasury, there are three major groups of participants that facilitate deals in the government bond markets:

- primary dealers – such as gilt-edged market makers (GEMMs)
- broker dealers
- inter-dealer brokers (IDBs).

7.1.1 Issuing Agency

The DMO is the issuing agency for the UK Government. It is an executive agency of the Treasury, making new issues of UK Government securities (gilt-edged securities or gilts). Once issued, the secondary market for dealing in gilts is overseen by two bodies, the DMO and the LSE.

The DMO is the body that enables certain LSE member firms to act as primary dealers, known as gilt-edged market makers (GEMMs). It then leaves it to the LSE to prescribe rules that apply when dealing takes place.

7.1.2 Gilt-Edged Market Makers (GEMMs)

A GEMM, once vetted by the DMO and registered with the LSE, becomes a primary dealer and is required to provide two-way quotes to customers (clients known directly to them) and other member firms of the LSE throughout the normal trading day. There is no requirement to use a particular system for making those quotes available to clients, and GEMMs are free to choose how to disseminate their prices.

The obligations of a GEMM can be summarised as follows:

- To make effective two-way prices to customers on demand, up to a size agreed with the DMO, thereby providing liquidity for customers wishing to trade.
- To participate actively in the DMO's gilt issuance programme, broadly by bidding competitively in all auctions and achieving allocations commensurate with their secondary market share – effectively informally agreeing to underwrite gilt auctions.
- To provide information to the DMO on closing prices, market conditions and the GEMM's positions and turnover.

The privileges of GEMM status include:

- exclusive rights to competitive bidding at gilt auctions and other DMO operations, either for the GEMM's own account or on behalf of clients
- an exclusive facility to trade as a counterparty of the DMO in any of its secondary market operations;
- exclusive access to gilt IDB screens.

A firm can register as a GEMM to provide quotes in:

- all gilt-edged securities
- gilt-edged securities excluding ILGs
- ILGs only.

There are exceptions to the requirement to customers, including the members of the LSE. The obligation does not include quoting to other GEMMs, fixed-interest market makers or gilt IDBs.

7.1.3 Broker-Dealers

These are non-GEMM LSE member firms that are able to buy or sell gilts as principal (dealer) or as agent (broker). When acting as a broker, the broker-dealer will be bound by the LSE's best execution rule, which is a part of FCA guidelines that has been subject to review and strengthened as a consequence of the FCA's implementation of the EU's Market Abuse Regime (see section 8) to get the best available price at the time.

When seeking a quote from a GEMM, the broker-dealer must identify at the outset if the deal is a small one, defined as less than £1 million nominal.

7.1.4 Gilt Inter-Dealer Brokers

Gilt IDBs arrange deals between GEMMs anonymously. They are not allowed to take principal positions and the identity of the market makers using the service remains anonymous at all times. The IDB will act as agent, but settle the transaction as if it were the principal. The IDB is only allowed to act as a broker between GEMMs, and has to be a separate company and not a division of a broker/dealer.

7.1.5 STRIPS

STRIPS is an acronym of separate trading of registered interest and principal securities and were mentioned in chapter 6 (section 4).

The key benefits of STRIPS are that investors can precisely match their liabilities, removing any 'reinvestment risk'.

Example

An institutional investor wants to fund the repayment of the principal on a £5 million liability due to be paid in five years' time. Using gilts, there are three major choices:

1. They could buy a £5 million nominal coupon-paying gilt, but the coupons on this would mean that it would generate more than £5 million.
2. They could buy less than £5 million nominal, attempting to arrive at £5 million in five years. However, they would have to estimate how the coupons over the life of the bond could be reinvested and what rate of return the coupons would provide – their estimate could well be wrong.
3. They could buy a £5 million strip.

STRIPS can precisely meet the liabilities of the investor, removing any reinvestment risk that is normally faced when covering liabilities with coupon-paying bonds. Furthermore, investors in gilt STRIPS need not worry about the risk that the issuer of the bonds will default – gilt-edged securities are considered to be free of any default risk (also known as credit risk).

7.2 Corporate Bond Markets

7.2.1 Corporate Bonds

Unlike the market for equities, the method of dealing in corporate bonds tends to be away from the major exchanges in what is commonly described as a decentralised dealer market. The dealers provide liquidity by being willing to buy or sell the bonds and effectively act as market makers. The systems that the dealers use to display their willingness to deal are numerous, with each being described as a separate 'pool' of liquidity.

7.2.2 Default

In the corporate bond market, unlike the government bond markets where it is assumed that no sovereign borrower will default, the determination of the likelihood that a corporate borrower may default is a vital part in the pricing mechanism for corporate bonds.

7.2.3 Credit Rating Agencies

Organisations such as Standard & Poor's (S&P), Moody's Investor Services and Fitch Ratings are credit rating agencies who provide a benchmarking system for corporate bonds. The highest grade corporate bonds are known as AAA or Aaa and these are bonds that these agencies have deemed the least likely to fail.

Lower-grade corporate bonds are perceived as more likely to default, when the borrower has to entice lenders with a higher coupon payment and higher yield to maturity. Indeed, bonds with a rating below BBB– (in the case of S&P and Fitch Ratings), or Baa3 (in the case of Moody's) are often referred to as 'junk bonds' or 'speculative bonds' which are non-investment-grade.

The primary difference between the corporate bond market and the equity market relates to the nature of the security being traded. A corporate bond usually has a specified income stream in the form of coupon payments which will be paid to the holder of the bond, and a bondholder has a more senior claim against the assets of the issuer in the case of a bankruptcy or restructuring.

Investors in equities may receive a dividend payment from the corporation but this is less certain and can fluctuate. Indeed, less mature companies may not even pay a dividend. The equity holder also has a greater risk that if the corporation which has issued the shares becomes insolvent or undergoes a restructuring there may be insufficient assets to be liquidated or reorganised and then distributed to shareholders. In such instances, shareholders may find that their equity stakes in a corporation have little or no residual value.

The primary function and role of market makers in corporate bonds is to provide liquidity to the marketplace and to act as a facilitator or agent in trades between the principals. Dealers are those that have been appointed by the corporate issuer to act as distributors on their behalf in the issuance and underwriting of bond issues. There is often a combination of such roles in large financial institutions.

7.3 Trading Methods for Bonds

Bond trading, including both corporate and government bonds, is either conducted between dealers, some of which is arranged by IDBs, or between dealers and their customers, like asset managers.

Dealer-to-dealer trading can occur in three ways:

- direct telephone contact
- indirect via an IDB voice broking the deal, or
- via an electronic market, known as an electronic trading platform, such as MTS or Brokertec.

Dealer-to-customer trading is done either by voice trading between the two parties, or via an electronic platform.

A proportion of corporate bond dealing takes place via the exchanges, eg, on the order book for retail bonds (ORB) on the LSE.

7.3.1 Trends in Trading Methods

The trading methods in the corporate and government bond markets are essentially driven by the liquidity of the instruments. Instruments issued in high volumes by G10 governments tend to be increasingly traded electronically, sometimes via IDBs. This is also true of liquid agency bonds and corporate bonds.

However, when the deals involve lower liquidity instruments, high volatility bonds or trades of unusually large size, the OTC trading is often via a 'request for quote' (RFQ) from the customer to the dealer. For deals between dealers, less commoditised bonds that are traded OTC include those bonds that are high-yield, many asset-backed securities and bonds issued from the emerging markets.

7.4 Quotation Methods

There are two major elements of a quote for a bond – the price and, as a result of the price, the yield. Most traders will be looking for particular yields and then adjust the price to achieve that yield.

When dealing in corporate bonds, or across different bond markets (such as different countries' government bonds), traders and researchers also look at the yield spreads that are available and anticipating changes in those spreads. For example, assessing whether the additional yield that is currently available for a BBB-rated sterling-denominated corporate bond over a gilt with similar maturity is likely to increase or decrease.

7.5 Hedging Bonds

The price of a bond is driven by a number of factors, such as credit rating and required yields. Clearly, the required yield will itself be driven by expected future interest rates. A key indicator of the markets' collective expectation of future interest rates is implicit within derivatives of bonds, such as bond futures, which are traded actively in high volumes. As a result, the prevailing price of bonds is driven by the price at which derivatives of those bonds are trading.

Futures contracts can be settled by a cash payment at the time of the contract's maturity or by the owner of a contract delivering certain bonds which are subject to a standardised definition or conversion factor. This gives rise to the practice among participants in the futures and cash markets for bonds of making continuous and precise calculations as to which particular bonds are the 'cheapest to deliver (CTD)' at the time of settlement of a futures position.

The relationship between the cash market for bonds and the futures markets in government bonds exemplifies the manner in which all cash and derivative markets are driven by a relatively simple arbitrage mechanism. The concept of cheapest to deliver is a vital component in this arbitrage strategy which will tend to eliminate price discrepancies arising between the trading of actual bonds in the cash market and the trading of bond futures. If pricing discrepancies should arise on a temporary basis, these will tend to be eliminated as in any arbitrage by selling the relatively more expensive item (the cash bond or the derivative depending on the particular circumstances), and buying an offsetting position in the corresponding alternate position of either the underlying asset or the futures contract.

The interaction between the cash price of bonds and the futures prices is a dynamic two-way process in which prices are constantly being adjusted through arbitrage and through the activities of 'hedgers' as well as speculators.

7.6 Stock Lending and CREST

The principle of stock lending or securities lending is to increase the return on stocks by lending them on a short-term basis.

Financial institution A seeks to borrow a stock from fund manager B. in return A pays B a fee as well as providing collateral to B which exceeds the market value of the stock. A can then use the borrowed stock in a variety of ways, eg, as a hedge against other market risk, to initiate a short position or to use as collateral in an entirely separate transaction. The collateral might be other bonds or equities, which is then held separately from other assets. The market value of the stock is reassessed every day, with the collateral being raised or lowered accordingly (if the adjustment is above certain thresholds).

Stock lending is conducted within a Securities Lending Agreement (SLA). One of the key parameters is that actual ownership of the stock passes to A and then back to B, even though it is only a loan. During the loan period, A has full ownership rights, including any voting rights, dividends or coupons. . If the security pays a dividend or coupon to A during the loan period, then A pays B the equivalent sum.

The main users of stock lending fall into the categories of lender and borrower.

- **Lenders** – these are typically asset managers with sufficient inventory of securities which can be lent, as well as custodial banks who hold securities on behalf of asset managers.
- **Borrowers** – these could be drawn from a much wider range of institutions. The primary purpose of borrowing is to cover short positions, so almost any active markets participant, who wishes to sell short a particular market, needs to borrow the security first, in order to sell it and later buy it back (hopefully at a lower price).

Certificateless Registry for Electronic Share Transfer (CREST) is the central securities depository (CSD) for UK and Irish markets. It is a same-day clearing system which holds securities in a paperless form and which can make dividend payments to shareholders.

Since there is no stamp duty in the UK on shares settled electronically via CREST, it instead collects a Stamp Duty Reserve Tax (SDRT) in its place on behalf of Her Majesty' Revenue and Customs (HMRC).

CREST is owned by Euroclear, but its members fall into two categories: members and sponsored members. The former tend to be large institutions such as nbpension funds or broker dealers, who are used by sponsored members to provide access to CREST.

8. Market Abuse Regime (MAR)

Learning Objective

10.2 Detail the market abuse regime and explain and contrast the role of the UK Listing Authority, ESMA, Takeover panel and London Stock Exchange in market regulation

The UK civil market abuse regime has recently undergone further development. On 3 July 2016 most of the requirements under the EU's Market Abuse Regulations (MAR) came into force. Although MAR runs alongside the European Directive on Criminal Sanctions for Market Abuse (CSMAD), the UK is not implementing this directive, so there will not be any changes to the UK's current criminal market abuse regime (see section 8.1 below).

The new MAR regime builds on most elements of the Market Abuse Directive (MAD) which it replaces. MAR widens the scope of the regime including more financial instruments and more trading venues.

It also extends market manipulation (a form of market abuse categorised under the previous legislation) to include attempted market manipulation and prohibits abusive behaviour in respect of benchmarks. More issuers, their staff and trading venues will therefore be subject to the sanctions under the new regime. MAR also differs in the level of its prescriptive detail.

The market abuse regime applies to the public at large and not only to the regulated sector. Continued updates to the UK market abuse regime have introduced important changes for publicly traded issuers, their advisors and senior management, those authorised under FSMA, those who recommend investments or investment strategies and those who participate in the investment markets.

The sanctions which may be imposed following a finding of market abuse are severe. Offenders may face unlimited financial penalties and, if they work in the financial services sector, they may have their livelihood removed by having their authorisation/approval withdrawn or a prohibition order made against them.

Regulations require firms in the UK to report transactions giving rise to suspicions of market abuse. Suspicious Transactions Order Reports (STORs) play a key role in the FCA's market abuse monitoring work. The FCA takes a serious view of firms which fail to report transactions in line with FCA rules or which do not have in place adequate internal transaction reporting procedures and systems.

Even in cases of market misconduct which do not necessarily fall within the definition of civil market abuse, the FCA can still take action against a firm or individual (if they are authorised to conduct investment business) based on a breach of its principles in the FCA Handbook.

8.1 Criminal Aspects of the Market Abuse Regulations (MAR)

The UK government decided to opt-out of the Criminal Sanctions Market Abuse Directive (CSMAD) due to the prior existence of sufficient legislation.

A person who engages in conduct amounting to market abuse may find that they are also be in breach of the provisions of the criminal law which runs in parallel to the amended FSMA 2000 market abuse regime. Sections 401 and 402 of FSMA 2000 give the FCA power to prosecute a number of offences under FSMA and other legislation.

The offences, for which the FCA can take criminal action, are broad. Some of the most important are:

- offences relating to breaches of the FCA Listing Rules, including that of offering new securities to the public in the UK before publishing a prospectus, if required by Listing Rules under Section 84, FSMA 2000 (FSMA 2000, s. 85(2))
- making misleading statements and market manipulation (Financial Services Act 2012, ss. 89–91)
- misleading the FCA (FSMA 2000, s. 398)
- insider dealing under Part V of the Criminal Justice Act (CJA) 1993
- breaches of prescribed regulations relating to money laundering.

When the FCA commences a criminal investigation, in many cases the FCA will use the regulatory enforcement process instead of, or alongside, its criminal powers. The FCA has stated that when it considers that behaviour justifies criminal rather than civil penalties, it will be prepared to pursue such cases through the criminal courts.

8.1.1 UK Markets Subject to MAR

MAR applies to a wider range of trading venues than the previous regime imposed by MAD in the UK, as it uses a wider definition of 'qualifying financial instrument'. For instance, emission allowances and trading on organised trading facilities (OTFs), which are to be introduced under MiFID II, come within MAR's scope.

MAR covers all financial instruments that are:

- admitted to trading on a regulated market – or for which a request for admission to trading has been made
- traded on an **multilateral trading facility** (MTF) – or for which a request for admission to trading has been made
- traded on an OTF, or
- not covered by any of the above, but whose price or value depends on or affects the price or value of such a financial instrument.

8.2 Types of Market Abuse

MAR provides that it is an offence to:

- engage or attempt to engage in insider dealing
- recommend that another person engage in insider dealing or induce another person to engage in insider dealing
- unlawfully disclose inside information, or
- engage or attempt to engage in market manipulation.

8.2.1 Insider Dealing

The regulations define engaging or attempting to engage in insider dealing as: using inside information in acquiring or disposing of financial instruments to which that information relates. Use of inside information to cancel or amend pre-existing orders or bids is also now caught under the new regulations.

An insider is regarded as any person who has inside information as a result of:

- their membership of an administrative, management or supervisory body of an issuer of QIs
- holding in the capital of an issuer of QIs
- having access to the information through the exercise of their employment, profession or duties
- their criminal activity
- other means which they know, or could reasonably be expected to know, is inside information.

8.2.2 Recommending that Another, or Inducing Another To, Engage in Insider Dealing

This offence fits closely alongside insider dealing and again it includes amendment or cancellation of orders or bids.

8.2.3 Unlawfully Disclosing Inside Information

It is an offence to disclose inside information otherwise than in the normal exercise of employment, a profession or duties. This offence includes onward disclosure of recommendations or inducements where the discloser knew or should have known the recommendation or inducement was based on inside information.

8.2.4 Engaging in or Attempting to Engage in Market Manipulation

This offence includes:

- entering into a transaction, placing an order to trade or any other behaviour which:
  - gives false or misleading signals as to the supply, demand, or price of financial instruments, related spot commodity contracts or an auctioned product based on emission allowances, or
  - secures the price of financial instruments, related spot commodity contracts or auctioned products based on emission allowances at an abnormal or artificial level
- entering into a transaction, placing an order to trade or any other activity or behaviour which employs a fictitious device or any other form of deception or contrivance
- disseminating information which gives false or misleading signals as to supply or demand or which secures price at an abnormal or artificial level, including the dissemination of rumours
- transmitting false or misleading information, or providing false or misleading inputs in relation to a benchmark, or any other behaviour which manipulates the calculation of a benchmark.

MAR captures attempted as well as actual market manipulation, such as where a transaction is intended for abusive purposes but is not successfully executed. This is not caught under MAD, as an order must actually be placed, or a transaction executed, for market manipulation to occur. There are concerns as to how this type of activity might be detected, particularly given the market requirement under MAR for persons who professionally arrange or execute trades in financial instruments to have systems ('effective arrangements') in place to detect and report suspicious or unsuccessful orders as well as transactions, which might amount to market abuse.

8.3 Exemptions to MAR

Although MAR retains the previously defined exemption (safe harbour) for buy-back and market stabilisation activities, the new regulations remove the discretion for competent authorities to allow the performance of certain acts which would otherwise be regarded as abuse, known as an 'accepted market practice' (AMP). Any AMPs would need to be agreed by the European Securities and Markets Authority (ESMA).

8.4 Penalties for Market Abuse

If the FCA is satisfied that a person is engaging in, or has engaged in market abuse, or has required or encouraged another person to do, it may:

- Impose an unlimited civil fine.
- Make a public statement that the person has engaged in market abuse.
- Apply to the court for an injunction to restrain threatened or continued market abuse.
- Require a person to disgorge profits made or losses avoided as a result of market abuse.
- Require the payment of compensation to victims.

In some cases, the FCA may rely on individual trading venues to take action and the FCA has agreed operating arrangements with such venues in relation to market conduct for this purpose.

8.5 The FCA's Approach to Implementation

8.5.1 Suspicious Transaction Orders Report (STOR)

An FCA-authorised firm which arranges or executes a transaction with or for a client in a QI admitted to trading on a prescribed market, and which has reasonable grounds to suspect that the transaction might constitute market abuse, is required to notify the FCA without delay. This includes all types of orders, including quotes.

8.5.2 Implementation of the New MAR

In implementing the new regulations the FCA has aimed to retain the breadth of the current regime as it exists in the UK – in terms of the market abuse offences and the markets covered by the regime – while incorporating the specific MAR offences and their additional scope.

Measures already used by the FCA to detect market abuse and prevent it from happening can include:

- **insiders' lists** – issuers and their advisers are required to keep lists of persons who have access to inside information
- **disclosure of managers' deals** – persons discharging managerial responsibility on behalf of an issuer are required to disclose details of their personal deals in the shares of the issuer and any related derivatives.
- **suspicious transaction orders reports** – firms arranging transactions must report those transactions to the FCA when there is a reasonable suspicion that market abuse might have taken place
- **research disclosures** – firms producing research will have to disclose information about research sources and methods, and also conflicts of interest that may impact on the impartiality of the research.

8.6 European Securities and Markets Authority (ESMA)

ESMA replaced the Committee of European Securities Regulators (CESR) in 2011. Its stated mission bears some similarity to that of the FCA, aiming to enhance the protection of investors and to promote stable and orderly financial markets.

With the advent of MiFID, which has led to an expansion in the scope for 'off-exchange' trading, the role of the major stock exchanges to monitor the full range of MTFs has arguably diminished, which impairs the LSE's ability to monitor practices in accordance with the regulations.

At present, as much as half of trading in some big-name stocks takes place away from exchanges, so surveillance staff only see a fraction of activity in many stocks.

In April 2010, the *Financial Times* reported that the CESR had expressed concern that national securities regulators in Europe were applying market abuse rules differently across the region. Part of their concern results from the proliferation of MTFs and off-exchange trading.

MAR 2016 strengthens the existing UK market abuse framework by extending its scope to new markets, new platforms and behaviours.

8.7 The Takeover Panel

As mentioned earlier, the UK supervisory authority that carries out the regulatory functions required under the EU Takeover Directive is the Takeover Panel, also known as the Panel on Takeovers and Mergers (or more simply 'the Panel' or 'POTAM'). The Panel's requirements are set out in The Takeover Code which consists of six general principles, and a number of detailed rules.

The Code is designed principally to ensure that shareholders are treated fairly and are not denied an opportunity to decide on the merits of a takeover. Furthermore, the Code ensures that shareholders of the same class are afforded equivalent treatment by an offeror. In short, the Code provides an orderly framework within which takeovers are conducted, and is designed to assist in promoting the integrity of the financial markets.

The European Takeovers Directive mandates that the Panel is put on a statutory footing. This was completed in the Companies Act 2006.

Whenever a transaction is made on the LSE or other London-based exchange that is greater than £10,000 the details of the transaction get passed on to the Panel for their evaluation, and a levy is charged of (currently) £1.00 on the transaction, which goes to the Panel as payment (this is known as the 'PTM levy').

8.8 UK Listing Authority (UKLA)

The UKLA is the body responsible for setting and administering the listing requirements and continuing obligations for plcs seeking and obtaining a full list on the LSE (see earlier sections 1.2.2 and 3.1.2).

8.8.1 The UKLA and Corporate Governance

The regulatory framework which has been implemented under the general MAR imposes robust regulations on the manner in which the securities industry operates and the FCA has considerable powers of enforcement.

In addition, there have been several initiatives in the UK over the last twenty years to improve corporate governance in relation to financial services. Numerous committees have reported, and from their recommendations a Code of Corporate Governance (2014) has been drawn up by the UKLA and is overseen by the Financial Reporting Council (FRC). Corporate governance is the system by which companies are directed and controlled. Boards of directors are responsible for the governance of their companies. The shareholders' role in governance is to appoint the directors and the auditors. The responsibilities of the board include setting the company's strategic aims, and also supervising and controlling the management assigned to achieve these aims. The board's actions are subject to rules and regulations and also to the above-mentioned control by the shareholders.

This system of control has been also used to tackle the agency theory problem, which is a management theory that identifies the problem when directors might not act in the shareholders' (or other stakeholders') best interests.

The UKLA requires companies to disclose in their annual reports both how they have applied the principles of good governance and whether they have complied with the provisions of the code of best practice. This is now more widely achieved through the principles of the Stewardship Code (which applies to institutional investors).

The Key Contents of the Combined Code

- Every listed company should be headed by an effective board, which should lead and control the company.
- The board should meet regularly.
- Directors should bring independent judgement to bear on issues of strategy.
- No one individual should have unfettered powers of decision.
- A decision to combine the posts of chairman and chief executive officer in one person should be publicly explained.
- There should be a strong and independent non-executive element on the board.
- The board should have a balance of executive and non-executive directors such that no small group of individuals can dominate the board's decision-making.
- There should be a formal and transparent procedure for appointment of new directors.
- All directors should submit themselves for re-election at least every three years.

Directors' Remuneration

- Levels of remuneration should be sufficient to attract and retain directors needed to run the company successfully.
- Remuneration should be structured to link rewards to corporate and individual performance.
- Remuneration committees should be responsible for this and should only include non-executive directors.

- There should be an objective of having service contracts with notice periods of a maximum of one year.
- The annual report should contain a statement of remuneration policy and details of the remuneration of each director.

In July 2018, a new Corporate Governance Code was introduced by the Financial Reporting Council (FRC); this updated the Code first seen in the early 1990s (the Cadbury report). At the time of writing (August 2018), it is too early to know if any amendments or alterations to the Code will be made and candidates should, therefore, research what it covers as it develops (eg, https://www.frc.org.uk/getattachment/88bd8c45-50ea-4841-95b0-d2f4f48069a2/2018-UK-Corporate-Governance-Code-FINAL.PDF).

8.9 London Stock Exchange and AIM

As an EU Regulation, MAR has direct effect across all EEA member states; therefore, MAR disclosure obligations apply to financial instruments admitted to all MTFs, as well as regulated markets. Accordingly, these obligations apply also to AIM companies admitted to trading on AIM.

The key disclosure obligations in MAR relate to the disclosure of inside information of deals by persons discharging managerial responsibilities (PDMRs) and closely associated persons. MAR also introduced mandatory close period rules. Under Article 19(11) of MAR, a close period is the period of 30 calendar days before the announcement of an interim or a year-end financial report, during which a PDMR is prohibited from conducting any transactions on their own account or for the account of a third party, directly or indirectly, relating to the shares or debt instruments of the issuer or to derivatives or other financial instruments linked to them.

The disclosure obligations under MAR are within the remit of FCA as the competent authority in the UK; however, the LSE has implemented regulatory procedures for AIM companies in order to comply with MAR.

The objective of MAR is to ensure market integrity and investor protection. The regulatory procedures will harmonise disclosure requirements applying to issuers across regulated markets and MTFs.

MAR applies to issuers on AIM, and includes disclosure obligations and closed period rules that apply to issuers that have agreed to or, have been approved for, admission to trading on an MTF; AIM is an MTF and, therefore, MAR applies.

AIM companies are required to maintain a list of all those persons working for them that have access to inside information.

9. Alternative Trading Venues

Learning Objective

10.3 Summarise the role of multilateral trading facilities (MTFs), systematic internalisers, and dark pools

Keeping abreast of developments in the various trading platforms in use in today's financial markets is a daunting challenge. There is a constant drive towards new IT architectures and software technologies, which means that the pace of innovation and the changes in the actual systems in effect, will have a tendency to make text books such as this which describe these systems outdated in relatively short time frames.

In understanding the evolution of trading platforms from the more conventional systems which were in place up until the mid-1990s, and which many non-professionals today still envisage as the model for work flow in markets, it is important to take a brief historical perspective.

In 1998 the SEC in the US authorised the introduction of electronic communication networks (ECNs). In essence, an ECN is a computerised trading platform which allows trading of various financial assets, primarily equities and currencies, to take place away from a specific venue such as a stock exchange. The primary motivation for the SEC to authorise the introduction of ECNs was to increase competition among trading firms by lowering transaction costs, giving clients full access to their order books, and offering order matching outside of traditional exchange hours.

Since an ECN exists as a large number of networked computers/work stations it effectively has no 'centre' or physical location but rather is decentralised and virtual. ECNs are sometimes also referred to as alternative trading networks or venues. However, the term 'venue' has to be understood in a looser sense than the common-sense notion of a specific place or location, because, as described a network is accessible from anywhere through an IT infrastructure and there is no obvious place (in the physical sense) where trades are executed for such a venue.

The original MiFID introduced rules to create harmonised competitive and transparent markets throughout the EU, with the objective of improving pre-trade and post-trade transparency. With regard to post-trade transparency, the intention was to improve price discovery and enable clients to verify that their brokers were complying with best execution rules, as well as standardising these requirements for equity trading conducted on a trading venue. MiFID also aimed to improve market data reporting, enabling regulators to monitor and ensure fair and orderly functioning of markets.

MiFID II has introduced new provisions to enhance controls around the prevention of market abuse and to increase transparency in markets. In particular, it has extended the scope of the regulatory requirements beyond equities, to include depositary receipts, ETFs, bonds, structured finance products, derivatives and emission allowances.

Transparency applies to financial instruments, or classes of financial instruments, that are admitted to trading or are traded on a trading venue. The concept of trading venues is extended to include regulated markets and, MTFs, as well as OTFs and systematic internalisers (SIs).

Transparency requirements can be separated into pre-trade and post-trade disclosure of the details of orders submitted to and transactions conducted on a trading venue, such as a regulated market, an MTF, or an OTF. Pre-trade transparency is designed to provide market participants with real-time trade data around firm quotes; post-trade transparency is designed to provide market participants with real-time trade data around executed trades.

9.1 Multilateral Trading Facilities (MTFs)

MTFs offer retail investors and investment firms an alternative venue to trading on formal exchanges. An MTF is, in short, an enabling system that brings together multiple parties (eg, retail investors or other investment firms) that are interested in buying and selling financial instruments. These systems can be crossing networks or matching engines that are operated by an investment firm or a market operator. Instruments may include shares, bonds and derivatives. This is done within the MTF operator's system. The investment firm operating the MTF has no discretion as to how interested parties may interact. These parties form a contract and the trade is executed under the system's rules or in accordance with the system's internal operating procedures.

The requirements that MiFID II introduces for investment firms operating an MTF expand the previous MiFID regime. These requirements have been aligned to those of regulated markets, so that an investment firm operating an MTF is required to have systems and controls in place to ensure that the performance of its activities is adequate, effective and appropriate.

MiFID II subjects regulated markets and MTFs to equivalent organisational requirements and similar regulatory oversight. These changes aim to ensure fair and orderly trading and efficient execution of orders, and will require published and non-discriminatory rules. MTF operators will be required to have specific arrangements in place to identify and manage conflicts of interest, with systems to recognise and mitigate operational risks and to manage the technical operation of the system.

A trading venue provides trade feeds on a non-discriminatory and transparent basis, upon request, to any authorised or recognised central counterparty (CCP) that wishes to clear transactions in financial instruments that are concluded on that trading venue.

MiFID II also introduces changes to pre- and post-trade transparency arrangements.

9.2 Organised Trading Facilities (OTFs)

MiFID II has introduced a new category of trading venue called OTFs. An OTF is a multilateral system that is not a regulated market or an MTF. Within an OTF, multiple third-party buying and selling interests in bonds, structured finance products, emission allowances or derivatives are able to interact in a way that results in a contract. Equities are not permitted to be traded through an OTF.

The introduction of OTFs means that many transactions that were previously categorised as 'off-venue' will come within a multilateral trading environment. This will increase overall market transparency and the quality of price discovery, investor protection and liquidity.

A key difference between OTFs and MTFs is the ability and requirements on an OTF to use discretion when matching buying and selling interests, providing that the use of discretion is in line with fair and orderly trading and with best execution obligations to clients. This helps to provide liquidity and price transparency in asset classes that have traditionally been less liquid and transparent.

This should help facilitate competition in these markets, where execution has traditionally been between large market participants, dealing in large sizes, bringing OTC contracts on venue should also bring better price transparency.

The requirements that apply to OTFs and their transactions are generally the same as those that apply to MTFs. This is because OTFs and MTFs are similar multilateral systems that bring together third-party buying and selling interests in financial instruments in a way that results in a contract.

As with MTFs, OTFs must establish clear rules and processes around trading. For example, an OTF operator must establish transparent rules and procedures for fair and orderly trading, and publish rules about which instruments can be traded on their venue. They must also establish and publish clear and non-discriminatory access rules, be able to suspend instruments from trading, and maintain resilient systems to facilitate the continuity of trading under stressed conditions.

OTFs are also subject to the same transparency requirements as regulated markets and MTFs. Pre- and post-trade transparency both apply to any order or transaction executed through the systems or under the rules of an OTF. According to the new pre-trade transparency regime, OTF operators have to publish the details of current bids and offers and the depth of trading interests of those prices. To comply with post-trade transparency rules, OTF operators have to make public the details of transactions as close to real time as is technically possible.

OTFs are also required to establish and maintain effective arrangements and procedures to enable the regular monitoring of compliance by members; at the same time, OTFs must monitor the transactions undertaken by their members using the venue's systems to identify breaches of the rules, disorderly trading conditions or conduct that may involve market abuse.

9.3 Systematic Internalisers (SIs)

An SI is, in broad terms, a qualifying investment firm which, on an organised, frequent, systematic and substantial basis, deals on its own account by executing client orders outside a regulated market, MTF or an OTF. The firm executes orders from its clients against its own book or against orders from other clients. MiFID II treats SIs as mini-exchanges, hence, for example, they will be subject to the pre-trade and post-trade transparency requirements that were outlined above.

For a firm to become an SI, it must trade on its own account on a 'frequent and systematic basis' when executing client orders outside a regulated market, an MTF or an OTF. It is considered that the terms 'frequent' and 'systematic' will be measured by the proportion and volume of OTC trades in financial instruments carried out by the firm executing client orders on its own on account.

The same legal entity cannot operate both an OTF and an SI.

9.4 Market Transparency

In economics, any market where information is freely available can be called transparent, eg, those involved know the capital assets available, how much capital is available and what the prices are, for example. This transparency is important as it will allow the financial markets to be efficient. It can mean that discounts are not available, that there is more volatility and a reduced need for expert advice as investors know, for example, the price and information.

Types of price transparency include the price:

- to be paid
- which will be charged.

Both have implications for pricing.

The stock market is a good example of a transparent, efficient market, however, hedge funds are famous for wanting secrecy in their transactions. Some hedge funds complain that they are hampered in their trades by others knowing their strategies due to transparency (even if it is incomplete transparency). This has led to major traders (such as hedge funds and pension funds) trying to find ways to trade where their intentions are not seen (limited or no transparency).

9.4.1 Dark Pools

A major way that traders have adapted is thorugh dark pool trading. In finance, dark pools (also known as 'black pool') are a private forum for trading derivatives, securities and other financial instruments. The liquidity of these markets is known as 'dark pool liquidity'. The main users of dark pool trades are financial institutions who do not wish their trades to be seen and possibly followed publicly on major exchanges – this way, they ensure that their trades (purchases or sales) are kept relatively private. The creation of dark pools has been helped by the development of alternative trading venues and computerised dealing systems (normally institutions access them through private contracts amongst the major market participants). Generally, dark pools cannot be accessed by an ordinary small investor (note: some brokers do offer such access but this is not the norm).

9.4.2 Reasons to Use a Dark Pool

The reasons for using dark pools is best seen by an example.

Example

Institutional investor A wishes to trade a large amount of stock in company QPR, say 2 million shares. Using a dark pool may well mean that the trade is not seen immediately and so the share price does not fall due to the large transaction. The institution, therefore, achieves a better price for the shares.

Remember, dark pool trades are not disclosed and there is no visible order book (they are eventually released, but when it is too late to affect the initial trades). If this were to be on a public exchange, then some traders may 'front run' the trades with the result being a reduction in the price before the institutional investor can complete its sale.

9.4.3 Types of Dark Pool

There are three major types of dark pool in the US, which has the most dark pools registered (over 40):

- **Broker-dealer owned** – these are set up by large broker-dealers for their clients and can include their own traders. Prices are taken from an order flow, eg, Credit Suisse's CrossFinder, Goldman Sachs' Sigma X, Citi's Citi Match and Citi Cross, and Morgan Stanley's MS Pool.
- **Agency broker or exchange-owned** – these act as agents only and not as principals. Here the prices are taken from the midpoint of an actual exchange, eg, Instinet, Liquidnet and ITG Posit, while exchange-owned dark pools include those offered by BATS Trading and NYSE Euronext.
- **Electronic market makers** – these are operated by independent operators, eg, Getco and Knight, and may well operate as principals in their own accounts.

Advantages

- The effect of large deals on the market is greatly reduced.
- Trades may be cheaper as the exchange fees are different (trades can use midpoint and, therefore, the spread is also different).
- A major advantage for institutional investors who utilise dark pools is that they do not give any indication of their market strategy and, therefore, do not influence the market. Many large managers are followed by smaller investors, where a trade by one institution may move a share price due to the following they have and because the identity of those trading is hidden until everything has been finalised. This means that it is no longer as transparent as it was.

Drawbacks

- The price on exchanges may no longer show what the actual market price is (as more trades are conducted out of market). For example, a sale of 10% of a stock by a large institution in a dark pool will not be seen by the market. This may result in market traders paying too much for that stock until it is seen by the market.
- In dark pools, the lack of transparency can mean that an institution's trade was made at the 'best price'.
- It is argued that some high frequency traders will use tactics which seek to unearth large hidden orders, allowing them to 'front run' and make an arbitrage profit.
- In many trades, it is thought that the actual size is very small (the average is said to be 200 shares) which appears to make such trades pointless (the reason is still to be researched fully).

Operation

Dark pools will frequently mirror traditional markets in the way orders, pricing and priorities are calculated. The real difference is that transactions are not revealed and so the degree of liquidity is kept hidden. Therefore, they do not need to operate iceberg orders (an iceberg order is where the real value of the order is split between the published part and a larger part, which is not published). It is also unlikely that dark pools will supply data to public market feeds (where trades are detailed) unless local laws make it compulsory to do so. This is intended to minimise the effect of any trades that have been made on the market.

The original dark pools came from brokers' order books and other off-market liquidity. (Note: these dark pools may have their own way of calculating liquidity, such as counting unfilled orders). They tend to be treated as OTC transactions, which means there is no requirement to disclose the details of the trades. Consequently, dark pools allow institutional investors to carry out deals without showing what they are actually doing. The use of electronic trading (ie, reduced human involvement) has meant that every trade is quickly analysed and large trades cause an almost immediate effect on the market (if seen).

Market Impact

As has been stated above, trading on a dark pool reduces the impact of large transactions on the market. However, as every trade needs to be financed, it is therefore likely that the finance will come from the major markets, eg, LSE and Nasdaq. This reduces, to some extent, the liquidity in these markets, and this can also slow down the speed of trades as reduced liquidity will mean it takes longer to find buyers.

In true and fair accounting, the lack of transparency may complicate the valuation of some types of assets, eg, those marked to market, creating questions as managers will be required to add their assumptions or expectations.

Controversy

Dark pools have caused some controversy as they are not regulated as completely as public markets (eg, conflicts of interest can be greater in dark pools).

Regulatory Statements

US

In 2009, the US Securities and Exchange Commission (SEC) proposed measures to make dark pools more transparent *'so investors get a clearer view of stock prices and liquidity'*. These involved making purchase and sales information available to the public and not just to pool participants.

In 2013, the Financial Industry Regulatory Authority (FINRA) stated it would be more closely monitoring dark pools and in 2014, stated it would make information from dark pools more freely available.

Barclays Fine

In January 2016, Barclays agreed to pay a fine of $35 million to the SEC and $70 million to the New York Attorney General for dark pool wrongdoings.

UBS Fine

In January 2015, the US regulators imposed a fine of $14.4 million on UBS Group AG's dark pool for failing to follow the rules designed to ensure stock trades are executed fairly.

EU Regulations

In January 2018, following the Markets in Financial Instruments Directive (MiFID II directive), the EU regulator (the European Securities and Markets Authority (ESMA)) announced that shares of hundreds of European companies, eg, Credit Suisse and Royal Dutch Shell, would be temporarily barred from being traded on dark pools (as the MiFID II rules on transparency came into effect). The changes brought in by MiFID II are intended to introduce caps on the volume of equities traded 'in the dark', therefore encouraging trades to be made on public exchanges. Initially, it is believed that London will be hardest hit (with more than 75% of FTSE 100 companies and more than 66% of the mid-cap index affected).

EU research has found that dark pools became ever more popular with fund managers as they perceived the potential advantages of trading on a non-transparent market.

This caused the regulators to be concerned that they were less able to monitor what was happening or to regulate what was happening (US legal action had highlighted certain problems). It was hoped that investors would be encouraged to trade on exchanges and venues that cater to large deals, or via off-exchange venues (systematic internalisers) run by banks and some market makers.

However, some analysts feared that the action would not succeed. Rebecca Healey, Head of EMEA Market Structure at equities trading venue Liquidnet, stated that *'there's a strong probability we're not going to see a return to public exchanges as the regulators intended'*.

The biggest impact was seen on UniCredit, Philips Lighting, TalkTalk and Euronext. According to data from the ESMA, it is believed that 7% of Euronext shares were traded on dark pools. Even relatively small companies, eg, Provident Financial, UBM, Foxtons, Pets at Home and Petra Diamonds were caught out by the changes.

Currently, London handles the largest amount of trading in equities in Europe (it is home to the two largest markets – LSE and Cboe Europe) plus over a dozen alternative trading venues and dark pools, eg, ITG.

Under MiFID II, dark pools face caps on the amount of trading that can be done. A limit of 4% of the total trading in any stock is permitted in a dark pool over any 12-month period, with a limit of only 8% across all dark pools. Once a cap is reached, all future trades are prohibited from that dark pool (or all dark pools if over 8%) for six months.

ESMA stated that the data it used to calculate the caps was not complete but *'it was of the utmost importance that the (dark pool) mechanism now takes effect'*. The month before the introduction of the rules, over 45% of trading was reported as being off-exchange deals (Thomson Reuters).

Note: some analysts have pointed out that London's dominance in the trades could impact on future calculations of caps, which are reviewed every six months.

Alexandra Hachmeister, Chief Regulatory Officer at Deutsche Börse said:

> *'the whole thinking was done with the assumption that the UK was part of the EU, every [threshold] we have, depending on Brexit, might have to be recalibrated.'*

Ping Pools

Today, dark pool systems are being challenged by new single-dealer platforms (known as 'ping pools'). They already account for 2.5% of US trades (dark pools by comparison represent 15% of the trades).

The main difference offered by a ping pool is that the brokers can ask questions about orders and know who is involved. Justin Schack, Managing Director and partner at Rosenblatt Securities, stated that:

> 'It is always more desirable if you are a market maker to know your counterparty.'

Another difference is that ping pools have fewer controls designed to offer transparency. Some regulators, eg, US regulators, demand that dark pools must publish who is using that particular pool and the way in which the pool operates (this is not required of ping pools).

This lack of transparency causes concern for some market participants.

9.4.1 Dark Pools of Liquidity

Dark pools refer to the non-displayed or hidden nature of the buy and sell orders that reside in a crossing platform. The term 'dark liquidity' can also be applied to all forms of non-displayed liquidity such as the order blotters of buy-side dealing desks.

One investment manager has described the appeal of dark liquidity pools as follows:

> 'A dark pool is a very simple way you can hopefully capture lots of liquidity and achieve a large proportion of your order being executed without displaying anything to the market.'

In the US, the influx of crossing networks and alternative venues, and the rapid adoption of electronic trading technologies, has been driving the growth of dark pools for several years.

As well as being a US phenomenon, the fragmentation of the market, which has been largely encouraged by the MiFID directives as well as the technological 'arms race', has led to the emergence of dark pools in Europe.

Even though there are few organised dark pools in Europe, there is dark liquidity. Dark liquidity is provided when exchanges offer iceberg orders which enable traders to have a lot more available to trade than is currently displayed on the screen or in an order book at any moment in time. The biggest sources of dark liquidity are within the investment banks and major brokers.

9.5 Summary of MTFs and Dark Pools

By making use of certain waivers for pre-trade transparency under MiFID, dark pools and MTFs are allowing institutions to execute large-volume trades away from the visible order book. As there is no pre-trade transparency there is no visible price formation. This is essentially what makes them dark.

The large transaction-size waiver (see below) on which the majority of trades in dark pools will rely is, in relative terms, not actually that large. The effect of the waiver therefore means that large institutions are increasingly able to conduct the majority of their trades in the dark through the new MTFs. There are a number of different models on which the new dark pool MTFs are based. While certain models offer a basic dark matching facility, certain systems provide a pass-through function that allows a user to send an order through to a light venue. For instance, the order can be passed through to a standard MTF or exchange if it cannot be filled in the dark pool. Brokers are now allowing combined access to liquidity in light and dark pools. This method of combined access ties in with the best execution obligations of both buy and sell side market participants.

It is uncertain what the long-term impact of MiFID II will be on dark pool trading activity, despite its introduction in January 2018; dark trading in Europe is still expected to be fundamentally altered by its implementation. The cap on dark pool volumes requires all institutional investors to consider how they interact with dark pool liquidity. These caps are implemented on the trading volume on any stock per individual venue at 4% of market volume, and at 8% maximum cap per stock on the dark pools market as a whole. At the time of writing, soon after the introduction of MiFID II, there has been an early adoption of SI status to preserve dark liquidity, but it is too early to say how permanent or pervasive this may become, or how it might impact on the transparency intended by the regulations.

However, dark trades that take pace using the large in scale (LIS) waiver are not subject to the volume cap, and these orders submitted to venues above certain sizes may be exempted from MiFID II's pre-trade transparency requirements under the LIS waiver.

Exercise 3

Explain what a 'systematic internaliser' (as defined in MiFID II) is and does.

The answer to this exercise can be found at the end of the chapter.

10. Structure of International Markets – Developed and Emerging

Learning Objective

10.4 Demonstrate an understanding of the structure of international markets: include both developed markets and emerging markets

10.1 Classification of International Markets

FTSE Russell, a joint venture, has developed a system for classifying the world's equity markets according to certain categories. Other financial information service companies such as Dow Jones in the US have devised similar systems.

10.2 Developed Countries

The following countries are classified by FTSE Russell as developed countries: Australia, Austria, Belgium, Luxembourg, Canada, Denmark, Finland, France, Germany, Hong Kong, Ireland, Israel, Italy, Japan, Netherlands, New Zealand, Norway, Portugal, Singapore, South Korea, Spain, Sweden, Switzerland, the UK and the US.

Developed countries have all met criteria adopted by the FTSE under the following categories:

- **Market and Regulatory Environment:**
  - high-income economies (as measured by the World Bank GNI Per Capita Ranking, 2015)
  - formal stock market regulatory authorities actively monitor market (eg, SEC, FCA, Securities and Futures Commission)
  - fair and non-prejudicial treatment of minority shareholders
  - selective or non-selective incidence of foreign ownership restrictions
  - no objections or significant restrictions or penalties applied on the repatriation of capital
  - free and well-developed equity market
  - free and well-developed FX market
  - non- or simple registration process for foreign investors.
- **Custody and Settlement:**
  - settlement – rare incidence of failed trades
  - custody-sufficient competition to ensure high quality custodian services
  - clearing and settlement – T+2 or shorter, T+3 or shorter for Frontier
  - settlement – free delivery available
  - custody – omnibus account facilities available to international investors.
- **Dealing Landscape:**
  - brokerage – sufficient competition to ensure high-quality broker services
  - liquidity versus sufficient broad market liquidity to support sizeable global investment
  - transaction costs – implicit and explicit costs to be reasonable and competitive
  - short sales permitted
  - stock lending permitted
  - off-exchange transactions permitted
  - efficient trading mechanism
  - transparency – market depth information/visibility and timely trade reporting process.
- **Derivatives:**
  - developed derivatives markets.

10.2.1 Advanced Emerging Countries

The following countries are classified by FTSE Russell as advanced emerging countries: Brazil, the Czech Republic, Greece, Hungary, Malaysia, Mexico, Poland, South Africa, Taiwan, Thailand and Turkey. Poland is expected to be promoted to developed market status from September 2018.

10.2.2 Secondary Emerging Countries

The following countries are classified by FTSE Russell as secondary emerging countries: Chile, China, Columbia, Egypt, India, Indonesia, Pakistan, Peru, Philippines, Qatar, Russia and the United Arab Emirates (UAE).

10.2.3 Frontier Markets

The term frontier markets is commonly used to describe the equity markets of the smaller and less accessible, but still 'investable', countries of the developing world. The frontier, or pre-emerging equity markets are typically pursued by investors seeking high, long-run return potential as well as low correlations with other markets. The implication of a country being labelled as frontier, or pre-emerging, is that the market is less liquid and significantly less correlated to developed and even traditional emerging markets.

10.3 MSCI World Index

The MSCI World is a stock market index of (at the time of writing) 1,653 'world' stocks. It is maintained by MSCI Inc., formerly Morgan Stanley Capital International, and is often used as a common benchmark for 'world' or 'global' stock funds.

The index includes a collection of stocks of all the developed markets in the world, as defined by MSCI. The index includes securities from 23 countries but excludes stocks from emerging economies making it less worldwide than the name suggests. A related index, the MSCI All Country World Index (ACWI), incorporates both developed and emerging countries.

10.4 United States

Since approximately 25% of global GDP is accounted for by the US, it is no surprise that two of its many exchanges, the NYSE (owned by ICE since 2013) and Nasdaq, comprise almost half of the world's total stock exchange activity. As well as trading domestic US stocks, these exchanges are also involved in the trading of shares in major international companies.

The NYSE is the largest stock exchange in the world as measured by its domestic market capitalisation and is significantly larger than any other exchange worldwide. Although it trails Nasdaq for the number of companies quoted on it, it is still larger in terms of the value of shares traded.

The NYSE trades in a continuous auction format, that is, member firms act as auctioneers in an open-outcry auction market environment in order to bring buyers and sellers together and to manage the actual auction. This makes it unique in world stock markets but, as more than 50% of its order flow is now delivered to the floor electronically, there are proposals to adopt a hybrid structure combining elements of open outcry and electronic markets.

Nasdaq, the National Association of Securities Dealers Automated Quotations, is an electronic stock exchange with (at the time of writing) 3,300 companies listed on it. It is the second largest stock exchange by market capitalisation and has the second largest trading volume.

There are a variety of companies traded on the exchange, but it is well known for being a high-tech exchange – that is, many of the companies listed on it are telecoms, media or technology companies; it is typically home to many new, high-growth, and volatile stocks.

Although it is an electronic exchange, trades are still undertaken through market makers who make a book in specific stocks, so that when a broker wants to purchase shares, they do so directly from the market maker.

The main depository in the US is the Depository Trust Company (DTC) which is responsible for corporate stocks and bonds, municipal bonds and money market instruments. The Federal Reserve Bank is still the depository for most US Government bonds and securities.

Transfer of securities held by DTC is by book entry, although shareholders have the right to request a physical certificate in many cases. However, about 85% of all shares are immobilised at DTC, and efforts are under way in the US to eliminate the requirement to issue physical certificates at the state level.

Equities settle at T+2, while US Government fixed-income stocks settle at T+1. Corporate, municipal and other fixed-income trades settle at T+2.

10.5 Japan

The Tokyo Stock Exchange (TSE) is one of five exchanges in Japan but is, undoubtedly, one of the more important world exchanges. The exchange has more than 2,000 listed companies, making it the third largest in the world. The exchange is home to the largest and best-known Japanese giants with a global presence, including Toyota, Honda and Mitsubishi.

The TSE uses an electronic, continuous auction system of trading. This means that brokers place orders online and when a buy and sell price match, the trade is automatically executed. Deals are made directly between buyer and seller, rather than through a market maker. The TSE uses price controls, so that the price of a stock cannot rise above or fall below a certain point throughout the day. These controls are used to prevent dramatic swings in prices that may lead to market uncertainty or stock crashes. If a major swing in price occurs, the exchange can stop trading on that stock for a specified period of time.

Settlement in Japan takes place at T+3 for both equities and corporate fixed-income trades, and at T+2 for Japanese Government bonds (JGBs), although this is likely to move towards T+1 settlement in 2018.

The Japan Securities Depository Centre (JASDEC) acts as the central securities depository (CSD) for equities. The Bank of Japan (BOJ) provides the central clearing system and depository for JGBs and Treasury bills.

Settlement within JASDEC is by book entry transfer, but without the simultaneous transfer of cash. However, these movements are co-ordinated through the TSE.

10.6 Germany

Deutsche Börse is the main German exchange and provides services that include securities and derivatives trading, transaction settlement, the provision of market information, as well as the development and operation of electronic trading systems.

The cash market comprises both floor trading and a fully electronic trading system. Both platforms provide efficient trading and optimum liquidity.

Xetra is Deutsche Börse's electronic trading system for the cash market and matches buy and sell orders from licensed traders in a central, fully electronic order book.

Floor trading takes place in Frankfurt. Each security is supported by a lead broker who fixes bid and ask prices and either executes incoming orders or manages them in an order book until they are executed, or deleted, or expire. Less liquid securities can thus also be traded efficiently on the trading floor.

Deutsche Börse also owns the international central securities depository, Clearstream, which provides integrated banking, custody and settlement services for the trading of fixed-interest securities and shares.

Clearstream performs clearing and settlement for the German market. At the end of March 2003, Eurex Clearing AG (part of the Deutsche Börse group) took on the role of CCP for German stocks traded on XETRA and Börse Frankfurt and held in collective safe custody.

Both equities and bonds now have a T+2 settlement cycle across all transactions involving German or foreign counterparties.

Clearstream Banking Frankfurt (CBF) acts as the central depository. Transfer is by book entry via one of two settlement processes, the Cascade system for domestic business, and through Clearstream for international users.

10.7 Developing Markets

There are many benefits to investing overseas. At a general level, these benefits arise from the fact that the world economy is not totally synchronised, most investment themes are global, many industries are either over- or under-represented in the UK and the UK equity market accounts for less than 10% of world stock market capitalisation. To be efficient then, a portfolio should be adequately diversified with no one geographical region or asset class monopolising it.

Although most overseas investment held by UK investors is in developed equity markets, emerging markets represent a rapidly increasingly proportion of UK overseas investment. The term 'emerging market' can be defined in various ways:

- markets in countries classified by the World Bank as low or middle income, and
- markets with a stock market capitalisation of less than 2% of the total world market capitalisation.

The attractions of investing in emerging markets are as follows:

- **Rapid economic growth** – developing nations tend to grow at faster rates of economic growth than developed nations as they attempt to catch up with rich country living standards by developing their infrastructure and financial systems. This process is assisted by domestic saving rates being generally higher than in developed nations and the embracing of world trade and foreign direct investment (FDI). Rapid economic growth tends to translate into rapid profits growth.
- **Low correlation of returns** – emerging markets offer significant diversification benefits when held with developed market investments, owing to the historically low correlation of returns between emerging and developed markets.
- **Attractive valuations** – emerging markets have historically traded at a discount to developed market valuations.

- **Industry representation** – investors are able to gain exposure to industries not represented in developed nations.
- **Inefficient pricing** – as emerging markets are not as well researched as their developed counterparts, pricing anomalies often appear.

However, there are also significant drawbacks:

- **Lack of transparency** – the quality and transparency of information is generally lower than for developed nations while accounting and other standards are generally not as comprehensive or as rigorously applied.
- **Regulation** – regulation is generally more lax in emerging than in developed markets and incidents of insider trading and fraud by local investors more prevalent. Corporate governance also tends to be lacking.
- **Volatility** – emerging market performances have been more volatile than that for developed markets owing to factors such as developing nations being less politically stable and more susceptible to banking and other financial crises.
- **Settlement and custodial problems** – the logistics of settling transactions and then arranging for custody of the securities purchased can be fraught with difficulty. In addition, property rights are not as well defined as in developed nations. However, these problems can be mitigated by using global depositary receipts (GDRs).
- **Liquidity** – as emerging markets are less liquid, or more concentrated, than their developed counterparts, investments in these markets tend not to be as readily marketable and, therefore, tend to trade on wider spreads.
- **Currencies** – emerging market currencies tend to be less stable than those of developed nations and periodically succumb to crises resulting from sudden significant outflows of overseas investor capital.
- **Controls on foreign ownership** – some developing nations impose restrictions on foreign ownership of particular industries.
- **Taxation** – emerging market returns may be subject to local taxes that may not be reclaimable under double taxation treaties.
- **Repatriation** – there may be severe problems in repatriating capital and/or income from investments made in some emerging markets.

10.8 The BRIC Markets

BRIC is an acronym for Brazil, Russia, India and China.

Goldman Sachs previously argued that, by 2050, the combined BRIC economies could eclipse the combined economies of the current richest countries of the world. These four countries currently account for more than a quarter of the world's land area and more than 40% of the world's population.

The annual growth rates in China and India, especially, are estimated to be between 6% and 7% per annum in 2017, when considered alongside the far less robust GDP growth rates which are forecasted for the G8 countries. This could mean that within 20 years the top ten economies ranked by GDP will look very different.

The Securities Market Structure

The manner in which the momentum for growth in the world economy is shifting is also reflected in the political structures which are emerging. Previously the semi-annual G7 summits and meetings of the respective finance ministers were the pivotal meetings for global policy coordination. However, the G20 summits which include all of the BRIC economies as well as those of the existing G7 and nations, such as Mexico and South Korea, are now becoming as important, if not more so, than the G7 gatherings.

Investing in these economies places investors at considerable risk however. In recent years, China has suffered significant crashes in its stock market and both Russia and Brazil have experienced recessionary pressures.

10.8.1 Investing in BRIC Economies

Certain collective investment vehicles are available to investors who wish to have investment exposure to the BRIC economies including specialised unit trusts and ETFs.

10.8.2 Exchanges in BRIC Economies

Brazil

The Bovespa Index (or Ibovespa) is an index of over 50 stocks that are traded on the BM&FBOVESPA exchange.

The index is composed by a theoretical portfolio of the stocks that accounted for 80% of the volume traded in the last 12 months and that were traded at least on 80% of the trading days. It is revised quarterly in order to keep its representativeness of the volumes traded and, on average, the components of Ibovespa represent 70% of all the stock value traded.

The Ibovespa is composed by the stocks that must meet the criteria as stipulated by the exchange:

- They should have been traded on the exchange in the past 12 months.
- To be included in the group of stocks whose negotiability indexes added represent 80% of the total value of all individual negotiability indexes.
- The trading share of the stock should be higher than 0.1% of the total share flow in the exchange.
- More than 80% of the shares of the stock must be traded on the exchange.

India

The Bombay Stock Exchange (BSE) is the oldest stock exchange in Asia. It has the largest number of listed companies in the world, with approximately 6,000. In August 2017, the equity market capitalisation of the companies listed on the BSE was US$1.8 trillion.

The listing requirements for the BSE are published at the exchange's website.

China

The Shanghai Stock Exchange (SSE) is one of the two stock exchanges operating independently in China; the other is the Shenzhen Stock Exchange. The SSE, founded in 1990, is the world's fifth largest stock market by market capitalisation at US$4.2 trillion as of August 2017. It is still not entirely open to foreign investors due to tight capital account controls exercised by the Chinese authorities.

A-shares are securities of Chinese incorporated companies that trade on either the Shanghai or Shenzhen stock exchanges. They are quoted in Chinese renminbi (RMB) or yuan. A-shares can be traded by residents of the People's Republic of China (PRC) or by international investors under the China qualified foreign institutional investors (QFII) regulations.

B-shares are securities of Chinese incorporated companies that trade on either the Shanghai or Shenzhen stock exchanges. They are quoted in US dollars (USD) on the Shanghai Stock Exchange (SSE) and in Hong Kong dollars (HKD) on the Shenzhen Stock Exchange. B-shares can be traded by non-residents of the PRC and also by residents of the PRC with appropriate foreign currency dealing accounts.

Russia

The Moscow Exchange Group is the largest in Russia. It operates trading markets in equities, bonds, derivatives, FX, money markets and precious metals. It also operates Russia's central securities depository, the National Settlement Depository and the country's largest clearing service provider, the National Clearing Centre.

The Moscow Exchange was created as a result of the 2011 merger of the Moscow Interbank Currency Exchange (MICEX) and the Russian Trading System (RTS) Stock Exchange. It is the main trading venue for Russian securities as well as a major venue for international trading participants willing to invest in the stocks and bonds of Russian companies.

The main market sector includes two main markets, each of which employs and offers specific procedures and instrument types.

- **Equity capital market** – offers trading in shares, depositary receipts, fund shares, and ETFs. Once a trade is executed in the main trading mode, it is settled two days after the trade has been conducted (ie, at T+2).
- **Debt capital market** – offers trading in Russian Federation Government bonds (OFZs), corporate bonds (including commercial papers), regional bonds, and municipal bonds. All bonds are traded in the main trading mode, and settled at T+0, except for OFZs, which are settled at T+1.

The main market sector accounts for over 80% of equities turnover and more than 99% of bonds trading volume on the Russian securities market. In the main market sector more than 1,400 securities from approximately 700 Russian issuers are available for trading every day.

11. Clearing, Settlement and Custody Process

Learning Objective

10.4 Demonstrate an understanding of: the clearing, settlement and custody process including the duties of central counterparty mechanisms and associated risks

11.1 Settlement

Settlement occurs after a deal has been executed. It is simply the transfer of ownership from the seller of the investment to the buyer, combined with the transfer of the cash consideration from the buyer to the seller. However, the process actually consists of several key stages, collectively described as clearing and settlement:

- **clearance** – the calculation of the obligations of the deal participants, the money to be paid and the securities to be transferred
- **settlement** – the final transfer of the securities (delivery) in exchange for the final transfer of funds (payment).

In any situation, the seller is unlikely to be willing to hand over legal title unless he is sure that the cash is flowing in the opposite direction, known as delivery versus payment (DvP). Similarly, the buyer is unlikely to be willing to hand over the cash without being sure that the legal ownership is passing in the other direction, known as cash against delivery (CAD).

There are two basic elements to the settlement of trades that can differ across different instruments and/or markets.

11.1.1 Timing of Settlement

Timing is normally based on a set number of business days after the trade is executed, known as 'rolling settlement'. The actual settlement dates are provided in the table on the following page.

Settlement System

There are a variety of settlement systems that are used in particular markets, for example, the majority of transactions in UK equities are settled via an electronic settlement facility, CREST, which since 2002 has been owned by Euroclear (about which more below). CREST has the status of a recognised clearing house (RCH) and is regulated by the BoE.

CREST clears the trade by matching the settlement details provided by the buyer and the seller. The transaction is then settled when CREST updates the register of the relevant company to transfer the shares to the buyer and, at the same time, CREST instructs the buyer's bank to transfer the appropriate amount of money to the seller's bank account.

In summary, to complete the settlement of a trade, CREST simultaneously:

- **updates the register of shareholders** – CREST maintains the so-called 'operator register' for UK companies' dematerialised shareholdings
- **issues a payment obligation** – CREST sends an instruction to the buyer's payment bank to pay for the shares
- **issues a receipt notification** – CREST notifies the seller's payment bank to expect payment.

The settlement process for OTC trades, which were discussed in section 6 of this chapter, will almost invariably not provide a clearing house or CCP mechanism to the trades. However, in the case of the CREST/Euroclear system there is a clearing house known as LCH.Clearnet which assumes responsibility for settling the transaction with each counterparty. The buyer and seller remain anonymous to each other. The role of a clearing house is discussed in greater detail below.

The settlement period for UK equities is normally on a T+2 basis, where T is the trade date and 2 is the number of business days after the trade date that the cash changes hands and the shares' registered title changes. In other words, if a trade is executed on a Wednesday, the cash and registered title will change hands two business days later, on the Friday. So, if the trade is executed on a Thursday, it will be on the following Monday that settlement will occur; this is referred to by the LSE as standard settlement. Standard settlement applies to all deals automatically executed on an LSE trading system, such as SETS.

The following table provides an overview of the settlement systems in the UK, the EU, the US and Japan:

Country/Region	Instruments settled	Settlement period	System name
UK	Listed equities and corporate bonds	T+2	CREST
	Government bonds (gilts)	T+1	CREST
EU (in particular, Germany)	Listed German equities	T+2 (cash settlement)	
	International bonds	T+2	
US	Listed equities	T+3	Depository Trust & Clearing Corporation (DTCC)
	Government bonds	T+1	DTCC
Japan	Listed equities and convertible bonds	T+2	Japan Securities Depository Center (JASDEC)

CREST allows shareholders and bondholders to hold assets in a dematerialised, ie, electronic, form, rather than holding physical share certificates. CREST also serves a number of other important functions, such as custodianship and assisting in the payments of dividends to shareholders and handling other corporate actions on behalf of the clients it represents.

The Securities Market Structure

CREST is also an 'electronic trade confirmation system' (ETC). When parties to a transaction make a deal, they both electronically confirm their sides of the transaction via file transfer. Both parties are required to submit confirmation details to CREST. In the event that transaction details do not match, CREST will highlight the issues and ensure that the problems are resolved as soon as is practicable.

Given that stamp duty is only payable on physical share certificates, there is no stamp duty payable on shares settled via CREST. There is, however, SDRT which is charged on electronic transfers only.

CREST holds all international stocks in a pool in a local depository such as Clearstream for German stocks and the DTCC for US stocks. CREST then issues a CREST Depository Interest (CDI) to each holder of the security, which can then be transferred in CREST, just like a UK equity. This is similar to the depositary receipts issued in other countries. However, restrictions apply to CDIs. Many are not withdrawable or depositable into/out of CREST. This is because a CDI is an electronic reflection of the underlying security held in the domestic (country of origin) market.

11.1.2 Depository Trust & Clearing Corporation (DTCC)

The electronic settlement system in the US is called DTCC. If a shareholder holds electronic stock in the US they will hold their securities electronically in DTCC. In reality they will hold the securities via a custodian, so the custodian's nominee details will appear on the DTCC register. This is known as holding stock in the 'domestic' market. Securities held this way can only be traded domestically, ie, in the market of the country of origin. If a shareholder wants to trade their securities outside of the US domestic market they can instruct their custodian to transfer their securities to the CREST account in DTCC. Restrictions apply, only securities that have a UK quote can be transferred to CREST's DTCC account. CREST is a member of DTCC. So once the securities have been transferred out of the original custodian's nominee name and into CREST's account in DTCC, the securities have now been 'cross bordered' into the UK market as CDIs. They can now be traded in the UK market, although not always withdrawn on to certificate or deposited into CREST.

11.2 Clearing

11.2.1 Clearing House – A CCP Mechanism

A clearing house is a financial institution that provides clearing and settlement services for financial and commodities derivatives and securities transactions. Before examining its method of operation it is important to consider counterparty risk.

11.2.2 Counterparty Risk

Counterparty risk is a general legal issue concerning the risk to each party, of any contractual arrangement, that the counterparty will not live up to its contractual obligations. In the specific financial context, counterparty risk is also known as 'default risk'. Since most financial transactions ultimately involve a contractual commitment, there is an important sense in which any and each transaction involving securities entails some element of counterparty risk.

The presence of a CCP clearing house provides a different level of protection against counterparty risk compared to OTC markets. Upon a transaction's acceptance by a clearing house, a CCP imposes itself as the legal counterparty to every trade. This substitution of counterparties is accomplished through the legal process of contract **novation**, which discharges the contract between the original trading counterparties and creates two new, legally binding contracts – one between each of the original trading counterparties and the clearing house.

A clearing house stands between two clearing firms (also known as 'member firms' or 'clearing participants') and its primary function is to reduce the risk of one (or more) clearing firms failing to honour its trade settlement obligations. A clearing house reduces the settlement risks by **netting** offsetting transactions between multiple counterparties, by requiring collateral deposits, or margin deposits, by providing independent valuation of trades and collateral, by monitoring the credit worthiness of the clearing firms, and in many cases, by providing a guarantee fund that can be used to cover losses that exceed a defaulting clearing firm's collateral on deposit.

Once a trade has been executed by two counterparties either on an exchange, or in the OTC markets, the trade can be handed over to a clearing house which then steps between the two original traders' clearing firms and assumes the legal counterparty risk for the trade. As the clearing house concentrates the risk of settlement failures into itself and is able to isolate the effects of a failure of a market participant, it also needs to be properly managed and capitalised in order to ensure its survival in the event of a significant adverse event, such as a large clearing firm defaulting or a market crash.

Clearing houses are capitalised with collateral from their clearing firms. In the event of a settlement failure, the clearing firm may be declared to be in default and clearing house default procedures may be utilised, which may include the orderly liquidation of the defaulting firm's positions and collateral. In the event of a significant clearing firm failure, the clearing house may draw on a guarantee fund in order to settle trades on behalf of the failed clearing firm.

11.2.3 Clearing Process

Buyers and sellers of derivative contracts do not create financial obligations to one another, but rather create obligations to the clearing house corporation through its member firms. A transaction in which investor A sells futures through ABC brokerage to XYZ brokerage for the account of investor B obligates ABC to the clearing organisation to perform under the terms of the contract, either to make delivery or to offset through an opposite and equal purchase of futures prior to the end of the trading period. In this way, the clearing house corporation acts as seller to the buyer at delivery.

The key safeguard in assuring performance on futures contracts is the clearing margin that clearing member firms must maintain with the clearing house against their position in each futures contract. Margins are set by the clearing corporation margin committee and directors. They are distinct from the margins that individual holders of commodities accounts are required to deposit with their brokers by exchange regulations.

Each clearing member's initial clearing margin deposits are made in relation to the net long or short position in each commodity. A long position is the buy side of a trade while a short position is the sell side. For example, to use a simple agricultural commodity for the futures contract, a clearing member firm with a short position of ten corn futures contracts, and a long position of five corn futures contracts, would be required to deposit margin money on the net short position of five corn contracts. Original margins are usually the same for all clearing members, although the directors are empowered to increase them in situations when particular risks develop.

Clearing margins may be posted in different forms or in combinations. For instance, in the US this could be:

- cash as evidenced by bank-issued margin certificates
- short-term government securities such as Treasury bills
- stock in the clearing corporation
- a letter of credit issued by an approved bank.

The margin deposited cannot be touched by the member firm until it is released by the clearing corporation. When a clearing member firm's position changes from day to day, the amount of margin required will also vary. One basic computation of the clearing corporation is the margin requirement for every clearing member after each trading session. A margin statement is provided each evening. In the event, the net position increases, additional margin must be deposited before the opening of the next day's market. When the net position in a commodity declines, excess margin money may be returned to the clearing member firm. Some firms prefer to keep surplus margin in reserve rather than draw it back on a daily basis.

Normally, initial margins are sufficient to cover daily maximum price fluctuations. When market prices move against a member's position, however, the standing margin is reduced to the extent of the price-change. The clearing corporation can call on a member to deposit additional margin money at any time within a trading session to cover adverse price changes. This is known as a 'variation margin call', and the member must pay the amount called for by wire transfer of funds within one hour. This amount is applied to the settlement for the day and does not go into the standing or initial margin account.

In this way, the clearing corporation maintains very tight control over margins as prices fluctuate.

Each day, the clearing corporation settles every account on its books. All futures accounts, long or short, whether traded during the most recent session or not, are adjusted daily as to gain or loss. The basis of adjustment is the difference between each delivery month's settlement price and the price at which a contract was made. The most common means of determining the settlement price is a simple average of the high and low prices in the closing range.

The role of clearing houses has expanded over time to include other functions including:

- transparent transaction processing
- post-trade management functions
- financial management of members' collateral deposits
- final settlement of outstanding obligations through financial payment or physical delivery
- the overall risk management of market participants
- a financial guarantee of performance of its contracts.

11.2.4 Clearing House Risks

An interesting question is how far does the clearing house's guarantee of performance extend? Under a net margin system, the clearing house collects margins from members only on their net exposure (their net long or net short position with the clearing house). This suggests that the clearing house's goal is not to guarantee all futures contracts, but only to protect clearing members from the default of other members.

11.2.5 Clearing in European Markets

The London Clearing House (LCH) is a leading, multi-asset class clearing house, serving a broad number of major exchanges and platforms, as well as a range of OTC markets.

LCH Group operates some of the largest clearing services operating in the financial markets today; this includes SwapClear, the clearing service for OTC interest rate swaps. Other clearing services include the FX clearing service, ForexClear, as well as CDSClear, the market's first credit derivatives clearing service to offer clearing of single-name CDSs referencing financial names.

All of these clearing services are situated within LCH Group's two clearing houses: LCH Ltd, which is a UK-based clearing house, and LCH SA, which is a clearing house registered and located in France. LCH Ltd, the UK-registered clearing house, offers clearing services that include SwapClear, ForexClear, RepoClear Ltd, EquityClear Ltd, CommodityClear Ltd and LCH's cleared Listed Rates business.

EuroCCP is a CCP that supports pan-European securities trading. It offers clearing and settlement services across Europe, and clears more than 6,000 securities.

EuroCCP adopts the novation concept, and substitutes itself for all counterparties, becoming the buyer to every seller and the seller to every buyer, therefore assuming counterparty risk and ensuring the settlement of trades in the event of a defaulting clearing member. It also ensures anonymity for all parties from the onset of a trade through to clearing and settlement. It provides clearing and settlement services for a number of platforms including Euronext (Amsterdam, Brussels, Lisbon, London, and Paris), the LSE, Sigma-X, SIX Swiss Exchange, and Turquoise.

EuroCCP is a company with limited liability, established in Amsterdam and owned by just five shareholders: ABN AMRO Clearing Investments, CBOE Europe Limited, DTCC Global Holdings, OMX, and Euronext each hold a 20% share.

ICE Clear Europe is one of the world's leading and most-diverse clearing houses. It provides CCP clearing and risk management services for interest rate, equity index, agricultural and energy derivatives, as well as European CDSs.

ICE Clear Europe is authorised as a CCP under the European Market Infrastructure Regulation (EMIR), having been recognised as a clearing house and CCP under FSMA, supervised by the Bank of England. It provides clearing services for futures and options contracts traded on ICE Futures Europe.

ICE Clear offers secure, capital-efficient clearing, risk management and physical delivery services through ICE Clear Europe. To help mitigate systemic risk, and protect the interests of its clearing members and customers, ICE Clear Europe holds $35 billion in its financial guarantee package (guarantee fund) and is regulated by the Bank of England in the UK and by the SEC and the CFTC in the US.

Eurex Clearing is one of the leading CCPs globally, assuring the safety and integrity of markets while providing innovation in risk management, clearing technology and client asset protection.

Eurex Clearing provides its services for derivatives, equities, bonds and the secured funding and securities financing market. Using the concept of novation, Eurex acts as the CCP between the buyer and the seller for all transactions. It serves approximately 200 clearing members in 19 countries, managing a collateral pool of €49 billion and clearing trades valued at €11 trillion every month.

Eurex Clearing is a company incorporated in Germany, and is also an authorised clearing house under EMIR.

12. The Role of International Central Securities Depositories

Learning Objective

10.4 Demonstrate an understanding of: the clearing, settlement and custody process including the duties of central counterparty mechanisms and associated risks, the role of international central securities depositories (ICSDs)

12.1 The Role of International Central Securities Depositories (ICSD)

An ICSD is a CSD that settles transactions in eurobonds. There are only three ICSDs; Clearstream, Euroclear and SIX SIS.

In addition to their dealings in eurobonds, these organisations also provide custody and settlement services in international securities and in various domestic securities, usually through direct or indirect (using local agents) links to local CSDs.

A CSD is an institution that holds financial instruments, including equities, bonds, money market instruments and mutual funds. It allows ownership of those instruments to be transferred, in electronic form, by updating electronic records often known as 'book-entry' records. The UK's CSD is Euroclear UK & Ireland, also known as CREST.

In general, each country will have only one CSD (although there are some that split equities, fixed-income, and funds into separate CSDs). The CSD will normally only have local financial institutions regulated in the country of the CSD as clients. In some cases, these organisations also carry out centralised comparison, and transaction processing such as clearing and settlement of securities. The physical securities may be immobilised by the depository, or securities may be dematerialised (so that they exist only as electronic records).

12.2 Functions of a CSD

12.2.1 Immobilisation

Immobilisation entails the use of securities in paper form and the use of depositories, which are electronically linked to a settlement system. Securities (either constituted by paper instruments or represented by paper certificates) are immobilised, in the sense that they are held by the depository at all times. In the historic transition from paper-based to electronic practice, immobilisation often serves as a transitional phase prior to dematerialisation which is the replacement of certificates altogether with electronic forms.

12.2.2 Safekeeping

Securities may be in dematerialised form, book-entry only form (with one or more 'global' certificates), or in physical form immobilised within the CSD.

12.2.3 Deposit and Withdrawal

Supporting deposits and withdrawals involves the relationship between the transfer agent and/or issuers and the CSD. It also covers the CSD's role within the underwriting process or listing of new issues in a market.

12.2.4 Corporate Action Processing

CSDs will perform all of the administrative tasks involved in processing dividends, interest, and principal processing, as well as corporate actions including proxy voting paying and transfer agents, as well as issuers that are involved in these processes, depending on the level of services provided by the CSD and its relationship with these entities.

12.2.5 Pledging

CSDs provide pledging of shares and securities. Each jurisdiction provides its own legal framework to protect the interest of the pledgor and pledgee.

12.2.6 Other Services

CSDs offer additional services aside from those considered core services, including securities lending and borrowing, matching, and repo settlement.

13. Custody of Assets

Learning Objective

10.4 Demonstrate an understanding of: the clearing, settlement and custody process including the duties of central counterparty mechanisms and associated risks, the role of international central securities depositories (ICSDs), the custody of assets & client money and relevance & impact of corporate actions

13.1 Role and Responsibility of a Custodian

The primary responsibility of the custodian is to ensure that the client's assets are fully protected at all times. Hence, it must provide robust safekeeping facilities for all valuables and documentation, ensuring that investments are only released from the custodian's care in accordance with authorised instructions from the client.

Importantly, the client's assets must be properly segregated from those of the custodian and appropriate legal arrangements must be in place to ensure that financial or external shock to the custodian does not expose the client's assets to claims from creditors or any other party.

13.1.1 Services Provided by Custodians

When an institutional investor invests in securities it will commonly employ the services of a custodian to administer these securities by:

- providing safe keeping of the investor's assets in the local market
- making appropriate arrangements for delivery and receipt of cash and securities to support settlement of the investor's trading activities in that market
- providing market information to the investor on developments and reforms within that market
- collecting dividend income, interest paid on debt securities and other income payments in the local market
- managing the client's cash flows
- monitoring and managing entitlements through corporate actions and voting rights held by the investor in the local market
- managing tax reclaims and other tax services in the local market
- ensuring that securities are registered and that transfer of legal title on securities transactions proceeds effectively
- ensuring that reporting obligations to the regulatory authorities, and to other relevant bodies, are discharged effectively.

An investor faces choices in selecting custody arrangements with regard to a portfolio of global assets. The possible paths can be summarised as follows:

- appointing a local custodian in each market in which they invest (often referred to as direct custody arrangements)
- appointing a global custodian to manage custody arrangements across the full range of foreign markets in which they have invested assets
- making arrangements to settle trades and hold securities and cash with a CSD within each market, or to go via an ICSD.

13.2 Global Custody

A global custodian provides investment administration for its clients, including processing cross-border securities trades and keeping financial assets secure (ie, providing safe custody) outside of the country where the investor is located.

The term 'global custody' came into common usage in the financial services world in the mid-1970s, when the Employee Retirement Income Security Act (ERISA) of 1974 was passed in the US. This legislation was designed to increase the protection given to US pension fund investors. The Act specified that US pension funds could not act as custodians of the assets held in their own funds. Instead, these assets had to be held in the safekeeping of another bank. ERISA went further to specify that only a US bank could provide custody services for a US pension fund.

Subsequently, use of the term global custody has evolved to refer to a broader set of responsibilities, encompassing settlement, safekeeping, cash management, record-keeping and asset servicing (for example, collecting dividend payments on shares and interest on bonds, reclaiming withholding tax, advising investor clients on their electing on corporate actions entitlements), and providing market information. Some investors may also use their global custodians to provide a wider suite of services, including investment accounting, treasury and FX, securities lending and borrowing, collateral management, and performance and risk analysis on the investor's portfolio.

Some global custodians maintain an extensive network of branches globally and can meet the local custody needs of their investor clients by employing their own branches as local custody providers. Citi, for example, maintains a proprietary branch network, covering 63 global markets. Consequently, Citi, acting as global custodian for an investor client, may opt to use its own branch to provide local custody in many locations where the investor holds assets.

In locations where a global custodian does not have its own branch, or in situations when it may find advantage by looking outside of its proprietary branch network, a global custodian may appoint an external agent bank to provide local custody services. For example, if Citi does not feel that there is a sound economic rationale for maintaining its own branches, it will employ external agents to act as its sub-custodian in these markets. Similarly, investment banks and global broker/dealers (eg, Morgan Stanley, Goldman Sachs and UBS) will also typically employ a network of agent banks to meet their needs for clearing, settlement, asset servicing and cash management in markets around the world where they have investment activities.

13.3 Sub-Custody

A sub-custodian is employed by a global custodian as its local agent to provide settlement and custody services for assets that it holds on behalf of investor clients in a foreign market. A sub-custodian effectively serves as the eyes and ears of the global custodian in the local market, providing a range of clearing, settlement and asset servicing duties. It will also typically provide market information relating to developments in the local market, and will lobby the market authorities for reforms that will make the market more appealing and an efficient target for foreign investment.

In selecting a sub-custodian, a global custodian may appoint:

- one of its own branches, in cases when this option is available
- a local agent bank that specialises in providing sub-custody in the market concerned
- a regional provider that can offer sub-custody to the global custodian across a range of markets in a region or globally.

13.4 Local Custodian

Agent banks that specialise in providing sub-custody in their home market are sometimes known as single-market providers. Stiff competition from larger regional or global competitors has meant that these are becoming a dying breed. However, some continue to win business in their local markets, often combining this service with offering global custody or master custody for institutional investors in their home markets.

A principal selling point is that they are local market specialists and that is what they do – hence they can remain focused on their local business without spreading their attentions broadly across a wide range of markets. A local specialist bank may be attractive in a market in which local practices tend to differ markedly from global standards, or when a provider's long-standing relationship with the local regulatory authorities and/or political elite leaves it particularly well placed to lobby for reforms on behalf of its cross-border clients.

Reciprocal arrangements may be influential in shaping the appointment of a local provider in some instances. Under such an arrangement, a global custodian (A) may appoint the local provider (B) to deliver sub-custody in its local market (market B). In return, the custodian (A) may offer sub-custody in its own home market (market A) for pension and insurance funds in market B that use provider B as their global custodian.

In summary, the strengths of a local custodian may include the following:

- They are country specialists.
- They can be the 'eyes and ears' of the global custodian or broker/dealer in the local market.
- They will have regular dealings with financial authorities and local politicians – may be well placed to lobby for reforms that will improve the efficiency of the local market.
- They have expert knowledge of local market practice, language and culture.
- They may offer opportunities for reciprocal business.

A local custody bank may be perceived to have the following disadvantages when compared with a regional custodian:

- Their credit rating may not match up to requirements laid down by some global custodians or global broker/dealers.
- They cannot leverage developments in technology and client service across multiple markets (unlike a regional custodian) – hence product and technology development may lag behind the regional custodians with which it competes.
- They may not be able to offer the price discounts that can be extended by regional custodians offering custody services across multiple markets.

13.5 Regional Custodian

A regional custodian is able to provide agent bank services across multiple markets in a region.

For example, Standard Chartered Bank and HSBC have both been offering regional custody and clearing in the Asia-Pacific and South Asian regions for many years, competing with Citi and some strong single market providers for business in this area.

Employing a regional custodian may offer a range of advantages to global custodian or global broker/dealer clients:

- Its credit rating may be higher than for single-market custodians.
- It can cross-fertilise good practice across multiple markets – lessons learned in one market may be applied, when appropriate, across other markets in its regional offering.
- It can leverage innovation in technology, product development and client service across multiple markets – delivering economies of scale benefits.
- It can offer standardised reporting, management information systems and market information across multiple markets in its regional offering.
- Economies of scale may support delivery of some or all product lines from a regional processing centre – offering potential cost savings and efficiency benefits.
- Its size and regional importance, plus the strength of its global client base, may allow a regional custodian to exert considerable leverage on local regulators, political authorities and infrastructure providers. This may be important in lobbying for reforms that support greater efficiency and security for foreign investors in that market.
- A global client may be able to secure price discounts by using a regional custodian across multiple markets.

In some situations, a regional provider may be perceived to have certain disadvantages when compared with a local custody bank:

- A regional custodian's product offering may be less well attuned to local market practice, service culture and investor needs than a well-established local provider.
- A regional custodian may spread its focus across a wider range of clients and a wider range of markets than a single market provider. Hence, a cross-border client may not receive the same level of attention, and the same degree of individualised service, as may be extended by a local custodian.
- Some regional custodians may lack the long track record, customer base and goodwill held by some local custodians in their own market.

13.6 Standard Form of a Custody Agreement

In order to formalise the custody arrangements outlined above, it is standard for the institutional investor and the global custodian to sign a custody agreement that details:

- the legal conditions under which the investor's assets are held by the global custodian, and are protected and segregated from the assets of the global custodian
- the responsibilities and obligations required of the global custodian under the custody relationship
- authority for the custodian to accept instructions from fund managers, in instances when an institutional investor employs investment managers to manage assets on its behalf.

The global custodians will negotiate a separate custody agreement with each institutional investor that it conducts business with. Given that these institutions may have markedly different investment strategies, allocating their assets across a different range of markets and investment instruments, the structure and content of the legal agreement may differ significantly from client to client.

A custody agreement is likely to address the following issues:

- the method through which the client's assets are received and held by the global custodian
- reporting obligations and deadlines
- guidelines for use of CSDs and other relevant use of financial infrastructure
- business contingency plans to cope with systemic malfunction or disaster
- liability in contract and claims for damages
- standards of service and care required under the custody relationship
- list of persons authorised to give instructions
- actions to be taken in response to instructions and actions to be taken without instructions.

Institutional investors and global custodians are required to adhere to the legal framework prevailing in the countries in which assets are invested.

The custody agreement will typically include provision on the part of the investor to conduct periodic reviews of the custodian's internal control environment in order to ensure that it has effective procedures in place to monitor and manage risk. These controls should ensure that the investor's assets are held securely and that procedures for accepting and acting on authorised instructions are in place.

The custody agreement will commonly detail the level of indemnity that the global custodian will provide to the client in instances of error or negligence on its own part, or the part of sub-custodians that it employs. It will also define the level of indemnity, if at all, that it will provide to clients against catastrophic events, default by a CSD or clearing house, theft or fraud, and a wide range of other contingencies.

13.7 Sub-Custody Agreement

When the global custodian employs a sub-custodian to provide custody on its behalf in a foreign market, it will sign a legal agreement with the sub-custody provider that will detail:

- the legal conditions under which client assets are held by the sub-custodian, and are protected and segregated from the assets of the sub-custodian
- the responsibilities and obligations required of the sub-custodian by the global custodian under the custody relationship.

Sub-custodian, global custodian and its foreign investor clients are bound by the legal regulations prevailing in the overseas market. Hence, while many provisions of the sub-custodian agreement will resemble those appearing in the investor-global custodian agreement outlined above, these provisions will be amended in certain instances to comply with local regulatory requirements and legal practice.

13.8 Service Level Agreement (SLA)

Detailed specifications pertaining to the standards of service required by an investor from its custodian are spelt out in a service level agreement (SLA). This lays down required standards for service areas including:

- record-keeping, maintenance of accurate and up-to-date documentation
- settlement on both recognised exchanges and in OTC markets
- communication and reporting
- processing of corporate actions – eg, rights issues and other capitalisation matters
- income processing, for example from dividends and coupon payments
- tax services
- cash management
- management information systems
- stock lending and borrowing
- market information and market knowledge
- standards of service expected from account officers and relationship managers that represent primary points of contact with the investor.

13.9 Selecting a Custodian

When selecting a global custodian, an institutional investor will typically invite statements of interest from suitable candidates. The investor may ask for further detail of services offered by applicants via a request for information (RFI). Eligible candidates will typically then be asked to complete a detailed request for proposal (RFP) submission as a preliminary stage in the appointment process. An RFP is a tendering process for buyers of global financial services.

Although the size and scope of the RFP will vary slightly from client to client, this will generally represent a lengthy questionnaire that will request background information on the custodian's staffing and IT capacity, its track record and experience in the custody area, the strength of its existing client base and assets under custody, its creditworthiness and its record of recent losses.

The RFP should be viewed as an early stage in the selection process, rather than a selection process in its own right. Typically, it will be used to screen out candidates that do not meet the client's selection criteria, and then to provide a springboard for further investigation at the site visit and/or interview stage.

13.10 Regulation and Legislation affecting Custodians

Legislation governing the responsibilities held by pension fund trustees and other fiduciaries can be important in shaping the procedures through which custodians are appointed and standards of service monitored. For example, standards of fiducial conduct laid down in the US in Section 404 of the ERISA or the 1995 UK Pensions Act, require pension fund trustees to be directly responsible for the appointment of custodians. This makes trustees liable for civil penalties if they rely on the skill or judgement of any person who is appointed (other than by the trustees) to exercise a prescribed function. To put it simply, this requires that pension fund trustees should have a direct legal relationship with their custodian, not an indirect one via the investment manager or any other appointed intermediary. Trustees must take full responsibility for appointing and monitoring the actions of custodians acting on behalf of their fund.

In their capacity as fiduciaries, pension fund trustees are generally required to uphold the following prudential standards:

- They must demonstrate that they have the necessary familiarity with the structure and aims of their pension scheme and have an appropriate level of training and skill to carry out their responsibilities to scheme members effectively.
- Fiduciaries have a responsibility to monitor and review the tasks that they delegate to third parties (including custodians and investment management companies) in order to ensure that these tasks are discharged effectively.
- The duty of loyalty demands that trustees administer their pension scheme solely in the best interests of the scheme members.
- Trustees must avoid undue risk in the way that they manage scheme assets, and appoint intermediaries to manage or administer scheme assets, on the scheme's behalf.

Also, legislation guiding safekeeping of client assets typically requires that a firm that holds safe custody investments with a custodian must have effective and transparent procedures in place for custodian selection and for monitoring performance. The frequency of these risk reviews should be dependent on the nature of the market and the type of services that the custodian delivers to the client.

Example Exam Question on the Securities Market Structure

Questions from this module frequently appear in the exam. Occasionally a longer question will arise but much of the time, questions have been set in Section A.

The following example act as practice questions from Section A.

Winter 2012

Discuss the risks of investing in emerging markets. (5 marks)

Discuss the main conditions that must be met by companies seeking admission to the alternative investment market (AIM). (5 marks)

Winter 2013

Discuss the choice that an IPO issuer has as to whether the offer will be 'Underwritten'. (5 marks)

Exercise Answers

Exercise 1

Outline one benefit and one potential drawback of a company obtaining a dual listing.

Answer

A key aim behind dual listing may be to improve the liquidity of a company's stock.

One potential drawback is that often it is found that much of a company's trade still gets carried out on one exchange. It may not therefore create the benefit to liquidity originally thought.

Exercise 2

Outline what you consider could be a benefit of OTC trading.

Answer

One key advantage of carrying out an OTC trade is the customised nature of the contract to specifically meet the counterparties' requirements (see section 6.3 for further information).

Exercise 3

Explain what a systematic internaliser (as defined in MiFID II) is and does.

Answer

- A systematic internaliser is, in broad terms, an investment firm making markets outside a regulated market or an MTF.
- The firm executes orders from its clients against its own book or against orders from other clients.
- MiFID treats systematic internalisers as mini-exchanges, hence, for example, they will be subject to the pre-trade and post-trade transparency requirements.

Glossary

Basis

The difference between the present cash price and the nearby futures price of an asset. Calculation is cash minus futures. Basis will be negative in a contango market, and positive in a backwardation market.

Bears

An investor who believes the market in general, or a particular investment, will fall.

Black-Scholes

An equation for valuing plain vanilla options developed by Fischer Black and Myron Scholes in 1973 for which they shared the Nobel Prize in Economics.

Bond

A debt security issued by an organisation such as a government or corporation. Bonds pay regular interest and repay their principal or face value at maturity. One of the most common underlying assets for derivative contracts.

Bull

An investor who believes the market in general, or a particular investment, will rise.

Call Option

A call option gives the owner the right but not the obligation to buy a pre-set amount of the underlying financial instrument at a pre-set price with a pre-set maturity date.

Cap

A financial contract giving the owner the right but not the obligation to borrow a pre-set amount of money at a pre-set interest rate with a pre-set maturity date. Equivalent to a call option.

Cash Settlement

Derivatives contracts which are settled at maturity (or before maturity at closeout) by an exchange of cash from the party who is out-of-the-money to the party who is in-the-money.

Collar

A combination of options in which the holder of the contract has bought an out-of-the money option call (or put) and sold an out-of-the-money put (or call). This locks in the effective minimum and maximum rates that the collar owner will transact in the underlying at expiry.

Commodity Swap

A contract in which counterparties agree to exchange payments related to indices, at least one of which (and possibly both of which) is a commodity index.

Contango (see also Backwardation)

Commodities or futures markets where shorter-dated contracts trade at a lower price than longer-dated contracts.

Contingent Liability

A potential liability for loss, over and above the amount invested, the amount of which cannot be established at the outset of a derivatives contract. For example, the seller of a future does not know how high the price could move against him – he is in a contingent liability situation.

Contracts for Difference (CFD)

A derivative contract which involves the exchange of the cash difference between the pre-agreed price and the closing price of an underlying instrument (such as a commodity, an index or a share price). A contract involving cash settlement.

Counterparty Risk

See Credit Risk.

Credit Risk

The exposure to loss associated with the payment default or failure on a payment due from a transaction/trade by a counterparty. It is also known as counterparty risk.

Currency Swap (see also interest rate swap)

An exchange of interest rate payments in different currencies on a pre-set notional amount and in reference to pre-determined interest rate indices in which the notional amounts might be exchanged at inception of the contract and then re-exchanged at the termination of the contract at pre-set exchange rates.

Delta

The sensitivity of the change in the option's price to changes in the price of the underlying asset.

Delivery

The settlement of a contract (such as a future) by delivery of the asset by the seller to the exchange clearing house. The long position holder takes delivery from the clearing house against payment.

Derivatives

Instruments whose price is derived from another asset. Examples include futures, options, foreign exchange (FX) forwards and swaps.

European-Style Option

An option that can be exercised only at expiry as opposed to an American Style option that can be exercised at any time from inception of the contract. European Style option contracts can be closed out early, mimicking the early exercise property of American style options in most cases.

Exchange-Traded Contracts

financial instruments listed on exchanges such as the Chicago Board of Trade.

Exchange Delivery Settlement Price (EDSP)

The price at which maturing futures are settled. It is an ICE Futures term.

Exchange For Physicals (EFP)

The exchange of a future's position for a physical position. Also known as 'against actuals' (AA).

Exercise

The decision by a holder of an option to take up their rights. In a call option, exercise involves buying the underlying asset; in a put option exercise involves selling the underlying asset.

Exercise Price (see also strike price)

The price at which a call's (put's) buyer can buy (or sell) the underlying instrument.

Exotic Derivatives

Any derivative contract that is not a plain vanilla contract and which is typically non-path dependent. Examples include barrier options, average rate and average strike options, lookback options and chooser options.

Fair Value

The theoretical price of a future, ie, cash price plus cost of carry.

Foreign Exchange (FX)

The name given to the general aspects of currency trading.

Forward

An OTC derivative on, for example, foreign exchange. Forward prices are based on the spot price and the interest rate differential of the two currencies, in the same way as exchange-traded FX futures.

Floor (see also Cap; Collar)

A financial contract giving the owner the right but not the obligation to lend a pre-set amount of money at a pre-set interest rate with a pre-set maturity date. It is equivalent to a put option.

Forward Contract

An over-the-counter (OTC) obligation to buy or sell a financial instrument or to make a payment at some point in the future. Examples include forward foreign exchange contracts in which one party is obligated to buy foreign exchange from another party at a fixed rate for delivery on a pre-set date.

Glossary

Forward rate agreements (FRAs)

A cash-settled obligation on interest rates for a pre-set period on a pre-set interest rate index with a forward start date. A 3×6 FRA on US dollar LIBOR is a contract between two parties obliging one to pay the other the difference between the fixed FRA rate and the floating LIBOR rate observed for that period.

Futures

An exchange-traded obligation to buy or sell a financial instrument or to make a payment at one of the exchange's fixed delivery dates, the details of which are transparent publicly on the trading floor. Contract settlement takes place through the exchange's clearinghouse.

Gamma

The degree of curvature in an option's price curve with respect to its underlying price. It is the rate of change of the delta (ie, delta of the delta) with respect to changes in the underlying price. Positive gamma is favourable. Negative gamma is damaging in a volatile market. Positive gamma is offset by negative theta (time decay). It grows most (ie, is most sensitive) in options which are at-the-money as time moves closer to expiry.

Gearing (or Leveraging)

An important feature of derivatives. Because only a small percentage of an asset's value is required when a contract is entered into (initial margin or premium) a small change in the underlying asset's value can lead to large percentage gains or losses relative to the initial investment. Also known as 'leverage'.

Hedge

A transaction that offsets an exposure to fluctuations in financial prices of some other contract or business risk. It may consist of cash instruments or derivatives.

Implied Volatility

Option pricing models rely upon an assumption of future volatility as well as the spot price, interest rates, the expiry date, the delivery date, the strike, etc. If all these parameters except for volatility are available as well as the option price, the volatility can be implied mathematically (eg, through the Black-Scholes equation).

In-the-money – Spot or Forward

An option with positive intrinsic value with respect to the prevailing market spot or forward rate. If the option were to mature immediately, the option holder would exercise it to capture its economic value.

Initial Margin

A good faith deposit (in the form of collateral or cash) lodged with the broker or clearing house against potential liabilities on an open position. It is returned when the position is closed out.

Interest Rate Swap

An exchange of cash flows based upon different interest rate denominated in the same currency on a pre-set notional amount with a pre-determined schedule of payments and calculations. Usually, one counterparty will received fixed flows in exchange for making floating payments.

Intrinsic Value

The economic value of an option, as distinct from its time value. For a call option to have intrinsic value, the strike must be less than the current spot or forward price. For a put option, the strike must be greater than the current spot or forward price. Intrinsic value cannot be less than zero.

Last Trading Day

The last day for trading futures with the current delivery month. All contracts outstanding/open at the end of the last trading day must be settled by delivery or by cash settlement.

London Interbank Offered Rate (LIBOR)

An interest rate benchmark. The average rate at which banks will lend for example, sterling, dollars, euros and yen to each other for periods such as one month and three months. Established by a daily survey by the British Bankers' Association (BBA) which also asks for bid rates enabling London Interbank Bid Rate (LIBID) to be calculated, which is how much banks will pay to borrow funds.

Long

The buyer of an asset is long the asset. Futures buyers are long the futures. Options buyers or holders are long the options.

Margin

Collateral paid to the clearing house by the counterparties to a derivatives transaction to guarantee their positions against loss. Initial margin is a security deposit that must be handed to the exchange clearing house by a broker (and to the broker by their client) for futures or short options. See also Variation Margin.

Multilateral Trading Facility (MTF)

See Electronic Communication Network.

Naked Option Writing

Selling options without having any offsetting exposure in the underlying cash instrument.

Netting

A system or agreement whereby all outstanding contracts of the same specification maturing, on the same date, between two counterparties can be settled on a net basis. This is an efficient way of reducing the number of settlements, the cost of settlement and counterparty risk.

Novation

The legal process when the exchange's clearing house becomes the counterparty to both the buyer and seller of futures contracts, substituting the original contract.

Open Outcry

Trading system where participants meet face-to-face and shout out their prices and trade sizes to the other traders on the floor. Used in many US exchanges.

Option

The right but not the obligation to buy (sell) a pre-determined amount of an underlying cash instrument at a pre-determined rate on a pre-determined expiration date.

Out-of-the-Money – Spot or Forward

An option with no intrinsic value with respect to the prevailing market spot or forward rate. If the option were to mature immediately, the option holder would let it expire. For a call price to have intrinsic value, the strike must be less than the current forward price. For a put price to have intrinsic value, the strike must be greater than the current forward price.

Over-the-Counter (OTC)

Any transaction that takes place between two counterparties directly, without involving an exchange. Contracts can be non-standardised, as negotiated between both counterparties.

Physical Delivery

Where the settlement of a futures contract is by delivery of the physical underlying asset. Certain futures (eg, copper) will run through to physical delivery for final settlement. Other futures (eg, stock index futures and short-term interest rate derivatives) are cash settled. Delivery is particularly important for commodities.

Premium

The price of an option, referring to the combination of intrinsic value and time value. It is paid by the buyer of an option contract to the seller, usually at the start of the contract.

Put Option (see also Option)

A financial contract giving the owner the right but not the obligation to sell a pre-set amount of the underlying financial instrument at a pre-set price with a pre-set maturity date.

Short

1. To need an asset.
2. Another term for selling futures or selling/writing call or put options.
3. To hold a net sold position.

Spot

The price in the cash market for delivery using the standard market convention. In the foreign exchange market, spot is delivered in most currencies for value two days from the transaction date.

Speculation

Taking positions in financial instruments without having an underlying exposure that offsets them.

Spread

1. In futures – buying and selling different months of the same asset (intra-market spread) with a view about changes in basis.
2. In futures – buying and selling futures in different assets (inter-market spread). For example, a fund manager could increase his effective weighting of US heating oil by buying NYMEX futures and simultaneously selling ICE Futures Gas Oil.
3. In options – see Vertical Spreads.
4. The difference between the bid and offer price.

Strike Price

The price at which the holder of an option exercises their right if it makes economic sense to do so at the appropriate expiry time.

Swap

An OTC hedging contract when exchanged cash flows are dependent on the price of an underlying commodity. This is normally used to hedge against the price of a commodity. Typically based upon the same principles as are used in financial OTC derivatives to exchange a series of payments with a counterparty, eg, fixed for floating interest rates, currency A for currency B and income from asset C for income from asset D.

Synthetic

Manufactured position, eg, a synthetic future can be created by buying a call and selling a put option on the future.

Theta

The sensitivity of an option's premium to changes in the time remaining to expiry, all other factors staying the same.

Tick (or Tick Size)

The smallest permitted variation between prices quoted to buy and sell on derivatives exchanges. For example, the tick for gold is 10 cents so prices of $990.00, $990.10, $990.20 can be quoted, but not $990.13.

Tick Value

The profit or loss that arises when prices move by one tick.

Vanilla

A derivative in its most simple form, with no unusual features of terms

Variation Margin

Margin is transferred from the account of the loser to the winner as prices move on a daily basis and positions are marked-to-market. The total accumulated variation margin equates to the profit or loss when a position is closed out.

Vega

The sensitivity of an option's premium to changes in implied volatility, all other factors staying the same.

Volatility

The measure of the probability of an asset's price moving. Usually calculated as annualised standard deviation. Volatility has an important impact on the pricing of options.

Warrant

1. A securitised option. An example is a security, which can be converted into shares in a company.
2. A document of title to goods, for example, warrants are used to satisfy the physical delivery of metals on the LME.

Syllabus Learning Map

Syllabus

Learning Outcome 01 Be able to assess the implications of macroeconomics and macroeconomic policy for financial markets		Chapter 1 Section
1.1	Evaluate Classical, Keynesian and Monetarist approaches in the context of macroeconomic government policy targets, instruments	1
1.2	Appraise the effectiveness of Classical, Keynesian and Monetarist approaches in the context of macroeconomic government policy targets, instruments	2
1.3	Analyse the impact of macroeconomics on the behaviour of markets, sectors, companies, and investment themes	3
1.4	Evaluate the effect of fiscal and monetary policy on inflation, interest rates, and exchange rates	4
1.5	Interpret macroeconomic statistics	5
1.6	Explain the role of financial markets and services within the economy	6

Learning Outcome 02 Be able to explain the structure and content of financial statements issued by companies and their impact on the valuation of securities		Chapter 2 Section
2.1	Explain the core accounting concepts: • dual aspect • money measurement • entity • going concern • asset management • accruals basis • matching principle • prudence • consistency and comparability • accounting for subsidiaries and overseas business	1
2.2	Explain the principles behind the construction of a balance sheet	2
2.3	Explain the principles behind the construction of an income statement	3
2.4	Explain the principles behind the construction of a cash flow statement	4
2.5	Summarise the financial statement accounting standards: • legal compliance • application and differences between UK GAAP, IFRS and IAS	5
2.6	Critically appraise a valuation based on a number of subjective assumptions • true and fair concept • apply a sceptical and critical approach	5.3

Learning Outcome 03 Be able to select and apply the principal accounting ratios, and explain their advantages and limitations, in the evaluation and comparison of financial statements		Chapter 3 Section
3.1	Apply the following profitability ratios: • return on capital employed • gross and net profit margins • asset turnover and gearing	1
3.2	Apply the following liquidity ratios: • working capital (current) ratio • quick (acid test) ratio	2
3.3	Apply receivables, payables and inventory ratios	3
3.4	Apply financial gearing ratios for: • debt/equity • interest cover • asset cover	4
3.5	Evaluate growth in sales, profitability, capital	5
3.6	Apply investor ratios: earnings per share including adjustments for capitalisation changes, corporate actions and post-balance sheet events	6
3.7	Calculate earnings yield, dividend yield and dividend cover	7
3.8	Interpret the implications and limitations of the analysis in the context of: • circumstances of the business • accounting policy and practice • distorting effects	8
3.9	Apply other interpretation tools: trend and common size statements	9

Learning Outcome 04 Be able to select and apply the techniques and concepts of the time value of money, compounding, discounting and annualising		Chapter 4 Section
4.1	Select and apply the techniques of time value of money, present value and discounted cash flow to investment scenarios	1
4.2	Select and apply discounting and compounding to: • perpetuities • continuous, annual and non-annual time periods	2
4.3	Select and apply standardised interest rate calculations: • APR • AER	3
4.4	Evaluate the effects of inflation on cash flows and determine the appropriate discount factor	4
4.5	Calculate and appraise annualisation techniques	5

Learning Outcome 05 Be able to evaluate critically the risks and returns offered by short-term, liquid instruments		Chapter 5 Section
5.1	Explain the types of cash deposits and their characteristics, including: • definition and key properties of cash • risk, price, and return • historic performance of cash • principal problems and liquidity issues, plus implications should liquidity fall • onshore deposit and savings accounts • offshore accounts and tax implications	2
5.2	Explain and evaluate the nature and use by investors of the money markets, money market participants, near cash and short-term money market instruments	3
5.3	Explain, calculate and appraise the investment performance of Treasury bills	4
5.4	Explain and evaluate the effect of inflation on the investment risk and return of short-term liquid instruments	5

Learning Outcome 06 Be able to evaluate critically the risks and returns offered by bonds		Chapter 6 Section
6.1	Explain the characteristics of bonds: • definition, types, and key properties of bonds • risk, price, and return • historic performance of bonds • principal problems and liquidity issues, plus implications should liquidity fall • maturities and redemption characteristics • coupons	1
6.2	Explain the characteristics of UK and overseas government bonds: • issuance • secondary markets • types of bond • repo market • borrowing/lending • trading and settlement	2

6.3	Explain the characteristics of UK and overseas corporate bonds: • markets • credit ratings • security • redemption • types of bond • fixed/floating coupon structures • covenants and sweeteners • domestic and Eurobond issuance • trading and settlement	3
6.4	Evaluate bond pricing using: • DCF evaluation • clean and dirty pricing of different types of bonds • index-linked issues and STRIPS	4
6.5	Apply the following methods in the calculation of bond returns, understanding their uses and limitation: • flat and running yield • gross and net redemption yield • grossed-up equivalent yield • real yields (inflation linked securities)	5
6.6	Evaluate the impact of interest rates on the term structure of a bond, including: • derivation of, and relationship between, yields, spot and forward rates • yield curves • liquidity preference and expectations theory • demand effects • interpretation of yield curves	6
6.7	Evaluate the risks of holding bonds and management of this risk, including: • interest rate, credit, inflation and other risks • sensitivity, duration and convexity	7

	Learning Outcome 07 Be able to calculate and evaluate critically the risks and returns offered by equities	Chapter 7 Section
7.1	Explain and appraise the characteristics of investing in listed equity: • definition and key properties of equities • risk, price, and return • historic performance of equities • principal problems and liquidity issues, plus implications should liquidity fall	1

Syllabus

7.2	Explain the types of listed equity: • characteristics • rights attached to classes of shares • issuance • equity-related investments	2
7.3	Explain and appraise the characteristics of investing in private equity: • definition and key properties of private equity • problems due to information asymmetry • risk, liquidity and return • performance of private equity • principal problems and liquidity issues, plus implications should liquidity fall	3

Learning Outcome 08 Be able to evaluate critically the risks and returns offered by property and alternative investments	Chapter 8 Section
8.1	Evaluate property as a component of a portfolio: • definition and the key properties of real estate • land, residential, commercial • risk, price, value, and return • historic performance of real estate • principal problems and liquidity issues, plus implications should liquidity fall	1
8.2	Explain the characteristics of property investment vehicles and their application in an investment portfolio: performance/risk/reward profiles of direct, indirect and buy-to-let investment approaches and appraisal methods	2
8.3	Explain and evaluate commodities as an investment vehicle: • definition and key properties of commodities • problems associated with particular types of commodity investment • distinguish between direct and indirect investments in commodities • performance of commodities • principal problems and liquidity issues, plus implications should liquidity fall • price discovery for commodities	3
8.4	Evaluate infrastructure funds as an investment vehicle: • definition and key properties of infrastructure funds • problems due to lumpiness and indivisibility • risk, liquidity and return • performance of infrastructure funds • principal problems and liquidity issues, plus implications should liquidity fall • ability of investors to gain access to infrastructure	4

8.5	Evaluate hedge funds as an investment vehicle: • definition and key properties of hedge funds • unique features of hedge funds • performance of hedge funds • charges of hedge funds • benefits of fund of funds • principal problems and liquidity issues, plus implications should liquidity fall	5
8.6	Evaluate enterprise investment schemes, venture capital trusts, woodland, bloodstock, collectibles as investment vehicles: • definition and key properties • problems due to lumpiness and indivisibility • risk, liquidity and return • performance • principal problems and liquidity issues, plus implications should liquidity fall • ability of investors to gain access at a reasonable price	6

Learning Outcome 09 **Be able to calculate and evaluate critically the risks and returns offered by derivative investments**	**Chapter 9 Section**
9.1	Explain derivatives market structures, features, and the regulatory and trading environment: • role, structure and regulation of global derivatives markets • role of regulators, other supervisory bodies • market terminology • key market participants and roles	1
9.2	Explain and appraise the range of derivative instruments and their key features: • financial derivatives • commodity derivatives • property derivatives • exotic derivatives • other derivatives	2

9.3	Explain and evaluate the principles, components, characteristics and risks of derivatives:
	• relationships to underlying
	• physically settled versus cash settled
	• derivatives strategies, risk/reward profiles and payoff diagrams
	• general pricing principles – futures, options
	• exercise of options, assignment of obligations, abandonment and expiry
	• types of contracts on equity, index, currency, bond and commodity assets
	• risks of derivatives:
	   ◦ legal
	   ◦ counterparty
	   ◦ settlement and dealing risks
	   ◦ market and other risks associated with derivative investing
		3

9.4	Explain and evaluate the characteristics and risks of margin and collateral: • purpose, types and application of collateral and margin • parties involved • processing, collection and payment • pricing factors and calculation • delivery and settlement	4, 5
9.5	Explain and evaluate the clearing and settlement of exchange traded and OTC derivatives: • definition and purpose of clearing and settlement • roles and relationships • risks and guarantees • central counterparty clearing • clearing of OTC transactions • transparency and confidentiality • counterparties • documentation • settlement of transactions	4

9.6	Explain the main types, characteristics, and pricing of exchange-traded derivatives:
	• convertibles, covered, and uncovered warrants:
	    ○ factors influencing pricing
	    ○ bases for calculation and actual calculation
	    ○ significance and uses
	• futures:
	    ○ factors influencing pricing
	    ○ bases for calculation
	    ○ significance and uses
	• options:
	    ○ factors influencing pricing
	    ○ bases for calculation and actual calculation
	    ○ significance and uses
		6

9.7	Describe and explain the trading of exchange traded derivatives: • main UK and international exchanges • trading platforms • mechanisms, procedures, and processes • wholesale trading facilities • standardisation of deals, contracts, and agreements • market transparency, reporting and monitoring • order/instruction flow and order type • input and matching, trade registration processes • maturity, expiry, margin, liquidity, exercise and delivery	6
9.8	Explain the main types, characteristics, risks, and pricing of OTC-traded derivatives: • forwards and forward rate agreements (FRAs) • OTC option products • contracts for difference • swaps - interest rate, currency, equity and commodity, bond • credit default swaps • credit derivatives • structured products	7
9.9	Describe and explain the trading of OTC-traded derivatives: • mechanisms, procedures, and processes • wholesale trading facilities • standard and bespoke deals, contracts, and agreements • market transparency, reporting and monitoring • order/instruction flow and order type • confirmation, maturity, expiry, margin, liquidity, exercise and delivery	7

Syllabus

Learning Outcome 10 Be able to explain the securities market structure, trading venues and custody and settlement processes		Chapter 10 Section
10.1	Describe and explain the trading of OTC-traded derivatives: • summarise primary, secondary & dual listing and explain the process of issuing and gaining admission to a recognised investment exchange • distinguish between the requirements of ISDX, the AIM market and the official list and issuing securities without a prospectus • discriminate between on exchange and over-the-counter (OTC) trading and detail the transparency obligations • illustrate markets for trading government and corporate bonds • stock lending and CREST	1–7
10.2	Detail the market abuse regime and explain and contrast the role of the UK Listing Authority, ESMA, Takeover panel and London Stock Exchange in market regulation	8
10.3	Summarise the role of multilateral trading facilities (MTFs), systematic internalisers, dark pools	9
10.4	Demonstrate an understanding of the structure of international markets: • include both developed markets and emerging markets • demonstrate an understanding of: the clearing, settlement and custody process including the duties of central counterparty mechanisms and associated risks, the role of International Central Securities Depositories (ICSDs), the custody of assets and client money and relevance and impact of corporate actions	10–13

Unit Summary

The aim of this unit is to enable candidates to think critically, apply, and communicate clearly in the context of:

- the analysis of macroeconomic government policy targets, instruments, and their effectiveness
- the impact of macroeconomics on the behaviour of markets, sectors, companies, and investment themes
- the analysis, interpretation and comparison of company information and financial statements in order to determine the prospects of a single company and investment class, as well as the relative prospects of different companies and investment classes
- the determination of prices and values for bonds and equities
- the evaluation, recommendation, and use of liquidity, bond, equity, and property based investments for wealth management and private client purposes
- the evaluation, recommendation, and use of alternatives and derivatives based investments for wealth management and private client purposes
- the analysis and comparison of market structure, trading venues, and financial indexes
- the analysis of the trading, clearing, settlement, lending, and custody process.

Assessment Structure

This is a three-hour examination of 100 marks comprising three sections:

- **Section A worth 20 marks:**
    - candidates answer FOUR questions from SIX, worth 5 marks each.

- **Section B worth 40 marks:**
    - candidates answer BOTH questions in this section worth 20 marks each.

- **Section C worth 40 marks:**
    - candidates answer ALL parts of the case study-based questions in this section.

Syllabus Structure

The syllabus is divided into learning outcomes. These are broken down into a series of assessment criteria.

Candidate Update

Candidates are reminded to check the Candidate Update area of the Institute's website (https://www.cisi.org/cisiweb2/cisi-website/study-with-us/candidate-update) on a regular basis for updates that could affect their examination as a result of industry change.

Reading List

Periodicals and Newspapers

1. Financial Times
2. FT Weekend
3. The Economist
4. Financial sections of The Times, The Daily Telegraph, Independent and Evening Standard
5. Bank of England Quarterly Bulletin
6. Bank of England Inflation Report (Quarterly)
7. Annual Debt and Reserves Management Report – The UK Treasury (Quarterly)
8. DMO Annual Review (The Debt Management Office)
9. Investors' Chronicle
10. Securities & Investment Review
11. Investment Week
12. Professional Investor (the quarterly journal of the CFA)
13. Money Management
14. What Investment?
15. Investment Adviser
16. Professional Adviser
17. Money Observer
18. Bloomberg Money

Books

1. *The Bond & Money Markets*; Choudhry M; Butterworth-Heinemann Finance 2001
2. *Mastering Derivatives Markets*; Francesca Taylor; FT Pitman/Prentice Hall
3. *Mastering Credit Derivatives*; Andrew Kasapi; FT/Prentice Hall
4. *Options, Futures and other Derivatives*; John C. Hull; Prentice Hall
5. *Interpreting Company Reports & Accounts*; Holmes, Sugden & Gee; FT/ Prentice Hall; 9th Edition 2004
6. *Investments: AND S&P*; Bodie Z, Kane A, Marcus AJ; McGraw Hill Higher Education; 7th Edition 2007
7. *Guide to Analysing Companies*; 4th Edition 2005; Vause B, Economist Publications
8. *An Investor's Guide to Analysing Companies and Valuing Shares*; Cahill M; FT Prentice Hall
9. *How to read the financial pages*; Brett M; Random House; 2003
10. *The Financial Times Guide to Using the Financial Pages*; Vaitilingham R; FT Prentice-Hall 2005, 5th Edition.
11. *The Intelligent Guide to Stockmarket Investment*; Keasey, K; Hudson, R; Little, K; Wiley 1998
12. *Investment Management*; Lofthouse S; J Wiley 2001
13. *An Introduction to Stock Exchange Investment*; Rutterford, J; Davison M; 3rd Edition; 2007
14. *A Guide to Stockpicking*; O'Connor G; Random House 1996
15. *Dictionary of Financial & Securities Terms*; Wilson, D; SII; 2002
16. *Investments* – 6th Edition, Prentice-Hall. By William Sharpe, Gordon Alexander and Jeffrey Bailey.
17. *Capital Markets - Institutions and Instruments.* 3rd Edition, Prentice-Hall. By Frank Fabozzi and Franco Modigliani.
18. *The Handbook of International Financial Terms.* Oxford University Press. By Peter Moles and Nicholas Terry

Websites

1. www.bankofengland.co.uk
2. www.dmo.gov.uk
3. www.euronext.com
4. www.fca.org.uk
5. www.ft.com
6. www.ftse.com
7. www.londonstockexchange.com
8. www.nsandi.com
9. www.trustnet.com
10. www.hm-treasury.gov.uk

CISI Chartered MCSI Membership can work for you...

Studying for a CISI qualification is hard work and we're sure you're putting in plenty of hours, but don't lose sight of your goal!

This is just the first step in your career; there is much more to achieve!

The securities and investments sector attracts ambitious and driven individuals. You're probably one yourself and that's great, but on the other hand you're almost certainly surrounded by lots of other people with similar ambitions.

So how can you stay one step ahead during these uncertain times?

Entry Criteria for Chartered MCSI Membership

As an ACSI and MCSI candidate, you can upgrade your membership status to Chartered MCSI. There are a number of ways of gaining the CISI Chartered MCSI membership.

A straightforward route requires candidates to have:
- a minimum of one year's ACSI or MCSI membership;
- passed a full Diploma; Certificate in Private Client Investment Advice & Management or Masters in Wealth Management award;
- passed IntegrityMatters with an A grade; and
- successfully logged and certified 12 months' CPD under the CISI's CPD Scheme.

Alternatively, experienced-based candidates are required to have:
- a minimum of one year's ACSI membership;
- passed IntegrityMatters with an A grade; and
- successfully logged and certified six years' CPD under the CISI's CPD Scheme.

Joining Fee:	Current Grade of Membership	Grade of Chartership	Upgrade Cost
	ACSI	Chartered MCSI	£85.00
	MCSI	Chartered MCSI	£30.00

By belonging to a Chartered professional body, members will benefit from enhanced status in the industry and the wider community. Members will be part of an organisation which holds the respect of government and the financial services sector, and can communicate with the public on a whole new level. There will be little doubt in consumers' minds that chartered members of the CISI are highly regarded and qualified professionals and, as a consequence, will be required to act as such.

The Chartered MCSI designation will provide you with full access to all member benefits, including Professional Refresher where there are currently over 100 modules available on subjects including Anti-Money Laundering, Information Security & Data Protection, Integrity & Ethics, and the UK Bribery Act. CISI TV is also available to members, allowing you to catch up on the latest CISI events, whilst earning valuable CPD.

Revision Express

You've bought the workbook... now test your knowledge before your exam.

Revision Express is an engaging online study tool to be used in conjunction with most CISI workbooks.

Key Features of Revision Express:
- Examination-focused – the content of Revision Express covers the key points of the syllabus
- Questions throughout to reaffirm understanding of the subject
- Special end-of-module practice exam to reflect as closely as possible the standard you will experience in your exam (please note, however, they are not the CISI exam questions themselves)
- Extensive glossary of terms
- Useful associated website links
- Allows you to study whenever you like, and on any device

IMPORTANT: The questions contained in Revision Express products are designed as aids to revision, and should not be seen in any way as mock exams.

Price per Revision Express module: £35
Price when purchased with the corresponding CISI workbook: £105

To purchase Revision Express:

call our Customer Support Centre on:
+44 20 7645 0777

or visit the CISI's online bookshop at:
cisi.org/bookshop

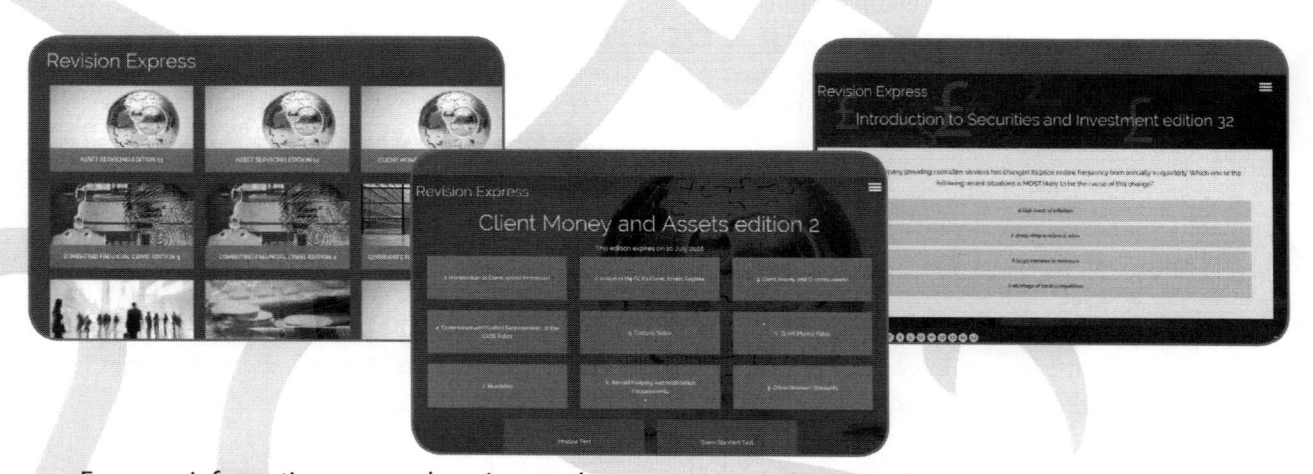

For more information on our elearning products, contact our Customer Support Centre on +44 20 7645 0777, or visit our website at cisi.org/elearning

Professional Refresher

Self-testing elearning modules to refresh your knowledge, meet regulatory and firm requirements, and earn CPD.

Professional Refresher is a training solution to help you remain up-to-date with industry developments, maintain regulatory compliance and demonstrate continuing learning.

This popular online learning tool allows self-administered refresher testing on a variety of topics, including the latest regulatory changes.

There are currently over 100 modules available which address UK and international issues. Modules are reviewed by practitioners frequently and new topics are added to the suite on a regular basis.

Benefits to firms:
- Learning and testing can form part of business T&C programme
- Learning and testing kept up-to-date and accurate by the CISI
- Relevant and useful – devised by industry practitioners
- Access to individual results available as part of management overview facility, 'Super User'
- Records of staff training can be produced for internal use and external audits
- Cost-effective – no additional charge for CISI members
- Available to non-members

Benefits to individuals:
- Comprehensive selection of topics across sectors
- Modules are regularly reviewed and updated by industry experts
- New topics added regularly
- Free for members
- Successfully passed modules are recorded in your CPD log as active learning
- Counts as structured learning for RDR purposes
- On completion of a module, a certificate can be printed out for your own records

The full suite of Professional Refresher modules is free to CISI members, or £250 for non-members. Modules are also available individually. To view a full list of Professional Refresher modules visit:

cisi.org/refresher

If you or your firm would like to find out more, contact our Client Relationship Management team:

+ 44 20 7645 0670
crm@cisi.org

For more information on our elearning products, contact our Customer Support Centre on +44 20 7645 0777, or visit our website at cisi.org/refresher

Professional Refresher

Free to CISI members

Top 5

SCORM COMPLIANT

Integrity & Ethics
- High Level View
- Ethical Behaviour
- An Ethical Approach
- Compliance vs Ethics

Anti-Money Laundering
- Introduction to Money Laundering
- UK Legislation and Regulation
- Money Laundering Regulations 2007
- Proceeds of Crime Act 2002
- Terrorist Financing
- Suspicious Activity Reporting
- Money Laundering Reporting Officer
- Sanctions

Financial Crime
- What Is Financial Crime?
- Insider Dealing and Market Abuse Introduction, Legislation, Offences and Rules
- Money Laundering Legislation, Regulations, Financial Sanctions and Reporting Requirements
- Money Laundering and the Role of the MLRO

Information Security and Data Protection
- Information Security: The Key Issues
- Latest Cybercrime Developments
- The Lessons From High-Profile Cases
- Key Identity Issues: Know Your Customer
- Implementing the Data Protection Act 1998
- The Next Decade: Predictions For The Future

UK Bribery Act
- Background to the Act
- The Offences
- What the Offences Cover
- When Has an Offence Been Committed?
- The Defences Against Charges of Bribery
- The Penalties

Latest Modules

Bonds
- Definition, Key Terms and Characteristics
- The Different Types of Bonds
- The Advantages and Disadvantages of Bonds
- Rating Bonds

General Data Protection Regulation (GDPR)
- Understanding the Terminology
- The Six Data Protection Principles
- Data Subject Rights
- Technical and Organisational Measures

Human Trafficking and the Modern Slavery Act 2015
- Human Trafficking and Modern Slavery
- Definitions and Scale of the Problem
- Detection and Prevention
- Statements

Long-term Care
- Setting the Scene
- State Provision
- Planned Changes
- Funding Your Own Care
- Effective Structuring

Managing in the Regulatory Environment
- Regulatory Framework and Expectations
- The Conduct Rules
- Obligations on Managers
- Personal Responsibilities
- Responsibilities for Managing Others
- If Things Go Wrong

Operations

Best Execution
- What Is Best Execution?
- Achieving Best Execution
- Order Execution Policies
- Information to Clients & Client Consent
- Monitoring, the Rules, and Instructions
- Best Execution for Specific Types of Firms

Approved Persons Regime
- The Basis of the Regime
- Fitness and Propriety
- The Controlled Functions
- Principles for Approved Persons
- The Code of Practice for Approved Persons

Corporate Actions
- Corporate Structure and Finance
- Life Cycle of an Event
- Mandatory Events
- Voluntary Events

Wealth

Client Assets and Client Money
- Protecting Client Assets and Client Money
- Ring-Fencing Client Assets and Client Money
- Due Diligence of Custodians
- Reconciliations
- Records and Accounts
- CASS Oversight

Investment Principles and Risk
- Diversification
- Factfind and Risk Profiling
- Investment Management
- Modern Portfolio Theory and Investing Styles
- Direct and Indirect Investments
- Socially Responsible Investment
- Collective Investments
- Investment Trusts
- Dealing in Debt Securities and Equities

Banking Standards
- Introduction and Background
- Strengthening Individual Accountability
- Reforming Corporate Governance
- Securing Better Outcomes for Consumers
- Enhancing Financial Stability

Suitability of Client Investments
- Assessing Suitability
- Risk Profiling
- Establishing Risk Appetite
- Obtaining Customer Information
- Suitable Questions and Answers
- Making Suitable Investment Selections
- Guidance, Reports and Record Keeping

International

Foreign Account Tax Compliance Act (FATCA)
- Foreign Financial Institutions
- Due Diligence Requirements
- Reporting
- Compliance

MiFID II
- The Organisations Covered by MiFID
- The Products Subject to MiFID's Guidelines
- The Origins of MiFID II
- The Products Covered by MiFID II
- Levels 1, 2, and 3 Implementation

UCITS
- The Original UCITS Directive
- UCITS III
- UCITS IV
- Non-UCITS Funds
- Future Developments

cisi.org/refresher

Feedback to the CISI

Have you found this workbook to be a valuable aid to your studies? We would like your views, so please email us at learningresources@cisi.org with any thoughts, ideas or comments.

Accredited Training Partners

Support for exam students studying for the Chartered Institute for Securities & Investment (CISI) qualifications is provided by several Accredited Training Partners (ATPs), including Fitch Learning and BPP. The CISI's ATPs offer a range of face-to-face training courses, distance learning programmes, their own learning resources and study packs which have been accredited by the CISI. The CISI works in close collaboration with its ATPs to ensure they are kept informed of changes to CISI exams so they can build them into their own courses and study packs.

CISI Workbook Specialists Wanted

Workbook Authors

Experienced freelance authors with finance experience, and who have published work in their area of specialism, are sought. Responsibilities include:
- Updating workbooks in line with new syllabuses and any industry developments
- Ensuring that the syllabus is fully covered

Workbook Reviewers

Individuals with a high-level knowledge of the subject area are sought. Responsibilities include:
- Highlighting any inconsistencies against the syllabus
- Assessing the author's interpretation of the workbook

Workbook Technical Reviewers

Technical reviewers to provide a detailed review of the workbook and bring the review comments to the panel. Responsibilities include:
- Cross-checking the workbook against the syllabus
- Ensuring sufficient coverage of each learning objective

Workbook Proofreaders

Proofreaders are needed to proof workbooks both grammatically and also in terms of the format and layout. Responsibilities include:
- Checking for spelling and grammar mistakes
- Checking for formatting inconsistencies

If you are interested in becoming a CISI external specialist call:
+44 20 7645 0609

or email:
externalspecialists@cisi.org

For bookings, orders, membership and general enquiries please contact our Customer Support Centre on +44 20 7645 0777, or visit our website at cisi.org